The History of the Decline and Fall of the Roman Empire

THE DECLINE AND FALL OF THE

ROMAN EMPIRE

VOL. III.

THE HISTORY

OF THE

DECLINE AND FALL OF THE
ROMAN EMPIRE

BY

EDWARD GIBBON

EDITED IN SEVEN VOLUMES

WITH INTRODUCTION, NOTES, APPENDICES, AND INDEX

BY

J. B. BURY, M.A.

HON. LITT D. OF DURHAM
FELLOW AND TUTOR OF TRINITY COLLEGE, DUBLIN
PROFESSOR OF MODERN HISTORY IN DUBLIN UNIVERSITY

VOL III

METHUEN & CO.
36 ESSEX STREET, W C
LONDON
1897
New Edition

CONTENTS OF THE THIRD VOLUME

CHAPTER XXV

*The Government and Death of Jovian—Election of Valentinian, who asso-
ciates his Brother Valens, and makes his final Division of the Eastern
and Western Empires—Revolt of Procopius—Civil and Ecclesiastical
Administration—Germany—Britain—Africa—The East—The Danube
—Death of Valentinian—His two Sons, Gratian and Valentinian II.,
succeed to the Western Empire*

A.D.		PAGE
363	State of the Church ...	1
	Jovian proclaims universal Toleration	3
	His progress from Antioch	4
364	Jovian, with his infant Son, assumes the Name and Ensigns of the Consulship	5
364	Death of Jovian	6
	Vacancy of the Throne	7
364	Election and Character of Valentinian	8
	He is acknowledged by the Army	8
	Associates his Brother Valens	10
364	The final Division of the Eastern and Western Empires	10
365	Revolt of Procopius	11
366	His Defeat and Death	14
373	Severe Inquisition into the Crime of Magic at Rome and Antioch	16
364-375.	The Cruelty of Valentinian and Valens	19
	Their Laws and Government	21
	Valentinian maintains the Religious Toleration	23
367-378.	Valens professes Arianism, and persecutes the Catholics	24
373	Death of Athanasius ...	26
	Just Idea of the Persecution of Valens	26
370	Valentinian restrains the Avarice of the Clergy ...	28
366-384	Ambition and Luxury of Damasus, Bishop of Rome	29
364-375.	Foreign Wars	31
365	I. GERMANY. The Alemanni invade Gaul	32
366	Their Defeat	33
368	Valentinian passes, and fortifies, the Rhine	34
371	The Burgundians	36
	The Saxons ...	37
	II BRITAIN. The Scots and Picts	40
343-366.	Their Invasion of Britain	43

A D   PAGE
367-370.   Restoration of Britain by Theodosius   44
366 III. AFRICA   Tyranny of Romanus   .   .   46
372 Revolt of Firmus   .   .   .   48
373 Theodosius recovers Africa   ..   .   48
376 He is executed at Carthage   50
    State of Africa   51
365-378   IV. THE EAST.   The Persian War   52
384 The Treaty of Peace   55
    Adventures of Para, King of Armenia   55
    V. THE DANUBE.   Conquest of Hermanric   57
366 The cause of the Gothic War   .   .   59
367, 368, 369   Hostilities and Peace   60
374 War of the Quadi and Sarmatians   62
375 The Expedition of Valentinian   64
    His Death   66
    The Emperors Gratian and Valentinian II   .   .   66

CHAPTER XXVI

Manners of the Pastoral Nations—Progress of the Huns, from China to Europe—Flight of the Goths—They pass the Danube—Gothic War—Defeat and Death of Valens—Gratian invests Theodosius with the Eastern Empire—His Character and Success—Peace and Settlement of the Goths

365 Earthquakes   69
376 The Huns and Goths   70
    The Pastoral Manners of the Scythians, or Tartars   71
    Diet   72
    Habitations   74
    Exercises   76
    Government   77
    Situation and Extent of Scythia, or Tartary   79
    Original Seat of the Huns   82
    Their Conquests in Scythia   82
201 Their Wars with the Chinese   83
141-87.   Decline and Fall of the Huns   84
100 Their Emigrations   87
    The White Huns of Sogdiana   87
    The Huns of the Volga   .   .   88
    Their Conquest of the Alani   89
375 Their Victories over the Goths   91
376 The Goths implore the Protection of Valens   .   93
    They are transported over the Danube into the Roman Empire   95
    Their Distress and Discontent   97
    Revolt of the Goths in Mæsia, and their first Victories .   99
    They penetrate into Thrace   101
377 Operations of the Gothic War   .   103
    Union of the Goths with the Huns, Alani, &c   .   .   105
378 Victory of Gratian over the Alemanni   107
    Valens marches against the Goths   109

A D
Battle of Hadrianople 111
The Defeat of the Romans 112
Death of the Emperor Valens 112
Funeral Oration of Valens and his Army 113
The Goths besiege Hadrianople 114
378, 379 They ravage the Roman Provinces 116
378 Massacre of the Gothic Youth in Asia ... 117
379 The Emperor Gratian invests Theodosius with the Empire of
the East 118
Birth and Character of Theodosius 120
379-382 His prudent and successful Conduct of the Gothic War . 122
Divisions, Defeat, and Submission of the Goths 124
381 Death and Funeral of Athanaric 126
386 Invasion and Defeat of the Gruthungi, or Ostrogoths .. 127
383-395. Settlement of the Goths in Thrace and Asia .. 129
Their hostile Sentiments 131

CHAPTER XXVII

Death of Gratian—Ruin of Arianism—St. Ambrose—First Civil War, against Maximus—Character, Administration, and Penance of Theodosius— Death of Valentinian II —Second Civil War, against Eugenius—Death of Theodosius

379-383. Character and Conduct of the Emperor Gratian 133
His Defects 133
383 Discontent of the Roman Troops 135
Revolt of Maximus in Britain 136
383 Flight and Death of Gratian 137
383-387. Treaty of Peace between Maximus and Theodosius ... 139
380 Baptism and orthodox Edicts of Theodosius 140
340-380. Arianism of Constantinople 142
378 Gregory Nazianzen accepts the Mission of Constantinople .. 144
380 Ruin of Arianism at Constantinople 146
381 „ „ in the East 147
The Council of Constantinople 148
Retreat of Gregory Nazianzen 150
380-394 Edicts of Theodosius against the Heretics 151
385 Execution of Priscillian and his Associates 153
375-397. Ambrose, Archbishop of Milan 155
385 His successful Opposition to the Empress Justina 156
387 Maximus invades Italy 161
Flight of Valentinian 162
Theodosius takes Arms in the Cause of Valentinian 163
388 Defeat and Death of Maximus 164
Virtues of Theodosius 166
Faults of Theodosius 168
387 The Sedition of Antioch 169
Clemency of Theodosius 171
390 Sedition and Massacre of Thessalonica 172
388 Influence and Conduct of Ambrose 174

CONTENTS

A D.		PAGE
390	Penance of Theodosius	175
388-391.	Generosity of Theodosius	177
391	Character of Valentinian	177
392	His Death	179
392-394.	Usurpation of Eugenius	180
	Theodosius prepares for War	181
394	His Victory over Eugenius	182
395	Death of Theodosius	185
	Corruption of the Times	186
	The Infantry lay aside their Armour	187

CHAPTER XXVIII

Final Destruction of Paganism—Introduction of the Worship of Saints, and Relics, among the Christians

		PAGE
378-395.	The Destruction of the Pagan Religion	188
	State of Paganism at Rome	189
384	Petition of the Senate for the Altar of Victory .	191
388	Conversion of Rome	193
381	Destruction of the Temples in the Provinces	195
	The Temple of Serapis at Alexandria	198
389	Its final Destruction	200
390	The Pagan Religion is prohibited	203
	Oppressed	205
390-420.	Finally extinguished	206
	The Worship of the Christian Martyrs . . .	208
	General Reflections	210
	I. Fabulous Martyrs and Relics .	210
	II. Miracles	210
	III. Revival of Polytheism	112
	IV Introduction of Pagan Ceremonies	214

CHAPTER XXIX

Final Division of the Roman Empire between the Sons of Theodosius—Reign of Arcadius and Honorius—Administration of Rufinus and Stilicho—Revolt and Defeat of Gildo in Africa

		PAGE
395	Division of the Empire between Arcadius and Honorius .	216
386-395.	Character and Administration of Rufinus	217
395	He oppresses the East	220
	He is disappointed by the Marriage of Arcadius	222
	Character of Stilicho, the Minister, and General of the Western Empire	224
385-408.	His Military Command	225
395	The Fall and Death of Rufinus	227
3/6	Discord of the two Empires	229
386-398.	Revolt of Gildo in Africa	231

CONTENTS

A D		PAGE
397	He is condemned by the Roman Senate ...	232
398	The African War	233
398	Defeat and Death of Gildo	235
398	Marriage and Character of Honorius	237

CHAPTER XXX

Revolt of the Goths—They plunder Greece—Two great Invasions of Italy by Alaric and Radagaisus—They are repulsed by Stilicho—The Germans over-run Gaul—Usurpation of Constantine in the West—Disgrace and Death of Stilicho

395	Revolt of the Goths	240
396 [395]	Alaric marches into Greece	241
397 [396]	He is attacked by Stilicho	244
	Escapes to Epirus	246
398	Alaric is declared Master general of the Eastern Illyricum	246
	Is proclaimed King of the Visigoths	248
400-403.	He invades Italy	248
403	Honorius flies from Milan	250
	He is pursued and besieged by the Goths	251
403 [402]	Battle of Pollentia	253
	Boldness and Retreat of Alaric	255
404	The triumph of Honorius at Rome	257
	The Gladiators abolished	258
	Honorius fixes his Residence at Ravenna	259
400	The Revolutions of Scythia	261
405	Emigration of the northern Germans	262
406 [405]	Radagaisus invades Italy	263
	,, besieges Florence	264
	,, threatens Rome	265
406	Defeat and Destruction of his Army by Stilicho	265
	The Remainder of the Germans invade Gaul	267
407	Desolation of Gaul	269
	Revolt of the British Army	271
	Constantine is acknowledged in Britain and Gaul	272
408	He reduces Spain	273
404-408.	Negotiation of Alaric and Stilicho	275
408	Debates of the Roman Senate	276
	Intrigues of the Palace	277
408	Disgrace and Death of Stilicho	279
408	His Memory persecuted	280
	The Poet Claudian among the Train of Stilicho's Dependents	282

CHAPTER XXXI

Invasion of Italy by Alaric—Manners of the Roman Senate and People—Rome is thrice besieged, and at length pillaged by the Goths—Death of Alaric—The Goths evacuate Italy—Fall of Constantine—Gaul and Spain are occupied by the Barbarians—Independence of Britain

408	Weakness of the Court of Ravenna	285
	Alaric marches to Rome	286

A D.		PAGE
	Hannibal at the Gates of Rome	288
	Genealogy of the Senators ..	289
	The Anician Family ..	290
	Wealth of the Roman Nobles	292
	Their Manners	294
	Character of the Roman Nobles, by Ammianus Marcellinus	295
	State and Character of the people of Rome	302
	Public Distribution of Bread, Bacon, Oil, Wine, &c	303
	Use of the public Baths	304
	Games and Spectacles	305
	Populousness of Rome	306
408	First Siege of Rome by the Goths	309
	Famine	309
	Plague ..	310
	Superstition	310
409	Alaric accepts a Ransom, and raises the Siege	311
	Fruitless Negotiations for Peace	313
	Change and Succession of Ministers	314
409	Second Siege of Rome by the Goths	317
	Attalus is created Emperor by the Goths and Romans .	318
410	He is degraded by Alaric ..	320
	Third Siege and Sack of Rome by the Goths	321
410	Respect of the Goths for the Christian Religion	322
	Pillage and Fire of Rome	323
	Captives and Fugitives	326
	Sack of Rome by the Troops of Charles V.	328
	Alaric evacuates Rome, and ravages Italy	330
408-412	Possession of Italy by the Goths .	331
410	Death of Alaric	332
412	Adolphus, King of the Goths, concludes a Peace with the Empire, and marches into Gaul	333
414	His Marriage with Placidia .	334
	The Gothic Treasures	336
410-417.	Laws for the Relief of Italy and Rome	337
413	Revolt and Defeat of Heraclian, Count of Africa	338
409-413.	Revolutions of Gaul and Spain	340
	Character and Victories of the General Constantius	341
411	Death of the Usurper Constantine	342
411-416.	Fall of the Usurpers, Jovinus, Sebastian, and Attalus	343
409	Invasion of Spain by the Suevi, Vandals, Alani, &c.	345
414	Adolphus, King of the Goths, marches into Spain	347
415	His Death	347
415-418	The Goths conquer and restore Spain	348
419	Their Establishment in Aquitain .	349
	The Burgundians	350
420, &c.	State of the Barbarians in Gaul	351
409	Revolt of Britain and Armorica	352
409-449.	State of Britain	353
418	Assembly of the Seven Provinces of Gaul	356

CONTENTS

CHAPTER XXXII

Arcadius Emperor of the East—Administration and Disgrace of Eutropius— Revolt of Gainas—Persecution of St. John Chrysostom—Theodosius II. Emperor of the East—His Sister Pulcheria—His Wife Eudocia— The Persian War, and Division of Armenia

A D		PAGE
395-1453.	The Empire of the East	358
395-408.	Reign of Arcadius	358
395-399.	Administration and Character of Eutropius	360
	His Venality and Injustice	362
	Ruin of Abundantius	363
	Destruction of Timasius	363
397	A cruel and unjust Law of Treason	365
399	Rebellion of Tribigild	366
	Fall of Eutropius	369
400	Conspiracy and Fall of Gainas	371
398	Election and Merit of St John Chrysostom	374
398-403	His Administration and Defects	375
403	Chrysostom is persecuted by the Empress Eudoxia	377
	Popular Tumults at Constantinople	378
404	Exile of Chrysostom	379
407	His Death	380
438	His Relics transported to Constantinople	381
408	Death of Arcadius	381
	His supposed Testament	382
408-415.	Administration of Anthemius	383
414-453.	Character and Administration of Pulcheria	384
	Education and Character of Theodosius the Younger	386
421-460.	Character and Adventures of the Empress Eudocia	387
422	The Persian War	390
431-440.	Armenia divided between the Persians and the Romans	391

CHAPTER XXXIII

Death of Honorius—Valentinian III. Emperor of the West—Administration of his Mother Placidia—Aetius and Boniface—Conquest of Africa by the Vandals

423	Last Years and Death of Honorius	394
423-425.	Elevation and Fall of the Usurper John	395
425-455.	Valentinian III. Emperor of the West	396
425-450.	Administration of his Mother Placidia	398
	Her two Generals, Aetius and Boniface	398
427	Error and Revolt of Boniface in Africa	399
428	He invites the Vandals	400
	Genseric King of the Vandals	401
429	He lands in Africa	401
	Reviews his Army	402
	The Moors	402
	The Donatists	403

CONTENTS

A.D.		PAGE
430	Tardy Repentance of Boniface	404
	Desolation of Africa	405
430	Siege of Hippo	406
430	Death of St Augustin	406
431	Defeat and Retreat of Boniface	407
432	His Death	408
431-439.	Progress of the Vandals in Africa	409
439	They surprise Carthage	410
	African Exiles and Captives	411
	Fable of the Seven Sleepers	412

CHAPTER XXXIV

The Character, Conquests, and Court of Attila, King of the Huns—Death of Theodosius the Younger—Elevation of Marcian to the Empire of the East

		PAGE
376-433.	The Huns	416
	Their Establishment in modern Hungary	416
433-453.	Reign of Attila	418
	His Figure and Character	418
	He discovers the Sword of Mars	419
	Acquires the Empire of Scythia and Germany	420
430-440	The Huns invade Persia	422
441, &c	They attack the Eastern Empire	423
	Ravage Europe as far as Constantinople	425
	The Scythian or Tartar Wars	426
	State of the Captives	427
446	Treaty of Peace between Attila and the Eastern Empire	430
	Spirit of the Azimuntines	431
	Embassies from Attila to Constantinople	433
448	The Embassy of Maximin to Attila	434
	The royal Village and Palace	437
	The Behaviour of Attila to the Roman Ambassadors	438
	The royal Feast	440
	Conspiracy of the Romans against the Life of Attila	442
	He reprimands and forgives the Emperor	442
450	Theodosius the Younger dies	444
	Is succeeded by Marcian	444

CHAPTER XXXV

Invasion of Gaul by Attila—He is repulsed by Aetius and the Visigoths—Attila invades and evacuates Italy—The Deaths of Attila, Aetius, and Valentinian the Third

		PAGE
450	Attila threatens both Empires, and prepares to invade Gaul	446
433-454.	Character and Administration of Aetius	447
	His Connexion with the Huns and Alani	448
419-451.	The Visigoths in Gaul under the Reign of Theodoric	450
435-439.	The Goths besiege Narbonne, &c	450
420-451.	The Franks in Gaul under the Merovingian Kings	453
	The Adventures of the Princess Honoria	455

CONTENTS

A D		PAGE
451	Attila invades Gaul and besieges Orleans	457
	Alliance of the Romans and Visigoths	459
	Attila retires to the plains of Champagne	461
	Battle of Châlons	464
	Retreat of Attila	465
452	Invasion of Italy by Attila	467
	Foundation of the Republic of Venice	469
	Attila gives peace to the Romans	471
453	The Death of Attila	474
	Destruction of his Empire	475
454	Valentinian murders the Patrician Aetius . .	476
	„ ravishes the Wife of Maximus ..	478
455	Death of Valentinian	479
	Symptoms of the Decay and Ruin of the Roman Government	479

MAP.

PAGE

Europe, c A D 450   ,   446

THE HISTORY

OF THE

DECLINE AND FALL OF THE ROMAN EMPIRE

CHAPTER XXV

The Government and Death of Jovian—Election of Valentinian, who associates his Brother Valens, and makes the final Division of the Eastern and Western Empires—Revolt of Procopius—Civil and Ecclesiastical Administration—Germany—Britain—Africa —The East—The Danube—Death of Valentinian—His two Sons, Gratian and Valentinian II., succeed to the Western Empire

THE death of Julian had left the public affairs of the empire in a very doubtful and dangerous situation. The Roman army was saved by an inglorious, perhaps a necessary, treaty;[1] and the first moments of peace were consecrated by the pious Jovian to restore the domestic tranquillity of the church and state. The indiscretion of his predecessor, instead of reconciling, had artfully fomented the religious war; and the balance which he affected to preserve between the hostile factions served only to perpetuate the contest, by the vicissitudes of hope and fear, by the rival claims of ancient possession and actual favour The Christians had forgotten the spirit of the Gospel, and the Pagans had imbibed the spirit of the church. In private families, the sentiments of nature were extinguished by the blind fury of zeal and revenge; the majesty of the laws was violated or abused; the cities of the East were stained with blood; and the most implacable enemies of the Romans were in the bosom of their country. Jovian was educated in the profession of Christianity; and, as he marched from Nisibis to Antioch, the banner of the Cross, the LABARUM of Constantine,

---

[1] The medals of Jovian adorn him with victories, laurel crowns, and prostrate captives. Ducange, Famil Byzantin., p. 52 Flattery is a foolish suicide; she destroys herself with her own hands.

which was again displayed at the head of the legions, announced
to the people the faith of their new emperor. As soon as he
ascended the throne, he transmitted a circular epistle to all the
governors of provinces: in which he confessed the divine truth,
and secured the legal establishment, of the Christian religion
The insidious edicts of Julian were abolished; the ecclesiastical
immunities were restored and enlarged; and Jovian condescended to lament that the distress of the times obliged him
to diminish the measure of charitable distributions[2] The
Christians were unanimous in the loud and sincere applause
which they bestowed on the pious successor of Julian. But
they were still ignorant what creed, or what synod, he would
choose for the standard of orthodoxy; and the peace of the
church immediately revived those eager disputes which had
been suspended during the season of persecution. The episcopal leaders of the contending sects, convinced, from experience, how much their fate would depend on the earliest
impressions that were made on the mind of an untutored
soldier, hastened to the court of Edessa or Antioch. The
highways of the East were crowded with Homoousian, and
Arian, and Semi-Arian, and Eunomian bishops, who struggled
to outstrip each other in the holy race; the apartments of the
palace resounded with their clamours; and the ears of the
prince were assaulted, and perhaps astonished, by the singular
mixture of metaphysical argument and passionate invective.[3]
The moderation of Jovian, who recommended concord and
charity and referred the disputants to the sentence of a future
council, was interpreted as a symptom of indifference; but his
attachment to the Nicene creed was at length discovered and
declared by the reverence which he expressed for the *celestial*[4]

[2] Jovian restored to the church τὸν αρχαῖον κοσμον; a forcible and comprehensive
expression (Philostorgius, l. viii. c 5, with Godefroy s Dissertations, p. 329
Sozomen, l. vi c. 3. [The phrase means the policy of Constantius, cp. Schiller,
ii 349]). The new law which condemned the rape or marriage of nuns (Cod.
Theod l. ix tit. xxv leg. 2) is exaggerated by Sozomen, who supposes that an
amorous glance, the adultery of the heart, was punished with death by the
evangelic legislator. [Jovian's Corcyræan inscription boasts that he destroyed
pagan temples Ελλήνων τεμενη και βωμοὺς ἐξαλαπαξαι, C I. G 8608.]
[3] Compare Socrates, l. iii. c 25, and Philostorgius, l. viii. c. 6, with Godefroy's
Dissertations, p 330
[4] The word *celestial* faintly expresses the impious and extravagant flattery of
the emperor to the archbishop, τῆς προς τὸν Θεὸν τῶν ὅλων ομοιωσεως. See the original
epistle in Athanasius, tom. ii p. 33 [Migne's Patr. Graec., vol. 26, p 813]. Gregory
Nazianzen (Orat. xxi p 392 [Migne, vol. 35, p. 1121]) celebrates the friendship of
Jovian and Athanasius The primate's journey was advised by the Egyptian
monks (Tillemont, Mém. Ecclés. tom viii. p. 221).

virtues of the great Athanasius. The intrepid veteran of the
faith, at the age of seventy, had issued from his retreat on the
first intelligence of the tyrant's death. The acclamations of the
people seated him once more on the archiepiscopal throne ; and
he wisely accepted, or anticipated, the invitation of Jovian.
The venerable figure of Athanasius, his calm courage, and insinuating eloquence, sustained the reputation which he had
already acquired in the courts of four successive princes.[5] As
soon as he had gained the confidence, and secured the faith, of
the Christian emperor, he returned in triumph to his diocese,
and continued, with mature counsels and undiminished vigour,
to direct, ten years longer,[6] the ecclesiastical government of till A.D. 373
Alexandria, Egypt, and the Catholic church. Before his
departure from Antioch, he assured Jovian that his orthodox
devotion would be rewarded with a long and peaceful reign.
Athanasius had reason to hope that he should be allowed either
the merit of a successful prediction or the excuse of a grateful,
though ineffectual, prayer.[7]

The slightest force, when it is applied to assist and guide the Jovian
natural descent of its object, operates with irresistible weight ; proclaims universal
and Jovian had the good fortune to embrace the religious toleration
opinions which were supported by the spirit of the times and
the zeal and numbers of the most powerful sect[8] Under his
reign, Christianity obtained an easy and lasting victory ; and, as
soon as the smile of royal patronage was withdrawn, the genius
of paganism, which had been fondly raised and cherished by the
arts of Julian, sunk irrecoverably in the dust. In many cities,
the temples were shut or deserted : the philosophers, who had

[5] Athanasius, at the court of Antioch, is agreeably represented by La Bléterie
(Hist. de Jovien, tom. 1. p. 121-148). he translates the singular and original con-
ferences of the emperor, the primate of Egypt, and the Arian deputies. The
Abbé is not satisfied with the coarse pleasantry of Jovian ; but his partiality for
Athanasius assumes, in *his* eyes, the character of justice.

[6] The true æra of his death is perplexed with some difficulties (Tillemont, Mém
Ecclés. tom. viii. p. 719-723). But the date (A.D. 373, May 2) which seems the
most consistent with history and reason is ratified by his authentic life Maffei,
Osservazioni Letterarie, tom iii. p. 81. [So Index of Heortastic Letters , the
Hist Aceph. gives 3rd May]

[7] See the observations of Valesius and Jortin (Remarks on Ecclesiastical
History, vol. iv. p. 38) on the original letter of Athanasius, which is preserved by
Theodoret (l. iv c. 3 [See Migne's Patr. Gr , vol 26, p 813]) In some Mss this
indiscreet promise is omitted ; perhaps by the Catholics, jealous of the prophetic
fame of their leader.

[8] Athanasius (apud Theodoret, l. iv. c 3) magnifies the number of the orthodox,
who composed the whole world, πάρεξ ὀλίγων τῶν τα 'Αρείου φρονουντων. This assertion was verified in the space of thirty or forty years.

abused their transient favour, thought it prudent to shave their beards and disguise their profession, and the Christians rejoiced, that they were now in a condition to forgive, or to revenge, the injuries which they had suffered under the preceding reign.[9] The consternation of the Pagan world was dispelled by a wise and gracious edict of toleration; in which Jovian explicitly declared that, although he should severely punish the sacrilegious rites of magic, his subjects might exercise, with freedom and safety, the ceremonies of the ancient worship. The memory of this law has been preserved by the orator Themistius, who was deputed by the senate of Constantinople to express their loyal devotion for the new emperor. Themistius expatiates on the clemency of the Divine Nature, the facility of human error, the rights of conscience, and the independence of the mind; and, with some eloquence, inculcates the principles of philosophical toleration, whose aid Superstition herself, in the hour of her distress, is not ashamed to implore. He justly observes that, in the recent changes, both religions had been alternately disgraced by the seeming acquisition of worthless proselytes, of those votaries of the reigning purple who could pass, without a reason and without a blush, from the church to the temple, and from the altars of Jupiter to the sacred table of the Christians [10]

His progress from Antioch A D 363, October

In the space of seven months, the Roman troops, who were now returned to Antioch, had performed a march of fifteen hundred miles; in which they had endured all the hardships of war, of famine, and of climate. Notwithstanding their services, their fatigues, and the approach of winter, the timid and impatient Jovian allowed only, to the men and horses, a respite of six weeks. The emperor could not sustain the indiscreet and malicious raillery of the people of Antioch.[11] He was impatient to possess the palace of Constantinople, and to prevent

---

[9] Socrates, l iii c 24. Gregory Nazianzen (Orat iv p 131) and Libanius (Orat Parentalis, c 148, p. 369) express the *living* sentiments of their respective factions.

[10] Themistius, Orat v p 63-71, edit Harduin, Paris, 1684. The Abbé de la Bléterie judiciously remarks (Hist de Jovien, tom 1 p. 199) that Sozomen has forgot the general toleration, and Themistius the establishment of the Catholic religion. Each of them turned away from the object which he disliked, and wished to suppress the part of the edict the least honourable, in his opinion, to the emperor Jovian [We cannot infer from Themistius that an edict of toleration was issued; the orator wished to induce Jovian to issue such an edict Cp. the fears of Libanius, *loc cit*, and Epitaph., p 614. So Schiller,Gesch der rom Kaiserzeit,ii 347]

[11] Οἱ δὲ ᾽Αντιοχεῖς οὐχ ἡδέως διέκειντο πρὸς αὐτόν ἀλλ᾽ ἀπεσκωπτον αὐτον ᾠδαῖς καὶ παρῳδίαις, καὶ τοῖς καλουμένοις φαμώσσοις (*famosis libellis*). Johan. Antiochen in Excerpt Valesian p 845 [Müller, F. G H. iv. p. 607]. The libels of Antioch may be admitted on very slight evidence.

the ambition of some competitor, who might occupy the vacant allegiance of Europe. But he soon received the grateful intelligence that his authority was acknowledged from the Thracian Bosphorus to the Atlantic ocean. By the first letters which he dispatched from the camp of Mesopotamia he had delegated the military command of Gaul and Illyricum to Malarich, a brave and faithful officer of the nation of the Franks, and to his father-in-law, Count Lucillian, who had formerly distinguished his courage and conduct in the defence of Nisibis. Malarich had declined an office to which he thought himself unequal ; and Lucillian was massacred at Rheims, in an accidental mutiny of the Batavian cohorts.[12] But the moderation of Jovinus, master-general of the cavalry, who forgave the intention of his disgrace, soon appeased the tumult and confirmed the uncertain minds of the soldiers. The oath of fidelity was administered and taken with loyal acclamations ; and the deputies of the Western armies [13] saluted their new sovereign as he descended from Mount Taurus to the city of Tyana, in Cappadocia. From Tyana he continued his hasty march to Ancyra, capital of the province of Galatia ; where Jovian assumed, with his infant son, the name and ensigns of the consulship.[14] Dadastana,[15] an obscure town, almost at an equal distance between Ancyra and Nice, was marked for the fatal term of his journey and his life   After indulging himself with a plentiful, perhaps an intemperate, supper, he retired to rest ; and the next morning the emperor Jovian was found dead in his bed. The cause of this sudden death was variously understood. By some it was ascribed to the consequences of an indigestion, occasioned either by the quantity of the wine, or the quality of the mushrooms, which he had swallowed in the evening. According to others, he was

A.D 364,
January 1

Death of
Jovian
Feb 17

[12] Compare Ammianus (xxv. 10), who omits the name of the Batavians, with Zosimus (l iii p. 197 [c. 35]), who removes the scene of action from Rheims to Sirmium

[13] Quos capita scholarum ordo castrensis appellat. Ammian. xxv. 10, and Vales ad locum.

[14] Cujus vagitus, pertinaciter reluctantis, ne in curuli sellâ veheretur ex more, id quod mox accidit protendebat   Augustus and his successors respectfully solicited a dispensation of age for the sons or nephews whom they raised to the consulship. But the curule chair of the first Brutus had never been dishonoured by an infant

[15] The Itinerary of Antoninus fixes Dadastana 125 [leg. 117] Roman miles from Nice ; 117 [leg 125] from Ancyra   Wesseling, Itinerar. p. 142.   The pilgrim of Bordeaux, by omitting some stages, reduces the whole space from 242 to 181 miles.   Wesseling, p 574. [Dadastana, border town between Bithynia and Galatia, seems before Diocletian to have been in Bithynia, but at this time was in Galatia. See Ramsay, Hist. Geography of Asia Minor, p. 241]

suffocated in his sleep by the vapour of charcoal; which extracted from the walls of the apartment the unwholesome moisture of the fresh plaister [16] But the want of a regular inquiry into the death of a prince, whose reign and person were soon forgotten, appears to have been the only circumstance which countenanced the malicious whispers of poison and domestic guilt.[17] The body of Jovian was sent to Constantinople, to be interred with his predecessors, and the sad procession was met on the road by his wife Charito, the daughter of Count Lucillian; who still wept the recent death of her father, and was hastening to dry her tears in the embraces of an Imperial husband. Her disappointment and grief were embittered by the anxiety of maternal tenderness. Six weeks before the death of Jovian, his infant son had been placed in the curule chair, adorned with the title of *Nobilissimus*, and the vain ensigns of the consulship Unconscious of his fortune, the royal youth, who, from his grandfather, assumed the name of Varronian, was reminded only by the jealousy of the government that he was the son of an emperor. Sixteen years afterwards he was still alive, but he had already been deprived of an eye; and his afflicted mother expected every hour that the innocent victim would be torn from her arms, to appease with his blood the suspicions of the reigning prince.[18]

Vacancy of the throne. Feb 17 26 After the death of Jovian, the throne of the Roman world remained ten days [19] without a master. The ministers and generals still continued to meet in council; to exercise their respective functions; to maintain the public order; and peaceably to conduct the army to the city of Nice in Bithynia, which

[16] See Ammianus (xxv. 10), Eutropius (x 18), who might likewise be present; Jerom (tom 1 p 26, ad Heliodorum [ep 60]), Orosius (vii 31), Sozomen (l vi c 6), Zosimus (l iii, p. 197, 198 [c. 35]), and Zonaras (tom ii. l xiii. p 28, 29 [c. 14]) We cannot expect a perfect agreement, and we shall not discuss minute differences

[17] Ammianus, unmindful of his usual candour and good sense, compares the death of the harmless Jovian to that of the second Africanus, who had excited the fears and resentment of the popular faction.

[18] Chrysostom, tom i p 336, 344, edit. Montfaucon The Christian orator attempts to comfort a widow by the examples of illustrious misfortunes; and observes that, of nine emperors (including the Cæsar Gallus) who had reigned in his time, only two (Constantine and Constantius) died a natural death Such vague consolations have never wiped away a single tear.

[19] Ten days appeared scarcely sufficient for the march and election But it may be observed. 1 That the generals might command the expeditious use of the public posts for themselves, their attendants, and messengers 2 That the troops, for the ease of the cities, marched in many divisions; and that the head of the column might arrive at Nice, when the rear halted at Ancyra.

was chosen for the place of the election.[20]   In a solemn assembly of the civil and military powers of the empire, the
diadem was again unanimously offered to the præfect Sallust.
He enjoyed the glory of a second refusal; and, when the virtues
of the father were alleged in favour of his son, the præfect,
with the firmness of a disinterested patriot, declared to the
electors that the feeble age of the one and the unexperienced
youth of the other were equally incapable of the laborious
duties of government.   Several candidates were proposed, and,
after weighing the objections of character or situation, they were
successively rejected; but, as soon as the name of Valentinian
was pronounced, the merit of that officer united the suffrages   Election and
of the whole assembly, and obtained the sincere approbation   character of
                                                                     Valentinian
of Sallust himself   Valentinian [21] was the son of count
Gratian,[22] a native of Cibalis, in Pannonia, who, from an [Vinkovce]
obscure condition, had raised himself, by matchless strength
and dexterity, to the military commands of Africa and Britain ;
from which he retired with an ample fortune and suspicious
integrity.   The rank and services of Gratian contributed, however, to smooth the first steps of the promotion of his son ; and
afforded him an early opportunity of displaying those solid and
useful qualifications which raised his character above the
ordinary level of his fellow-soldiers.   The person of Valentinian was tall, graceful, and majestic.   His manly countenance,
deeply marked with the impression of sense and spirit, inspired
his friends with awe, and his enemies with fear : and, to second
the efforts of his undaunted courage, the son of Gratian had
inherited the advantages of a strong and healthy constitution.
By the habits of chastity and temperance, which restrain the
appetites and invigorate the faculties, Valentinian preserved
his own, and the public, esteem.   The avocations of a military
life had diverted his youth from the elegant pursuits of
literature ; he was ignorant of the Greek language and the
arts of rhetoric ; but, as the mind of the orator was never dis-

---

[20] Ammianus, xxvi. 1   Zosimus, l iii. p. 198 [c 36]   Philostorgius, l viii c
8, and Godefroy, Dissertat p 334.   Philostorgius, who appears to have obtained
some curious and authentic intelligence, ascribes the choice of Valentinian to the
præfect Sallust [Secundus ; not Sallust], the master-general Arintheus, Dagalaiphus
count of the domestics, and the Patrician Datianus, whose pressing recommenda-
tions from Ancyra had a weighty influence in the election.
   [21] Ammianus (xxx 7, 9), and the younger Victor [Epit. 45], have furnished the
portrait of Valentinian ; which naturally precedes and illustrates the history of his
reign.   [Additional material in Symmachus, Or. 1., cp. Appendix 1.]
   [22] [Inscription in memory of Gratian C. I L 8, 7014.]

concerted by timid perplexity, he was able, as often as the occasion prompted him, to deliver his decided sentiments with bold and ready elocution. The laws of martial discipline were the only laws that he had studied; and he was soon distinguished by the laborious diligence and inflexible severity with which he discharged and enforced the duties of the camp. In the time of Julian he provoked the danger of disgrace by the contempt which he publicly expressed for the reigning religion;[23] and it should seem from his subsequent conduct that the indiscreet and unseasonable freedom of Valentinian was the effect of military spirit rather than of Christian zeal. He was pardoned, however, and still employed by a prince who esteemed his merit ·[24] and in the various events of the Persian war he improved the reputation which he had already acquired on the banks of the Rhine. The celerity and success with which he executed an important commission recommended him to the favour of Jovian, and to the honourable command of the second *school*, or company, of Targetteers, of the domestic guards. In the march from Antioch, he had reached his quarters at Ancyra, when he was unexpectedly summoned without guilt, and without intrigue, to assume, in the forty-third year of his age, the absolute government of the Roman empire.

He is acknow-
ledged by the
army,
A D 364,
February 26
[or 25]

The invitation of the ministers and generals at Nice was of little moment, unless it were confirmed by the voice of the army. The aged Sallust, who had long observed the irregular fluctuations of popular assemblies, proposed, under pain of death, that none of those persons whose rank in the service might excite a party in their favour should appear in public, on the day of the inauguration. Yet such was the prevalence of ancient superstition that a whole day was voluntarily added to this dangerous interval, because it happened to be the intercalation of the Bissextile.[25] At length, when the hour was supposed

[23] At Antioch, where he was obliged to attend the emperor to the temple, he struck a priest, who had presumed to purify him with lustral water (Sozomen, l vi c. 6 Theodoret, l. iii c. 15 [*leg*. 12]) Such public defiance might become Valentinian; but it could leave no room for the unworthy delation of the philosopher Maximus, which supposes some more private offence (Zosimus, l iv p. 200, 201 [c. 2]).

[24] Socrates, l. iv A previous exile to Melitene, or Thebais (the first might be possible), is interposed by Sozomen (l vi c 6) and Philostorgius (l. vii. c. 7, with Godefroy's Dissertations, p 293)

[25] Ammianus, in a long, because unseasonable, digression (xxvi. 1 and Valesius ad locum), rashly supposes that he understands an astronomical question of which his readers are ignorant. It is treated with more judgment and propriety by Censorinus (de Die Natali, c 20) and Macrobius (Saturnal. l i cap. 12-16). The

to be propitious, Valentinian showed himself from a lofty tribunal; the judicious choice was applauded, and the new prince was solemnly invested with the diadem and the purple, amidst the acclamations of the troops, who were disposed in martial order round the tribunal. But, when he stretched forth his hand to address the armed multitude, a busy whisper was accidentally started in the ranks, and insensibly swelled into a loud and imperious clamour, that he should name, without delay, a colleague in the empire. The intrepid calmness of Valentinian obtained silence and commanded respect, and he thus addressed the assembly: "A few minutes since it was in *your* power, fellow-soldiers, to have left me in the obscurity of a private station. Judging, from the testimony of my past life, that I deserved to reign, you have placed me on the throne It is now *my* duty to consult the safety and interest of the republic The weight of the universe is undoubtedly too great for the hands of a feeble mortal. I am conscious of the limits of my abilities and the uncertainty of my life; and far from declining, I am anxious to solicit, the assistance of a worthy colleague. But, where discord may be fatal, the choice of a faithful friend requires mature and serious deliberation. That deliberation shall be *my* care. Let *your* conduct be dutiful and consistent. Retire to your quarters; refresh your minds and bodies; and expect the accustomed donative on the accession of a new emperor." [26] The astonished troops, with a mixture of pride, of satisfaction, and of terror, confessed the voice of their master. Their angry clamours subsided into silent reverence; and Valentinian, encompassed with the eagles of the legions and the various banners of the cavalry and infantry, was conducted, in warlike pomp, to the palace of Nice. As he was sensible, however, of the importance of preventing some rash declaration of the soldiers, he consulted the assembly of the chiefs: and their real sentiments were concisely expressed by the generous freedom of Dagalaiphus. "Most excellent prince," said that officer, "if you consider only your family, you have a brother; if you love the republic, look round for the most deserving of the Romans." [27] The emperor, who suppressed his

appellation of *Bissextile*, which marks the inauspicious year (Augustin ad Januarium, Epist 119), is derived from the *repetition* of the *sixth* day of [*i e* before] the calends of March. [Both 24th Feb. and 25th Feb. were called *A D. vi. Kal. Mart*]

[26] Valentinian's first speech is full in Ammianus (xxvi 2); concise and sententious in Philostorgius (l. viii c. 8)

[27] Si tuos amas, Imperator optime, habes fratrem; si Rempublicam, quære quem vestias. Ammian xxvi 4. In the division of the empire, Valentinian retained that sincere counsellor for himself (c 6)

and associates his
brother
Valens
A D 364,
March 28

displeasure, without altering his intention, slowly proceeded from Nice to Nicomedia and Constantinople. In one of the suburbs of that capital,[28] thirty days after his own elevation, he bestowed the title of Augustus on his brother Valens; and, as the boldest patriots were convinced that their opposition, without being serviceable to their country, would be fatal to themselves, the declaration of his absolute will was received with silent submission. Valens was now in the thirty-sixth year of his age; but his abilities had never been exercised in any employment, military or civil; and his character had not inspired the world with any sanguine expectations. He possessed, however, one quality, which recommended him to Valentinian, and preserved the domestic peace of the empire · a devout and grateful attachment to his benefactor, whose superiority of genius, as well as of authority, Valens humbly and cheerfully acknowledged in every action of his life [29]

The final
division of
the eastern
and western
empires
A D 364,
June
[July]

Before Valentinian divided the provinces, he reformed the administration of the empire. All ranks of subjects, who had been injured or oppressed under the reign of Julian, were invited to support their public accusations The silence of mankind attested the spotless integrity of the præfect Sallust;[30] and his own pressing solicitations that he might be permitted to retire from the business of the state were rejected by Valentinian with the most honourable expressions of friendship and esteem But among the favourites of the late emperor there were many who had abused his credulity or superstition, and who could no longer hope to be protected either by favour or justice.[31] The greater part of the ministers of the palace and the governors of the provinces were removed from their respective stations; yet the eminent merit of some officers was distinguished from the obnoxious crowd; and, notwithstanding the opposite clamours of zeal and resentment, the

---

[28] In suburbano, Ammianus, xxvi 4 The famous *Hebdomon*, or field of Mars, was distant from Constantinople either seven stadia or seven miles. See Valesius and his brother, ad loc , and Ducange, Const l ii p. 140, 141, 172, 173. [On the Propontis not at Blachernae, where Ducange put it See above, vol. ii. Appendix 9, p 546]

[29] Participem quidem legitimum potestatis; sed in modum apparitoris morigerum, ut progrediens aperiet textus Ammian xxvi 4 [Formally Valens was fully co-ordinate, cp Symmachus, Orat i, 11, Augustum pari iure confirmans]

[30] Notwithstanding the evidence of Zonaras, Suidas, and the Paschal Chronicle, M de Tillemont (Hist. des Empereurs, tom. v. p. 671) *wishes* to disbelieve these stories, si avantageuses à un païen

[31] Eunapius celebrates and exaggerates the sufferings of Maximus (p 82, 83 [Commelin's ed 1616; p 102, ed 1596]); yet he allows that this sophist or magician, the guilty favourite of Julian and the personal enemy of Valentinian, was dismissed on the payment of a small fine.

whole proceedings of this delicate inquiry appear to have been conducted with a reasonable share of wisdom and moderation.[32] The festivity of a new reign received a short and suspicious interruption from the sudden illness of the two princes ; but, as soon as their health was restored, they left Constantinople in the beginning of the spring. In the castle or palace of Mediana, only three miles from Naissus, they executed the solemn and final division of the Roman empire [33] Valentinian bestowed on his brother the rich præfecture of the *East*, from the Lower Danube to the confines of Persia ; whilst he reserved for his immediate government the warlike præfectures of *Illyricum, Italy* and *Gaul*, from the extremity of Greece to the Caledonian rampart ; and from the rampart of Caledonia to the foot of Mount Atlas. The provincial administration remained on its former basis, but a double supply of generals and magistrates was required for two councils and two courts : the division was made with a just regard to their peculiar merit and situation, and seven master-generals were soon created, either of the cavalry or infantry. When this important business had been amicably transacted, Valentinian and Valens embraced for the last time. The emperor of the West established his temporary residence at Milan ; and the emperor of the East returned to Constantinople, to assume the dominion of fifty provinces, of whose language he was totally ignorant [34]

The tranquillity of the East was soon disturbed by rebellion ; and the throne of Valens was threatened by the daring attempts of a rival, whose affinity to the Emperor Julian [35] was his sole merit, and had been his only crime. Procopius had been hastily promoted from the obscure station of a tribune and a notary to the joint command of the army of Mesopotamia ; the public opinion already named him as the successor of a prince who was destitute of natural heirs ; and a vain rumour was propagated by his friends, or his enemies, that Julian, before the altar of the Moon, at Carrhæ, had privately invested Procopius with the

Revolt of Procopius A D 365, September 28

[32] The loose assertions of a general disgrace (Zosimus, l iv p. 201 [c 2]) are detected and refuted by Tillemont (tom v p 21)

[33] Ammianus, xxvi 5

[34] Ammianus says, in general terms, subagrestis ingenii, nec bellicis nec liberalibus studiis eruditus. Ammian xxxi. 14. The orator Themistius, with the genuine impertinence of a Greek, wished for the first time to speak the Latin language, the dialect of his sovereign, την διάλεκτον κρατούσαν Orat vi. p. 71.

[35] The uncertain degree of alliance, or consanguinity, is expressed by the words ἀνεψιός, cognatus, consobrinus (see Valesius ad Ammian xxiii 3) The mother of Procopius might be a sister of Basilina and Count Julian, the mother and uncle of the apostate. Ducange, Fam Byzantin. p 49.

Imperial purple.[36]   He endeavoured, by his dutiful and submissive behaviour, to disarm the jealousy of Jovian ; resigned,
without a contest, his military command ; and retired, with his
wife and family, to cultivate the ample patrimony which he
possessed in the province of Cappadocia   These useful and
innocent occupations were interrupted by the appearance of an
officer, with a band of soldiers, who, in the name of his new
sovereigns, Valentinian and Valens, was dispatched to conduct
the unfortunate Procopius either to a perpetual prison or an
ignominious death. His presence of mind procured him a longer
respite and a more splendid fate. Without presuming to dispute the royal mandate, he requested the indulgence of a few
moments to embrace his weeping family ; and, while the
vigilance of his guards was relaxed by a plentiful entertainment, he dexterously escaped to the sea-coast of the Euxine,
from whence he passed over to the country of Bosphorus.   In
that sequestered region he remained many months, exposed to
the hardships of exile, of solitude, and of want : his melancholy
temper brooding over his misfortunes, and his mind agitated by
the just apprehension that, if any accident should discover his
name, the faithless Barbarians would violate, without much
scruple, the laws of hospitality. In a moment of impatience
and despair, Procopius embarked in a merchant vessel, which
made sail for Constantinople ; and boldly aspired to the rank of
a sovereign, because he was not allowed to enjoy the security
of a subject. At first he lurked in the villages of Bithynia,
continually changing his habitation, and his disguise.[37] By
degrees he ventured into the capital, trusted his life and fortune
to the fidelity of two friends, a senator and an eunuch, and
conceived some hopes of success from the intelligence which he
obtained of the actual state of public affairs. The body of the
people was infected with a spirit of discontent: they regretted
the justice and the abilities of Sallust, who had been imprudently
dismissed from the præfecture of the East. They despised the
character of Valens, which was rude without vigour and feeble
without mildness. They dreaded the influence of his father-in-

[36] Ammian xxiii 3, xxvi 6   He mentions the report with much hesitation ·
susurravit obscurior fama ; nemo enim dicti auctor exstitit verus   It serves, however, to mark that Procopius was a pagan   Yet his religion does not appear to
have promoted, or obstructed, his pretensions.

[37] One of his retreats was a country-house of Eunomius, the heretic. The
master was absent, innocent, ignorant ; yet he narrowly escaped a sentence of
death, and was banished into the remote parts of Mauritania (Philostorg l iv. c,
5, 8, and Godefroy's Dissert p 369-378)

law, the Patrician Petronius, a crue. and rapacious minister, who rigorously exacted all the arrears of tribute that might remain unpaid since the reign of the emperor Aurelian. The circumstances were propitious to the designs of an usurper. The hostile measures of the Persians required the presence of Valens in Syria; from the Danube to the Euphrates the troops were in motion; and the capital was occasionally filled with the soldiers who passed, or repassed, the Thracian Bosphorus. Two cohorts of Gauls were persuaded to listen to the secret proposals of the conspirators; which were recommended by the promise of a liberal donative; and, as they still revered the memory of Julian, they easily consented to support the hereditary claim of his proscribed kinsman. At the dawn of day they were drawn up near the baths of Anastasia; [38] and Procopius, clothed in a purple garment, more suitable to a player than to a monarch, appeared, as if he rose from the dead, in the midst of Constantinople. The soldiers, who were prepared for his reception, saluted their trembling prince with shouts of joy and vows of fidelity. Their numbers were soon increased by a sturdy band of peasants, collected from the adjacent country; and Procopius, shielded by the arms of his adherents, was successively conducted to the tribunal, the senate, and the palace. During the first moments of his tumultuous reign, he was astonished and terrified by the gloomy silence of the people; who were either ignorant of the cause or apprehensive of the event. But his military strength was superior to any actual resistance · the malcontents flocked to the standard of rebellion; the poor were excited by the hopes, and the rich were intimidated by the fear, of a general pillage; and the obstinate credulity of the multitude was once more deceived by the promised advantages of a revolution. The magistrates were seized; the prisons and arsenals broke open; the gates, and the entrance of the harbour, were diligently occupied; and, in a few hours, Procopius became the absolute, though precarious, master of the Imperial city. The usurper improved this unexpected success with some degree of courage and dexterity He artfully propagated the rumours and opinions the most favourable to his interest; while he deluded the populace by giving audience to the frequent, but imaginary, ambassadors of distant nations. The large bodies of troops stationed in the cities of Thrace and the fortresses of the Lower Danube were gradually involved in the guilt of rebellion:

---

[38] [Sister of Constantius The site seems not to have been determined.]

and the Gothic princes consented to supply the sovereign of Constantinople with the formidable strength of several thousand auxiliaries. His generals passed the Bosphorus, and subdued, without an effort, the unarmed but wealthy provinces of Bithynia and Asia. After an honourable defence, the city and island of Cyzicus yielded to his power; the renowned legions of the Jovians and Herculians embraced the cause of the usurper whom they were ordered to crush; and, as the veterans were continually augmented with new levies, he soon appeared at the head of an army whose valour, as well as numbers, were not unequal to the greatness of the contest The son of Hormisdas,[39] a youth of spirit and ability, condescended to draw his sword against the lawful emperor of the East; and the Persian prince was immediately invested with the ancient and extraordinary powers of a Roman Proconsul. The alliance of Faustina, the widow of the emperor Constantius, who intrusted herself and her daughter to the hands of the usurper, added dignity and reputation to his cause. The princess Constantia, who was then about five years of age, accompanied in a litter the march of the army. She was shewn to the multitude in the arms of her adopted father; and, as often as she passed through the ranks, the tenderness of the soldiers was inflamed into martial fury:[40] they recollected the glories of the house of Constantine, and they declared, with loyal acclamation, that they would shed the last drop of their blood in the defence of the royal infant.[41]

In the meanwhile, Valentinian was alarmed and perplexed by the doubtful intelligence of the revolt of the East The difficulties of a German war forced him to confine his immediate care to the safety of his own dominions; and, as every channel of communication was stopt or corrupted, he listened, with doubtful anxiety, to the rumours which were industriously spread, that the defeat and death of Valens had left Procopius

Marginal notes:
[Nov, Dec]
[Jovii et victores]
His defeat and death. A D 366, May 28 [leg 27]

---

[39] Hormisdæ maturo juveni, Hormisdæ regalis illius filio, potestatem Proconsulis detulit; et civilia, more veterum, et bella recturo. Ammian xxvi. 8. The Persian prince escaped with honour and safety, and was afterwards (A D. 380) restored to the same extraordinary office of proconsul of Bithynia (Tillemont, Hist. des Empercurs, tom. v. p. 204). I am ignorant whether the race of Sassan was propagated I find (A D. 514) a pope Hormisdas; but he was a native of Frusino, in Italy (Pagi, Brev. Pontific. tom 1 p. 247).

[40] The infant rebel was afterwards the wife of the Emperor Gratian; but she died young and childless See Ducange, Fam Byzantin p 48, 59

[41] Sequimini culminis summi prosapiam was the language of Procopius, who affected to despise the obscure birth and fortuitous election of the upstart Pannonian. Ammian. xxvi 7.

sole master of the eastern provinces Valens was not dead.
but, on the news of the rebellion, which he received at Cæsarea,
he basely despaired of his life and fortune ; proposed to negotiate with the usurper, and discovered his secret inclination
to abdicate the Imperial purple.   The timid monarch was
saved from disgrace and ruin by the firmness of his ministers,
and their abilities soon decided in his favour the event of the
civil war.   In a season of tranquillity, Sallust had resigned
without a murmur ; but, as soon as the public safety was attacked, he ambitiously solicited the pre-eminence of toil and
danger ; and the restoration of that virtuous minister to the
præfecture of the East was the first step which indicated the
repentance of Valens and satisfied the minds of the people.
The reign of Procopius was apparently supported by powerful
armies and obedient provinces.   But many of the principal
officers, military as well as civil, had been urged, either by
motives of duty or interest, to withdraw themselves from the
guilty scene ; or to watch the moment of betraying and deserting the cause of the usurper.   Lupicinus advanced, by hasty
marches, to bring the legions of Syria to the aid of Valens.
Arintheus, who, in strength, beauty, and valour, excelled all
the heroes of the age, attacked with a small troop a superior
body of the rebels   When he beheld the faces of the soldiers
who had served under his banner, he commanded them, with a
loud voice, to seize and deliver up their pretended leader ; and
such was the ascendant of his genius that this extraordinary
order was instantly obeyed.[42]   Arbetio, a respectable veteran of
the great Constantine, who had been distinguished by the
honours of the consulship, was persuaded to leave his retirement, and once more to conduct an army into the field.   In the
heat of action, calmly taking off his helmet, he shewed his
grey hairs, and venerable countenance ; saluted the soldiers of
Procopius by the endearing names of children and companions,
and exhorted them, no longer to support the desperate cause of
a contemptible tyrant ; but to follow their old commander, who
had so often led them to honour and victory.   In the two

---

[42] Et dedignatus hominem superare certamine despicabilem, auctoritatis et
celsi fiduciâ corporis, ipsis hostibus jussit suum vincire rectorem · atque ita
turmarum antesignanus umbratilis comprensus suorum manibus. The strength
and beauty of Arintheus, the new Hercules, are celebrated by St. Basil, who
supposes that God had created him as an inimitable model of the human species
The painters and sculptors could not express his figure the historians appeared
fabulous when they related his exploits (Ammian. xxvi [8] and Vales. ad loc).

engagements of Thyatıra [43] ana Nacolia, the unfortunate Procopius was deserted by his troops, who were seduced by the
instructions and example of their perfidious officers. After
wandering some time among the woods and mountains of
Phrygia, he was betrayed by his desponding followers, conducted
to the Imperial camp, and immediately beheaded. He suffered
the ordinary fate of an unsuccessful usurper; but the acts of
cruelty which were exercised by the conqueror, under the forms
of legal justice, excited the pity and indignation of mankind.[44]

Severe in-
quisition
into the
crime of
magic at
Rome and
Antioch
A.D. 373,
&c.

Such indeed are the common and natural fruits of despotism
and rebellion. But the inquisition into the crime of magic,
which, under the reign of the two brothers, was so rigorously
prosecuted both at Rome and Antioch, was interpreted as the
fatal symptom either of the displeasure of heaven or of the depravity of mankind.[45] Let us not hesitate to indulge a liberal
pride that in the present age the enlightened part of Europe
has abolished [46] a cruel and odious prejudice, which reigned in
every climate of the globe and adhered to every system of
religious opinions.[47] The nations and the sects of the Roman
world admitted with equal credulity and similar abhorrence the
reality of that infernal art [48] which was able to control the

[43] The same field of battle is placed by Ammianus in Lycia, and by Zosimus
at Thyatira, which are at the distance of 150 miles from each other   But Thyatira
alluitur *Lyco* (Plin. Hist Natur. v 31   Cellarius, Geograph Antiq. t. ii. p 79);
and the transcribers might easily convert an obscure river into a well-known
province   [Ammianus does not mention the battle of Thyatira, and merely says
ire tendebat ad Lyciam   Nacolia is now Seidi Ghazi]

[44] The adventures, usurpation, and fall of Procopius are related, in a regular
series, by Ammianus (xxvi. 6, 7, 8, 9, 10) and Zosimus (l. iv p. 203-210 [c 4-8]).
They often illustrate, and seldom contradict, each other   Themistius (Orat. vii p
91, 95) adds some base panegyric ; and Eunapius (p 83, 84 [Muller iv. p 26, 27])
some malicious satire   [For date of defeat see Idatius Fast cons , ed Mommsen,
Chron. Min 1 p 241   See also account in Symmachus, Or 1 17 *sqq*]

[45] Libanius de ulciscend Julian nece, c ix p 158, 159. The sophist deplores
the public frenzy, but he does not (after their deaths) impeach the justice of the
emperors   [Milman observes, "The persecution against philosophers and their
libraries was carried on with so much fury that from this time (A D 374) the
names of the Gentile philosophers became almost extinct, and the Christian philosophy and religion, especially in the East, established their ascendancy"]

[46] The French and English lawyers of the present age allow the *theory*, and
deny the *practice*, of witchcraft   Denisart, Recueil des Décisions de Jurisprudence,
au mot *Sorciers*, t iv. p 553   Blackstone's Commentaries, vol. iv p 60. As
private reason always prevents or outstrips public wisdom, the presiden· Montesquieu (Esprit des Loix, l xii. c 5, 6) rejects the *existence* of magic.

[47] See Oeuvres de Bayle, tom. iii p 567-589   The sceptic of Rotterdam exhibits, according to his custom, a strange medley of loose knowledge and lively wit.

[48] The pagans distinguished between good and bad magic, the Theurgic and
the Goetic (Hist de l'Académie, &c., t vii p 25)   But they could not have
defended this obscure distinction against the acute logic of Bayle   In the Jewish
and Christian system *all* demons are infernal spirits, and *all* commerce with them
is idolatry, apostacy, &c , which deserves death and damnation   [For ancient
magic, consult L F. A Maury, La magie et l'astrologie dans l'antiquité, 1860]

eternal order of the planets and the voluntary operations of the human mind. They dreaded the mysterious power of spells and incantations, of potent herbs, and execrable rites; which could extinguish or recall life, inflame the passions of the soul, blast the works of creation, and extort from the reluctant demons the secrets of futurity They believed, with the wildest inconsistency, that this preternatural dominion of the air, of earth, and of hell, was exercised, from the vilest motives of malice or gain, by some wrinkled hags and itinerant sorcerers, who passed their obscure lives in penury and contempt [49] The arts of magic were equally condemned by the public opinion and by the laws of Rome; but, as they tended to gratify the most imperious passions of the heart of man, they were continually proscribed, and continually practised.[50] An imaginary cause is capable of producing the most serious and mischievous effects. The dark predictions of the death of an emperor, or the success of a conspiracy, were calculated only to stimulate the hopes of ambition and to dissolve the ties of fidelity; and the intentional guilt of magic was aggravated by the actual crimes of treason and sacrilege.[51] Such vain terrors disturbed the peace of society and the happiness of individuals; and the harmless flame which insensibly melted a waxen image might derive a powerful and pernicious energy from the affrighted fancy of the person whom it was maliciously designed to represent.[52] From the infusion of those herbs which were

[49] The Candia of Horace (Carm 1 v. od. 5 with Dacier's and Sanadon's illustrations) is a vulgar witch The Erichtho of Lucan (Pharsal vi 430-830) is tedious, disgusting, but sometimes sublime She chides the delay of the Furies, and threatens, with tremendous obscurity, to pronounce their real names, to reveal the true infernal countenance of Hecate, to invoke the secret powers that lie *below* hell, &c.

[50] Genus hominum potentibus infidum, sperantibus fallax, quod in civitate nostrâ et vetabitur semper et retinebitur. Tacit Hist. i. 22. See Augustin. de Civitate Dei, l. viii c. 19, and the Theodosian Code, l. ix. tit. xvi. with Godefroy's Commentary.

[51] The persecution of Antioch was occasioned by a criminal consultation. The twenty-four letters of the alphabet were arranged round a magic tripod; and a dancing ring, which had been placed in the centre, pointed to the first four letters in the name of the future emperor, Θ. E O Δ. Theodorus (perhaps with many others who owned the fatal syllables) was executed. Theodosius succeeded. Lardner (Heathen Testimonies, vol iv p. 353-372) has copiously and fairly examined this dark transaction of the reign of Valens.

[52] Limus ut hic durescit, et hæc ut cera liquescit
    Uno eodemque igni———— Virgil. Bucolic viii. 80
    Devovet absentes, simulacraque cerea figit
            Ovid. in Epist Hypsip ad Jason [Her. vi.] 91.
Such vain incantations could affect the mind and increase the disease of Germanicus. Tacit. Annal ii 69.

supposed to possess a supernatural influence it was an easy step
to the use of more substantial poison ; and the folly of mankind
sometimes became the instrument, and the mask, of the most
atrocious crimes. As soon as the zeal of informers was encouraged by the ministers of Valens and Valentinian, they could
not refuse to listen to another charge, too frequently mingled
in the scenes of domestic guilt ; a charge of a softer and less
malignant nature, for which the pious, though excessive, rigour
of Constantine had recently decreed the punishment of death.[53]
This deadly and incoherent mixture of treason and magic, of
poison and adultery, afforded infinite gradations of guilt and
innocence, of excuse and aggravation, which in these proceedings
appear to have been confounded by the angry or corrupt
passions of the judges.   They easily discovered that the degree
of their industry and discernment was estimated, by the Imperial court, according to the number of executions that were
furnished from their respective tribunals.   It was not without
extreme reluctance that they pronounced a sentence of ac-
quittal ; but they eagerly admitted such evidence as was stained
with perjury, or procured by torture, to prove the most improbable charges against the most respectable characters.   The
progress of the inquiry continually opened new subjects of criminal prosecution ; the audacious informer, whose falsehood was
detected, retired with impunity ; but the wretched victim, who
discovered his real or pretended accomplices, was seldom permitted to receive the price of his infamy.   From the extremity
of Italy and Asia, the young and the aged were dragged in
chains to the tribunals of Rome and Antioch.   Senators,
matrons, and philosophers expired in ignominious and cruel
tortures   The soldiers, who were appointed to guard the
prisons, declared, with a murmur of pity and indignation, that
their numbers were insufficient to oppose the flight or resistance
of the multitude of captives.   The wealthiest families were
ruined by fines and confiscations ; the most innocent citizens
trembled for their safety ; and we may form some notion of
the magnitude of the evil from the extravagant assertion of an
ancient writer that, in the obnoxious provinces, the prisoners,
the exiles, and the fugitives formed the greatest part of the
inhabitants.[54]

[53] See Heineccius Antiquitat. Juris Roman. tom. ii. p. 353, &c.   Cod Theodosian l. ix tit 7 with Godefroy's Commentary
[54] The cruel persecution of Rome and Antioch is described, and most probably
exaggerated, by Ammianus (xxviii 1, xxix. 1, 2), and Zosimus (l. iv p 216-218

When Tacitus describes the deaths of the innocent and illustrious Romans, who were sacrificed to the cruelty of the first Cæsars, the art of the historian, or the merit of the sufferers, excite in our breasts the most lively sensations of terror, of admiration, and of pity. The coarse and undistinguishing pencil of Ammianus has delineated his bloody figures with tedious and disgusting accuracy. But, as our attention is no longer engaged by the contrast of freedom and servitude, of recent greatness and of actual misery, we should turn with horror from the frequent executions which disgraced, both at Rome and Antioch, the reign of the two brothers.[55] Valens was of a timid,[56] and Valentinian of a choleric, disposition.[57] An anxious regard to his personal safety was the ruling principle of the administration of Valens. In the condition of a subject, he had kissed, with trembling awe, the hand of the oppressor; and, when he ascended the throne, he reasonably expected that the same fears which had subdued his own mind would secure the patient submission of his people. The favourites of Valens obtained, by the privilege of rapine and confiscation, the wealth which his economy would have refused.[58] They urged, with persuasive eloquence, *that*, in all cases of treason, suspicion is equivalent to proof; *that* the power, supposes the intention, of mischief, *that* the intention is not less criminal than the act, and *that* a subject no longer deserves to live, if his life may threaten the safety, or disturb the repose, of his sovereign. The judgment of Valentinian was sometimes deceived and his confidence abused; but he would have silenced the informers with a contemptuous smile, had they presumed to alarm his fortitude by the sound of danger. They

(margin note: The cruelty of Valentinian and Valens A.D 364-375*)*

[c. 13]). The philosopher Maximus, with some justice, was involved in the charge of magic (Eunapius in Vit Sophist. p. 88, 89 [ed Commelin, 1616]); and young Chrysostom, who had accidently found one of the proscribed books, gave himself for lost Tillemont, Hist. des Empereurs, tom v p 340

[55] Consult the six last books of Ammianus, and more particularly the portraits of the two royal brothers (xxv. 8, 9, xxxi. 14). Tillemont has collected (tom. v. p. 12-18, p. 127-133) from all antiquity their virtues and vices

[56] The younger Victor asserts [Epit. 46] that he was valde timidus yet he behaved, as almost every man would do, with decent resolution at the *head* of an army. The same historian attempts to prove that his anger was harmless Ammianus observes [31, 14] with more candour and judgment, incidentia crimina ad contemptam vel læsam principis amplitudinem trahens, in sanguinem sæviebat.

[57] Cum esset ad acerbitatem naturæ calore propensior . poenas per ignes augebat et gladios. Ammian. xxv 8. See xxvii. 7

[58] I have transferred the reproach of avarice from Valens to his servants. Avarice more properly belongs to ministers than to kings; in whom that passion is commonly extinguished by absolute possession.

praised his inflexible love of justice; and, in the pursuit of justice, the emperor was easily tempted to consider clemency as a weakness and passion as a virtue. As long as he wrestled with his equals, in the bold competition of an active and ambitious life, Valentinian was seldom injured, and never insulted, with impunity if his prudence was arraigned, his spirit was applauded, and the proudest and most powerful generals were apprehensive of provoking the resentment of a fearless soldier. After he became master of the world, he unfortunately forgot that, where no resistance can be made, no courage can be exerted; and, instead of consulting the dictates of reason and magnanimity, he indulged the furious emotions of his temper at a time when they were disgraceful to himself and fatal to the defenceless objects of his displeasure. In the government of his household, or of his empire, slight, or even imaginary, offences, a hasty word, a casual omission, an involuntary delay, were chastised by a sentence of immediate death. The expressions which issued the most readily from the mouth of the emperor of the West were, "Strike off his head"; "Burn him alive"; "Let him be beaten with clubs till he expires";[59] and his most favoured ministers soon understood that, by a rash attempt to dispute, or suspend, the execution of his sanguinary commands, they might involve themselves in the guilt and punishment of disobedience. The repeated gratification of this savage justice hardened the mind of Valentinian against pity and remorse, and the sallies of passion were confirmed by the habits of cruelty.[60] He could behold with calm satisfaction the convulsive agonies of torture and death: he reserved his friendship for those faithful servants whose temper was the most congenial to his own. The merit of Maximin, who had slaughtered the noblest families of Rome, was rewarded with the royal approbation and the præfecture of Gaul. Two fierce and enormous bears, distinguished by the appellations of *Innocence* and *Mica Aurea*, could alone deserve to share the favour

---

[59] He sometimes expressed a sentence of death with a tone of pleasantry: "Abi, Comes, et muta ei caput, qui sibi mutari provinciam cupit". A boy, who had slipped too hastily a Spartan hound; an armourer, who had made a polished cuirass that wanted some grains of the legitimate weight, &c, were the victims of his fury.

[60] The innocents of Milan were an agent and three apparitors, whom Valentinian condemned for signifying a legal summons   Ammianus (xxvii. 7) strangely supposes that all who had been unjustly executed were worshipped as martyrs by the Christians. His impartial silence does not allow us to believe that the great chamberlain Rhodanus was burnt alive for an act of oppression (Chron Paschal p. 302 [i. 558, ed Bonn])

of Maximin. The cages of those trusty guards were always placed near the bed-chamber of Valentinian, who frequently amused his eyes with the grateful spectacle of seeing them tear and devour the bleeding limbs of the malefactors who were abandoned to their rage. Their diet and exercises were carefully inspected by the Roman emperor; and, when *Innocence* had earned her discharge by a long course of meritorious service, the faithful animal was again restored to the freedom of her native woods.[61]

But in the calmer moments of reflection, when the mind of Valens was not agitated by fear, or that of Valentinian by rage, the tyrant resumed the sentiments, or at least the conduct, of the father of his country. The dispassionate judgment of the Western emperor could clearly perceive, and accurately pursue, his own and the public interest; and the sovereign of the East, who imitated with equal docility the various examples which he received from his elder brother, was sometimes guided by the wisdom and virtue of the præfect Sallust. Both princes invariably retained, in the purple, the chaste and temperate simplicity which had adorned their private life; and, under their reign, the pleasures of the court never cost the people a blush or a sigh. They gradually reformed many of the abuses of the times of Constantius, judiciously adopted and improved the designs of Julian and his successor; and displayed a style and spirit of legislation which might inspire posterity with the most favourable opinion of their character and government. It is not from the master of *Innocence* that we should expect the tender regard for the welfare of his subjects which prompted Valentinian to condemn the exposition of new-born infants;[62] and to establish fourteen skilful physicians, with stipends and privileges, in the fourteen quarters of Rome. The good sense of an illiterate soldier founded an useful and liberal institution for the education of youth, and the support of declining science.[63] It was his intention that the arts of rhetoric

Their laws and government

[61] Ut bene meritam in silvas jussit abiri *Innoxiam.* Ammian xix 3, and Valesius ad locum

[62] See the Code of Justinian, l viii. tit lii. leg 2   Unusquisque sobolem suam nutriat.   Quod si exponendam putaverit animadversioni quæ constituta est subjacebit   For the present I shall not interfere in the dispute between Noodt and Bankershoek; how far, or how long, this unnatural practice had been condemned or abolished by law, philosophy, and the more civilized state of society. [C. Theod ix 14, 1]

[63] These salutary institutions are explained in the Theodosian Code, l. xiii t. iii. *De professoribus et Medicis*, and l xiv. tit. ix. *De Studiis liberalibus Urbis Romæ.* Besides our usual guide (Godefroy), we may consult Giannone (Istoria di Napoli. tom. 1 p 105-111), who has treated the interesting subject with the zeal and curiosity of a man of letters who studies his domestic history

and grammar should be taught in the Greek and Latin
languages in the metropolis of every province; and as the
size and dignity of the school was usually proportioned to the
importance of the city, the academies of Rome and Constantinople claimed a just and singular pre-eminence. The fragments of the literary edicts of Valentinian imperfectly represent
the school of Constantinople, which was gradually improved by
subsequent regulations.   That school consisted of thirty-one
professors in different branches of learning.   One philosopher,
and two lawyers; five sophists and ten grammarians for the
Greek, and three orators and ten grammarians for the Latin
tongue; besides seven scribes, or, as they were then styled,
antiquarians, whose laborious pens supplied the public library
with fair and correct copies of the classic writers. The rule of
conduct, which was prescribed to the students, is the more
curious, as it affords the first outlines of the form and discipline
of a modern university.   It was required that they should
bring proper certificates from the magistrates of their native
province. Their names, professions, and places of abode were
regularly entered in a public register   The studious youth
were severely prohibited from wasting their time in feasts or
in the theatre; and the term of their education was limited to
the age of twenty. The præfect of the city was empowered
to chastise the idle and refractory, by stripes or expulsion; and
he was directed to make an annual report to the master of the
offices, that the knowledge and abilities of the scholars might
be usefully applied to the public service. The institutions of
Valentinian contributed to secure the benefits of peace and
plenty; and the cities were guarded by the establishment of
the *Defensors*,[64] freely elected as the tribunes and advocates
of the people, to support their rights and to expose their
grievances before the tribunals of the civil magistrates, or even
at the foot of the Imperial throne. The finances were diligently
administered by two princes, who had been so long accustomed
to the rigid economy of a private fortune; but in the receipt
and application of the revenue a discerning eye might observe
some difference between the government of the East and of
the West. Valens was persuaded that royal liberality can be
supplied only by public oppression, and his ambition never
aspired to secure, by their actual distress, the future strength

[64] Cod Theodos 1 1 tit xi with Godefroy's *Paratitlon*, which diligently gleans
from the rest of the code.

and prosperity of his people.   Instead of increasing the weight of taxes, which, in the space of forty years, had been gradually doubled, he reduced, in the first years of his reign, one-fourth of the tribute of the East.[65]   Valentinian appears to have been less attentive and less anxious to relieve the burthens of his people.   He might reform the abuses of the fiscal administration; but he exacted, without scruple, a very large share of the private property; as he was convinced that the revenues, which supported the luxury of individuals, would be much more advantageously employed for the defence and improvement of the state   The subjects of the East, who enjoyed the present benefit, applauded the indulgence of their prince.   The solid, but less splendid, merit of Valentinian was felt and acknowledged by the subsequent generation [6]

But the most honourable circumstance of the character of Valentinian is the firm and temperate impartiality which he uniformly preserved in an age of religious contention.   His strong sense, unenlightened, but uncorrupted, by study, declined, with respectful indifference, the subtle questions of theological debate   The government of the *Earth* claimed his vigilance and satisfied his ambition, and, while he remembered that he was the disciple of the church, he never forgot that he was the sovereign of the clergy.   Under the reign of an apostate, he had signalised his zeal for the honour of Christianity: he allowed to his subjects the privilege which he had assumed for himself; and they might accept, with gratitude and confidence, the general toleration which was granted by a prince addicted to passion, but incapable of fear or of disguise.[67] The Pagans, the Jews, and all the various sects which acknowledged the divine authority of Christ were protected by the laws from arbitrary power or popular insult: nor was any mode

Valentinian maintains the religious toleration A.D 364-375

[65] Three lines from Ammianus (xxvi 14) countenance a whole oration of Themistius (viii p. 101-120), full of adulation, pedantry, and common-place morality.   The eloquent M Thomas (tom i. p 366-396) has amused himself with celebrating the virtues and genius of Themistius, who was not unworthy of the age in which he lived

[66] Zosimus, l. iv. p. 202 [c. 3]   Ammian xxv 9   His reformation of costly abuses might entitle him to the praise of: in provinciales admodum parcus, tributorum ubique molliens sarcinas   By some, his frugality was styled avarice (Jerom Chron. p. 186)

[67] Testes sunt leges a me in exordio Imperii mei datæ: quibus unicuique quod animo imbibisset colendi libera facultas tributa est   Cod Theodos l. ix tit xvi leg 9.   To this declaration of Valentinian we may add the various testimonies of Ammianus (xxx 9), Zosimus (l iv. p. 204 [c 3]), and Sozomen (l vi. c.7, 21) Baronius would naturally blame such rational toleration (Annal Eccles. A.D. 370, No. 129-132, A.D. 376, No. 3, 4).

of worship prohibited by Valentinian, except those secret and
criminal practices which abused the name of religion for the
dark purposes of vice and disorder. The art of magic, as it
was more cruelly punished, was more strictly proscribed; but
the emperor admitted a formal distinction to protect the
ancient methods of divination, which were approved by the
senate and exercised by the Tuscan haruspices He had
condemned, with the consent of the most rational Pagans,
the licence of nocturnal sacrifices; but he immediately admitted
the petition of Prætextatus, proconsul of Achaia, who represented that the life of the Greeks would become dreary and
comfortless, if they were deprived of the invaluable blessing
of the Eleusinian mysteries. Philosophy alone can boast (and
perhaps it is no more than the boast of philosophy), that her
gentle hand is able to eradicate from the human mind the latent
and deadly principle of fanaticism. But this truce of twelve
years, which was enforced by the wise and vigorous government
of Valentinian, by suspending the repetition of mutual injuries,
contributed to soften the manners, and abate the prejudices,
of the religious factions.

Valens pro-
fesses Arian-
ism, and
persecutes
the Catho-
lics
A.D 367-378

The friend of toleration was unfortunately placed at a distance
from the scene of the fiercest controversies. As soon as the
Christians of the West had extricated themselves from the
snares of the creed of Rimini, they happily relapsed into the
slumber of orthodoxy; and the small remains of the Arian party
that still subsisted at Sirmium or Milan might be considered
rather as objects of contempt than of resentment But in the
provinces of the East, from the Euxine to the extremity of
Thebais, the strength and numbers of the hostile factions were
more equally balanced: and this equality, instead of recommending the counsels of peace, served only to perpetuate the
horrors of religious war. The monks and bishops supported
their arguments by invectives; and their invectives were sometimes followed by blows. Athanasius still reigned at Alexandria;
the thrones of Constantinople and Antioch were occupied by
Arian prelates, and every episcopal vacancy was the occasion
of a popular tumult The Homoousians were fortified by the
reconciliation of fifty-nine Macedonian, or Semi-Arian, bishops;
but their secret reluctance to embrace the divinity of the Holy
Ghost clouded the splendour of the triumph . and the declaration of Valens, who, in the first years of his reign, had imitated
the impartial conduct of his brother, was an important victory
on the side of Arianism. The two brothers had passed their

private life in the condition of catechumens; but the piety of Valens prompted him to solicit the sacrament of baptism, before he exposed his person to the dangers of a Gothic war. He naturally addressed himself to Eudoxus,[68] bishop of the Imperial city; and, if the ignorant monarch was instructed by that Arian pastor in the principles of heterodox theology, his misfortune, rather than his guilt, was the inevitable consequence of his erroneous choice. Whatever had been the determination of the emperor, he must have offended a numerous party of his Christian subjects, as the leaders both of the Homoousians and of the Arians believed that, if they were not suffered to reign, they were most cruelly injured and oppressed. After he had taken this decisive step, it was extremely difficult for him to preserve either the virtue or the reputation of impartiality. He never aspired, like Constantius, to the fame of a profound theologian; but, as he had received with simplicity and respect the tenets of Eudoxus, Valens resigned his conscience to the direction of his ecclesiastical guides, and promoted, by the influence of his authority, the re-union of the *Athanasian heretics* to the body of the catholic church. At first, he pitied their blindness, by degrees he was provoked at their obstinacy; and he insensibly hated those sectaries to whom he was an object of hatred.[69] The feeble mind of Valens was always swayed by the persons with whom he familiarly conversed; and the exile or imprisonment of a private citizen are the favours the most readily granted in a despotic court. Such punishments were frequently inflicted on the leaders of the Homoousian party; and the misfortune of fourscore ecclesiastics of Constantinople, who, perhaps accidentally, were burnt on shipboard, was imputed to the cruel and premeditated malice of the emperor and his Arian ministers. In every contest, the catholics (if we may anticipate that name) were obliged to pay the penalty of their own faults, and of those of their adversaries. In every election, the claims of the Arian candidate obtained the preference; and, if they were opposed by the majority of the people, he was usually supported by the authority of the civil magistrate, or even by the terrors of a military force. The enemies of Athanasius attempted to disturb

---

[68] Eudoxus was of a mild and timid disposition. When he baptised Valens (A.D. 367), he must have been extremely old, since he had studied theology fifty-five years before, under Lucian, a learned and pious martyr. Philostorg. l. ii. c. 14-16, l. iv. c. 4, with Godefroy, p. 82, 206, and Tillemont, Mém. Eccles. tom. v. p. 474-480, &c

[69] Gregory Nazianzen (Orat. xxv [=33] p. 432 [ap. Migne, vol. 36, p. 217 *sqq.*]) insults the persecuting spirit of the Arians, as an infallible symptom of error and heresy

the last years of his venerable age , and his temporary retreat to his father's sepulchre has been celebrated as a fifth exile. But the zeal of a great people who instantly flew to arms, intimidated the præfect , and the archbishop was permitted to end his life in peace and in glory, after a reign of forty-seven years.

Death of
Athanasius
A.D. 373,
May 2 The death of Athanasius was the signal of the persecution of Egypt ; and the Pagan minister of Valens, who forcibly seated the worthless Lucius on the archiepiscopal throne, purchased the favour of the reigning party by the blood and sufferings of their Christian brethren.   The free toleration of the heathen and Jewish worship was bitterly lamented, as a circumstance which aggravated the misery of the catholics and the guilt of the impious tyrant of the East.[70]

Just idea of
his perse
cution The triumph of the orthodox party has left a deep stain of persecution on the memory of Valens ; and the character of a prince who derived his virtues, as well as his vices, from a feeble understanding and a pusillanimous temper scarcely deserves the labour of an apology. Yet candour may discover some reasons to suspect that the ecclesiastical ministers of Valens often exceeded the orders, or even the intentions, of their master ; and that the real measure of facts has been very liberally magnified by the vehement declamation and easy credulity of his antagonists [71] 1.   The silence of Valentinian may suggest a probable argument, that the partial severities, which were exercised in the name and provinces of his colleague, amounted only to some obscure and inconsiderable deviations from the established system of religious toleration : and the judicious historian, who has praised the equal temper of the elder brother, has not thought himself obliged to contrast the tranquillity of the West with the cruel persecution of the East.[72] 2. Whatever credit may be allowed to vague and distant reports, the character, or at least the behaviour, of Valens may be most distinctly seen in his personal transactions with the eloquent Basil, archbishop of Cæsarea, who had succeeded Athanasius in the management of

---

[70] This sketch of the ecclesiastical government of Valens is drawn from Socrates (l. iv), Sozomen (l. vi), Theodoret (l. iv), and the immense compilations of Tillemont (particularly tom. vi viii and ix).

[71] Dr Jortin (Remarks on Ecclesiastical History, vol iv. p. 78) has already conceived and intimated the same suspicion

[72] This reflection is so obvious and forcible that Orosius (l vii. c 32, 33) delays the persecution till after the death of Valentinian. Socrates, on the other hand, supposes (l iii [leg iv] c 32) that it was appeased by a philosophical oration, which Themistius pronounced in the year 374 (Orat vii p 154, in Latin only [Greek in Dindorf's ed]) Such contradictions diminish the evidence, and reduce the term, of the persecution of Valens.

the Trinitarian cause.[73]　The circumstantial narrative has been
composed by the friends and admirers of Basil; and, as soon as
we have stripped away a thick coat of rhetoric and miracle, we
shall be astonished by the unexpected mildness of the Arian
tyrant, who admired the firmness of his character, or was
apprehensive, if he employed violence, of a general revolt in the
province of Cappadocia.　The archbishop, who asserted, with
inflexible pride,[74] the truth of his opinions and the dignity of
his rank, was left in the free possession of his conscience and his
throne.　The emperor devoutly assisted at the solemn service
of the cathedral; and, instead of a sentence of banishment,
subscribed the donation of a valuable estate for the use of an
hospital which Basil had lately founded in the neighbourhood
of Cæsarea [75]　3.　I am not able to discover that any law (such
as Theodosius afterwards enacted against the Arians) was published by Valens against the Athanasian sectaries; and the
edict which excited the most violent clamours may not appear
so extremely reprehensible.　The emperor had observed that
several of his subjects, gratifying their lazy disposition under
the pretence of religion, had associated themselves with the
monks of Egypt; and he directed the count of the East to drag
them from their solitude; and to compel those deserters of
society to accept the fair alternative of renouncing their temporal possessions or of discharging the public duties of men and
citizens.[76]　The ministers of Valens seem to have extended the
sense of this penal statute, since they claimed a right of enlisting
the young and able-bodied monks in the Imperial armies.　A
detachment of cavalry and infantry, consisting of three thousand
men, marched from Alexandria into the adjacent desert of

[73] Tillemont, whom I follow and abridge, has extracted (Mém Ecclés tom
viii p 153-167) the most authentic circumstances from the Panegyrics of the two
Gregories the brother, and the friend, of Basil　The letters of Basil himself
(Dupin, Bibliothèque Ecclésiastique, tom. ii. p 155-180) do not present the image
of a very lively persecution.

[74] Basilius Cæsariensis episcopus Cappadociæ clarus habetur. . . qui multa
continentiæ et ingenii bona uno superbiæ malo perdidit.　This irreverent passage
is perfectly in the style and character of St. Jerom.　It does not appear in
Scaliger's edition of his Chronicle , but Isaac Vossius found it in some old Mss.
which had not been reformed by the monks [ad ann 2392, cp. note in Migne's
edition, 8, p 699].

[75] This noble and charitable foundation (almost a new city) surpassed in merit,
if not in greatness, the pyramids, or the walls of Babylon　It was principally
intended for the reception of lepers (Greg. Nazianzen, Orat xx [=43] p 439[c 63])

[76] Cod. Theodos. l. xii. tit. 1 leg. 63　Godefroy (tom iv p. 409-413) performs
the duty of a commentator and advocate.　Tillemont (Mém Ecclés. tom. viii. p.
808) supposes a second law to excuse his orthodox friends, who had misrepresented
the edict of Valens and suppressed the liberty of choice.

Nitria,[77] which was peopled by five thousand monks. The soldiers were conducted by Arian priests, and it is reported that a considerable slaughter was made in the monasteries which disobeyed the commands of their sovereign.[78]

Valentinian restrains the avarice of the clergy A.D 370

The strict regulations which have been framed by the wisdom of modern legislators to restrain the wealth and avarice of the clergy may be originally deduced from the example of the emperor Valentinian. His edict[79] addressed to Damasus, bishop of Rome, was publicly read in the churches of the city. He admonished the ecclesiastics and monks not to frequent the houses of widows and virgins; and menaced their disobedience with the animadversion of the civil judge. The director was no longer permitted to receive any gift, or legacy, or inheritance, from the liberality of his spiritual daughter; every testament contrary to this edict was declared null and void; and the illegal donation was confiscated for the use of the treasury. By a subsequent regulation it should seem that the same provisions were extended to nuns and bishops; and that all persons of the ecclesiastical order were rendered incapable of receiving any testamentary gifts, and strictly confined to the natural and legal rights of inheritance. As the guardian of domestic happiness and virtue, Valentinian applied this severe remedy to the growing evil In the capital of the empire, the females of noble and opulent houses possessed a very ample share of independent property: and many of those devout females had embraced the doctrines of Christianity, not only with the cold assent of the understanding, but with the warmth of affection, and perhaps with the eagerness of fashion. They sacrificed the pleasures of dress and luxury; and renounced, for the praise of chastity, the soft endearments of conjugal society. Some ecclesiastic, of real or apparent sanctity, was chosen to direct their timorous conscience and to amuse the vacant tenderness of their heart: and the unbounded confidence which they hastily bestowed was often abused by knaves and enthusiasts; who hastened from the

[77] See D'Anville, Description de l'Egypte, p 74   Hereafter I shall consider the monastic institutions.

[78] Socrates, l. iv. c. 24, 25. Orosius, L vii. c. 33   Jerom in Chron. p 189, and tom ii p. 212   The monks of Egypt performed many miracles, which prove the truth of their faith   Right, says Jortin (Remarks, vol iv. p 79), but what proves the truth of those miracles?

[79] Cod   Theodos. l xvi. tit. ii. leg 20, Godefroy (tom vi p 49), after the example of Baronius, impartially collects all that the fathers have said on the subject of this important law, whose spirit was long afterwards revived by the emperor Frederic II, Edward I of England, and other Christian princes who reigned after the twelfth century.

extremities of the East to enjoy, on a splendid theatre, the privileges of the monastic profession. By their contempt of the world, they insensibly acquired its most desirable advantages ; the lively attachment, perhaps, of a young and beautiful woman, the delicate plenty of an opulent household, and the respectful homage of the slaves, the freedmen, and the clients of a senatorial family. The immense fortunes of the Roman ladies were gradually consumed in lavish alms and expensive pilgrimages ; and the artful monk, who had assigned himself the first or possibly the sole place in the testament of his spiritual daughter, still presumed to declare, with the smooth face of hypocrisy, that *he* was only the instrument of charity and the steward of the poor The lucrative, but disgraceful, trade [80] which was exercised by the clergy to defraud the expectations of the natural heirs had provoked the indignation of a superstitious age: and two of the most respectable of the Latin fathers very honestly confess that the ignominious edict of Valentinian was just and necessary ; and that the Christian priests had deserved to lose a privilege which was still enjoyed by comedians, charioteers, and the ministers of idols. But the wisdom and authority of the legislator are seldom victorious in a contest with the vigilant dexterity of private interest: and Jerom or Ambrose might patiently acquiesce in the justice of an ineffectual or salutary law. If the ecclesiastics were checked in the pursuit of personal emolument, they would exert a more laudable industry to increase the wealth of the church, and dignify their covetousness with the specious names of piety and patriotism. [81]

Damasus, bishop of Rome, who was constrained to stigmatize the avarice of his clergy by the publication of the law of Valentinian, had the good sense or the good fortune to engage in his service the zeal and abilities of the learned Jerom ; and the grateful saint has celebrated the merit and purity of a very

Ambition and luxury of Damasus bishop of Rome A D 366 384

---

[80] The expressions which I have used are temperate and feeble, if compared with the vehement invectives of Jerom (tom 1 p 13, 45, 144, &c). In *his* turn, he was reproached with the guilt which he imputed to his brother monks: and the *Sceleratus*, the *Versipellis*, was publicly accused as the lover of the widow Paula (tom ii p 363). He undoubtedly possessed the affections both of the mother and the daughter ; but he declares that he never abused his influence to any selfish or sensual purpose.

[81] Pudet dicere, sacerdotes idolorum, mimi et aurigæ, et scorta, hæreditates capiunt ; solis *clericis* ac *monachis* hâc [hoc] lege prohibetur Et non prohibetur a persecutoribus, sed a principibus Christianis Nec de lege queror , sed dolco cur *meruerimus* hanc legem. Jerom (tom. 1 p 13) discreetly insinuates the secret policy of his patron Damasus.

ambiguous character.[82]   But the splendid vices of the church of
Rome, under the reign of Valentinian and Damasus, have been
curiously observed by the historian Ammianus, who delivers his
impartial sense in these expressive words : " The præfecture of
Juventius [83] was accompanied with peace and plenty · but the
tranquillity of his government was soon disturbed by a bloody
sedition of the distracted people   The ardour of Damasus and
Ursinus, to seize the episcopal seat, surpassed the ordinary
measure of human ambition.   They contended with the rage
of party , the quarrel was maintained by the wounds and death
of their followers ; and the præfect, unable to resist or to appease
the tumult, was constrained, by superior violence, to retire into
the suburbs.   Damasus prevailed . the well-disputed victory
remained on the side of his faction ; one hundred and thirty-
seven dead bodies [84] were found in the *Basilica* of Sicininus,[85]
where the Christians hold their religious assemblies ; and it was
long before the angry minds of the people resumed their accustomed tranquillity.   When I consider the splendour of the
capital, I am not astonished that so valuable a prize should
inflame the desires of ambitious men, and produce the fiercest
and most obstinate contests.   The successful candidate is secure
that he will be enriched by the offerings of matrons , [86] that, as
soon as his dress is composed with becoming care and elegance,
he may proceed, in his chariot, through the streets of Rome ; [87]
and that the sumptuousness of the Imperial table will not equal
the profuse and delicate entertainments provided by the taste,
and at the expense, of the Roman pontiffs.   How much more

[82] Three words of Jerom, *sanctæ memoriæ Damasus* (tom ii p. 109) wash
away all his stains, and blind the devout eyes of Tillemont (Mém. Ecclés tom.
viii. p 386-424).   [A collection of the epigrams of Damasus has been edited by Ihm]
[83] [Read Viventius with the Mss]
[84] Jerom himself is forced to allow, crudelissimæ interfectiones diversi sexus
perpetratæ (in Chron p 186)   But an original *libel* or petition of two presbyters
of the adverse party has unaccountably escaped   They affirm that the doors of
the Basilica were burnt, and that the roof was untiled , that Damasus marched at
the head of his own clergy, grave-diggers, charioteers, and hired gladiators;
that none of *his* party were killed, but that one hundred and sixty dead bodies were
found.   This petition is published by the P Sirmond, in the first volume of his
works
[85] The *Basilica* of Sicininus, or Liberius, is probably the church of Sancta
Maria Maggiore, on the Esquiline hill   Baronius, A D 367, No 3, and Donatus,
Roma Antiqua et Nova. l iv. c. 3, p 462.   [It is disputed whether the *Basilica
Liberiana* was a new building or a reconstruction of the Basi¹ ca Sicinina]
[86] The enemies of Damasus styled him *Auriscalpius Matronarum*, the ladies'
ear-scratcher
[87] Gregory Nazianzen (Orat xxvii [= 42] p 526 [c. 24]) describes the pride and
luxury of the prelates who reigned in the imperial cities ; their gilt car, fiery steeds,
numerous train, &c   The crowd gave way as to a wild beast.

rationally (continues the honest Pagan) would those pontiffs consult their true happiness, if, instead of alleging the greatness of the city as an excuse for their manners, they would imitate the exemplary life of some provincial bishops, whose temperance and sobriety, whose mean apparel and downcast looks, recommended their pure and modest virtue to the Deity and his true worshippers." [88] The schism of Damasus and Ursinus was extinguished by the exile of the latter ; and the wisdom of the præfect Prætextatus [89] restored the tranquillity of the city Prætextatus was a philosophic Pagan, a man of learning, of taste, and politeness ; who disguised a reproach in the form of a jest, when he assured Damasus that, if he could obtain the bishopric of Rome, he himself would immediately embrace the Christian religion.[90] This lively picture of the wealth and luxury of the popes in the fourth century becomes the more curious as it represents the intermediate degree between the humble poverty of the apostolic fisherman and the royal state of a temporal prince whose dominions extend from the confines of Naples to the banks of the Po.

When the suffrage of the generals and of the army com- Foreign mitted the sceptre of the Roman empire to the hands of A D Valentinian, his reputation in arms, his military skill and 364-375 experience, and his rigid attachment to the forms, as well as spirit, of ancient discipline, were the principal motives of their judicious choice. The eagerness of the troops who pressed him to nominate his colleague was justified by the dangerous situation of public affairs ; and Valentinian himself was conscious that the abilities of the most active mind were unequal to the defence

[88] Ammian. xxvii 3. Perpetuo Numini, verisque ejus cultoribus The incomparable pliancy of a Polytheist !

[89] Ammianus, who makes a fair report of his præfecture (xxvii. 9), styles him præclaræ indolis gravitatisque senator (xxii 7, and Vales ad loc) A curious inscription (Gruter MCII. No 2) records, in two columns, his religious and civil honours In one line he was Pontiff of the Sun, and of Vesta, Augur, Quindecemvir, Hierophant, &c , &c In the other, 1 Quæstor candidatus, more probably titular. 2. Prætor 3. Corrector of Tuscany and Umbria 4 Consular of Lusitania. 5. Proconsul of Achaia 6 Præfect of Rome 7 Prætorian præfect of Italy. 8. Of Illyricum [This is incorrect: the writer states that he was Præt. Præf. Italiae et Illyrici,—which formed one prefecture. See above, vol 11. Appendix 15.] 9 Consul elect ; but he died before the beginning of the year 385 See Tillemont, Hist des Empereurs, tom v p 241, 736. [See C. I L 6, 1778. Cp. 1777 and 1779, of which the latter contains a most remarkable iambic and pagan poem to his wife Paulina.]

[90] Facite me Romanæ urbis episcopum ; et ero protinus Christianus (Jerom, tom. 11. p. 165). It is more than probable that Damasus would not have purchased his conversion at such a price.

of the distant frontiers of an invaded monarchy. As soon as
the death of Julian had relieved the Barbarians from the terror
of his name, the most sanguine hopes of rapine and conquest
excited the nations of the East, and of the North, and of the
A D 364-375 South. Their inroads were often vexatious, and sometimes
formidable ; but, during the twelve years of the reign of
Valentinian, his firmness and vigilance protected his own
dominions ; and his powerful genius seemed to inspire and
direct the feeble counsels of his brother. Perhaps the method
of annals would more forcibly express the urgent and divided
cares of the two emperors , but the attention of the reader,
likewise, would be distracted by a tedious and desultory narrative. A separate view of the five great theatres of war : I.
Germany ; II. Britain ; III. Africa ; IV. The East ; and, V.
The Danube ; will impress a more distinct image of the military
state of the empire under the reigns of Valentinian and Valens.

I GERMANY   I. The ambassadors of the Alemanni had been offended by
The Alemanni
invade Gaul the harsh and haughty behaviour of Ursacius, master of the
A.D 365   offices ;[91] who, by an act of unseasonable parsimony, had diminished the value, as well as the quantity, of the presents to which
they were entitled, either from custom or treaty, on the accession
of a new emperor. They expressed, and they communicated to
their countrymen, their strong sense of the national affront.
The irascible minds of the chiefs were exasperated by the suspicion of contempt ; and the martial youth crowded to their
standard. Before Valentinian could pass the Alps, the villages of
A.D. 366,   Gaul were in flames ; before his general Dagalaiphus could
January   encounter the Alemanni, they had secured the captives and the
spoil in the forests of Germany   In the beginning of the ensuing
year, the military force of the whole nation, in deep and solid
columns, broke through the barrier of the Rhine, during the
severity of a northern winter. Two Roman counts were defeated
and mortally wounded ; and the standard of the Heruli and Batavians fell into the hands of the conquerors, who displayed, with
insulting shouts and menaces, the trophy of their victory. The
standard was recovered ; but the Batavians had not redeemed
the shame of their disgrace and flight in the eyes of their severe
judge. It was the opinion of Valentinian that his soldiers must
learn to fear their commander, before they could cease to fear
the enemy. The troops were solemnly assembled ; and the

---

[91] Ammian xxvi. 5. Valesius adds a long and good note on the master of the
offices. [For the chronology of these campaigns, see Reiche, Chronologie der
sechs letzten Bücher des Amm. Marc , 1889]

trembling Batavians were inclosed within the circle of the Imperial army. Valentinian then ascended his tribunal; and, as if he disdained to punish cowardice with death, he inflicted a stain of indelible ignominy on the officers whose misconduct and pusillanimity were found to be the first occasion of the defeat. The Batavians were degraded from their rank, stripped of their arms, and condemned to be sold for slaves to the highest bidder. At this tremendous sentence the troops fell prostrate on the ground, deprecated the indignation of their sovereign, and protested that, if he would indulge them in another trial, they would approve themselves not unworthy of the name of Romans, and of his soldiers. Valentinian, with affected reluctance, yielded to their entreaties: the Batavians resumed their arms, and, with their arms, the invincible resolution of wiping away their disgrace in the blood of the Alemanni.[92] The principal command was declined by Dagalaiphus; and that experienced general, who had represented, perhaps with too much prudence, the extreme difficulties of the undertaking, had the mortification, before the end of the campaign, of seeing his rival Jovinus convert those difficulties into a decisive advantage over the scattered forces of the Barbarians. At the head of a well-disciplined army of cavalry, infantry, and light troops, Jovinus advanced, with cautious and rapid steps, to Scarponna,[93] in the territory of Metz, where he surprised a large division of the Alemanni, before they had time to run to their arms: and flushed his soldiers with the confidence of an easy and bloodless victory. Another division, or rather army, of the enemy, after the cruel and wanton devastation of the adjacent country, reposed themselves on the shady banks of the Moselle. Jovinus, who had viewed the ground with the eyes of a general, made his silent approach through a deep and woody vale, till he could distinctly perceive the indolent security of the Germans. Some were bathing their huge limbs in the river; others were combing their long and flaxen hair; others again were swallowing large draughts of rich and delicious wine. On a sudden they heard the sound of the Roman trumpet; they saw the enemy in their camp. Astonishment produced disorder; disorder was followed by flight and

Their defeat [A.D. 366]

[Charpeigne]

[92] Ammian. xxvii 1 Zosimus, l. iv. p. 208 [c 9]. The disgrace of the Batavians is suppressed by the contemporary soldier, from a regard for military honour, which could not affect a Greek rhetorician of the succeeding age

[93] See D'Anville, Notice de l'Ancienne Gaule, p 587 The name of the Moselle, which is not specified by Ammianus, is clearly understood by Mascou (Hist of the ancient Germans, vii 2). [Dagalaiphus *did* take the command, but was recalled to enter on the consulate as colleague of Gratian.]

dismay; and the confused multitude of the bravest warriors was
pierced by the swords and javelins of the legionaries and auxiliaries. The fugitives escaped to the third and most considerable
camp, in the Catalaunian plains, near Châlons in Champagne · the
straggling detachments were hastily recalled to their standard;
and the Barbarian chiefs, alarmed and admonished by the fate
of their companions, prepared to encounter, in a decisive battle,
the victorious forces of the lieutenant of Valentinian. The
bloody and obstinate conflict lasted a whole summer's day,
with equal valour, and with alternate success. The Romans at
length prevailed, with the loss of about twelve hundred men.
Six thousand of the Alemanni were slain, four thousand were
wounded; and the brave Jovinus, after chasing the flying remnant of their host as far as the banks of the Rhine, returned to

July

Paris, to receive the applause of his sovereign and the ensigns
of the consulship for the ensuing year.[94] The triumph of the
Romans was indeed sullied by their treatment of the captive
king, whom they hung on a gibbet without the knowledge of
their indignant general. This disgraceful act of cruelty which

[?A D 368]

might be imputed to the fury of the troops, was followed by the
deliberate murder of Withicab, the son of Vadomair; a German
prince, of a weak and sickly constitution, but of a daring and
formidable spirit. The domestic assassin was instigated and
protected by the Romans;[95] and the violation of the laws of
humanity and justice betrayed their secret apprehension of the
weakness of the declining empire. The use of the dagger is
seldom adopted in public councils, as long as they retain any
confidence in the power of the sword.

Valentin-
ian passes
and forti-
fies the
Rhine,
A D. 368

[Easter,
March 23 ?]

While the Alemanni appeared to be humbled by their recent
calamities, the pride of Valentinian was mortified by the unexpected surprisal of Moguntiacum, or Mentz, the principal city
of the Upper Germany. In the unsuspicious moment of a
Christian festival, Rando, a bold and artful chieftain, who had
long meditated his attempt, suddenly passed the Rhine; entered
the defenceless town, and retired with a multitude of captives
of either sex   Valentinian resolved to execute severe vengeance on the whole body of the nation. Count Sebastian, with

---

[94] The battles are described by Ammianus (xxvii. 2), and by Zosimus (l. iv. p
209 [c. 9]), who supposes Valentinian to have been present. ·
[95] Studio solicitante nostrorum, occubuit. Ammian. xxvii 10 [This murder
did not happen in 366, as might be inferred from the text, but (1) beginning of 368
(Sievers), or (2) summer 368 (Reiche), or (3) autumn 368 (Maurer) Tillemont
put it at end of 367, and also the surprisal of Mainz, with which it was doubtless
connected. But cp. Reiche, p. 23.]

the bands of Italy and Illyricum, was ordered to invade their country, most probably on the side of Rhætia. The emperor in person, accompanied by his son Gratian, passed the Rhine at [368 A D] the head of a formidable army, which was supported on both flanks by Jovinus and Severus, the two masters-general of the cavalry and infantry of the West. The Alemanni, unable to prevent the devastation of their villages, fixed their camp on a lofty, and almost inaccessible, mountain, in the modern duchy of Wirtemberg, and resolutely expected the approach of the Romans. The life of Valentinian was exposed to imminent danger by the intrepid curiosity with which he persisted to explore some secret and unguarded path. A troop of Barbarians suddenly rose from their ambuscade : and the emperor, who vigorously spurred his horse down a steep and slippery descent, was obliged to leave behind him his armour-bearer, and his helmet, magnificently enriched with gold and precious stones. At the signal of the general assault, the Roman troops encompassed and ascended the mountain of Solicinium on three [? Sülchen-different sides   Every step which they gained increased their Rotten-burg] ardour and abated the resistance of the enemy : and, after their united forces had occupied the summit of the hill, they impetuously urged the Barbarians down the northern descent where Count Sebastian was posted to intercept their retreat. After this signal victory, Valentinian returned to his winter-quarters at Treves ; where he indulged the public joy by the exhibition of splendid and triumphal games.[96] But the wise monarch, instead of aspiring to the conquest of Germany, confined his attention to the important and laborious defence of the Gallic frontier, against an enemy whose strength was renewed by a stream of daring volunteers, which incessantly flowed from the most distant tribes of the North.[97] The banks of the Rhine, from its source to the straits of the ocean, were closely planted with strong castles and convenient towers ; new works, and new arms, were invented by the ingenuity of a prince who was skilled in the mechanical

[96] The expedition of Valentinian is related by Ammianus (xxvii. 10), and celebrated by Ausonius (Mosell. 421, &c.), who foolishly supposes that the Romans were ignorant of the sources of the Danube   [As Smith points out, Ausonius only says, "unknown to Roman annals," Latiis ignotum annalibus]
[97] Immanis enim natio, jam inde ab incunabulis primis varietate casuum imminuta ; ita sæpius adolescit, ut fuisse longis sæculis æstimetur intacta. Ammian. xxviii. 5   The Count de Buat (Hist des Peuples de l'Europe, tom vi p. 370) ascribes the fecundity of the Alemanni to their easy adoption of strangers   [For the activity of Valentinian in the defence of the frontiers cp an inscription on the construction of the Castra of Salva (365-367 A D), in Ephem Epig. 2, p. 389, also C. I. L. 3, 5670 a and 3771.]

arts; and his numerous levies of Roman and Barbarian youth were severely trained in all the exercises of war. The progress of the work, which was sometimes opposed by modest representations, and sometimes by hostile attempts, secured the tranquillity of Gaul during the nine subsequent years of the administration of Valentinian.[98]

The Bur
gundians.
A D 371
[370] That prudent emperor, who diligently practised the wise maxims of Diocletian, was studious to foment and excite the intestine divisions of the tribes of Germany About the middle of the fourth century, the countries, perhaps of Lusace and Thuringia, on either side of the Elbe were occupied by the vague dominion of the BURGUNDIANS; a warlike and numerous people of the Vandal race,[99] whose obscure name insensibly swelled into a powerful kingdom, and has finally settled on a flourishing province. The most remarkable circumstance in the ancient manners of the Burgundians appears to have been the difference of their civil and ecclesiastical constitution. The appellation of *Hendinos* was given to the king or general, and the title of *Sinistus* to the high priest, of the nation The person of the priest was sacred, and his dignity perpetual; but the temporal government was held by a very precarious tenure. If the events of war accused the courage or conduct of the king, he was immediately deposed; and the injustice of his subjects made him responsible for the fertility of the earth and the regularity of the seasons, which seemed to fall more properly within the sacerdotal department.[100] The disputed possession of some salt-pits [101] engaged the Alemanni and the Burgundians in frequent contests: the latter were easily tempted by the secret solicitations and liberal offers of the emperor; and their fabulous descent from the Roman soldiers who had formerly been left to garrison the fortresses of Drusus was admitted with

[98] Ammian xxviii 2 Zosimus, l iv. p. 214 [c 16] The younger Victor mentions the mechanical genius of Valentinian, nova arma meditari, fingere terrâ seu limo simulacra [Epit. 45].

[99] Bellicosos et pubis immensæ viribus affluentes, et ideo metuendos finitimis universis. Ammian. xxviii 5 [Pliny represented them as a subdivision of the Vandalic branch. They were closely allied to the Goths and Vandals]

[100] I am always apt to suspect historians and travellers of improving extraordinary facts into general laws Ammianus ascribes a similar custom to Egypt: and the Chinese have imputed it to the Tatsin, or Roman empire (de Guignes, Hist. des Huns, tom. ii part i. p 79).

[101] Salinarum finiumque causâ Alemannis sæpe jurgabant Ammian xxviii 5 Possibly they disputed the possession of the *Sala*, a river which produced salt, and which had been the object of ancient contention Tacit Annal. xiii 57, and Lipsius ad loc.

mutual credulity, as it was conducive to mutual interest.[102]
An army of fourscore thousand Burgundians soon appeared on
the banks of the Rhine; and impatiently required the support
and subsidies which Valentinian had promised : but they were
amused with excuses and delays, till at length, after a fruitless
expectation, they were compelled to retire.   The arms and
fortifications of the Gallic frontier checked the fury of their
just resentment; and their massacre of the captives served to
embitter the hereditary feud of the Burgundians and the Alemanni.   The inconstancy of a wise prince may, perhaps, be
explained by some alteration of circumstances , and perhaps
it was the original design of Valentinian to intimidate rather
than to destroy, as the balance of power would have been
equally overturned by the extirpation of either of the German
nations.   Among the princes of the Alemanni, Macrianus, who,
with a Roman name, had assumed the arts of a soldier and a
statesman, deserved his hatred and esteem.   The emperor him- [A.D 371]
self, with a light and unencumbered band, condescended to
pass the Rhine, marched fifty miles into the country, and would
infallibly have seized the object of his pursuit, if his judicious
measures had not been defeated by the impatience of the
troops.   Macrianus was afterwards admitted to the honour of a
personal conference with the emperor; and the favours which
he received fixed him, till the hour of his death, a steady and
sincere friend of the republic.[103]

The land was covered by the fortifications of Valentinian ; The Saxons
but the sea-coast of Gaul and Britain was exposed to the depredations of the Saxons.   That celebrated name, in which we
have a dear and domestic interest, escaped the notice of Tacitus ;
and in the maps of Ptolemy it faintly marks the narrow neck
of the Cimbric peninsula and three small islands towards the
mouth of the Elbe.[104]   This contracted territory, the present

[102] Jam inde temporibus priscis sobolem se esse Romanam Burgundii sciunt
and the vague tradition gradually assumed a more regular form   Oros l. vii c
32.   It is annihilated by the decisive authority of Pliny, who composed the history
of Drusus, and served in Germany (Plin Secund Epist iii. 5) within sixty years
after the death of that hero.   *Germanorum genera* quinque , Vindili, quorum pars
Burgundiones, &c   Hist Natur iv. 28

[103] The wars and negotiations relative to the Burgundians and Alemanni are
distinctly related by Ammianus Marcellinus (xxviii 5, xxix 4, xxx 3).   Orosius
(l vii c 32) and the Chronicles of Jerom and Cassiodorius fix some dates and add
some circumstances.

[104] Επι τον αυχενα της Κιμβρικῆς χερσονήσου, Σάξονες   At the northern extremity
of the peninsula (the Cimbric promontory of Pliny, iv 27) Ptolemy fixes the
remnant of the *Cimbri*.   He fills the interval between the *Saxons* and the Cimbri
with six obscure tribes, who were united, as early as the sixth century, under the
national appellation of *Danes*. See Cluver. German. Antiq l. iii. c. 21, 22, 23.

Duchy of Sleswig, or perhaps of Holstein, was incapable of pouring forth the inexhaustible swarms of Saxons who reigned over the ocean, who filled the British island with their language, their laws, and their colonies, and who so long defended the liberty of the North against the arms of Charlemagne.[105] The solution of this difficulty is easily derived from the similar manners and loose constitution of the tribes of Germany; which were blended with each other by the slightest accidents of war or friendship. The situation of the native Saxons disposed them to embrace the hazardous professions of fishermen and pirates; and the success of their first adventures would naturally excite the emulation of their bravest countrymen, who were impatient of the gloomy solitude of their woods and mountains   Every tide might float down the Elbe whole fleets of canoes, filled with hardy and intrepid associates, who aspired to behold the unbounded prospect of the ocean and to taste the wealth and luxury of unknown worlds   It should seem probable, however, that the most numerous auxiliaries of the Saxons were furnished by the nations who dwelt along the shores of the Baltic.   They possessed arms and ships, the art of navigation, and the habits of naval war; but the difficulty of issuing through the northern columns of Hercules (which during several months of the year are obstructed with ice) confined their skill and courage within the limits of a spacious lake [106]   The rumour of the successful armaments which sailed from the mouth of the Elbe would soon provoke them to cross the narrow isthmus of Sleswig and to launch their vessels on the great sea.   The various troops of pirates and adventurers who fought under the same standard were insensibly united in a permanent society, at first of rapine, and afterwards of government.   A military confederation was gradually moulded into a national body, by the gentle operation of marriage and consanguinity, and the adjacent tribes, who solicited the alliance, accepted the name and laws, of the Saxons.   If the fact were not established by the most unquestionable evidence, we should appear to abuse the credulity of our readers by the description of the vessels in which the Saxon pirates ventured to sport in the waves of the German

[105] M d'Anville (Etablissement des Etats de l'Europe, &c, p 19-26) has marked the extensive limits of the Saxony of Charlemagne
[106] The fleet [sic] of Drusus had failed in their attempt to pass, or even to approach, the Sound (styled, from an obvious resemblance, the columns of Hercules); and the naval enterprise was never resumed (Tacit de Moribus German c 34). The knowledge which the Romans acquired of the naval powers of the Baltic (c. 44, 45) was obtained by their land journeys in search of amber.

Ocean, the British Channel, and the Bay of Biscay. The keel of their large flat-bottomed boats was framed of light timber, but the sides and upper work consisted only of wicker, with a covering of strong hides.[107] In the course of their slow and distant navigations, they must always have been exposed to the danger, and very frequently to the misfortune, of shipwreck; and the naval annals of the Saxons were undoubtedly filled with the accounts of the losses which they sustained on the coasts of Britain and Gaul. But the daring spirit of the pirates braved the perils, both of the sea and of the shore; their skill was confirmed by the habits of enterprise; the meanest of their mariners was alike capable of handling an oar, of rearing a sail, or of conducting a vessel; and the Saxons rejoiced in the appearance of a tempest, which concealed their design, and dispersed the fleets of the enemy.[108] After they had acquired an accurate knowledge of the maritime provinces of the West, they extended the scene of their depredations, and the most sequestered places had no reason to presume on their security. The Saxon boats drew so little water that they could easily proceed fourscore or an hundred miles up the great rivers; their weight was so inconsiderable that they were transported on waggons from one river to another; and the pirates who had entered the mouth of the Seine or of the Rhine, might descend, A D. 371 with the rapid stream of the Rhone, into the Mediterranean Under the reign of Valentinian, the maritime provinces of Gaul were afflicted by the Saxons. a military count was stationed for the defence of the sea-coast, or Armorican limit; and that officer, who found his strength, or his abilities, unequal to the task, implored the assistance of Severus, master-general of the infantry. The Saxons, surrounded and out-numbered, were forced to relinquish their spoil, and to yield a select band of their tall and robust youth to serve in the Imperial armies. They stipulated only a safe and honourable retreat: and the

[107] Quin et Aremoricus piratam *Saxona* tractus
Sperabat , cui pelle salum sulcare Britannum
Ludus et assuto glaucum mare findere lembo.
Sidon in Panegyr Avit 369
The genius of Cæsar imitated, for a particular service, these rude, but light vessels, which were likewise used by the natives of Britain (Comment de Bell Civil i 51, and Guichardt, Nouveaux Mémoires Militaires, tom ii p 41, 42) The British vessels would now astonish the genius of Cæsar

[108] The best original account of the Saxon pirates may be found in Sidonius Apollinaris (l viii epist. 6, p 223, edit. Sirmond), and the best commentary in the Abbé du Bos (Hist. Critique de la Monarchie Françoise, &c , tom i l i c 16, p 148-155. See likewise p 77, 78). [The Saxons seem to have made a settlement in the north of Gaul.]

condition was readily granted by the Roman general; who meditated an act of perfidy,[109] imprudent as it was inhuman, while a Saxon remained alive, and in arms, to revenge the fate of his countrymen The premature eagerness of the infantry, who were secretly posted in a deep valley, betrayed the ambuscade; and they would perhaps have fallen the victims of their own treachery, if a large body of cuirassiers, alarmed by the noise of the combat, had not hastily advanced to extricate their companions and to overwhelm the undaunted valour of the Saxons Some of the prisoners were saved from the edge of the sword, to shed their blood in the amphitheatre; and the orator Symmachus complains that twenty-nine of those desperate savages, by strangling themselves with their own hands, had disappointed the amusement of the public. Yet the polite and philosophic citizens of Rome were impressed with the deepest horror, when they were informed that the Saxons consecrated to the gods the tythe of their *human* spoil; and that they ascertained by lot the objects of the barbarous sacrifice [110]

II BRITAIN The Scots and Picts II. The fabulous colonies of Egyptians and Trojans, of Scandinavians and Spaniards, which flattered the pride, and amused the credulity, of our rude ancestors, have insensibly vanished in the light of science and philosophy.[111] The present age is satisfied with the simple and rational opinion that the islands of Great Britain and Ireland were gradually peopled from the adjacent continent of Gaul From the coast of Kent to the extremity of Caithness and Ulster, the memory of a Celtic origin was distinctly preserved, in the perpetual resemblance of language, of religion, and of manners . and the peculiar characters of the British tribes might be naturally ascribed to the influence of accidental and local circumstances.[112] The Roman province was

[109] Ammian. (xxviii 5) justifies this breach of faith to pirates and robbers: and Orosius (l. vii. c 32) more clearly expresses their real guilt; virtute atque agilitate terribiles.

[110] Symmachus (l. ii epist. 46) still presumes to mention the sacred names of Socrates and philosophy Sidonius, bishop of Clermont, might condemn (l. viii. epist 6 [§ 15]) with *less* inconsistency the human sacrifices of the Saxons.

[111] In the beginning of the last century the learned Cambden was obliged to undermine, with respectful scepticism, the romance of *Brutus* the Trojan, who is now buried in silent oblivion with *Scota*, the daughter of Pharaoh, and her numerous progeny Yet I am informed that some champions of the *Milesian colony* may still be found among the original natives of Ireland A people dissatisfied with their present condition grasp at any visions of their past or future glory.

[112] Tacitus, or rather his father-in-law Agricola, might remark the German or Spanish complexion of some British tribes But it was their sober, deliberate opinion: "In universum tamen æstimanti Gallos vicinum solum occupâsse credibile est Eorum sacra deprehendas sermo haud multum diversus (in Vit.

reduced to the state of civilized and peaceful servitude: the rights of savage freedom were contracted to the narrow limits of Caledonia. The inhabitants of that northern region were divided, as early as the reign of Constantine, between the two great tribes of the Scots and of the Picts,[113] who have since experienced a very different fortune. The power, and almost the memory, of the Picts have been extinguished by their successful rivals; and the Scots, after maintaining for ages the dignity of an independent kingdom, have multiplied, by an equal and voluntary union, the honours of the English name. The hand of nature had contributed to mark the ancient distinction of the Scots and Picts. The former were the men of the hills, and the latter those of the plain. The eastern coast of Caledonia may be considered as a level and fertile country, which, even in a rude state of tillage, was capable of producing a considerable quantity of corn; and the epithet of *cruitnich*, or wheat-eaters, expressed the contempt, or envy, of the carnivorous highlander. The cultivation of the earth might introduce a more accurate separation of property and the habits of a sedentary life, but the love of arms and rapine was still the ruling passion of the Picts; and their warriors, who stripped themselves for a day of battle, were distinguished, in the eyes of the Romans, by the strange fashion of painting their naked bodies with gaudy colours and fantastic figures. The western part of Caledonia irregularly rises into wild and barren hills, which scarcely repay the toil of the husbandman and are most profitably used for the pasture of cattle. The highlanders were condemned to the occupations of shepherds and hunters, and, as they seldom were fixed to any permanent habitation, they acquired the expressive name of Scots, which, in the Celtic tongue, is said to be equivalent to that of *wanderers* or *vagrants*. The inhabitants of a barren land were urged to seek a fresh supply of food in the waters. The

Agricol. c. xi)'' Cæsar had observed their common religion (Comment. de Bello Gallico, vi 13); and in his time the emigration from the Belgic Gaul was a recent, or at least an historical, event (v. 10) Cambden, the British Strabo, has modestly ascertained our genuine antiquities (Britannia, vol i Introduction, p ii-xxxi).

[113] In the dark and doubtful paths of Caledonian antiquity, I have chosen for my guides two learned and ingenious Highlanders, whom their birth and education had peculiarly qualified for that office See Critical Dissertations on the Origin, Antiquities, &c, of the Caledonians, by Dr John Macpherson, London, 1768, in 4to; and Introduction to the History of Great Britain and Ireland, by James Macpherson, Esq, London, 1773, in 4to, third edit Dr Macpherson was a minister in the Isle of Sky and it is a circumstance honourable for the present age that a work, replete with erudition and criticism, should have been composed in the most remote of the Hebrides [See Appendix 2.]

deep lakes and bays which intersect their country are plentifully
stored with fish ; and they gradually ventured to cast their nets
in the waves of the ocean.   The vicinity of the Hebrides, so
profusely scattered along the western coast of Scotland, tempted
their curiosity and improved their skill ; and they acquired by
slow degrees, the art, or rather the habit, of managing their
boats in a tempestuous sea and of steering their nocturnal course
by the light of the well-known stars.   The two bold headlands
of Caledonia almost touch the shores of a spacious island, which
obtained, from its luxuriant vegetation, the epithet of *Green* ;
and has preserved, with a slight alteration, the name of Erin, or
Ierne, or Ireland.   It is *probable* that in some remote period of
antiquity the fertile plains of Ulster received a colony of hungry
Scots ; and that the strangers of the North, who had dared to
encounter the arms of the legions, spread their conquests over the
savage and unwarlike natives of a solitary island.   It is *certain*,
that, in the declining age of the Roman empire, Caledonia,
Ireland, and the Isle of Man, were inhabited by the Scots, and
that the kindred tribes, who were often associated in military
enterprise, were deeply affected by the various accidents of their
mutual fortunes   They long cherished the lively tradition of
their common name and origin, and the missionaries of the Isle
of Saints, who diffused the light of Christianity over North
Britain, established the vain opinion that their Irish countrymen
were the natural as well as spiritual fathers of the Scottish race.
The loose and obscure tradition has been preserved by the venerable Bede, who scattered some rays of light over the darkness
of the eighth century.   On this slight foundation, a huge super-
structure of fable was gradually reared, by the bards and the
monks ; two orders of men who equally abused the privilege of
fiction.   The Scottish nation, with mistaken pride, adopted their
Irish genealogy · and the annals of a long line of imaginary
kings have been adorned by the fancy of Boethius and the classic
elegance of Buchanan.[114]

[114] The Irish descent of the Scots has been revived, in the last moments of its
decay, and strenuously supported, by the Rev Mr Whitaker (Hist of Manchester, vol 1 p 430, 431 ; and Genuine History of the Britons asserted, &c , p
154-293)   Yet he acknowledges, 1   *That* the Scots of Ammianus Marcellinus
(A D 340) were already settled in Caledonia ; and that the Roman authors do not
afford any hints of their emigration from another country   2   *That all* the
accounts of such emigrations, which have been asserted, or received, by Irish
bards, Scotch historians, or English antiquaries (Buchanan, Cambden, Usher,
Stillingfleet, &c), are totally fabulous   3   *That* three of the Irish tribes which
are mentioned by Ptolemy (A D 150) were of Caledonian extraction   4   *That* a
younger branch of Caledonian princes, of the house of Fingal, acquired and

Six years after the death of Constantine, the destructive _{Their invasion} inroads of the Scots and Picts required the presence of his _{A.D 343-366} youngest son, who reigned in the western empire. Constans visited his British dominions; but we may form some estimate of the importance of his achievements by the language of panegyric, which celebrates only his triumph over the elements; or, in other words, the good fortune of a safe and easy passage from the port of Boulogne to the harbour of Sandwich.[115] The calamities which the afflicted provincials continued to experience, from foreign war and domestic tyranny, were aggravated by the feeble and corrupt administration of the eunuchs of Constantius; and the transient relief which they might obtain from the virtues of Julian was soon lost by the absence and death of their benefactor. The sums of gold and silver which had been painfully collected, or liberally transmitted, for the payment of the troops were intercepted by the avarice of the commanders; discharges, or, at least, exemptions, from the military service were publicly sold; the distress of the soldiers, who were injuriously deprived of their legal and scanty subsistence, provoked them to frequent desertion; the nerves of discipline were relaxed, and the highways were infested with robbers [116] The oppression of the good and the impunity of the wicked equally contributed to diffuse through the island a spirit of discontent and revolt; and every ambitious subject, every desperate exile, might entertain a reasonable hope of subverting the weak and distracted government of Britain. The hostile tribes of the North, who detested the pride and power of the King of the World, suspended their domestic feuds; and the Barbarians of the land and sea, the Scots, the Picts, and the Saxons, spread themselves, with rapid and irresistible fury, from the wall of Antoninus to the

possessed the monarchy of Ireland.   After these concessions, the remaining difference between Mr. Whitaker and his adversaries is minute and obscure. The *genuine history* which he produces of a Fergus, the cousin of Ossian, who was transplanted (A.D 320) from Ireland to Caledonia, is built on a conjectural supplement to the Erse poetry, and the feeble evidence of Richard of Cirencester, a monk of the fourteenth century.   The lively spirit of the learned and ingenious antiquarian has tempted him to forget the nature of a question, which he so *vehemently* debates, and so *absolutely* decides   [It is now generally admitted that the Scots of Scotland were immigrants from (the north-east of) Ireland   See Appendix 2]

115 Hyeme tumentes ac sævientes undas calcâstis Oceani sub remis vestris;   . insperatam imperatoris faciem Britannus expavit   Julius Firmicus Maternus de errore Profan. Relig. p. 464, edit. Gronov. ad calcem Minuc Fel   See Tillemont (Hist des Empereurs, tom. iv p 336).

116 Libanius, Orat Parent c xxvix p. 264.   This curious passage has escaped the diligence of our British antiquaries.

shores of Kent. Every production of art and nature, every object of convenience or luxury, which they were incapable of creating by labour or procuring by trade, was accumulated in the rich and fruitful province of Britain.[117] A philosopher may deplore the eternal discord of the human race, but he will confess that the desire of spoil is a more rational provocation than the vanity of conquest. From the age of Constantine to that of the Plantagenets, this rapacious spirit continued to instigate the poor and hardy Caledonians : but the same people, whose generous humanity seems to inspire the songs of Ossian, was disgraced by a savage ignorance of the virtues of peace and of the laws of war. Their southern neighbours have felt, and perhaps exaggerated, the cruel depredations of the Scots and Picts :[118] and a valiant tribe of Caledonia, the Attacotti,[119] the enemies, and afterwards the soldiers, of Valentinian, are accused, by an eye-witness, of delighting in the taste of human flesh. When they hunted the woods for prey, it is said that they attacked the shepherd rather than his flock ; and that they curiously selected the most delicate and brawny parts, both of males and females, which they prepared for their horrid repasts[120] If, in the neighbourhood of the commercial and literary town of Glasgow, a race of cannibals has really existed, we may contemplate, in the period of the Scottish history, the opposite extremes of savage and civilized life. Such reflections tend to enlarge the circle of our ideas · and to encourage the pleasing hope that New Zealand may produce, in some future age, the Hume of the Southern Hemisphere.

Restoration of Britain by Theodosius [Dux Britanniarum] A D 366 370

Every messenger who escaped across the British channel conveyed the most melancholy and alarming tidings to the ears of Valentinian ; and the emperor was soon informed that the two

[117] The Caledonians praised and coveted the gold, the steeds, the lights, &c , of the *stranger* See Dr Blair's Dissertation on Ossian, vol. ii. p 343 ; and Mr. Macpherson's Introduction, p 242-286

[118] Lord Lyttleton has circumstantially related (History of Henry II. vol. i. p 182), and Sir David Dalrymple has slightly mentioned (Annals of Scotland, vol i p 69), a barbarous inroad of the Scots, at a time (A D 1137) when law, religion, and society must have softened their primitive manners

[119] Attacotti bellicosa hominum natio   Ammian xxvii 8   Cambden (Introduct p clii) has restored their true name in the text of Jerom   The bands of Attacotti, which Jerom had seen in Gaul, were afterwards stationed in Italy and Illyricum (Notitia, S viii xxix. xl)

[120] Cum ipse adolescentulus in Galliâ viderim Attacottos (or Scotos) gentem Britannicam humanis vesci carnibus , et cum per silvas porcorum greges, et armentorum pecudumque repetiant, pastorum *nates* et feminarum *papillas* solere abscindere ; et has solas ciborum delicias arbitrari.   Such is the evidence of Jerom (tom. ii p 75), whose veracity I find no reason to question.

military commanders of the province had been surprised and
cut off by the Barbarians. Severus, count of the domestics, was
hastily dispatched, and as suddenly recalled, by the court of
Treves. The representations of Jovinus served only to indicate
the greatness of the evil ; and after a long and serious consultation, the defence, or rather the recovery, of Britain was intrusted
to the abilities of the brave Theodosius. The exploits of that
general, the father of a line of emperors, have been celebrated,
with peculiar complacency, by the writers of the age : but his
real merit deserved their applause ; and his nomination was
received, by the army and province, as a sure presage of approaching victory He seized the favourable moment of navigation, and securely landed the numerous and veteran bands of
the Heruli and Batavians, the Jovians and the Victors. In his
march from Sandwich to London, Theodosius defeated several
parties of the barbarians, released a multitude of captives, and,
after distributing to his soldiers a small portion of the spoil,
established the fame of disinterested justice by the restitution
of the remainder to the rightful proprietors. The citizens of
London, who had almost despaired of their safety, threw open
their gates ; and, as soon as Theodosius had obtained from the
court of Treves the important aid of a military lieutenant and a
civil governor, he executed, with wisdom and vigour, the laborious task of the deliverance of Britain.[121] The vagrant soldiers
were recalled to their standard ; an edict of amnesty dispelled
the public apprehensions ; and his cheerful example alleviated
the rigour of martial discipline. The scattered and desultory
warfare of the Barbarians, who infested the land and sea, deprived him of the glory of a signal victory ; but the prudent
spirit and consummate art of the Roman general were displayed ^{A D 368
and 369}
in the operations of two campaigns, which successively rescued
every part of the province from the hands of a cruel and rapacious
enemy. The splendour of the cities and the security of the
fortifications were diligently restored by the paternal care
of Theodosius : who with a strong hand confined the trembling
Caledonians to the northern angle of the island ; and perpetuated, by the name and settlement of the new province of
Valentia, the glories of the reign of Valentinian.[122] The voice

[121] [Theodosius had the task too of suppressing a tyrant, Valentinus ; Amm
xxxviii. 3.]
[122] Ammianus has concisely represented (xx. 1, xxvi. 4, xxvii 8, xxviii 3) the
whole series of the British war [It is generally said that the name Valentia was
in honour of Valentinian But would it not, in that case, be Valentiniana ? It
seems more likely that it was a compliment to Valens on the part of his
brother.]

of poetry and panegyric may add, perhaps with some degree of truth, that the unknown legions of Thule were stained with the blood of the Picts; that the oars of Theodosius dashed the waves of the Hyperborean ocean, and that the distant Orkneys were the scene of his naval victory over the Saxon pirates.[123] He left the province with a fair, as well as splendid, reputation and was immediately promoted to the rank of master-general of the cavalry, by a prince who could applaud without envy the merit of his servants. In the important station of the upper Danube, the conqueror of Britain checked and defeated the armies of the Alemanni before he was chosen to suppress the revolt of Africa.

III. AFRICA
Tyranny of
Romanus
A D 366,
&c.

III. The prince who refuses to be the judge, instructs his people to consider him as the accomplice, of his ministers. The military command of Africa had been long exercised by Count Romanus, and his abilities were not inadequate to his station: but, as sordid interest was the sole motive of his conduct, he acted, on most occasions, as if he had been the enemy of the province and the friend of the Barbarians of the desert. The three flourishing cities of Oea, Leptis, and Sabrata, which, under the name of Tripoli, had long constituted a federal union,[124] were obliged, for the first time, to shut their gates against a hostile invasion : several of their most honourable citizens were surprised and massacred; the villages, and even the suburbs, were pillaged; and the vines and fruit-trees of that rich territory were extirpated by the malicious savages of Getulia. The unhappy provincials implored the protection of Romanus; but they soon found that their military governor was not less cruel and rapacious than the Barbarians. As they were incapable of furnishing the four thousand camels, and the exorbitant pre-

---

[123] Horrescit ratibus . . impervia Thule.
Ille . nec falso nomine Pictos
Edomuit Scotumque vago mucrone secutus
Fregit Hyperboreas remis audacibus undas
Claudian, in iii Cons Honorii, vei 53, &c.
————Maduerunt Saxone fuso
Orcades incaluit Pictorum sanguine Thule
Scotorum cumulos flevit glacialis Ierne.
In iv Cons. Hon ver. 31, &c.
See likewise Pacatus (in Panegyr Vet xii 5) But it is not easy to appreciate the intrinsic value of flattery and metaphor. Compare the *British* victories of Bolanus (Statius Silv v. 2) with his real character (Tacit in Vit Agricol c. 16).

[124] Ammianus frequently mentions their concilium annuum, legitimum, &c Leptis and Sabrata are long since ruined; but the city of Oea, the native country of Apuleius, still flourishes under the provincial denomination of *Tripoli*. See Cellarius (Geograph Antiqua, tom. ii part ii p. 81), D'Anville (Géographie Ancienne, tom. iii p. 71, 72), and Marmol (Afrique, tom ii p 562).

sent, which he required before he would march to the assistance of Tripoli, his demand was equivalent to a refusal, and he might justly be accused as the author of the public calamity In the annual assembly of the three cities, they nominated two deputies, to lay at the feet of Valentinian the customary offering of a gold victory; and to accompany this tribute of duty, rather than of gratitude, with their humble complaint that they were ruined by the enemy and betrayed by their governor. If the severity of Valentinian had been rightly directed, it would have fallen on the guilty head of Romanus. But the Count, long exercised in the arts of corruption, had dispatched a swift and trusty messenger to secure the venal friendship of Remigius, master of the offices. The wisdom of the Imperial council was deceived by artifice; and their honest indignation was cooled by delay. At length, when the repetition of complaint had been justified by the repetition of public misfortunes, the notary Palladius was sent from the court of Treves, to examine the state of Africa, and the conduct of Romanus. The rigid impartiality of Palladius was easily disarmed: he was tempted to reserve for himself a part of the public treasure which he brought with him for the payment of the troops; and from the moment that he was conscious of his own guilt, he could no longer refuse to attest the innocence and merit of the Count. The charge of the Tripolitans was declared to be false and frivolous; and Palladius himself was sent back from Treves to Africa, with a special commission to discover and prosecute the authors of this impious conspiracy against the representatives of the sovereign. His inquiries were managed with so much dexterity and success that he compelled the citizens of Leptis, who had sustained a recent siege of eight days, to contradict the truth of their own decrees and to censure the behaviour of their own deputies. A bloody sentence was pronounced, without hesitation, by the rash and headstrong cruelty of Valentinian. The president of Tripoli, who had presumed to pity the distress of the province, was publicly executed at Utica; four distinguished citizens were put to death as the accomplices of the imaginary fraud; and the tongues of two others were cut out by the express order of the emperor. Romanus, elated by impunity and irritated by resistance, was still continued in the military command; till the Africans were provoked by his avarice to join the rebellious standard of Firmus, the Moor.[125]

[125] Ammian. xviii 6. Tillemont (Hist. des Empereurs, tom. v p 25, 676) has discussed the chronological difficulties of the history of Count Romanus. [Attacks

Revolt of
Firmus
A.D 372

His father Nabal was one of the richest and most powerful of the Moorish princes, who acknowledged the supremacy of Rome   But, as he left, either by his wives or concubines, a very numerous posterity, the wealthy inheritance was eagerly disputed; and Zamma, one of his sons, was slain in a domestic quarrel by his brother Firmus   The implacable zeal with which Romanus prosecuted the legal revenge of this murder could be ascribed only to a motive of avarice, or personal hatred: but, on this occasion, his claims were just; his influence was weighty, and Firmus clearly understood that he must either present his neck to the executioner or appeal from the sentence of the Imperial consistory to his sword and to the people.[126]   He was received as the deliverer of his country, and, as soon as it appeared that Romanus was formidable only to a submissive province, the tyrant of Africa became the object of universal contempt.   The ruin of Cæsarea, which was plundered and burnt by the licentious Barbarians, convinced the refractory cities of the danger of resistance, the power of Firmus was established, at least in the provinces of Mauritania and Numidia, and it seemed to be his only doubt, whether he should assume the diadem of a Moorish king or the purple of a Roman emperor. But the imprudent and unhappy Africans soon discovered that, in this rash insurrection, they had not sufficiently consulted their own strength or the abilities of their leader.   Before he could procure any certain intelligence that the emperor of the West had fixed the choice of a general, or that a fleet of transports was collected at the mouth of the Rhone, he was suddenly in-

Theodosius
recovers Afri-
ca. A D
373

formed that the great Theodosius, with a small band of veterans, had landed near Igilgilis, or Gigeri, on the African coast; and the timid usurper sunk under the ascendant of virtue and military genius.   Though Firmus possessed arms and treasures, his despair of victory immediately reduced him to the use of

of the barbarians on the Tripolitan towns are fixed by Reiche, op. cit , to winter 363 and summer 365; Valentinian dispatches Nestorius and others to protect Africa, winter 365 (Amm xxvi 5, 14); Tripolis again invaded, summer 366; commission of Palladius, end of 366; embassy from Leptis, and return of Palladius, winter 367, second visit of Palladius to Africa, spring 368, Firmus rebels, winter 371; Theodosius arrives, summer 372 (between May and June 372 and Feb. 373. Sievers, Studien, p 288).]

[126] The chronology of Ammianus is loose and obscure and Orosius (l vii c 33, p 551, edit. Havercamp) seems to place the revolt of Firmus after the deaths of Valentinian and Valens. [Not so; Gibbon has misread Orosius] Tillemont (Hist. des Emp tom v p 691) endeavours to pick his way The patient and sure-footed mule of the Alps may be trusted in the most slippery paths. [Sievers and Reiche agree that the revolt was suppressed in 373, Cagnat prefers the date 374, L'armée romaine d'Afrique, p. 78]

those arts which, in the same country and in a similar situation, had formerly been practised by the crafty Jugurtha. He attempted to deceive, by an apparent submission, the vigilance of the Roman general; to seduce the fidelity of his troops; and to protract the duration of the war, by successively engaging the independent tribes of Africa to espouse his quarrel or to protect his flight. Theodosius imitated the example, and obtained the success, of his predecessor Metellus. When Firmus, in the character of a suppliant, accused his own rashness and humbly solicited the clemency of the emperor, the lieutenant of Valentinian received and dismissed him with a friendly embrace; but he diligently required the useful and substantial pledges of a sincere repentance; nor could he be persuaded, by the assurances of peace, to suspend, for an instant, the operations of an active war. A dark conspiracy was detected by the penetration of Theodosius; and he satisfied, without much reluctance, the public indignation, which he had secretly excited. Several of the guilty accomplices of Firmus were abandoned, according to ancient custom, to the tumult of a military execution; many more, by the amputation of both their hands, continued to exhibit an instructive spectacle of horror, the hatred of the rebels was accompanied with fear; and the fear of the Roman soldiers was mingled with respectful admiration. Amidst the boundless plains of Getulia, and the innumerable valleys of Mount Atlas, it was impossible to prevent the escape of Firmus; and, if the usurper could have tired the patience of his antagonist, he would have secured his person in the depth of some remote solitude, and expected the hopes of a future revolution. He was subdued by the perseverance of Theodosius; who had formed an inflexible determination that the war should end only by the death of the tyrant, and that every nation of Africa which presumed to support his cause should be involved in his ruin. At the head of a small body of troops, which seldom exceeded three thousand five hundred men, the Roman general advanced with a steady prudence, devoid of rashness or of fear, into the heart of a country where he was sometimes attacked by armies of twenty thousand Moors. The boldness of his charge dismayed the irregular Barbarians; they were disconcerted by his seasonable and orderly retreats; they were continually baffled by the unknown resources of the military art; and they felt and confessed the just superiority which was assumed by the leader of a civilized nation. When Theodosius entered the extensive dominions of Igmazen, king of the Isaflenses, the haughty savage

required, in words of defiance, his name and the object of his
expedition. "I am," replied the stern and disdainful count,
"I am the general of Valentinian, the lord of the world; who
has sent me hither to pursue and punish a desperate robber.
Deliver him instantly into my hands, and be assured that, if
thou dost not obey the commands of my invincible sovereign,
thou, and the people over whom thou reignest, shall be utterly
extirpated." As soon as Igmazen was satisfied that his enemy
had strength and resolution to execute the fatal menace, he
consented to purchase a necessary peace by the sacrifice of a
guilty fugitive. The guards that were placed to secure the
person of Firmus deprived him of the hopes of escape; and the
Moorish tyrant, after wine had extinguished the sense of danger,
disappointed the insulting triumph of the Romans by strangling
himself in the night. His dead body, the only present which
Igmazen could offer to the conqueror, was carelessly thrown
upon a camel; and Theodosius, leading back his victorious troops
to Sitifi, was saluted by the warmest acclamations of joy and
loyalty.[127]

He is executed
at Carthage
A D 376

Africa had been lost by the vices of Romanus; it was restored
by the virtues of Theodosius. and our curiosity may be usefully
directed to the inquiry of the respective treatment which the
two generals received from the Imperial court. The authority
of Count Romanus had been suspended by the master-general
of the cavalry; and he was committed to safe and honourable
custody till the end of the war His crimes were proved by the
most authentic evidence; and the public expected, with some
impatience, the decree of severe justice. But the partial

[leg Mero-
baudes]

and powerful favour of Mellobaudes encouraged him to challenge
his legal judges, to obtain repeated delays for the purpose of
procuring a crowd of friendly witnesses, and, finally, to cover
his guilty conduct by the additional guilt of fraud and forgery.
About the same time, the restorer of Britain and Africa, on a
vague suspicion that his name and services were superior to the
rank of a subject, was ignominiously beheaded at Carthage.
Valentinian no longer reigned, and the death of Theodosius,
as well as the impunity of Romanus, may justly be imputed to
the arts of the ministers who abused the confidence, and deceived
the inexperienced youth, of his sons.[128]

[127] Ammian. xxix 5 The text of this long chapter (fifteen quarto pages) is
broken and corrupted, and the narrative is perplexed by the want of chronological
and geographical landmarks [For the revolt, cp. also Pacatus, 5]
[128] Ammianus, xxviii 4 Orosius, l vii c 33, p. 551, 552. Jerom, in Chron.
374. [For confusion of Merobaudes and Mellobaudes, cp p 67 and App. 4]

If the geographical accuracy of Ammianus had been fortun- State of
ately bestowed on the British exploits of Theodosius, we should Africa
have traced, with eager curiosity, the distinct and domestic
footsteps of his march.   But the tedious enumeration of the
unknown and uninteresting tribes of Africa may be reduced to
the general remark that they were all of the swarthy race of
the Moors; that they inhabited the back settlements of the
Mauritanian and Numidian provinces, the country, as they have
since been termed by the Arabs, of dates and of locusts;[129] and
that, as the Roman power declined in Africa, the boundary of
civilized manners and cultivated land was insensibly contracted.
Beyond the utmost limits of the Moors, the vast and inhospitable
desert of the South extends above a thousand miles to the
banks of the Niger.   The ancients, who had a very faint and
imperfect knowledge of the great peninsula of Africa, were
sometimes tempted to believe that the torrid zone must ever
remain destitute of inhabitants · [130] and they sometimes amused
their fancy by filling the vacant space with headless men, or
rather monsters;[131] with horned and cloven-footed satyrs;[132]
with fabulous centaurs;[133] and with human pygmies, who waged
a bold and doubtful warfare against the cranes.[134]   Carthage

[129] Leo Africanus (in the Viaggi di Ramusio, tom 1 fol 78-83) has traced a
curious picture of the people and the country, which are more minutely described
in the Afrique de Marmol, tom III p 1-54
[130] This uninhabitable zone was gradually reduced, by the improvements of
ancient geography, from forty-five to twenty-four, or even sixteen, degrees of
latitude.   See a learned and judicious note of Dr Robertson, Hist of America,
vol 1. p 426
[131] Intra, si credere libet, vix jam homines et magis semiferi   . Blemmyes,
Satyri, &c   Pomponius Mela, 1 4, p 26, edit Voss. in 8vo. Pliny *philosophically*
explains (vi 35) the irregularities of nature, which he had *credulously* admitted
(v. 8)
[132] If the satyr was the Orang-outang, the great human ape (Buffon, Hist.
Nat tom xiv p 43, &c), one of that species might actually be shown alive at
Alexandria in the reign of Constantine   Yet some difficulty will still remain
about the conversation which St. Anthony held with one of these pious savages
in the desert of Thebais (Jerom, in Vit Paul Eremit tom i. p 238)
[133] St. Anthony likewise met one of *these* monsters, whose existence was seriously
asserted by the emperor Claudius.   The public laughed; but his præfect of
Egypt had the address to send an artful preparation, the embalmed corpse of an
Hippocentaur, which was preserved almost a century afterwards in the Imperial
palace.   See Pliny (Hist Natur vii. 3), and the judicious observations of Fréret
(Mémoires de l'Acad. tom. vii p. 321, &c).
[134] The fable of the pygmies is as old as Homer (Iliad, iii 6).   The pygmies of
India and Æthiopia were (trispithami) twenty-seven inches high   Every spring
their cavalry (mounted on rams and goats) marched in battle array to destroy the
cranes' eggs, aliter (says Pliny) futuris gregibus non resisti   Their houses were
built of mud, feathers, and egg-shells. See Pliny (vi 35, vii. 2), and Strabo (l. ii.
p. 121 [§ 1, 9])

would have trembled at the strange intelligence that the countries on either side of the equator were filled with innumerable nations, who differed only in their colour from the ordinary appearance of the human species; and the subjects of the Roman empire might have anxiously expected that the swarms of Barbarians which issued from the North would soon be encountered from the South by new swarms of Barbarians, equally fierce, and equally formidable. These gloomy terrors would indeed have been dispelled by a more intimate acquaintance with the character of their African enemies. The inaction of the negroes does not seem to be the effect either of their virtue or of their pusillanimity. They indulge, like the rest of mankind, their passions and appetites; and the adjacent tribes are engaged in frequent acts of hostility.[185] But their rude ignorance has never invented any effectual weapons of defence or of destruction; they appear incapable of forming any extensive plans of government or conquest; and the obvious inferiority of their mental faculties has been discovered and abused by the nations of the temperate zone. Sixty thousand blacks are annually embarked from the coast of Guinea, never to return to their native country; but they are embarked in chains:[136] and this constant emigration, which, in the space of two centuries, might have furnished armies to overrun the globe, accuses the guilt of Europe and the weakness of Africa.

IV. The ignominious treaty which saved the army of Jovian had been faithfully executed on the side of the Romans. and, as they had solemnly renounced the sovereignty and alliance of Armenia and Iberia, those tributary kingdoms were exposed, without protection, to the arms of the Persian monarch.[187] Sapor entered the Armenian territories at the head of a formidable host of cuirassiers, of archers, and of mercenary foot; but it was the invariable practice of Sapor to mix war and

IV THE EAST. The Persian war A D. 365-378

---

[135] The third and fourth volumes of the valuable Histoire des Voyages describe the present state of the negroes The nations of the sea-coast have been polished by European commerce, and those of the inland country have been improved by Moorish colonies

[136] Histoire Philosophique et Politique, &c , tom iv. p. 192

[137] The evidence of Ammianus is original and decisive (xxvii. 12) Moses of Chorene (l. iii. c. 17, p 249, and c. 34 p 269) and Procopius (de Bell. Persico, l i. c. 5, p. 17, edit. Louvre) have been consulted; but those historians, who confound distinct facts, repeat the same events, and introduce strange stories, must be used with diffidence and caution. [The account in the text of the war about Armenia is vitiated by numerous confusions. The only good sources are Faustus and Ammian. See above, vol. ii. App. 18.]

negotiation, and to consider falsehood and perjury as the most powerful instruments of regal policy. He affected to praise the prudent and moderate conduct of the king of Armenia; and the unsuspicious Tiranus was persuaded, by the repeated assurances [Arshak] of insidious friendship, to deliver his person into the hands of a faithless and cruel enemy. In the midst of a splendid entertainment, he was bound in chains of silver, as an honour due to the blood of the Arsacides; and, after a short confinement in the Tower of Oblivion at Ecbatana,[138] he was released from the miseries of life, either by his own dagger or by that of an [367 A D] assassin. The kingdom of Armenia was reduced to the state of a Persian province; the administration was shared between a distinguished satrap and a favourite eunuch; and Sapor marched, without delay, to subdue the martial spirit of the Iberians. Sauromaces, who reigned in that country by the permission of the emperors, was expelled by a superior force; and, as an insult on the majesty of Rome, the King of kings placed a diadem on the head of his abject vassal Aspacuras. The city of Artogerassa [139] was the only place of Armenia which presumed to resist the effort of his arms. The treasure deposited in that strong fortress tempted the avarice of Sapor; but the danger of Olympias, the wife, or widow, of the Armenian king, excited [Pharandzem] the public compassion, and animated the desperate valour of her subjects and soldiers. The Persians were surprised and repulsed under the walls of Artogerassa, by a bold and well-concerted sally of the besieged. But the forces of Sapor were continually renewed and increased; the hopeless courage of the garrison was exhausted; the strength of the walls yielded to the assault; and the proud conqueror, after wasting the rebellious city with fire and sword, led away captive an unfortunate queen, who, in a more auspicious hour, had been the destined bride of the son of Constantine.[140] Yet, if Sapor already triumphed in the easy conquest of two dependent kingdoms, he soon felt that a country is unsubdued, as long as the minds of the people are actuated by an hostile and contumacious spirit. The satraps, whom he was obliged to trust, embraced the first opportunity

---

[138] [Castle of Aniush (Ammian calls it Agabana), in Susiana; exact locality is uncertain. For the events (Gibbon makes Arshak into Tiran) see Faustus, iv. 54]

[139] Perhaps Artagera, or Ardis [= Ardakers], under whose walls Gaius, the grandson of Augustus, was wounded   This fortress was situate above Amida, near one of the sources of the Tigris   See d'Anville, Géographie Ancienne, tom. ii., p. 106

[140] Tillemont (Hist des Empereurs, tom v p 701) proves from chronology that Olympias must have been the mother of Para. [The wife was Pharandzēm, not Olympias; Faustus, iv. 55]

of regaining the affection of their countrymen and of signalizing
their immortal hatred to the Persian name   Since the conversion of the Armenians and Iberians, those nations considered
the Christians as the favourites, and the Magians as the adversaries, of the Supreme Being, the influence of the clergy over
a superstitious people was uniformly exerted in the cause of
Rome; and, as long as the successors of Constantine disputed
with those of Artaxerxes the sovereignty of the intermediate
provinces, the religious connexion always threw a decisive advantage into the scale of the empire.   A numerous and active
[Pap]   party acknowledged Para, the son of Tiranus, as the lawful
sovereign of Armenia; and his title to the throne was deeply
rooted in the hereditary succession of five hundred years   By
the unanimous consent of the Iberians, the country was
equally divided between the rival princes; and Aspacuras, who
owed his diadem to the choice of Sapor, was obliged to declare
that his regard for his children, who were detained as hostages
by the tyrant, was the only consideration which prevented him
from openly renouncing the alliance of Persia.   The emperor
Valens, who respected the obligations of the treaty, and who
was apprehensive of involving the East in a dangerous war, ventured, with slow and cautious measures, to support the Roman
party in the kingdoms of Iberia and Armenia.   Twelve legions
[A.D 372] established the authority of Sauromaces on the banks of the
Cyrus.   The Euphrates was protected by the valour of Arintheus.   A powerful army, under the command of Count Trajan,
and of Vadomair, king of the Alemanni, fixed their camp on the
confines of Armenia.   But they were strictly enjoined not to
commit the first hostilities, which might be understood as a
breach of the treaty: and such was the implicit obedience of
the Roman general that they retreated, with exemplary patience,
under a shower of Persian arrows, till they had clearly acquired
[A D 373   a just title to an honourable and legitimate victory.   Yet these
Battle of
Vagabanta] appearances of war insensibly subsided in a vain and tedious
negotiation.   The contending parties supported their claims by
mutual reproaches of perfidy and ambition; and it should seem
that the original treaty was expressed in very obscure terms,
since they were reduced to the necessity of making their incon-
clusive appeal to the partial testimony of the generals of the
two nations who had assisted at the negotiations.[141]   The in-

---

[141] Ammianus (xxvii 12, xxix. 1, xxx. 1, 2) has described the events, without
the dates, of the Persian war.   Moses of Chorene (Hist Armen. 1 iii c. 28, p.
261, c 31, p 266, c. 35, p 271) affords some additional facts; but it is extremely
difficult to separate truth from fable.

vasion of the Goths and Huns, which soon afterwards shook the
foundations of the Roman empire, exposed the provinces of Asia
to the arms of Sapor But the declining age, and perhaps the
infirmities, of the monarch suggested new maxims of tranquillity
and moderation. His death, which happened in the full [A D 380]
maturity of a reign of seventy years, changed in a moment the [379] [Summer]
court and councils of Persia ; and their attention was most probably engaged by domestic troubles, and the distant efforts of a
Carmanian war.[142] The remembrance of ancient injuries was
lost in the enjoyment of peace. The kingdoms of Armenia and [The treaty]
Iberia were permitted, by the mutual, though tacit, consent of [A D 384] [of peace]
both empires, to resume their doubtful neutrality. In the first
years of the reign of Theodosius, a Persian embassy arrived at
Constantinople, to excuse the unjustifiable measures of the
former reign ; and to offer, as the tribute of friendship, or even
of respect, a splendid present of gems, of silk, and of Indian
elephants.[143]

In the general picture of the affairs of the East under the [Adventures]
reign of Valens, the adventures of Para form one of the most [of Para, king] [of Armenia]
striking and singular objects. The noble youth, by the per-
suasion of his mother Olympias, had escaped through the Per [Pharandzem]
sian host that besieged Artogerassa, and implored the protection [A D 367]
of the emperor of the East By his timid councils, Para was
alternately supported, and recalled, and restored, and betrayed. [restored] [A D 369]
The hopes of the Armenians were sometimes raised by the
presence of their natural sovereign ; and the ministers of Valens
were satisfied that they preserved the integrity of the public
faith, if their vassal was not suffered to assume the diadem and
title of King. But they soon repented of their own rashness
They were confounded by the reproaches and threats of the
Persian monarch. They found reason to distrust the cruel and
inconstant temper of Para himself, who sacrificed, to the
slightest suspicions, the lives of his most faithful servants ; and [A D 371]
held a secret and disgraceful correspondence with the assassin
of his father and the enemy of his country. Under the specious

---

[142] Artaxerxes was the successor and brother (*the cousin-german*) of the great
Sapor ; and the guardian of his son Sapor III (Agathias, l. iv p. 136, edit.
Louvre [c. 26, p. 263, ed Bonn]). See the Universal History, vol, xi. p. 86, 161.
The authors of that unequal work have compiled the Sassanian dynasty with
erudition and diligence · but it is a preposterous arrangement to divide the Roman
and Oriental accounts into two distinct histories [The first year of Ardeshir,
successor of Sapor, was reckoned from 19 Aug 379, Noldeke, Gesch der Perser
und Araber, &c , p 418. For dates of his successors see Appendix 5]

[143] Pacatus in Panegyr Vet. xii 22, and Orosius, l vii. c 34. Ictumque tum
foedus est, quo universus Oriens usque ad nunc (A. D. 416) tranquillissimè fruitur.

pretence of consulting with the emperor on the subject of their common interest, Para was persuaded to descend from the mountains of Armenia, where his party was in arms, and to trust his independence and safety to the discretion of a perfidious court   The king of Armenia, for such he appeared in his own eyes and in those of his nation, was received with due honours by the governors of the provinces through which he passed ; but, when he arrived at Tarsus in Cilicia, his progress was stopped under various pretences ; his motions were watched with respectful vigilance ; and he gradually discovered that he was a prisoner in the hands of the Romans.   Para suppressed his indignation, dissembled his fears, and, after secretly preparing his escape, mounted on horseback with three hundred of his faithful followers.   The officer stationed at the door of his apartment immediately communicated his flight to the consular of Cilicia, who overtook him in the suburbs, and endeavoured, without success, to dissuade him from prosecuting his rash and dangerous design.   A legion was ordered to pursue the royal fugitive ; but the pursuit of infantry could not be very alarming to a body of light cavalry ; and upon the first cloud of arrows that was discharged into the air they retreated with precipitation to the gates of Tarsus.   After an incessant march of two days and two nights, Para and his Armenians reached the banks of the Euphrates ; but the passage of the river, which they were obliged to swim, was attended with some delay and some loss   The country was alarmed ; and the two roads, which were only separated by an interval of three miles, had been occupied by a thousand archers on horseback, under the command of a count and a tribune.   Para must have yielded to superior force, if the accidental arrival of a friendly traveller had not revealed the danger, and the means of escape   A dark and almost impervious path securely conveyed the Armenian troop through the thicket ; and Para had left behind him the count and the tribune, while they patiently expected his approach along the public highways.   They returned to the Imperial court to excuse their want of diligence or success : and seriously alleged that the king of Armenia, who was a skilful magician, had transformed himself and his followers, and passed before their eyes under a borrowed shape.   After his return to his native kingdom, Para still continued to profess himself the friend and ally of the Romans ; but the Romans had injured him too deeply ever to forgive, and the secret sentence of his death was signed in the council of Valens   The execution of the bloody deed was committed to the subtle prudence of Count Trajan; and he had the merit of insinuating himself into the confidence of the credulous prince, that he might find an opportunity of stabbing him to the heart. Para was invited to a Roman banquet, which had been prepared with all the pomp and sensuality of the East: the hall resounded with cheerful music, and the company was already heated with wine; when the count retired for an instant, drew his sword, and gave the signal of the murder. A robust and desperate Barbarian instantly rushed on the king of Armenia; and, though he bravely defended his life with the first weapon that chance offered to his hand, the table of the A D 374 Imperial general was stained with the royal blood of a guest, and an ally. Such were the weak and wicked maxims of the Roman administration, that, to attain a doubtful object of political interest, the laws of nations and the sacred rights of hospitality were inhumanly violated in the face of the world.[144]

V. During a peaceful interval of thirty years, the Romans V THE DAN UBE Con- secured their frontiers, and the Goths extended their dominions quests of The victories of the great Hermanric,[145] king of the Ostrogoths, Hermanric and the most noble of the race of the Amali, have been compared, by the enthusiasm of his countrymen, to the exploits of Alexander: with this singular, and almost incredible, difference, that the martial spirit of the Gothic hero, instead of being supported by the vigour of youth, was displayed with glory and success in the extreme period of human life; between the age of fourscore and one hundred and ten years. The independent tribes were persuaded, or compelled, to acknowledge the king of the Ostrogoths as the sovereign of the Gothic nation · the chiefs of the Visigoths, or Thervingi, renounced the royal title, and assumed the more humble appellation of *Judges*,[146] and, among those judges, Athanaric, Fritigern, and Alavivus were the most illustrious, by their personal merit, as well as by their vicinity to the Roman provinces. These domestic conquests,

[144] See in Ammianus (xxx 1) the adventures of Para [Pap is the true name, Faustus, B H passim] Moses of Chorene calls him Tiridates, and tells a long and not improbable story of his son Gnelus, who afterwards made himself popular in Armenia, and provoked the jealousy of the reigning king (l. iii. c. 21, &c, p 253, &c). [Knel was nephew of Arshak, who killed him and married his wife Pharandzēm. Faustus, iv. 15]

[145] The concise account of the reign and conquests of Hermanric, seems to be one of the valuable fragments which Jornandes (c 28) borrowed from the Gothic histories of Ablavius, or Cassiodorus.

[146] [Dahn agrees that the Visigoths belonged to a (loose) confederacy of which Hermanric was chief, Kon der Germanen, ii 90. But he doubts the legitimacy of inferring from the case of Athanaric (called Judge by Themistius, Or. X., and Ammian) that the other chiefs were called Judges (v 10)]

which increased the military power of Hermanric, enlarged his
ambitious designs. He invaded the adjacent countries of the
North ; and twelve considerable nations, whose names and limits
cannot be accurately defined, successively yielded to the superiority of the Gothic arms [147] The Heruli, who inhabited the
marshy lands near the lake Mæotis, were renowned for their
strength and agility ; and the assistance of their light infantry
was eagerly solicited, and highly esteemed, in all the wars of
the Barbarians. But the active spirit of the Heruli was subdued by the slow and steady perseverance of the Goths ; and,
after a bloody action, in which the king was slain, the remains
of that warlike tribe became an useful accession to the camp of
Hermanric. He then marched against the Venedi ; unskilled
in the use of arms, and formidable only by their numbers, which
filled the wide extent of the plains of modern Poland. The
victorious Goths, who were not inferior in numbers, prevailed in
the contest, by the decisive advantages of exercise and discipline. After the submission of the Venedi, the conqueror advanced, without resistance, as far as the confines of the *Æstii ;* [148]
an ancient people, whose name is still preserved in the province
of Esthonia   Those distant inhabitants of the Baltic coast were
supported by the labours of agriculture, enriched by the trade
of amber, and consecrated by the peculiar worship of the Mother
of the Gods. But the scarcity of iron obliged the Æstian
warriors to content themselves with wooden clubs , and the
reduction of that wealthy country is ascribed to the prudence,
rather than to the arms, of Hermanric. His dominions, which
extended from the Danube to the Baltic, included the native
seats, and the recent acquisitions, of the Goths ; and he reigned
over the greatest part of Germany and Scythia with the authority
of a conqueror, and sometimes with the cruelty of a tyrant. But
he reigned over a part of the globe incapable of perpetuating
and adorning the glory of its heroes. The name of Hermanric is almost buried in oblivion , his exploits are imperfectly
known ; and the Romans themselves appeared unconscious of

[147] M. de Buat (Hist. des Peuples de l'Europe, t vi p. 311-329) investigates,
with more industry than success, the nations subdued by the arms of Hermanric
He denies the existence of the *Vissnobroncæ*, on account of the immoderate length
of their name   Yet the French envoy to Ratisbon, or Dresden, must have
traversed the country of the *Mediomatrici*

[148] The edition of Grotius (Jornandes, p 642 [xviii § 120]) exhibits the name
of *Æstri*   But reason and the Ambrosian Ms have restored the *Æstii*, whose
manners and situation are expressed by the pencil of Tacitus (Germania, c. 45)

the progress of an aspiring power, which threatened the liberty
of the North and the peace of the empire.[149]

The Goths had contracted an hereditary attachment for the The cause of the Gothic war A D 366
Imperial house of Constantine, of whose power and liberality
they had received so many signal proofs. They respected the
public peace ; and, if an hostile band sometimes presumed to
pass the Roman limit, their irregular conduct was candidly
ascribed to the ungovernable spirit of the Barbarian youth.
Their contempt for two new and obscure princes, who had been
raised to the throne by a popular election, inspired the Goths
with bolder hopes, and, while they agitated some design of
marching their confederate force under the national standard,[150]
they were easily tempted to embrace the party of Procopius,
and to foment, by their dangerous aid, the civil discord of the
Romans.   The public treaty might stipulate no more than ten
thousand auxiliaries ; but the design was so zealously adopted
by the chiefs of the Visigoths that the army which passed the
Danube amounted to the number of thirty thousand men.[151]
They marched with the proud confidence that their invincible
valour would decide the fate of the Roman empire ; and the
provinces of Thrace groaned under the weight of the Barbarians,
who displayed the insolence of masters and the licentiousness of
enemies.   But the intemperance which gratified their appetites
retarded their progress, and, before the Goths could receive
any certain intelligence of the defeat and death of Procopius,
they perceived, by the hostile state of the country, that the
civil and military powers were resumed by his successful rival.
A chain of posts and fortifications, skilfully disposed by Valens,
or the generals of Valens, resisted their march, prevented their
retreat, and intercepted their subsistence.   The fierceness of the
Barbarians was tamed and suspended by hunger ; they indignantly threw down their arms at the feet of the conqueror, who
offered them food and chains ; the numerous captives were
distributed in all the cities of the East ; and the provincials,
who were soon familiarized with their savage appearance, ventured, by degrees, to measure their own strength with these

[149] Ammianus (xxxi. 3) observes, in general terms . Ermenrichi . . . nobilissimi
Regis, et, per multa variaque fortiter facta, vicinis gentibus formidati, &c.

[150] Valens . . . docetur relationibus Ducum, gentem Gothorum, eâ tempestate
intactam ideoque sævissimam conspirantem in unum, ad pervadendam parari
collimitia Thraciarum   Ammian xxvi 6

[151] M. de Buat (Hist des Peuples de l'Europe, tom vi. p. 332) has curiously
ascertained the real number of these auxiliaries.   The 3000 of Ammianus, and the
10,000 of Zosimus, were only the first divisions of the Gothic army.

formidable adversaries, whose name had so long been the object
of their terror.   The king of Scythia (and Hermanric alone
could deserve so lofty a title) was grieved and exasperated by
this national calamity.   His ambassadors loudly complained, at
the court of Valens, of the infraction of the ancient and solemn
alliance which had so long subsisted between the Romans and
the Goths.   They alleged that they had fulfilled the duty of
allies by assisting the kinsman and successor of the emperor
Julian, they required the immediate restitution of the noble
captives ; and they urged a very singular claim, that the Gothic
generals, marching in arms and in hostile array, were entitled
to the sacred character and privileges of ambassadors   The
decent but peremptory refusal of these extravagant demands
was signified to the Barbarians by Victor, master-general of the
cavalry ; who expressed, with force and dignity, the just complaints of the Emperor of the East.[152]   The negotiation was
interrupted ; and the manly exhortations of Valentinian
encouraged his timid brother to vindicate the insulted majesty
of the empire.[153]

Hostilities
and peace.
A D 367, 368,
369

The splendour and magnitude of this Gothic war are celebrated by a contemporary historian ;[154] but the events scarcely
deserve the attention of posterity, except as the preliminary
steps of the approaching decline and fall of the empire.   Instead of leading the nations of Germany and Scythia to the
banks of the Danube, or even to the gates of Constantinople,
the aged monarch of the Goths resigned to the brave Athanaric
the danger and glory of a defensive war, against an enemy who
wielded with a feeble hand the powers of a mighty state.   A
bridge of boats was established upon the Danube ; the presence
of Valens animated his troops, and his ignorance of the art of
war was compensated by personal bravery and a wise deference
to the advice of Victor and Arintheus, his masters-general of
the cavalry and infantry   The operations of the campaign were

[152] The march and subsequent negotiation are described in the Fragments of
Eunapius (Excerpt Legat p 18, edit. Louvre [fr 37 F. H G iv])   The provincials, who afterwards became familiar with the Barbarians, found that their strength
was more apparent than real.   They were tall of stature; but their legs were
clumsy, and their shoulders were narrow.

[153] Valens enim, ut consulto placuerat fratri, cujus regebatur arbitrio, arma
concussit in Gothos ratione justâ permotus   Ammianus (xxvii 4) then proceeds
to describe, not the country of the Goths, but the peaceful and obedient province
of Thrace, which was not affected by the war.

[154] Eunapius, in Excerpt Legat p 18, 19 [18].   The Greek sophist must have
considered as one and the same war the whole series of Gothic history till the
victories and peace of Theodosius.

conducted by their skill and experience; but they found it
impossible to drive the Visigoths from their strong posts in the
mountains : and the devastation of the plains obliged the
Romans themselves to repass the Danube on the approach of
winter. The incessant rains, which swelled the waters of the
river, produced a tacit suspension of arms, and confined the
emperor Valens, during the whole course of the ensuing
summer, to his camp of Marcianopolis. The third year of the
war was more favourable to the Romans and more pernicious
to the Goths. The interruption of trade deprived the Barbarians of the objects of luxury which they already confounded
with the necessaries of life ; and the desolation of a very extensive
tract of country threatened them with the horrors of famine.
Athanaric was provoked, or compelled, to risk a battle, which
he lost, in the plains ; and the pursuit was rendered more
bloody by the cruel precaution of the victorious generals, who
had promised a large reward for the head of every Goth that
was brought into the Imperial camp. The submission of the
Barbarians appeased the resentment of Valens and his council ;
the emperor listened with satisfaction to the flattering and
eloquent remonstrance of the senate of Constantinople, which
assumed, for the first time, a share in the public deliberations ;
and the same generals, Victor and Arintheus, who had successfully directed the conduct of the war, were empowered to
regulate the conditions of peace. The freedom of trade, which
the Goths had hitherto enjoyed, was restricted to two cities on
the Danube; the rashness of their leaders was severely punished
by the suppression of their pensions and subsidies; and the
exception, which was stipulated in favour of Athanaric alone,
was more advantageous than honourable to the Judge of the
Visigoths. Athanaric, who, on this occasion, appears to have
consulted his private interest, without expecting the orders of
his sovereign, supported his own dignity, and that of his tribe,
in the personal interview which was proposed by the ministers
of Valens. He persisted in his declaration that it was impossible for him, without incurring the guilt of perjury, ever to
set his foot on the territory of the empire , and it is more than
probable that his regard for the sanctity of an oath was confirmed by the recent and fatal examples of Roman treachery.
The Danube, which separated the dominions of the two independent nations, was chosen for the scene of the conference.
The Emperor of the East and the Judge of the Visigoths, accompanied by an equal number of armed followers, advanced

in their respective barges to the middle of the stream. After the ratification of the treaty, and the delivery of hostages, Valens returned in triumph to Constantinople; and the Goths remained in a state of tranquillity about six years; till they were violently impelled against the Roman empire by an innumerable host of Scythians, who appeared to issue from the frozen regions of the North [155]

War of the Quadi and Sarmatians A.D. 374

The Emperor of the West, who had resigned to his brother the command of the Lower Danube, reserved for his immediate care the defence of the Rhætian and Illyrian provinces, which spread so many hundred miles along the greatest of the European rivers. The active policy of Valentinian was continually employed in adding new fortifications to the security of the frontier; but the abuse of this policy provoked the just resentment of the Barbarians. The Quadi complained that the ground for an intended fortress had been marked out on their territories, and their complaints were urged with so much reason and moderation that Equitius, master-general of Illyricum, consented to suspend the prosecution of the work, till he should be more clearly informed of the will of his sovereign. This fair occasion of injuring a rival, and of advancing the fortune of his son, was eagerly embraced by the inhuman Maximin, the præfect, or rather tyrant, of Gaul. The passions of Valentinian were impatient of control; and he credulously listened to the assurances of his favourite that, if the government of Valeria, and the direction of the work, were intrusted to the zeal of his son Marcellinus, the emperor should no longer be importuned with the audacious remonstrances of the Barbarians. [156] The subjects of Rome, and the natives of Germany, were insulted by the arrogance of a young and worthless minister, who considered his rapid elevation as the proof and reward of his superior merit. He affected, however, to receive the modest application of Gabinius, king of the Quadi, with some attention and regard; but this artful civility

[Marcellianus]

---

[155] The Gothic war is described by Ammianus (xxvii. 5), Zosimus (l. iv. p. 211-214 [c. 10]), and Themistius (Orat. x. p. 129-141). The orator Themistius was sent from the senate of Constantinople to congratulate the victorious emperor; and his servile eloquence compares Valens on the Danube to Achilles in the Scamander. Jornandes forgets a war peculiar to the Visi-Goths, and inglorious to the Gothic name (Mascou's Hist. of the Germans, vii. 3).

[156] [The measures taken for the security of Valeria are illustrated by an inscription found near Gran (C. I. L. 3, 3653), which records the construction of a *burgum* named Commercium. In 377 A.D. Frigeridus was dux of Valeria, and his name is preserved inscribed on several tiles, C. I. L. 3, 3761. Cp. also Mommsen, Hermes, 17, p. 523.]

concealed a dark and bloody design, and the credulous prince was persuaded to accept the pressing invitation of Marcellinus. I am at a loss how to vary the narrative of similar crimes; or how to relate that, in the course of the same year, but in remote parts of the empire, the inhospitable table of two Imperial generals was stained with the royal blood of two guests and allies, inhumanly murdered by their order and in their presence. The fate of Gabinius and of Para was the same: but the cruel death of their sovereign was resented in a very different manner by the servile temper of the Armenians and the free and daring spirit of the Germans. The Quadi were much declined from that formidable power which, in the time of Marcus Antoninus, had spread terror to the gates of Rome. But they still possessed arms and courage; their courage was animated by despair, and they obtained the usual reinforcement of the cavalry of their Sarmatian allies. So improvident was the assassin Marcellinus that he chose the moment when the bravest veterans had been drawn away to suppress the revolt of Firmus; and the whole province was exposed, with a very feeble defence, to the rage of the exasperated Barbarians. They invaded Pannonia in the season of harvest, unmercifully destroyed every object of plunder which they could not easily transport; and either disregarded or demolished the empty fortifications. The princess Constantia, the daughter of the emperor Constantius and the grand-daughter of the great Constantine, very narrowly escaped. That royal maid, who had innocently supported the revolt of Procopius, was now the destined wife of the heir of the Western empire. She traversed the peaceful province with a splendid and unarmed train. Her person was saved from danger, and the republic from disgrace, by the active zeal of Messalla, governor of the provinces. As soon as he was informed that the village, where she stopped only to dine, was almost encompassed by the Barbarians, he hastily placed her in his own chariot, and drove full speed till he reached the gates of Sirmium, which were at the distance of six and twenty miles. Even Sirmium might not have been secure, if the Quadi and Sarmatians had diligently advanced during the general consternation of the magistrates and people. Their delay allowed Probus, the Prætorian præfect, sufficient time to recover his own spirits and to revive the courage of the citizens He skilfully directed their strenuous efforts to repair and strengthen the decayed fortifications, and procured the seasonable and effectual

assistance of a company of archers, to protect the capital of the
Illyrian provinces   Disappointed in their attempts against the
walls of Sirmium, the indignant Barbarians turned their arms
against the master-general of the frontier, to whom they unjustly
attributed the murder of their king   Equitius could bring into
the field no more than two legions , but they contained the
veteran strength of the Mæsian and Pannonian bands.   The
obstinacy with which they disputed the vain honours of rank and
precedency was the cause of their destruction ; and, while they
acted with separate forces and divided councils, they were
surprised and slaughtered by the active vigour of the Sarmatian
horse   The success of this invasion provoked the emulation of
the bordering tribes; and the province of Mæsia would infallibly have been lost, if young Theodosius, the duke, or
military commander, of the frontier, had not signalized, in the
defeat of the public enemy, an intrepid genius, worthy of his
illustrious father, and of his future greatness.[157]

The expedi-
tion

A.D. 375

The mind of Valentinian, who then resided at Treves, was
deeply affected by the calamities of Illyricum ; but the lateness
of the season suspended the execution of his designs till the
ensuing spring.   He marched in person, with a considerable
part of the forces of Gaul, from the banks of the Moselle : and
to the suppliant ambassadors of the Sarmatians, who met him
on the way, he returned a doubtful answer that, as soon as he
reached the scene of action, he should examine and pronounce.
When he arrived at Sirmium, he gave audience to the deputies
of the Illyrian provinces ; who loudly congratulated their own
felicity under the auspicious government of Probus, his Prætorian præfect [158]   Valentinian, who was flattered by these
demonstrations of their loyalty and gratitude, imprudently asked

[157] Ammianus (xxix. 6) and Zosimus (l. iv. p. 219, 220 [c. 16]) carefully mark
the origin and progress of the Quadic and Sarmatian war. [Cp Ranke, Welt-
geschichte, iv. 1, 168. But the victory of Theodosius was probably won after his
recall in 378 A D   So Richter, Westrom. Reich, 691, Sievers, Stud., 294; Kaufmann, Philologus, 31, 472, sqq.   The authority is Theodoret, v. 5, 6, and perhaps
Pacatus, Panag 9, 10]
[158] Ammianus (xxx. 5), who acknowledges the merit, has censured, with becoming asperity, the oppressive administration, of Petronius Probus   When Jerom
translated and continued the Chronicle of Eusebius (A D. 380   See Tillemont,
Mém Eccles tom. vii. p 53, 626), he expressed the truth, or at least the public
opinion of his country, in the following words   "Probus P. P. Illyrici iniquissimis
tributorum exactionibus, ante provincias quas regebat, qu...m a Barbaris vasta-
rentur, erasit" (Chron. edit. Scaliger, p. 187   Animadvers p 259).   The saint
afterwards formed an intimate and tender friendship with the widow of Probus;
and the name of Count Equitius, with less propriety, but without much injustice,
has been substituted in the text.

the deputy of Epirus, a Cynic philosopher of intrepid sincerity,[159] whether he was freely sent by the wishes of the province? "With tears and groans am I sent (replied Iphicles) by a reluctant people." The emperor paused: but the impunity of his ministers established the pernicious maxim that they might oppress his subjects without injuring his service. A strict inquiry into their conduct would have relieved the public discontent. The severe condemnation of the murder of Gabinius was the only measure which could restore the confidence of the Germans and vindicate the honour of the Roman name. But the haughty monarch was incapable of the magnanimity which dares to acknowledge a fault. He forgot the provocation, remembered only the injury, and advanced into the country of the Quadi with an insatiate thirst of blood and revenge. The extreme devastation and promiscuous massacre of a savage war were justified, in the eyes of the emperor, and perhaps in those of the world, by the cruel equity of retaliation;[160] and such was the discipline of the Romans, and the consternation of the enemy, that Valentinian repassed the Danube without the loss of a single man. As he had resolved to complete the destruction of the Quadi by a second campaign, he fixed his winter-quarters at Bregetio, on the Danube, near the [O-Szőny] Hungarian city of Presburg. While the operations of war were suspended by the severity of the weather, the Quadi made an humble attempt to deprecate the wrath of their conqueror; and, at the earnest persuasion of Equitius, their ambassadors were introduced into the Imperial council. They approached the throne with bended bodies and dejected countenances; and, without daring to complain of the murder of their king, they affirmed, with solemn oaths, that the late invasion was the crime of some irregular robbers, which the public council of the nation condemned and abhorred. The answer of the emperor left them but little to hope from his clemency or compassion. He reviled, in the most intemperate language, their baseness, their ingratitude, their insolence.—His eyes, his voice, his colour, his gestures, expressed the violence of his ungoverned fury; and, while his whole frame was agitated with convulsive passion, a large

---

[159] Julian (Orat vi. p. 198) represents his friend Iphicles as a man of virtue and merit, who had made himself ridiculous and unhappy by adopting the extravagant dress and manners of the Cynics

[160] Ammian. xxx 5. Jerom, who exaggerates the misfortune of Valentinian, refuses him even this last consolation of revenge. Genitali vastato solo, et *inultam* patriam derelinquens (tom. i. p 26 [ep 60]).

blood-vessel suddenly burst in his body; and Valentinian fell speechless into the arms of his attendants. Their pious care immediately concealed his situation from the crowd; but, in a few minutes, the Emperor of the West expired in an agony of pain, retaining his senses till the last, and struggling, without success, to declare his intentions to the generals and ministers who surrounded the royal couch. Valentinian was about fifty-four years of age; and he wanted only one hundred days to accomplish the twelve years of his reign.[161]

The polygamy of Valentinian is seriously attested by an ecclesiastical historian.[162] "The empress Severa (I relate the fable) admitted into her familiar society the lovely Justina, the daughter of an Italian governor; her admiration of those naked charms which she had often seen in the bath was expressed with such lavish and imprudent praise that the emperor was tempted to introduce a second wife into his bed; and his public edict extended to all the subjects of the empire the same domestic privilege which he had assumed for himself." But we may be assured, from the evidence of reason as well as history, that the two marriages of Valentinian, with Severa, and with Justina, were *successively* contracted; and that he used the ancient permission of divorce, which was still allowed by the laws, though it was condemned by the church. Severa was the mother of Gratian, who seemed to unite every claim which could entitle him to the undoubted succession of the Western empire. He was the eldest son of a monarch, whose glorious reign had confirmed the free and honourable choice of his fellow-soldiers. Before he had attained the ninth year of his age, the royal youth received from the hands of his indulgent father the purple robe and diadem, with the title of Augustus: the election was solemnly ratified by the consent and applause of the armies of Gaul;[163] and the name of Gratian was added to

Sidenotes:
and death of Valentinian

A D 375, November 17

The emperors Gratian and Valentinian II.

[A.D 368]

[A.D 367, Aug 24]

---

[161] See, on the death of Valentinian, Ammianus (xxx 6), Zosimus (l iv p. 221 [c 17]), Victor (in Epitom. [45]), Socrates (l. iv. c 31), and Jerom (in Chron. p. 187, and tom. 1. p. 26, ad Heliodor) There is much variety of circumstances among them, and Ammianus is so eloquent that he writes nonsense.

[162] Socrates (l iv. c 31) is the only original witness of this foolish story, so repugnant to the laws and manners of the Romans that it scarcely deserves the formal and elaborate dissertation of M. Bonamy (Mém de l'Académie, tom xxx p 394-405) Yet I would preserve the natural circumstance of the bath, instead of following Zosimus, who represents Justina as an old woman, the widow of Magnentius. [For the divorce of Valeria Severa Marina, and marriage with Aviana Justina, cp Richter, Das west-romische Reich, p. 278]

[163] Ammianus (xxvii. 6) describes the form of this military election and *august* investiture. Valentinian does not appear to have consulted, or even informed, the senate of Rome. [Date Idatius, Fasti Cons]

the names of Valentinian and Valens, in all the legal transactions of the Roman government.   By his marriage with the
grand-daughter of Constantine, the son of Valentinian acquired [Constantia,
all the hereditary rights of the Flavian family; which, in a $\begin{smallmatrix}\text{daughter of}\\\text{Constantius}\end{smallmatrix}$
series of three Imperial generations, were sanctified by time, $^{ii\ ]}$
religion, and the reverence of the people.   At the death of his
father, the royal youth was in the seventeenth year of his age ;
and his virtues already justified the favourable opinion of the
army and people.   But Gratian resided, without apprehension,
in the palace of Treves ; whilst, at the distance of many
hundred miles, Valentinian suddenly expired in the camp of
Bregetio.   The passions, which had been so long suppressed by
the presence of a master, immediately revived in the imperial
council ; and the ambitious design of reigning in the name of
an infant, was artfully executed by Mellobaudes and Equitius, [leg Mero-
who commanded the attachment of the Illyrian and Italian $^{\text{baudes]}}$
bands.   They contrived the most honourable pretences to
remove the popular leaders and the troops of Gaul, who might
have asserted the claims of the lawful successor ; they suggested the necessity of extinguishing the hopes of foreign and
domestic enemies by a bold and decisive measure.   The
empress Justina, who had been left in a palace about one
hundred miles from Bregetio, was respectfully invited to appear
in the camp, with the son of the deceased emperor.   On the
sixth day after the death of Valentinian, the infant prince of
the same name, who was only four years old, was shewn in the
arms of his mother to the legions ; and solemnly invested by
military acclamation with the titles and ensigns of supreme
power.   The impending dangers of a civil war were seasonably
prevented by the wise and moderate conduct of the emperor
Gratian.   He cheerfully accepted the choice of the army ;
declared that he should always consider the son of Justina as
a brother, not as a rival ; and advised the empress, with her
son Valentinian, to fix their residence at Milan, in the fair and
peaceful province of Italy ; while he assumed the more arduous
command of the countries beyond the Alps.   Gratian dissembled his resentment till he could safely punish, or disgrace,
the authors of the conspiracy ; and, though he uniformly
behaved with tenderness and regard to his infant colleague,
he gradually confounded, in the administration of the Western
empire, the office of a guardian with the authority of a
sovereign.   The government of the Roman world was exercised
in the united names of Valens and his two nephews ; but the

feeble emperor of the East, who succeeded to the rank of his elder brother, never obtained any weight or influence in the councils of the West.[164]

[164] Ammianus, xxx 10. Zosimus, l iv p 222, 223, [c 19]. Tillemont has proved (Hist des Empereurs, tom v p 707-709) that Gratian *reigned* in Italy, Africa, and Illyricum. I have endeavoured to express his authority over his brother's dominions, as he used it, in an ambiguous style.

CHAPTER XXVI

Manners of the Pastoral Nations—Progress of the Huns, from China to Europe—Flight of the Goths—They pass the Danube—Gothic war—Defeat and Death of Valens—Gratian invests Theodosius with the Eastern Empire—His Character and Success—Peace and Settlement of the Goths

IN the second year of the reign of Valentinian and Valens, on the morning of the twenty-first day of July, the greatest part of the Roman world was shaken by a violent and destructive earthquake. The impression was communicated to the waters; the shores of the Mediterranean were left dry, by the sudden retreat of the sea; great quantities of fish were caught with the hand; large vessels were stranded on the mud, and a curious spectator [1] amused his eye, or rather his fancy, by contemplating the various appearance of valleys and mountains, which had never, since the formation of the globe, been exposed to the sun. But the tide soon returned, with the weight of an immense and irresistible deluge, which was severely felt on the coast of Sicily, of Dalmatia, of Greece, and of Egypt; large boats were transported, and lodged on the roofs of houses, or at the distance of two miles from the shore; the people, with their habitations, were swept away by the waters; and the city of Alexandria annually commemorated the fatal day on which fifty thousand persons had lost their lives in the inundation. This calamity, the report of which was magnified from one province to another, astonished and terrified the subjects of Rome; and their affrighted imagination enlarged the real extent of a momentary evil. They recollected the preceding earthquakes, which had subverted the cities of Palestine and Bithynia; they considered these alarming strokes as the prelude only of still more dreadful calamities, and their fearful vanity was disposed to confound the symptoms of a declining empire and a

Earthquakes
A D 365, July
21st

---

[1] Such is the bad taste of Ammianus (xxvi. 10) that it is not easy to distinguish his facts from his metaphors   Yet he positively affirms that he saw the rotten carcase of a ship, ad *secundum lapidem*, at Methone, or Modon, in Peloponnesus.

sinking world.[2] It was the fashion of the times to attribute
every remarkable event to the particular will of the Deity; the
alterations of nature were connected, by an invisible chain, with
the moral and metaphysical opinions of the human mind; and
the most sagacious divines could distinguish, according to the
colour of their respective prejudices, that the establishment of
heresy tended to produce an earthquake, or that a deluge was
the inevitable consequence of the progress of sin and error. Without presuming to discuss the truth or propriety of these lofty
speculations, the historian may content himself with an observation, which seems to be justified by experience, that man has
much more to fear from the passions of his fellow-creatures
than from the convulsions of the elements.[3] The mischievous
effects of an earthquake or deluge, a hurricane, or the eruption
of a volcano, bear a very inconsiderable proportion to the
ordinary calamities of war, as they are now moderated by the
prudence or humanity of the princes of Europe, who amuse
their own leisure, and exercise the courage of their subjects,
in the practice of the military art.   But the laws and manners
of modern nations protect the safety and freedom of the vanquished soldier; and the peaceful citizen has seldom reason to
complain that his life, or even his fortune, is exposed to the
rage of war.   In the disastrous period of the fall of the Roman
empire, which may justly be dated from the reign of Valens, the
happiness and security of each individual were personally
attacked; and the arts and labours of ages were rudely defaced
by the Barbarians of Scythia and Germany.   The invasion of
the Huns precipitated on the provinces of the West the Gothic
nation, which advanced, in less than forty years, from the
Danube to the Atlantic, and opened a way, by the success of
their arms, to the inroads of so many hostile tribes, more savage
than themselves.   The original principle of motion was concealed
in the remote countries of the North, and the curious observa-

The Huns and
Goths A D
876

---

[2] The earthquakes and inundations are variously described by Libanius (Orat.
de ulciscendâ Juliani nece, c x in Fabricius, Bibl Graec. tom vii p 158, with
a learned note of Olearius), Zosimus (l iv p 221 [c. 18]), Sozomen (l vi. c. 2), Cedrenus (p 310, 314), and Jerom (in Chron. p 186, and t i p 250, in Vit Hilarion)
Epidaurus must have been overwhelmed, had not the prudent citizens placed St
Hilarion, an Egyptian monk, on the beach   He made the sign of the cross; the
mountain wave stopped, bowed, and returned   [The earthquakes in Greece mentioned by Zosimus belong to A D 375]

[3] Dicæarchus, the Peripatetic, composed a formal treatise, to prove this obvious
truth, which is not the most honourable to the human species. Cicero, de
Officiis, ii. 5

tion of the pastoral life of the Scythians,[4] or Tartars,[5] will illustrate the latent cause of these destructive emigrations.

The different characters that mark the civilized nations of the globe may be ascribed to the use, and the abuse, of reason; which so variously shapes, and so artificially composes, the manners and opinions of an European or a Chinese. But the operation of instinct is more sure and simple than that of reason · it is much easier to ascertain the appetites of a quadruped than the speculations of a philosopher; and the savage tribes of mankind, as they approach nearer to the condition of animals, preserve a stronger resemblance to themselves and to each other. The uniform stability of their manners is the natural consequence of the imperfection of their faculties. Reduced to a similar situation, their wants, their desires, their enjoyments, still continue the same; and the influence of food or climate, which, in a more improved state of society, is suspended or subdued by so many moral causes, most powerfully contributes to form and to maintain the national character of Barbarians. In every age, the immense plains of Scythia or Tartary have been inhabited by vagrant tribes of hunters and shepherds, whose indolence refuses to cultivate the earth, and whose restless spirit disdains the confinement of a sedentary life. In every age, the Scythians and Tartars have been renowned for their invincible courage and rapid conquests. The thrones of Asia have been repeatedly overturned by the shepherds of the North; and their arms have spread terror and devastation over the most fertile and warlike countries of Europe.[6] On this occasion, as well as on many others, the sober historian is forcibly awakened from a pleasing vision, and is compelled,

The pastoral manners of the Scythians, or Tartars

---

[4] The original Scythians of Herodotus (l iv c. 47-57, 99-101) were confined by the Danube and the Palus Mæotis, within a square of 4000 stadia (400 Roman miles). See d'Anville (Mém de l'Académie, tom xxxv p 573-591) Diodorus Siculus (tom i, l ii p. 155, edit Wesseling) has marked the gradual progress of the *name* and nation.

[5] The *Tatars*, or Tartars, were a primitive tribe, the rivals, and at length the subjects, of the Moguls In the victorious armies of Zingis Khan, and his successors, the Tartars formed the vanguard; and the name, which first reached the ears of foreigners, was applied to the whole nation (Fréret, in the Hist. de l'Académie, tom xviii p. 60) In speaking of all, or any, of the northern shepherds of Europe, or Asia, I indifferently use the appellations of *Scythians* or *Tartars*

[6] Imperium Asiæ *ter* quæsivere: ipsi perpetuo ab alieno imperio aut intacti aut invicti mansere. Since the time of Justin (ii 2), they have multiplied this account Voltaire, in a few words (tom x. p 64, Hist Générale, c. 156), has abridged the Tartar conquests

Oft o'er the trembling nations from afar
Has Scythia breath'd the living cloud of war.

with some reluctance, to confess that the pastoral manners which have been adorned with the fairest attributes of peace and innocence are much better adapted to the fierce and cruel habits of a military life. To illustrate this observation, I shall now proceed to consider a nation of shepherds and of warriors, in the three important articles of, I. Their diet; II. Their habitations; and, III. Their exercises The narratives of antiquity are justified by the experience of modern times; [7] and the banks of the Borysthenes, of the Volga, or of the Selinga, will indifferently present the same uniform spectacle of similar and native manners [8]

Diet

I. The corn, or even the rice, which constitutes the ordinary and wholesome food of a civilized people, can be obtained only by the patient toil of the husbandman. Some of the happy savages who dwell between the tropics are plentifully nourished by the liberality of nature; but in the climates of the North a nation of shepherds is reduced to their flocks and herds. The skilful practitioners of the medical art will determine (if they are able to determine) how far the temper of the human mind may be affected by the use of animal or of vegetable food; and whether the common association of carnivorous and cruel deserves to be considered in any other light than that of an innocent, perhaps a salutary, prejudice of humanity.[9] Yet, if it be true that the sentiment of compassion is imperceptibly weakened by the sight and practice of domestic cruelty, we may observe that the horrid objects which are disguised by the arts of European refinement are exhibited, in their naked and

[7] The fourth book of Herodotus affords a curious, though imperfect, portrait of the Scythians. Among the moderns, who describe the uniform scene, the Khan of Khowaresm, Abulghazi Bahadur, expresses his native feelings; and his Genealogical History of the Tartars has been copiously illustrated by the French and English editors. Carpin, Ascelin, and Rubruquis (in the Hist. des Voyages, tom vii) represent the Moguls of the fourteenth century To these guides I have added Gerbillon, and the other Jesuits (Description de la Chine, par du Halde, tom iv), who accurately surveyed the Chinese Tartary; and that honest and intelligent traveller, Bell of Antermony (two volumes in 4to, Glasgow, 1763).

[8] The Uzbecks are the most altered from their primitive manners; 1, by the profession of the Mahometan religion, and, 2, by the possession of the cities and harvests of the great Bucharia

[9] Il est certain que les grands mangeurs de viande sont en général cruels et féroces plus que les autres hommes. Cette observation est de tous les lieux, et de tous les tems la barbare Angloise est connue, &c Emile de Rousseau, tom i p 274. Whatever we may think of the general observation, we shall not easily allow the truth of his example. The good-natured complaints of Plutarch, and the pathetic lamentations of Ovid, seduce our reason, by exciting our sensibility

most disgusting simplicity, in the tent of a Tartarian shepherd. The ox or the sheep are slaughtered by the same hand from which they were accustomed to receive their daily food ; and the bleeding limbs are served, with very little preparation, on the table of their unfeeling murderer. In the military profession, and especially in the conduct of a numerous army, the exclusive use of animal food appears to be productive of the most solid advantages. Corn is a bulky and perishable commodity ; and the large magazines, which are indispensably necessary for the subsistence of our troops, must be slowly transported by the labour of men or horses. But the flocks and herds, which accompany the march of the Tartars, afford a sure and increasing supply of flesh and milk ; in the far greater part of the uncultivated waste, the vegetation of the grass is quick and luxuriant ; and there are few places so extremely barren that the hardy cattle of the North cannot find some tolerable pasture. The supply is multiplied and prolonged by the undistinguishing appetite and patient abstinence of the Tartars. They indifferently feed on the flesh of those animals that have been killed for the table or have died of disease. Horse-flesh, which in every age and country has been proscribed by the civilized nations of Europe and Asia, they devour with peculiar greediness ; and this singular taste facilitates the success of their military operations. The active cavalry of Scythia is always followed, in their most distant and rapid incursions, by an adequate number of spare horses, who may be occasionally used, either to redouble the speed, or to satisfy the hunger, of the Barbarians. Many are the resources of courage and poverty. When the forage round a camp of Tartars is almost consumed, they slaughter the greatest part of their cattle, and preserve the flesh either smoked or dried in the sun. On the sudden emergency of a hasty march, they provide themselves with a sufficient quantity of little balls of cheese, or rather of hard curd, which they occasionally dissolve in water ; and this unsubstantial diet will support, for many days, the life, and even the spirits, of the patient warrior. But this extraordinary abstinence, which the Stoic would approve and the hermit might envy, is commonly succeeded by the most voracious indulgence of appetite. The wines of a happier climate are the most grateful present, or the most valuable commodity, that can be offered to the Tartars ; and the only example of their industry seems to consist in the art of extracting from mares' milk a fermented liquor, which possesses a very strong power of intoxication. Like the animals of prey, the savages, both of the

old and new world, experience the alternate vicissitudes of famine
and plenty, and their stomach is enured to sustain, without
much inconvenience, the opposite extremes of hunger and of
intemperance.

Habitations   II.   In the ages of rustic and martial simplicity, a people of
soldiers and husbandmen are dispersed over the face of an extensive and cultivated country, and some time must elapse before
the warlike youth of Greece or Italy could be assembled under
the same standard, either to defend their own confines or to
invade the territories of the adjacent tribes.   The progress of
manufactures and commerce insensibly collects a large multitude within the walls of a city; but these citizens are no longer
soldiers; and the arts which adorn and improve the state of
civil society corrupt the habits of a military life.   The pastoral
manners of the Scythians seem to unite the different advantages
of simplicity and refinement.   The individuals of the same tribe
are constantly assembled, but they are assembled in a camp;
and the native spirit of these dauntless shepherds is animated by
mutual support and emulation.   The houses of the Tartars are
no more than small tents, of an oval form, which afford a cold
and dirty habitation for the promiscuous youth of both sexes.
The palaces of the rich consist of wooden huts, of such a size
that they may be conveniently fixed on large waggons and drawn
by a team perhaps of twenty or thirty oxen.   The flocks and
herds, after grazing all day in the adjacent pastures, retire, on the
approach of night, within the protection of the camp.   The
necessity of preventing the most mischievous confusion, in such
a perpetual concourse of men and animals, must gradually introduce, in the distribution, the order, and the guard of the encampment, the rudiments of the military art.   As soon as the
forage of a certain district is consumed, the tribe, or rather army,
of shepherds makes a regular march to some fresh pastures;
and thus acquires, in the ordinary occupations of the pastoral life,
the practical knowledge of one of the most important and difficult
operations of war.   The choice of stations is regulated by the
difference of the seasons · in the summer, the Tartars advance
towards the North, and pitch their tents on the banks of a river,
or, at least, in the neighbourhood of a running stream   But in
the winter they return to the South, and shelter their camp
behind some convenient eminence, against the winds which are
chilled in their passage over the bleak and icy regions of Siberia.
These manners are admirably adapted to diffuse, among the
wandering tribes, the spirit of emigration and conquest.   The

connexion between the people and their territory is of so frail a
texture that it may be broken by the slightest accident. The
camp, and not the soil, is the native country of the genuine
Tartar. Within the precincts of that camp, his family, his companions, his property are always included ; and in the most distant marches he is still surrounded by the objects which are
dear, or valuable, or familiar in his eyes. The thirst of rapine,
the fear or the resentment of injury, the impatience of servitude, have, in every age, been sufficient causes to urge the tribes
of Scythia boldly to advance into some unknown countries, where
they might hope to find a more plentiful subsistence or a less
formidable enemy. The revolutions of the North have frequently determined the fate of the South ; and, in the conflict
of hostile nations, the victor and the vanquished have alternately
drove and been driven, from the confines of China to those of
Germany.[10] These great emigrations, which have been sometimes executed with almost incredible diligence, were rendered
more easy by the peculiar nature of the climate. It is well
known that the cold of Tartary is much more severe than in
the midst of the temperate zone might reasonably be expected :
this uncommon rigour is attributed to the height of the plains,
which rise, especially towards the East, more than half a mile
above the level of the sea ; and to the quantity of saltpetre
with which the soil is deeply impregnated.[11] In the winter-
season, the broad and rapid rivers, that discharge their waters
into the Euxine, the Caspian, or the Icy Sea, are strongly frozen ;
the fields are covered with a bed of snow ; and the fugitive or
victorious tribes may securely traverse, with their families, their

[10] These Tartar emigrations have been discovered by M. de Guignes (Histoire
des Huns, tom. i. ii), a skilful and laborious interpreter of the Chinese language;
who has thus laid open new and important scenes in the history of mankind.
[The account of the Hiung-nu (= " Hiung slaves ") and their relations to China,
which Gibbon has derived from De Guignes, is on the whole accurate. I have
compared it with the work of a living Chinese scholar, Mr. E. H. Parker, A Thousand Years of the Tartars, 1895. But this episode ceases to be relevant, when we
recognize that there is no good ground for identifying the Hiung-nu with the Huns ;
in fact, that identification rested entirely on the resemblance of name between the
two nomad peoples. Sir H. Howorth decided against the theory, on the ground
that the Hiung-nu are certainly Turks, while he regards the Huns as Ugrians. But
see Appendix 6.]

[11] A plain in the Chinese Tartary, only eighty leagues from the great wall, was
found by the missionaries to be three thousand geometrical paces above the level
of the sea. Montesquieu, who has used, and abused, the relations of travellers,
deduces the revolutions of Asia from this important circumstance that heat and
cold, weakness and strength, touch each other without any temperate zone (Esprit
des Loix, l. xvii. c. 3).

waggons, and their cattle, the smooth and hard surface of an immense plain

III. The pastoral life, compared with the labours of agriculture and manufactures, is undoubtedly a life of idleness; and, as the most honourable shepherds of the Tartar race devolve on their captives the domestic management of the cattle, their own leisure is seldom disturbed by any servile and assiduous cares. But this leisure, instead of being devoted to the soft enjoyments of love and harmony, is usefully spent in the violent and sanguinary exercise of the chase. The plains of Tartary are filled with a strong and serviceable breed of horses, which are easily trained for the purposes of war and hunting. The Scythians of every age have been celebrated as bold and skilful riders; and constant practice had seated them so firmly on horseback that they were supposed by strangers to perform the ordinary duties of civil life, to eat, to drink, and even to sleep, without dismounting from their steeds. They excel in the dexterous management of the lance; the long Tartar bow is drawn with a nervous arm; and the weighty arrow is directed to its object with unerring aim and irresistible force. These arrows are often pointed against the harmless animals of the desert, which increase and multiply in the absence of their most formidable enemy · the hare, the goat, the roebuck, the fallow-deer, the stag, the elk, and the antelope The vigour and patience both of the men and horses are continually exercised by the fatigues of the chase; and the plentiful supply of game contributes to the subsistence, and even luxury, of a Tartar camp. But the exploits of the hunters of Scythia are not confined to the destruction of timid or innoxious beasts; they boldly encounter the angry wild boar, when he turns against his pursuers, excite the sluggish courage of the bear, and provoke the fury of the tiger, as he slumbers in the thicket. Where there is danger, there may be glory; and the mode of hunting which opens the fairest field to the exertions of valour may justly be considered as the image and as the school of war. The general hunting-matches, the pride and delight of the Tartar princes, compose an instructive exercise for their numerous cavalry. A circle is drawn, of many miles in circumference, to encompass the game of an extensive district; and the troops that form the circle regularly advance towards a common centre; where the captive animals, surrounded on every side, are abandoned to the darts of the hunters. In this march, which frequently continues many days, the cavalry are obliged to climb the hills, to swim the rivers, and to wind through the valleys, without interrupting the prescribed order of their gradual progress. They acquire the habit of directing their eye, and their steps, to a remote object; of preserving their intervals; of suspending, or accelerating, their pace, according to the motions of the troops on their right and left, and of watching and repeating the signals of their leaders. Their leaders study, in this practical school, the most important lesson of the military art: the prompt and accurate judgment of ground, of distance, and of time. To employ against a human enemy the same patience and valour, the same skill and discipline, is the only alteration which is required in real war; and the amusements of the chase serve as a prelude to the conquest of an empire.[12]

The political society of the ancient Germans has the appear- Government ance of a voluntary alliance of independent warriors. The tribes of Scythia, distinguished by the modern appellation of *Hords*, assume the form of a numerous and increasing family; which, in the course of successive generations, has been propagated from the same original stock. The meanest and most ignorant of the Tartars preserve, with conscious pride, the inestimable treasure of their genealogy; and, whatever distinctions of rank may have been introduced by the unequal distribution of pastoral wealth, they mutually respect themselves, and each other, as the descendants of the first founder of the tribe. The custom, which still prevails, of adopting the bravest and most faithful of the captives may countenance the very probable suspicion that this extensive consanguinity is, in a great measure, legal and fictitious. But the useful prejudice, which has obtained the sanction of time and opinion, produces the effects of truth; the haughty Barbarians yield a cheerful and voluntary obedience to the head of their blood; and their chief or *mursa*, as the representative of their great father, exercises the authority of a judge, in peace, and of a leader, in war. In the original state of the pastoral world, each of the *mursas* (if we may continue to use a modern appellation) acted as the independent chief of a large and separate family; and the limits

---

[12] Petit de la Croix (Vie de Gengiscan, l. iii c 7) represents the full glory and extent of the Mogul chase. The Jesuits Gerbillon and Verbiest followed the emperor Kamhi when he hunted in Tartary (Duhalde, Description de la Chine, tom. iv p. 81, 290, &c., folio edit). His grandson, Kienlong, who unites the Tartar discipline with the laws and learning of China, describes (Éloge de Moukden, p. 273-285), as a poet, the pleasures which he had often enjoyed, as a sportsman

of their peculiar territories were gradually fixed by superior force or mutual consent. But the constant operation of various and permanent causes contributed to unite the vagrant Hords into national communities, under the command of a supreme head. The weak were desirous of support, and the strong were ambitious of dominion ; the power, which is the result of union, oppressed and collected the divided forces of the adjacent tribes ; and, as the vanquished were freely admitted to share the advantages of victory, the most valiant chiefs hastened to range themselves and their followers under the formidable standard of a confederate nation. The most successful of the Tartar princes assumed the military command, to which he was entitled by the superiority either of merit or of power. He was raised to the throne by the acclamations of his equals ; and the title of *Khan* expresses, in the language of the North of Asia, the full extent of the regal dignity. The right of hereditary succession was long confined to the blood of the founder of the monarchy ; and at this moment all the Khans, who reign from Crimea to the wall of China, are the lineal descendants of the renowned Zingis.[13] But, as it is the indispensable duty of a Tartar sovereign to lead his warlike subjects into the field, the claims of an infant are often disregarded ; and some loyal kinsman, distinguished by his age and valour, is intrusted with the sword and sceptre of his predecessor. Two distinct and regular taxes are levied on the tribes, to support the dignity of their national monarch and of their peculiar chief; and each of those contributions amounts to the tythe both of their property and of their spoil. A Tartar sovereign enjoys the tenth part of the wealth of his people; and, as his own domestic riches of flocks and herds increase in a much larger proportion, he is able plentifully to maintain the rustic splendour of his court, to reward the most deserving, or the most favoured, of his followers, and to obtain, from the gentle influence of corruption, the obedience which might be sometimes refused to the stern mandates of authority. The manners of his subjects, accustomed, like himself, to blood and rapine, might excuse, in their eyes, such partial acts of tyranny

[13] See the second volume of the Genealogical History of the Tartars, and the list of the Khans, at the end of the life of Gengis, or Zingis. Under the reign of Timur, or Tamerlane, one of his subjects, a descendant of Zingis, still bore the regal appellation of Khan , and the conqueror of Asia contented himself with the title of Emir, or Sultan. Abulghazi, p v. c. 4 D'Herbelot, Bibliothèque Orientale, p. 878.

as would excite the horror of a civilized people; but the power of a despot has never been acknowledged in the deserts of Scythia. The immediate jurisdiction of the Khan is confined within the limits of his own tribe; and the exercise of his royal prerogative has been moderated by the ancient institution of a national council. The Coroultai,[14] or Diet, of the Tartars was regularly held in the spring and autumn, in the midst of a plain; where the princes of the reigning family and the mursas of the respective tribes may conveniently assemble on horseback, with their martial and numerous trains; and the ambitious monarch, who reviewed the strength, must consult the inclination, of an armed people. The rudiments of a feudal government may be discovered in the constitution of the Scythian or Tartar nations; but the perpetual conflict of these hostile nations has sometimes terminated in the establishment of a powerful and despotic empire. The victor, enriched by the tribute, and fortified by the arms, of dependent kings, has spread his conquests over Europe or Asia; the successful shepherds of the North have submitted to the confinement of arts, of laws, and of cities; and the introduction of luxury, after destroying the freedom of the people, has undermined the foundations of the throne.[15]

The memory of past events cannot long be preserved, in the frequent and remote emigrations of illiterate Barbarians. The modern Tartars are ignorant of the conquests of their ancestors;[16] and our knowledge of the history of the Scythians is derived from their intercourse with the learned and civilized nations of the South, the Greeks, the Persians, and the Chinese. The Greeks, who navigated the Euxine, and planted their colonies along the sea-coast, made the gradual and imperfect discovery of Scythia; from the Danube, and the confines of Thrace, as far as the frozen Mæotis, the seat of eternal winter, *Situation and extent of Scythia, or Tartary*

[14] See the Diets of the ancient Huns (de Guignes, tom II p 26), and a curious description of those of Zingis (Vie de Gengiscan, l 1 c 6, l.½ iv c 11) Such assemblies are frequently mentioned in the Persian history of Timur; though they served only to countenance the resolutions of their master ["Every New Year the Zenghi (title of the king) held a great religious festival at what the Chinese call Dragon City: it was evidently much the same kind of affair as the Mongol *couroultai* of Marco Polo's time" Parker, p. 19]

[15] Montesquieu labours to explain a difference which has not existed between the liberty of the Arabs and the *perpetual* slavery of the Tartars (Esprit des Loix, l xvii c. 5; l xviii c 19, &c)

[16] Abulghazi Khan, in the two first parts of his Genealogical History, relates the miserable fables and traditions of the Uzbek Tartars concerning the times which preceded the reign of Zingis

and Mount Caucasus, which, in the language of poetry, was described as the utmost boundary of the earth. They celebrated, with simple credulity, the virtues of the pastoral life [17] They entertained a more rational apprehension of the strength and numbers of the warlike Barbarians,[18] who contemptuously baffled the immense armament of Darius, the son of Hystaspes.[19] The Persian monarchs had extended their western conquests to the banks of the Danube and the limits of European Scythia The eastern provinces of their empire were exposed to the Scythians of Asia : the wild inhabitants of the plains beyond the Oxus and the Jaxartes, two mighty rivers, which direct their course towards the Caspian Sea. The long and memorable quarrel of Iran and Touran is still the theme of history or romance ; the famous, perhaps the fabulous, valour of the Persian heroes, Rustan and Asfendiar, was signalized in the defence of their country against the Afrasiabs of the North ; [20] and the invincible spirit of the same Barbarians resisted, on the same ground, the victorious arms of Cyrus and Alexander.[21] In the eyes of the Greeks and Persians, the real geography of Scythia was bounded, on the East, by the mountains of Imaus, or Caf ; and their distant prospect of the extreme and inaccessible parts of Asia was clouded by ignorance or perplexed by fiction. But those inaccessible regions are the ancient residence of a powerful and civilized nation,[22] which ascends, by a probable tradition, above

[17] In the thirteenth book of the Iliad Jupiter turns away his eyes from the bloody fields of Troy to the plains of Thrace and Scythia. He would not, by changing the prospect, behold a more peaceful or innocent scene.

[18] Thucydides, l ii c 97

[19] See the fourth book of Herodotus. When Darius advanced into the Moldavian desert, between the Danube and the Dniester, the king of the Scythians sent him a mouse, a frog, a bird, and five arrows, a tremendous allegory '

[20] These wars and heroes may be found under their respective *titles* in the Bibliothèque Orientale of d'Herbelot. They have been celebrated in an epic poem of sixty thousand rhymed couplets by Ferdusi, the Homer of Persia. See the History of Nadir Shah, p 145, 165. The public must lament that Mr Jones has suspended the pursuit of oriental learning

[21] The Caspian Sea, with its rivers and adjacent tribes, are laboriously illustrated in the Examen Critique des Historiens d'Alexandre, which compares the true geography and the errors produced by the vanity or ignorance of the Greeks

[22] The original seat of the nation appears to have been in the North-west of China, in the provinces of Chensi and Chansi Under the two first dynasties, the principal town was still a moveable camp : the villages were thinly scattered , more land was employed in pasture than in tillage , the exercise of hunting was ordained to clear the country from wild beasts, Petcheli (where Pekin stands) was a desert, and the southern provinces were peopled with Indian savages The dynasty of the *Han* (before Christ 206) gave the empire its actual form and extent

forty centuries ; [23] and which is able to verify a series of near two thousand years, by the perpetual testimony of accurate and contemporary historians.[24] The annals of China [25] illustrate the state and revolutions of the pastoral tribes, which may still be distinguished by the vague appellation of Scythians, or Tartars ; the vassals, the enemies, and sometimes the conquerors, of a great empire; whose policy has uniformly opposed the blind and impetuous valour of the Barbarians of the North. From the mouth of the Danube to the sea of Japan, the whole longitude of Scythia is about one hundred and ten degrees, which, in that parallel, are equal to more than five thousand miles. The latitude of these extensive deserts cannot be so easily or so accurately measured ; but, from the fortieth degree, which touches the wall of China, we may securely advance above a thousand miles to the northward, till our progress is stopped by the excessive cold of Siberia. In that dreary climate, instead of the animated picture of a Tartar camp, the smoke which issues from the earth, or rather from the snow, betrays the subterraneous dwellings of the Tongouses and the Samoiedes : the want of horses and oxen is imperfectly supplied by the use of reindeer and of large dogs ; and the conquerors

[23] The æra of the Chinese monarchy has been variously fixed, from 2952 to 2132 years before Christ ; and the year 2637 has been chosen for the lawful epoch by the authority of the present emperor The difference arises from the uncertain duration of the two first dynasties : and the vacant space that lies beyond them as far as the real, or fabulous, times of Fohi, or Hoangti Sematsien dates his authentic chronology from the year 841 . the thirty-six eclipses of Confucius (thirty-one of which have been verified) were observed between the years 722 and 480 before Christ The *historical period* of China does not ascend above the Greek Olympiads.

[24] After several ages of anarchy and despotism, the dynasty of the Han (before Christ 206) was the æra of the revival of learning. The fragments of ancient literature were restored , the characters were improved and fixed, and the future preservation of books was secured by the useful inventions of ink, paper, and the art of printing Ninety-seven years before Christ Sematsien published the first history of China. His labours were illustrated and continued by a series of one hundred and eighty historians. The substance of their works is still extant, and the most considerable of them are now deposited in the king of France's library.

[25] China has been illustrated by the labours of the French , of the missionaries at Pekin, and Messrs Freret and de Guignes at Paris The substance of the three preceding notes is extracted from The *Chou-king* with the preface and notes of M. de Guignes, Paris, 1770; the *Tong-Kien-Kang-Mou* translated by the P de Mailla, under the name of Hist Générale de la Chine, tom i. p. xliv -cc ; the Mémoires sur la Chine, Paris, 1776, &c , tom. i p. 1-323, tom ii p 5-364; the Histoire des Huns, tom. i p 1-131, tom v p 345-362; and the Mémoires de l'Académie des Inscriptions, tom. x. p. 377-402, tom. xv. p. 495-564, tom xviii p. 178-295, tom xxxvi. p. 164-238.

of the earth insensibly degenerate into a race of deformed and diminutive savages, who tremble at the sound of arms.[2b]

Original seat of the Huns

The Huns, who under the reign of Valens threatened the empire of Rome, had been formidable, in a much earlier period, to the empire of China.[27] Their ancient, perhaps their original, seat was an extensive, though dry and barren, tract of country, immediately on the north side of the great wall. Their place is at present occupied by the forty-nine Hords or Banners of the Mongous, a pastoral nation, which consists of about two hundred

[Under Megh der, c. B C 200]

thousand families.[28] But the valour of the Huns had extended the narrow limits of their dominions; and their rustic chiefs,

[Tengri Kudu Zenghi] Their conquests in Scythia

who assumed the appellation of *Tanjou*, gradually became the conquerors, and the sovereigns, of a formidable empire. Towards the East, their victorious arms were stopped only by the ocean; and the tribes, which are thinly scattered between the Amoor and the extreme peninsula of Corea, adhered with reluctance to the standard of the Huns. On the West, near the head of the Irtish and in the valleys of Imaus, they found a more ample space, and more numerous enemies. One of the

[Zenghi] [Kirghiz]

lieutenants of the Tanjou subdued in a single expedition twenty-six nations; the Igours,[29] distinguished above the Tartar race by the use of letters, were in the number of his vassals, and by the strange connexion of human events, the flight of one of those vagrant tribes recalled the victorious Parthians from the invasion of Syria.[30] On the side of the North, the ocean was assigned as the limit of the power of the Huns. Without enemies to resist their progress or witnesses to contradict their vanity, they might securely achieve a real, or imaginary, conquest of the frozen regions of Siberia. The *Northern Sea* was fixed as the remote boundary of their empire. But the name of that sea, on whose shores the patriot Sovou embraced the life of a shepherd

[26] See the Histoire Générale des Voyages, tom. xviii. and the Genealogical History, vol. ii. p. 620-664

[27] M. de Guignes (tom. ii p 1-124) has given the original history of the ancient Hiong-nou, or Huns. The Chinese geography of their country (tom. i part ii. p. iv.-lxiii) seems to comprise a part of their conquests

[28] See in Duhalde (tom. iv. p 18-65) a circumstantial description with a correct map of the country of the Mongous

[29] The Igours, or Vigours [Ouigours], were divided into three branches hunters, shepherds, and husbandmen; and the last class was despised by the two former. See Abulghazi, part ii. c 7.

[30] Mémoires de l'Académie des Inscriptions, tom xxv p. 17-33. The comprehensive view of M. de Guignes has compared these distant events

and an exile,[31] may be transferred, with much more probability, to the Baikal, a capacious basin, above three hundred miles in length, which disdains the modest appellation of a lake,[32] and which actually communicates with the seas of the North, by the long course of the Angara, the Tonguska, and the Jenissea. The submission of so many distant nations might flatter the pride of the Tanjou, but the valour of the Huns could be re- [Zenghi] warded only by the enjoyment of the wealth and luxury of the empire of the South.   In the third century before the Christian [By Meng æra, a wall of fifteen hundred miles in length was constructed, B C] Tien, c 200 to defend the frontiers of China against the inroads of the Huns;[33] but this stupendous work, which holds a conspicuous place in the map of the world, has never contributed to the safety of an unwarlike people.   The cavalry of the Tanjou frequently consisted of two or three hundred thousand men, formidable by the matchless dexterity with which they managed their bows and their horses; by their hardy patience in supporting the inclemency of the weather; and by the incredible speed of their march, which was seldom checked by torrents or precipices, by the deepest rivers or by the most lofty mountains.   They spread themselves at once over the face of [Their wars the country; and their rapid impetuosity surprised, astonished, Chinese, ant and disconcerted the grave and elaborate tactics of a Chinese Christ 201 army   The emperor Kaoti,[34] a soldier of fortune, whose per- [Han Kao Tsu sonal merit had raised him to the throne, marched against the Han dynas Huns with those veteran troops which had been trained in the ty)] civil wars of China.   But he was soon surrounded by the Bar- barians; and after a siege of seven days, the monarch, hopeless [Near Ta of relief, was reduced to purchase his deliverance by an Shan Si] ignominious capitulation.   The successors of Kaoti, whose lives were dedicated to the arts of peace or the luxury of the palace,

[31] The fame of Sovou, or So-ou, his merit, and his singular adventures are still celebrated in China. See the Eloge de Moukden, p. 20, and notes, p. 241-247, and Mémoires sur la Chine, tom. iii p. 317-360.
[32] See Isbrand Ives, in Harris's collection, vol. ii. p. 931; Bell's Travels, vol. i. p. 247-254, and Gmelin, in the Hist. Générale des Voyages, tom xviii. p. 283-329   They all remark the vulgar opinion that the *holy sea* grows angry and tempestuous if any one presumes to call it a *lake*   This grammatical nicety often excites a dispute between the absurd superstition of the mariners and the absurd obstinacy of travellers
[33] The construction of the wall of China is mentioned by Duhalde (tom ii. p 45) and de Guignes (tom ii. p. 59).
[34] See the life of Lieoupang, or Kaoti, in the Hist. de la Chine, published at Paris, 1777, &c , tom. i p 442-522   This voluminous work is the translation (by the P. de Mailla) of the *Tong-Kien Kang-Mou*, the celebrated abridgment of the great History of Semakouang (A D 1084) and his continuators.

submitted to a more permanent disgrace. They too hastily confessed the insufficiency of arms and fortifications. They were too easily convinced that, while the blazing signals announced on every side the approach of the Huns, the Chinese troops, who slept with the helmet on their head and the cuirass on their back, were destroyed by the incessant labour of ineffectual marches.[35] A regular payment of money and silk was stipulated as the condition of a temporary and precarious peace ; and the wretched expedient of disguising a real tribute under the names of a gift or a subsidy was practised by the emperors of China, as well as by those of Rome. But there still remained a more disgraceful article of tribute, which violated the sacred feelings of humanity and nature. The hardships of the savage life, which destroy in their infancy the children who are born with a less healthy and robust constitution, introduce a remarkable disproportion between the numbers of the two sexes. The Tartars are an ugly, and even deformed race ; and, while they consider their own women as the instruments of domestic labour, their desires, or rather their appetites, are directed to the enjoyment of more elegant beauty. A select band of the fairest maidens of China was annually devoted to the rude embraces of the Huns ; [36] and the alliance of the haughty Tanjous was secured by their marriage with the genuine, or adopted, daughters of the Imperial family, which vainly attempted to escape the sacrilegious pollution. The situation of these unhappy victims is described in the verses of a Chinese princess, who laments that she had been condemned by her parents to a distant exile, under a Barbarian husband ; who complains that sour milk was her only drink, raw flesh her only food, a tent her only palace ; and who expresses, in a strain of pathetic simplicity, the natural wish that she were transformed into a bird, to fly back to her dear country ; the object of her tender and perpetual regret.[37]

[Zenghis]

Decline and fall of the Huns

The conquest of China has been twice achieved by the pastoral tribes of the North : the forces of the Huns were not

[35] See a free and ample memorial presented by a Mandarin to the emperor Venti [Wên Ti] (before Christ 180-157) in Duhalde (tom ii p. 412-426) ; from a collection of State papers marked with the red pencil by Kamhi himself (p. 384-612) Another memorial from the minister of war (Kang Mou, t. ii p 555) supplies some curious circumstances of the manners of the Huns

[36] A supply of women is mentioned as a customary article of treaty and tribute (Hist de la conquête de la Chine par les Tartares Mantcheoux, tom. i, p 186, 187, with the note of the editor)

[37] De Guignes, Hist des Huns, tom. ii. p 62.

inferior to those of the Moguls, or of the Mantcheoux; and
their ambition might entertain the most sanguine hopes of
success. But their pride was humbled, and their progress was
checked, by the arms and policy of Vouti,[38] the fifth emperor of [Wu Ti]
the powerful dynasty of the Han. In his long reign of fifty- Ant Christ
four years, the Barbarians of the southern provinces submitted 141 87
to the laws and manners of China; and the ancient limits of the
monarchy were enlarged, from the great river of Kiang to the
port of Canton   Instead of confining himself to the timid
operations of a defensive war, his lieutenants penetrated many
hundred miles into the country of the Huns. In those boundless deserts, where it is impossible to form magazines and
difficult to transport a sufficient supply of provisions, the armies
of Vouti were repeatedly exposed to intolerable hardships : and,
of one hundred and forty thousand soldiers, who marched
against the Barbarians, thirty thousand only returned in safety
to the feet of their master. These losses, however, were compensated by splendid and decisive success. The Chinese generals improved the superiority which they derived from the
temper of their arms, their chariots of war, and the service of
their Tartar auxiliaries. The camp of the Tanjou was surprised [Zenghi]
in the midst of sleep and intemperance; and, though the
monarch of the Huns bravely cut his way through the ranks of
the enemy, he left above fifteen thousand of his subjects on the
field of battle. Yet this signal victory, which was preceded and
followed by many bloody engagements, contributed much less
to the destruction of the power of the Huns than the effectual
policy which was employed to detach the tributary nations from
their obedience. Intimidated by the arms, or allured by the Ant. Christ
promises, of Vouti and his successors, the most considerable 70
tribes, both of the East and of the West, disclaimed the [Especially
authority of the Tanjou. While some acknowledged them- the Nomads
selves the allies or vassals of the empire, they all became the of Kuldja]
implacable enemies of the Huns: and the numbers of that
haughty people, as soon as they were reduced to their native
strength, might, perhaps, have been contained within the walls
of one of the great and populous cities of China [39] The deser-

---

[38] See the reign of the emperor Vouti, in the Kang-Mou, t. iii p 1-98. His
various and inconsistent character seems to be impartially drawn
[39] This expression is used in the memorial to the emperor Venti (Duhalde,
tom ii. p 417)   Without adopting the exaggerations of Marco-Polo and Isaac
Vossius, we may rationally allow for Pekin two millions of inhabitants. The
cities of the South, which contain the manufactures of China, are still more
populous

tion of his subjects, and the perplexity of a civil war, at length
compelled the Tanjou himself to renounce the dignity of an
independent sovereign and the freedom of a warlike and high-
spirited nation. He was received at Sigan, the capital of the
monarchy, by the troops, the Mandarins, and the emperor himself, with all the honours that could adorn and disguise the
triumph of Chinese vanity.[40] A magnificent palace was prepared for his reception ; his place was assigned above all the
princes of the royal family ; and the patience of the Barbarian
king was exhausted by the ceremonies of a banquet, which consisted of eight courses of meat, and of nine solemn pieces of
music.   But he performed, on his knees, the duty of a respectful homage to the emperor of China ; pronounced, in his own
name, and in the name of his successors, a perpetual oath of
fidelity ; and gratefully accepted a seal, which was bestowed as
the emblem of his regal dependence.   After this humiliating
submission, the Tanjous sometimes departed from their allegiance, and seized the favourable moments of war and rapine ;
but the monarchy of the Huns gradually declined, till it was
broken, by civil dissension, into two hostile and separate kingdoms   One of the princes of the nation was urged, by fear and
ambition, to retire towards the South with eight hords, which
composed between forty and fifty thousand families. He
obtained, with the title of Tanjou, a convenient territory on the
verge of the Chinese provinces ; and his constant attachment to
the service of the empire was secured by weakness and the
desire of revenge   From the time of this fatal schism, the Huns
of the North continued to languish about fifty years ; till they
were oppressed on every side by their foreign and domestic
enemies.   The proud inscription [41] of a column, erected on a
lofty mountain, announced to posterity that a Chinese army
had marched seven hundred miles into the heart of their
country.   The Sienpi,[42] a tribe of Oriental Tartars, retaliated
the injuries which they had formerly sustained ; and the power
of the Tanjous, after a reign of thirteen hundred years, was

[Khnganja]

Ant. Christ
51
[Shan Ti]

A.D 48

[A D 87]

A D 93
[End of the
kingdom of
the Northern
Zenghis]

[40] See the Kang-Mou, tom III p 150, and the subsequent events under the
proper years. This memorable festival is celebrated in the Eloge de Moukden,
and explained in a note by the P. Gaubil, p. 89, 90

[41] This inscription was composed on the spot by Pankou, President of the
Tribunal of History (Kang-Mou, tom. III p. 392) Similar monuments have
been discovered in many parts of Tartary (Histoire des Huns, tom. II. p 122).
[Parker, p 100]

[42] M. de Guignes (tom I p 189) has inserted a short account of the Sienpi,

utterly destroyed before the end of the first century of the Christian æra.[43]

The fate of the vanquished Huns was diversified by the various influence of character and situation.[44]   Above one hundred thousand persons, the poorest, indeed, and the most pusillanimous of the people, were contented to remain in their native country, to renounce their peculiar name and origin, and to mingle with the victorious nation of the Sienpi. Fifty-eight hords, about two hundred thousand men, ambitious of a more honourable servitude, retired towards the South; implored the protection of the emperors of China; and were permitted to inhabit, and to guard, the extreme frontiers of the province of Chansi and the territory of Ortous. But the most warlike and powerful tribes of the Huns maintained, in their adverse fortune, the undaunted spirit of their ancestors.   The western world was open to their valour; and they resolved, under the conduct of their hereditary chieftains, to discover and subdue some remote country, which was still inaccessible to the arms of the Sienpi and to the laws of China.[45] The course of their emigration soon carried them beyond the mountains of Imaus, and the limits of the Chinese geography; but *we* are able to distinguish the two great divisions of these formidable exiles, which directed their march towards the Oxus, and towards the Volga. The first of these colonies established their dominion in the fruitful and extensive plains of Sogdiana, on the eastern side of the Caspian: where they preserved the name of Huns, with the epithet of Euthalites or Nepthalites.[46] Their manners were softened, and even their features were insensibly improved, by the mildness of the climate and their long residence in a flourishing province [47] which might still retain a faint

(margin note: Their emigrations A D 100, &c)

(margin note: The white Huns of Sogdiana)

[43] The æra of the Huns is placed, by the Chinese, 1210 years before Christ. But the series of their kings does not commence till the year 230 (Hist des Huns, tom. ii. p. 21, 123). [The southern Zenghis continued till nearly the end of the second cent A D; Parker, p 102]

[44] The various accidents, the downfall, and flight of the Huns are related in the Khan-Mou, tom iii p. 88, 91, 95, 139, &c. The small numbers of each hord may be ascribed to their losses and divisions

[45] M de Guignes has skilfully traced the footsteps of the Huns through the vast deserts of Tartary (tom ii. p 123, 277, &c, 325, &c)

[46] [The Ephthalites were not part of the Hiung-nu, but seem to have been the Yüeh-chih, who possessed part of "the long straggling province now known as Kan Suh"; were conquered by Meghder, were driven westward by his successor before 162 B C, and divided Bactria with the Parthians. See Parker, p. 29, 30]

[47] Mohammed, Sultan of Carizme, reigned in Sogdiana, when it was invaded (A D 1218) by Zingis and his Moguls.   The Oriental Historians (see d'Herbelot, Petit de la Croix, &c) celebrate the populous cities which he ruined, and the

impression of the arts of Greece.[48]   The *white* Huns, a name
which they derived from the change of their complexions, soon
abandoned the pastoral life of Scythia   Gorgo, which, under
the appellation of Carizme, has since enjoyed a temporary
splendour, was the residence of the king, who exercised a legal
authority over an obedient people.   Their luxury was maintained by the labour of the Sogdians; and the only vestige of
their ancient barbarism was the custom which obliged all the
companions, perhaps to the number of twenty, who had shared
the liberality of a wealthy lord, to be buried alive in the same
grave.[49]   The vicinity of the Huns to the provinces of Persia
involved them in frequent and bloody contests with the power
of that monarchy.   But they respected, in peace, the faith of
treaties; in war, the dictates of humanity; and their memorable victory over Peroses, or Firuz, displayed the moderation, as
The Huns of   well as the valour, of the Barbarians.   The *second* division of
the Volga   their countrymen,[50] the Huns, who gradually advanced towards
the North-west, were exercised by the hardships of a colder
climate and a more laborious march   Necessity compelled them
to exchange the silks of China for the furs of Siberia; the imperfect rudiments of civilized life were obliterated; and the
native fierceness of the Huns was exasperated by their intercourse with the savage tribes, who were compared, with some
propriety, to the wild beasts of the desert   Their independent
spirit soon rejected the hereditary succession of the Tanjous;
and, while each hord was governed by its peculiar mursa, their
tumultuary council directed the public measures of the whole
nation.   As late as the thirteenth century, their transient
residence on the Eastern banks of the Volga was attested by the
name of Great Hungary.[51]   In the winter, they descended with

fruitful country which he desolated   In the next century, the same provinces
of Chorasmia and Mawaralnahr were described by Abulfeda (Hudson, Geograph
Minor tom iii)   Their actual misery may be seen in the Genealogical History
of the Tartars, p 423-469.

[48] Justin (xli 6) has left a short abridgment of the Greek kings of Bactriana.
To their industry I should ascribe the new and extraordinary trade, which trans-
ported the merchandises of India into Europe, by the Oxus, the Caspian, the
Cyrus, the Phasis, and the Euxine.   The other ways, both of the land and
sea, were possessed by the Seleucides and the Ptolemies   See l'Esprit des
Loix, l xxi

[49] Procopius de Bell Persico, l 1 c 3, p 9.

[50] [There is no evidence that the Huns of the Volga had migrated from the
borders of China.]

[51] In the thirteenth century, the monk Rubruquis (who traversed the immense
plain of Kipzak, in his journey to the court of the Great Khan) observed the
remarkable name of *Hungary*, with the traces of a common language and origin,
Hist. des Voyages, tom vii p 269

their flocks and herds towards the mouth of that mighty river ;
and their summer excursions reached as high as the latitude of
Saratoff, or perhaps the conflux of the Kama. Such at least
were the recent limits of the black Calmucks,[52] who remained
about a century under the protection of Russia ; and who have
since returned to their native seats on the frontiers of the
Chinese empire. The march and the return of those wandering
Tartars, whose united camp consists of fifty thousand tents or
families, illustrate the distant emigrations of the ancient Huns [53]

It is impossible to fill the dark interval of time, which elapsed, *Their con-
after the Huns of the Volga were lost in the eyes of the Chinese, quest of the
Alani* and before they shewed themselves to those of the Romans.
There is some reason, however, to apprehend, that the same
force which had driven them from their native seats, still continued to impel their march towards the frontiers of Europe.
The power of the Sienpi, their implacable enemies, which
extended above three thousand miles from East to West,[54]
must have gradually oppressed them by the weight and terror
of a formidable neighbourhood ; and the flight of the tribes of
Scythia would inevitably tend to increase the strength, or to
contract the territories, of the Huns. The harsh and obscure
appellations of those tribes would offend the ear, without informing the understanding, of the reader; but I cannot suppress
the very natural suspicion, *that* the Huns of the North derived
a considerable reinforcement from the ruin of the dynasty of the
South, which, in the course of the third century, submitted to
the dominion of China ; *that* the bravest warriors marched away
in search of their free and adventurous countrymen ; *and* that, as
they had been divided by prosperity, they were easily reunited by

---

[52] Bell (vol. i. p 29-34), and the editors of the Genealogical History (p. 539),
have described the Calmucks of the Volga in the beginning of the present
century.

[53] This great transmigration of 300,000 Calmucks, or Torgouts, happened in
the year 1771. The original narrative of Kien-long, the reigning emperor of
China, which was intended for the inscription of a column, has been translated
by the missionaries of Pekin (Mémoire sur la Chine, tom 1 p. 401-418) The
emperor affects the smooth and specious language of the Son of Heaven and the
Father of his People.

[54] The Kang-Mou (tom. iii p. 447) ascribes to their conquest a space of 14,000
lis. According to the present standard, 200 *lis* (or more accurately 193) are equal
to one degree of latitude ; and one English mile consequently exceeds three miles
of China But there are strong reasons to believe that the ancient *li* scarcely
equalled one-half of the modern. See the elaborate researches of M. d'Anville,
a geographer who is not a stranger in any age, or climate of the globe Mémoires de l'Acad tom. ii p. 125-502 Mesures Itinéraires, p 154-167.

the common hardships of their adverse fortune.[55] The Huns, with their flocks and herds, their wives and children, their dependents and allies, were transported to the West of the Volga, and they boldly advanced to invade the country of the Alani, a pastoral people who occupied, or wasted, an extensive tract of the deserts of Scythia. The plains between the Volga and the Tanais were covered with the tents of the Alani, but their name and manners were diffused over the wide extent of their conquests; and the painted tribes of the Agathyrsi and Geloni were confounded among their vassals. Towards the North, they penetrated into the frozen regions of Siberia, among the savages who were accustomed, in their rage or hunger, to the taste of human flesh; and their Southern inroads were pushed as far as the confines of Persia and India. The mixture of Sarmatic and German blood had contributed to improve the features of the Alani, to whiten their swarthy complexions, and to tinge their hair with a yellowish cast, which is seldom found in the Tartar race. They were less deformed in their persons, less brutish in their manners, than the Huns, but they did not yield to those formidable Barbarians in their martial and independent spirit; in the love of freedom, which rejected even the use of domestic slaves, and in the love of arms, which considered war and rapine as the pleasure and the glory of mankind. A naked scymetar, fixed in the ground, was the only object of their religious worship; the scalps of their enemies formed the costly trappings of their horses; and they viewed, with pity and contempt, the pusillanimous warriors, who patiently expected the infirmities of age and the tortures of lingering disease.[56] On the banks of the Tanais, the military power of the Huns and the Alani, encountered each other with equal valour, but with unequal success. The Huns prevailed in [A.D 372-37] the bloody contest: the king of the Alani was slain; and the remains of the vanquished nation were dispersed by the ordinary alternative of flight or submission.[57] A colony of exiles found a

[55] See the Histoire des Huns, tom. ii. p 125-144 The subsequent history (p 145-277) of three or four Hunnic dynasties evidently proves that their martial spirit was not impaired by a long residence in China

[56] Utque hominibus quietis et placidis otium est voluptabile, ita illos pericula juvant et bella. Judicatur ibi beatus qui in proelio profudent animam senescentes etiam et fortuitis mortibus mundo digressos, ut degeneres et ignavos conviciis atrocibus insectantur. We must think highly of the conquerors of ⟍ such men

[57] On the subject of the Alani, see Ammianus (xxxi 2), Jornandes (de Rebus Geticis, c. 24), M. de Guignes (Hist. des Huns, tom. ii. p 279), and the Genealogical History of the Tartars (tom. ii p. 617).

secure refuge in the mountains of Caucasus, between the Euxine and the Caspian; where they still preserve their name and their independence.   Another colony advanced, with more intrepid courage, towards the shores of the Baltic; associated themselves with the Northern tribes of Germany; and shared the spoil of the Roman provinces of Gaul and Spain.   But the greatest part of the nation of the Alani embraced the offers of an honourable and advantageous union; and the Huns, who esteemed the valour of their less fortunate enemies, proceeded, with an increase of numbers and confidence, to invade the limits of the Gothic empire.

The great Hermanric, whose dominions extended from the Baltic to the Euxine, enjoyed, in the full maturity of age and reputation, the fruit of his victories, when he was alarmed by the formidable approach of an host of unknown enemies,[58] on whom his barbarous subjects might, without injustice, bestow the epithet of Barbarians.   The numbers, the strength, the rapid motions, and the implacable cruelty of the Huns were felt and dreaded and magnified by the astonished Goths; who beheld their fields and villages consumed with flames and deluged with indiscriminate slaughter.   To these real terrors they added the surprise and abhorrence which were excited by the shrill voice, the uncouth gestures, and the strange deformity, of the Huns.   These savages of Scythia were compared (and the picture had some resemblance) to the animals who walk very awkwardly on two legs; and to the misshapen figures, the *Termini*, which were often placed on the bridges of antiquity.   They were distinguished from the rest of the human species by their broad shoulders, flat noses, and small black eyes, deeply buried in the head; and, as they were almost destitute of beards, they never enjoyed either the manly graces of youth or the venerable aspects of age.[59]   A fabulous origin was assigned worthy of their form and manners; that the witches of Scythia, who, for their foul and deadly practices, had been driven from society, had

Their victories over the Goths A.D. 375

[58] As we are possessed of the authentic history of the Huns, it would be impertinent to repeat, or to refute, the fables, which misrepresent their origin and progress, their passage of the mud or water of the Mæotis, in pursuit of an ox or stag, les Indes qu'ils avoient découvertes, &c Zosimus, l iv. p 224 [c. 20; after Eurapius], Sozomen, l vi. c. 37, Procopius [*leg* Paulus], Hist Miscell. c 5 [*leg.* Bk. 12 (p 933, ap Migne, vol 95)], Jornandes, c. 24, Grandeur et Décadence, &c, des Romains, c. 17

[59] Prodigiosæ formæ, et pandi; ut bipedes existimes bestias; vel quales in commarginandis pontibus, effigiati stipites dolantur incompti.   Ammian xxxi 1. Jornandes (c. 24) draws a strong caricature of a Calmuck face.   Species pavendâ nigredine . . quædam deformis offa, non facies, habensque magis puncta quam lumina.   See Buffon, Hist. Naturelle, tom. iii. p. 380.

copulated in the desert with infernal spirits; and that the Huns were the offspring of this execrable conjunction.[60] The tale, so full of horror and absurdity, was greedily embraced by the credulous hatred of the Goths, but, while it gratified their hatred, it increased their fear; since the posterity of demons and witches might be supposed to inherit some share of the preternatural powers, as well as of the malignant temper, of their parents. Against these enemies, Hermanric prepared to exert the united forces of the Gothic state; but he soon discovered that his vassal tribes, provoked by oppression, were much more inclined to second, than to repel, the invasion of the Huns. One of the chiefs of the Roxolani[61] had formerly deserted the standard of Hermanric, and the cruel tyrant had condemned the innocent wife of the traitor to be torn asunder by wild horses. The brother of that unfortunate woman seized the favourable moment of revenge The aged king of the Goths languished some time after the dangerous wound which he received from their daggers; but the conduct of the war was retarded by his infirmities, and the public councils of the nation were distracted by a spirit of jealousy and discord. His death, which has been imputed to his own despair, left the reins of government in the hands of Withimer, who, with the doubtful aid of some Scythian mercenaries, maintained the unequal contest against the arms of the Huns and the Alani, till he was [A D 374.5 ?] defeated and slain in a decisive battle. The Ostrogoths submitted to their fate; and the royal race of the Amali will hereafter be found among the subjects of the haughty Attila. But the person of Witheric, the infant king, was saved by the diligence of Alatheus and Saphrax: two warriors of approved valour and fidelity; who, by cautious marches, conducted the independent remains of the nation of the Ostrogoths towards [Danastris] the Danastus, or Dniester, a considerable river, which now separates the Turkish dominions from the empire of Russia. On the banks of the Dniester the prudent Athanaric, more attentive to his own than to the general safety, had fixed the camp of the Visigoths, with the firm resolution of opposing the victorious

[60] This execrable origin, which Jornandes (c. 24) describes with the rancour of a Goth, might be originally derived from a more pleasing fable of the Greeks. (Herodot l. iv c. 9, &c)

[61] The Roxolani may be the fathers of the 'Ρῶς, the *Russians* (d'Anville, Empire de Russie, p 1-10), whose residence (A D 862) about Novgorod Veliki cannot be very remote from that which the Geographer of Ravenna (i 12, iv 4. 46. v. 28, 30) assigns to the Roxolani (A D 886) [Rosomoni is the name in Jordanes, Get. 24. A connexion with Ρῶς is utterly wild]

Barbarians whom he thought it less advisable to provoke. The
ordinary speed of the Huns was checked by the weight of baggage, and the encumbrance of captives ; but their military skill
deceived, and almost destroyed, the army of Athanaric. While
the judge of the Visigoths defended the banks of the Dniester,
he was encompassed and attacked by a numerous detachment of
cavalry, who, by the light of the moon, had passed the river in
a fordable place ; and it was not without the utmost efforts of
courage and conduct that he was able to effect his retreat
towards the hilly country. The undaunted general had already
formed a new and judicious plan of defensive war; and the
strong lines, which he was preparing to construct between the
mountains, the Pruth, and the Danube, would have secured the
extensive and fertile territory that bears the modern name of
Walachia from the destructive inroads of the Huns.[62] But the
hopes and measures of the judge of the Visigoths were soon
disappointed by the trembling impatience of his dismayed
countrymen ; who were persuaded by their fears that the interposition of the Danube was the only barrier that could save
them from the rapid pursuit and invincible valour of the Barbarians of Scythia. Under the command of Fritigern and
Alavivus,[63] the body of the nation hastily advanced to the banks
of the great river, and implored the protection of the Roman
emperor of the East. Athanaric himself, still anxious to avoid
the guilt of perjury, retired with a band of faithful followers
into the mountainous country of Caucaland ; which appears to
have been guarded, and almost concealed, by the impenetrable
forests of Transylvania.[64]

After Valens had terminated the Gothic war with some appear- The Goths
ance of glory and success, he made a progress through his implore the protection of
dominions of Asia, and at length fixed his residence in the Valens A D 376
capital of Syria. The five years [65] which he spent at Antioch

[62] The text of Ammianus seems to be imperfect or corrupt ; but the nature of
the ground explains, and almost defines, the Gothic rampart Mémoires de
l'Académie, &c tom xxviii p 444-462. [The fortification, according to Wietersheim and Hodgkin, was " between the mountains of Transylvania and the river
Sereth ".]

[63] M de Buat (Hist des Peuples de l'Europe, t vi p 407) has conceived a
strange idea that Alavivus was the same person as Ulphilas the Gothic bishop
and that Ulphilas, the grandson of a Cappadocian captive, became a temporal
prince of the Goths

[64] Ammianus (xxxi 3) and Jornandes (de Rebus Geticis, c 24) describe the
subversion of the Gothic empire by the Huns [For Caucaland see below, p 126]

[65] The chronology of Ammianus is obscure and imperfect. Tillemont has
laboured to clear and settle the Annals of Valens. [See Reiche, op. cit. p 29 sqq.]

[A.D 372
spring -377
spring] were employed to watch, from a secure distance, the hostile designs of the Persian monarch, to check the depredations of the Saracens and Isaurians;[66] to enforce, by arguments more prevalent than those of reason and eloquence, the belief of the Arian theology, and to satisfy his anxious suspicions by the promiscuous execution of the innocent and the guilty. But the attention of the emperor was most seriously engaged by the important intelligence which he received from the civil and military officers who were intrusted with the defence of the Danube. He was informed that the North was agitated by a furious tempest; that the irruption of the Huns, an unknown and monstrous race of savages, had subverted the power of the Goths; and that the suppliant multitudes of that warlike nation, whose pride was now humbled in the dust, covered a space of many miles along the banks of the river   With out-stretched arms and pathetic lamentations, they loudly deplored their past misfortunes and their present danger; acknowledged that their only hope of safety was in the clemency of the Roman government, and most solemnly protested that, if the gracious liberality of the emperor would permit them to cultivate the waste lands of Thrace, they should ever hold themselves bound, by the strongest obligations of duty and gratitude, to obey the laws, and to guard the limits, of the republic.   These assurances were confirmed by the ambassadors of the Goths, who impatiently expected, from the mouth of Valens, an answer that must finally determine the fate of their unhappy countrymen.   The emperor of the East was no longer

A D 375,
Nov 17 guided by the wisdom and authority of his elder brother, whose death happened towards the end of the preceding year: and, as the distressful situation of the Goths required an instant and peremptory decision, he was deprived of the favourite resource of feeble and timid minds; who consider the use of dilatory and ambiguous measures as the most admirable efforts of consummate prudence.   As long as the same passions and interests subsist among mankind, the questions of war and peace, of justice and policy, which were debated in the councils of antiquity, will frequently present themselves as the subject of modern deliberation.   But the most experienced statesman of Europe has never been summoned to consider the propriety or the danger of admitting or rejecting an innumerable multitude

---

[66] Zosimus, l iv p 223 [c 20]   Sozomen, l vi c 38   The Isaurians, each winter, infested the roads of Asia Minor, as far as the neighbourhood of Constantinople. Basil, Epist ccl apud Tillemont, Hist des Empereurs, tom. v. p. 106

of Barbarians, who are driven by despair and hunger to solicit a
settlement on the territories of a civilized nation.   When that
important proposition, so essentially connected with the public
safety, was referred to the ministers of Valens, they were perplexed and divided; but they soon acquiesced in the flattering
sentiment which seemed the most favourable to the pride, the
indolence, and the avarice of their sovereign.   The slaves, who
were decorated with the titles of præfects and generals, dissembled or disregarded the terrors of this national emigration,
so extremely different from the partial and accidental colonies
which had been received on the extreme limits of the empire.
But they applauded the liberality of fortune, which had
conducted, from the most distant countries of the globe, a
numerous and invincible army of strangers, to defend the
throne of Valens, who might now add to the royal treasures
the immense sums of gold supplied by the provincials to
compensate their annual proportion of recruits.   The prayers of
the Goths were granted, and their service was accepted by the
Imperial court : and orders were immediately dispatched to the
civil and military governors of the Thracian diocese, to make
the necessary preparations for the passage and subsistence of a
great people, till a proper and sufficient territory could be
allotted for their future residence.   The liberality of the
emperor was accompanied, however, with two harsh and rigorous conditions, which prudence might justify on the side of the
Romans but which distress alone could extort from the indignant
Goths.   Before they passed the Danube, they were required to
deliver their arms ; and it was insisted that their children should
be taken from them and dispersed through the provinces of
Asia, where they might be civilized by the arts of education
and serve as hostages to secure the fidelity of their parents.

During this suspense of a doubtful and distant negotiation, They are
the impatient Goths made some rash attempts to pass the transported
Danube, without the permission of the government whose over the Dan-
protection they had implored.   Their motions were strictly pire
observed by the vigilance of the troops which were stationed
along the river, and their foremost detachments were defeated
with considerable slaughter ; yet such were the timid councils
of the reign of Valens that the brave officers who had served
their country in the execution of their duty were punished by
the loss of their employments and narrowly escaped the loss of
their heads.   The Imperial mandate was at length received for
transporting over the Danube the whole body of the Gothic

nation;[67] but the execution of this order was a task of labour
and difficulty.   The stream of the Danube, which in those parts
is above a mile broad,[68] had been swelled by incessant rains,
and, in this tumultuous passage, many were swept away and
drowned by the rapid violence of the current.   A large fleet of
vessels, of boats, and of canoes was provided; many days and
nights they passed and repassed with indefatigable toil; and
the most strenuous diligence was exerted by the officers of
Valens that not a single Barbarian, of those who were reserved
to subvert the foundations of Rome, should be left on the
opposite shore.   It was thought expedient that an accurate
account should be taken of their numbers; but the persons
who were employed soon desisted, with amazement and
dismay, from the prosecution of the endless and impracticable
task;[69] and the principal historian of the age most seriously
affirms that the prodigious armies of Darius and Xerxes, which
had so long been considered as the fables of vain and credulous
antiquity, were now justified, in the eyes of mankind, by the
evidence of fact and experience.   A probable testimony has
fixed the number of the Gothic warriors at two hundred thousand men; and, if we can venture to add the just proportion of
women, of children, and of slaves, the whole mass of people
which composed this formidable emigration must have amounted
to near a million of persons, of both sexes and of all ages.   The
children of the Goths, those at least of a distinguished rank,
were separated from the multitude.   They were conducted,
without delay, to the distant seats assigned for their residence
and education; and, as the numerous train of hostages or captives
passed through the cities, their gay and splendid apparel, their
robust and martial figure, excited the surprise and envy of the
Provincials.   But the stipulation, the most offensive to the
Goths and the most important to the Romans, was shamefully

---

[67] The passage of the Danube is exposed by Ammianus (xxxi 3, 4), Zosimus (l.
iv p. 223, 224), Eunapius (in Excerpt Legat p 19, 20), and Jornandes (c. 25, 26)
Ammianus declares (c. 5) that he means only ipsas rerum digerere *summitate*
But he often takes a false measure of their importance; and his superfluous
prolixity is disagreeably balanced by his unseasonable brevity.

[68] Chishull, a curious traveller, has remarked the breadth of the Danube, which
he passed to the south of Bucharest, near the conflux of the Argish [Argèche] (p.
77)   He admires the beauty and spontaneous plenty of Mæsia, or Bulgaria.

[69] Quem si [*leg.* qui] scire velit, Libyci velit æquoris idem
    Scire [*leg.* discere] quam multæ Zephyro truduntur [*leg.* turbentur] harenæ.
Ammianus has inserted, in his prose, these lines of Virgil (Georgic. l. ii. [105-6]),
originally designed by the poet to express the impossibility of numbering the
different sorts of vines. See Plin Hist Natur l. xiv

eluded. The Barbarians, who considered their arms as the ensigns of honour and the pledges of safety, were disposed to offer a price which the lust or avarice of the Imperial officers was easily tempted to accept. To preserve their arms, the haughty warriors consented, with some reluctance, to prostitute their wives or their daughters; the charms of a beauteous maid, or a comely boy, secured the connivance of the inspectors; who sometimes cast an eye of covetousness on the fringed carpets and linen garments of their new allies,[70] or who sacrificed their duty to the mean consideration of filling their farms with cattle and their houses with slaves. The Goths, with arms in their hands, were permitted to enter the boats; and, when their strength was collected on the other side of the river, the immense camp which was spread over the plains and the hills of the Lower Mœsia assumed a threatening and even hostile aspect. The leaders of the Ostrogoths, Alatheus and Saphrax, the guardians of their infant king, appeared soon afterwards on the Northern banks of the Danube; and immediately dispatched their ambassadors to the court of Antioch, to solicit, with the same professions of allegiance and gratitude, the same favour which had been granted to the suppliant Visigoths. The absolute refusal of Valens suspended their progress, and discovered the repentance, the suspicions, and the fears of the Imperial council.

An undisciplined and unsettled nation of Barbarians required the firmest temper and the most dexterous management. The daily subsistence of near a million of extraordinary subjects could be supplied only by constant and skilful diligence, and might continually be interrupted by mistake or accident. The insolence or the indignation of the Goths, if they conceived themselves to be the objects either of fear or of contempt, might urge them to the most desperate extremities; and the fortune of the state seemed to depend on the prudence, as well as the integrity, of the generals of Valens. At this important crisis, the military government of Thrace was exercised by Lupicinus and Maximus, in whose venal minds the slightest hope of private emolument outweighed every consideration of public advantage; and whose guilt was only alleviated by their incapacity of discerning the pernicious effects of their rash and

Their distress and discontent

---

[70] Eunapius and Zosimus curiously specify these articles of Gothic wealth and luxury. Yet it must be presumed that they were the manufactures of the provinces; which the Barbarians had acquired as the spoils of war, or as the gifts or merchandise of peace [Another frag. of Eunapius (55) describes a *later* crossing of Goths, in reign of Theodosius, c. 382 A.D.]

criminal administration.   Instead of obeying the orders of
their sovereign and satisfying with decent liberality the
demands of the Goths, they levied an ungenerous and
oppressive tax on the wants of the hungry Barbarians   The
vilest food was sold at an extravagant price , and, in the room
of wholesome and substantial provisions, the markets were
filled with the flesh of dogs, and of unclean animals, who had
died of disease.   To obtain the valuable acquisition of a pound
of bread, the Goths resigned the possession of an expensive,
though serviceable, slave; and a small quantity of meat was
greedily purchased with ten pounds of a precious, but useless,
metal.[71]   When their property was exhausted, they continued
this necessary traffic by the sale of their sons and daughters;
and notwithstanding the love of freedom, which animated
every Gothic breast, they submitted to the humiliating maxim
that it was better for their children to be maintained in a servile
condition than to perish in a state of wretched and helpless independence.   The most lively resentment is excited by the
tyranny of pretended benefactors, who sternly exact the debt
of gratitude which they have cancelled by subsequent injuries :
a spirit of discontent insensibly arose in the camp of the
Barbarians, who pleaded, without success, the merit of their
patient and dutiful behaviour; and loudly complained of the
inhospitable treatment which they had received from their new
allies.   They beheld around them the wealth and plenty of a
fertile province, in the midst of which they suffered the
intolerable hardships of artificial famine.   But the means of
relief, and even of revenge, were in their hands; since the
rapaciousness of their tyrants had left, to an injured people,
the possession and the use of arms.   The clamours of a
multitude, untaught to disguise their sentiments, announced
the first symptoms of resistance, and alarmed the timid and
guilty minds of Lupicinus and Maximus.   Those crafty
ministers, who substituted the cunning of temporary expedients
to the wise and salutary counsels of general policy, attempted
to remove the Goths from their dangerous station on the
frontiers of the empire, and to disperse them in separate

[71] *Decem libras;* the word *silver* must be understood.   Jornandes betrays the
passions and prejudices of a Goth.   The servile Greeks, Eunapius and Zosimus,
disguise the Roman oppression and execrate the perfidy of the Barbarians.
Ammianus, a patriot historian, slightly, and reluctantly, touches on the odious
subject.   Jerom, who wrote almost on the spot, is fair, though concise.   Per
avaritiam Maximi ducis ad rebellionem fame *coacti* sunt (in **Chron.**).

quarters of cantonment through the interior provinces.   As they were conscious how ill they had deserved the respect, or confidence, of the Barbarians, they diligently collected, from every side, a military force, that might urge the tardy and reluctant march of a people who had not yet renounced the title, or the duties, of Roman subjects.   But the generals of Valens, while their attention was solely directed to the discontented Visigoths, imprudently disarmed the ships and fortifications which constituted the defence of the Danube.   The fatal oversight was observed and improved by Alatheus and Saphrax, who anxiously watched the favourable moment of escaping from the pursuit of the Huns.   By the help of such rafts and vessels as could be hastily procured, the leaders of the Ostrogoths transported, without opposition, their king and their army; and boldly fixed an hostile and independent camp on the territories of the empire.[72]

Under the name of judges, Alavivus and Fritigern were the leaders of the Visigoths in peace and war; and the authority which they derived from their birth was ratified by the free consent of the nation.   In a season of tranquillity, their power might have been equal, as well as their rank; but, as soon as their countrymen were exasperated by hunger and oppression, the superior abilities of Fritigern assumed the military command, which he was qualified to exercise for the public welfare.   He restrained the impatient spirit of the Visigoths, till the injuries and the insults of their tyrants should justify their resistance in the opinion of mankind; but he was not disposed to sacrifice any solid advantages for the empty praise of justice and moderation.   Sensible of the benefits which would result from the union of the Gothic powers under the same standard, he secretly cultivated the friendship of the Ostrogoths; and, while he professed an implicit obedience to the orders of the Roman generals, he proceeded by slow marches towards Marcianopolis, the capital of the Lower Mæsia, about seventy miles from the banks of the Danube.   On that fatal spot, the flames of discord and mutual hatred burst forth into a dreadful conflagration.   Lupicinus had invited the Gothic chiefs to a splendid entertainment; and their martial train remained under arms at the entrance of the palace.   But the gates of the city were strictly guarded; and the Barbarians were sternly excluded from the use of a plentiful market, to which they

Revolt of the Goths in Mæsia, and their first victories

[Shumla]

[A.D. 377]

---

[72] Ammian. xxxi. 4, 5.

asserted their equal claim of subjects and allies. Their humble prayers were rejected with insolence and derision; and, as their patience was now exhausted, the townsmen, the soldiers, and the Goths were soon involved in a conflict of passionate altercation and angry reproaches. A blow was imprudently given; a sword was hastily drawn; and the first blood that was spilt in this accidental quarrel became the signal of a long and destructive war. In the midst of noise and brutal intemperance, Lupicinus was informed, by a secret messenger, that many of his soldiers were slain and despoiled of their arms; and, as he was already inflamed by wine and oppressed by sleep, he issued a rash command that their death should be revenged by the massacre of the guards of Fritigern and Alavivus. The clamorous shouts and dying groans apprised Fritigern of his extreme danger; and, as he possessed the calm and intrepid spirit of a hero, he saw that he was lost if he allowed a moment of deliberation to the man who had so deeply injured him. "A trifling dispute," said the Gothic leader, with a firm but gentle tone of voice, "appears to have arisen between the two nations; but it may be productive of the most dangerous consequences, unless the tumult is immediately pacified by the assurance of our safety and the authority of our presence." At these words, Fritigern and his companions drew their swords, opened their passage through the unresisting crowd which filled the palace, the streets, and the gates of Marcianopolis, and, mounting their horses, hastily vanished from the eyes of the astonished Romans. The generals of the Goths were saluted by the fierce and joyful acclamations of the camp; war was instantly resolved, and the resolution was executed without delay; the banners of the nation were displayed according to the custom of their ancestors; and the air resounded with the harsh and mournful music of the Barbarian trumpet.[73] The weak and guilty Lupicinus, who had dared to provoke, who had neglected to destroy, and who still presumed to despise, his formidable

[73] Vexillis de *more* sublatis, auditisque *triste sonantibus classicis* Ammian xxxi. 5. These are the *rauca cornua* of Claudian (in Rufin. ii. 57), the large horns of the *Uri*, or wild bull, such as have been more recently used by the Swiss Cantons of Uri and Underwald (Simler de Republicâ Helvet l. ii. p. 201, edit. Fuselin Tigur. 1734) The military horn is finely, though perhaps casually, introduced in an original narrative of the battle of Nancy (A.D 1477). "Attendant le combat le dit |cor fut corné par trois fois, tant que le vent du souffleur pouvoit durer . ce qui esbahit fort Monsieur de Bourgoigne , *car déja à Morat l'avoit ouy.*" (See the Pièces Justificatives, in the 4to edition of Philippe de Comines, tom. iii. p. 493.)

enemy, marched against the Goths, at the head of such a military force as could be collected on this sudden emergency. The Barbarians expected his approach about nine miles from Marcianopolis; and on this occasion the talents of the general were found to be of more prevailing efficacy than the weapons and discipline of the troops. The valour of the Goths was so ably directed by the genius of Fritigern that they broke, by a close and vigorous attack, the ranks of the Roman legions. Lupicinus left his arms and standards, his tribunes and his bravest soldiers, on the field of battle; and their useless courage served only to protect the ignominious flight of their leader. "That successful day put an end to the distress of the Barbarians and the security of the Romans: from that day, the Goths, renouncing the precarious condition of strangers and exiles, assumed the character of citizens and masters, claimed an absolute dominion over the possessors of land, and held, in their own right, the northern provinces of the empire, which are bounded by the Danube." Such are the words of the Gothic historian,[74] who celebrates, with rude eloquence, the glory of his countrymen. But the dominion of the Barbarians was exercised only for the purposes of rapine and destruction. As they had been deprived, by the ministers of the emperor, of the common benefits of nature and the fair intercourse of social life, they retaliated the injustice on the subjects of the empire; and the crimes of Lupicinus were expiated by the ruin of the peaceful husbandmen of Thrace, the conflagration of their villages, and the massacre, or captivity, of their innocent families. The report of the Gothic victory was soon diffused over the adjacent country; and, while it filled the minds of the Romans with terror and dismay, their own hasty prudence contributed to increase the forces of Fritigern and the calamities of the province. Some time before the great emigration, a numerous body of Goths, under the command of Suerid and Colias, had been received into the protection and service of the empire.[75] They were encamped under the walls of Hadrianople. but the ministers of Valens were anxious to remove them beyond the Hellespont, at a distance from the dangerous temptation which might so easily

They penetrate into Thrace

---

[74] Jornandes de Rebus Geticis, c. 26, p 648, edit Grot   These *splendidi panni* (they are comparatively such) are undoubtedly transcribed from the larger histories of Priscus, Ablavius, or Cassiodorius.

[75] Cum populis suis longe ante suscepti.   We are ignorant of the precise date and circumstances of their transmigration.

be communicated by the neighbourhood, and the success, of
their countrymen. The respectful submission with which they
yielded to the order of their march might be considered as a
proof of their fidelity ; and their moderate request of a sufficient
allowance of provisions, and of a delay of only two days, was
expressed in the most dutiful terms   But the first magistrate
of Hadrianople, incensed by some disorders which had been
committed at his country-house, refused this indulgence ; and
arming against them the inhabitants and manufacturers of a
populous city, he urged, with hostile threats, their instant
departure   The Barbarians stood silent and amazed, till they
were exasperated by the insulting clamours, and missile
weapons, of the populace : but, when patience or contempt was
fatigued, they crushed the undisciplined multitude, inflicted
many a shameful wound on the backs of their flying enemies,
and despoiled them of the splendid armour [76] which they were
unworthy to bear. The resemblance of their sufferings and
their actions soon united this victorious detachment to the
nation of the Visigoths ; the troops of Colias and Suerid expected the approach of the great Fritigern, ranged themselves
under his standard, and signalized their ardour in the siege of
Hadrianople.   But the resistance of the garrison informed the
Barbarians that, in the attack of regular fortifications, the
efforts of unskilful courage are seldom effectual.   Their
general acknowledged his error, raised the siege, declared that
" he was at peace with stone walls," [77] and revenged his disappointment on the adjacent country   He accepted, with
pleasure, the useful reinforcement of hardy workmen, who
laboured in the gold mines of Thrace [78] for the emolument, and
under the lash, of an unfeeling master : [79] and these new
associates conducted the Barbarians, through the secret paths,
to the most sequestered places, which had been chosen to

[76] An Imperial manufacture of shields, &c., was established at Hadrianople , and
the populace were headed by the *Fabricenses*, or workmen (Vales ad Ammian
xxxi 6)
[77] Pacem sibi esse cum parietibus memorans. Amm xxxi. 7
[78] These mines were in the country of the Bessi, in the ridge of mountains, the
Rhodope, that runs between Philippi and Philippopolis , two Macedonian cities,
which derived their name and origin from the father of Alexander   From the
mines of Thrace he annually received the value, not the weight, of a thousand
talents (200,000 l), a revenue which paid the phalanx, and corrupted the orators
of Greece   See Diodor Siculus, tom ii l xvi. p 88, edit Wesseling. Godefroy's
Commentary on the Theodosian Code, tom. iii p. 496   Cellarius, Geograph.
Antiq. tom i p 676, 857.   D'Anville, Géographie Ancienne, tom i p. 336
[79] As those unhappy workmen often ran away, Valens had enacted severe laws
to drag them from their hiding-places   Cod Theodosian l. x. tit. xix. leg 5, 7.

secure the inhabitants, the cattle, and the magazines of corn. With the assistance of such guides, nothing could remain impervious or inaccessible; resistance was fatal; flight was impracticable; and the patient submission of helpless innocence seldom found mercy from the Barbarian conqueror. In the course of these depredations, a great number of the children of the Goths, who had been sold into captivity, were restored to the embraces of their afflicted parents; but these tender interviews, which might have revived and cherished in their minds some sentiments of humanity, tended only to stimulate their native fierceness by the desire of revenge. They listened, with eager attention, to the complaints of their captive children, who had suffered the most cruel indignities from the lustful or angry passions of their masters; and the same cruelties, the same indignities, were severely retaliated on the sons and daughters of the Romans.[80]

The imprudence of Valens and his ministers had introduced into the heart of the empire a nation of enemies; but the Visigoths might even yet have been reconciled, by the manly confession of past errors and the sincere performance of former engagements These healing and temperate measures seemed to concur with the timorous disposition of the sovereign of the East; but, on this occasion alone, Valens was brave, and his unseasonable bravery was fatal to himself and to his subjects. His declared his intention of marching from Antioch to Constantinople, to subdue this dangerous rebellion ; and, as he was not ignorant of the difficulties of the enterprise, he solicited the assistance of his nephew, the emperor Gratian, who commanded all the forces of the West. The veteran troops were hastily recalled from the defence of Armenia; that important frontier was abandoned to the discretion of Sapor; and the immediate conduct of the Gothic war was intrusted, during the absence of Valens, to his lieutenants Trajan and Profuturus, two generals who indulged themselves in a very false and favourable opinion of their own abilities. On their arrival in Thrace, they were joined by Richomer, count of the domestics; and the auxiliaries of the West, that marched under his banner, were composed of the Gallic legions, reduced indeed by a spirit of desertion to the vain appearances of strength and numbers. In a council of war, which was influenced by pride rather than

Operations of the Gothic war A.D 377

---

[80] See Ammianus, xxxi. 5, 6   The historian of the Gothic war loses time and space by an unseasonable recapitulation of the ancient inroads of the Barbarians.

by reason, it was resolved to seek and to encounter the Barbarians, who lay encamped in the spacious and fertile meadows
near the most southern of the six mouths of the Danube.[81]
Their camp was surrounded by the usual fortification of
waggons ;[82] and the Barbarians, secure within the vast circle
of the inclosure, enjoyed the fruits of their valour and the
spoils of the province. In the midst of riotous intemperance,
the watchful Fritigern observed the motions, and penetrated
the designs, of the Romans. He perceived that the numbers
of the enemy were continually increasing, and, as he understood their intention of attacking his rear as soon as the
scarcity of forage should oblige him to remove his camp, he
recalled to their standard his predatory detachments which
covered the adjacent country. As soon as they descried the
flaming beacons,[83] they obeyed, with incredible speed, the
signal of their leader; the camp was filled with the martial
crowd of Barbarians; their impatient clamours demanded the
battle, and their tumultuous zeal was approved and animated
by the spirit of their chiefs. The evening was already far
advanced, and the two armies prepared themselves for the
approaching combat, which was deferred only till the dawn of
day. While the trumpets sounded to arms, the undaunted
courage of the Goths was confirmed by the mutual obligation
of a solemn oath, and, as they advanced to meet the enemy,
the rude songs, which celebrated the glory of their forefathers,
were mingled with their fierce and dissonant outcries, and
opposed to the artificial harmony of the Roman shout. Some
military skill was displayed by Fritigern to gain the advantage
of a commanding eminence, but the bloody conflict, which
began and ended with the light, was maintained, on either
side, by the personal and obstinate efforts of strength, valour,
and agility. The legions of Armenia supported their fame in

[Battle of Ad
Salices A D
377]

---

[81] The Itinerary of Antoninus (p 226, 227, edit Wesseling) marks the situation
of this place about sixty miles north of Tomi, Ovid's exile · and the name of *Salices*
(the willows) expresses the nature of the soil   [The Romans " succeeded in clearing
first the Rhodope country, and then the line of the Balkans, of the Gothic army "
(Hodgkin, 1 261)]

[82] This circle of waggons, the *Carrago*, was the usual fortification of the
Barbarians (Vegetius de Re Militari, l iii c 10. Valesius ad Ammian xxvi 7)
The practice and the name were preserved by their descendants, as late as the
fifteenth century   The *Charroy*, which surrounded the *Ost*, is a word familiar to
the readers of Froissard or Comines

[83] Statim ut accensi malleoli [*ib.*]   I have used the literal sense of real torches or
beacons: but I almost suspect that it is only one of those turgid metaphors, those
false ornaments, that perpetually disfigure the style of Ammianus.

arms; but they were oppressed by the irresistible weight of
the hostile multitude; the left wing of the Romans was thrown
into disorder, and the field was strewed with their mangled
carcasses. This partial defeat was balanced, however, by
partial success; and when the two armies, at a late hour of
the evening, retreated to their respective camps, neither of
them could claim the honours, or the effects, of a decisive
victory. The real loss was more severely felt by the Romans,
in proportion to the smallness of their numbers; but the Goths
were so deeply confounded and dismayed by this vigorous, and
perhaps unexpected, resistance that they remained seven days
within the circle of their fortifications Such funeral rites as
the circumstances of time and place would admit were piously
discharged to some officers of distinguished rank; but the
indiscriminate vulgar was left unburied on the plain. Their
flesh was greedily devoured by the birds of prey, who, in that
age, enjoyed very frequent and delicious feasts; and several
years afterwards the white and naked bones which covered the
wide extent of the fields presented to the eyes of Ammianus
a dreadful monument of the battle of Salices.[84]

The progress of the Goths had been checked by the doubt- Union of the
ful event of that bloody day; and the Imperial generals, whose Goths with
army would have been consumed by the repetition of such a the Huns, Alani, &c
contest, embraced the more rational plan of destroying the
Barbarians by the wants and pressure of their own multitudes.
They prepared to confine the Visigoths in the narrow angle of
land between the Danube, the desert of Scythia, and the
mountains of Hæmus, till their strength and spirit should be
insensibly wasted by the inevitable operation of famine The
design was prosecuted with some conduct and success; the
Barbarians had almost exhausted their own magazines, and the
harvests of the country, and the diligence of Saturninus, the
master-general of the cavalry, was employed to improve the
strength, and to contract the extent, of the Roman fortifications His labours were interrupted by the alarming intelligence that new swarms of Barbarians had passed the
unguarded Danube, either to support the cause, or to imitate

[84] Indicant nunc usque albentes ossibus campi Ammian. xxxi 7 The
historian might have viewed these plains either as a soldier or as a traveller. But
his modesty has suppressed the adventures of his own life subsequent to the Persian
wars of Constantius and Julian We are ignorant of the time when he quitted the
service and retired to Rome, where he appears to have composed his History of
his own Times

the example, of Fritigern.   The just apprehension, that he
himself might be surrounded, and overwhelmed, by the arms
of hostile and unknown nations, compelled Saturninus to
relinquish the siege of the Gothic camp : and the indignant
Visigoths, breaking from their confinement, satiated their
hunger and revenge, by the repeated devastation of the fruitful
country, which extends above three hundred miles from the
banks of the Danube to the straits of the Hellespont [85]   The
sagacious Fritigern had successfully appealed to the passions,
as well as to the interest, of his Barbarian allies ; and the love
of rapine and the hatred of Rome seconded, or even prevented,
the eloquence of his ambassadors.   He cemented a strict and
useful alliance with the great body of his countrymen, who
obeyed Alatheus and Saphrax as the guardians of their infant
king ; the long animosity of rival tribes was suspended by the
sense of their common interest ; the independent part of the
nation was associated under one standard ; and the chiefs of
the Ostrogoths appear to have yielded to the superior genius
of the general of the Visigoths.   He obtained the formidable

[Taifali]

aid of the Taifalæ, whose military renown was disgraced and
polluted by the public infamy of their domestic manners.
Every youth, on his entrance into the world, was united by
the ties of honourable friendship, and brutal love, to some
warrior of the tribe ; nor could he hope to be released from
this unnatural connexion, till he had approved his manhood
by slaying, in single combat, a huge bear, or a wild boar of
the forest [86]   But the most powerful auxiliaries of the Goths
were drawn from the camp of those enemies who had expelled
them from their native seats.   The loose subordination, and
extensive possessions, of the Huns and the Alani delayed the
conquests, and distracted the councils, of that victorious people.
Several of the hords were allured by the liberal promises of
Fritigern , and the rapid cavalry of Scythia added weight and
energy to the steady and strenuous efforts of the Gothic infantry.   The Sarmatians, who could never forgive the successor
of Valentinian, enjoyed and increased the general confusion ;
and a seasonable irruption of the Alemanni into the provinces

[85] Ammianus, xxxi 8.
[86] Hanc Taifalorum gentem turpem, et obscenæ vitæ flagitiis ita accipimus
mersam , ut apud eos nefandi concubitus fœdere copulentur mares puberes, ætatis
viriditatem in eorum pollutis usibus consumpturi.   Porro, si qui jam adultus
aprum exceperit solus, vel interemit ursum immanem, colluvione liberatur incesti.
Ammian xxxi 9   Among the Greeks likewise, more especially among the Cretans,
the holy bands of friendship were confirmed, and sullied, by unnatural love.

of Gaul engaged the attention, and diverted the forces, of the emperor of the West.[87]

One of the most dangerous inconveniences of the introduction of the Barbarians into the army and the palace, was sensibly felt in their correspondence with their hostile countrymen, to whom they imprudently, or maliciously, revealed the weakness of the Roman empire. A soldier, of the life-guards of Gratian, was of the nation of the Alemanni, and of the tribe of the Lentienses, who dwelt beyond the lake of Constance. Some domestic business obliged him to request a leave of absence. In a short visit to his family and friends, he was exposed to their curious inquiries; and the vanity of the loquacious soldier tempted him to display his intimate acquaintance with the secrets of the state and the designs of his master. The intelligence that Gratian was preparing to lead the military force of Gaul and of the West to the assistance of his uncle Valens pointed out to the restless spirit of the Alemanni the moment, and the mode, of a successful invasion. The enterprise of some light detachments, who, in the month of February, passed the Rhine upon the ice, was the prelude of a more important war. The boldest hopes of rapine, perhaps of conquest, outweighed the consideration of timid prudence or national faith. Every forest and every village poured forth a band of hardy adventurers; and the great army of the Alemanni, which, on their approach, was estimated at forty thousand men by the fears of the people, was afterwards magnified to the number of seventy thousand by the vain and credulous flattery of the Imperial court. The legions which had been ordered to march into Pannonia were immediately recalled or detained for the defence of Gaul; the military command was divided between Nanienus and Mellobaudes; and the youthful emperor, though he respected the long experience and sober wisdom of the former, was much more inclined to admire and to follow the martial ardour of his colleague; who was allowed to unite the incompatible characters of count of the domestics and of king of the Franks. His rival Priarius, king of the Alemanni, was guided, or rather impelled, by the same headstrong valour; and, as their troops were animated by the spirit of their leaders, they met, they saw, they encountered, each other, near the town of Argentaria, or

Victory of Gratian over the Alemanni
A D 378, May

---

[87] Ammian xvvi. 8, 9.   Jerom (tom 1 p 26) enumerates the nations, and marks a calamitous period of twenty years   This epistle to Heliodorus was composed in the year 397 (Tillemont, Mém. Ecclés. tom. xii. p 645) [Ep 60, ap. Migne, i. p. 600.]

[Horburg, near Colmar]

Colmar,[88] in the plains of Alsace. The glory of the day was justly ascribed to the missile weapons and well-practised evolutions of the Roman soldiers; the Alemanni, who long maintained their ground, were slaughtered with unrelenting fury; five thousand only of the Barbarians escaped to the woods and mountains; and the glorious death of their king on the field of battle saved him from the reproaches of the people, who are always disposed to accuse the justice, or policy, of an unsuccessful war. After this signal victory, which secured the peace of Gaul and asserted the honour of the Roman arms, the emperor Gratian appeared to proceed without delay on his Eastern expedition; but, as he approached the confines of the Alemanni, he suddenly inclined to the left, surprised them by his unexpected passage of the Rhine, and boldly advanced into the heart of their country. The Barbarians opposed to his progress the obstacles of nature and of courage; and still continued to retreat from one hill to another, till they were satisfied, by repeated trials, of the power and perseverance of their enemies. Their submission was accepted as a proof, not indeed of their sincere repentance, but of their actual distress; and a select number of their brave and robust youth was exacted from the faithless nation, as the most substantial pledge of their future moderation. The subjects of the empire, who had so often experienced that the Alemanni could neither be subdued by arms nor restrained by treaties, might not promise themselves any solid or lasting tranquillity: but they discovered, in the virtues of their young sovereign, the prospect of a long and auspicious reign. When the legions climbed the mountains, and scaled the fortifications, of the Barbarians, the valour of Gratian was distinguished in the foremost ranks; and the gilt and variegated armour of his guards was pierced and shattered by the blows which they had received in their constant attachment to the person of their sovereign. At the age of nineteen, the son of Valentinian seemed to possess the talents of peace and war; and his personal success against the Alemanni was interpreted as a sure presage of his Gothic triumphs.[89]

---

[88] The field of battle, *Argentaria* or *Argentovaria*, is accurately fixed by M d'Anville (Notice de l'Ancienne Gaul, p 96-99) at twenty-three Gallic leagues, or thirty-four and a half Roman miles, to the south of Strasburg From its ruins the adjacent town of *Colmar* has arisen

[89] The full and impartial narrative of Ammianus (xxi 10) may derive some additional light from the Epitome of Victor, the Chronicle of Jerom, and the History of Orosius (l vii c 33, p 552, edit Havercamp)

While Gratian deserved and enjoyed the applause of his sub-^{Valens}
jects, the emperor Valens, who, at length, had removed his ^{marches}
court and army from Antioch, was received by the people of ^{Goths A D}
Constantinople as the author of the public calamity.   Before he ^{June 11}
had reposed himself ten days in the capital, he was urged, by
the licentious clamours of the Hippodrome, to march against
the Barbarians whom he had invited into his dominions : and
the citizens, who are always brave at a distance from any real
danger, declared, with confidence, that, if they were supplied
with arms, *they* alone would undertake to deliver the province
from the ravages of an insulting foe.[90]   The vain reproaches of
an ignorant multitude hastened the downfall of the Roman
empire ; they provoked the desperate rashness of Valens, who
did not find, either in his reputation or in his mind, any motives
to support with firmness the public contempt.   He was soon
persuaded, by the successful achievements of his lieutenants, to
despise the power of the Goths, who, by the diligence of Fritigern, were now collected in the neighbourhood of Hadrianople
The march of the Taifalæ had been intercepted by the valiant
Frigerid ; the king of those licentious Barbarians was slain in [A D 377]
battle ; and the suppliant captives were sent into distant exile
to cultivate the lands of Italy which were assigned for their
settlement in the vacant territories of Modena and Parma.[91]
The exploits of Sebastian,[92] who was recently engaged in the
service of Valens and promoted to the rank of master-general of
the infantry, were still more honourable to himself and useful to
the republic.   He obtained the permission of selecting three
hundred soldiers from each of the legions ; and this separate
detachment soon acquired the spirit of discipline and the exercise
of arms, which were almost forgotten under the reign of Valens.
By the vigour and conduct of Sebastian, a large body of the

[90] Moratus paucissimos dies, seditione popularium levium pulsus Ammian.
xxvi 11   Socrates (l iv. c. 38) supplies the dates and some circumstances [And
cp. Eunapius, p. 46, ed. Muller]
[91] Vivosque omnes circa Mutinam, Regiumque, et Parmam, Italica oppida,
rura culturos exterminavit. Ammianus, xxxi 9   Those cities and districts, about
ten years after the colony of the Taifalæ [Taifali], appear in a very desolate state.
See Muratori, Dissertazioni sopra le Antichità Italiana, tom. i Dissertat. xxi. p
354.   [Frigeridus fortified the pass of Succi (between Sofia and Philippopolis), but
his incompetent successor Maurus sustained a defeat there, Amm xx. 4, 18,
Hodgkin, i. 266 ; see below, p 115]
[92] Ammian xxvi 11   Zosimus, l. iv. p. 228-230 [23]   The latter expatiates on
the desultory exploits of Sebastian, and dispatches, in a few lines, the important
battle of Hadrianople. According to the ecclesiastical critics, who hate Sebastian,
the praise of Zosimus is disgrace (Tillemont, Hist des Empereurs, tom v. p 121)
His prejudice and ignorance undoubtedly render him a very questionable judge of
merit.

Goths was surprised in their camp: and the immense spoil
which was recovered from their hands filled the city of Hadrianople and the adjacent plain   The splendid narratives which
the general transmitted of his own exploits alarmed the Imperial
court by the appearance of superior merit; and, though he
cautiously insisted on the difficulties of the Gothic war, his
valour was praised, his advice was rejected; and Valens, who
listened with pride and pleasure to the flattering suggestions of
the eunuchs of the palace, was impatient to seize the glory of
an easy and assured conquest.   His army was strengthened by
a numerous reinforcement of veterans; and his march from
Constantinople to Hadrianople was conducted with so much
military skill that he prevented the activity of the Barbarians,
who designed to occupy the intermediate defiles and to intercept
either the troops themselves or their convoys of provisions.   The
camp of Valens, which he pitched under the walls of Hadrianople, was fortified, according to the practice of the Romans,
with a ditch and rampart; and a most important council was
summoned, to decide the fate of the emperor and of the empire.
The party of reason and of delay was strenuously maintained by
Victor, who had corrected, by the lessons of experience, the
native fierceness of the Sarmatian character; while Sebastian,
with the flexible and obsequious eloquence of a courtier, represented every precaution and every measure that implied a
doubt of immediate victory as unworthy of the courage and
majesty of their invincible monarch.   The ruin of Valens was
precipitated by the deceitful arts of Fritigern and the prudent
admonitions of the emperor of the West.   The advantages of
negotiating in the midst of war were perfectly understood by
the general of the Barbarians; and a Christian ecclesiastic
was dispatched, as the holy minister of peace, to penetrate, and
to perplex, the councils of the enemy.   The misfortunes, as
well as the provocations, of the Gothic nation were forcibly and
truly described by their ambassador; who protested, in the
name of Fritigern, that he was still disposed to lay down his
arms, or to employ them only in the defence of the empire if he
could secure, for his wandering countrymen, a tranquil settle-
[The *province* of Thrace] ment on the waste lands of Thrace and a sufficient allowance of
corn and cattle.   But he added, in a whisper of confidential
friendship), that the exasperated Barbarians were averse to these
reasonable conditions, and that Fritigern was doubtful whether
he could accomplish the conclusion of the treaty, unless he found
himself supported by the presence and terrors of an Imperial

army.   About the same time Count Richomer returned from the West, to announce the defeat and submission of the Alemanni ; to inform Valens that his nephew advanced by rapid marches at the head of the veteran and victorious legions of Gaul ; and to request, in the name of Gratian and of the republic, that every dangerous and decisive measure might be suspended, till the junction of the two emperors should ensure the success of the Gothic war.   But the feeble sovereign of the East was actuated only by the fatal illusions of pride and jealousy.   He disdained the importunate advice ; he rejected the humiliating aid ; he secretly compared the ignominious, or at least the inglorious, period of his own reign with the fame of a beardless youth : and Valens rushed into the field, to erect his imaginary trophy, before the diligence of his colleague could usurp any share of the triumphs of the day.

On the ninth of August, a day which has deserved to be marked among the most inauspicious of the Roman Calendar,[93] the emperor Valens, leaving, under a strong guard, his baggage and military treasure, marched from Hadrianople to attack the Goths, who were encamped about twelve miles from the city.[94] By some mistake of the orders, or ignorance of the ground, the right wing, or column of cavalry, arrived in sight of the enemy, whilst the left was still at a considerable distance ; the soldiers were compelled, in the sultry heat of summer, to precipitate their pace ; and the line of battle was formed with tedious confusion and irregular delay.   The Gothic cavalry had been detached to forage in the adjacent country ; and Fritigern still continued to practise his customary arts.   He dispatched messengers of peace, made proposals, required hostages, and wasted the hours, till the Romans, exposed without shelter to the burning rays of the sun, were exhausted by thirst, hunger, and intolerable fatigue.   The emperor was persuaded to send an ambassador to the Gothic camp ; the zeal of Richomer, who alone had courage to accept the dangerous commission, was applauded : and the count of the domestics, adorned with

Marginal note: Battle of Hadrianople. A D 378, August 9th

[93] Ammianus (xxxi 12, 13) almost alone describes the councils and actions which were terminated by the fatal battle of Hadrianople.   We might censure the vices of his style, the disorder and perplexity of his narrative, but we must now take leave of this impartial historian, and reproach is silenced by our regret for such an irreparable loss.   [The most recent investigation of the Battle of Hadrianople is by Judeich, in the Deutsche Ztsch f Geschichtswissenschaft, 1891, p 1, *sqq*]

[94] The difference of the eight miles of Ammianus, and the twelve of Idatius, can only embarrass those critics (Valesius ad loc.) who suppose a great army to be a mathematical point, without space or dimensions   [The Goths had come from N.E. corner of the province of Haemimontus ; cp Hodgkin, 1 269]

the splendid ensigns of his dignity, had proceeded some way in the space between the two armies when he was suddenly re-called by the alarm of battle. The hasty and imprudent attack was made by Bacurius the Iberian, who commanded a body of archers and targetteers; and, as they advanced with rashness, they retreated with loss and disgrace. In the same moment, the flying squadrons of Alatheus and Saphrax, whose return was anxiously expected by the general of the Goths, descended like a whirlwind from the hills, swept across the plain, and added new terrors to the tumultuous, but irresistible, charge of the Barbarian host. The event of the battle of Hadrianople,

The defeat of the Romans

so fatal to Valens and to the empire, may be described in a few words. the Roman cavalry fled; the infantry was aban-doned, surrounded, and cut in pieces. The most skilful evolu-tions, the firmest courage, are scarcely sufficient to extricate a body of foot, encompassed, on an open plain, by superior numbers of horse; but the troops of Valens, oppressed by the weight of the enemy and their own fears, were crowded into a narrow space, where it was impossible for them to extend their ranks, or even to use, with effect, their swords and javelins. In the midst of tumult, of slaughter, and of dismay, the emperor, deserted by his guards and wounded, as it was supposed, with an arrow, sought protection among the Lancearii

[Palatine troops]

and the Mattiarii, who still maintained their ground with some appearance of order and firmness. His faithful generals, Trajan and Victor, who perceived his danger, loudly exclaimed that all was lost unless the person of the emperor could be saved. Some troops, animated by their exhortation, advanced to his relief: they found only a bloody spot, covered with a heap of broken arms and mangled bodies, without being able to dis-cover their unfortunate prince, either among the living or the dead. Their search could not indeed be successful, if there is any truth in the circumstances with which some historians have

Death of the emperor Valens

related the death of the emperor. By the care of his attend-ants, Valens was removed from the field of battle to a neighbour-ing cottage, where they attempted to dress his wound and to provide for his future safety. But this humble retreat was instantly surrounded by the enemy; they tried to force the door; they were provoked by a discharge of arrows from the roof, till at length, impatient of delay, they set fire to a pile of dry faggots, and consumed the cottage with the Roman emperor and his train. Valens perished in the flames,[94a] and a

[94a] [See Claudian, B. G., 61, absumptique igne Valentis.]

youth, who dropt from the window, alone escaped, to attest the melancholy tale and to inform the Goths of the inestimable prize which they had lost by their own rashness. A great number of brave and distinguished officers perished in the battle of Hadrianople, which equalled in the actual loss, and far surpassed in the fatal consequences, the misfortune which Rome had formerly sustained in the field of Cannæ.[95] Two master-generals of the cavalry and infantry, two great officers of the palace and thirty-five tribunes were found among the slain; and the death of Sebastian might satisfy the world that he was the victim, as well as the author, of the public calamity. Above two-thirds of the Roman army were destroyed; and the darkness of the night was esteemed a very favourable circumstance, as it served to conceal the flight of the multitude and to protect the more orderly retreat of Victor and Richomer, who alone, amidst the general consternation, maintained the advantage of calm courage and regular discipline.[96]

While the impressions of grief and terror were still recent in the minds of men, the most celebrated rhetorician of the age composed the funeral oration of a vanquished army and of an unpopular prince, whose throne was already occupied by a stranger. "There are not wanting," says the candid Libanius, "those who arraign the prudence of the emperor,[96a] or who impute the public misfortune to the want of courage and discipline in the troops. For my own part, I reverence the memory of their former exploits · I reverence the glorious death which they bravely received, standing, and fighting in their ranks: I reverence the field of battle, stained with *their* blood and the blood of the Barbarians. Those honourable marks have been already washed away by the rains; but the lofty monuments of their bones, the bones of generals, of centurions, and of valiant warriors, claim a longer period of duration. The

Funeral oration of Valens and his army

[95] Nec ulla, annalibus, præter Cannensem pugnam ita ad internecionem res legitur gesta Ammian. xxxi. 13. According to the grave Polybius, no more than 370 horse and 3000 foot escaped from the field of Cannæ: 10,000 were made prisoners , and the number of the slain amounted to 5630 horse and 70,000 foot (Polyb l. iii p. 371, edit Casaubon, in 8vo [c 117]) Livy (xxii. 49) is somewhat less bloody: he slaughters only 2700 horse and 40,000 foot The Roman army was supposed to consist of 87,200 effective men (xxii 36).

[96] We have gained some faint light from Jerom (t. i p 26 [Ep 60, 16] and in Chron p. 188 [ad ann. 2393]), Victor (in Epitome [47]), Orosius (l vii c 33, p 554), Jornandes (c 27), Zosimus (l iv, p 230 [24]), Socrates (l iv, c 38), Sozomen (l vi. c. 40), Idatius (in Chron). But their united evidence, if weighed against Ammianus alone, is light and unsubstantial

[96a] [*Legendum* generals; the original is τῶν στρατηγῶν.

[*leg* em-
peror]
king himself fought and fell in the foremost ranks of the battle. His attendants presented him with the fleetest horses of the Imperial stable, that would soon have carried him beyond the pursuit of the enemy. They vainly pressed him to reserve his important life for the future service of the republic. He still declared that he was unworthy to survive so many of the bravest and most faithful of his subjects; and the monarch was nobly buried under a mountain of the slain. Let none, therefore, presume to ascribe the victory of the Barbarians to the fear, the weakness, or the imprudence, of the Roman troops. The chiefs and the soldiers were animated by the virtue of their ancestors, whom they equalled in discipline and the arts of war. Their generous emulation was supported by the love of glory, which prompted them to contend at the same time with heat and thirst, with fire and the sword; and cheerfully to embrace an honourable death as their refuge against flight and infamy. The indignation of the gods has been the only cause of the success of our enemies." The truth of history may disclaim some parts of this panegyric, which cannot strictly be reconciled with the character of Valens or the circumstances of the battle; but the fairest commendation is due to the eloquence, and still more to the generosity, of the sophist of Antioch.[97]

The Goths be
siege Hadria
nople
The pride of the Goths was elated by this memorable victory; but their avarice was disappointed by the mortifying discovery that the richest part of the Imperial spoil had been within the walls of Hadrianople. They hastened to possess the reward of their valour; but they were encountered by the remains of a vanquished army with an intrepid resolution, which was the effect of their despair and the only hope of their safety. The walls of the city and the ramparts of the adjacent camp were lined with military engines, that threw stones of an enormous weight; and astonished the ignorant Barbarians by the noise and velocity, still more than by the real effects, of the discharge. The soldiers, the citizens, the provincials, the domestics of the palace, were united in the danger and in the defence; the furious assault of the Goths was repulsed; their secret arts of treachery and treason were discovered; and, after an obstinate conflict of many hours, they retired to their tents; convinced, by experience, that it would be far more advisable to observe the treaty which their sagacious leader had tacitly stipulated with the fortifications of great and populous cities.

[97] Libanius de ulciscend Julian Nece, c 3 in Fabricius, Bibliot. Græc tom. vii. p. 146-148.

After the hasty and impolitic massacre of three hundred deserters, an act of justice extremely useful to the discipline of the Roman armies, the Goths indignantly raised the siege of Hadrianople. The scene of war and tumult was instantly converted into a silent solitude; the multitude suddenly disappeared; the sacred paths of the wood and mountains were marked with the footsteps of the trembling fugitives, who sought a refuge in the distant cities of Illyricum and Macedonia; and the faithful officers of the household and the treasury cautiously proceeded in search of the emperor, of whose death they were still ignorant. The tide of the Gothic inundation rolled from the walls of Hadrianople to the suburbs of Constantinople. The Barbarians were surprised with the splendid appearance of the capital of the East, the height and extent of the walls, the myriads of wealthy and affrighted citizens who crowded the ramparts, and the various prospect of the sea and land. While they gazed with hopeless desire on the inaccessible beauties of Constantinople, a sally was made from one of the gates by a party of Saracens,[98] who had been fortunately engaged in the service of Valens. The cavalry of Scythia was forced to yield to the admirable swiftness and spirit of the Arabian horses; their riders were skilled in the evolutions of irregular war; and the Northern Barbarians were astonished, and dismayed, by the inhuman ferocity of the Barbarians of the South. A Gothic soldier was slain by the dagger of an Arab; and the hairy, naked savage, applying his lips to the wound, expressed a horrid delight, while he sucked the blood of his vanquished enemy.[99] The army of the Goths, laden with the spoils of the wealthy suburbs and the adjacent territory, slowly moved from the Bosphorus to the mountains which form the western boundary of Thrace The important pass of Succi was betrayed by the fear, or the misconduct, of Maurus; and the Barbarians, who no longer had any resistance to apprehend from the scattered and vanquished troops of the East, spread

[98] Valens had gained, or rather purchased, the friendship of the Saracens, whose vexatious inroads were felt on the borders of Phœnicia, Palestine, and Egypt. The Christian faith had been lately introduced among a people, reserved, in a future age, to propagate another religion (Tillemont, Hist des Empereurs, t v. p. 104, 106, 141. Mém Eccl t. vii p 593).
[99] Crinitus quidam, nudus omnia præter pubem, subraucum et lugubre strepens. Ammian xxxi. 16, and Vales, ad loc. The Arabs often fought naked; a custom which may be ascribed to their sultry climate and ostentatious bravery. The description of this unknown savage is the lively portrait of Derar, a name so dreadful to the Christians of Syria. See Ockley's Hist. of the Saracens, vol i p. 72, 84, 87.

themselves over the face of a fertile and cultivated country, as far as the confines of Italy and the Hadriatic Sea [100]

They ravage the Roman provinces A.D 378, 379

The Romans, who so coolly and so concisely mention the acts of *justice* which were exercised by the legions,[101] reserve their compassion and their eloquence for their own sufferings, when the provinces were invaded and desolated by the arms of the successful Barbarians. The simple circumstantial narrative (did such a narrative exist) of the ruin of a single town, of the misfortunes of a single family,[102] might exhibit an interesting and instructive picture of human manners; but the tedious repetition of vague and declamatory complaints would fatigue the attention of the most patient reader. The same censure may be applied, though not perhaps in an equal degree, to the profane and the ecclesiastical writers of this unhappy period; that their minds were inflamed by popular and religious animosity; and that the true size and colour of every object is falsified by the exaggerations of their corrupt eloquence. The vehement Jerom [103] might justly deplore the calamities inflicted by the Goths and their barbarous allies on his native country of Pannonia and the wide extent of the provinces, from the walls of Constantinople to the foot of the Julian Alps; the rapes, the massacres, the conflagrations; and, above all, the profanation of the churches, that were turned into stables, and the contemptuous treatment of the relics of holy martyrs. But the Saint is surely transported beyond the limits of nature and history, when he affirms "that, in those desert countries, nothing was left except the sky and the earth; that, after the destruction of the cities and the extirpation of the human race, the land was overgrown with thick forests and inextricable brambles;

[100] The series of events may still be traced in the last pages of Ammianus (xxxi 15, 16) Zosimus (l. iv p 227, 231 [22, 24]), whom we are now reduced to cherish, misplaces the sally of the Arabs before the death of Valens. Eunapius (in Excerpt Legat p. 20 [fr 42, F. H. G. iv. p. 32]) praises the fertility of Thrace, Macedonia, &c

[101] Observe with how much indifference Cæsar relates, in the Commentaries of the Gallic war *that* he put to death the whole senate of the Veneti, who had yielded to his mercy (iii 16), *that* he laboured to extirpate the whole nation of the Eburones (vi. 31 *sqq*), *that* forty thousand persons were massacred at Bourges by the just revenge of his soldiers, who spared neither age nor sex (vii 27), &c.

[102] Such are the accounts of the sack of Magdeburg, by the ecclesiastic and the fisherman, which Mr. Harte has transcribed (Hist of Gustavus Adolphus, vol. i p 313-320), with some apprehension of violating the *dignity* of history

[103] Et vastatis urbibus, hominibusque interfectis, solitudinem et *raritatem* bestiarum quoque fieri, *et volat 'turn, piscumque* testis Illyricum est, testis Thracia, testis in quo ortus sum solum (Pannonia), ubi præter cælum et terram, et crescentes vepres, et condensa sylvarum *cuncta perierunt* Tom vii. p. 250 ad i Cap. Sophonias; and tom i p 26. [Ep. 60, 16]

and that the universal desolation, announced by the prophet Zephaniah, was accomplished, in the scarcity of the beasts, the birds, and even of the fish ". These complaints were pronounced about twenty years after the death of Valens; and the Illyrian provinces, which were constantly exposed to the invasion and passage of the Barbarians, still continued, after a calamitous period of ten centuries, to supply new materials for rapine and destruction. Could it even be supposed that a large tract of country had been left without cultivation and without inhabitants, the consequences might not have been so fatal to the inferior productions of animated nature. The useful and feeble animals, which are nourished by the hand of man, might suffer and perish, if they were deprived of his protection; but the beasts of the forest, his enemies, or his victims, would multiply in the free and undisturbed possession of their solitary domain. The various tribes that people the air, or the waters, are still less connected with the fate of the human species, and it is highly probable that the fish of the Danube would have felt more terror and distress from the approach of a voracious pike than from the hostile inroad of a Gothic army.

Whatever may have been the just measure of the calamities of Europe, there was reason to fear that the same calamities would soon extend to the peaceful countries of Asia The sons of the Goths had been judiciously distributed through the cities of the East; and the arts of education were employed to polish and subdue the native fierceness of their temper. In the space of about twelve years, their numbers had continually increased; and the children, who, in the first emigration, were sent over the Hellespont, had attained, with rapid growth, the strength and spirit of perfect manhood.[104] It was impossible to conceal from their knowledge the events of the Gothic war; and, as those daring youths had not studied the language of dissimulation, they betrayed their wish, their desire, perhaps their intention, to emulate the glorious example of their fathers. The danger of the times seemed to justify the jealous suspicions of the provincials; and these suspicions were admitted as unquestionable evidence that the Goths of Asia had formed a secret and dangerous conspiracy against the public safety. The death of Valens had left the East without a sovereign;

Massacre of the Gothic youth in Asia A D 378

---

[104] Eunapius (in Excerpt Legat p 20 [F H G iv. p 32]) foolishly supposes a preternatural growth of the young Goths, that he may introduce Cadmus's armed men, who sprung from the dragon's teeth, &c Such was the Greek eloquence of the times.

and Julius, who filled the important station of master-general of the troops, with a high reputation of diligence and ability, thought it his duty to consult the senate of Constantinople; which he considered, during the vacancy of the throne, as the representative council of the nation. As soon as he had obtained the discretionary power of acting as he should judge most expedient for the good of the republic, he assembled the principal officers; and privately concerted effectual measures for the execution of his bloody design. An order was immediately promulgated that, on a stated day, the Gothic youth should assemble in the capital cities of their respective provinces; and, as a report was industriously circulated that they were summoned to receive a liberal gift of lands and money, the pleasing hope allayed the fury of their resentment and perhaps suspended the motions of the conspiracy. On the appointed day, the unarmed crowd of the Gothic youth was carefully collected in the square, or Forum; the streets and avenues were occupied by the Roman troops; and the roofs of the houses were covered with archers and slingers. At the same hour, in all the cities of the East, the signal was given of indiscriminate slaughter; and the provinces of Asia were delivered, by the cruel prudence of Julius, from a domestic enemy, who, in a few months, might have carried fire and sword from the Hellespont to the Euphrates.[105] The urgent consideration of the public safety may undoubtedly authorise the violation of every positive law. How far that, or any other, consideration may operate to dissolve the natural obligations of humanity and justice is a doctrine of which I still desire to remain ignorant.

The emperor Gratian invests Theodosius with the empire of the East A D 379, Jan 19   The emperor Gratian was far advanced on his march towards the plains of Hadrianople when he was informed, at first by the confused voice of fame, and afterwards by the more accurate reports of Victor and Richomer, that his impatient colleague had been slain in battle, and that two-thirds of the Roman army were exterminated by the sword of the victorious Goths. Whatever resentment the rash and jealous vanity of his uncle might deserve, the resentment of a generous mind is easily subdued by the softer emotions of grief and compassion and even the sense of pity was soon lost in the serious and alarming consideration of the state of the republic. Gratian was too late to assist,

---

[105] Ammianus evidently approves this execution, efficacia velox et salutaris, which concludes his work (xxxi 16). Zosimus, who is curious and copious (l iv p 233-236 [26]), mistakes the date, and labours to find the reason why Julius did not consult the emperor Theodosius, who had not yet ascended the throne of the East.

he was too weak to revenge his unfortunate colleague : and the valiant and modest youth felt himself unequal to the support of a sinking world. A formidable tempest of the Barbarians of Germany seemed ready to burst over the provinces of Gaul ; and the mind of Gratian was oppressed and distracted by the administration of the Western Empire. In this important crisis, the government of the East and the conduct of the Gothic war required the undivided attention of a hero and a statesman A subject invested with such ample command would not long have preserved his fidelity to a distant benefactor ; and the Imperial council embraced the wise and manly resolution of conferring an obligation rather than of yielding to an insult. It was the wish of Gratian to bestow the purple as the reward of virtue ; but, at the age of nineteen, it is not easy for a prince, educated in the supreme rank, to understand the true characters of his ministers and generals. He attempted to weigh, with an impartial hand, their various merits and defects ; and, whilst he checked the rash confidence of ambition, he distrusted the cautious wisdom which despaired of the republic. As each moment of delay diminished something of the power and resources of the future sovereign of the East, the situation of the times would not allow a tedious debate. The choice of Gratian was soon declared in favour of an exile, whose father, only three years before, had suffered, under the sanction of *his* authority, an unjust and ignominious death. The great Theodosius, a name celebrated in history and dear to the Catholic church,[106] was summoned to the Imperial court, which had gradually retreated from the confines of Thrace to the more secure station of Sirmium. Five months after the death of Valens, the emperor Gratian produced before the assembled troops *his* colleague and *their* master ; who, after a modest, perhaps a sincere, resistance, was compelled to accept, amidst the general acclamations, the diadem, the purple, and the equal title of Augustus.[107] The provinces of Thrace, Asia, and

[106] A life of Theodosius the Great was composed in the last century (Paris, 1679, in 4to ; 1680, in 12mo), to inflame the mind of the young Dauphin with Catholic zeal. The author, Fléchier, afterwards bishop of Nismes, was a celebrated preacher ; and his history is adorned, or tainted, with pulpit-eloquence ; but he takes his learning from Baronius, and his principles from St Ambrose and St Augustin   [For recent works cp. Appendix 1]

[107] The birth, character, and elevation of Theodosius, are marked in Picatus (in Panegyr Vet xii 10, 11, 12), Themistius (Orat xiv. p 182), Zosimus (l iv p 231 [24]), Augustin (de Civitat Dei, v 25), Orosius (l. vii c 34), Sozomen (l vii c. 2), Socrates (l. v. c 2), Theodoret (l v c 5), Philostorgius (l ix c 17, with Godefroy, p 393), the Epitome of Victor [48], and the Chronicles of Prosper, Idatius, and Marcellinus, in the Thesaurus Temporum of Scaliger. [Eunap. fr. 48.]

Egypt, over which Valens had reigned, were resigned to the administration of the new emperor; but, as he was specially intrusted with the conduct of the Gothic war, the Illyrian præfecture was dismembered; and the two great dioceses of Dacia and Macedonia were added to the dominions of the Eastern empire.[108]

Birth and character of Theodosius   The same province, and, perhaps, the same city,[109] which had given to the throne the virtues of Trajan and the talents of Hadrian, was the original seat of another family of Spaniards, who, in a less fortunate age, possessed, near fourscore years, the declining empire of Rome[110] They emerged from the obscurity of municipal honours by the active spirit of the elder Theodosius, a general whose exploits in Britain and Africa have formed one of the most splendid parts of the annals of Valen-

[born c 346] tinian.   The son of that general, who likewise bore the name of Theodosius, was educated, by skilful preceptors, in the liberal studies of youth; but he was instructed in the art of war by the tender care and severe discipline of his father.[111]   Under the standard of such a leader, young Theodosius sought glory and knowledge, in the most distant scenes of military action; enured his constitution to the difference of seasons and climates; distinguished his valour by sea and land; and observed the various warfare of the Scots, the Saxons, and the Moors.   His own merit, and the recommendation of the conqueror of Africa,

[A D 373] soon raised him to a separate command; and in the station of Duke of Mæsia, he vanquished an army of Sarmatians; saved the province; deserved the love of the soldiers; and provoked the envy of the court[112]   His rising fortunes were soon blasted

[A D 376] by the disgrace and execution of his illustrious father; and

---

[108] Tillemont, Hist. des Empereurs, tom v. p 716, &c   [Soz. vii 4]

[109] *Italica*, founded by Scipio Africanus for his wounded veterans of *Italy* The ruins still appear, about a league above Seville, on the opposite bank of the river.   See the Hispania Illustrata of Nonius, a short, though valuable treatise C. xvii p 64-67.

[110] I agree with Tillemont (Hist des Empereurs, tom v p 726) in suspecting the royal pedigree, which remained a secret till the promotion of Theodosius. Even after that event the silence of Pacatus outweighs the venal evidence of Themistius, Victor, and Claudian, who connect the family of Theodosius with the blood of Trajan and Hadrian

[111] Pacatus compares, and consequently prefers, the youth of Theodosius to the military education of Alexander, Hannibal, and the second Africanus, who, like him, had served under their fathers (xii 8)

[112] Ammianus (xxix 6) mentions this victory of Theodosius Junior Dux Mæsiæ, prima etiam tum lanugine juvenis, princeps postea perspectissimus.   The same fact is attested by Themistius and Zosimus; but Theodoret (l v. c. 5), who adds some curious circumstances, strangely applies it to the time of the interregnum. [Theodoret refers to another campaign in A.D. 378, see Appendix 7]

Theodosius obtained, as a favour, the permission of retiring to a
private life in his native province of Spain. He displayed a firm
and temperate character in the ease with which he adapted
himself to this new situation   His time was almost equally
divided between the town and country: the spirit which had
animated his public conduct was shewn in the active and affectionate performance of every social duty; and the diligence of
the soldier was profitably converted to the improvement of his
ample patrimony,[113] which lay between Valladolid and Segovia,
in the midst of a fruitful district still famous for a most exquisite
breed of sheep.[114]   From the innocent but humble labours of
his farm Theodosius was transported, in less than four months,
to the throne of the Eastern empire;[115] and the whole period of
the history of the world will not perhaps afford a similar example
of an elevation, at the same time, so pure and so honourable.
The princes who peaceably inherit the sceptre of their fathers
claim and enjoy a legal right, the more secure as it is absolutely
distinct from the merits of their personal characters. The
subjects, who, in a monarchy or a popular estate, acquire the
possession of supreme power, may have raised themselves, by
the superiority either of genius or virtue, above the heads of
their equals; but their virtue is seldom exempt from ambition;
and the cause of the successful candidate is frequently stained
by the guilt of conspiracy or civil war. Even in those governments which allow the reigning monarch to declare a colleague
or a successor, his partial choice, which may be influenced by the
blindest passions, is often directed to an unworthy object. But
the most suspicious malignity cannot ascribe to Theodosius, in
his obscure solitude of Caucha, the arts, the desires, or even the
hopes, of an ambitious statesman; and the name of the Exile
would long since have been forgotten, if his genuine and
distinguished virtues had not left a deep impression in the Imperial court. During the season of prosperity, he had been neglected; but, in the public distress, his superior merit was
universally felt and acknowledged. What confidence must
have been reposed in his integrity, since Gratian could trust
that a pious son would forgive, for the sake of the republic, the

113 Pacatus (in Panegyr. Vet. xii 9) prefers the rustic life of Theodosius to that
of Cincinnatus ; the one was the effect of choice, the other of poverty
114 M. d'Anville (Géographie Ancienne, tom i p 25) has fixed the situation of
Caucha, or Coca, in the old province of Gallicia, where Zosimus [iv 24] and Idatius
[in Cont. Chron Hieron] have placed the birth, or patrimony, of Theodosius
115 [Recalled from exile some months before his investiture he won a victory
over the Sarmatians ; see above, c xxv. note 157   Cp. Ifland, p. 59.]

murder of his father! What expectations must have been formed of his abilities to encourage the hope that a single man could save, and restore, the empire of the East! Theodosius

was invested with the purple in the thirty-third year of his age. The vulgar gazed with admiration on the manly beauty of his face, and the graceful majesty of his person, which they were pleased to compare with the pictures and medals of the emperor Trajan; whilst intelligent observers discovered, in the qualities of his heart and understanding, a more important resemblance to the best and greatest of the Roman princes.

It is not without the most sincere regret that I must now take leave of an accurate and faithful guide, who has composed the history of his own times without indulging the prejudices and passions which usually affect the mind of a contemporary. Ammianus Marcellinus, who terminates his useful work with the defeat and death of Valens, recommends the more glorious subject of the ensuing reign to the youthful vigour and eloquence of the rising generation.[116]   The rising generation was not disposed to accept his advice or to imitate his example;[117] and, in the study of the reign of Theodosius, we are reduced to illustrate the partial narrative of Zosimus by the obscure hints of fragments and chronicles, by the figurative style of poetry or panegyric, and by the precarious assistance of the ecclesiastical writers who, in the heat of religious faction, are apt to despise the profane virtues of sincerity and moderation. Conscious of these disadvantages, which will continue to involve a considerable portion of the decline and fall of the Roman empire, I shall proceed with doubtful and timorous steps. Yet I may boldly pronounce that the battle of Hadrianople was never revenged by any signal or decisive victory of Theodosius over the Barbarians; and the expressive silence of his venal orators may be confirmed by the observation of the condition and circumstances of the times. The fabric of a mighty state, which has been

[116] Let us hear Ammianus himself Hæc, ut miles quondam et Græcus, a principatu Cæsaris Nervæ exorsus, adusque Valentis interitum, pro virium explicavi mensurâ : nunquam, ut arbitror, sciens, silentio ausus corrumpere vel mendacio Scribant reliqua potiores ætate doctrinisque florentes. Quos id, si libuerit, aggressuros, procudere linguas ad majores moneo stilos. Ammian. xxxi. 16. The first thirteen books, a superficial epitome of two hundred and fifty-seven years, are now lost ; the last eighteen, which contain no more than twenty-five years, still preserve the copious and authentic history of his own times [Cp. vol. 2, Appendix 1.]

[117] Ammianus was the last subject of Rome who composed a profane history in the Latin language. The East, in the next century, produced some rhetorical historians, Zosimus, Olympiodorus, Malchus, Candidus, &c See Vossius de Historicis Græcis, l. ii c. 18, de Historicis Latinis, l. ii c. 10, &c.

reared by the labours of successive ages, could not be overturned by the misfortune of a single day, if the fatal power of
the imagination did not exaggerate the real measure of the
calamity. The loss of forty thousand Romans, who fell in
the plains of Hadrianople, might have been soon recruited in
the populous provinces of the East, which contained so many
millions of inhabitants. The courage of a soldier is found to
be the cheapest, and most common, quality of human nature;
and sufficient skill to encounter an undisciplined foe might
have been speedily taught by the care of the surviving centurions. If the Barbarians were mounted on the horses, and
equipped with the armour, of their vanquished enemies, the
numerous studs of Cappadocia and Spain would have supplied
new squadrons of cavalry; the thirty-four arsenals of the empire
were plentifully stored with magazines of offensive and defensive
arms; and the wealth of Asia might still have yielded an ample
fund for the expenses of the war. But the effects which were
produced by the battle of Hadrianople on the minds of the
Barbarians, and of the Romans, extended the victory of the
former, and the defeat of the latter, far beyond the limits of a
single day. A Gothic chief was heard to declare, with insolent
moderation, that, for his own part, he was fatigued with
slaughter; but that he was astonished how a people who fled
before him like a flock of sheep could still presume to dispute
the possession of their treasures and provinces [118] The same
terrors which the name of the Huns had spread among the
Gothic tribes were inspired, by the formidable name of the
Goths, among the subjects and soldiers of the Roman empire.[119]
If Theodosius, hastily collecting his scattered forces, had led
them into the field to encounter a victorious enemy, his army
would have been vanquished by their own fears; and his rashness could not have been excused by the chance of success.
But the *great* Theodosius, an epithet which he honourably
deserved on this momentous occasion, conducted himself as
the firm and faithful guardian of the republic. He fixed his
headquarters at Thessalonica, the capital of the Macedonian [Spring A D 379]
diocese;[120] from whence he could watch the irregular motions

[118] Chrysostom, tom i p 344, edit Montfaucon. I have verified and examined
this passage; but I should never, without the aid of Tillemont (Hist. des Emp.
tom v. p 152), have detected an historical anecdote, in a strange medley of
moral and mystic exhortations, addressed by the preacher of Antioch to a young
widow
[119] Eunapius, in Excerpt Legation p. 21 [F. H. G. iv p 32]
[120] See Godefroy's Chronology of the Laws Codex Theodos. tom. i. Prole-
gomen p xcix.-civ. [Cp. Cod. Theod. x. 1, 12.]

of the Barbarians, and direct the operations of his lieutenants, from the gates of Constantinople to the shores of the Hadriatic. The fortifications and garrisons of the cities were strengthened; and the troops, among whom a sense of order and discipline was revived, were insensibly emboldened by the confidence of their own safety From these secure stations, they were encouraged to make frequent sallies on the Barbarians, who infested the adjacent country; and, as they were seldom allowed to engage without some decisive superiority either of ground or of numbers, their enterprises were, for the most part, successful; and they were soon convinced, by their own experience, of the possibility of vanquishing their *invincible* enemies [121] The detachments of these separate garrisons were gradually united into small armies; the same cautious measures were pursued, according to an extensive and well-concerted plan of operations; the events of each day added strength and spirit to the Roman arms; and the artful diligence of the emperor, who circulated the most favourable reports of the success of the war, contributed to subdue the pride of the Barbarians and to animate the hopes and courage of his subjects. If, instead of this faint and imperfect outline, we could accurately represent the counsels and actions of Theodosius, in four successive campaigns, there is reason to believe that his consummate skill would deserve the applause of every military reader. The republic had formerly been saved by the delays of Fabius: and, while the splendid trophies of Scipio in the field of Zama attract the eyes of posterity, the camps and marches of the Dictator among the hills of Campania may claim a juster proportion of the solid and independent fame which the general is not compelled to share either with fortune or with his troops. Such was likewise the merit of Theodosius; and the infirmities of his body, which most unseasonably languished under a long and dangerous disease, could not oppress the vigour of his mind or divert his attention from the public service.[122]

[A.D 380]

Divisions, defeat, and submission of the Goths A D 379-382

The deliverance and peace of the Roman provinces [123] was the work of prudence rather than of valour. the prudence of

[121] [They were assisted by a pestilence. Cp. Ambrose, Epist. 15, ap Migne, 16, p 955]
[122] Most writers insist on the illness and long repose of Theodosius at Thessalonica: Zosimus, to diminish his glory, Jornandes, to favour the Goths; and the ecclesiastical writers, to introduce his baptism
[123] Compare Themistius (Orat. xiv p 181) with Zosimus (l iv p 232 [25]), Joinandes (c xxvii, p 649), and the prolix Commentary of M de Buat (Hist des Peuples, &c, tom vi p 477-552) The Chronicles of Idatius and Marcellinus allude, in general terms, to magna certamina, *magna multaque* prælia The two epithets are not easily reconciled [For chronology, cp Appendix 8]

Theodosius was seconded by fortune; and the emperor never failed to seize, and to improve, every favourable circumstance. As long as the superior genius of Fritigern preserved the union, and directed the motions, of the Barbarians, their power was not inadequate to the conquest of a great empire. The death of that hero, the predecessor and master of the renowned Alaric, relieved an impatient multitude from the intolerable yoke of discipline and discretion. The Barbarians, who had been restrained by his authority, abandoned themselves to the dictates of their passions; and their passions were seldom uniform or consistent. An army of conquerors was broken into many disorderly bands of savage robbers; and their blind and irregular fury was not less pernicious to themselves than to their enemies.[124] Their mischievous disposition was shewn in the destruction of every object which they wanted strength to remove or taste to enjoy; and they often consumed, with improvident rage, the harvests or the granaries, which soon afterwards became necessary for their own subsistence. A spirit of discord arose among the independent tribes and nations, which had been united only by the bands of a loose and voluntary alliance. The troops of the Huns and the Alani would naturally upbraid the flight of the Goths who were not disposed to use with moderation the advantages of their fortune; the ancient jealousy of the Ostrogoths and the Visigoths could not long be suspended; and the haughty chiefs still remembered the insults and injuries which they had reciprocally offered, or sustained, while the nation was seated in the countries beyond the Danube. The progress of domestic faction abated the more diffusive sentiment of national animosity; and the officers of Theodosius were instructed to purchase with liberal gifts and promises the retreat, or service, of the discontented party. The acquisition of Modar, a prince of the royal blood of the Amali, gave a bold and faithful champion to the cause of Rome. The illustrious deserter soon obtained the rank of master-general, with an important command; surprised an army of his countrymen who [In Thrace] were immersed in wine and sleep; and, after a cruel slaughter of the astonished Goths, returned with an immense spoil, and four thousand waggons, to the Imperial camp.[125]   In the hands

---

[124] [Some bands made raids into Epirus (Nicopolis capitulated to them; Eunapius, fr 50), and Greece (which was defended by one Theodore, C I A iii 636)]

[125] Zosimus (l. iv p 232 [25]) styles him a Scythian, a name which the more recent Greeks seem to have appropriated to the Goths [See Gregory Naz. Ep. 136; Ifland, Kaiser Theodosios der Grosse, p 70   There is no authority for the statement that he was "of the royal blood of the Amali".]

of a skilful politician, the most different means may be successfully applied to the same ends . and the peace of the empire,
which had been forwarded by the divisions, was accomplished
Death and
funeral of
Athanaric
A D 381,
Jan 25
by the re-union of the Gothic nation   Athanaric, who had been
a patient spectator of these extraordinary events, was at length
driven, by the chance of arms, from the dark recesses of the
woods of Caucaland.[126] He no longer hesitated to pass the
Danube , and a very considerable part of the subjects of Fritigern, who already felt the inconveniences of anarchy, were
easily persuaded to acknowledge for their king a Gothic Judge,
whose birth they respected and whose abilities they had
frequently experienced.   But age had chilled the daring spirit
of Athanaric ; and, instead of leading his people to the field of
battle and victory, he wisely listened to the fair proposal of an
honourable and advantageous treaty.   Theodosius, who was
acquainted with the merit and power of his new ally, condescended to meet him at the distance of several miles from
[Jan. 11]
Constantinople ; and entertained him in the Imperial city, with
the confidence of a friend and the magnificence of a monarch
"The Barbarian prince observed, with curious attention, the
variety of objects which attracted his notice, and at last broke
out into a sincere and passionate exclamation of wonder.   I now
behold (said he) what I never could believe, the glories of this
stupendous capital ! and, as he cast his eyes around, he viewed,
and he admired, the commanding situation of the city, the
strength and beauty of the walls and public edifices, the
capacious harbour, crowded with innumerable vessels, the
perpetual concourse of distant nations, and the arms and discipline of the troops.   Indeed (continued Athanaric), the emperor
of the Romans is a god upon earth ; and the presumptuous man,
who dares to lift his hand against him, is guilty of his own
blood." [127]   The Gothic king did not long enjoy this splendid
and honourable reception ; and, as temperance was not the
virtue of his nation, it may justly be suspected that his mortal
disease was contracted amidst the pleasures of the Imperial

---

[126] [Hauha-land (== Highland) acc to Zeuss.   Somewhere in Siebenbürgen ?]
[127] The reader will not be displeased to see the original words of Jornandes or
the author whom he transcribed   Regiam urbem ingressus est, miransque, En,
inquit, cerno quod sæpe incredulus audiebam, faman videlicet tantæ urbis.   Et
huc illuc oculos volvens, nunc situm urbis commeatumque navium, nunc mœnia
clara prospectans, miratur , populosque diversarum gentium, quasi fonte in uno
e diversis partibus scaturriente undâ, sic quoque militem ordinatum aspiciens
Deus, inquit, est sine dubio terrenus [*leg.* sine dub. terr est] imperator, et quisquis
adversus eum manum movent, ipse sui sanguinis reus existit.   Jornandes (c.
xxviii. p. 650) proceeds to mention his death and funeral.

banquets. But the policy of Theodosius derived more solid benefit from the death, than he could have expected from the most faithful services, of his ally. The funeral of Athanaric was performed with solemn rites in the capital of the East; a stately monument was erected to his memory; and his whole army, won by the liberal courtesy and decent grief of Theodosius, enlisted under the standard of the Roman empire.[128] The submission of so great a body of the Visigoths was productive of the most salutary consequences; and the mixed influence of force, of reason, and of corruption became every day more powerful and more extensive. Each independent chieftain hastened to obtain a separate treaty, from the apprehension that an obstinate delay might expose *him*, alone and unprotected, to the revenge, or justice, of the conqueror. The general, or rather the final, capitulation of the Goths may be dated four years, one month, and twenty-five days, after the defeat and death of the emperor Valens.[129] A D 382, Oct. 3

The provinces of the Danube had been already relieved from the oppressive weight of the Gruthungi, or Ostrogoths, by the voluntary retreat of Alatheus and Saphrax; whose restless spirit had prompted them to seek new scenes of rapine and glory. Invasion and defeat of the Gruthungi, or Ostrogoths A D 386 [leg 380], October Their destructive course was pointed towards the West; but we must be satisfied with a very obscure and imperfect knowledge of their various adventures. The Ostrogoths impelled several of the German tribes on the provinces of Gaul; concluded, and soon violated, a treaty with the emperor Gratian; advanced into the unknown countries of the North; and, after an interval of more than four years, returned, with accumulated force, to the banks of the Lower Danube. [Gratian at Sirmium Sept, A D 380] Their troops were recruited with the fiercest warriors of Germany and Scythia; and the soldiers, or at least the historians, of the empire no longer recognized the name and countenances of their former enemies [130] The general, who commanded the military and naval powers of the Thracian frontier, soon perceived that his superiority would be disadvantageous to the public service; and that the Barbarians, awed by the presence of his fleet and

128 Jornandes, c. xxviii p. 650   Even Zosimus (l iv p 246 [34]) is compelled to approve the generosity of Theodosius, so honourable to himself, and so beneficial to the public

129 The short, but authentic, hints in the *Fasti* of Idatius (Chron Scaliger, p. 52) are stained with contemporary passion   The fourteenth oration of Themistius is a compliment to Peace, and the consul Saturninus (A D. 383)   [Cp. Seeck, Hermes, xi. p. 67.]

130 Ἔθνος τὸ [leg. τι] Σκυθικὸν πᾶσιν ἄγνωστον. Zosimus,l iv. p 252 [38].

legions, would probably defer the passage of the river till the
approaching winter. The dexterity of the spies whom he sent
into the Gothic camp allured the Barbarians into a fatal snare.
They were persuaded that, by a bold attempt, they might
surprise, in the silence and darkness of the night, the sleeping
army of the Romans, and the whole multitude was hastily
embarked in a fleet of three thousand canoes [131] The bravest
of the Ostrogoths led the van; the main body consisted of the
remainder of their subjects and soldiers; and the women and
children securely followed in the rear. One of the nights without a moon had been selected for the execution of their design;
and they had almost reached the southern bank of the Danube,
in the firm confidence that they should find an easy landing
and an unguarded camp. But the progress of the Barbarians
was suddenly stopped by an unexpected obstacle: a triple line
of vessels, strongly connected with each other, and which
formed an impenetrable chain of two miles and a half along
the river. While they struggled to force their way in the
unequal conflict, their right rank was overwhelmed by the
irresistible attack of a fleet of gallies, which were urged down
the stream by the united impulse of oars and of the tide. The
weight and velocity of those ships of war broke, and sank,
and dispersed, the rude and feeble canoes of the Barbarians;
their valour was ineffectual; and Alatheus, the king, or general,
of the Ostrogoths, perished with his bravest troops either by
the sword of the Romans or in the waves of the Danube. The
last division of this unfortunate fleet might regain the opposite
shore; but the distress and disorder of the multitude rendered
them alike incapable either of action or counsel; and they
soon implored the clemency of the victorious enemy. On this
occasion, as well as on many others, it is a difficult task to
reconcile the passions and prejudices of the writers of the age
of Theodosius. The partial and malignant historian who mis-
represents every action of his reign affirms that the emperor
did not appear in the field of battle till the Barbarians had
been vanquished by the valour and conduct of his lieutenant

---

[131] I am justified, by reason and example, in applying this Indian name to the
μονόξυλα of the Barbarians, the single trees hollowed into the shape of a boat,
πλήθει μονοξύλων ἐμβιβάσαντες. Zosimus, l iv p 253 [38]
   Ausi Danuvium quondam tranare Gruthungi
   In lintres fregere nemus· ter mille ruebant
   Per fluvium plenœ cuneis immanibus alni
         Claudian, in iv. Cons. Hon 623

Promotus.[132] The flattering poet, who celebrated, in the court of Honorius, the glory of the father and of the son, ascribes the victory to the personal prowess of Theodosius ; and almost insinuates that the King of the Ostrogoths was slain by the hand of the emperor.[133] The truth of history might perhaps be found in a just medium between these extreme and contradictory assertions. [Triumph of Theodosius A D 386, Oct 12]

The original treaty, which fixed the settlement of the Goths, ascertained their privileges and stipulated their obligations, would illustrate the history of Theodosius and his successors. The series of their history has imperfectly preserved the spirit and substance of this singular agreement[134] The ravages of war and tyranny had provided many large tracts of fertile but uncultivated land for the use of those Barbarians who might not disdain the practice of agriculture. A numerous colony of the Visigoths was seated in Thrace ; the remains of the Ostrogoths were planted in Phrygia and Lydia ; their immediate wants were supplied by a distribution of corn and cattle ; and their future industry was encouraged by an exemption from tribute,[135] during a certain term of years   The Barbarians would have deserved to feel the cruel and perfidious policy of the Imperial court, if they had suffered themselves to be dispersed through the provinces.   They required, and they obtained, the sole possession of the villages and districts assigned for their residence ; they still cherished and propagated their native manners and language ; asserted, in the bosom of despotism, the freedom of their domestic government ; and acknowledged the sovereignty of the emperor, without submitting to the inferior jurisdiction of the laws and magistrates of Rome. The hereditary chiefs of the tribes and families were still permitted to command their followers in peace and war ; but the royal dignity was abolished ; and the generals of the [Settlement of the Goths in Thrace and Asia. A D 383 395]

[132] Zosimus, l. iv p 252-255 [38] He too frequently betrays his poverty of judgment by disgracing the most serious narratives with trifling and incredible circumstances. [He duplicates the invasion of Odothæus, cp. iv. 35 with 38.]

[133] ———— Odothæi Regis *optima*
    Rettulit————   Ver. 632 [*ib*].
The *optima* were the spoils which a Roman general could only win from the king, or general, of the enemy whom he had slain with his own hands , and no more than three such examples are celebrated in the victorious ages of Rome. [Had Odothæus been slain by Theodosius, Claudian would not have been content to insinuate it.]

[134] See Themistius, Orat. xvi. p 211.   Claudian (in Eutrop. l ii. 152) mentions the Phrygian colony :
    ———— Ostrogothis colitur mistisque Gruthungis
        Phryx ager ————
and then proceeds to name the rivers of Lydia, the Pactolus and Hermus.
[135] [So Mr. Hodgkin, who discusses the treaty at length ; i. p. 312.]

Goths were appointed and removed at the pleasure of the
emperor. An army of forty thousand Goths was maintained
for the perpetual service of the empire of the East ; and those
haughty troops, who assumed the title of *Fœderati*, or allies,
were distinguished by their gold collars, liberal pay, and
licentious privileges. Their native courage was improved by
the use of arms and the knowledge of discipline ; and, while
the republic was guarded, or threatened, by the doubtful sword
of the Barbarians, the last sparks of the military flame were
finally extinguished in the minds of the Romans [136] Theodosius
had the address to persuade his allies that the conditions of
peace which had been extorted from him by prudence and
necessity were the voluntary expressions of his sincere friendship for the Gothic nation [137] A different mode of vindication
or apology was opposed to the complaints of the people ; who
loudly censured these shameful and dangerous concessions.[138]
The calamities of the war were painted in the most lively
colours ; and the first symptoms of the return of order, of
plenty, and security, were diligently exaggerated. The
advocates of Theodosius could affirm, with some appearance
of truth and reason, that it was impossible to extirpate so
many warlike tribes, who were rendered desperate by the loss
of their native country ; and that the exhausted provinces
would be revived by a fresh supply of soldiers and husbandmen.
The Barbarians still wore an angry and hostile aspect ; but the
experience of past times might encourage the hope that they
would acquire the habits of industry and obedience ; that their
manners would be polished by time, education, and the influence
of Christianity ; and that their prosperity would insensibly
blend with the great body of the Roman people [139]

---

[136] Compare Jornandes (c xx. 27), who marks the condition and number of the
Gothic *Fœderati*, with Zosimus (l. iv. p. 258 [40]), who mentions their golden
collars, and Pacatus (in Panegyr. Vet xii. 37), who applauds, with false or
foolish joy, their bravery and discipline. [The first extant text in which *Fœderati*
is used of the Goths is Cod Theod. vii 13, 16 A D. 406, cp. Hodgkin, 1 314]

[137] Amator pacis generisque Gothorum, is the praise bestowed by the Gothic
historian (c xxiv), who represents his nation as innocent, peaceable men, slow to
anger, and patient of injuries. According to Livy, the Romans conquered the world
in their own defence

[138] Besides the partial invectives of Zosimus (always discontented with the
Christian reigns), see the grave representations which Synesius addresses to the
emperor Arcadius (de Regno, p 25, 26, edit Petav). The philosophic bishop of
Cyrene was near enough to judge ; and he was sufficiently removed from the
temptation of fear or flattery

[139] Themistius (Orat. xvi p 211, 212) composes an elaborate and rational
apology [partly translated by Mr Hodgkin, 1 316 *sqq.*], which is not, however,

Notwithstanding these specious arguments and these sanguine expectations, it was apparent to every discerning eye that the Goths would long remain the enemies, and might soon become the conquerors, of the Roman empire.   Their rude and insolent behaviour expressed their contempt of the citizens and provincials, whom they insulted with impunity.[140]   To the zeal and valour of the Barbarians Theodosius was indebted for the success of his arms ; but their assistance was precarious ; and they were sometimes seduced by a treacherous and inconstant disposition to abandon his standard at the moment when their service was the most essential.   During the civil war against Maximus, a great number of Gothic deserters retired into the morasses of Macedonia, wasted the adjacent provinces, and obliged the intrepid monarch to expose his person, and exert his power, to suppress the rising flame of rebellion.[141]   The public apprehensions were fortified by the strong suspicion that these tumults were not the effect of accidental passion, but the result of deep and premeditated design.   It was generally believed that the Goths had signed the treaty of peace with an hostile and insidious spirit ; and that their chiefs had previously bound themselves, by a solemn and secret oath, never to keep faith with the Romans ; to maintain the fairest shew of loyalty and friendship, and to watch the favourable moment of rapine, of conquest and of revenge.   But, as the minds of the Barbarians were not insensible to the power of gratitude, several of the Gothic leaders sincerely devoted themselves to the service of the empire, or, at least, of the emperor ; the whole nation was insensibly divided into two opposite factions, and much sophistry was employed in conversation and dispute, to compare the obligations of their first and second engagements   The Goths, who considered themselves as the friends of peace, of justice, and of Rome, were directed by the authority of Fravitta, a valiant and honourable youth, distinguished above the rest of his countrymen by the politeness of his manners, the liberality of his sentiments, and the mild virtues of social life.   But the more

exempt from the puerilities of Greek rhetoric   Orpheus could *only* charm the wild beasts of Thrace , but Theodosius enchanted the men and women whose predecessors in the same country had torn Orpheus in pieces, &c.

[140] Constantinople was deprived, half a day, of the public allowance of bread, to expiate the murder of a Gothic soldier : κινοῦντες τὸ Σκυθικόν was the guilt of the people.   Libanius, Orat. xii. p 394, edit. Morel

[141] Zosimus, l iv p 267-271 [48, 49]   He tells a long and ridiculous story of the adventurous prince who roved the country with only five horsemen, of a spy whom they detected, whipped, and killed in an old woman's cottage, &c   [Guldenpenning, p. 196.]

numerous faction adhered to the fierce and faithless Priulf, who inflamed the passions, and asserted the independence, of his warlike followers. On one of the solemn festivals, when the chiefs of both parties were invited to the Imperial table, they were insensibly heated by wine, till they forgot the usual restraints of discretion and respect; and betrayed, in the presence of Theodosius, the fatal secret of their domestic disputes. The emperor, who had been the reluctant witness of this extraordinary controversy, dissembled his fears and resentment, and soon dismissed the tumultuous assembly. Fravitta, alarmed and exasperated by the insolence of his rival, whose departure from the palace might have been the signal of a civil war, boldly followed him; and, drawing his sword, laid Priulf dead at his feet. Their companions flew to arms; and the faithful champion of Rome would have been oppressed by superior numbers, if he had not been protected by the seasonable interposition of the Imperial guards.[142] Such were the scenes of Barbaric rage which disgraced the palace and table of the Roman emperor; and, as the impatient Goths could only be restrained by the firm and temperate character of Theodosius, the public safety seemed to depend on the life and abilities of a single man[143]

---

[142] Compare Eunapius (in Excerpt. Legat p 21, 22 [fr 60, F H G iv p 41]) with Zosimus (l. iv. p 279 [56]) The difference of circumstances and names must undoubtedly be applied to the same story. Fravitta, or Travitta, was afterwards consul (A D 401), and still continued his faithful service to the eldest son of Theodosius (Tillemont, Hist des Empereurs, tom v p 467) ["Priulf" is called Eriulph by Eunapius. The conspiracy seems to have been formed by the Arian Goths. Fravitta was a leader of pagan Goths. The date seems to be during the preparation for the war with Eugenius. Cp. Güldenpenning, p. 218.]

[143] Les Goths ravagèrent tout depuis le Danube jusqu'au Bosphore, exterminèrent Valens et son armée; et ne repassèrent le Danube que pour abandonner l'affreuse solitude qu'ils avoient faite (Œuvres de Montesquieu, tom iii p 479; Considérations sur les Causes de la Grandeur et de la Décadence des Romains, c. xvii.) The president Montesquieu seems ignorant that the Goths, after the defeat of Valens, never abandoned the Roman territory It is now thirty years, says Claudian (de Bello Getico [Gothico, Birt and Koch], 166 [leg. 169], &c, A D 404 [rather 402])

> Ex quo jam patrios gens hæc oblita Triones,
> Atque Istrum transvecta semel, vestigia fixit
> Threicio funesta solo ————

The error is inexcusable; since it disguises the principal and immediate cause of the fall of the Western Empire of Rome

CHAPTER XXVII

Death of Gratian—Ruin of Arianism—St. Ambrose—First Civil War, against Maximus—Character, Administration, and Penance of Theodosius—Death of Valentinian II.—Second Civil War, against Eugenius—Death of Theodosius

THE fame of Gratian, before he had accomplished the twentieth year of his age, was equal to that of the most celebrated princes. His gentle and amiable disposition endeared him to his private friends, the graceful affability of his manners engaged the affection of the people: the men of letters, who enjoyed the liberality, acknowledged the taste and eloquence, of their sovereign; his valour and dexterity in arms were equally applauded by the soldiers; and the clergy considered the humble piety of Gratian as the first and most useful of his virtues. The victory of Colmar had delivered the West from a formidable invasion; and the grateful provinces of the East ascribed the merits of Theodosius to the author of *his* greatness and of the public safety. Gratian survived those memorable events only four or five years; but he survived his reputation; and, before he fell a victim to rebellion, he had lost, in a great measure, the respect and confidence of the Roman world.

The remarkable alteration of his character or conduct may not be imputed to the arts of flattery which had besieged the son of Valentinian from his infancy; nor to the headstrong passions which that gentle youth appears to have escaped. A more attentive view of the life of Gratian may perhaps suggest the true cause of the disappointment of the public hopes. His apparent virtues, instead of being the hardy productions of experience and adversity, were the premature and artificial fruits of a royal education. The anxious tenderness of his father was continually employed to bestow on him those advantages which he might perhaps esteem the more highly, as he himself had been deprived of them; and the most skilful masters of every science and of every art had laboured to form the mind and

Character and conduct of the emperor Gratian. A.D. 379 383

His defects

body of the young prince.[1] The knowledge which they painfully communicated was displayed with ostentation and celebrated with lavish praise   His soft and tractable disposition
received the fair impression of their judicious precepts, and the
absence of passion might easily be mistaken for the strength of
reason.   His preceptors gradually rose to the rank and consequence of ministers of state;[2] and, as they wisely dissembled
their secret authority, he seemed to act with firmness, with
propriety and with judgment, on the most important occasions
of his life and reign.   But the influence of this elaborate
instruction did not penetrate beyond the surface; and the
skilful preceptors, who so accurately guided the steps of their
royal pupil, could not infuse into his feeble and indolent character the vigorous and independent principle of action which
renders the laborious pursuit of glory essentially necessary to
the happiness, and almost to the existence, of the hero.   As
soon as time and accident had removed those faithful counsellors
from the throne, the emperor of the West insensibly descended
to the level of his natural genius; abandoned the reins of
government to the ambitious hands which were stretched forwards to grasp them; and amused his leisure with the most
frivolous gratifications.   A public sale of favour and injustice
was instituted, both in the court and in the provinces, by the
worthless delegates of his power, whose merit it was made
[A D 380]   *sacrilege* to question.[3] The conscience of the credulous prince
was directed by saints and bishops,[4] who procured an Imperial
edict to punish as a capital offence, the violation, the neglect, or

---

[1] Valentinian was less attentive to the religion of his son, since he entrusted [c.
A D. 364] the education of Gratian to Ausonius, a professed Pagan (Mém. de
l'Académie des Inscriptions, tom xv. p. 125-138)   [But in his poem the
Ephemeris (before 367 A D ; Schenkl, Pref to his ed of Ausonius in M H. G)
he poses not only as a Christian, but as an orthodox Christian]   The poetical
fame of Ausonius condemns the taste of his age.

[2] [Decimus Magnus] Ausonius was successively promoted to the Prætorian præfecture of Italy (A D 377) and of Gaul (A D 378), cp Aus ii 2, 42, præfectus Gallis
et Libyæ et Latio, and was at length invested with the consulship (A D. 379).   He
expressed his gratitude in a servile and insipid piece of flattery (Actio Gratiarum,
p 699-736) which has survived more worthy productions   [This statement as to
the præfectures of Ausonius is not quite accurate, cp. Appendix 1]

[3] Disputare de principali judicio non oportet   Sacri egii enim instar est
dubitare, an is dignus sit, quem elegerit imperator   Codex Justinian 1 ix tit
xxix leg 3 [2, ed Kruger]   This convenient law was revived and promulgated
after the death of Gratian by the feeble court of Milan.

[4] Ambrose composed, for his instruction, a theological treatise on the faith of
the Trinity, and Tillemont (Hist des Empereurs, tom v p. 158, 169) ascribes
to the archbishop the merit of Gratian's intolerant laws

even the ignorance of the divine law.[5] Among the various arts [A D 380]
which had exercised the youth of Gratian, he had applied himself with singular inclination and success to manage the horse, to draw the bow, and to dart the javelin ; and these qualifications, which might be useful to a soldier, were prostituted to the viler purposes of hunting. Large parks were enclosed for the Imperial pleasures, and plentifully stocked with every species of wild beasts; and Gratian neglected the duties, and even the dignity, of his rank, to consume whole days in the vain display of his dexterity and boldness in the chase. The pride and wish of the Roman emperor to excell in an art in which he might be surpassed by the meanest of his slaves reminded the numerous spectators of the examples of Nero and Commodus; but the chaste and temperate Gratian was a stranger to their monstrous vices ; and his hands were stained only with the blood of animals.[6]

The behaviour of Gratian, which degraded his character in Disconten the eyes of mankind, could not have disturbed the security of troops A D his reign, if the army had not been provoked to resent their 383 peculiar injuries. As long as the young emperor was guided by the instructions of his masters, he professed himself the friend and pupil of the soldiers ; many of his hours were spent in the familiar conversation of the camp ; and the health, the comforts, the rewards, the honours, of his faithful troops appeared to be the object of his attentive concern. But, after Gratian more freely indulged his prevailing taste for hunting and shooting, he naturally connected himself with the most dexterous ministers of his favourite amusement. A body of the Alani was received into the military and domestic service of the palace ; and the admirable skill which they were accustomed to display in the unbounded plains of Scythia was exercised, on a more narrow theatre, in the parks and inclosures of Gaul. Gratian admired the talents and customs of these favourite guards, to whom alone he entrusted the defence of his person : and, as if he meant to insult the public opinion, he frequently shewed himself to the soldiers and people, with the dress and arms, the long bow, the

[5] Qui divinæ legis sanctitatem [aut] nesciendo omittunt [leg confundunt] aut negligendo violant et offendunt, sacrilegium committunt. Codex Justinian. l. ix. it xxix leg 1   Theodosius indeed may claim his share in the merit of this comprehensive law

[6] Ammianus (xxxi. 10) and the younger Victor [Epit 47] acknowledge the virtues of Gratian, and accuse, or rather lament, his degenerate taste   The odious parallel of Commodus is saved by "licet incruentus"; and perhaps Philostorgius (l x c 10, and Godefroy, p. 412) had guarded with some similar reserve the comparison of Nero.

sounding quiver, and the fur garments of a Scythian warrior. The unworthy spectacle of a Roman prince who had renounced the dress and manners of his country filled the minds of the legions with grief and indignation.[7]   Even the Germans, so strong and formidable in the armies of the empire, affected to disdain the strange and horrid appearance of the savages of the North, who, in the space of a few years, had wandered from the banks of the Volga to those of the Seine.   A loud and licentious murmur was echoed through the camps and garrisons of the West; and, as the mild indolence of Gratian neglected to extinguish the first symptoms of discontent, the want of love and respect was not supplied by the influence of fear.   But the subversion of an established government is always a work of some real, and of much apparent, difficulty, and the throne of Gratian was protected by the sanctions of custom, law, religion, and the nice balance of the civil and military powers, which had been established by the policy of Constantine.   It is not very important to inquire from what causes the revolt of Britain was produced.   Accident is commonly the parent of disorder; the seed of rebellion happened to fall on a soil which was supposed to be more fruitful than any other in tyrants and usurpers;[8] the legions of that sequestered island had been long famous for a spirit of presumption and arrogance;[9] and the name of Maximus was proclaimed by the tumultuary but unanimous voice both of the soldiers and of the provincials.   The emperor, or the rebel, for his title was not yet ascertained by fortune, was a native of Spain, the countryman, the fellow-soldier, and the rival of Theodosius, whose elevation he had not seen without some emotions of envy and resentment   The events of his life had long since fixed him in Britain; and I should not be unwilling to find some evidence for the marriage which he is said to have contracted with the daughter of a wealthy lord of Caernarvonshire.[10]   But this provincial rank might justly be con-

Revolt of [Magnus] Maximus in Britain

[7] Zosimus (l. iv. p 247 [c 35]) and the younger Victor [ib] ascribe the revolution to the favour of the Alani and the discontent of the Roman troops   Dum exercitum neghgeret, et paucos ex Alanis, quos ingenti auro ad se transtulerat, anteferret veteri ac Romano militi

[8] Britannia fertilis provincia tyrannorum, is a memorable expression used by Jerom in the Pelagian controversy, and variously tortured in the disputes of our national antiquaries.   The revolutions of the last age appeared to justify the image of the sublime Bossuet, " cette isle, plus orageuse que les mers qui l'environnent ".

[9] Zosimus says of the British soldiers, τῶν ἄλλων ἁπαντων πλεον αὐθαδειᾳ καὶ θυμῶ νικωμένους [ib]   Ausonius describes Maximus as *armigeri sub nomine lixa*, Ord. urb. nob. l 70]

[10] Helena the daughter of Eudda. Her chapel may still be seen at Caersegont, now Caer-narvon (Carte's Hist of England, vol. i. p 168, from Rowland's

sidered as a state of exile and obscurity; and, if Maximus had
obtained any civil or military office, he was not invested with
the authority either of governor or general.[11]   His abilities, and
even his integrity, are acknowledged by the partial writers of
the age; and the merit must indeed have been conspicuous,
that could extort such a confession in favour of the vanquished
enemy of Theodosius.   The discontent of Maximus might incline him to censure the conduct of his sovereign, and to encourage, perhaps without any views of ambition, the murmurs
of the troops.   But in the midst of the tumult he artfully, or
modestly, refused to ascend the throne; and some credit appears
to have been given to his own positive declaration that he was
compelled to accept the dangerous present of the Imperial
purple.[12]

But there was a danger likewise in refusing the empire; and from the moment that Maximus had violated his allegiance to his lawful sovereign, he could not hope to reign, or even to live, if he confined his moderate ambition within the narrow limits of Britain.   He boldly and wisely resolved to prevent the designs of Gratian; the youth of the island crowded to his standard, and he invaded Gaul with a fleet and army, which were long afterwards remembered as the emigration of a considerable part of the British nation.[13]   The emperor, in his peaceful residence of Paris, was alarmed by their hostile approach; and the darts which he idly wasted on lions and bears might have been employed more honourably against the rebels   But his feeble efforts announced his degenerate spirit

Mona Antiqua)   The prudent reader may not perhaps be satisfied with such Welsh evidence
[11] Cambden (vol. 1 introduct. p. ci) appoints him governor of Britain; and the father of our antiquities is followed, as usual, by his blind progeny   Pacatus and Zosimus had taken some pains to prevent this error, or fable, and I shall protect myself by their decisive testimonies   Regali habitu *exulem* suum illi exules orbes induerunt (in Panegyr Vet. xii. 23), and the Greek historian, still less equivocally, αυτὸς (Maximus) δὲ οὐδὲ εἰς αρχὴν ἔντιμον ἔτυχε προελθών (l. iv. p 248 [c. 35])
[12] Sulpicius Severus, Dialog ii 7, Orosius, l. vii. c. 34, p. 556   They both acknowledge (Sulpicius had been his subject) his innocence and merit   It is singular enough that Maximus should be less favourably treated by Zosimus, the partial adversary of his rival
[13] Archbishop Usher (Antiquitat Britan. Eccles p 107, 108) has diligently collected the legends of the island and the continent   The whole emigration consisted of 30,000 soldiers, and 100,000 plebeians, who settled in Bretagne. Their destined brides, St Ursula with 11,000 noble, and 60,000 plebeian, virgins, mistook their way, landed at Cologne, and were all most cruelly murdered by the Huns.   But the plebeian sisters have been defrauded of their equal honours; and, what is still harder, John Trithemius presumes to mention the *children* of these British *virgins*

and desperate situation, and deprived him of the resources which he still might have found in the support of his subjects and allies. The armies of Gaul, instead of opposing the march of Maximus, received him with joyful and loyal acclamations ; and the shame of the desertion was transferred from the people to the prince. The troops whose station more immediately attached them to the service of the palace abandoned the standard of Gratian the first time that it was displayed in the neighbourhood of Paris. The emperor of the West fled towards Lyons, with a train of only three hundred horse ; and in the cities along the road, where he hoped to find a refuge, or at least a passage, he was taught, by cruel experience, that every gate is shut against the unfortunate. Yet he might still have reached in safety the dominions of his brother, and soon have returned with the forces of Italy and the East, if he had not suffered himself to be fatally deceived by the perfidious governor of the Lyonese province. Gratian was amused by protestations of doubtful fidelity and the hopes of a support which could not be effectual, till the arrival of Andragathius, the general of the cavalry of Maximus, put an end to his suspense. That resolute officer executed without remorse the orders, or the intentions, of the usurper. Gratian, as he rose from supper, was delivered into the hands of the assassin ; and his body was denied to the pious and pressing entreaties of his brother Valentinian.[14] The death of the emperor was followed by that of his powerful general Mellobaudes, the king of the Franks ; who maintained, to the last moment of his life, the ambiguous reputation which is the just recompense of obscure and subtle policy[15] These executions might be necessary to the public safety ; but the successful usurper, whose power was acknowledged by all the provinces of the West, had the merit and the satisfaction of boasting that, except those who had perished by the chance of war, his triumph was not stained by the blood of the Romans.[16]

A D 383, Aug 25

[leg Mero baudes]

---

[14] Zosimus (l iv p 248, 249 [c 35]) has transported the death of Gratian from Lugdunum in Gaul (Lyons) to Singidunum in Mœsia Some hints may be extracted from the Chronicles ; some lies may be detected in Sozomen (l vii c 13) and Socrates (l v c 11) Ambrose is our most authentic evidence (tom 1 Enarrat in Psalm lxi p 961 [ed Migne, 1 p 1173], tom 11. epist. xxiv. p 888 [ib. 11. 1035], &c , and de Obitu Valentinian Consolat No 28, p. 1182 [ib 11. 1368])

[15] Pacatus (xii 28) celebrates his fidelity, while his treachery is marked in Prosper's Chronicle, as the cause of the ruin of Gratian Ambrose, who has occasion to exculpate himself, only condemns the death of Vallio, a faithful servant of Gratian (tom. 11 epist xxiv p 891, edit Benedict [Migne, 11. p. 1039]).

[16] He protested, nullum ex adversariis nisi in acie occubuisse Sulp. Severus, in Vit B. Martin c 23 The orator of Theodosius bestows reluctant, and therefore weighty, praise on his clemency Si cui ille, pro ceteris sceleribus suis, *minus crudelis* fuisse videtur (Panegyr. Vet xii 28).

The events of this revolution had passed in such rapid Treaty of peace between Maximus and Theodosius A.D. 383-387 succession that it would have been impossible for Theodosius to march to the relief of his benefactor, before he received the intelligence of his defeat and death. During the season of sincere grief, or ostentatious mourning, the Eastern emperor was interrupted by the arrival of the principal chamberlain of Maximus; and the choice of a venerable old man, for an office which was usually exercised by eunuchs, announced to the court of Constantinople the gravity and temperance of the British usurper. The ambassador condescended to justify, or excuse, the conduct of his master, and to protest in specious language that the murder of Gratian had been 'perpetrated, without his knowledge or consent, by the precipitate zeal of the soldiers. But he proceeded, in a firm and equal tone, to offer Theodosius the alternative of peace or war. The speech of the ambassador concluded with a spirited declaration that, although Maximus, as a Roman and as the father of his people, would choose rather to employ his forces in the common defence of the republic, he was armed and prepared, if his friendship should be rejected, to dispute in a field of battle the empire of the world. An immediate and peremptory answer was required; but it was extremely difficult for Theodosius to satisfy, on this important occasion, either the feelings of his own mind or the expectations of the public. The imperious voice of honour and gratitude called aloud for revenge. From the liberality of Gratian he had received the Imperial diadem: his patience would encourage the odious suspicion that he was more deeply sensible of former injuries than of recent obligations; and, if he accepted the friendship, he must seem to share the guilt, of the assassin. Even the principles of justice and the interest of society would receive a fatal blow from the impunity of Maximus; and the example of successful usurpation would tend to dissolve the artificial fabric of government, and once more to replunge the empire in the crimes and calamities of the preceding age. But, as the sentiments of gratitude and honour should invariably regulate the conduct of an individual, they may be overbalanced in the mind of a sovereign by the sense of superior duties; and the maxims both of justice and humanity must permit the escape of an atrocious criminal, if an innocent people would be involved in the consequences of his punishment. The assassin of Gratian had usurped, but he actually possessed, the most warlike provinces of the empire; the East was exhausted by the misfortunes, and even by the success, of the

Gothic war; and it was seriously to be apprehended that, after the vital strength of the republic had been wasted in a doubtful and destructive contest, the feeble conqueror would remain an easy prey to the Barbarians of the North.   These weighty considerations engaged Theodosius to dissemble his resentment and to accept the alliance of the tyrant.   But he stipulated that Maximus should content himself with the possession of the countries beyond the Alps.   The brother of Gratian was confirmed and secured in the sovereignty of Italy, Africa, and the Western Illyricum; and some honourable conditions were inserted in the treaty, to protect the memory and the laws of the deceased emperor.[17]   According to the custom of the age, the images of the three Imperial colleagues were exhibited to the veneration of the people: nor should it be lightly supposed that, in the moment of a solemn reconciliation, Theodosius secretly cherished the intention of perfidy and revenge.[18]

Baptism and
orthodox
edicts of
Theodosius
A.D 380,
Feb 28   The contempt of Gratian for the Roman soldiers had exposed him to the fatal effects of their resentment.   His profound veneration for the Christian clergy was rewarded by the applause and gratitude of a powerful order, which has claimed, in every age, the privilege of dispensing honours both on earth and in heaven.[19]   The orthodox bishops bewailed his death and their own irreparable loss; but they were soon comforted by the discovery that Gratian had committed the sceptre of the East to the hands of a prince whose humble faith and fervent zeal were supported by the spirit and abilities of a more vigorous character.   Among the benefactors of the church, the fame of Constantine has been rivalled by the glory of Theodosius.   If Constantine had the advantage of erecting the standard of the cross, the emulation of his successor assumed the merit of subduing the Arian heresy and of abolishing the worship of idols in the Roman world   Theodosius was the first of the emperors baptized in the true faith of the Trinity   Although he was born of a Christian family, the maxims, or at least the practice, of the age encouraged him to

[17] Ambrose mentions the laws of Gratian, quas non abrogavit hostis (tom. ii. epist xvi p 827)

[18] Zosimus, l. iv p 251, 252 [c 37]   We may disclaim his odious suspicions, but we cannot reject the treaty of peace which the friends of Theodosius have absolutely forgotten or slightly mentioned.   [His name, afterwards erased, can be discovered along with Valent ii and Theodosius on an inscription, C I L 8, 27]

[19] Their oracle, the archbishop of Milan, assigns to his pupil Gratian an high and respectable place in heaven (tom ii de Obit Val Consol p 1193)

delay the ceremony of his initiation; till he was admonished of
the danger of delay by the serious illness which threatened his
life towards the end of the first year of his reign. Before he
again took the field against the Goths, he received the sacrament of baptism [20] from Acholius, the orthodox bishop of
Thessalonica; [21] and, as the emperor ascended from the holy
font, still glowing with the warm feelings of regeneration, he
dictated a solemn edict, which proclaimed his own faith and
prescribed the religion of his subjects. " It is our pleasure (such
is the Imperial style) that all the nations which are governed [Feb 28]
by our clemency and moderation should steadfastly adhere to
the religion which was taught by St. Peter to the Romans;
which faithful tradition has preserved; and which is now professed by the pontiff Damasus, and by Peter, bishop of
Alexandria, a man of apostolic holiness. According to the
discipline of the apostles and the doctrine of the gospel, let us
believe the sole deity of the Father, the Son, and the Holy
Ghost; under an equal majesty and a pious Trinity. We
authorize the followers of this doctrine to assume the title of
Catholic Christians; and, as we judge that all others are
extravagant madmen, we brand them with the infamous name
of Heretics; and declare that their conventicles shall no longer
usurp the respectable appellation of churches. Besides the
condemnation of Divine justice, they must expect to suffer the
severe penalties which our authority, guided by heavenly
wisdom, shall think proper to inflict upon them " [22] The faith
of a soldier is commonly the fruit of instruction rather than of
inquiry; but, as the emperor always fixed his eyes on the
visible land-marks of orthodoxy, which he had so prudently
constituted, his religious opinions were never affected by the
specious texts, the subtle arguments, and the ambiguous creeds of
the Arian doctors. Once indeed he expressed a faint inclination
to converse with the eloquent and learned Eunomius, who lived
in retirement at a small distance from Constantinople [22a] But
the dangerous interview was prevented by the prayers of the

[20] For the baptism of Theodosius, see Sozomen (l vii. c. 4), Socrates (l v c 6)
and Tillemont (Hist. des Empereurs, tom v p. 728)
[21] Ascolius, or Acholius [so Ambrose, Ascholius in Socr. and Sozomen], was
honoured by the friendship and the praises of Ambrose; who styles him, murus
fidei atque sanctitatis (tom. ii epist. xv. p. 820), and afterwards celebrates his
speed and diligence in running to Constantinople, Italy, &c. (epist. xvi p. 822), a
virtue which does not appertain either to a *wall*, or a *bishop*.
[22] Codex Theodos. l. xvi. tit i leg 2, with Godefroy's Commentary, tom. vi.
p. 5-9. Such an edict deserved the warmest praises of Baronius, auream sanctionem
edictum pium et salutare —Sic itur ad astra
[22a] [See above, p. 12, n 37.]

empress Flaccilla, who trembled for the salvation of her husband ;
and the mind of Theodosius was confirmed by a theological
argument, adapted to the rudest capacity. He had lately
bestowed on his eldest son Arcadius the name and honours of
Augustus ; and the two princes were seated on a stately throne
to receive the homage of their subjects. A bishop, Amphilochius
of Iconium, approached the throne, and, after saluting with due
reverence the person of his sovereign, he accosted the royal
youth with the same familiar tenderness which he might have
used towards a plebeian child. Provoked by this insolent
behaviour, the monarch gave orders that the rustic priest
should be instantly driven from his presence. But, while the
guards were forcing him to the door, the dexterous polemic had
time to execute his design, by exclaiming with a loud voice,
"Such is the treatment, O emperor! which the King of
heaven has prepared for those impious men who affect to
worship the Father but refuse to acknowledge the equal
majesty of his divine Son ". Theodosius immediately embraced
the bishop of Iconium, and never forgot the important lesson
which he had received from this dramatic parable [23]

Arianism of Constantino- ple A D 340-380 Constantinople was the principal seat and fortress of Arianism ; and, in a long interval of forty years,[24] the faith of the
princes and prelates who reigned in the capital of the East
was rejected in the purer schools of Rome and Alexandria.
The archiepiscopal throne of Macedonius, which had been
polluted with so much Christian blood, was successively filled
[Demophilus] by Eudoxus and Damophilus. Their diocese enjoyed a free
importation of vice and error from every province of the
empire, the eager pursuit of religious controversy afforded a
new occupation to the busy idleness of the metropolis ; and we
[Gregory Nyssen] may credit the assertion of an intelligent observer, who describes, with some pleasantry, the effects of their loquacious
zeal. "This city," says he, "is full of mechanics and slaves,
who are all of them profound theologians, and preach in the
shops and in the streets. If you desire a man to change a piece
of silver, he informs you wherein the Son differs from the
Father ; if you ask the price of a loaf, you are told by way of

[23] Sozomen, l vii c 6 Theodoret, l. v c. 16 Tillemont is displeased (Mém.
Ecclés tom vi p 627, 628) with the terms of "rustic bishop," "obscure city"
Yet I must take leave to think that both Amphilochius and Iconium were objects
of inconsiderable magnitude in the Roman empire

[24] Sozomen, l vii c. 5. Socrates, l v c 7 Marcellin in Chron The account
of forty years must be dated from the election or intrusion of Eusebius, who
wisely exchanged the bishopric of Nicomedia for the throne of Constantinople

reply that the Son is inferior to the Father; and, if you enquire whether the bath is ready, the answer is that the Son was made out of nothing."[25] The heretics of various denominations subsisted in peace under the protection of the Arians of Constantinople; who endeavoured to secure the attachment of those obscure sectaries; while they abused, with unrelenting severity, the victory which they had obtained over the followers of the council of Nice. During the partial reigns of Constantius and Valens, the feeble remnant of the Homoousians was deprived of the public and private exercise of their religion; and it has been observed, in pathetic language, that the scattered flock was left without a shepherd, to wander on the mountains, or to be devoured by rapacious wolves.[26] But, as their zeal, instead of being subdued, derived strength and vigour from oppression, they seized the first moments of imperfect freedom, which they acquired by the death of Valens, to form themselves into a regular congregation under the conduct of an episcopal pastor. Two natives of Cappadocia, Basil and Gregory Nazianzen,[27] were distinguished above all their contemporaries [28] by the rare union of profane eloquence and of orthodox piety. These orators, who might sometimes be compared, by themselves and by the public, to the most celebrated of the ancient Greeks, were united by the ties of the strictest friendship. They had cultivated, with equal ardour, the same liberal studies in the schools of Athens; they had retired, with equal devotion, to the same solitude in the deserts of Pontus; and every spark of emulation, or envy, appeared to be totally extinguished in the holy and ingenuous breasts of Gregory and Basil. But the exaltation of Basil, from a private life to the archiepiscopal throne of Cæsarea, dis-

Gregory Nazianzen

[25] See Jortin's Remarks on Ecclesiastical History, vol. iv. p. 71   The thirty-third [27th ap. Migne] Oration of Gregory Nazianzen affords indeed some similar ideas, even some still more ridiculous; but I have not yet found the *words* of this remarkable passage, which I allege on the faith of a correct and liberal scholar [But see Appendix 9.]

[26] See the thirty-second [42nd ap Migne] Oration of Gregory Nazianzen, and the account of his own life, which he has composed in 1800 iambics. Yet every physician is prone to exaggerate the inveterate nature of the disease which he has cured.

[27] I confess myself deeply indebted to the *two* lives of Gregory Nazianzen, composed, with very different views, by Tillemont (Mém, Ecclés. tom iv p. 305-560, 692-731) and Le Clerc (Bibliothèque Universelle, tom. xviii. p 1-128) [Ullmann, Gregor von Nazianz, 1825, Bénoit, S. Grégoire de Nazianze, 1884]

[28] Unless Gregory Nazianzen mistook thirty years in his own age, he was born, as well as his friend Basil, about the year 329. The preposterous chronology of Suidas has been graciously received; because it removes the scandal of Gregory's father, a saint likewise, begetting children, after he became a bishop (Tillem Mém. Ecclés. tom ix. p 693-697).

covered to the world, and perhaps to himself, the pride of his character ; and the first favour which he condescended to bestow on his friend was received, and perhaps was intended, as a cruel insult.[29] Instead of employing the superior talents of Gregory in some useful and conspicuous station, the haughty prelate selected, among the fifty bishoprics of his extensive province, the wretched village of Sasima,[30] without water, without verdure, without society, situate at the junction of [Hassa Keui?] three highways, and frequented only by the incessant passage of rude and clamorous waggoners. Gregory submitted with reluctance to this humiliating exile ; he was ordained bishop of Sasima ; but he solemnly protests that he never consummated his spiritual marriage with this disgusting bride   He [Neuizi] afterwards consented to undertake the government of his native church of Nazianzus,[31] of which his father had been bishop above five-and-forty years. But, as he was still conscious that he deserved another audience and another theatre, he Accepts the mission of accepted, with no unworthy ambition, the honourable invitation Constantino- which was addressed to him from the orthodox party of Con-
ple A.D 378,
November [or stantinople. On his arrival in the capital, Gregory was enter-
Jan. 379]
tained in the house of a pious and charitable kinsman ; the most spacious room was consecrated to the uses of religious worship ; and the name of *Anastasia* was chosen to express the resurrection of the Nicene faith. This private conventicle was

---

[29] Gregory's Poem on his own Life contains some beautiful lines (tom ii p 8), which burst from the heart, and speak the pangs of injured and lost friendship

$$. . . \pi \acute{o}\nu o\iota \; \kappa o\iota\nu o\iota \; \lambda \acute{o}\gamma \omega\nu,$$
$$\text{'}O\mu \acute{o}\sigma\tau\epsilon\gamma \acute{o}s \; \tau\epsilon \; \kappa a\iota \; \sigma\upsilon\nu\acute{\epsilon}\sigma\tau\iota os \; \beta \acute{\iota}os,$$
$$N o\hat{\upsilon}s \; \epsilon \acute{\iota}s \; \acute{\epsilon}\nu \; \acute{a}\mu\phi o\hat{\iota}\nu \; . \; . \; .$$
$$\Delta\iota\epsilon\sigma\kappa\acute{\epsilon}\delta a\sigma\tau a\iota \; \pi a\nu\tau a, \; \acute{\epsilon}\rho\rho\iota-\tau a\iota \; \chi a\mu a\acute{\iota},$$
$$A\mathring{\upsilon}\rho a\iota \; \phi\acute{\epsilon}\rho o\upsilon\sigma a\iota \; \tau a s \; \pi a\lambda a\iota a s \; \acute{\epsilon}\lambda\pi\acute{\iota}\delta a s \; [477\text{-}483]$$

in the Midsummer Night's Dream, Helena addresses the same pathetic complaint to her friend Hermia

Is all the counsel that we two have shared,
The sister's vows, &c.

Shakespeare had never read the poems of Gregory Nazianzen, he was ignorant of the Greek language , but his mother-tongue, the language of Nature, is the same in Cappadocia and in Britain.
[30] This unfavourable portrait of Sasima is drawn by Gregory Nazianzen (tom ii. de Vitâ suâ, p 7, 8 [Migne, 3, p 1059]) Its precise situation, forty-nine miles from Archelais [Ak Serai], and thirty-two from Tyana, is fixed in the Itinerary of Antoninus (p 144, edit Wesseling)
[31] The name of Nazianzus has been immortalized by Gregory ; but his native town, under the Greek or Roman title of Diocæsarea (Tillemont, Mém Ecclés. tom ix p. 692), is mentioned by Pliny (vi 3), Ptolemy, and Hierocles (Itinerar. Wesseling, p. 709) It appears to have been situate on the edge of Isauria. [ἡ Διοκαισαρέων ὀλίγη πόλις, as Gregory calls Nazianzus, is more northerly than Gibbon supposed, lying on the road from Iconium to Tyana , about six hours due east of Archelais ; Ramsay, Asia Minor, 285]

afterwards converted into a magnificent church; and the credulity of the succeeding age was prepared to believe the miracles and visions, which attested the presence, or at least the protection, of the Mother of God.[32] The pulpit of the Anastasia was the scene of the labours and triumphs of Gregory Nazianzen; and, in the space of two years, he experienced all the spiritual adventures which constitute the prosperous or adverse fortunes of a missionary.[33] The Arians, who were provoked by the boldness of his enterprise, represented his doctrine as if he had preached three distinct and equal Deities; and the devout populace was excited to suppress, by violence and tumult, the irregular assemblies of the Athanasian heretics. From the cathedral of St. Sophia there issued a motley crowd "of common beggars, who had forfeited their claim to pity; of monks, who had the appearance of goats or satyrs; and of women, more terrible than so many Jezebels". The doors of the Anastasia were broke open; much mischief was perpetrated, or attempted, with sticks, stones, and firebrands; and, as a man lost his life in the affray, Gregory, who was summoned the next morning before the magistrate, had the satisfaction of supposing that he publicly confessed the name of Christ. After he was delivered from the fear and danger of a foreign enemy, his infant church was disgraced and distracted by intestine faction. A stranger who assumed the name of Maximus [34] and the cloak of a Cynic philosopher, insinuated himself into the confidence of Gregory, deceived and abused his favourable opinion, and, forming a secret connexion with some bishops of Egypt, attempted by a clandestine ordination to supplant his patron in the episcopal seat of Constantinople. These mortifications might sometimes tempt the Cappadocian missionary to regret his obscure solitude. But his fatigues were rewarded by the daily increase of his fame and his congregation; and he enjoyed the pleasure of observing that the greater part of his

[32] See Ducange, Constant. Christiana, l iv p 141, 142. The θεια δυναμις of Sozomen (l. vii. c 5) is interpreted o mean the Virgin Mary [The site of the Church of Anastasia, S.W. of the Hippodrome, is marked now by the mosque of Mehmed Pasha Djemi; see Paspa'ês, Βυȝαντιναι Μελεται, 369]

[33] Tillemont (Mém. Ecclés. tom ix. p 432, &c) diligently collects, enlarges and explains the oratorical and poetical hints o Gregory himself.

[34] He pronounced an oration (tom 1. Orat xxiii p 409 [= xxv Migne, p 1197 sqq]) in his praise; but after their quarrel the name of Maximus was changed into that of Heron (see Jerom, tom 1. in Catalog. Script Eccles. p. 301) I touch slightly on these obscure and personal squabbles [For an account of Maximus, see Hodgkin, 1 346 sqq. Cp. also J. Draseke, Z. f. Wiss. Theologie, 36 (1893), p. 290 sqq]

numerous audience retired from his sermons satisfied with the eloquence of the preacher[35] or dissatisfied with the manifold imperfections of their faith and practice.[36]

Ruin of Arianism at Constantinople. A.D. 380, Nov. 26

The Catholics of Constantinople were animated with joyful confidence by the baptism and edict of Theodosius; and they impatiently waited the effects of his gracious promise. Their hopes were speedily accomplished; and the emperor, as soon as he had finished the operations of the campaign, made his

[Nov. 24]

public entry into the capital at the head of a victorious army. The next day after his arrival, he summoned Damophilus to his presence, and offered that Arian prelate the hard alternative of subscribing the Nicene creed, or of instantly resigning, to the orthodox believers, the use and possession of the episcopal palace, the cathedral of St. Sophia, and all the churches of Constantinople. The zeal of Damophilus, which in a Catholic saint would have been justly applauded, embraced, without hesitation, a life of poverty and exile,[37] and his removal was immediately followed by the purification of the Imperial City. The Arians might complain, with some appearance of justice, that an inconsiderable congregation of sectaries should usurp the hundred churches, which they were insufficient to fill; whilst the far greater part of the people was cruelly excluded from every place of religious worship. Theodosius was still inexorable: but, as the angels who protected the Catholic cause were only visible to the eyes of faith, he prudently reinforced those heavenly legions with the more effectual aid of temporal and carnal weapons; and the church of St. Sophia[38] was occupied by a large body of the Imperial guards. If the mind of Gregory was susceptible of pride, he must have felt a very lively satisfaction, when the emperor conducted him through the streets in solemn triumph; and, with his own hand, respectfully placed him on the archiepiscopal throne of

[35] Under the modest emblem of a dream, Gregory (tom. ii. carmen ix. p. 78 [ed. Migne, 3, p. 1254]) describes his own success with some human complacency. Yet it should seem, from his familiar conversation with his auditor St. Jerom (tom. i. Epist. ad Nepotian, p. 14 [ep. 52; Migne, i. p. 534]), that the preacher understood the true value of popular applause.

[36] Lachrymæ auditorum, laudes tuæ sint, is the lively and judicious advice of St. Jerom [*ib.*].

[37] Socrates (l. v. c. 7) and Sozomen (l. vii. c. 5) relate the evangelical words and actions of Damophilus without a word of approbation. He considered, says Socrates, that it is difficult to *resist* the powerful; but it was easy, and would have been profitable, to *submit*. [Date of entry of Theodosius, 14th Nov., Idacius, Fast. C.; but 24th Nov., acc. to Pasch. Chron. and Socrates, v. 6, which Clinton accepts and Hodgkin supports.]

[38] [Not St. Sophia, which was not yet the chief church, but the Church of the Twelve Apostles; s. P. n. b. v. . ii. p. 1.]

Constantinople. But the saint (who had not subdued the imperfections of human virtue) was deeply affected by the mortifying consideration that his entrance into the fold was that of a wolf, rather than of a shepherd; that the glittering arms, which surrounded his person, were necessary for his safety; and that he alone was the object of the imprecations of a great party, whom, as men and citizens, it was impossible for him to despise. He beheld the innumerable multitude, of either sex and of every age, who crowded the streets, the windows, and the roofs of the houses; he heard the tumultuous voice of rage, grief, astonishment, and despair; and Gregory fairly confesses that, on the memorable day of his installation, the capital of the East wore the appearance of a city taken by storm, and in the hands of a Barbarian conqueror.[39] About six weeks afterwards, Theodosius declared his resolution of expelling, from all the churches of his dominions, the bishops and their clergy who should obstinately refuse to believe, or at least to profess, the doctrine of the council of Nice. His lieutenant Sapor was armed with the ample powers of a general law, a special commission, and a military force;[40] and this ecclesiastical revolution was conducted with so much discretion and vigour that the religion of the emperor was established, without tumult or bloodshed, in all the provinces of the East. The writings of the Arians, if they had been permitted to exist,[41] would perhaps contain the lamentable story of the persecution which afflicted the church under the reign of the impious Theodosius; and the sufferings of *their* holy confessors might claim the pity of the disinterested reader. Yet there is reason to imagine that the violence of zeal and revenge was, in some measure, eluded by the want of resistance; and that, in their adversity, the Arians displayed much less firmness than had been exerted by the orthodox party under the reigns of Constantius and Valens. The moral character and conduct of the hostile sects appear to have been governed

In the East.
A D 381,
January 10

[39] See Gregory Nazianzen, tom ii de Vitâ suâ, p. 21, 22 [l 1331 *sqq.*] For the sake of posterity, the bishop of Constantinople records a stupendous prodigy. In the month of November, it was a cloudy morning, but the sun broke forth when the procession entered the church

[40] Of the three ecclesiastical historians, Theodoret alone (l v c. 2) has mentioned this important commission of Sapor, which Tillemont (Hist des Empereurs, tom v p 728) judiciously removes from the reign of Gratian to that of Theodosius

[41] I do not reckon Philostorgius, though he mentions (l ix c. 19) the expulsion of Damophilus. The Eunomian historian has been carefully strained through an orthodox sieve.

by the same common principles of nature and religion; but a
very material circumstance may be discovered, which tended
to distinguish the degrees of their theological faith. Both
parties in the schools, as well as in the temples, acknowledged
and worshipped the divine majesty of Christ; and, as we are
always prone to impute our own sentiments and passions to the
Deity, it would be deemed more prudent and respectful to
exaggerate, than to circumscribe, the adorable perfections of
the Son of God   The disciple of Athanasius exulted in the
proud confidence that he had entitled himself to the divine
favour; while the follower of Arius must have been tormented
by the secret apprehension that he was guilty, perhaps, of an
unpardonable offence, by the scanty praise, and parsimonious
honours, which he bestowed on the Judge of the World.   The
opinions of Arianism might satisfy a cold and speculative mind;
but the doctrine of the Nicene Creed, most powerfully recommended by the merits of faith and devotion, was much better
adapted to become popular and successful in a believing age.

The council of Constan-tinople A D 381, May [sat till July 9]   The hope that truth and wisdom would be found in the
assemblies of the orthodox clergy induced the emperor to
convene, at Constantinople, a synod of one hundred and fifty
bishops, who proceeded, without much difficulty or delay, to
complete the theological system which had been established
in the council of Nice   The vehement disputes of the fourth
century had been chiefly employed on the nature of the Son of
God; and the various opinions, which were embraced concerning the *Second*, were extended and transferred, by a natural
analogy, to the *Third*, person of the Trinity.[42]   Yet it was found,
or it was thought, necessary, by the victorious adversaries of
Arianism, to explain the ambiguous language of some respectable doctors; to confirm the faith of the Catholics; and to
condemn an unpopular and inconsistent sect of Macedonians,
who freely admitted that the Son was consubstantial to the
Father, while they were fearful of seeming to acknowledge the
existence of *Three* Gods.   A final and unanimous sentence was
pronounced to ratify the equal Deity of the Holy Ghost, the
mysterious doctrine has been received by all the nations and

---

[42] Le Clerc has given a curious extract (Bibliothèque Universelle. tom xviii p.
91-105) of the theological sermons which Gregory Nazianzen pronounced at
Constantinople against the Arians, Eunomians, Macedonians, &c   He tells the
Macedonians, who deified the Father and the Son, without the Holy Ghost, that
they might as well be styled *Tritheists* as *Ditheists*   Gregory himself was almost a
Tritheist; and his monarchy of heaven resembles a well-regulated aristocracy.

all the churches of the Christian world; and their grateful
reverence has assigned to the bishops of Theodosius the second
rank among the general councils [43]   Their knowledge of
religious truth may have been preserved by tradition, or it
may have been communicated by inspiration; but the sober
evidence of history will not allow much weight to the personal
authority of the fathers of Constantinople. In an age when
the ecclesiastics had scandalously degenerated from the model
of apostolical purity, the most worthless and corrupt were always
the most eager to frequent, and disturb, the episcopal assemblies.
The conflict and fermentation of so many opposite interests and
tempers inflamed the passions of the bishops; and their ruling
passions were the love of gold and the love of dispute.   Many
of the same prelates who now applauded the orthodox piety
of Theodosius had repeatedly changed, with prudent flexibility,
their creeds and opinions; and in the various revolutions of
the church and state, the religion of their sovereign was the
rule of their obsequious faith.   When the emperor suspended
his prevailing influence, the turbulent synod was blindly impelled
by the absurd or selfish motives of pride, hatred, and resentment.
The death of Meletius, which happened at the council of
Constantinople, presented the most favourable opportunity of
terminating the schism of Antioch, by suffering his aged rival,
Paulinus, peaceably to end his days in the episcopal chair.
The faith and virtues of Paulinus were unblemished.   But
his cause was supported by the Western churches; and the
bishops of the synod resolved to perpetuate the mischiefs of
discord by the hasty ordination of a perjured candidate,[44]
rather than to betray the imagined dignity of the East, which
had been illustrated by the birth and death of the Son of God.
Such unjust and disorderly proceedings forced the gravest
members of the assembly to dissent and to secede; and the
clamorous majority, which remained masters of the field of

[43] The first general council of Constantinople now triumphs in the Vatican ·
but the popes had long hesitated, and their hesitation perplexes, and almost
staggers, the humble Tillemont (Mém Ecclés tom. ix. p 499, 500). [It had no
good claim to be ecumenical, for the 150 bishops present were entirely from the
eastern provinces of the Empire. It put forward no new doctrines, but simply
reasserted the Nicene Creed. See Gwatkin, Studies of Arianism, p 262]

[44] Before the death of Meletius, six or eight of his most popular ecclesiastics,
among whom was Flavian, had *abjured*, for the sake of peace, the bishopric of
Antioch (Sozomen, l vii. c 3, 11. Socrates, l. v c 5). Tillemont thinks it his
duty to disbelieve the story; but he owns that there are many circumstances in the
life of Flavian which *seem* inconsistent with the praises of Chrysostom and the
character of a saint (Mém. Ecclés tom. x. p. 541)   [Gregory of Nyssa pronounced
the funeral oration on Meletius.]

battle, could be compared only to wasps or magpies, to a flight
of cranes, or to a flock of geese [45]

    A suspicion may possibly arise that so unfavourable a picture

of ecclesiastical synods has been drawn by the partial hand of
some obstinate heretic or some malicious infidel.   But the name
of the sincere historian who has conveyed this instructive lesson
to the knowledge of posterity must silence the impotent murmurs of superstition and bigotry.   He was one of the most
pious and eloquent bishops of the age ; a saint and a doctor of
the church ; the scourge of Arianism, and the pillar of the orthodox faith ; a distinguished member of the council of Constantinople, in which, after the death of Meletius, he exercised the
functions of president : in a word—Gregory Nazianzen himself.
The harsh and ungenerous treatment which he experienced,[46]
instead of derogating from the truth of his evidence, affords an
additional proof of the spirit which actuated the deliberations
of the synod.   Their unanimous suffrage had confirmed the
pretensions which the bishop of Constantinople derived from
the choice of the people and the approbation of the emperor.
But Gregory soon became the victim of malice and envy   The
bishops of the East, his strenuous adherents, provoked by his
moderation in the affairs of Antioch, abandoned him, without
support, to the adverse faction of the Egyptians ; who disputed
the validity of his election, and rigorously asserted the obso-

lete canon that prohibited the licentious practice of episcopal
translations.   The pride, or the humility, of Gregory prompted
him to decline a contest which might have been imputed to
ambition and avarice ; and he publicly offered, not without some
mixture of indignation, to renounce the government of a church
which had been restored, and almost created, by his labours.
His resignation was accepted by the synod, and by the emperor,
with more readiness than he seems to have expected.   At the
time, when he might have hoped to enjoy the fruits of his victory, his episcopal throne was filled by the senator Nectarius ;

---

[45] Consult Gregory Nazianzen, de Vitâ suâ, tom 11. p 25-28 [1509 *sqq.*]   His
general and particular opinion of the clergy and their assemblies may be seen in
verse and prose (tom 1. orat 1 p 33 [= or. 11 Migne], epist lv. [= ep cxxx Migne,
111. p. 225] p. 814, tom. ii carmen x. [*leg.* xi] p. 81 [Migne, *ib.* p. 1227]). Such
passages are faintly marked by Tillemont, and fairly produced by Le Clerc

[46] See Gregory, tom 11 de Vitâ suâ, p 28-31 [1680 *sqq*].   The fourteenth
[22nd], twenty-seventh [36th], and thirty-second [42nd] orations were pronounced
in the several stages of this business.   The peroration of the last (tom. i. p. 528)
in which he takes a solemn leave of men and angels, the city and the emperor,
the East and the West, &c , is pathetic, and almost sublime

and the new archbishop, accidentally recommended by his easy temper and venerable aspect, was obliged to delay the ceremony of his consecration, till he had previously dispatched the rites of his baptism [47] After this remarkable experience of the ingratitude of princes and prelates, Gregory retired once more to his obscure solitude of Cappadocia ; where he employed the remainder of his life, about eight years, in the exercises of poetry and devotion. The title of Saint has been added to his name ; but the tenderness of his heart [48] and the elegance of his genius reflect a more pleasing lustre on the memory of Gregory Nazianzen

[Died A D 389-90]

It was not enough that Theodosius had suppressed the insolent reign of Arianism, or that he had abundantly revenged the injuries which the Catholics sustained from the zeal of Constantius and Valens. The orthodox emperor considered every heretic as a rebel against the supreme powers of heaven, and of earth ; and each of those powers might exercise their peculiar jurisdiction over the soul and body of the guilty. The decrees of the council of Constantinople had ascertained the true standard of the faith ; and the ecclesiastics who governed the conscience of Theodosius suggested the most effectual methods of persecution. In the space of fifteen years, he promulgated at least fifteen severe edicts against the heretics ; [49] more especially against those who rejected the doctrine of the Trinity ; and to deprive them of every hope of escape, he sternly enacted that, if any laws or rescripts should be alleged in their favour, the judges should consider them as the illegal productions either of fraud or forgery. The penal statutes were directed against the ministers, the assemblies, and the persons, of the heretics ; and the passions of the legislator were expressed in the language of declamation and invective. I. The heretical teachers, who usurped the sacred titles of Bishops

Edicts of Theodosius against the heretics A.D 380-394

---

[47] The whimsical ordination of Nectarius is attested by Sozomen (l vii c 8) ; but Tillemont observes (Mém Ecclés tom ix p 719), Après tout, ce narré de Sozomène est si honteux pour tous ceux qu'il y mêle, et surtout pour Théodose, qu'il vaut mieux travailler à le détruire, qu'à le soutenir , an admirable canon of criticism

[48] I can only be understood to mean that such was his natural temper , when it was not hardened, or inflamed, by religious zeal From his retirement [at Arianzus, a farm close to the village of Karbala (now Καλβαρή, Turk Gelvere), 2½ hours south of Nazianzus, containing "a church full of relics of S Gregory". Ramsay, Asia Minor, 285], he exhorts Nectarius to prosecute the heretics of Constantinople

[49] See the Theodosian Code, l xvi tit. v leg 6-23, with Godefroy's commentary on each law, and his general summary, or *Paratitlon*, tom. vi p 104-110.

or Presbyters, were not only excluded from the privileges
and emoluments so liberally granted to the orthodox clergy,
but they were exposed to the heavy penalties of exile and
confiscation, if they presumed to preach the doctrine, or to
practise the rites, of their *accursed* sects. A fine of ten pounds
of gold (above four hundred pounds sterling) was imposed on
every person who should dare to confer, or receive, or promote,
an heretical ordination and it was reasonably expected that,
if the race of pastors could be extinguished, their helpless flocks
would be compelled by ignorance and hunger to return within
the pale of the Catholic church. II. The rigorous prohibition
of conventicles was carefully extended to every possible circumstance in which the heretics could assemble with the intention
of worshipping God and Christ according to the dictates of their
conscience   Their religious meetings, whether public or secret,
by day or by night, in cities or in the country, were equally
proscribed by the edicts of Theodosius; and the building or
ground which had been used for that illegal purpose was
forfeited to the Imperial domain. III. It was supposed that
the error of the heretics could proceed only from the obstinate
temper of their minds; and that such a temper was a fit object
of censure and punishment. The anathemas of the church
were fortified by a sort of civil excommunication, which separated them from their fellow-citizens by a peculiar brand of
infamy; and this declaration of the supreme magistrate tended
to justify, or at least to excuse, the insults of a fanatic populace.
The sectaries were gradually disqualified for the possession of
honourable or lucrative employments; and Theodosius was
satisfied with his own justice, when he decreed that, as the
Eunomians distinguished the nature of the Son from that of
the Father, they should be incapable of making their wills or
of receiving any advantage from testamentary donations. The
guilt of the Manichæan heresy was esteemed of such magnitude
that it could be expiated only by the death of the offender;
and the same capital punishment was inflicted on the Audians,
or *Quartodecimans,*[50] who should dare to perpetrate the atrocious
crime of celebrating, on an improper day, the festival of Easter.
Every Roman might exercise the right of public accusation;
but the office of *Inquisitors* of the Faith, a name so deservedly

[Law against
Manichæans
and Quarto-
decimans,
A D 382,
March 31]

---

[50] They always kept their Easter, like the Jewish Passover, on the fourteenth
day of the first moon after the vernal equinox, and thus pertinaciously opposed
to the Roman church and Nicene synod, which had *fixed* Easter to a Sunday.
Bingham's Antiquities, l xx c. 5, vol ii. p. 309, fol. edit.

abhorred, was first instituted under the reign of Theodosius. Yet we are assured that the execution of his penal edicts was seldom enforced ; and that the pious emperor appeared less desirous to punish than to reclaim, or terrify, his refractory subjects.[51]

The theory of persecution was established by Theodosius, whose justice and piety have been applauded by the saints ; but the practice of it, in the fullest extent, was reserved for his rival and colleague Maximus, the first, among the Christian princes, who shed the blood of his Christian subjects on account of their religious opinions   The cause of the Priscillianists,[52] a recent sect of heretics, who disturbed the provinces of Spain, was transferred, by appeal, from the synod of Bourdeaux to the Imperial consistory of Treves ; and, by the sentence of the Prætorian præfect, seven persons were tortured, condemned, and executed.   The first of these was Priscillian[53] himself, bishop of Avila,[54] in Spain ; who adorned the advantages of birth and fortune by the accomplishments of eloquence and learning. Two presbyters and two deacons accompanied their beloved master in his death, which they esteemed as a glorious martyrdom ; and the number of religious victims was completed by the execution of Latronian, a poet, who rivalled the fame of the ancients ; and of Euchrocia, a noble matron of Bourdeaux, the

Execution
of Priscil
lian and his
associates
A D 385

[51] Sozomen, l, vii. c 12

[52] See the Sacred History of Sulpicius Severus (l. ii. p 437-452, edit. Ludg Bat. 1647 [c. 46-51]), a correct and original writer.   Dr. Lardner (Credibility, &c part ii. vol ix. p. 256-350) has laboured this article, with pure learning, good sense, and moderation.   Tillemont (Mém Ecclés. tom viii. p. 491-527) has raked together all the dirt of the fathers ; an useful scavenger ! [It has been debated how far Priscillian is to be regarded as a heretic.   J. H Lubkert, De haeresi Priscillianistarum, 1840, followed by Bernays, held that he was condemned, not as a heretic, but as a lawbreaker.   Since then some remains of his own writings (eleven Tractates) were discovered (1885) in a Wurzburg Ms of ⅚ cent., and edited (1889) by G Schepss.   His religious position has been investigated by F. Paret, Priscillianus ein Reformator des vierten Jahrhunderts, 1891.   It seems clear that Priscillian's point of view was undogmatic , and he was certainly heretical in so far as he made use of apocryphal books   See too Schepss, Priscillian, 1886.   Cp Jerome's notice, de vir. ill. c. 21, and Orosius, Commonitorium de errore Priscillianistarum et Origenistarum, published by Schepss at end of his ed of Priscillian]

[53] Sulpicius Severus mentions the arch-heretic with esteem and pity.   Felix profecto, si non pravo studio corrupisset optimum ingenium ; prorsus multa in eo animi et corporis bona cerneres (Hist. Sacra, l ii p 439[c. 46]).   Even Jerom (tom i. in Script. Eccles. p. 302) speaks with temper of Priscillian and Latronian. [They suffered in 385, Prosper, Epit. Chron. ; but Idatius gives 387]

[54] The bishopric (in Old Castile) is now worth 20,000 ducats a year (Busching's Geography, vol. ii. p. 308) and is therefore much less likely to produce the author of a new heresy.

widow of the orator Delphidius [55] Two bishops, who had embraced the sentiments of Priscillian, were condemned to a
distant and dreary exile; [56] and some indulgence was shown to
the meaner criminals who assumed the merit of an early repentance. If any credit could be allowed to confessions extorted
by fear or pain, and to vague reports, the offspring of malice
and credulity, the heresy of the Priscillianists would be found to
include the various abominations of magic, of impiety, and of
lewdness. [57] Priscillian, who wandered about the world in the
company of his spiritual sisters, was accused of praying stark-
naked in the midst of the congregation; and it was confidently
asserted that the effects of his criminal intercourse with the
daughter of Euchrocia had been suppressed by means still more
odious and criminal. But an accurate, or rather a candid,
inquiry will discover that, if the Priscillianists violated the
laws of nature, it was not by the licentiousness, but by the
austerity, of their lives. They absolutely condemned the use
of the marriage-bed; and the peace of families was often disturbed by indiscreet separations. They enjoined, or recommended, a total abstinence from all animal food; and their
continual prayers, fasts, and vigils inculcated a rule of strict
and perfect devotion   The speculative tenets of the sect, concerning the person of Christ and the nature of the human soul,
were derived from the Gnostic and Manichæan system; and
this vain philosophy, which had been transported from Egypt
to Spain, was ill adapted to the grosser spirits of the West.
The obscure disciples of Priscillian suffered, languished, and
gradually disappeared · his tenets were rejected by the clergy
and people, but his death was the subject of a long and
vehement controversy; while some arraigned, and others applauded, the justice of his sentence   It is with pleasure that
we can observe the humane inconsistency of the most illustrious
saints and bishops, Ambrose of Milan, [58] and Martin of Tours; [59]

[55] Exprobabatur mulieri viduæ nimia religio, et diligentius culta divinitas (Pacat
in Panegyr. Vet xii. 29). Such was the idea of a humane, though ignorant,
polytheist
[56] One of them was sent in Syllinam insulam quæ ultra Britanniam est   What
must have been the ancient condition of the rocks of Scilly (Cambden's Britannia,
vol. ii p. 1519)?
[57] The scandalous calumnies of Augustin, Pope Leo, &c, which Tillemont
swallows like a child, and Lardner refutes like a man, may suggest some candid
suspicions in favour of the older Gnostics.
[58] Ambros tom ii epist xxiv p 891
[59] In the Sacred History, and the Life of St Martin, Sulpicius Severus uses some
caution, but he declares himself more freely in the Dialogues (iii 15). Martin
was reproved, however, by his own conscience, and by an angel, nor could he
afterwards perform miracles with so much ease,

who, on this occasion, asserted the cause of toleration. They
pitied the unhappy men, who had been executed at Treves;
they refused to hold communication with their episcopal
murderers; and, if Martin deviated from that generous resolution, his motives were laudable, and his repentance was exemplary. The bishops of Tours and Milan pronounced, without
hesitation, the eternal damnation of heretics; but they were
surprised, and shocked, by the bloody image of their temporal
death, and the honest feelings of nature resisted the artificial
prejudices of theology. The humanity of Ambrose and Martin
was confirmed by the scandalous irregularity of the proceedings
against Priscillian and his adherents. The civil and ecclesiastical
ministers had transgressed the limits of their respective provinces. The secular judge had presumed to receive an appeal,
and to pronounce a definitive sentence, in a matter of faith and
episcopal jurisdiction. The bishops had disgraced themselves
by exercising the function of accusers in a criminal prosecution.
The cruelty of Ithacius,[60] who beheld the tortures, and solicited
the death, of the heretics, provoked the just indignation of
mankind; and the vices of that profligate bishop were admitted
as a proof that his zeal was instigated by the sordid motives of
interest. Since the death of Priscillian, the rude attempts of
persecution have been refined and methodized in the holy
office, which assigns their distinct parts to the ecclesiastical and
secular powers. The devoted victim is regularly delivered by
the priest to the magistrate, and by the magistrate to the
executioner; and the inexorable sentence of the church, which
declares the spiritual guilt of the offender, is expressed in the
mild language of pity and intercession.

Among the ecclesiastics, who illustrated the reign of Theo- Ambrose,
dosius, Gregory Nazianzen was distinguished by the talents of archbishop
of Milan
an eloquent preacher; the reputation of miraculous gifts added A D 374 397
weight and dignity to the monastic virtues of Martin of Tours;[61]
but the palm of episcopal vigour and ability was justly claimed
by the intrepid Ambrose.[62] He was descended from a noble

---

[60] The Catholic Presbyter (Sulp Sever l. ii p. 448 [c. 50]) and the Pagan
Orator (Pacat in Panegyr Vet xii. 29) reprobate, with equal indignation, the
character and conduct of Ithacius.

[61] The life of St Martin, and the Dialogues concerning his miracles, contain
facts adapted to the grossest barbarism, in a style not unworthy of the Augustan
age. So natural is the alliance between good taste and good sense that I am
always astonished by this contrast

[62] The short and superficial life of St Ambrose by his deacon Paulinus
(Appendix ad edit Benedict p. i-xv) has the merit of original evidence Tillemont
(Mém. Ecclés tom. x. p 78-306) and the Benedictine editors (p. xxxi-lxiii) have
laboured with their usual diligence,

family of Romans; his father had exercised the important office
of Prætorian præfect of Gaul; and the son, after passing through
[born c 340] the studies of a liberal education, attained, in the regular gradation of civil honours, the station of consular of Liguria, a province which included the Imperial residence of Milan. At the
age of thirty-four, and before he had received the sacrament of
baptism, Ambrose, to his own surprise, and to that of the world,
[A.D. 374] was suddenly transformed from a governor to an archbishop.
Without the least mixture, as it is said, of art or intrigue, the
whole body of the people unanimously saluted him with the
episcopal title; the concord and perseverance of their acclamations were ascribed to a præternatural impulse; and the
reluctant magistrate was compelled to undertake a spiritual
office, for which he was not prepared by the habits and occupations of his former life. But the active force of his genius soon
qualified him to exercise, with zeal and prudence, the duties of
his ecclesiastical jurisdiction; and, while he cheerfully renounced
the vain and splendid trappings of temporal greatness, he condescended, for the good of the church, to direct the conscience
of the emperors and to control the administration of the
empire. Gratian loved and revered him as a father; and the
[De Fide elaborate treatise on the faith of the Trinity was designed for
A D 378] the instruction of the young prince. After his tragic death,
at a time when the empress Justina trembled for her own safety
and for that of her son Valentinian, the archbishop of Milan was
dispatched, on two different embassies, to the court of Treves.
He exercised, with equal firmness and dexterity, the powers of
his spiritual and political characters; and perhaps contributed,
by his authority and eloquence, to check the ambition of Maximus and to protect the peace of Italy.[63] Ambrose had devoted
his life and his abilities to the service of the church. Wealth
was the object of his contempt; he had renounced his private
patrimony, and he sold, without hesitation, the consecrated
plate for the redemption of captives The clergy and people of
Milan were attached to their archbishop; and he deserved the
esteem, without soliciting the favour or apprehending the displeasure, of his feeble sovereigns.

His successful   The government of Italy, and of the young emperor, naturally
opposition to
the   empress devolved to his mother Justina, a woman of beauty and spirit,
Justina.
A D 385, but who, in the midst of an orthodox people, had the misfortune
April 3—
April 10

[63] Ambrose himself (tom II. epist xxiv p 888-891) gives the emperor a very
spirited account of his own embassy.

of professing the Arian heresy, which she endeavoured to instil
into the mind of her son.   Justina was persuaded that a Roman
emperor might claim, in his own dominions, the public exercise
of his religion; and she proposed to the archbishop, as a
moderate and reasonable concession, that he should resign the
use of a single church, either in the city or suburbs of Milan
But the conduct of Ambrose was governed by very different
principles.[64]   The palaces of the earth might indeed belong to
Cæsar; but the churches were the houses of God; and, within
the limits of his diocese, he himself, as the lawful successor of
the apostles, was the only minister of God.   The privileges of
Christianity, temporal as well as spiritual, were confined to the
true believers; and the mind of Ambrose was satisfied that his
own theological opinions were the standard of truth and orthodoxy.   The archbishop, who refused to hold any conference or
negotiation with the instruments of Satan, declared, with
modest firmness, his resolution to die a martyr rather than to
yield to the impious sacrilege; and Justina, who resented the
refusal as an act of insolence and rebellion, hastily determined
to exert the Imperial prerogative of her son.   As she desired to
perform her public devotions on the approaching festival of
Easter, Ambrose was ordered to appear before the council.   He
obeyed the summons with the respect of a faithful subject, but
he was followed, without his consent, by an innumerable people:
they pressed, with impetuous zeal, against the gates of the
palace; and the affrighted ministers of Valentinian, instead of
pronouncing a sentence of exile on the archbishop of Milan,
humbly requested that he would interpose his authority, to protect the person of the emperor and to restore the tranquillity
of the capital.   But the promises which Ambrose received and
communicated were soon violated by a perfidious court, and
during six of the most solemn days which Christian piety has
set apart for the exercise of religion the city was agitated by the
irregular convulsions of tumult and fanaticism.   The officers of
the household were directed to prepare, first the Porcian, and
afterwards, the new *Basilica*, for the immediate reception of the
emperor and his mother.   The splendid canopy and hangings of
the royal seat were arranged in the customary manner; but it
was found necessary to defend them, by a strong guard, from

[64] His own representation of his principles and conduct (tom ii. epist xx. xxi.
xxii p 852-880) is one of the curious monuments of ecclesiastical antiquity.   It
contains two letters to his sister Marcellina, with a petition of Valentinian, and the
sermon *de Basilicis non tradendis*

the insults of the populace. The Arian ecclesiastics who ventured to shew themselves in the streets were exposed to the most imminent danger of their lives; and Ambrose enjoyed the merit and reputation of rescuing his personal enemies from the hands of the enraged multitude.

But, while he laboured to restrain the effects of their zeal, the pathetic vehemence of his sermons continually inflamed the angry and seditious temper of the people of Milan. The characters of Eve, of the wife of Job, of Jezebel, of Herodias, were indecently applied to the mother of the emperor; and her desire to obtain a church for the Arians was compared to the most cruel persecutions which Christianity had endured under the reign of Paganism. The measures of the court served only to expose the magnitude of the evil. A fine of two hundred pounds of gold was imposed on the corporate body of merchants and manufacturers: an order was signified, in the name of the emperor, to all the officers, and inferior servants, of the courts of justice, that, during the continuance of the public disorders, they should strictly confine themselves to their houses. and the ministers of Valentinian imprudently confessed that the most respectable part of the citizens of Milan was attached to the cause of their archbishop. He was again solicited to restore peace to his country, by a timely compliance with the will of his sovereign The reply of Ambrose was couched in the most humble and respectful terms, which might, however, be interpreted as a serious declaration of civil war. "His life and fortune were in the hands of the emperor; but he would never betray the church of Christ or degrade the dignity of the episcopal character. In such a cause, he was prepared to suffer whatever the malice of the dæmon could inflict; and he only wished to die in the presence of his faithful flock, and at the foot of the altar; *he* had not contributed to excite, but it was in the power of God alone to appease, the rage of the people: he deprecated the scenes of blood and confusion which were likely to ensue; and it was his fervent prayer that he might not survive to behold the ruin of a flourishing city and perhaps the desolation of all Italy." [65] The obstinate bigotry of Justina would have endangered the

---

[65] Retz had a similar message from the queen, to request that he would appease the tumult of Paris. It was no longer in his power, &c A quoi j'ajoutai tout ce que vous pouvez vous imaginer de respect, de douleur, de regret, et de soumission, &c (Mémoires, tom 1 p. 140) Certainly I do not compare either the causes or the men ; yet the coadjutor himself had some idea (p. 84) of imitating St Ambrose.

empire of her son, if, in this contest with the church and
people of Milan, she could have depended on the active
obedience of the troops of the palace. A large body of Goths
had marched to occupy the *Basilica* which was the object of
the dispute: and it might be expected from the Arian
principles and barbarous manners of these foreign mercenaries
that they would not entertain any scruples in the execution
of the most sanguinary orders. They were encountered, on
the sacred threshold, by the archbishop, who, thundering
against them a sentence of excommunication, asked them, in
the tone of a father and a master, Whether it was to invade
the house of God that they had implored the hospitable protection of the republic?   The suspense of the Barbarians
allowed some hours for a more effectual negotiation; and the
empress was persuaded, by the advice of her wisest counsellors,
to leave the Catholics in possession of all the churches of Milan;
and to dissemble, till a more convenient season, her intentions
of revenge.   The mother of Valentinian could never forgive
the triumph of Ambrose; and the royal youth uttered a
passionate exclamation that his own servants were ready to
betray him into the hands of an insolent priest.

The laws of the empire, some of which were inscribed with A.D 386
the name of Valentinian, still condemned the Arian heresy,
and seemed to excuse the resistance of the Catholics.   By the
influence of Justina an edict of toleration was promulgated
in all the provinces which were subject to the court of Milan;
the free exercise of their religion was granted to those who
professed the faith of Rimini; and the emperor declared that
all persons who should infringe this sacred and salutary constitution should be capitally punished as the enemies of the
public peace.[66] The character and language of the archbishop
of Milan may justify the suspicion that his conduct soon afforded
a reasonable ground, or at least a specious pretence, to the
Arian ministers, who watched the opportunity of surprising
him in some act of disobedience to a law which he strangely
represents as a law of blood and tyranny. A sentence of
easy and honourable banishment was pronounced, which enjoined Ambrose to depart from Milan without delay; whilst
it permitted him to choose the place of his exile and the number
of his companions. But the authority of the saints who have

---

[66] Sozomen alone (l. vii c. 13) throws this luminous fact into a dark and
perplexed narrative.

preached and practised the maxims of passive loyalty appeared to Ambrose of less moment than the extreme and pressing danger of the church. He boldly refused to obey; and his refusal was supported by the unanimous consent of his faithful people.[67] They guarded by turns the person of their archbishop; the gates of the cathedral and the episcopal palace were strongly secured; and the Imperial troops, who had formed the blockade, were unwilling to risk the attack, of that impregnable fortress. The numerous poor, who had been relieved by the liberality of Ambrose, embraced the fair occasion of signalizing their zeal and gratitude; and, as the patience of the multitude might have been exhausted by the length and uniformity of nocturnal vigils, he prudently introduced into the church of Milan the useful institution of a loud and regular psalmody. While he maintained this arduous contest, he was instructed by a dream to open the earth in a place where the remains of two martyrs, Gervasius and Protasius,[68] had been deposited above three hundred years. Immediately under the pavement of the church two perfect skeletons were found,[69] with the heads separated from their bodies, and a plentiful effusion of blood. The holy relics were presented, in solemn pomp, to the veneration of the people; and every circumstance of this fortunate discovery was admirably adapted to promote the designs of Ambrose. The bones of the martyrs, their blood, their garments, were supposed to contain a healing power; and their præternatural influence was communicated to the most distant objects, without losing any part of its original virtue. The extraordinary cure of a blind man,[70] and the

[67] Excubabat pia plebs in ecclesiâ mori parata cum episcopo suo . Nos adhuc frigidi excitabamur tamen civitate attonitâ atque turbatâ. Angustin Confession l ix c 7

[68] Tillemont, Mém Ecclés tom ii p 78 498 Many churches in Italy, Gaul, &c , were dedicated to these unknown martyrs, of whom St Gervase seems to have been more fortunate than his companion

[69] Invenimus miræ magnitudinis viros duos, ut prisca ætas ferebat Tom. ii. epist xxii p 875 [Mr Hodgkin, who discusses the discovery, seems disposed to entertain the idea that Ambrose may have practised a pious fraud ; i 440.] The size of these skeletons was fortunately, or skilfully, suited to the popular prejudice of the gradual increase of the human stature , which has prevailed in every age since the time of Homer
Grandiaque effossis mirabitur ossa sepulchris

[70] Ambros tom ii epist. xxii p 875 Augustin Confes. l ix. c 7, de Civitat Dei, l. xxii c 8 Paulin in Vitâ St Ambros c 14, in Append Benedict. p 4. The blind man's name was Severus , he touched the holy garment, recovered his sight, and devoted the rest of his life (at least twenty-five years) to the service of the church I should recommend this miracle to our divines if it did not prove the worship of relics, as well as the Nicene creed.

reluctant confessions of several dæmoniacs, appeared to justify
the faith and sanctity of Ambrose; and the truth of those
miracles is attested by Ambrose himself, by his secretary
Paulinus, and by his proselyte, the celebrated Augustin, who,
at that time, professed the art of rhetoric in Milan.   The
reason of the present age may possibly approve the incredulity
of Justina and her Arian court; who derided the theatrical
representations which were exhibited by the contrivance, and
at the expense, of the archbishop.[71]   Their effect, however,
on the minds of the people was rapid and irresistible; and
the feeble sovereign of Italy found himself unable to contend
with the favourite of heaven.   The powers likewise of the
earth interposed in the defence of Ambrose; the disinterested
advice of Theodosius was the general result of piety and
friendship; and the mask of religious zeal concealed the
hostile and ambitious designs of the tyrant of Gaul [72]

The reign of Maximus might have ended in peace and Maximus invades Italy
prosperity, could he have contented himself with the possession A.D. 387, August
of three ample countries, which now constitute the three most
flourishing kingdoms of modern Europe.   But the aspiring
usurper, whose sordid ambition was not dignified by the love
of glory and of arms, considered his actual forces as the instruments only of his future greatness, and his success was the
immediate cause of his destruction   The wealth which he
extorted [73] from the oppressed provinces of Gaul, Spain, and
Britain was employed in levying and maintaining a formidable
army of Barbarians, collected, for the most part, from the
fiercest nations of Germany.   The conquest of Italy was the
object of his hopes and preparations; and he secretly meditated
the ruin of an innocent youth, whose government was abhorred
and despised by his Catholic subjects.   But, as Maximus wished
to occupy, without resistance, the passes of the Alps, he
received, with perfidious smiles, Domninus of Syria, the ambassador of Valentinian, and pressed him to accept the aid of a
considerable body of troops for the service of a Pannonian
war.   The penetration of Ambrose had discovered the snares

---

[71] Paulin in Vit St Ambros c 5 [15], in Append Benedict p 5

[72] Tillemont, Mém Ecclés tom x. p 190, 750   He partially allows the
mediation of Theodosius, and capriciously rejects that of Maximus, though it is
attested by Prosper [not the true Prosper, but Chron Gall. ap Mommsen, Chron.
Min 1 p 648; cp Rufin, 11. 16], Sozomen, and Theodoret.

[73] The modest censure of Sulpicius (Dialog III. 15) inflicts a much deeper wound
than the feeble declamation of Pacatus (xii 25, 26)

of an enemy under the professions of friendship;[74] but the Syrian Domninus was corrupted, or deceived, by the liberal favour of the court of Treves ; and the council of Milan obstinately rejected the suspicion of danger, with a blind confidence which was the effect, not of courage, but of fear. The march of the auxiliaries was guided by the ambassador; and they were admitted, without distrust, into the fortresses of the Alps   But the crafty tyrant followed, with hasty and silent footsteps, in the rear; and, as he diligently intercepted all intelligence of his motions, the gleam of armour and the dust excited by the troops of cavalry first announced the hostile approach of a stranger to the gates of Milan.   In this extremity, Justina and her son might accuse their own imprudence and the perfidious arts of Maximus; but they wanted time, and force and resolution to stand against the Gauls and Germans, either in the field or within the walls of a large and disaffected city.   Flight was their only hope, Aquileia their only refuge; and, as Maximus now displayed his genuine character, the brother of Gratian might expect the same fate from the hands of the same assassin.   Maximus entered Milan in triumph ; and, if the wise archbishop refused a dangerous and criminal connexion with the usurper, he might indirectly contribute to the success of his arms by inculcating, from the pulpit, the duty of resignation rather than that of resistance.[75]   The unfortunate Justina reached Aquileia in safety; but she distrusted the strength of the fortifications; she dreaded the event of a siege ; and she resolved to implore the protection of the great Theodosius, whose power and virtue were celebrated in all the countries of the West.   A vessel was secretly provided to transport the Imperial family; they embarked with precipitation in one of the obscure harbours of Venetia or Istria; traversed the whole extent of the Hadriatic and Ionian seas; turned the extreme promontory of Peloponnesus ; and, after a long but successful navigation, reposed themselves in the port

Flight of Valentinian of Thessalonica   All the subjects of Valentinian deserted the cause of a prince who, by his abdication, had absolved them **[Laibach]** from the duty of allegiance ; and, if the little city of Æmona, on the verge of Italy, had not presumed to stop the career of

---

[74] Esto tutior adversus hominem, pacis involucro tegentem, was the wise caution of Ambrose (tom ii. p. 891) after his return from his second embassy [A D 386-7]

[75] Baronius (A D 387, No 63) applies to this season of public distress some of the penitential sermons of the archbishop

his inglorious victory, Maximus would have obtained, without a struggle, the sole possession of the western empire

Instead of inviting his royal guests to the palace of Constantinople, Theodosius had some unknown reasons to fix their residence at Thessalonica; but these reasons did not proceed from contempt or indifference, as he speedily made a visit to that city, accompanied by the greatest part of his court and senate. After the first tender expressions of friendship and sympathy, the pious emperor of the East gently admonished Justina that the guilt of heresy was sometimes punished in this world as well as in the next; and that the public profession of the Nicene faith would be the most efficacious step to promote the restoration of her son, by the satisfaction which it must occasion both on earth and in heaven. The momentous question of peace or war was referred, by Theodosius, to the deliberation of his council; and the arguments which might be alleged on the side of honour and justice had acquired, since the death of Gratian, a considerable degree of additional weight. The persecution of the Imperial family, to which Theodosius himself had been indebted for his fortune, was now aggravated by recent and repeated injuries. Neither oaths nor treaties could restrain the boundless ambition of Maximus; and the delay of vigorous and decisive measures, instead of prolonging the blessings of peace, would expose the eastern empire to the danger of an hostile invasion. The Barbarians, who had passed the Danube, had lately assumed the character of soldiers and subjects, but their native fierceness was yet untamed; and the operations of a war which would exercise their valour and diminish their numbers might tend to relieve the provinces from an intolerable oppression. Notwithstanding these specious and solid reasons, which were approved by a majority of the council, Theodosius still hesitated whether he should draw the sword in a contest which could no longer admit any terms of reconciliation; and his magnanimous character was not disgraced by the apprehensions which he felt for the safety of his infant sons and the welfare of his exhausted people. In this moment of anxious doubt, while the fate of the Roman world depended on the resolution of a single man, the charms of the princess Galla most powerfully pleaded the cause of her brother Valentinian [76] The heart of Theodosius was softened

Theodosius takes arms in the cause of Valentinian A.D. 387

---

[76] The flight of Valentinian and the love of Theodosius for his sister are related by Zosimus (l. iv. p 263, 264 [c 43]). Tillemont produces some weak and

by the tears of beauty, his affections were insensibly engaged by the graces of youth and innocence ; the art of Justina managed and directed the impulse of passion ; and the celebration of the royal nuptials was the assurance and signal of the civil war. The unfeeling critics, who consider every amorous weakness as an indelible stain on the memory of a great and orthodox emperor, are inclined, on this occasion, to dispute the suspicious evidence of the historian Zosimus. For my own part, I shall frankly confess that I am willing to find, or even to seek, in the revolutions of the world some traces of the mild and tender sentiments of domestic life ; and, amidst the crowd of fierce and ambitious conquerors, I can distinguish, with peculiar complacency, a gentle hero, who may be supposed to receive his armour from the hands of love. The alliance of the Persian king was secured by the faith of treaties ; the martial Barbarians were persuaded to follow the standard, or to respect the frontiers, of an active and liberal monarch ; and the dominions of Theodosius, from the Euphrates to the Hadriatic, resounded with the preparations of war both by land and sea The skilful disposition of the forces of the East seemed to multiply their numbers, and distracted the attention of Maximus He had reason to fear that a chosen body of troops, under the command of the intrepid Arbogastes, would direct their march along the banks of the Danube and boldly penetrate through the Rhætian provinces into the centre of Gaul. A powerful fleet was equipped in the harbours of Greece and Epirus, with an apparent design that, as soon as a passage had been opened by a naval victory, Valentinian and his mother should land in Italy, proceed, without delay, to Rome, and occupy the majestic seat of religion and empire. In the meanwhile, Theodosius himself advanced at the head of a brave and disciplined army, to encounter his unworthy rival, who, after the siege of Æmona, had fixed his camp in the neighbourhood of Siscia, a city of Pannonia, strongly fortified by the broad and rapid stream of the Save.

Defeat and death of Maximus A.D 388, June August
The veterans, who still remembered the long resistance and successive resources of the tyrant Magnentius, might prepare themselves for the labours of three bloody campaigns. But the contest with his successor, who, like him, had usurped the throne of the West, was easily decided in the term of two

ambiguous evidence to antedate the second marriage of Theodosius (Hist. des Empereurs, tom v p. 740), and consequently to refute ces contes de Zosime, qui seroient trop contraires à la piété de Théodose.

months [77] and within the space of two hundred miles. The superior genius of the emperor of the East might prevail over the feeble Maximus; who, in this important crisis, shewed himself destitute of military skill or personal courage; but the abilities of Theodosius were seconded by the advantage which he possessed of a numerous and active cavalry. The Huns, the Alani, and, after their example, the Goths themselves, were formed into squadrons of archers; who fought on horseback and confounded the steady valour of the Gauls and Germans by the rapid motions of a Tartar war. After the fatigue of a long march, in the heat of summer, they spurred their foaming horses into the waters of the Save, swam the river in the presence of the enemy, and instantly charged and routed the troops who guarded the high ground on the opposite side. Marcellinus, the tyrant's brother, advanced to support them with the select cohorts which were considered as the hope and strength of the army. The action, which had been interrupted by the approach of night, was renewed in the morning; and, after a sharp conflict, the surviving remnant of the bravest soldiers of Maximus threw down their arms at the feet of the conqueror. Without suspending his march to receive the loyal acclamations of the citizens of Æmona, Theodosius pressed forwards, to terminate the war by the death or captivity of his rival, who fled before him with the diligence of fear. From the summit of the Julian Alps, he descended with such incredible speed into the plain of Italy that he reached Aquileia on the evening of the first day; and Maximus, who found himself encompassed on all sides, had scarcely time to shut the gates of the city. But the gates could not long resist the effort of a victorious enemy; and the despair, the disaffection, the indifference of the soldiers and people, hastened the downfall of the wretched Maximus. He was dragged from his throne, rudely stripped of the Imperial ornaments, the robe, the diadem, and the purple slippers; and conducted, like a malefactor, to the camp and presence of Theodosius, at a place about three miles from Aquileia. The behaviour of the emperor was not intended to insult, and he shewed some disposition to pity and forgive, the tyrant of the West, who had never been his personal enemy and was now become the object of his contempt. Our sympathy is the most forcibly excited by the misfortunes to which we are exposed; and the spectacle of a proud competitor, now prostrate

[77] See Godefroy's Chronology of the Laws, Cod Theodos tom 1 p 119.

at his feet, could not fail of producing very serious and solemn thoughts in the mind of the victorious emperor.   But the feeble emotion of involuntary pity was checked by his regard for

public justice and the memory of Gratian; and he abandoned the victim to the pious zeal of the soldiers, who drew him out of the Imperial presence and instantly separated his head from his body.   The intelligence of his defeat and death was received with sincere, or well-dissembled, joy. his son Victor, on whom he had conferred the title of Augustus, died by the order, perhaps by the hand, of the bold Arbogastes; and all the military plans of Theodosius were successfully executed.   When he had thus terminated the civil war with less difficulty and bloodshed than he might naturally expect, he employed the winter months of his residence at Milan to restore the state of

the afflicted provinces; and early in the spring he made, after the example of Constantine and Constantius, his triumphal entry into the ancient capital of the Roman empire.[78]

The orator, who may be silent without danger, may praise without difficulty and without reluctance;[79] and posterity will confess that the character of Theodosius[80] might furnish the subject of a sincere and ample panegyric.   The wisdom of his laws, and the success of his arms, rendered his administration respectable in the eyes both of his subjects and of his enemies. He loved and practised the virtues of domestic life, which seldom hold their residence in the palaces of kings.   Theodosius was chaste and temperate; he enjoyed, without excess, the sensual and social pleasures of the table; and the warmth of his amorous passions was never diverted from their lawful objects. The proud titles of Imperial greatness were adorned by the tender names of a faithful husband, an indulgent father; his

[78] Besides the hints which may be gathered from chronicles and ecclesiastical history, Zos (l iv p 259-267 [c. 44-47]), Oros (l vii c 35) and Pacatus (in Pan Vet xii 30-47) supply the loose and scanty materials of this civil war Ambrose (tom ii epist. xl p 952, 953) darkly alludes to the well-known events of a magazine surprised, an action at Pœtovio, a Sicilian, perhaps a naval, victory, &c. Ausonius (p 256, edit Toll [Ord Urb Nob 66 *sqq*]) applauds the peculiar merit, and good fortune, of Aquileia   [For the son of Maximus, Flavius Victor, see C I L 5, 8032 and Eckhel, 8, 66   The victory *in Sicilia* must have been on sea, over the fleet of Andragathius , cp Oros *loc. cit*]

[79] Quam promptum laudare principem, tam tutum silu sse de principe (Pacat. in Pan Vet. xii 2)   Latinus Pacatus Drepanius, a native of Gaul, pronounced this oration at Rome (A.D. 388)   He was afterwards proconsul of Africa ; and his friend Ausonius praises him as a poet, second only to Virgil   See Tille-mont, Hist des Emper tom v. p 303.

[80] See the fair portrait of Theodosius by the younger Victor , the strokes are distinct, and the colours are mixed   The praise of Pacatus is too vague. and Claudian always seems afraid of exalting the father above the son

uncle was raised, by his affectionate esteem, to the rank of a second parent; Theodosius embraced, as his own, the children of his brother and sister; and the expressions of his regard were extended to the most distant and obscure branches of his numerous kindred. His familiar friends were judiciously selected from among those persons who, in the equal intercourse of private life, had appeared before his eyes without a mask; the consciousness of personal and superior merit enabled him to despise the accidental distinction of the purple; and he proved by his conduct that he had forgotten all the injuries, while he most gratefully remembered all the favours and services, which he had received before he ascended the throne of the Roman empire. The serious, or lively, tone of his conversation was adapted to the age, the rank, or the character, of his subjects whom he admitted into his society; and the affability of his manners displayed the image of his mind. Theodosius respected the simplicity of the good and virtuous; every art, every talent, of an useful, or even of an innocent, nature was rewarded by his judicious liberality; and, except the heretics whom he persecuted with implacable hatred, the diffusive circle of his benevolence was circumscribed only by the limits of the human race. The government of a mighty empire may assuredly suffice to occupy the time and the abilities of a mortal; yet the diligent prince, without aspiring to the unsuitable reputation of profound learning, always reserved some moments of his leisure for the instructive amusement of reading. History, which enlarged his experience, was his favourite study. The annals of Rome, in the long period of eleven hundred years, presented him with a various and splendid picture of human life; and it has been particularly observed that, whenever he perused the cruel acts of Cinna, of Marius, or of Sylla, he warmly expressed his generous detestation of those enemies of humanity and freedom. His disinterested opinion of past events was usefully applied as the rule of his own actions; and Theodosius has deserved the singular commendation that his virtues always seemed to expand with his fortune; the season of his prosperity was that of his moderation; and his clemency appeared the most conspicuous after the danger and success of the civil war. The Moorish guards of the tyrant had been massacred in the first heat of the victory; and a small number of the most obnoxious criminals suffered the punishment of the law. But the emperor shewed himself much more attentive to relieve the innocent than to chastise the guilty. The oppressed subjects of the West, who would have deemed themselves happy in the restoration of their lands, were astonished to receive a sum of money equivalent to their losses; and the liberality of the conqueror supported the aged mother, and educated the orphan daughters, of Maximus.[81] A character thus accomplished might almost excuse the extravagant supposition of the orator Pacatus, that, if the elder Brutus could be permitted to revisit the earth, the stern republican would abjure, at the feet of Theodosius, his hatred of kings; and ingenuously confess that such a monarch was the most faithful guardian of the happiness and dignity of the Roman people.[82]

Faults of Theodosius

Yet the piercing eye of the founder of the republic must have discerned two essential imperfections, which might, perhaps, have abated his recent love of despotism. The virtuous mind of Theodosius was often relaxed by indolence,[83] and it was sometimes inflamed by passion.[84] In the pursuit of an important object, his active courage was capable of the most vigorous exertions; but, as soon as the design was accomplished or the danger was surmounted, the hero sunk into inglorious repose; and, forgetful that the time of a prince is the property of his people, resigned himself to the enjoyment of the innocent, but trifling, pleasures of a luxurious court. The natural disposition of Theodosius was hasty and choleric; and, in a station where none could resist and few would dissuade the fatal consequence of his resentment, the humane monarch was justly alarmed by the consciousness of his infirmity, and of his power. It was the constant study of his life to suppress or regulate the intemperate sallies of passion; and the success of his efforts enhanced the merit of his clemency. But the painful virtue which claims the merit of victory is exposed to the danger of defeat; and the reign of a wise and merciful prince was polluted by an act of cruelty which would stain the annals of Nero or Domitian. Within the space of three years, the inconsistent historian of Theodosius must relate the generous pardon of the citizens of

[81] Ambros tom ii epist xl. p 955. [The interpretation of this passage is not certain. The daughters of an *inimicus* and the mother of a *hostis* are mentioned Are the *hostis* and *inimicus* the same, viz , Maximus?] Pacatus, from the want of skill, or of courage, omits this glorious circumstance.

[82] Pacat in Panegyr. Vet. vii 20.

[83] Zosimus, l iv p 271, 272 [c 50]. His partial evidence is marked by an air of candour and truth. He observes these vicissitudes of sloth and activity, not as a vice, but as a singularity, in the character of Theodosius.

[84] This choleric temper is acknowledged, and excused, by Victor [Epit 48]. Sed habes (says Ambrose, in decent and manly language, to his sovereign) naturæ impetum, quem si quis lenire velit, cito vertes ad misericordiam : si quis stimulet, in magis exsuscitas, ut eum revocare vix possis (tom ii. epist ii p 998) Theod. (Claud in iv. Cons Hon. 266, &c) exhorts his son to moderate his anger.

Antioch and the inhuman massacre of the people of Thessalonica.

The lively impatience of the inhabitants of Antioch was never The sedition of Antioch. satisfied with their own situation, or with the character or con- A.D. 387 duct of their successive sovereigns. The Arian subjects of Theodosius deplored the loss of their churches ; and, as three rival bishops disputed the throne of Antioch, the sentence which decided their pretensions excited the murmurs of the two unsuccessful congregations. The exigencies of the Gothic war, and the inevitable expense that accompanied the conclusion of the peace, had constrained the emperor to aggravate the weight of the public impositions ; and the provinces of Asia, as they had not been involved in the distress, were the less inclined to contribute to the relief, of Europe. The auspicious period now approached of the tenth year of his reign ; a festival more grateful to the soldiers, who received a liberal donative, than to the subjects, whose voluntary offerings had been long since converted into an extraordinary and oppressive burthen. The edicts of taxation interrupted the repose and pleasures of Antioch ; and the tribunal of the magistrate was besieged by a suppliant crowd ; who, in pathetic, but, at first, in respectful language, solicited the redress of their grievances. They were gradually incensed by the pride of their haughty rulers, who treated their complaints as a criminal resistance ; their satirical wit degenerated into sharp and angry invectives ; and, from the subordinate powers of government, the invectives of the people insensibly rose to attack the sacred character of the emperor himself. Their fury, provoked by a feeble opposition, discharged Feb 26 [March 4] itself on the images of the Imperial family, which were erected as objects of public veneration in the most conspicuous places of the city. The statues of Theodosius, of his father, of his wife Flaccilla, of his two sons, Arcadius and Honorius, were insolently thrown down from their pedestals, broken in pieces, or dragged with contempt through the streets ; and the indignities which were offered to the representations of Imperial majesty, sufficiently declared the impious and treasonable wishes of the populace. The tumult was almost immediately suppressed by the arrival of a body of archers ; and Antioch had leisure to reflect on the nature and consequences of her crime.[85] According

---

[85] The Christians and Pagans agreed in believing that the sedition of Antioch was excited by the dæmons A gigantic woman (says Sozomen, l vii c 23) paraded the streets with a scourge in her hand An old man (says Libanius, Orat xii p. 396 [or xix in Reiske's ed., vol. 7, p. 626 *seq.*]) transformed himself into a youth, then a boy, &c.

to the duty of his office, the governor of the province dispatched a faithful narrative of the whole transaction, while the trembling citizens intrusted the confession of their crime, and the assurance of their repentance, to the zeal of Flavian their bishop and to the eloquence of the senator Hilarius, the friend, and most probably the disciple, of Libanius, whose genius, on this melancholy occasion, was not useless to his country.[86]   But the two capitals, Antioch and Constantinople, were separated by the distance of eight hundred miles; and, notwithstanding the diligence of the Imperial posts, the guilty city was severely punished by a long and dreadful interval of suspense.   Every rumour agitated the hopes and fears of the Antiochians, and they heard with terror that their sovereign, exasperated by the insult which had been offered to his own statues, and, more especially, to those of his beloved wife, had resolved to level with the ground the offending city; and to massacre, without distinction of age or sex, the criminal inhabitants;[87] many of whom were actually driven by their apprehensions to seek a refuge in the mountains of Syria and the adjacent desert.   At

March 22length, twenty-four days after the sedition, the general Hellebicus and Cæsarius, master of the offices, declared the will of

[arrive March 29]the emperor and the sentence of Antioch.   That proud capital was degraded from the rank of a city; and the metropolis of the East, stripped of its lands, its privileges, and its revenues, was subjected, under the humiliating denomination of a village, to the jurisdiction of Laodicea.[88]   The baths, the circus, and the theatres were shut; and, that every source of plenty and pleasure might at the same time be intercepted, the distribution of corn was abolished by the severe instructions of Theodosius. His commissioners then proceeded to inquire into the guilt of individuals; of those who had perpetrated, and of those who had not prevented, the destruction of the sacred statues.   The tribunal of Hellebicus and Cæsarius, encompassed with armed soldiers, was erected in the midst of the Forum   The noblest and most wealthy of the citizens of Antioch appeared before

[86] Zosimus, in his short and disingenuous account (l. iv p 258, 259 [c 41]), is certainly mistaken in sending Libanius himself to Constantinople. His own orations fix him at Antioch

[87] Libanius (Orat i p 6, edit Venet) declares that, under such a reign, the fear of a massacre was groundless and absurd, especially in the emperor's absence, for his presence, according to the eloquent slave, might have given a sanction to the most bloody acts.

[88] Laodicea, on the sea coast, sixty-five miles from Antioch (see Noris, Epoch. Syro-Maced Dissert iii. p. 230).   The Antiochians were offended that the dependent city of Seleucia should presume to intercede for them

them in chains; the examination was assisted by the use of torture, and their sentence was pronounced or suspended, according to the judgment of these extraordinary magistrates. The houses of the criminals were exposed to sale, their wives and children were suddenly reduced, from affluence and luxury, to the most abject distress; and a bloody execution was expected to conclude the horrors of a day [89] which the preacher of Antioch, the eloquent Chrysostom, has represented as a lively image of the last and universal judgment of the world. But the ministers of Theodosius performed, with reluctance, the cruel task which had been assigned them; they dropped a gentle tear over the calamities of the people; and they listened with reverence to the pressing solicitations of the monks and hermits, who descended in swarms from the mountains.[90]   Hellebicus and Cæsarius were persuaded to suspend the execution of their sentence; and it was agreed [March 31] that the former should remain at Antioch, while the latter returned, with all possible speed, to Constantinople; and [C departs April 1] presumed once more to consult the will of his sovereign   The resentment of Theodosius had already subsided; the deputies [Clemency of Theodosius] of the people, both the bishop and the orator, had obtained a favourable audience; and the reproaches of the emperor were [C arrives at Cple. April 8 10] the complaints of injured friendship rather than the stern menaces of pride and power.   A free and general pardon was granted to the city and citizens of Antioch; the prison-doors [c April 17] were thrown open; the senators who despaired of their lives recovered the possession of their houses and estates; and the capital of the East was restored to the enjoyment of her ancient dignity and splendour.   Theodosius condescended to praise the senate of Constantinople, who had generously interceded for their distressed brethren; he rewarded the eloquence of Hilarius with the government of Palestine; and dismissed the bishop of Antioch with the warmest expressions of his respect and gratitude.   A thousand new statues arose to [April 25 [Easter the clemency of Theodosius; the applause of his subjects was Sunday] ratified by the approbation of his own heart; and the emperor

---

[89] As the days of the tumult depend on the *moveable* festival of Easter, they can only be determined by the previous determination of the year   The year 387 has been preferred, after a laborious inquiry, by Tillemont (Hist des Emp. tom v p. 741-744) and Montfaucon (Chrysostom, tom. xiii. p 105-110)   [So Guldenpenning and Ifland, but Baronius and Clinton give 388.   Cp Arnold Hug, Studien aus dem classischen Alterthum, p. 54]

[90] Chrysostom opposes *their* courage, which was not attended with much risk, to the cowardly flight of the Cynics.

confessed that, if the exercise of justice is the most important duty, the indulgence of mercy is the most exquisite pleasure, of a sovereign.[91]

Sedition and massacre of Thessalonica. A.D 390 The sedition of Thessalonica is ascribed to a more shameful cause,[91a] and was productive of much more dreadful consequences. That great city, the metropolis of all the Illyrian provinces, had been protected from the dangers of the Gothic war by strong fortifications and a numerous garrison. Botheric, the general of those troops, and, as it should seem from his name, a Barbarian, had among his slaves a beautiful boy, who excited the impure desires of one of the charioteers of the Circus. The insolent and brutal lover was thrown into prison by the order of Botheric; and he sternly rejected the importunate clamours of the multitude, who, on the day of the public games, lamented the absence of their favourite, and considered the skill of a charioteer as an object of more importance than his virtue. The resentment of the people was embittered by some previous disputes; and, as the strength of the garrison had been drawn away for the service of the Italian war, the feeble remnant, whose numbers were reduced by desertion, could not save the unhappy general from their licentious fury. Botheric, and several of his principal officers, were inhumanly murdered; their mangled bodies were dragged about the streets; and the emperor, who then resided at Milan, was surprised by the intelligence of the audacious and wanton cruelty of the people of Thessalonica. The sentence of a dispassionate judge would have inflicted a severe punishment on the authors of the crime; and the merit of Botheric might contribute to exasperate the grief and indignation of his master. The fiery and choleric temper of Theodosius was impatient of the dilatory forms of a judicial enquiry; and he hastily resolved that the blood of his lieutenant should be expiated by the blood of the guilty people. Yet his mind still fluctuated between the counsels of clemency and of revenge; the zeal of the bishops had almost extorted from the reluctant emperor the promise of a general

[91] The sedition of Antioch is represented in a lively, and almost dramatic, manner by two orators, who had their respective shares of interest and merit. See Libanius (Orat. xiv. xv [*leg.* xii. xiii.] p 389-420, edit Morel, Orat i p 1-14, Venet. 1754 and the twenty orations of St Chrysostom, *ai Statuts* (tom ii p 1-225, edit Montfaucon) I do not pretend to much personal acquaintance with Chrysostom; but Tillem. (Hist des Emper tom v p. 263 283) and Hermant (Vie de St. Chrysostome, tom. i. p 137-224) had read him with pious curiosity and diligence. [The dates which A. Hug (Antiochia und der Aufstand des Jahres 387 n. Chr.) has endeavoured to establish are added in the margin above]
[91a] ["Cause" in sense of occasion But the true cause was discontent at the practice of quartering barbarian soldiers in Antioch. Cp. John Malalas, p. 347]

pardon; his passion was again inflamed by the flattering suggestions of his minister Rufinus; and, after Theodosius had despatched the messengers of death, he attempted, when it was too late, to prevent the execution of his orders. The punishment of a Roman city was blindly committed to the undistinguishing sword of the Barbarians; and the hostile preparations were concerted with the dark and perfidious artifice of an illegal conspiracy. The people of Thessalonica were treacherously invited, in the name of their sovereign, to the games of the Circus; and such was their insatiate avidity for those amusements that every consideration of fear, or suspicion, was disregarded by the numerous spectators. As soon as the assembly was complete, the soldiers, who had secretly been [April] posted round the Circus, received the signal, not of the races, but of a general massacre. The promiscuous carnage continued three hours, without discrimination of strangers or natives, of age or sex, of innocence or guilt; the most moderate accounts state the number of the slain at seven thousand;[92] and it is affirmed by some writers, that more than fifteen thousand victims were sacrificed to the manes of Botheric A foreign merchant, who had probably no concern in his murder, offered his own life and all his wealth, to supply the place of *one* of his two sons; but, while the father hesitated with equal tenderness, while he was doubtful to choose and unwilling to condemn, the soldiers determined his suspense by plunging their daggers at the same moment into the breasts of the defenceless youths. The apology of the assassins that they were obliged to produce the prescribed number of heads serves only to increase, by an appearance of order and design, the horrors of the massacre which was executed by the commands of Theodosius. The guilt of the emperor is aggravated by his long and frequent residence at Thessalonica. The situation of the unfortunate city, the aspect of the streets and buildings, the dress and faces of the inhabitants, were familiar and even present to his imagination; and Theodosius possessed a quick and lively sense of the existence of the people whom he destroyed.[93]

[92] [Theodoret, v 17, on the authority of Philostorgius?]
[93] The original evidence of Ambrose (tom. ii. epist. li. p 998), Augustin (de Civitat. Dei, v. 26), and Paulinus (in Vit. Ambros. c. 24) is delivered in vague expressions of horror and pity It is illustrated by the subsequent and unequal testimonies of Sozomen (l. vii. c. 25), Theodoret (l. v. c. 17), Theophanes (Chronograph p 62), Cedrenus (p. 317 [p 556, ed Bonn]), and Zonaras (tom. ii. l. xiii. p 34 [c 18]) Zosimus *alone*, the partial enemy of Theodosius, most unaccountably passes over in silence the worst of his actions. [Further, Rufinus, ii. 18; Moses Choren. iii. 37; and Malalas, p. 347.]

Influence and
conduct of
Ambrose
A D 388 The respectful attachment of the emperor for the orthodox clergy had disposed him to love and admire the character of Ambrose; who united all the episcopal virtues in the most eminent degree. The friends and ministers of Theodosius imitated the example of their sovereign; and he observed, with more surprise than displeasure, that all his secret counsels were immediately communicated to the archbishop, who acted from the laudable persuasion that every measure of civil government may have some connexion with the glory of God and the interest of the true religion. The monks and populace of [Aug 1,
A D 388] Callinicum, an obscure town on the frontier of Persia, excited by their own fanaticism and by that of their bishop, had tumult-uously burnt a conventicle of the Valentinians and a synagogue of the Jews. The seditious prelate was condemned by the magistrate of the province either to rebuild the synagogue or to repay the damage, and this moderate sentence was confirmed by the emperor. But it was not confirmed by the archbishop of Milan.[94] He dictated an epistle of censure and reproach, more suitable, perhaps, if the emperor had received the mark of circumcision and renounced the faith of his baptism   Ambrose considers the toleration of the Jewish, as the persecution of the Christian, religion; boldly declares that he himself and every true believer would eagerly dispute with the bishop of Callini-cum the merit of the deed and the crown of martyrdom; and laments, in the most pathetic terms, that the execution of the sentence would be fatal to the fame and salvation of Theodo-sius.   As this private admonition did not produce an immediate effect, the archbishop, from his pulpit,[95] publicly addressed the emperor on his throne;[96] nor would he consent to offer the oblation of the altar, till he had obtained from Theodosius a solemn and positive declaration, which secured the impunity of the bishop and monks of Callinicum   The recantation of Theo-dosius was sincere;[97] and, during the term of his residence

[94] See the whole transaction in Ambrose (tom ii epist. xl xli p. 946-956) and his biographer Paulinus (c. 23).   Bayle and Barbeyrac (Morales des Pères, c xvii p 325, &c) have justly condemned the archbishop   [The sentence was that the bishop should rebuild the synagogue *and* pay the value of the destroyed treasures]

[95] His sermon is a strange allegory of Jeremiah's rod, of an almond-tree, of the woman who washed and anointed the feet of Christ   But the peroration is direct and personal

[96] Hodie, Episcope, de me proposuisti.   Ambrose modestly confessed it but he sternly reprimanded Timasius, general of the horse and foot, who had presumed to say that the monks of Callinicum deserved punishment.

[97] Yet, five years afterwards, when Theodosius was absent from his spiritual guide, he tolerated the Jews and condemned the destruction of their synagogue Cod Theodos. l. xvi tit viii leg. 9, with Godefroy's commentary, tom vi. p 225

at Milan, his affection for Ambrose was continually increased by the habits of pious and familiar conversation.

When Ambrose was informed of the massacre of Thessalonica,[97a] his mind was filled with horror and anguish. He retired into the country to indulge his grief, and to avoid the presence of Theodosius. But, as the archbishop was satisfied that a timid silence would render him the accomplice of his guilt, he represented, in a private letter, the enormity of the crime; which could only be effaced by the tears of penitence. The episcopal vigour of Ambrose was tempered by prudence; and he contented himself with signifying[98] an indirect sort of excommunication, by the assurance that he had been warned in a vision not to offer the oblation in the name or in the presence of Theodosius; and by the advice that he would confine himself to the use of prayer, without presuming to approach the altar of Christ or to receive the holy eucharist with those hands that were still polluted with the blood of an innocent people. The emperor was deeply affected by his own reproaches and by those of his spiritual father; and, after he had bewailed the mischievous and irreparable consequences of his rash fury, he proceeded, in the accustomed manner, to perform his devotions in the great church of Milan. He was stopped in the porch by the archbishop; who, in the tone and language of an ambassador of Heaven, declared to his sovereign that private contrition was not sufficient to atone for a public fault or to appease the justice of the offended Deity. Theodosius humbly represented that, if he had contracted the guilt of homicide, David, the man after God's own heart, had been guilty, not only of murder, but of adultery. " You have imitated David in his crime, imitate then his repentance," was the reply of the undaunted Ambrose. The rigorous conditions of peace and pardon were accepted; and the public penance of the emperor Theodosius has been recorded as one of the most honourable events in the annals of the church. According to the mildest rules of ecclesiastical discipline which were established in the fourth century the crime of homicide was expiated by the penitence of twenty years;[99] and, as it was

---

[97a] [A letter from the Bishop of Thessalonica, informing Ambrose, was published (from a Bodl cod.) by Gaisford in Theodoret, v. 18, genuineness uncertain.]

[98] Ambros. tom. ii epist li. p 997-1001. His Epistle is a miserable rhapsody on a noble subject. Ambrose could act better than he could write. His compositions are destitute of taste, or genius, without the spirit of Tertullian, the copious elegance of Lactantius, the lively wit of Jerom, or the grave energy of Augustin.

[99] According to the discipline of St Basil (Canon lvi) the voluntary homicide was *four* years a mourner; *five* an hearer; *seven* in a prostrate state, and *four* in

impossible, in the period of human life, to purge the accumulated guilt of the massacre of Thessalonica, the murderer
should have been excluded from the holy communion till the
hour of his death. But the archbishop, consulting the maxims
of religious policy, granted some indulgence to the rank of his
illustrious penitent, who humbled in the dust the pride of the
diadem ; and the public edification might be admitted as a
weighty reason to abridge the duration of his punishment. It
was sufficient that the emperor of the Romans, stripped of the
ensigns of royalty, should appear in a mournful and suppliant
postuie ; and that, in the midst of the church of Milan, he
should humbly solicit, with sighs and tears, the pardon of his
sins.[100] In this spiritual cure, Ambrose employed the various
methods of mildness and severity.   After a delay of about
eight months, Theodosius was restored to the communion of
the faithful; and the edict, which interposes a salutary interval
of thirty days between the sentence and the execution, may be
accepted as the worthy fiuits of his repentance.[101]   Posterity
has applauded the virtuous firmness of the archbishop; and the
example of Theodosius may prove the beneficial influence of
those principles which could force a monarch, exalted above
the apprehension of human punishment, to respect the laws,
and ministers, of an invisible Judge   "The prince," says
Montesquieu, "who is actuated by the hopes and fears of
religion, may be compared to a lion, docile only to the voice,
and tractable to the hand, of his keeper." [102]   The motions
of the royal animal will therefore depend on the inclination
and interest of the man who has acquired such dangerous
authority over him ; and the priest who holds in his hand the
conscience of a king may inflame or moderate his sanguinary
passions.   The cause of humanity, and that of persecution,
have been asserted by the same Ambrose, with equal energy
and with equal success.

a standing posture.   I have the original (Beveridge, Pandect. tom ii p 47-151)
and a translation (Chardon, Hist. des Sacremens, tom iv, p 219-277) of the
Canonical Epistles of St Basil.
   [100] The penance of Theodosius is authenticated by Ambrose (tom. vi de Obit.
Theodos c 34 p 1207), Augustin (de Civitat Dei, v 26), and Paulinus (in Vit.
Ambros c 24)   Socrates is ignorant , Sozomen (l vii. c 25) concise [but places it
after revolt of Eugenius] , and the copious narrative of Theodoret (L v c 18) must
be used with precaution
   [101] Codex Theodos l ix. tit xl leg. 13   The date and circumstances of this
law are perplexed with difficulties , but I feel myself inclined to favour the honest
efforts of Tillemont (Hist. des Emp tom. v. p 721) and Pagi (Critica, tom i. p
578).
   [102] Un prince qui aime la religion, et qui la craint, est un lion qui cède à la
main qui le flatte, ou à la voix qui l'appaise Esprit des Lois, l xxiv. c. 2.

After the defeat and death of the tyrant of Gaul, the Roman Generosity of Theodosius world was in the possession of Theodosius. He derived from A D 388-391 the choice of Gratian his honourable title to the provinces of the East; he had acquired the West by the right of conquest; and the three years which he spent in Italy were usefully employed to restore the authority of the laws, and to correct the abuses, which had prevailed with impunity under the usurpation of Maximus and the minority of Valentinian. The name of Valentinian was regularly inserted in the public acts; but the tender age, and doubtful faith, of the son of Justina appeared to require the prudent care of an orthodox guardian; and his specious ambition might have excluded the unfortunate youth, without a struggle and almost without a murmur, from the administration, and even from the inheritance, of the empire. If Theodosius had consulted the rigid maxims of interest and policy, his conduct would have been justified by his friends; but the generosity of his behaviour on this memorable occasion has extorted the applause of his most inveterate enemies. He seated Valentinian on the throne of Milan; and, without stipulating any present or future advantages, restored him to the absolute dominion of all the provinces from which he had been driven by the arms of Maximus. To the restitution of his ample patrimony, Theodosius added the free and generous gift of the countries beyond the Alps, which his successful valour had recovered from the assassin of Gratian.[103] Satisfied with the glory which he had acquired, by revenging the death of his benefactor and delivering the West from the yoke of tyranny, the emperor returned from Milan to Constantinople; and, in the peaceful possession of the East, insensibly relapsed into his former habits of luxury and indolence. Theodosius discharged his obligation to the brother, he indulged his conjugal tenderness to the sister, of Valentinian; and posterity, which admires the pure and singular glory of his elevation, must applaud his unrivalled generosity in the use of victory.

The empress Justina did not long survive her return to Italy; Character of Valentinian. and, though she beheld the triumph of Theodosius, she was A D 391 not allowed to influence the government of her son.[104] The

---

[103] Τοῦτο περὶ τοὺς εὐεργέτας καθῆκον ἐδόξεν εἶναι, is the niggard praise of Zosimus himself (l. iv p 267 [c 48]) Augustin says, with some happiness of expression, Valentinianum . misericordissima veneratione restituit

[104] Sozomen, l. vii c 14 His chronology is very irregular [She seems to have died just before the defeat of Maximus, Rufinus, Hist Ecc ii 17 Cp. Chron. Gall (Pseudo-Prosper) 452, ap. Mommsen, Chr. Min i. p. 648. Otherwise Zosimus, iv. 47.]

pernicious attachment to the Arian sect, which Valentinian had imbibed from her example and instructions, was soon erased by the lessons of a more orthodox education. His growing zeal for the faith of Nice and his filial reverence for the character and authority of Ambrose disposed the Catholics to entertain the most favourable opinion of the virtues of the young emperor of the West.[105] They applauded his chastity and temperance, his contempt of pleasure, his application to business, and his tender affection for his two sisters; which could not, however, seduce his impartial equity to pronounce an unjust sentence against the meanest of his subjects. But this amiable youth, before he had accomplished the twentieth year of his age, was oppressed by domestic treason; and the empire was again involved in the horrors of a civil war. Arbogastes,[106] a gallant soldier of the nation of the Franks, held the second rank in the service of Gratian. On the death of his master, he joined the standard of Theodosius; contributed, by his valour and military conduct, to the destruction of the tyrant; and was appointed, after the victory, master-general of the armies of Gaul. His real merit and apparent fidelity had gained the confidence both of the prince and people; his boundless liberality corrupted the allegiance of the troops; and, whilst he was universally esteemed as the pillar of the state, the bold and crafty Barbarian was secretly determined either to rule or to ruin the empire of the West. The important commands of the army were distributed among the Franks; the creatures of Arbogastes were promoted to all the honours and offices of the civil government; the progress of the conspiracy removed every faithful servant from the presence of Valentinian; and the emperor, without power and without intelligence, insensibly sunk into the precarious and dependent condition of a captive.[107] The indignation which he expressed, though it might arise only from the rash and impatient temper of youth, may be candidly ascribed to the generous spirit of a

[105] See Ambrose (tom. ii de Obit. Valentinian c. 15, &c p 1178, c 36, &c p 1184) When the young emperor gave an entertainment, he fasted himself, he refused to see an handsome actress, &c Since he ordered his wild beasts to be killed, it is ungenerous in Philostorgius (l xi c. 1) to reproach him with the love of that amusement.

[106] Zosimus (l iv p 275 [c. 53]) praises the enemy of Theodosius. But he is detested by Socrates (l v c 25) and Orosius (l vii c. 35) [Acc to John of Antioch (Muller, F. H G. iv fr. 187), Arbogast was son of Bauto, and nephew of Richomer]

[107] Gregory of Tours (l ii c 9, p 165, in the second volume of the Historians of France) has preserved a curious fragment of Sulpicius Alexander, an historian far more valuable than himself.

prince who felt that he was not unworthy to reign.   He
secretly invited the archbishop of Milan to undertake the
office of a mediator, as the pledge of his sincerity and the
guardian of his safety.   He contrived to apprise the emperor
of the East of his helpless situation; and he declared that,
unless Theodosius could speedily march to his assistance, he
must attempt to escape from the palace, or rather prison, of
Vienna in Gaul, where he had imprudently fixed his residence
in the midst of the hostile faction.   But the hopes of relief
were distant and doubtful; and, as every day furnished some
new provocation, the emperor, without strength or counsel,
too hastily resolved to risk an immediate contest with his
powerful general.   He received Arbogastes on the throne; and,
as the count approached with some appearance of respect,
delivered to him a paper, which dismissed him from all his
employments.   "My authority," replied Arbogastes with insulting coolness, "does not depend on the smile, or the frown,
of a monarch"; and he contemptuously threw the paper on the
ground.[108]   The indignant monarch snatched at the sword of
one of the guards, which he struggled to draw from its scabbard;
and it was not without some degree of violence that he was
prevented from using the deadly weapon against his enemy,
or against himself.   A few days after this extraordinary His death
quarrel, in which he had exposed his resentment and his May 15
weakness, the unfortunate Valentinian was found strangled in
his apartment; and some pains were employed to disguise
the manifest guilt of Arbogastes, and to persuade the world
that the death of the young emperor had been the voluntary
effect of his own despair.[109]   His body was conducted with
decent pomp to the sepulchre of Milan; and the archbishop
pronounced a funeral oration, to commemorate his virtue and his
misfortunes.[110]   On this occasion, the humanity of Ambrose
tempted him to make a singular breach in his theological
system, and to comfort the weeping sisters of Valentinian, by

[108] [He tore it in bits with his nails, according to John of Antioch, loc. cit.]
[109] Godefroy (Dissertat ad Philostorg p. 429-434) has diligently collected all
the circumstances of the death of Valentinian II   The variations and the ignorance of contemporary writers prove that it was secret.   [Mr Hodgkin discusses
the evidence (Italy and her Invaders, i. p. 590, note F), which he thinks does not
exclude the hypothesis of suicide, though he agrees that there was probably foul
play   The passage in Epiphanius, De Mens. 20 (which gives the date) is the
most important : εὑρεθεὶς ἄφνω εν τῷ παλατίῳ πεπνιγημένος, ὡς λογος.]
[110] De Obitu Valentinian tom. ii. p. 1173-1196   He is forced to speak a discreet
and obscure language, yet he is much bolder than any layman, or perhaps any
other ecclesiastic, would have dared to be.

the firm assurance that their pious brother, though he had not received the sacrament of baptism, was introduced, without difficulty, into the mansions of eternal bliss [111]

Usurpation
of Eugenius
A.D 392-394 The prudence of Arbogastes had prepared the success of his ambitious designs; and the provincials, in whose breasts every sentiment of patriotism or loyalty was extinguished, expected, with tame resignation, the unknown master, whom the choice of a Frank might place on the Imperial throne. But some remains of pride and prejudice still opposed the elevation of Arbogastes himself; and the judicious Barbarian thought it more advisable to reign under the name of some dependent Roman. He bestowed the purple on the rhetorician Eugenius; [112] whom he had already raised from the place of his domestic secretary to the rank of master of the offices.[112a] In the course both of his private and public service, the count had always approved the attachment and abilities of Eugenius; his learning and eloquence, supported by the gravity of his manners, recommended him to the esteem of the people; and the reluctance with which he seemed to ascend the throne may inspire a favourable prejudice of his virtue and moderation. The ambassadors of the new emperor were immediately despatched to the court of Theodosius, to communicate, with affected grief, the unfortunate accident of the death of Valentinian; and, without mentioning the name of Arbogastes, to request that the monarch of the East would embrace, as his lawful colleague, the respectable citizen who had obtained the unanimous suffrage of the armies and provinces of the West [113] Theodosius was justly provoked that the perfidy of a Barbarian should have destroyed, in a moment, the labours and the fruit of his former victory; and he was excited by the tears of his beloved wife [114] to revenge the fate of her unhappy brother and once more to assert by

---

[111] See c 51, p 1188, c 75, p 1193   Dom. Chardon (Hist. des Sacremens, tom. 1 p. 86), who owns that St Ambrose most strenuously maintains the *indispensable* necessity of baptism, labours to reconcile the contradiction.

[112] Quem [*leg.* hunc] sibi Germanus famulum delegerat evul, is the contemptuous expression of Claudian (iv Cons Hon 74)   Eugenius professed Christianity; but his secret attachment to Paganism (Sozomen, l vii c 22   Philostorg l vi c 2) is probable in a grammarian, and would secure the friendship of Zosimus (l iv p 276, 277 [c 54])   [Gibbon has not sufficiently insisted on the paganism as part of the political programme of Eugenius (cp chap xxviii n 60)]

[112a] [This inference from Philostorgius (vi 2, μαγιστρος) is not certain]

[113] Zosimus (l. iv p 278 [c 55]) mentions this embassy, but he is diverted by another story from relating the event   [But see c. 57 ad init.]

[114] Συνετάραξεν ἡ τουτου γαμετη Γαλλα τα βασιλεια τὸν αδελφον ὁλοφυρομενη   Zosim l iv p 277 [*ib*].   He afterwards says (p 280 [c 57]) that Galla died in childbed, and intimates that the affliction of her husband was extreme, but short.

arms the violated majesty of the throne. But, as the second conquest of the West was a task of difficulty and danger, he dismissed, with splendid presents and an ambiguous answer, the ambassadors of Eugenius; and almost two years were consumed in the preparations of the civil war. Before he formed any decisive resolution, the pious emperor was anxious to discover the will of Heaven; and, as the progress of Christianity had silenced the oracles of Delphi and Dodona, he consulted an Egyptian monk, who possessed, in the opinion of the age, the gift of miracles and the knowledge of futurity. Eutropius, one of the favourite eunuchs of the palace of Constantinople, embarked for Alexandria, from whence he sailed up the Nile as far as the city of Lycopolis, or of Wolves, in the remote province of Thebais.[115] In the neighbourhood of that city, and on the summit of a lofty mountain, the holy John [116] had constructed, with his own hands, an humble cell, in which he had dwelt above fifty years, without opening his door, without seeing the face of a woman, and without tasting any food that had been prepared by fire or any human art. Five days of the week he spent in prayer and meditation; but on Saturdays and Sundays he regularly opened a small window, and gave audience to the crowd of suppliants who successively flowed from every part of the Christian world. The eunuch of Theodosius approached the window with respectful steps, proposed his questions concerning the event of the civil war, and soon returned with a favourable oracle, which animated the courage of the emperor by the assurance of a bloody but infallible victory.[117] The accomplishment of the prediction was forwarded by all the means that human prudence could supply. The industry of the two master-generals, Stilicho and Timasius, was directed to recruit the numbers, and to revive the discipline, of the Roman legions. The formidable troops of Barbarians marched under the ensigns of their national chieftains. The

[margin: Theodosius prepares for war]

[margin: [starts May June 394]]

---

[115] Lycopolis is the modern Siut, or Osiot, a town of Said, about the size of St Denys, which drives a profitable trade with the kingdom of Sennaar, and has a very convenient fountain, "cujus potu signa virginitatis eripiuntur'. See D'Anville, Description de l'Egypte, p 181 Abulfeda, Descript Ægypt p. 14, and the curious annotations, p. 25, 92, of his editor Michaelis.

[116] The life of John of Lycopolis is described by his two friends, Rufinus (l. 11 c. 1 p 449) and Palladius (Hist Lausiac c. 43, p 738) in Rosweyde's great Collection of the Vitæ Patrum. [See Acta Sctorum, 27 Mart. 111 693 *sqq.*] Tillemont (Mém Ecclés. tom. x p 718, 720) has settled the Chronology.

[117] Sozomen, l. vii. c. 22. Claudian (in Eutrop l i. 312) mentions the eunuch's journey: but he most contemptuously derides the Egyptian dreams and the oracles of the Nile.

Iberian, the Arab, and the Goth, who gazed on each other with mutual astonishment, were enlisted in the service of the same prince ; and the renowned Alaric acquired, in the school of Theodosius, the knowledge of the art of war which he afterwards so fatally exerted for the destruction of Rome.[118]

His victory over Eugenius A D 394, September 6

The emperor of the West, or, to speak more properly, his general Arbogastes, was instructed by the misconduct and misfortune of Maximus, how dangerous it might prove to extend the line of defence against a skilful antagonist, who was free to press or to suspend, to contract or to multiply, his various methods of attack.[119] Arbogastes fixed his station on the confines of Italy · the troops of Theodosius were permitted to occupy without resistance the provinces of Pannonia as far as the foot of the Julian Alps ; and even the passages of the mountains were negligently, or perhaps artfully, abandoned to the bold invader. He descended from the hills, and beheld, with some astonishment, the formidable camp of the Gauls and Germans that covered with arms and tents the open

[Wipbach]

country which extends to the walls of Aquileia and the banks of the Frigidus,[120] or Cold River.[121] This narrow theatre of the war, circumscribed by the Alps and the Hadriatic, did not allow much room for the operations of military skill ; the spirit of Arbogastes would have disdained a pardon ; his guilt extinguished the hope of a negotiation ; and Theodosius was impatient to satisfy his glory and revenge by the chastisement of the assassins of Valentinian. Without weighing the

---

[118] Zosimus, l. iv. p 280 [c 57] Socrates, L vii 10 Alaric himself (de Bell Getico, 524) dwells with more complacency on his early exploits against the Romans

. . . Tot Augustos Hebro qui teste fugavi.

Yet his vanity could scarcely have proved this *plurality* of flying emperors

[119] Claudian (in iv Cons. Honor. 77, &c) contrasts the military plans of the two usurpers

. . Novitas audere priorem
Suadebat , cautumque dabant exempla sequentem.
Hic nova moliri praeceps hic quaerere tutus
Providus. Hic fusis , collectis viribus ille.
Hic vagus excurrens , hic intra claustra reductus ;
Dissimiles, sed morte pares . . .

[120] The Frigidus, a small though memorable stream in the country of Goretz, now called the Vipao [Wipbach], falls into the Sontius, or Lisonzo, above Aquileia, some miles from the Hadriatic. See D'Anville's Ancient and Modern Maps, and the Italia Antiqua of Cluverius (tom. 1 p. 188). [Mr. Hodgkin thinks the battle was fought near Heidenschafft, 1 p 578]

[121] Claudian's wit is intolerable the snow was dyed red ; the cold river smoked ; and the channel must have been choked with carcases, if the current had not been swelled with blood.

natural and artificial obstacles that opposed his efforts, the
emperor of the East immediately attacked the fortifications [Sept 5]
of his rivals, assigned the post of honourable danger to the
Goths, and cherished a secret wish that the bloody conflict
might diminish the pride and numbers of the conquerors.
Ten thousand of those auxiliaries, and Bacurius, general of the
Iberians, died bravely on the field of battle.   But the victory
was not purchased by their blood; the Gauls maintained their
advantage; and the approach of night protected the disorderly
flight, or retreat, of the troops of Theodosius.   The emperor
retired to the adjacent hills; where he passed a disconsolate
night, without sleep, without provisions, and without hopes; [122]
except that strong assurance which, under the most desperate
circumstances, the independent mind may derive from the
contempt of fortune and of life.   The triumph of Eugenius
was celebrated by the insolent and dissolute joy of his camp;
whilst the active and vigilant Arbogastes secretly detached
a considerable body of troops, to occupy the passes of the mountains, and to encompass the rear of the Eastern army.   The
dawn of day discovered to the eyes of Theodosius the ex- [Sept 6]
tent and the extremity of his danger: but his apprehensions
were soon dispelled by a friendly message from the leaders
of those troops, who expressed their inclination to desert the
standard of the tyrant.   The honourable and lucrative rewards,
which they stipulated as the price of their perfidy, were
granted without hesitation; and, as ink and paper could not
easily be procured, the emperor subscribed, on his own tablets,
the ratification of the treaty.   The spirit of his soldiers was
revived by this seasonable reinforcement; and they again marched
with confidence, to surprise the camp of a tyrant whose principal
officers appeared to distrust either the justice or the success of
his arms.   In the heat of the battle, a violent tempest,[123]

---

[122] Theodoret affirms that St John and St Philip appeared to the waking, or
sleeping, emperor, on horseback, &c.   This is the first instance of apostolic chivalry,
which afterwards became so popular in Spain and in the Crusades

[123] Te propter, gelidis Aquilo de monte procellis
Obruit adversas acies, revolutaque tela
Vertit in auctores, et turbine reppulit hastas.
O nimium dilecte Deo, cui fundit ab antris
Æolus armatas hyemes, cui militat Æther,
Et conjurati veniunt ad classica venti.

These famous lines of Claudian (in III. Cons Honor. 93, &c A D 396) are alleged
by his contemporaries, Augustin and Orosius; who suppress the Pagan deity of
Æolus, and add some circumstances from the information of eye-witnesses.   Within four months after the victory, it was compared by Ambrose to the miraculous
victories of Moses and Joshua.

such as is often felt among the Alps, suddenly arose from the East. The army of Theodosius was sheltered by their position from the impetuosity of the wind, which blew a cloud of dust in the faces of the enemy, disordered their ranks, wrested their weapons from their hands, and diverted or repelled their ineffectual javelins. This accidental advantage was skilfully improved; the violence of the storm was magnified by the superstitious terrors of the Gauls; and they yielded without shame to the invisible powers of heaven, who seemed to militate on the side of the pious emperor. His victory was decisive; and the deaths of his two rivals were distinguished only by the difference of their characters. The rhetorician Eugenius, who had almost acquired the dominion of the world, was reduced to implore the mercy of the conqueror; and the unrelenting soldiers separated his head from his body, as he lay prostrate at the feet of Theodosius. Arbogastes, after the loss of a battle in which he had discharged the duties of a soldier and a general, wandered several days among the mountains. But, when he was convinced that his cause was desperate, and his escape impracticable, the intrepid Barbarian imitated the example of the ancient Romans, and turned his sword against his own breast. The fate of the empire was determined in a narrow corner of Italy, and the legitimate successor of the house of Valentinian embraced the archbishop of Milan, and graciously received the submission of the provinces of the West. Those provinces were involved in the guilt of rebellion; while the inflexible courage of Ambrose alone had resisted the claims of successful usurpation. With a manly freedom, which might have been fatal to any other subject, the archbishop rejected the gifts of Eugenius, declined [to Florence] his correspondence, and withdrew himself from Milan, to avoid the odious presence of a tyrant, whose downfall he predicted in discreet and ambiguous language. The merit of Ambrose was applauded by the conqueror, who secured the attachment of the people by his alliance with the church; and the clemency of Theodosius is ascribed to the humane intercession of the archbishop of Milan [124]

[124] The events of this civil war are gathered from Ambrose (tom ii epist lvii. p. 1022 [cp Ep 57]), Paulinus (in Vit. Ambros c 26-34), Augustin (de Civitat Dei, v 26), Orosius (l vii. c. 35), Sozomen (l. vii. c 24), Theodoret (l. v. c. 24), Zosimus (l iv p 281, 282 [c. 58]), Claudian (in iii Cons. Hon. 63-105, in iv. Cons. Hon 70-117), and the Chronicles published by Scaliger. [See also Philostorg. xi 2, Socrates, v 25; Victor, *Epit.*, and cp. Sievers, *Studien*, p 326 *sqq.* Cp Appendix 10]

After the defeat of Eugenius, the merit, as well as the authority, of Theodosius was cheerfully acknowledged by all the inhabitants of the Roman world. The experience of his past conduct encouraged the most pleasing expectations of his future reign; and the age of the emperor, which did not exceed fifty years, seemed to extend the prospect of the public felicity. His death, only four months after his victory, was considered by the people as an unforeseen and fatal event, which destroyed in a moment the hopes of the rising generation. But the indulgence of ease and luxury had secretly nourished the principles of disease.[125] The strength of Theodosius was unable to support the sudden and violent transition from the palace to the camp; and the increasing symptoms of a dropsy announced the speedy dissolution of the emperor. The opinion, and perhaps the interest, of the public had confirmed the division of the Eastern and Western empires; and the two royal youths, Arcadius and Honorius, who had already obtained, from the tenderness of their father, the title of Augustus, were destined to fill the thrones of Constantinople and of Rome. Those princes were not permitted to share the danger and glory of the civil war;[126] but, as soon as Theodosius had triumphed over his unworthy rivals, he called his younger son Honorius to enjoy the fruits of the victory and to receive the sceptre of the West from the hands of his dying father. The arrival of Honorius at Milan was welcomed by a splendid exhibition of the games of the Circus; and the emperor, though he was oppressed by the weight of his disorder, contributed by his presence to the public joy. But the remains of his strength were exhausted by the painful effort which he made to assist at the spectacles of the morning. Honorius supplied, during the rest of the day, the place of his father; and the great Theodosius expired in the ensuing night. Notwithstanding the recent animosities of a civil war, his death was universally lamented. The Barbarians, whom he had vanquished, and the churchmen, by whom he had been subdued, celebrated with loud and sincere applause, the qualities of the deceased emperor which appeared the most valuable in their eyes. The Romans were terrified by the impending dangers of a

---

[125] This disease, ascribed by Socrates (l v c 26) to the fatigues of war, is represented by Philostorgius (l xi c 2) as the effect of sloth and intemperance : for which Photius calls him an impudent liar (Godefroy, Dissert p 438).

[126] Zosimus supposes that the boy Honorius accompanied his father (l iv. p. 280 [c 58]) Yet the quanto flagrabant pectora voto, is all that flattery would allow to a contemporary poet ; who clearly describes the emperor's refusal and the journey of Honorius, *after* the victory (Claudian in iii Cons. 78-125)

feeble and divided administration ; and every disgraceful moment of the unfortunate reigns of Arcadius and Honorius revived the memory of their irreparable loss

Corruption of
the times

In the faithful picture of the virtues of Theodosius, his imperfections have not been dissembled , the act of cruelty, and the habits of indolence, which tarnished the glory of one of the greatest of the Roman princes An historian, perpetually adverse to the fame of Theodosius, has exaggerated his vices and their pernicious effects ; he boldly asserts that every rank of subjects imitated the effeminate manners of their sovereign ; that every species of corruption polluted the course of public and private life ; and that the feeble restraints of order and decency were insufficient to resist the progress of that degenerate spirit which sacrifices, without a blush, the consideration of duty and interest to the base indulgence of sloth and appetite.[127] The complaints of contemporary writers, who deplore the increase of luxury and depravation of manners, are commonly expressive of their peculiar temper and situation. There are few observers who possess a clear and comprehensive view of the revolutions of society ; and who are capable of discovering the nice and secret springs of action which impel, in the same uniform direction, the blind and capricious passions of a multitude of individuals. If it can be affirmed, with any degree of truth, that the luxury of the Romans was more shameless and dissolute in the reign of Theodosius than in the age of Constantine, perhaps, or of Augustus, the alteration cannot be ascribed to any beneficial improvements, which had gradually increased the stock of national riches. A long period of calamity or decay must have checked the industry, and diminished the wealth, of the people ; and their profuse luxury must have been the result of that indolent despair which enjoys the present hour and declines the thoughts of futurity. The uncertain condition of their property discouraged the subjects of Theodosius from engaging in those useful and laborious undertakings which require an immediate expense and promise a slow and distant advantage. The frequent examples of ruin and desolation tempted them not to spare the remains of a patrimony which might, every hour, become the prey of the rapacious Goth And the mad prodigality which prevails in the confusion of a shipwreck or a siege may serve to explain the progress of luxury amidst the misfortunes and terrors of a sinking nation.

[127] Zosimus, l iv p 244 [c. 33].

The effeminate luxury which infected the manners of courts
and cities had instilled a secret and destructive poison into the
camps of the legions; and their degeneracy has been marked
by the pen of a military writer who had accurately studied the
genuine and ancient principles of Roman discipline. It is the
just and important observation of Vegetius that the infantry
was invariably covered with defensive armour, from the foundation of the city to the reign of the emperor Gratian. The
relaxation of discipline and the disuse of exercise rendered
the soldiers less able, and less willing, to support the fatigues
of the service; they complained of the weight of the armour,
which they seldom wore; and they successfully obtained the
permission of laying aside both their cuirasses and their helmets.
The heavy weapons of their ancestors, the short sword and the
formidable *pilum*, which had subdued the world, insensibly
dropped from their feeble hands   As the use of the shield
is incompatible with that of the bow, they reluctantly marched
into the field; condemned to suffer either the pain of wounds
or the ignominy of flight, and always disposed to prefer the
more shameful alternative. The cavalry of the Goths, the
Huns and the Alani had felt the benefits, and adopted the
use, of defensive armour; and, as they excelled in the management of missile weapons, they easily overwhelmed the naked
and trembling legions, whose heads and breasts were exposed,
without defence, to the arrows of the Barbarians. The loss
of armies, the destruction of cities, and the dishonour of the
Roman name ineffectually solicited the successors of Gratian
to restore the helmets and cuirasses of the infantry. The
enervated soldiers abandoned their own and the public defence;
and their pusillanimous indolence may be considered as the
immediate cause of the downfall of the empire.[128]

[128] Vegetius, de Re Militari, l. 1 c. 10. The series of calamities which he marks
compel us to believe that the Hero to whom he dedicates his book is the last and
most inglorious of the Valentinians. [This view is maintained by O. Seeck
(Hermes, 11, 61 *sqq*), who contests the usual identification with Theodosius i Theodosius 11 has also been conjectured   The minor limit for the date of the *Epitome
rei Militaris* is A D 450 (determined by the entry in some Mss. Fl Eutropius
emendavi sine exemplario Constantinopolim Valentiniano Aug vii et Abieni).
The work is by no means critical or trustworthy   Cp Forster, de fide Vegetii,
1879]

CHAPTER XXVIII

Final Destruction of Paganism—Introduction of the Worship of Saints, and Relics, among the Christians.

The destruction of the Pagan religion A.D 378-395

THE ruin of Paganism,[1] in the age of Theodosius, is perhaps the only example of the total extirpation of any ancient and popular superstition; and may therefore deserve to be considered as a singular event in the history of the human mind   The Christians, more especially the clergy, had impatiently supported the prudent delays of Constantine and the equal toleration of the elder Valentinian; nor could they deem their conquest perfect or secure, as long as their adversaries were permitted to exist.   The influence which Ambrose and his brethren had acquired over the youth of Gratian and the piety of Theodosius was employed to infuse the maxims of persecution into the breasts of their Imperial proselytes.   Two specious principles of religious jurisprudence were established, from whence they deduced a direct and rigorous conclusion against the subjects of the empire who still adhered to the ceremonies of their ancestors: *that* the magistrate is, in some measure, guilty of the crimes which he neglects to prohibit or to punish; and, *that* the idolatrous worship of fabulous deities and real dæmons is the most abominable crime against the supreme majesty of the Creator   The laws of Moses and the examples of Jewish history [2] were hastily, perhaps erroneously, applied by the clergy to the mild and universal reign of Christianity.[3]   The zeal of the emperors was excited to

---

1 [Beugnot, Histoire de la déstruction du paganisme, 1835, Chastel, Hist de la déstr du pag dans l'empire d'orient, 1850, Lasaulx, Der Untergang des Hellenismus, 1854, G Boissier, La fin du paganisme (2 vols), 1891.]

2 St. Ambrose (tom ii de Obit Theodos p 1208) expressly praises and recommends the zeal of Josiah in the destruction of idolatry   The language of Julius Firmicus Maternus on the same subject (de Errore Profan Relig p 467, edit Gronov) is piously inhuman.   Nec filio jubet (the Mosaic Law) parci, nec fratri, et per amatam conjugem gladium vindicem ducit, &c.

3 Bayle (tom ii. p 406, in his Commentaire Philosophique) justifies and limits these intolerant laws by the temporal reign of Jehovah over the Jews,   The attempt is laudable.

vindicate their own honour, and that of the Deity; and the temples of the Roman world were subverted, about sixty years after the conversion of Constantine.

From the age of Numa to the reign of Gratian the Romans State of preserved the regular succession of the several colleges of the Paganism at Rome sacerdotal order.[4] Fifteen PONTIFFS exercised their supreme jurisdiction over all things and persons that were consecrated to the service of the gods; and the various questions which perpetually arose in a loose and traditionary system were submitted to the judgment of their holy tribunal. Fifteen grave and learned AUGURS observed the face of the heavens, and prescribed the actions of heroes, according to the flight of birds Fifteen keepers of the Sybilline books (their name of QUINDECEMVIRS was derived from their number) occasionally consulted the history of future, and as it should seem, of contingent, events. Six VESTALS devoted their virginity to the guard of the sacred fire and of the unknown pledges of the duration of Rome; which no mortal had been suffered to behold with impunity.[5] Seven EPULOS[6] prepared the table of the gods, conducted the solemn procession, and regulated the ceremonies of the annual festival. The three FLAMENS[7] of Jupiter, of Mars, and of Quirinus, were considered as the peculiar ministers of the three most powerful deities who watched over the fate of Rome and of the universe. The KING of the SACRIFICES represented the person of Numa, and of his successors, in the religious functions which could be performed only by royal hands. The confraternities of the SALIANS, the LUPERCALS, &c., practised such rites as might extort a smile of contempt from every reasonable man, with a lively confidence of recommending themselves to the favour of the immortal gods The authority

---

[4] See the outlines of the Roman hierarchy in Cicero (de Legibus, ii 7, 8), Livy (i 20), Dionysius Halicarnassensis (l ii p 119-129, edit Hudson), Beaufort (République Romaine, tom i. p 1-90), and Moyle (vol. i. p. 10-55). The last is the work of an English Whig, as well as of a Roman antiquary. [The number of Pontiffs and Augurs first reached fifteen in the time of Sulla. A sixteenth Augur was added by Julius Cæsar The emperor (after A D 29) had power to create additional Augurs]

[5] These mystic and perhaps imaginary symbols have given birth to various fables and conjectures It seems probable that the Palladium was a small statue (three cubits and a half high) of Minerva, with a lance and distaff, that it was usually inclosed in a seria, or barrel, and that a similar barrel was placed by its side to disconcert curiosity or sacrilege. See Mezeriac (Comment sur les Epîtres d'Ovide, tom i p 60-66) and Lipsius (tom iii p 610, de Vestâ, &c c 10)

[6] [Cp Lucan, i 602 The Epulo was called Septemvir epulonum]

[7] [In the later Republic there were also a number of minor Flamens; in all fifteen For some of the names, see Varro, L L. vii 44]

which the Roman priests had formerly obtained in the counsels
of the republic was gradually abolished by the establishment
of monarchy and the removal of the seat of empire. But the
dignity of their sacred character was still protected by the
laws and manners of their country; and they still continued,
more especially the college of pontiffs, to exercise in the capital,
and sometimes in the provinces, the rights of their ecclesiastical
and civil jurisdiction.   Their robes of purple, chariots of state,
and sumptuous entertainments attracted the admiration of the
people; and they received, from the consecrated lands and the
public revenue, an ample stipend, which liberally supported
the splendour of the priesthood and all the expenses of the
religious worship of the state.   As the service of the altar was
not incompatible with the command of armies, the Romans,
after their consulships and triumphs, aspired to the place of
pontiff or of augur; the seats of Cicero[8] and Pompey were
filled, in the fourth century, by the most illustrious members
of the senate; and the dignity of their birth reflected additional splendour on their sacerdotal character.   The fifteen
priests who composed the college of pontiffs enjoyed a more
distinguished rank as the companions of their sovereign; and
the Christian emperors condescended to accept the robe and ensigns which were appropriated to the office of supreme pontiff.
But, when Gratian ascended the throne, more scrupulous, or
more enlightened, he sternly rejected those profane symbols;[9]
[c A D 375?] applied to the service of the state, or of the church, the
revenues of the priests and vestals; abolished their honours
and immunities; and dissolved the ancient fabric of Roman
superstition, which was supported by the opinions and habits
of eleven hundred years.[10]   Paganism was still the constitutional
religion of the senate.   The hall, or temple, in which they
assembled, was adorned by the statue and altar of Victory;[11]
a majestic female standing on a globe, with flowing garments,
expanded wings, and a crown of laurel in her outstretched

[8] Cicero frankly (ad Atticum, l ii epist 5) or indirectly (ad Familiar l xv
epist 4) confesses, that the *Augurate* is the supreme object of his wishes   Pliny
is proud to tread in the footsteps of Cicero (l. iv. epist 8), and the chain of
tradition might be continued from history and marbles.

[9] Zosimus, l iv p 249, 250 [c. 36]   I have suppressed the foolish pun about
Pontifex and *Maximus*   [Cp Hodgkin, 1 400. For probable date (375 A.D) see
Mommsen, Staatsrecht, ii² p 1108   In an inscr of 370 A.D Gratian is Pont
Max , C I L vi 1175]

[10] [Compare C I L 6, 749   antra facit sumptusque tuos nec Roma requirit]

[11] This statue was transported from Tarentum to Rome, placed in the *Curia
Julia* by Cæsar, and decorated by Augustus with the spoils of Egypt.

hand [12]   The senators were sworn on the altar of the goddess to observe the laws of the emperor and of the empire ; and a solemn offering of wine and incense was the ordinary prelude of their public deliberations.[13]   The removal of this ancient monument was the only injury which Constantius had offered [A D 357] to the superstition of the Romans.   The altar of Victory was again restored by Julian, tolerated by Valentinian, and once [A D 360-3] more banished from the senate by the zeal of Gratian.[14]   But [A D 382] the emperor yet spared the statues of the gods, which were exposed to the public veneration , four hundred and twenty-four temples, or chapels, still remained to satisfy the devotion of the people ; and in every quarter of Rome the delicacy of the Christians was offended by the fumes of idolatrous sacrifice.[15]

But the Christians formed the least numerous party in the senate of Rome ; [16] and it was only by their absence that they could express their dissent from the legal, though profane, acts of a Pagan majority   In that assembly, the dying embers of freedom were, for a moment, revived and inflamed by the breath of fanaticism.   Four respectable deputations were successively voted to the Imperial court [17] to represent the grievances of the priesthood and the senate ; and to solicit the restoration of the altar of Victory.   The conduct of this important business was entrusted to the eloquent Symmachus,[18] a wealthy and noble senator, who united the sacred characters of pontiff and augur with the civil dignities of proconsul of Africa and præfect of the city.   The breast of Symmachus was animated

Petition of the senate for the altar of Victory A D 384

[12] Prudentius ([in Symm.] l ii in initio) has drawn a very awkward portrait of Victory ; but the curious reader will obtain more satisfaction from Montfaucon's Antiquities (tom. i. p. 341).

[13] See Suetonius (in August. c. 35) and the Exordium of Pliny's Panegyric.

[14] These facts are mutually allowed by the two advocates, Symmachus and Ambrose.

[15] The *Notitia Urbis*, more recent than Constantine, does not find one Christian church worthy to be named among the edifices of the city   Ambrose (tom. ii. epist xvii. p. 825) deplores the public scandals of Rome, which continually offended the eyes, the ears, and the nostrils of the faithful

[16] Ambrose repeatedly affirms, in contradiction to common sense (Moyle's Works, vol. ii. p. 147), that the Christians had a majority in the senate

[17] The *first* (A D. 382) to Gratian, who refused them audience.   The *second* (A D 384) to Valentinian, when the field was disputed by Symmachus and Ambrose.   The *third* (A.D. 388 [so Guldenpenning, p 172 (A.D 388-9); but Seeck puts it in 391, *Chronol. Symmach* in M G H Auct Ant vi p lviii See Prosper, de Prom. Dei, iii 38]) to Theodosius, and the *fourth* (A.D. 392 [Ambrose, ep 57]) to Valentinian.   Lardner (Heathen Testimonies, vol iv. p 372-399) fairly represents the whole transaction

[18] Symmachus, who was invested with all the civil and sacerdotal honours, represented the emperor under the two characters of *Pontifex Maximus* and *Princeps Senatus*.   See the proud inscription at the head of his works.

by the warmest zeal for the cause of expiring Paganism ; and
his religious antagonists lamented the abuse of his genius,
and the inefficacy of his moral virtues [19]   The orator, whose
petition is extant to the emperor Valentinian, was conscious
of the difficulty and danger of the office which he had assumed.
He cautiously avoids every topic which might appear to reflect
on the religion of his sovereign ; humbly declares that prayers
and entreaties are his only arms ; and artfully draws his arguments from the schools of rhetoric rather than from those of
philosophy.   Symmachus endeavours to seduce the imagination
of a young prince, by displaying the attributes of the goddess
of victory ; he insinuates that the confiscation of the revenues,
which were consecrated to the service of the gods, was a
measure unworthy of his liberal and disinterested character ;
and he maintains that the Roman sacrifices would be deprived
of their force and energy, if they were no longer celebrated
at the expense, as well as in the name, of the republic.   Even
scepticism is made to supply an apology for superstition   The
great and incomprehensible *secret* of the universe eludes the
enquiry of man.   Where reason cannot instruct, custom may
be permitted to guide ; and every nation seems to consult
the dictates of prudence by a faithful attachment to those
rites and opinions which have received the sanction of ages
If those ages have been crowned with glory and prosperity,
if the devout people has frequently obtained the blessings
which they have solicited at the altars of the gods, it must
appear still more advisable to persist in the same salutary
practice ; and not to risk the unknown perils that may attend any
rash innovations.   The test of antiquity and success was applied
with singular advantage to the religion of Numa ; and Rome
herself, the celestial genius that presided over the fates of the
city, is introduced by the orator to plead her own cause before
the tribunal of the emperors   "Most excellent princes," says
the venerable matron, "fathers of your country ! pity and
respect my age, which has hitherto flowed in an uninterrupted
course of piety.   Since I do not repent, permit me to continue
in the practice of my ancient rites.   Since I am born free,
allow me to enjoy my domestic institutions   This religion

[19] As if any one, says Prudentius (in Symmach 1 639), should dig in the mud
with an instrument of gold and ivory   Even saints, and polemic saints, treat this
adversary with respect and civility [One of the chief pagan Senators was Flavianus,
Præt. Præf of Italy   There is extant a virulent attack on him of unknown
authorship printed in the Revue Archéologique, 1868, June   Cp. Mommsen, in
Hermes, vol 4, 1870, p 350 *sqq*]

has reduced the world under my laws. These rites have repelled Hannibal from the city, and the Gauls from the capitol.
Were my grey hairs reserved for such intolerable disgrace? I
am ignorant[20] of the new system that I am required to adopt; but
I am well assured that the correction of old age is always an
ungrateful and ignominious office."[21]   The fears of the people
supplied what the discretion of the orator had suppressed; and
the calamities which afflicted, or threatened, the declining
empire were unanimously imputed, by the Pagans, to the new
religion of Christ and of Constantine.

But the hopes of Symmachus were repeatedly baffled by the
firm and dexterous opposition of the archbishop of Milan; who
fortified the emperors against the fallacious eloquence of the Conversion of
advocate of Rome. In this controversy, Ambrose condescends A.D 388, &c.
to speak the language of a philosopher, and to ask, with some
contempt, why it should be thought necessary to introduce an
imaginary and invisible power, as the cause of those victories
which were sufficiently explained by the valour and discipline
of the legions? He justly derides the absurd reverence for
antiquity which could only tend to discourage the improvements of art and to replunge the human race into their original
barbarism. From thence gradually rising to a more lofty and
theological tone, he pronounces that Christianity alone is the
doctrine of truth and salvation, and that every mode of
Polytheism conducts its deluded votaries, through the paths
of error, to the abyss of eternal perdition.[22]   Arguments like
these, when they were suggested by a favourite bishop, had
power to prevent the restoration of the altar of Victory; but
the same arguments fell, with much more energy and effect,
from the mouth of a conqueror; and the gods of antiquity

---

[20] [*Videro.*]

[21] See the fifty-fourth epistle of the tenth book of Symmachus [=x. iii. ed Seeck]
In the form and disposition of his ten books of epistles, he imitated the younger
Pliny, whose rich and florid style he was supposed, by his friends, to equal or
excel (Macrob. Saturnal. l v. c 1)   But the luxuriancy of Symmachus consists of
barren leaves, without fruits, and even without flowers   Few facts, and few
sentiments, can be extracted from his verbose correspondence.

[22] See Ambrose (tom. ii. epist. xvii. xviii. p. 825-833).   The former of these
epistles is a short caution, the latter is a formal reply to the petition or *libel* of
Symmachus.   The same ideas are more copiously expressed in the poetry, if it
may deserve that name, of Prudentius, who composed his two books against
Symmachus (A D 404) while that Senator was still alive   It is whimsical enough
that Montesquieu (Considérations, &c c xix. tom iii p. 487) should overlook the
two professed antagonists of Symmachus; and amuse himself with descanting on
the more remote and indirect confutations of Orosius, St. Augustin, and Salvian

were dragged in triumph at the chariot-wheels of Theodosius [23] In a full meeting of the senate, the emperor proposed, according to the forms of the republic, the important question, Whether the worship of Jupiter or that of Christ should be the religion of the Romans ? [24]   The liberty of suffrages, which he affected to allow, was destroyed by the hopes and fears that his presence inspired ; and the arbitrary exile of Symmachus was a recent admonition that it might be dangerous to oppose the wishes of the monarch.   On a regular division of the senate, Jupiter was condemned and degraded by the sense of a very large majority, and it is rather surprising that any members should be found bold enough to declare by their speeches and votes that they were still attached to the interest of an abdicated deity.[25]   The hasty conversion of the senate must be attributed either to supernatural or to sordid motives ; and many of these reluctant proselytes betrayed, on every favourable occasion, their secret disposition to throw aside the mask of odious dissimulation.   But they were gradually fixed in the new religion, as the cause of the ancient became more hopeless ; they yielded to the authority of the emperor, to the fashion of the times, and to the entreaties of their wives and children,[26] who were instigated and governed by the clergy of Rome and the monks of the East   The edifying example of the Anician family was soon imitated by the rest of the nobility : the Bassi, the Paullini, the Gracchi, embraced the Christian religion ; and "the luminaries of the world, the venerable assembly of Catos (such are the high-flown expressions of Prudentius), were impatient to strip themselves of their pontifical garment : to cast

---

[23] See Prudentius (in Symmach. l. 1 545, &c)   The Christian agrees with the Pagan Zosimus (l iv p. 283 [c 59]) in placing this visit of Theodosius after the *second* civil war, gemini bis victor cæde Tyranni (l 1 410)   But the time and circumstances are better suited to his first triumph

[24] [This can hardly be inferred from the lines of Prudentius]

[25] Prudentius, after proving that the sense of the senate is declared by a legal majority, proceeds to say (609, &c).

> Adspice quam pleno subsellia nostra Senatu
> Decernant infame Jovis pulvinar, et omne
> Idolium longe purgatâ ex urbe fugandum.
> Qui vocat egregii sententia Principis, illuc
> Libera, cum pedibus, tum corde, frequentia transit

Zosimus ascribes to the conscript fathers an heathenish courage, which few of them are found to possess

[26] Jerom specifies the pontiff Albinus, who was surrounded with such a believing family of children and grand-children as would have been sufficient to convert even Jupiter himself, an extraordinary proselyte ! (tom 1. ad Lætam, p 54 [*iuvenem* is the reading of the Mss ; and the correction *Iovem* is unwarranted   Ep 107, Migne, Hieron 1. p 868])

the skin of the old serpent; to assume the snowy robes of baptismal innocence; and to humble the pride of the consular fasces before the tombs of the martyrs".[27]   The citizens, who subsisted by their own industry, and the populace, who were supported by the public liberality, filled the churches of the Lateran and Vatican with an incessant throng of devout proselytes.   The decrees of the senate, which proscribed the worship of idols, were ratified by the general consent of the Romans;[28] the splendour of the capitol was defaced, and the solitary temples were abandoned to ruin and contempt.[29] Rome submitted to the yoke of the Gospel; and the vanquished provinces had not yet lost their reverence for the name and authority of Rome.

The filial piety of the emperors themselves engaged them to proceed, with some caution and tenderness, in the reformation of the eternal city.   Those absolute monarchs acted with less regard to the prejudices of the provincials.   The pious labour, which had been suspended near twenty years since the death of Constantius,[30] was vigorously resumed, and finally accomplished, by the zeal of Theodosius.   Whilst that warlike prince yet struggled with the Goths, not for the glory, but for the safety, of the republic, he ventured to offend a considerable party of his subjects, by some acts which might perhaps secure the protection of Heaven, but which must seem rash and unseasonable in the eye of human prudence.   The success of his first experiments against the Pagans encouraged the pious emperor to reiterate and enforce his edicts of proscription; the same laws which had been originally published in the provinces of the East were applied, after the defeat of Maximus, to the whole extent of the Western empire; and every victory of the

Destruction of the temples in the provinces A D 381, &c

---

[27] Exsultare Patres videas, pulcherrima mundi
    Lumina; conciliumque senum gestire Catonum
    Candidiore togâ niveum pietatis amictum
    Sumere, et exuvias deponere pontificales.
The fancy of Prudentius is warmed and elevated by victory

[28] Prudentius, after he has described the conversion of the senate and people, asks, with some truth and confidence,
    Et dubitamus adhuc Romam, tibi, Christe, dicatam
        In leges transisse tuas?

[29] Jerom exults in the desolation of the capitol, and the other temples of Rome (tom i. p 54 [ep. 107], tom ii. p. 95).

[30] Libanius (Orat pro Templis, p. 10, Genev 1634, published by James Godefroy, and now extremely scarce) accuses Valentinian and Valens of prohibiting sacrifices   Some partial order may have been issued by the Eastern emperor; but the idea of any general law is contradicted by the silence of the Code and the evidence of ecclesiastical history.

orthodox Theodosius contributed to the triumph of the Christian and Catholic faith.[31] He attacked superstition in her most vital part by prohibiting the use of sacrifices, which he declared to be criminal as well as infamous; and, if the terms of his edicts more strictly condemned the impious curiosity which examined the entrails of the victims,[32] every subsequent explanation tended to involve, in the same guilt, the general practice of *immolation*, which essentially constituted the religion of the Pagans. As the temples had been erected for the purpose of sacrifice, it was the duty of a benevolent prince to remove from his subjects the dangerous temptation of offending against the laws which he had enacted. A special commission was granted to Cynegius, the Prætorian præfect of the East, and afterwards to the counts Jovius and Gaudentius, two officers of distinguished rank in the West; by which they were directed to shut the temples, to seize or destroy the instruments of idolatry, to abolish the privileges of the priests, and to confiscate the consecrated property for the benefit of the emperor, of the church, or of the army.[33] Here the desolation might have stopped, and the naked edifices, which were no longer employed in the service of idolatry, might have been protected from the destructive rage of fanaticism Many of those temples were the most splendid and beautiful monuments of Grecian architecture: and the emperor himself was interested not to deface the splendour of his own cities or to diminish the value of his own possessions. Those stately edifices might be suffered to remain as so many lasting trophies of the victory of Christ. In the decline of the arts, they might be usefully converted into magazines, manufactures, or places of public assembly; and perhaps, when the walls of the temple had been sufficiently purified by holy rites, the worship of the true Deity might be allowed to expiate the ancient guilt of idolatry. But, as long as they subsisted, the Pagans fondly cherished the secret hope that an auspicious revolution, a second Julian, might again restore the altars of the gods; and the earnestness with which

---

[31] See his laws in the Theodosian Code, l. xvi. tit. x leg 7-11

[32] Homer's sacrifices are not accompanied with any inquisition of entrails (see Feithius, Antiquitat. Homer l i c 10, 16). The Tuscans, who produced the first *Haruspices*, subdued both the Greeks and the Romans (Cicero de Divinatione, ii. 23).

[33] Zosimus, l iv p 245, 249 [c 37]. Theodoret, l. v. c. 21 Idatius in Chron. Prosper Aquitan. [De promissionibus et prædictionibus Dei] l. iii, c. 38, apud Baronium, Annal. Eccles. A D 389, No. 52. Libanius (pro Templis, p 10) labours to prove that the commands of Theodosius were not direct and positive.

they addressed their unavailing prayers to the throne [34] increased the zeal of the Christian reformers to extirpate, without mercy, the root of superstition.   The laws of the emperors exhibit some symptoms of a milder disposition ; [35] but their cold and languid efforts were insufficient to stem the torrent of enthusiasm and rapine, which was conducted, or rather impelled, by the spiritual rulers of the church.   In Gaul, the holy Martin, bishop of Tours,[36] marched at the head of his faithful monks, to destroy the idols, the temples, and the consecrated trees of his extensive diocese ; and in the execution of this arduous task, the prudent reader will judge whether Martin was supported by the aid of miraculous powers or of carnal weapons   In Syria, the divine and excellent Marcellus,[37] as he is styled by Theodoret, a bishop animated with apostolic fervour, resolved to level with the ground the stately temples within the diocese of Apamea.   His attack was resisted by the skill and solidity with which the temple of Jupiter had been constructed.   The building was seated on an eminence ; on each of the four sides, the lofty roof was supported by fifteen massy columns, sixteen feet in circumference , and the large stones, of which they were composed, were firmly cemented with lead and iron.   The force of the strongest and sharpest tools had been tried without effect.   It was found necessary to undermine the foundations of the columns, which fell down as soon as the temporary wooden props had been consumed with fire ; and the difficulties of the enterprise are described under the allegory of a black dæmon, who retarded, though he could not defeat, the operations of the Christian engineers.   Elated with victory, Marcellus took the field in person against the powers of darkness ; a numerous troop of soldiers and gladiators marched under the episcopal banner, and he successively attacked the villages and

[34] Cod Theodos l. xvi tit x. leg 8, 18   There is room to believe that this temple of Edessa, which Theodosius wished to save for civil uses, was soon afterwards a heap of ruins (Libanius pro Templis, p 26, 27, and Godefroy's notes, p. 59).

[35] See this curious oration of Libanius pro Templis, pronounced, or rather composed, about the year 390.   I have consulted, with advantage, Dr. Lardner's version and remarks (Heathen Testimonies, vol iv p. 135-163).   [περι τῶν ιερῶν, or xxviii., Reiske, ii 155 sqq , composed between 385 (Cod. Th xvi 10, 9, cp. Lib. 163, &c) and 391 (Cod Th xvi 10, 10, cp Lib 180, 182)   But 388 may be the prior limit, cp. Sievers, Das Leben des Libanius, p 192]

[36] See the life of Martin, by Sulpicius Severus, c. 9-14   The saint once mistook (as Don Quixote might have done) an harmless funeral for an idolatrous procession, and imprudently committed a miracle

[37] Compare Sozomen (l vii c. 15) with Theodoret (l v. c. 21).   Between them, they relate the crusade and death of Marcellus.

country temples of the diocese of Apamea. Whenever any resistance or danger was apprehended, the champion of the faith, whose lameness would not allow him either to fight or fly, placed himself at a convenient distance, beyond the reach of darts   But this prudence was the occasion of his death; he was surprised and slain by a body of exasperated rustics; and the synod of the province pronounced, without hesitation, that the holy Marcellus had sacrificed his life in the cause of God.   In the support of this cause, the monks, who rushed with tumultuous fury from the desert, distinguished themselves by their zeal and diligence.   They deserved the enmity of the Pagans; and some of them might deserve the reproaches of avarice and intemperance· of avarice, which they gratified with holy plunder, and of intemperance, which they indulged at the expense of the people, who foolishly admired their tattered garments, loud psalmody, and artificial paleness.[38]   A small number of temples was protected by the fears, the venality, the taste, or the prudence, of the civil and ecclesiastical governors   The temple of the celestial Venus at Carthage, whose sacred precincts formed a circumference of two miles, was judiciously converted into a Christian church;[39] and a similar consecration has preserved inviolate the majestic dome of the Pantheon at Rome.[40] But, in almost every province of the Roman world, an army of fanatics, without authority and without discipline, invaded the peaceful inhabitants; and the ruin of the fairest structures of antiquity still displays the ravages of *those* Barbarians, who alone had time and inclination to execute such laborious destruction.

The temple of Serapis in Alexandria   In this wide and various prospect of devastation, the spectator may distinguish the ruins of the temple of Serapis, at Alexandria[41]   Serapis does not appear to have been one of the native gods, or monsters, who sprung from the fruitful soil of super-

[38] Libanius pro Templis, p 10-13   He rails at these black-garbed men, the Christian monks, who eat more than elephants   Poor elephants! *they* are temperate animals

[39] Prosper Aquitan. l iii. c. 38, apud Baronium; Annal Eccles A D 389, No. 58, &c.   The temple had been shut some time, and the access to it was overgrown with brambles

[40] Donatus, Roma Antiqua et Nova, l iv. c 4, p 468   This consecration was performed by Pope Boniface IV   I am ignorant of the favourable circumstances which had preserved the Pantheon above two hundred years after the reign of Theodosius

[41] Sophronius composed a recent and separate history (Jerom, in Script Eccles. tom i. p 303), which had furnished materials to Socrates (l v c. 16), Theodoret (l v c. 22), and Rufinus (l ii. c 22)   Yet the last, who had been at Alexandria before and after the event, may deserve the credit of an original witness

stitious Egypt.[42]   The first of the Ptolemies had been commanded, by a dream, to import the mysterious stranger from
the coast of Pontus, where he had been long adored by the
inhabitants of Sinope; but his attributes and his reign were so
imperfectly understood that it became a subject of dispute,
whether he represented the bright orb of day or the gloomy
monarch of the subterraneous regions.[43]   The Egyptians, who
were obstinately devoted to the religion of their fathers, refused
to admit this foreign deity within the walls of their cities [44]
But the obsequious priests, who were seduced by the liberality
of the Ptolemies, submitted, without resistance, to the power
of the god of Pontus; an honourable and domestic genealogy
was provided; and this fortunate usurper was introduced into
the throne and bed of Osiris,[45] the husband of Isis, and the
celestial monarch of Egypt   Alexandria, which claimed
his peculiar protection, gloried in the name of the city of
Serapis.   His temple,[46] which rivalled the pride and magnificence of the capitol, was erected on the spacious summit of an
artificial mount, raised one hundred steps above the level of the
adjacent parts of the city; and the interior cavity was strongly
supported by arches, and distributed into vaults and subterraneous apartments.   The consecrated buildings were surrounded
by a quadrangular portico; the stately halls, and exquisite
statues, displayed the triumph of the arts; and the treasures of
ancient learning were preserved in the famous Alexandrian
library, which had arisen with new splendour from its ashes.[47]

[42] Gerard Vossius (Opera, tom. v. p. 80, and de Idololatriâ, l 1 c 29) strives to
support the strange notion of the Fathers, that the patriarch Joseph was adored
in Egypt as the bull Apis and the god Serapis.
[43] Origo dei nondum nostris celebrata   Ægyptiorum antistites *sic* memorant,
&c, Tacit. Hist. iv. 83   The Greeks, who had travelled into Egypt, were alike
ignorant of this new deity. [Cp. Mahaffy, Empire of the Ptolemies, p 72-74]
[44] Macrobius, Saturnal l. 1. c. 7.   Such a living fact decisively proves his
foreign extraction
[45] At Rome Isis and Serapis were united in the same temple   The precedency
which the queen assumed may seem to betray her unequal alliance with the
stranger of Pontus. But the superiority of the female sex was established in
Egypt as a civil and religious institution (Diodor Sicul. tom. 1 l 1, p 31, edit
Wesseling), and the same order is observed in Plutarch's Treatise of Isis and
Osiris, whom he identifies with Serapis
[46] Ammianus (xxii. 16)   The Expositio totius Mundi (p. 8, in Hudson's
Geograph Minor. tom iii) and Rufinus (l ii c 22) celebrate the *Serapeum*, as
one of the wonders of the world
[47] See Mémoires de l'Acad des Inscriptions, tom. ix p. 397-416   The *old*
library of the Ptolemies was *totally* consumed in Cæsar's Alexandrian war. Marc
Antony gave the whole collection of Pergamus (200,000 volumes) to Cleopatra, as
the foundation of the *new* library of Alexandria   [See Appendix 11]

After the edicts of Theodosius had severely prohibited the sacrifices of the Pagans, they were still tolerated in the city and temple of Serapis, and this singular indulgence was imprudently ascribed to the superstitious terrors of the Christians themselves · as if they had feared to abolish those ancient rites which could alone secure the inundations of the Nile, the harvests of Egypt, and the subsistence of Constantinople [48]

Its final destruction A.D 389 [391] At that time [49] the archiepiscopal throne of Alexandria was filled by Theophilus,[50] the perpetual enemy of peace and virtue ; a bold, bad man, whose hands were alternately polluted with gold and with blood. His pious indignation was excited by the honours of Serapis; and the insults which he offered to an ancient chapel of Bacchus [51] convinced the Pagans that he meditated a more important and dangerous enterprise. In the tumultuous capital of Egypt, the slightest provocation was sufficient to inflame a civil war. The votaries of Serapis, whose strength and numbers were much inferior to those of their antagonists, rose in arms at the instigation of the philosopher Olympius,[52] who exhorted them to die in the defence of the altars of the gods. These Pagan fanatics fortified themselves in the temple, or rather fortress, of Serapis ; repelled the besiegers by daring sallies and a resolute defence ; and, by the inhuman cruelties which they exercised on their Christian prisoners, obtained the last consolation of despair. The efforts of the prudent magistrate were usefully exerted for the establishment of a truce till the answer of Theodosius should determine the fate of Serapis The two parties assembled, without arms, in the principal square ; and the Imperial rescript was publicly read. But, when a sentence of destruction against the idols of Alexandria was pronounced, the Christians set up a shout of joy and exultation, whilst the unfortunate Pagans, whose fury had given way to consternation, retired with hasty

---

[48] Libanius (pro Templis, p 21) indiscreetly provokes his Christian masters by this insulting remark.

[49] We may choose between the date of Marcellinus (A D 389) or that of Prosper (A D 391) Tillemont (Hist des Emp tom v p 310, 756) prefers the former, and Pagi the latter [which is probably right; so Gothofredus, ad Cod Th xvi 10, 11; Guldenpenning, p. 189 Clinton decides for end of 390 A.D]

[50] Tillemont, Mém Ecclés tom xi p 441-500 The ambiguous situation of Theophilus,—a *saint*, as the friend of Jerom ; a *devil*, as the enemy of Chrysostom—produces a sort of impartiality ; yet, upon the whole, the balance is justly inclined against him

[51] [A Mithreum cp Socrates, l. c]

[52] Lardner (Heathen Testimonies, vol. iv. p 411) has alleged a beautiful passage from Suidas, or rather from Damascius, which shews the devout and virtuous Olympius, not in the light of a warrior, but of a prophet

and silent steps, and eluded, by their flight or obscurity, the resentment of their enemies. Theophilus proceeded to demolish the temple of Serapis, without any other difficulties than those which he found in the weight and solidity of the materials ; but these obstacles proved so insuperable that he was obliged to leave the foundations and to content himself with reducing the edifice itself to a heap of rubbish ; a part of which was soon afterwards cleared away, to make room for a church erected in honour of the Christian martyrs. The valuable library of Alexandria was pillaged or destroyed ; and, near twenty years afterwards, the appearance of the empty shelves excited the regret and indignation of every spectator whose mind was not totally darkened by religious prejudice.[53] The compositions of ancient genius, so many of which have irretrievably perished, might surely have been excepted from the wreck of idolatry, for the amusement and instruction of succeeding ages ; and either the zeal or the avarice of the archbishop[54] might have been satiated with the rich spoils which were the reward of his victory. While the images and vases of gold and silver were carefully melted, and those of a less valuable metal were contemptuously broken and cast into the streets, Theophilus laboured to expose the frauds and vices of the ministers of the idols ; their dexterity in the management of the loadstone ; their secret methods of introducing an human actor into a hollow statue, and their scandalous abuse of the confidence of devout husbands and unsuspecting females[55] Charges like these may seem to deserve some degree of credit, as they are not repugnant to the crafty and interested spirit of superstition. But the same spirit is equally prone to the base practice of insulting and calumniating a fallen enemy ; and our belief is

[53] [Unde quamlibet hodieque in templis extent, quae et] nos vidimus, armaria librorum, quibus direptis exinanita ea a nostris hominibus nostris temporibus memorant [memorent]. Orosius, 1 vi. c 15, p 421, edit. Havercamp [p. 216, ed Zangemeister] Though a bigot, and a controversial writer, Orosius seems to blush   [See Appendix 11]

[54] Eunapius, in the lives of Antonius [*leg* Antoninus] and Ædesius, execrates the sacrilegious rapine of Theophilus. Tillemont (Mém Ecclés tom xiii p 453) quotes an epistle of Isidore of Pelusium, which reproaches the primate with the *idolatrous* worship of gold, the auri *sacra* fames.

[55] Rufinus names the priest of Saturn, who, in the character of the god, familiarly conversed with many pious ladies of quality ; till he betrayed himself, in a moment of transport, when he could not disguise the tone of his voice. The authentic and impartial narrative of Æschines (see Bayle, Dictionnaire Critique, SCAMANDRE) and the adventure of Mundus (Joseph. Antiquitat. Judaic 1 xviii. c. 3, p. 877, edit. Havercamp) may prove that such amorous frauds have been practised with success

naturally checked by the reflection that it is much less difficult to invent a fictitious story than to support a practical fraud. The colossal statue of Serapis [56] was involved in the ruin of his temple and religion. A great number of plates of different metals, artificially joined together, composed the majestic figure of the Deity, who touched on either side the walls of the sanctuary. The aspect of Serapis, his sitting posture, and the sceptre which he bore in his left hand, were extremely similar to the ordinary representations of Jupiter. He was distinguished from Jupiter by the basket, or bushel, which was placed on his head; and by the emblematic monster, which he held in his right hand: the head and body of a serpent branching into three tails, which were again terminated by the triple heads of a dog, a lion, and a wolf. It was confidently affirmed that, if any impious hand should dare to violate the majesty of the god, the heavens and the earth would instantly return to their original chaos. An intrepid soldier, animated by zeal and armed with a weighty battle-axe, ascended the ladder; and even the Christian multitude expected, with some anxiety, the event of the combat.[57] He aimed a vigorous stroke against the cheek of Serapis; the cheek fell to the ground; the thunder was still silent, and both the heavens and the earth continued to preserve their accustomed order and tranquillity. The victorious soldier repeated his blows; the huge idol was overthrown, and broken in pieces; and the limbs of Serapis were ignominiously dragged through the streets of Alexandria. His mangled carcase was burnt in the Amphitheatre, amidst the shouts of the populace; and many persons attributed their conversion to this discovery of the impotence of their tutelar deity. The popular modes of religion that propose any visible and material objects of worship have the advantage of adapting and familiarising themselves to the senses of mankind; but this advantage is counterbalanced by the various and inevitable accidents to which the faith of the idolater is exposed. It is scarcely possible that, in every dis-

---

[56] See the images of Serapis, in Montfaucon (tom. ii. p. 297), but the description of Macrobius (Saturnal. l. i. c. 20) is much more picturesque and satisfactory.

[57] Sed fortes tremuere manus, motique verendâ
  Majestate loci, si robora sacra ferirent
  In sua credebant redituras membra secures.

(Lucan. iii. 429.) " Is it true (said Augustus to a veteran of Italy, at whose house he supped) that the man who gave the first blow to the golden statue of Anaitis was instantly deprived of his eyes, and of his life?"   "*I* was that man (replied the clear-sighted veteran), and you now sup on one of the legs of the goddess." (Plin. Hist. Natur. xxxiii. 24.)

position of mind, he should preserve his implicit reverence for
the idols or the relics which the naked eye and the profane
hand are unable to distinguish from the most common productions of art or nature ; and, if, in the hour of danger, their
secret and miraculous virtue does not operate for their own
preservation, he scorns the vain apologies of his priest, and
justly derides the object, and the folly, of his superstitious
attachment.[58]   After the fall of Serapis, some hopes were still
entertained by the Pagans that the Nile would refuse his
annual supply to the impious masters of Egypt ; and the extraordinary delay of the inundation seemed to announce the
displeasure of the river-god.   But this delay was soon compensated by the rapid swell of the waters.   They suddenly
rose to such an unusual height as to comfort the discontented
party with the pleasing expectation of a deluge ; till the
peaceful river again subsided to the well-known and fertilising
level of sixteen cubits, or about thirty English feet [59]

The temples of the Roman empire were deserted, or destroyed ; The Pagan
but the ingenious superstition of the Pagans still attempted to religion is
elude the laws of Theodosius, by which all sacrifices had been prohibited,
severely prohibited.   The inhabitants of the country, whose A.D. 390
conduct was less exposed to the eye of malicious curiosity,
disguised their *religious*, under the appearance of *convivial*,
meetings   On the days of solemn festivals, they assembled in
great numbers under the spreading shade of some consecrated
trees ; sheep and oxen were slaughtered and roasted ; and this
rural entertainment was sanctified by the use of incense, and by
the hymns which were sung in honour of the gods.   But it was
alleged that, as no part of the animal was made a burnt-offering,
as no altar was provided to receive the blood, and as the previous
oblation of salt cakes and the concluding ceremony of libations
were carefully omitted, these festal meetings did not involve the
guests in the guilt, or penalty, of an illegal sacrifice.[60]   Whatever might be the truth of the facts or the merit of the dis-

[58] The history of the Reformation affords frequent examples of the sudden
change from superstition to contempt

[59] Sozomen, l vii c 20.   I have supplied the measure.   The same standard of
the inundation, and consequently of the cubit, has uniformly subsisted since the
time of Herodotus   See Fréret, in the Mém de l'Académie des Inscriptions,
tom. xvi p 344-353   Greaves's Miscellaneous Works, vol i p. 233.   The
Egyptian cubit is about twenty-two inches of the English measure.

[60] Libanius (pro Templis, p 15, 16, 17) pleads their cause with gentle and insinuating rhetoric.   From the earliest age, such feasts had enlivened the country ;
and those of Bacchus (Georgic ii. 380) had produced the theatre of Athens.   See
Godefroy, ad loc Liban. and Codex Theodos. tom vi p 284.

tinction,[61] these vain pretences were swept away by the last
edict of Theodosius; which inflicted a deadly wound on the
superstition of the Pagans.[62]   This prohibitory law is expressed
in the most absolute and comprehensive terms.   "It is our will
and pleasure," says the emperor, "that none of our subjects,
whether magistrates or private citizens, however exalted or
however humble may be their rank and condition, shall presume,
in any city or in any place, to worship an inanimate idol by the
sacrifice of a guiltless victim."   The act of sacrificing and the
practice of divination by the entrails of the victim are declared
(without any regard to the object of the enquiry) a crime of
high-treason against the state; which can be expiated only by
the death of the guilty.   The rites of Pagan superstition, which
might seem less bloody and atrocious, are abolished, as highly
injurious to the truth and honour of religion; luminaries,
garlands, frankincense, and libations of wine, are specially
enumerated and condemned; and the harmless claims of the
domestic genius, of the household gods, are included in this
rigorous proscription.   The use of any of these profane and
illegal ceremonies subjects the offender to the forfeiture of the
house or estate where they have been performed; and, if he has
artfully chosen the property of another for the scene of his
impiety, he is compelled to discharge, without delay, a heavy
fine of twenty-five pounds of gold, or more than one thousand
pounds sterling.   A fine, not less considerable, is imposed on
the connivance of the secret enemies of religion, who shall
neglect the duty of their respective stations, either to reveal or
to punish the guilt of idolatry.   Such was the persecuting spirit
of the laws of Theodosius, which were repeatedly enforced by
his sons and grandsons, with the loud and unanimous applause
of the Christian world.[63]

[61] Honorius tolerated these rustic festivals (A.D. 399).   "Absque ullo sacrificio,
atque ullâ superstitione damnabili."   But nine years afterwards he found it necessary to reiterate and enforce the same proviso (Codex Theodos. l. xvi. tit. x. leg.
17, 19).   [The ordinance of certain heathen feasts in Campania, published by
Imperial sanction in 387 A.D., is very instructive, proving that Paganism of a kind
was tolerated by Theodosius.   See Schiller, ii. p. 435.]
[62] Cod. Theodos. l. xvi. tit. x. leg. 12.   Jortin (Remarks on Eccles. History,
vol. iv. p. 134) censures, with becoming asperity, the style and sentiments of this
intolerant law.
[63] Such a charge should not be lightly made; but it may surely be justified by
the authority of St. Augustin, who thus addresses the Donatists: "Quis nostrûm,
quis vestrûm non laudat leges ab Imperatoribus datas adversus sacrificia Pagan-
orum?   Et certe longe ibi pœna severior constituta est; illius quippe impietatis
capitale supplicium est."   Epist. xciii. No. 10, quoted by Le Clerc (Bibliothèque
Choisie, tom. viii. p. 277), who adds some judicious reflections on the intolerance
of the victorious Christians.

In the cruel reigns of Decius and Diocletian, Christianity had <small>oppressed</small> been proscribed, as a revolt from the ancient and hereditary religion of the empire; and the unjust suspicions which were entertained of a dark and dangerous faction were, in some measure, countenanced by the inseparable union and rapid conquests of the Catholic church.   But the same excuses of fear and ignorance cannot be applied to the Christian emperors, who violated the precepts of humanity and of the gospel.   The experience of ages had betrayed the weakness, as well as folly, of Paganism; the light of reason and of faith had already exposed, to the greatest part of mankind, the vanity of idols; and the declining sect, which still adhered to their worship, might have been permitted to enjoy, in peace and obscurity, the religious customs of their ancestors.   Had the Pagans been animated by the undaunted zeal which possessed the minds of the primitive believers, the triumph of the church must have been stained with blood; and the martyrs of Jupiter and Apollo might have embraced the glorious opportunity of devoting their lives and fortunes at the foot of their altars   But such obstinate zeal was not congenial to the loose and careless temper of polytheism.   The violent and repeated strokes of the orthodox princes were broken by the soft and yielding substance against which they were directed; and the ready obedience of the Pagans protected them from the pains and penalties of the Theodosian Code.[64]   Instead of asserting that the authority of the gods was superior to that of the emperor, they desisted, with a plaintive murmur, from the use of those sacred rites which their sovereign had condemned.   If they were sometimes tempted, by a sally of passion or by the hopes of concealment, to indulge their favourite superstition, their humble repentance disarmed the severity of the Christian magistrate; and they seldom refused to atone for their rashness by submitting, with some secret reluctance, to the yoke of the Gospel.   The churches were filled with the increasing multitude of these unworthy proselytes, who had conformed, from temporal motives, to the reigning religion; and, whilst they devoutly imitated the postures, and recited the prayers, of the faithful, they satisfied their conscience by the silent and sincere invocation of the gods of antiquity.[65]   If the Pagans wanted patience to suffer, they

---

[64] Orosius, l vii. c 28, p 537.   Augustin (Enarrat in Psal. cxl apud Lardner, Heathen Testimonies, vol. iv. p 458) insults their cowardice   "Quis eorum comprehensus est in sacrificio (cum his legibus ista prohiberentur) et non negavit?"
[65] Libanius (pro Templis, p. 17, 18) mentions, without censure, the occasional conformity, and as it were theatrical play, of these hypocrites.

wanted spirit to resist ; and the scattered myriads, who deplored
the ruin of the temples, yielded, without a contest, to the
fortune of their adversaries.   The disorderly opposition [66] of the
peasants of Syria, and the populace of Alexandria, to the rage
of private fanaticism was silenced by the name and authority of
the emperor.   The Pagans of the West, without contributing to
the elevation of Eugenius, disgraced, by their partial attachment, the cause and character of the usurper.   The clergy
vehemently exclaimed that he aggravated the crime of rebellion
by the guilt of apostasy ; that, by his permission, the altar of
Victory was again restored , and that the idolatrous symbols of
Jupiter and Hercules were displayed in the field against the
invincible standard of the cross.   But the vain hopes of the
Pagans were soon annihilated by the defeat of Eugenius ; and
they were left exposed to the resentment of the conqueror, who
laboured to deserve the favour of heaven by the extirpation of
idolatry.[67]

and finally
extinguished.
A D 390-420,
&c. A nation of slaves is always prepared to applaud the clemency
of their master, who, in the abuse of absolute power, does not
proceed to the last extremes of injustice and oppression.   Theodosius might undoubtedly have proposed to his Pagan subjects
the alternative of baptism or of death ; and the eloquent Libanius has praised the moderation of a prince, who never enacted,
by any positive law, that all his subjects should immediately
embrace and practise the religion of their sovereign [68]   The
profession of Christianity was not made an essential qualification
for the enjoyment of the civil rights of society, nor were any
peculiar hardships imposed on the sectaries who credulously
received the fables of Ovid and obstinately rejected the miracles
of the Gospel.   The palace, the schools, the army, and the
senate were filled with declared and devout Pagans ; they obtained, without distinction. the civil and military honours of the
empire   Theodosius distinguished his liberal regard for virtue
and genius, by the consular dignity which he bestowed on Sym-

[66] Libanius concludes his apology (p. 32) by declaring to the emperor that,
unless he expressly warrants the destruction of the temples, ἴσθι τοὺς τῶν ἀγρῶν δεσ-
πότας, καὶ αὐτοῖς, καὶ τῷ νόμῳ βοηθήσαντας, the proprietors will defend themselves
and the laws.

[67] Paulinus, in Vit Ambros c 26. Augustin de Civitat Dei, l. v. c 26
Theodoret, l v c 24

[68] Libanius suggests the form of a persecuting edict, which Theodosius might
enact (pro Templis, p. 32)   a rash joke, and a dangerous experiment.   Some
princes would have taken his advice

machus,[69] and by the personal friendship which he expressed
to Libanius;[70] and the two eloquent apologists of Paganism
were never required either to change or to dissemble their
religious opinions. The Pagans were indulged in the most
licentious freedom of speech and writing; the historical and
philosophical remains of Eunapius, Zosimus,[71] and the fanatic
teachers of the school of Plato, betray the most furious animosity, and contain the sharpest invectives, against the sentiments and conduct of their victorious adversaries. If these
audacious libels were publicly known, we must applaud the good
sense of the Christian princes who viewed, with a smile of contempt, the last struggles of superstition and despair.[72] But the
Imperial laws which prohibited the sacrifices and ceremonies of
Paganism were rigidly executed; and every hour contributed to
destroy the influence of a religion which was supported by
custom rather than by argument. The devotion of the poet or
the philosopher may be secretly nourished by prayer, meditation, and study; but the exercise of public worship appears to
be the only solid foundation of the religious sentiments of the
people, which derive their force from imitation and habit. The
interruption of that public exercise may consummate, in the
period of a few years, the important work of a national revolution   The memory of theological opinions cannot long be preserved without the artificial helps of priests, of temples, and of
books.[73] The ignorant vulgar, whose minds are still agitated by
the blind hopes and terrors of superstition, will be soon per-

[69] Denique pro meritis terrestribus æqua rependens
Munera, sacricolis summos impertit honores

. . . . .
Ipse magistratum tibi consulis, ipse tribunal
Contulit   Prudent. in Symmach i. 617, &c.
[70] Libanius (pro Templis, p 32) is proud that Theodosius should thus distinguish
a man, who even in his *presence* would swear by Jupiter   Yet this presence seems
to be no more than a figure of rhetoric
[71] Zosimus, who styles himself Count and Ex-advocate of the Treasury, reviles,
with partial and indecent bigotry, the Christian princes, and even the father of his
sovereign   His work must have been privately circulated, since it escaped the invectives of the ecclesiastical historians prior to Evagrius (l iii c. 40-42), who lived
towards the end to the sixth century [For date of Zosimus, see above, vol ii.
App. 1]
[72] Yet the Pagans of Africa complained that the times would not allow them to
answer with freedom the City of God, nor does St Augustin (v 26) deny the
charge
[73] The Moors of Spain, who secretly preserved the Mahometan religion above
a century, under the tyranny of the Inquisition, possessed the Koran, with the
peculiar use of the Arabic tongue See the curious and honest story of their expulsion in Geddes (Miscellanies, vol. i. p. 1-198).

suaded by their superiors to direct their vows to the reigning deities of the age ; and will insensibly imbibe an ardent zeal for the support and propagation of the new doctrine, which spiritual hunger at first compelled them to accept.   The generation that arose in the world after the promulgation of the Imperial laws was attracted within the pale of the Catholic church : and so rapid, yet so gentle, was the fall of Paganism that only twenty-eight years after the death of Theodosius the faint and minute vestiges were no longer visible to the eye of the legislator.[74]

The worship of the Christian Martyrs The ruin of the Pagan religion is described by the sophists as a dreadful and amazing prodigy which covered the earth with darkness and restored the ancient dominion of chaos and of night   They relate, in solemn and pathetic strains, that the temples were converted into sepulchres, and that the holy places, which had been adorned by the statues of the gods, were basely polluted by the relics of Christian martyrs.   "The monks" (a race of filthy animals, to whom Eunapius is tempted to refuse the name of men) "are the authors of the new worship, which, in the place of one of those deities, who are conceived by the understanding, has substituted the meanest and most contemptible slaves.   The heads, salted and pickled, of those infamous malefactors, who for the multitude of their crimes have suffered a just and ignominious death ; their bodies, still marked by the impression of the lash, and the scars of those tortures which were inflicted by the sentence of the magistrate ; such" (continues Eunapius) "are the gods which the earth produces in our days ; such are the martyrs, the supreme arbitrators of our prayers and petitions to the Deity, whose tombs are now consecrated as the objects of the veneration of the people "[75]   Without approving the malice, it is natural enough to share the surprise, of the Sophist, the spectator of a revolution which raised those obscure victims of the laws of Rome to the rank of celestial and invisible protectors of the Roman empire.   The grateful respect of the Christians for the martyrs of the faith was exalted, by time and victory, into religious adoration ; and the most illustrious of the saints and prophets were deservedly associated to the honours of the martyrs.   One hundred and fifty years after the glorious deaths of St. Peter and St. Paul,

[74] Paganos qui supersunt, quanquam jam nullos esse credamus, &c. Cod Theodos l xvi tit x leg 22, A D. 423   The younger Theodosius was afterwards satisfied that his judgment had been somewhat premature.

[75] See Eunapius, in the life of the sophist Ædesius [p 65, ed. Commelin] ; in that of Eustathius he foretells the ruin of Paganism, καὶ τι μυθῶδες, καὶ ἀειδὲς σκότος τυραννήσει τὰ ἐπι γῆς κάλλιστα.

the Vatican and the Ostian road were distinguished by the tombs, or rather by the trophies, of those spiritual heroes.[76] In the age which followed the conversion of Constantine, the emperors, the consuls, and the generals of armies devoutly visited the sepulchres of a tent-maker and a fisherman;[77] and their venerable bones were deposited under the altars of Christ, on which the bishops of the royal city continually offered the unbloody sacrifice.[78] The new capital of the eastern world, unable to produce any ancient and domestic trophies, was enriched by the spoils of dependent provinces. The bodies of St. Andrew, St Luke, and St. Timothy, had reposed, near three hundred years, in the obscure graves from whence they were sent, in solemn pomp, to the church of the Apostles, which the magnificence of Constantine had founded on the banks of the Thracian Bosphorus.[79] About fifty years afterwards, the same banks were honoured by the presence of Samuel, the judge and prophet of the people of Israel. His ashes, deposited in a golden vase and covered with a silken veil, were delivered by the bishops into each other's hands. The relics of Samuel were received by the people with the same joy and reverence which they would have shown to the living prophet; the highways, from Palestine to the gates of Constantinople, were filled with an uninterrupted procession; and the emperor Arcadius himself, at the head of the most illustrious members of the clergy and senate, advanced to meet his extraordinary guest, who had always deserved and claimed the homage of kings.[80] The example of Rome and Constantinople confirmed the faith and discipline of the Catholic world The honours of the saints and martyrs, after a feeble and ineffectual murmur of profane

---

[76] Caius (apud Euseb Hist. Eccles l. ll. c. 25), a Roman presbyter, who lived in the time of Zephyrinus (A.D. 202-219), is an early witness of this superstitious practice.

[77] Chrysostom. Quod Christus sit Deus. Tom i. nov. edit. No 9. I am indebted for this quotation to Benedict the XIV.th's pastoral letter on the jubilee of the year 1750. See the curious and entertaining letters of M Chais, tom. iii.

[78] Male facit ergo Romanus episcopus? qui, super mortuorum hominum, Petri et Pauli, secundum nos, ossa veneranda . . offert Domino sacrificia, et tumulos eorum Christi arbitratur altaria. Jerom tom ii advers Vigilant. p 153 [c. 8, ed. Migne, ii p. 346]

[79] Jerom (tom ii p 122 [c Vigil c 5]) bears witness to these translations, which are neglected by the ecclesiastical historians The passion of St. Andrew at Patræ is described in an epistle from the clergy of Achaia, which Baronius (Annal. Eccles A D 60, No. 35) wishes to believe and Tillemont is forced to reject. St. Andrew was adopted as the spiritual founder of Constantinople (Mém Ecclés. tom i. p 317-323, 588-594).

[80] Jerom (tom. ii p 122) pompously describes the translation of Samuel, which is noticed in the chronicles of the times

reason,[81] were universally established; and in the age of Ambrose and Jerom, something was still deemed wanting to the sanctity of a Christian church, till it had been consecrated by some portion of holy relics, which fixed and inflamed the devotion of the faithful.

General reflections

In the long period of twelve hundred years which elapsed between the reign of Constantine and the reformation of Luther the worship of saints and relics corrupted the pure and perfect simplicity of the Christian model; and some symptoms of degeneracy may be observed even in the first generations which adopted and cherished this pernicious innovation.

I. Fabulous martyrs and relics

I. The satisfactory experience that the relics of saints were more valuable than gold or precious stones [82] stimulated the clergy to multiply the treasures of the church. Without much regard for truth or probability, they invented names for skeletons and actions for names. The fame of the apostles, and of the holy men who had imitated their virtues, was darkened by religious fiction. To the invincible band of genuine and primitive martyrs, they added myriads of imaginary heroes, who had never existed except in the fancy of crafty or credulous legendaries; and there is reason to suspect that Tours might not be the only diocese in which the bones of a malefactor were adored instead of those of a saint.[83] A superstitious practice, which tended to increase the temptations of fraud and credulity, insensibly extinguished the light of history and of reason in the Christian world.

II. Miracles

II. But the progress of superstition would have been much less rapid and victorious, if the faith of the people had not been assisted by the seasonable aid of visions and miracles, to ascertain the authenticity and virtue of the most suspicious relics. In the reign of the younger Theodosius, Lucian,[84] a presbyter of

[81] The presbyter Vigilantius, the protestant of his age, firmly, though ineffectually, withstood the superstition of monks, relics, saints, fasts, &c, for which Jerom compares him to the Hydra, Cerberus, the Centaurs, &c, and considers him only as the organ of the dæmon (tom. ii. p 120-126) Whoever will peruse the controversy of St. Jerom and Vigilantius, and St Augustin's account of the miracles of St. Stephen, may speedily gain some idea of the spirit of the Fathers [Cp App. 12]

[82] M. de Beausobre (Hist. du Manichéisme, tom. ii p 648) has applied a worldly sense to the pious observation of the clergy of Smyrna who carefully preserved the relics of St Polycarp the martyr

[83] Martin of Tours (see his Life, c 8, by Sulpicius Severus) extorted this confession from the mouth of the dead man. The error is allowed to be natural; the discovery is supposed to be miraculous. Which of the two was likely to happen most frequently?

[84] Lucian composed in Greek his original narrative, which has been translated by Avitus, and published by Baronius (Annal Eccles A D. 415, No. 7-16). The

Jerusalem, and the ecclesiastical minister of the village of Caphargamala, about twenty miles from the city, related a very singular dream, which, to remove his doubts, had been repeated on three successive Saturdays. A venerable figure stood before him, in the silence of the night, with a long beard, a white robe, and a gold rod ; announced himself by the name of Gamaliel, and revealed to the astonished presbyter that his own corpse, with the bodies of his son Abibas, his friend Nicodemus, and the illustrious Stephen, the first martyr of the Christian faith, were secretly buried in the adjacent field   He added, with some impatience, that it was time to release himself and his companions from their obscure prison ; that their appearance would be salutary to a distressed world ; and that they had made choice of Lucian to inform the bishop of Jerusalem of their situation and their wishes. The doubts and difficulties which still retarded this important discovery were successively removed by new visions ; and the ground was opened by the bishop, in the presence of an innumerable multitude. The coffins of Gamaliel, of his son, and of his friend were found in regular order ; but when the fourth coffin, which contained the remains of Stephen, was shown to the light, the earth trembled, and an odour, such as that of paradise, was smelt, which instantly cured the various diseases of seventy-three of the assistants. The companions of Stephen were left in their peaceful residence of Caphargamala ; but the relics of the first martyr were transported in solemn procession to a church constructed in their honour on Mount Sion, and the minute particles of those relics, a drop of blood,[85] or the scrapings of a bone, were acknowledged in almost every province of the Roman world to possess a divine and miraculous virtue.   The grave and learned Augustin,[86] whose understanding scarcely admits the excuse of credulity, has attested the innumerable prodigies which were performed in Africa by the relics of St Stephen; and this marvellous narrative is inserted in the elaborate work of the City of God, which the

Benedictine editors of St. Augustin have given (at the end of the work de Civitate Dei) two several copies, with many various readings. It is the character of falsehood to be loose and inconsistent.   The most incredible parts of the legend are smoothed and softened by Tillemont (Mém. Ecclés tom. ii p 9, &c.).

[85] A phial of St Stephen's blood was annually liquefied at Naples, till he was superseded by St. Januarius (Ruinart Hist. Persecut. Vandal. p. 529)

[86] Augustin composed the two and twenty books de Civitate Dei in the space of thirteen years, A D. 413-426 (Tillemont, Mém. Ecclés tom xiv p 608, &c.)   His learning is too often borrowed, and his arguments are too often his own ; but the whole work claims the merit of a magnificent design, vigorously, and not unskilfully, executed.

bishop of Hippo designed as a solid and immortal proof of the truth of Christianity. Augustin solemnly declares that he has selected those miracles only which were publicly certified by the persons who were either the objects, or the spectators, of the power of the martyr. Many prodigies were omitted or forgotten; and Hippo had been less favourably treated than the other cities of the province. And yet the bishop enumerates above seventy miracles, of which three were resurrections from the dead, in the space of two years and within the limits of his own diocese.[87] If we enlarge our view to all the dioceses and all the saints of the Christian world, it will not be easy to calculate the fables and the errors which issued from this inexhaustible source. But we may surely be allowed to observe that a miracle, in that age of superstition and credulity, lost its name and its merit, since it could scarcely be considered as a deviation from the ordinary and established laws of nature.

III Revival of Polytheism

III. The innumerable miracles of which the tombs of the martyrs were the perpetual theatre revealed to the pious believer the actual state and constitution of the invisible world; and his religious speculations appeared to be founded on the firm basis of fact and experience. Whatever might be the condition of vulgar souls, in the long interval between the dissolution and the resurrection of their bodies, it was evident that the superior spirits of the saints and martyrs did not consume that portion of their existence in silent and inglorious sleep [88] It was evident (without presuming to determine the place of their habitation or the nature of their felicity) that they enjoyed the lively and active consciousness of their happiness, their virtue, and their powers; and that they had already secured the possession of their eternal reward. The enlargement of their intellectual faculties surpassed the measure of the human imagination; since it was proved by *experience* that they were capable of hearing and understanding the various petitions of their numerous votaries; who, in the same moment of time, but in the most distant parts of the world, invoked the name and assistance of

---

[87] See Augustin, de Civitat. Dei, l xxii c 22, and the Appendix, which contains two books of St. Stephen's miracles, by Evodius, bishop of Uzalis   Freculphus (apud Basnage, Hist des Juifs, tom viii. p. 249) has preserved a Gallic or Spanish proverb, "Whoever pretends to have read all the miracles of St Stephen, he lies"

[88] Burnet (de Statu Mortuorum, p 56-84) collects the opinions of the fathers, as far as they assert the sleep, or repose, of human souls till the day of judgment   He afterwards exposes (p 91, &c) the inconveniencies which must arise, if they possessed a more active and sensible existence.

Stephen or of Martin [89]   The confidence of their petitioners was founded on the persuasion that the saints, who reigned with Christ, cast an eye of pity upon earth; that they were warmly interested in the prosperity of the Catholic church; and that the individuals, who imitated the example of their faith and piety, were the peculiar and favourite objects of their most tender regard.   Sometimes, indeed, their friendship might be influenced by considerations of a less exalted kind: they viewed, with partial affection, the places which had been consecrated by their birth, their residence, their death, their burial, or the possession of their relics.   The meaner passions of pride, avarice, and revenge may be deemed unworthy of a celestial breast; yet the saints themselves condescended to testify their grateful approbation of the liberality of their votaries; and the sharpest bolts of punishment were hurled against those impious wretches who violated their magnificent shrines or disbelieved their supernatural power.[90]   Atrocious, indeed, must have been the guilt, and strange would have been the scepticism, of those men, if they had obstinately resisted the proofs of a divine agency which the elements, the whole range of the animal creation, and even the subtle and invisible operations of the human mind were compelled to obey.[91]   The immediate, and almost instantaneous, effects, that were supposed to follow the prayer or the offence, satisfied the Christians of the ample measure of favour and authority which the saints enjoyed in the presence of the Supreme God; and it seemed almost superfluous to inquire whether they were continually obliged to intercede before the throne of grace, or whether they might not be permitted to exercise, according to the dictates of their benevolence and justice, the delegated powers of their subordinate ministry. The imagination, which had been raised by a painful effort to the contemplation and worship of the Universal Cause, eagerly

[89] Vigilantius placed the souls of the prophets and martyrs either in the bosom of Abraham (in loco refrigerii) or else under the altar of God.   Nec posse suis tumulis et ubi voluerunt adesse præsentes.   But Jerom (tom ii p 122) sternly refutes this *blasphemy*   Tu Deo leges pones?   Tu apostolis vincula injicies, ut usque ad diem judicii teneantur custodiâ, nec sint cum Domino suo; de quibus scriptum est, Sequuntur Agnum quocunque vadit   Si Agnus ubique, ergo, et hi, qui cum Agno sunt, ubique esse credendi sunt.   Et cum diabolus et dæmones toto vagentur in orbe, &c.

[90] Fleury, Discours sur l'Hist Ecclésiastique, iii. p 80

[91] At Minorca, the relics of St Stephen converted, in eight days, 540 Jews, with the help, indeed, of some severities, such as burning the synagogue, driving the obstinate infidels to starve among the rocks, &c.   See the original letter of Severus, bishop of Minorca (ad calcem St. Augustin de Civ. Dei), and the judicious remarks of Basnage (tom. viii. p. 245-251).

embraced such inferior objects of adoration as were more proportioned to its gross conceptions and imperfect faculties.   The
sublime and simple theology of the primitive Christians was
gradually corrupted; and the MONARCHY of heaven, already
clouded by metaphysical subtleties, was degraded by the introduction of a popular mythology, which tended to restore the
reign of polytheism.[92]

IV Intro-
duction of
Pagan cere-
monies

IV. As the objects of religion were gradually reduced to the
standard of the imagination, the rites and ceremonies were
introduced that seemed most powerfully to affect the senses of
the vulgar   If, in the beginning of the fifth century,[93] Tertullian or Lactantius [94] had been suddenly raised from the dead,
to assist at the festival of some popular saint or martyr, [95] they
would have gazed with astonishment and indignation on the
profane spectacle, which had succeeded to the pure and spiritual
worship of a Christian congregation.   As soon as the doors of
the church were thrown open, they must have been offended by
the smoke of incense, the perfume of flowers, and the glare of
lamps and tapers, which diffused, at noon-day, a gaudy, superfluous, and, in their opinion, a sacrilegious light.   If they
approached the balustrade of the altar, they made their way
through the prostrate crowd, consisting, for the most part, of
strangers and pilgrims, who resorted to the city on the vigil of
the feast; and who already felt the strong intoxication of
fanaticism, and, perhaps, of wine. ˙ Their devout kisses were imprinted on the walls and pavement of the sacred edifice; and
their fervent prayers were directed, whatever might be the
language of their church, to the bones, the blood, or the ashes
of the saints, which were usually concealed by a linen or silken
veil from the eyes of the vulgar.   The Christians frequented the
tombs of the martyrs, in the hope of obtaining, from their
powerful intercession, every sort of spiritual, but more especially

[92] Mr Hume (Essays, vol ii p 434) observes, like a philosopher, the natural
flux and reflux of polytheism and theism

[93] D'Aubigné (see his own Mémoires, p 156-160) frankly offered, with the consent
of the Huguenot ministers, to allow the first 400 years as the rule of faith.   The
Cardinal du Perron haggled for forty years more, which were indiscreetly given.
Yet neither party would have found their account in this foolish bargain.

[94] The worship practised and inculcated by Tertullian, Lactantius, Arnobius,
&c , is so *extremely* pure and spiritual that their declamations against the Pagan,
sometimes glance against the Jewish, ceremonies.

[95] Faustus the Manichæan accuses the Catholics of idolatry.   Vertitis idola in
martyres .   quos votis similibus colitis. M de Beausobre (Hist. Critique du
Manichéisme, tom. ii p. 629-700), a protestant, but a philosopher, has represented,
with candour and learning, the introduction of *Christian idolatry* in the fourth
and fifth centuries,

of temporal, blessings.   They implored the preservation of their
health or the cure of their infirmities; the fruitfulness of their
barren wives or the safety and happiness of their children.
Whenever they undertook any distant or dangerous journey,
they requested that the holy martyrs would be their guides and
protectors on the road; and, if they returned without having
experienced any misfortune, they again hastened to the tombs
of the martyrs, to celebrate, with grateful thanksgivings, their
obligations to the memory and relics of those heavenly patrons.
The walls were hung round with symbols of the favours which
they had received; eyes, and hands, and feet, of gold and
silver; and edifying pictures, which could not long escape the
abuse of indiscreet or idolatrous devotion, represented the image,
the attributes, and the miracles of the tutelar saint.   The same
uniform original spirit of superstition might suggest, in the most
distant ages and countries, the same methods of deceiving the
credulity, and of affecting the senses, of mankind; [96] but it
must ingenuously be confessed that the ministers of the Catholic
church imitated the profane model which they were impatient
to destroy.   The most respectable bishops had persuaded
themselves that the ignorant rustics would more cheerfully
renounce the superstitions of Paganism, if they found some
resemblance, some compensation, in the bosom of Christianity.
The religion of Constantine achieved, in less than a century, the
final conquest of the Roman empire: but the victors themselves
were insensibly subdued by the arts of their vanquished
rivals. [97]

[96] The resemblance of superstition, which could not be imitated, might be
traced from Japan to Mexico   Warburton had seized this idea, which he distorts,
by rendering it too general and absolute (Divine Legation, vol. iv p 126, &c.).

[97] The imitation of Paganism is the subject of Dr. Middleton's agreeable letter
from Rome.   Warburton's animadversions obliged him to connect (vol iii. p. 120-
132) the history of the two religions, and to prove the antiquity of the Christian
copy.   [Compare transformation of birthday of Mithra into that of Christ;
Mommsen, C. I. L. i p 409.]

CHAPTER XXIX

*Final Division of the Roman Empire between the Sons of Theodo-
sius—Reign of Arcadius and Honorius—Administration of
Rufinus and Stilicho—Revolt and Defeat of Gildo in Africa*

Division of
the empire
between
Arcadius and
Honorius.
A.D. 395,
January 17
THE genius of Rome expired with Theodosius; the last of the
successors of Augustus and Constantine, who appeared in the
field at the head of their armies, and whose authority was
universally acknowledged throughout the whole extent of the
empire. The memory of his virtues still continued, however,
to protect the feeble and inexperienced youth of his two sons.
After the death of their father, Arcadius and Honorius were
saluted, by the unanimous consent of mankind, as the lawful
emperors of the East, and of the West; and the oath of fidelity
was eagerly taken by every order of the state; the senates of
old and new Rome, the clergy, the magistrates, the soldiers,
and the people. Arcadius, who then was about eighteen years
of age, was born in Spain, in the humble habitation of a private
family. But he received a princely education in the palace of
Constantinople; and his inglorious life was spent in that peaceful and splendid seat of royalty, from whence he appeared to
reign over the provinces of Thrace, Asia Minor, Syria, and
Egypt, from the Lower Danube to the confines of Persia and
[Born A.D. 384, Æthiopia. His younger brother, Honorius, assumed, in the
Sept. 9]
eleventh year of his age, the nominal government of Italy,
Africa, Gaul, Spain, and Britain; and the troops which guarded
the frontiers of his kingdom were opposed, on one side, to the
Caledonians, and on the other, to the Moors. The great and
martial præfecture of Illyricum was divided between the two
princes; the defence and possession of the provinces of
Noricum, Pannonia, and Dalmatia, still belonged to the western
empire; but the two large dioceses of Dacia and Macedonia,
which Gratian had intrusted to the valour of Theodosius, were
for ever united to the empire of the East. The boundary in
Europe was not very different from the line which now
separates the Germans and the Turks; and the respective
and fifth

advantages of territory, riches, populousness, and military strength, were fairly balanced and compensated in this final and permanent division of the Roman empire. The hereditary sceptre of the sons of Theodosius appeared to be the gift of nature, and of their father ; the generals and ministers had been accustomed to adore the majesty of the royal infants ; and the army and people were not admonished of their rights and of their power by the dangerous example of a recent election. The gradual discovery of the weakness of Arcadius and Honorius, and the repeated calamities of their reign, were not sufficient to obliterate the deep and early impressions of loyalty. The subjects of Rome, who still reverenced the persons or rather the names of their sovereigns, beheld, with equal abhorrence, the rebels who opposed, and the ministers who abused, the authority of the throne.

Theodosius had tarnished the glory of his reign by the elevation of Rufinus : an odious favourite, who, in an age of civil and religious faction, has deserved, from every party, the imputation of every crime. The strong impulse of ambition and avarice[1] had urged Rufinus to abandon his native country, an obscure corner of Gaul,[2] to advance his fortune in the capital of the East ; the talent of bold and ready elocution[3] qualified him to succeed in the lucrative profession of the law ; and his success in that profession was a regular step to the most honourable and important employments of the state. He was raised, by just degrees, to the station of master of the offices. In the exercise of his various functions, so essentially connected with the whole system of civil government, he acquired the confidence of a monarch, who soon discovered his diligence and capacity in business, and who long remained ignorant of the pride, the malice, and the covetousness of his disposition. These vices were concealed beneath the mask of profound dissimulation ;[4] his passions were subservient only to the passions of his master ; yet, in the horrid massacre of Thes-

Character and adminis- tration of Rufinus A D 386-395

---

[1] Alecto, envious of the public felicity, convenes an infernal synod   Megæra recommends her pupil Rufinus, and excites him to deeds of mischief, &c   But there is as much difference between Claudian's fury and that of Virgil, as between the characters of Turnus and Rufinus.

[2] It is evident (Tillemont, Hist des Emp. tom. v p 770), though de Marca is ashamed of his countryman, that Rufinus was born at Elusa, the metropolis of Novempopulania, now a small village of Gascony (d'Anville, Notice de l'Ancienne Gaule, p 219)

[3] Philostorgius, l xi c 3, with Godefroy's Dissert. p. 440

[4] A passage of Suidas is expressive of his profound dissimulation · βαθυγνωμων ανθρωπος και κρυψινους.   [F H. G iv. p 42]

salonica, the cruel Rufinus inflamed the fury, without imitating the repentance, of Theodosius. The minister, who viewed with proud indifference the rest of mankind, never forgave the appearance of an injury ; and his personal enemies had forfeited in his opinion the merit of all public services. Promotus, the master-general of the infantry, had saved the empire from the invasion of the Ostrogoths ; but he indignantly supported the pre-eminence of a rival whose character and profession he despised ; and, in the midst of a public council, the impatient soldier was provoked to chastise with a blow the indecent pride of the favourite   This act of violence was represented to the emperor as an insult which it was incumbent on *his* dignity to resent   The disgrace and exile of Promotus were signified by a peremptory order to repair, without delay, to a military station on the banks of the Danube ; and the death of that general (though he was slain in a skirmish with the Barbarians) was imputed to the perfidious arts of Rufinus.[5] The sacrifice of an hero gratified his revenge ; the honours of the consulship elated his vanity ; but his power was still imperfect and precarious, as long as the important posts of præfect of the East and of præfect of Constantinople were filled by Tatian [6] and his son Proculus ; whose united authority balanced, for some time, the ambition and favour of the master of the offices   The two præfects were accused of rapine and corruption in the administration of the laws and finances. For the trial of these illustrious offenders, the emperor constituted a special commission ; several judges were named to share the guilt and reproach of injustice ; but the right of pronouncing sentence was reserved to the president alone, and that president was Rufinus himself. The father, stripped of the præfecture of the East, was thrown into a dungeon ; but the son, conscious that few ministers can be found innocent where an enemy is their judge, had secretly escaped ; and Rufinus must have been satisfied with the least obnoxious victim, if despotism had not condescended to employ the basest and most ungenerous artifice. The prosecution was conducted with an appearance of equity and moderation, which flattered

[5] Zosimus, l iv. p 272, 273 [c. 51].

[6] Zosimus, who describes the fall of Tatian and his son (l v p 273, 274 [c. 52]), asserts their innocence ; and even *his* testimony may outweigh the charges of their enemies (Cod Theodos tom iv. p 489) who accuse them of oppressing the *Curiæ* The connexion of Tatian with the Arians, while he was præfect of Egypt (A D. 373), inclines Tillemont to believe that he was guilty of every crime (Hist. des Emp tom v p. 360   Mém. Ecclés. tom. vi. p 589). [Rufinus was probably not guilty of the death of Promotus, The silence of Claudian outweighs the charge of Zosimus]

Tatian with the hope of a favourable event; his confidence was
fortified by the solemn assurances and perfidious oaths of the
president, who presumed to interpose the sacred name of
Theodosius himself; and the unhappy father was at last persuaded to recall, by a private letter, the fugitive Proculus. He
was instantly seized, examined, condemned, and beheaded, in
one of the suburbs of Constantinople, with a precipitation which
disappointed the clemency of the emperor. Without respecting
the misfortunes of a consular senator, the cruel judges of Tatian
compelled him to behold the execution of his son; the fatal
cord was fastened round his own neck; but, in the moment when
he expected, and perhaps desired, the relief of a speedy death,
he was permitted to consume the miserable remnant of his old
age in poverty and exile.[7] The punishment of the two præfects
might perhaps be excused by the exceptionable parts of their
own conduct; the enmity of Rufinus might be palliated by the
jealous and unsociable nature of ambition. But he indulged a
spirit of revenge, equally repugnant to prudence and to justice,
when he degraded their native country of Lycia from the rank
of Roman provinces; stigmatized a guiltless people with a mark
of ignominy; and declared that the countrymen of Tatian and
Proculus should ever remain incapable of holding any employment of honour or advantage under the Imperial government.[8]
The new præfect of the East (for Rufinus instantly succeeded to
the vacant honours of his adversary) was not diverted, however,
by the most criminal pursuits, from the performance of the
religious duties which in that age were considered as the most
essential to salvation. In the suburb of Chalcedon, surnamed
the *Oak*, he had built a magnificent villa; to which he devoutly
added a stately church, consecrated to the apostles St. Peter
and St. Paul, and continually sanctified by the prayers and

---

[7] . . . Juvenum rorantia colla
Ante patrum vultus strictâ cecidere securi;
Ibat grandævus nato moriente superstes
Post trabeas exul

in Rufin 1 248 [246-9]

The *facts* of Zosimus explain the *allusions* of Claudian; but his classic interpreters
were ignorant of the fourth century. The *fatal cord* I found, with the help of
Tillemont, in a sermon of St. Asterius of Amasea

[8] This odious law is recited, and repealed, by Arcadius (A D 396), in the
Theodosian Code, l. ix tit. xxxviii leg 9 The sense, as it is explained by
Claudian (in Rufin 1 234 [232]) and Godefroy (tom. iii. p. 279), is perfectly clear.

. . Exscindere cives
Funditus et nomen gentis delere laborat.

The scruples of Pagi and Tillemont can arise only from their zeal for the glory of
Theodosius

penance of a regular society of monks   A numerous, and almost
general, synod of the bishops of the eastern empire was summoned to celebrate, at the same time, the dedication of the
church and the baptism of the founder.   This double ceremony
was performed with extraordinary pomp ; and, when Rufinus was
purified, in the holy font, from all the sins that he had hitherto
committed, a venerable hermit of Egypt rashly proposed himself as the sponsor of a proud and ambitious statesman.[9]

He oppresses
the East.
A D 395

The character of Theodosius imposed on his minister the task
of hypocrisy, which disguised, and sometimes restrained, the
abuse of power ; and Rufinus was apprehensive of disturbing the
indolent slumber of a prince, still capable of exerting the abilities
and the virtue which had raised him to the throne.[10]   But the
absence, and soon afterwards the death, of the emperor confirmed the absolute authority of Rufinus over the person and
dominions of Arcadius : a feeble youth, whom the imperious
præfect considered as his pupil rather than his sovereign.   Regardless of the public opinion, he indulged his passions without
remorse and without resistance ; and his malignant and rapacious
spirit rejected every passion that might have contributed to his
own glory or the happiness of the people.   His avarice,[11] which
seems to have prevailed in his corrupt mind over every other
sentiment, attracted the wealth of the East by the various arts
of partial, and general, extortion : oppressive taxes, scandalous
bribery, immoderate fines, unjust confiscations, forced or fictitious
testaments, by which the tyrant despoiled of their lawful inheritance the children of strangers, or enemies ; and the public
sale of justice, as well as of favour, which he instituted in the

---

[9] Ammonius .   . Rufinum propriis manibus suscepit sacro fonte mundatum
See Rosweyde's Vitæ Patrum, p 947 [ed. 2, A D. 1628]. Sozomen (l viii c 17)
mentions the church and monastery, and Tillemont (Mém Ecclés tom iv p 593)
records this synod, in which St Gregory of Nyssa performed a conspicuous part.
[10] Montesquieu (Esprit des Loix, l. xii c 12) praises one of the laws of Theodosius, addressed to the præfect Rufinus (l ix tit iv. leg unic), to discourage the
prosecution of treasonable, or sacrilegious, words   A tyrannical statute always
proves the existence of tyranny; but a laudable edict may only contain the
specious professions, or ineffectual wishes, of the prince, or his ministers   This, I
am afraid, is a just though mortifying canon of criticism.
[11] . . . fluctibus auri
    Expleri ille calor nequit . . .

    Congestæ cumulantur opes ; orbisque rapinas [ruinas]
    Accipit una domus . . .
This character (Claudian in Rufin. i. 184[183]-220) is confirmed by Jerom, a
disinterested witness (dedecus insatiabilis avaritiæ, tom. i. ad Heliodor. p 26 [Ep
60]), by Zosimus (l. v p. 286 [c 1]), and by Suidas, who copied the history of
Eunapius [fr 63, F H G iv p 42].

palace of Constantinople. The ambitious candidate eagerly solicited, at the expense of the fairest part of his patrimony, the honours and emoluments of some provincial government; the lives and fortunes of the unhappy people were abandoned to the most liberal purchaser; and the public discontent was sometimes appeased by the sacrifice of an unpopular criminal, whose punishment was profitable only to the præfect of the East, his accomplice and his judge. If avarice were not the blindest of the human passions, the motives of Rufinus might excite our curiosity; and we might be tempted to inquire, with what view he violated every principle of humanity and justice, to accumulate those immense treasures which he could not spend without folly nor possess without danger. Perhaps he vainly imagined that he laboured for the interest of an only daughter, on whom he intended to bestow his royal pupil and the august rank of Empress of the East Perhaps he deceived himself by the opinion that his avarice was the instrument of his ambition. He aspired to place his fortune on a secure and independent basis, which should no longer depend on the caprice of the young emperor; yet he neglected to conciliate the hearts of the soldiers and people, by the liberal distribution of those riches which he had acquired with so much toil, and with so much guilt. The extreme parsimony of Rufinus left him only the reproach and envy of ill-gotten wealth; his dependents served him without attachment; the universal hatred of mankind was repressed only by the influence of servile fear. The fate of Lucian proclaimed to the East that the præfect whose industry was much abated in the despatch of ordinary business was active and indefatigable in the pursuit of revenge. Lucian, the son of the præfect Florentius, the oppressor of Gaul, and the enemy of Julian, had employed a considerable part of his inheritance, the fruit of rapine and corruption, to purchase the friendship of Rufinus and the high office of Count of the East. But the new magistrate imprudently departed from the maxims of the court and of the times; disgraced his benefactor, by the contrast of a virtuous and temperate administration; and presumed to refuse an act of injustice, which might have tended to the profit of the emperor's uncle Arcadius was easily persuaded to resent the supposed insult; and the præfect of the East resolved to execute in person the cruel vengeance which he meditated against this ungrateful delegate of his power. He performed with incessant speed the journey of seven or eight hundred miles from Constantinople to Antioch, entered the capital of Syria at the dead

of night, and spread universal consternation among a people
ignorant of his design but not ignorant of his character. The
count of the fifteen provinces of the East was dragged, like the
vilest malefactor, before the arbitrary tribunal of Rufinus. Notwithstanding the clearest evidence of his integrity, which was
not impeached even by the voice of an accuser, Lucian was condemned, almost without a trial, to suffer a cruel and ignominious
punishment. The ministers of the tyrant, by the order, and in
the presence, of their master, beat him on the neck with leather
thongs, armed at the extremities with lead; and, when he fainted
under the violence of the pain, he was removed in a close litter,
to conceal his dying agonies from the eyes of the indignant city.
No sooner had Rufinus perpetrated this inhuman act, the sole
object of his expedition, than he returned, amidst the deep and
silent curses of a trembling people, from Antioch to Constantinople; and his diligence was accelerated by the hope of accom-
plishing, without delay, the nuptials of his daughter with the
emperor of the East.[12]

He is disap-
pointed by
the marriage
of Arcadius.
A.D. 395,
April 27

But Rufinus soon experienced that a prudent minister should
constantly secure his royal captive by the strong, though invisible, chain of habit; and that the merit, and much more
easily the favour, of the absent are obliterated in a short time
from the mind of a weak and capricious sovereign. While the
præfect satiated his revenge at Antioch, a secret conspiracy of
the favourite eunuchs, directed by the great chamberlain Eutropius, undermined his power in the palace of Constantinople.
They discovered that Arcadius was not inclined to love the
daughter of Rufinus, who had been chosen, without his consent,
for his bride; and they contrived to substitute in her place the
fair Eudoxia, the daughter of Bauto,[13] a general of the Franks
in the service of Rome; and who was educated, since the
death of her father, in the family of the sons of Promotus.
The young emperor, whose chastity had been strictly guarded
by the pious care of his tutor Arsenius,[14] eagerly listened

---

[12] . . . Cetera segnis,
  Ad facinus velox; penitus regione remotas
  Impiger ire vias.
This allusion of Claudian (in Rufin. i. [239-]241) is again explained by the circum-
stantial narrative of Zosimus (l. v p. 288, 289 [c. 2])

[13] Zosimus (l. iv p. 243 [c. 33]) praises the valour, prudence and integrity of
Bauto the Frank. See Tillemont, Hist. des Empereurs, tom. v p. 771

[14] Arsenius escaped from the palace of Constantinople, and passed fifty-five
years in rigid penance in the monasteries of Egypt. See Tillemont, Mém. Ecclés.
tom. xiv. p. 676-702; and Fleury, Hist. Ecclés. tom. v. p 1, &c., but the latter,
for want of authentic materials, has given too much credit to the legend of
Metaphrastes.

to the artful and flattering descriptions of the charms of Eudoxia; he gazed with impatient ardour on her picture, and he understood the necessity of concealing his amorous designs from the knowledge of a minister who was so deeply interested to oppose the consummation of his happiness. Soon after the return of Rufinus, the approaching ceremony of the royal nuptials was announced to the people of Constantinople, who prepared to celebrate, with false and hollow acclamations, the fortune of his daughter   A splendid train of eunuchs and officers issued, in hymeneal pomp, from the gates of the palace; bearing aloft the diadem, the robes and the inestimable ornaments of the future empress. The solemn procession passed through the streets of the city, which were adorned with garlands and filled with spectators; but, when it reached the house of the sons of Promotus, the principal eunuch respectfully entered the mansion, invested the fair Eudoxia with the Imperial robes, and conducted her in triumph to the palace and bed of Arcadius.[15]   The secrecy and success with which this conspiracy against Rufinus had been conducted imprinted a mark of indelible ridicule on the character of a minister who had suffered himself to be deceived in a post where the arts of deceit and dissimulation constitute the most distinguished merit. He considered, with a mixture of indignation and fear, the victory of an aspiring eunuch, who had secretly captivated the favour of his sovereign; and the disgrace of his daughter, whose interest was inseparably connected with his own, wounded the tenderness, or, at least, the pride, of Rufinus. At the moment when he flattered himself that he should become the father of a line of kings, a foreign maid, who had been educated in the house of his implacable enemies, was introduced into the Imperial bed; and Eudoxia soon displayed a superiority of sense and spirit, to improve the ascendant which her beauty must acquire over the mind of a fond and youthful husband. The emperor would soon be instructed to hate, to fear and to destroy the powerful subject whom he had injured; and the consciousness of guilt deprived Rufinus of every hope, either of safety or comfort, in the retirement of a private life. But he still possessed the most effectual means of defending his

---

[15] This story (Zosimus, l v p 290 [c. 3]) proves that the hymeneal rites of antiquity were still practised, without idolatry, by the Christians of the East, and the bride was *forcibly* conducted from the house of her parents to that of her husband. Our form of marriage requires, with less delicacy, the express and public consent of a virgin.

dignity, and perhaps of oppressing his enemies. The præfect still exercised an uncontrolled authority over the civil and military government of the East , and his treasures, if he could resolve to use them, might be employed to procure proper instruments for the execution of the blackest designs that pride, ambition, and revenge could suggest to a desperate statesman. The character of Rufinus seemed to justify the accusations that he conspired against the person of his sovereign to seat himself on the vacant throne ; and that he had secretly invited the Huns and the Goths to invade the provinces of the empire and to increase the public confusion. The subtle præfect, whose life had been spent in the intrigues of the palace, opposed, with equal arms, the artful measures of the eunuch Eutropius ; but the timid soul of Rufinus was astonished by the hostile approach of a more formidable rival, of the great Stilicho, the general, or rather the master, of the empire of the West.[16]

Character of Stilicho, the minister, and general, of the Western empire   The celestial gift which Achilles obtained, and Alexander envied, of a poet worthy to celebrate the actions of heroes has been enjoyed by Stilicho in a much higher degree than might have been expected from the declining state of genius and of art. The muse of Claudian,[17] devoted to his service, was always prepared to stigmatize his adversaries, Rufinus or Eutropius, with eternal infamy ; or to paint, in the most splendid colours, the victories and virtues of a powerful benefactor. In the review of a period indifferently supplied with authentic materials, we cannot refuse to illustrate the annals of Honorius from the invectives or the panegyrics of a contemporary writer ; but, as Claudian appears to have indulged the most ample privilege of a poet and a courtier, some criticism will be requisite to translate the language of fiction or exaggeration into the truth and simplicity of historic prose. His silence concerning the family of Stilicho may be admitted as a proof that his patron was neither able nor desirous to boast a long series of illustrious progenitors ; and the slight mention of his father, an officer of Barbarian cavalry in the service of Valens, seems to countenance the assertion that the general who so long commanded the armies of Rome was descended from the savage and perfidious

---

[16] Zosimus (l v p 290 [c 47]), Orosius (l vii c 37), and the Chronicle of Marcellinus [Marcellinus used Orosius; but adds the words *in Græciam*, and *missis clam pecuniis*, from some other source] Claudian (in Rufin. ii. 7-100) paints, in lively colours, the distress and guilt of the præfect.

[17] Stilicho, directly or indirectly, is the perpetual theme of Claudian. The youth and private life of the hero are vaguely expressed in the poem on his first consulship, 35-140.

race of the Vandals.[18] If Stilicho had not possessed the external advantages of strength and stature, the most flattering bard, in the presence of so many thousand spectators, would have hesitated to affirm that he surpassed the measure of the demigods of antiquity ; and that, whenever he moved, with lofty steps, through the streets of the capital, the astonished crowd made room for the stranger, who displayed, in a private condition, the awful majesty of a hero.   From his earliest youth he embraced the profession of arms , his prudence and valour were soon distinguished in the field ; the horsemen and archers of the East admired his superior dexterity ; and in each degree of his military promotions the public judgment always prevented and approved the choice of the sovereign.   He was named by Theodosius to ratify a solemn treaty with the monarch of Persia ; [A D 383] he supported, during that important embassy, the dignity of the Roman name ; and, after his return to Constantinople, his merit was rewarded by an intimate and honourable alliance with the Imperial family.   Theodosius had been prompted by a pious motive of fraternal affection to adopt for his own the daughter of his brother Honorius ; the beauty and accomplishments of Serena [19] were universally admired by the obsequious court ; and Stilicho obtained the preference over a crowd of rivals, who am- [A D 384] bitiously disputed the hand of the princess and the favour of her adoptive father.[20]   The assurance that the husband of Serena would be faithful to the throne, which he was permitted to approach, engaged the emperor to exalt the fortunes and to employ the abilities of the sagacious and intrepid Stilicho.   He rose, through the successive steps of master of the horse and count of the domestics, to the supreme rank of master-general His military of all the cavalry and infantry of the Roman, or at least of the command Western, empire ; [21] and his enemies confessed that he invariably disdained to barter for gold the rewards of merit, or to defraud A D. 385-408

[18] Vandalorum, imbellis, avaræ, perfidæ, et dolosæ, gentis, genere editus Orosius, L vii. c. 38. Jerom (tom 1 ad Gerontiam, p. 93) calls him a Semi-Barbarian

[19] Claudian, in an imperfect poem, has drawn a fair, perhaps a flattering, portrait of Serena. That favourite niece of Theodosius was born, as well as her sister Thermantia, in Spain ; from whence, in their earliest youth, they were honourably conducted to the palace of Constantinople.

[20] Some doubt may be entertained whether this adoption was legal or only metaphorical (see Ducange, Fam. Byzant p 75). An old inscription gives Stilicho the singular title of *Pro-gener Divi Theodosii* [See Appendix 13]

[21] Claudian (Laus Serenæ, 190, 193) expresses, in poetic language, the "dilectus equorum," and . ￮ " gemino mox idem culmine [inde e germine] duxit agmina " The inscription aou￮, "count of the domestics," an important command, which Stilicho, in the height of his grandeur, might prudently retain.

the soldiers of the pay and gratifications which they deserved or claimed from the liberality of the state.[22]   The valour and conduct which he afterwards displayed in the defence of Italy against the arms of Alaric and Radagaisus may justify the fame of his early achievements ; and, in an age less attentive to the laws of honour or of pride, the Roman generals might yield the pre-eminence of rank to the ascendant of superior genius [23]   He lamented and revenged the murder of Promotus, his rival and his friend ; and the massacre of many thousands of the flying Bastarnæ is represented by the poet as a bloody sacrifice which the Roman Achilles offered to the manes of another Patroclus The virtues and victories of Stilicho deserved the hatred of Rufinus ; and the arts of calumny might have been successful, if the tender and vigilant Serena had not protected her husband against his domestic foes, whilst he vanquished in the field the enemies of the empire.[24]   Theodosius continued to support an unworthy minister, to whose diligence he delegated the government of the palace and of the East; but, when he marched against the tyrant Eugenius, he associated his faithful general to the labours and glories of the civil war , and, in the last moments of his life, the dying monarch recommended to Stilicho the care of his sons, and of the republic.[25]   The ambition and the abilities of Stilicho were not unequal to the important trust ; and he claimed the guardianship of the two empires during the minority of Arcadius and Honorius [26]   The first measure of his adminis-

[22] The beautiful lines of Claudian (in i. Cons Stilich ii 113) display *his* genius ; but the integrity of Stilicho (in the military administration) is much more firmly established by the unwilling evidence of Zosimus (l v. p 345 [c. 34]).

[23]   . . Si bellica moles [nubes]
Ingrueret, quamvis annis et jure minori,
Cedere grandævos equitum peditumque magistros
Adspiceres ———

Claudian, Laus Seren p 196, &c.
A modern general would deem their submission either heroic patriotism or abject servility

[24] Compare the poem on the first consulship (i 95[94]-115) with the *Laus Serenæ* (227-237 [236], where it unfortunately breaks off)   We may perceive the deep inveterate malice of Rufinus

[25]   .   Quem *fratribus* ipse
Discedens clipeumque [*leg* clipeum] defensoremque dedisti
Yet the nomination (iv Cons Hon 443) was private (iii Cons. Hon 142), cunctos discedere . .   jubet ; and may therefore be suspected   Zosimus and Suidas apply to Stilicho and Rufinus the same equal title of Ἐπίτροποι, guardians, or procurators.

[26] The Roman law distinguishes two sorts of *minority*, which expired at the age of fourteen and of twenty-five.   The one was subject to the *tutor*, or guardian, of the person ;   the other to the *curator*, or trustee, of the estate (Heineccius, Antiquitat. Rom. ad Jurisprudent. pertinent. L i. tit. xvii xxiii p. 218-232).   But these legal ideas were never accurately transferred into the constitution of an elective monarchy.

tration, or rather of his reign, displayed to the nations the vigour and activity of a spirit worthy to command.   He passed the Alps in the depth of winter ; descended the stream of the Rhine from the fortress of Basel to the marshes of Batavia ; reviewed the state of the garrisons ; repressed the enterprises of the Germans ; and, after establishing along the banks a firm and honourable peace, returned with incredible speed to the palace of Milan.[27]   The person and court of Honorius were subject to the master-general of the West ;   and the armies and provinces of Europe obeyed, without hesitation, a regular authority, which was exercised in the name of their young sovereign.   Two rivals only remained to dispute the claims, and to provoke the vengeance, of Stilicho.   Within the limits of Africa, Gildo, the Moor, maintained a proud and dangerous independence ; and the minister of Constantinople asserted his equal reign over the emperor and the empire of the East.

The impartiality which Stilicho affected, as the common guardian of the royal brothers, engaged him to regulate the equal division of the arms, the jewels, and the magnificent wardrobe and furniture of the deceased emperor.[28]   But the most important object of the inheritance consisted of the numerous legions, cohorts and squadrons of Romans or Barbarians, whom the event of the civil war had united under the standard of Theodosius   The various multitudes of Europe and Asia, exasperated by recent animosities, were overawed by the authority of a single man ; and the rigid discipline of Stilicho protected the lands of the citizen from the rapine of the licentious soldier [29]   Anxious, however, and impatient to relieve Italy from the presence of this formidable host, which could be useful only on the frontiers of the empire, he listened to the just requisition of the minister of Arcadius, declared his intention of re-conducting in person the troops of the East, and dexterously employed the rumour of a Gothic tumult to conceal his private designs of ambition and revenge.[30]   The guilty soul of

The fall and death of Rufinus   A D 395, Nov 27

---

[27] See Claudian (i. Cons Stilich. i. 188-242), but he must allow more than fifteen days for the journey and return between Milan and Leyden

[28] I. Cons Stilich. ii 88-94   Not only the robes and diadems of the deceased emperor, but even the helmets, sword-hilts, belts, cuirasses, &c., were enriched with pearls, emeralds, and diamonds.

[29] . . . Tantoque remoto
Principe, mutatas orbis non sensit habenas
This high commendation (i Cons Stil i 149) may be justified by the fears of the dying emperor (de Bell. Gildon 292-301), and the peace and good order which were enjoyed after his death (i Cons. Stil. i 150-168)

[30] Stilicho's march, and the death of Rufinus, are described by Claudian (in

Rufinus was alarmed by the approach of a warrior and a rival, whose enmity he deserved; he computed with increasing terror the narrow space of his life and greatness: and, as the last hope of safety, he interposed the authority of the emperor Arcadius Stilicho, who appears to have directed his march along the sea coast of the Hadriatic, was not far distant from the city of Thessalonica, when he received a peremptory message to recall the troops of the East and to declare that *his* nearer approach would be considered by the Byzantine court as an act of hostility. The prompt and unexpected obedience of the general of the West convinced the vulgar of his loyalty and moderation; and, as he had already engaged the affection of the Eastern troops, he recommended to their zeal the execution of his bloody design, which might be accomplished in his absence with less danger, perhaps, and with less reproach. Stilicho left the command of the troops of the East to Gainas the Goth, on whose fidelity he firmly relied; with an assurance, at least, that the hardy Barbarian would never be diverted from his purpose by any consideration of fear or remorse. The soldiers were easily persuaded to punish the enemy of Stilicho and of Rome; and such was the general hatred which Rufinus had excited that the fatal secret, communicated to thousands, was faithfully preserved during the long march from Thessalonica to the gates of Constantinople. As soon as they had resolved his death, they condescended to flatter his pride; the ambitious præfect was seduced to believe that those powerful auxiliaries might be tempted to place the diadem on his head; and the treasures which he distributed with a tardy and reluctant hand were accepted by the indignant multitude as an insult rather than as a gift. At the distance of a mile from the capital, in the field of Mars, before the palace of Hebdomon,[31] the troops halted; and the emperor, as well as his minister, advanced according to ancient custom respectfully to salute the power which supported their throne. As Rufinus passed along the ranks and disguised with studied courtesy his innate haughtiness, the wings insensibly wheeled from the right and left and inclosed the devoted victim within the circle of their arms. Before he could reflect on the danger of his situation Gainas gave the signal of death; a daring and forward soldier plunged his sword into the breast of the

Rufin. l. ii. 101-453), Zosimus (l v p 296, 297 [c 7]), Sozomen (l. viii c. 1), Socrates (l vi c. 1), Philostorgius (l. xi c. 3, with Godefroy, p. 441), and the Chronicle of Marcellinus. [See Appendix 14.]

[31] [See above, p. 10, n. 28, and vol. ii. App. 9.]

guilty præfect, and Rufinus fell, groaned and expired at the feet
of the affrighted emperor. If the agonies of a moment could
expiate the crimes of a whole life, or if the outrages inflicted on
a breathless corpse could be the object of pity, our humanity
might perhaps be affected by the horrid circumstances which
accompanied the murder of Rufinus. His mangled body was
abandoned to the brutal fury of the populace of either sex, who
hastened in crowds from every quarter of the city to trample on
the remains of the haughty minister at whose frown they had
so lately trembled. His right hand was cut off and carried
through the streets of Constantinople in cruel mockery to extort contributions for the avaricious tyrant, whose head was
publicly exposed, borne aloft on the point of a long lance.[32]
According to the savage maxims of the Greek republics his innocent family would have shared the punishment of his crimes.
The wife and daughter of Rufinus were indebted for their safety
to the influence of religion. *Her* sanctuary protected them
from the raging madness of the people ; and they were permitted to spend the remainder of their lives in the exercises of
Christian devotion in the peaceful retirement of Jerusalem.[33]

The servile poet of Stilicho applauds, with ferocious joy, this Discord of
horrid deed, which, in the execution, perhaps, of justice, the two empires.
violated every law of nature and society, profaned the majesty A.D 396, &c.
of the prince, and renewed the dangerous examples of military
licence. The contemplation of the universal order and harmony
had satisfied Claudian of the existence of the Deity ; but the
prosperous impunity of vice appeared to contradict his moral
attributes ; and the fate of Rufinus was the only event which
could dispel the religious doubts of the poet.[34] Such an act
might vindicate the honour of Providence ; but it did not much
contribute to the happiness of the people. In less than three
months they were informed of the maxims of the new adminis-

---

[32] The *dissection* of Rufinus, which Claudian performs with the savage coolness
of an anatomist (in Rufin ii 405-415), is likewise specified by Zosimus [ib] and
Jerom (tom. i. p. 26)

[33] The Pagan Zosimus mentions their sanctuary and pilgrimage The sister of
Rufinus, Sylvania, who passed her life at Jerusalem, is famous in monastic history.
1. The studious virgin had diligently, and even repeatedly, perused the commentators on the Bible, Origen, Gregory, Basil, &c , to the amount of five millions of
lines. 2 At the age of threescore, she could boast that she had never washed her
hands, face, or any part of her whole body, except the tips of her fingers to receive
communion   See the Vitæ Patrum, p 779, 977. [For the confiscation of the
property of Rufinus, cp. Symmachus, ep vi 14]

[34] See the beautiful exordium of his invective against Rufinus, which is curiously
discussed by the sceptic Bayle, Dictionnaire Critique, RUFIN Not E

tration by a singular edict, which established the exclusive
right of the treasury over the spoils of Rufinus, and silenced,
under heavy penalties, the presumptuous claims of the subjects
of the Eastern empire, who had been injured by his rapacious
tyranny [35] Even Stilicho did not derive from the murder of his
rival the fruit which he had proposed; and, though he gratified
his revenge, his ambition was disappointed. Under the name
of a favourite, the weakness of Arcadius required a master; but
he naturally preferred the obsequious arts of the eunuch Eutropius, who had obtained his domestic confidence; and the
emperor contemplated, with terror and aversion, the stern
genius of a foreign warrior. Till they were divided by the
jealousy of power, the sword of Gainas and the charms of
Eudoxia supported the favour of the great chamberlain of the
palace; the perfidious Goth, who was appointed master-general
of the East, betrayed, without scruple, the interest of his benefactor; and the same troops who had so lately massacred the
enemy of Stilicho were engaged to support, against him, the
independence of the throne of Constantinople. The favourites
of Arcadius fomented a secret and irreconcileable war against a
formidable hero who aspired to govern and to defend the two
empires of Rome and the two sons of Theodosius They incessantly laboured, by dark and treacherous machinations, to
deprive him of the esteem of the prince, the respect of the
people, and the friendship of the Barbarians. The life of
Stilicho was repeatedly attempted by the dagger of hired
assassins; and a decree was obtained, from the senate of Constantinople, to declare him an enemy of the republic and to
confiscate his ample possessions in the provinces of the East.
At a time when the only hope of delaying the ruin of the
Roman name depended on the firm union, and reciprocal aid,
of all the nations to whom it had been gradually communicated,
the subjects of Arcadius and Honorius were instructed, by their
respective masters, to view each other in a foreign, and even
hostile, light; to rejoice in their mutual calamities, and to embrace, as their faithful allies, the Barbarians whom they excited
to invade the territories of their countrymen [36] The natives of
Italy affected to despise the servile and effeminate Greeks of

[35] See the Theodosian Code, l iv. tit. xlii leg 14, 15   The new ministers
attempted, with inconsistent avarice, to seize the spoils of their predecessor and to
provide for their own future security
[36] See Claudian (1 Cons Stilich l 1 275, 292, 296, l ii 83) and Zosimus (l v.
p. 302 [c. 11])

Byzantium, who presumed to imitate the dress, and to usurp the dignity, of Roman senators;[37] and the Greeks had not yet forgot the sentiments of hatred and contempt which their polished ancestors had so long entertained for the rude inhabitants of the West. The distinction of two governments, which soon produced the separation of two nations, will justify my design of suspending the series of the Byzantine history, to prosecute, without interruption, the disgraceful, but memorable, reign of Honorius.

The prudent Stilicho, instead of persisting to force the inclinations of a prince and people who rejected his government, wisely abandoned Arcadius to his unworthy favourites; and his reluctance to involve the two empires in a civil war displayed the moderation of a minister who had so often signalized his military spirit and abilities. But, if Stilicho had any longer endured the revolt of Africa, he would have betrayed the security of the capital and the majesty of the Western emperor to the capricious insolence of a Moorish rebel. Gildo,[38] the brother of the tyrant Firmus, had preserved and obtained, as the reward of his apparent fidelity, the immense patrimony which was forfeited by treason; long and meritorious service, in the armies of Rome, raised him to the dignity of a military count; the narrow policy of the court of Theodosius had adopted the mischievous expedient of supporting a legal government by the interest of a powerful family; and the brother of Firmus was invested with the command of Africa. His ambition soon usurped the administration of justice and of the finances, without account and without control; and he maintained, during a reign of twelve years, the possession of an office from which it was impossible to remove him without the danger of a civil war. During those twelve years, the province of Africa groaned under the dominion of a tyrant who seemed to unite the unfeeling temper of a stranger with the partial resentments of domestic faction   The forms of law were often

Revolt of Gildo in Africa A D 386 398

---

[37] Claudian turns the consulship of the eunuch Eutropius into a national reflection (l ii 134 [135])

Plaudentem cerne senatum
Et Byzantinos proceres *Graiosque* Quirites
O patribus plebes, O digni consule patres

It is curious to observe the first symptoms of jealousy and schism between old and new Rome, between the Greeks and Latins.

[38] Claudian may have exaggerated the vices of Gildo, but his Moorish extraction, his notorious actions, and the complaints of St Augustin may justify the poet's invectives   Baronius (Annal. Eccles A D 398, No 35-56) has treated the African rebellion with skill and learning

superseded by the use of poison, and, if the trembling guests, who were invited to the table of Gildo, presumed to express their fears, the insolent suspicion served only to excite his fury, and he loudly summoned the ministers of death. Gildo alternately indulged the passions of avarice and lust ;[39] and, if his *days* were terrible to the rich, his *nights* were not less dreadful to husbands and parents The fairest of their wives and daughters were prostituted to the embraces of the tyrant, and afterwards abandoned to a ferocious troop of Barbarians and assassins, the black, or swarthy, natives of the desert, whom Gildo considered as the only guardians of his throne. In the civil war between Theodosius and Eugenius, the count, or rather the sovereign, of Africa maintained a haughty and suspicious neutrality ; refused to assist either of the contending parties with troops or vessels, expected the declaration of fortune, and reserved for the conqueror the vain professions of his allegiance. Such professions would not have satisfied the master of the Roman world; but the death of Theodosius, and the weakness and discord of his sons, confirmed the power of the Moor ; who condescended, as a proof of his moderation, to abstain from the use of the diadem and to supply Rome with the customary tribute, or rather subsidy, of corn In every division of the empire, the five provinces of Africa were invariably assigned to the West ; and Gildo had consented to govern that extensive country in the name of Honorius ; but his knowledge of the character and designs of Stilicho soon engaged him to address his homage to a more distant and feeble sovereign. The ministers of Arcadius embraced the cause of a perfidious rebel, and the delusive hope of adding the numerous cities of Africa to the empire of the East tempted them to assert a claim which they were incapable of supporting either by reason or by arms.[40]

He is condemned by the Roman Senate. A.D 397

When Stilicho had given a firm and decisive answer to the pretensions of the Byzantine court, he solemnly accused the

[39] Instat terribilis vivis, morientibus hæres,
Virginibus raptor, thalamis obscœnus adulter
Nulla quies · oritur præda cessante libido,
Divitibusque dies et nox metuenda mariti
. . . Mauris clarissima quæque
Fastidita datur. . [De B G 165 *sqq* and 189]
Baronius condemns, still more severely, the licentiousness of Gildo, as his wife, his daughter, and his sister were examples of perfect chastity The adulteries of the African soldiers are checked by one of the Imperial laws

[40] Inque tuam sortem numerosas transtulit urbes. Claudian (de Bell. Gildonico, 220-324) has touched, with political delicacy, the intrigues of the Byzantine court which are likewise mentioned by Zosimus (l. v. p. 302 [c. 11]).

tyrant of Africa before the tribunal which had formerly judged the kings and nations of the earth ; and the image of the republic was revived, after a long interval, under the reign of Honorius. The emperor transmitted an accurate and ample detail of the complaints of the provincials and the crimes of Gildo to the Roman senate ; and the members of that venerable assembly were required to pronounce the condemnation of the rebel. Their unanimous suffrage declared him the enemy of the republic ; and the decree of the senate added a sacred and legitimate sanction to the Roman arms.[41] A people who still remembered that their ancestors had been the masters of the world would have applauded, with conscious pride, the representation of ancient freedom ; if they had not long since been accustomed to prefer the solid assurance of bread to the unsubstantial visions of liberty and greatness. The subsistence of Rome depended on the harvests of Africa ; and it was evident that a declaration of war would be the signal of famine. The præfect Symmachus, who presided in the deliberations of the senate, admonished the ministers of his just apprehension that, as soon as the revengeful Moor should prohibit the exportation of corn, the tranquillity, and perhaps the safety, of the capital would be threatened by the hungry rage of a turbulent multitude.[42] The prudence of Stilicho conceived and executed without delay the most effectual measure for the relief of the Roman people. A large and seasonable supply of corn, collected in the inland provinces of Gaul, was embarked on the rapid stream of the Rhone, and transported, by an easy navigation, from the Rhone to the Tiber. During the whole term of the African war, the granaries of Rome were continually filled, her dignity was vindicated from the humiliating dependence, and the minds of an immense people were quieted by the calm confidence of peace and plenty.[43]

The cause of Rome and the conduct of the African war were entrusted, by Stilicho, to a general active and ardent to avenge his private injuries on the head of the tyrant. The spirit of discord which prevailed in the house of Nabal had excited a

The African war A.D 398

---

[41] Symmachus (l iv. epist. 4. [5, Seeck]) expresses the judicial forms of the senate , and Claudian (i. Cons. Stilich L 1 325, &c) seems to feel the spirit of a Roman. [Cp Seeck, in his ed of Symmachus, p lxvii *sqq*]

[42] Claudian finely displays these complaints of Symmachus in a speech of the goddess of Rome before the throne of Jupiter (de Bell. Gildon 28-128).

[43] See Claudian (in Eutrop. 1 1 401, &c : Cons Stil. l. 1. 306, &c. ii Cons. Stilich 91, &c.).

deadly quarrel between two of his sons, Gildo and Mascezel.[44]
The usurper pursued, with implacable rage, the life of his
younger brother, whose courage and abilities he feared; and
Mascezel, oppressed by superior power, took refuge in the
court of Milan; where he soon received the cruel intelligence
that his two innocent and helpless children had been murdered
by their inhuman uncle. The affliction of the father was suspended only by the desire of revenge. The vigilant Stilicho
already prepared to collect the naval and military forces of the
Western empire; and he had resolved, if the tyrant should be
able to wage an equal and doubtful war, to march against him
in person. But, as Italy required his presence, and as it might
be dangerous to weaken the defence of the frontier, he judged
it more advisable that Mascezel should attempt this arduous
adventure, at the head of a chosen body of Gallic veterans, who
had lately served under the standard of Eugenius. These
troops, who were exhorted to convince the world that they
could subvert, as well as defend, the throne of an usurper,
consisted of the *Jovian*, the *Herculian*, and the *Augustan* legions;
of the *Nervian* auxiliaries; of the soldiers who displayed in their
banners the symbol of a *lion*, and of the troops which were
distinguished by the auspicious names of *Fortunate* and *Invincible*. Yet such was the smallness of their establishments,
or the difficulty of recruiting, that these *seven* bands,[45] of high
dignity and reputation in the service of Rome, amounted to no
more than five thousand effective men.[46] The fleet of gallies
and transports sailed in tempestuous weather from the port of
Pisa, in Tuscany, and steered their course to the little island of
[Caprera]   Capraria, which had borrowed that name from the wild goats,
its original inhabitants, whose place was now occupied by a new
colony of a strange and savage appearance. "The whole island
(says an ingenious traveller of those times) is filled, or rather
defiled, by men who fly from the light   They call themselves

---

[44] He was of a mature age, since he had formerly (A D 373) served against his
brother Firmus (Ammian xxix 5). Claudian, who understood the court of Milan,
dwells on the injuries, rather than the merits, of Mascezel (de Bell Gild. 389-414)
The Moorish war was not worthy of Honorius or Stilicho, &c.

[45] Claudian, Bell. Gild 415-423   The change of discipline allowed him to use
indifferently the names of *Legio, Cohors, Manipulus*. See the *Notitia Imperii*, S.
38, 40

[46] Orosius (L vii c 36, p 565) qualifies this account with an expression of doubt
(ut aiunt), and it scarcely coincides with the δυναμεις αδρας of Zosimus (l. v p 303
[c 11]) Yet Claudian, after some declamation about Cadmus's soldiers, frankly
owns that Stilicho sent a small army, lest the rebel should fly, ne timeare times
(i. Cons. Stilich. l. i. 314, &c)

Monks, or solitaries, because they choose to live alone, without any witnesses of their actions. They fear the gifts of fortune, from the apprehension of losing them ; and, lest they should be miserable, they embrace a life of voluntary wretchedness How absurd is their choice ! how perverse their understanding ! to dread the evils, without being able to support the blessings, of the human condition. Either this melancholy madness is the effect of disease, or else the consciousness of guilt urges these unhappy men to exercise on their own bodies the tortures which are inflicted on fugitive slaves by the hand of justice." [47] Such was the contempt of a profane magistrate for the monks of Capraria, who were revered, by the pious Mascezel, as the chosen servants of God.[48] Some of them were persuaded, by his entreaties, to embark on board the fleet ; and it is observed, to the praise of the Roman general, that his days and nights were employed in prayer, fasting, and the occupation of singing psalms. The devout leader, who, with such a reinforcement, appeared confident of victory, avoided the dangerous rocks of Corsica, coasted along the eastern side of Sardinia, and secured his ships against the violence of the south wind, by casting anchor in the safe and capacious harbour of Cagliari, at the distance of one hundred and forty miles from the African shores.[49]

Gildo was prepared to resist the invasion with all the forces of Africa By the liberality of his gifts and promises, he endeavoured to secure the doubtful allegiance of the Roman soldiers, whilst he attracted to his standard the distant tribes of Gætulia and Æthiopia. He proudly reviewed an army of seventy thousand men, and boasted, with the rash presumption which is the forerunner of disgrace, that his numerous cavalry would trample under their horses' feet the troops of Mascezel and involve, in a cloud of burning sand, the natives of the cold regions of Gaul and Germany.[50] But the Moor who commanded the

Defeat and death of Gildo A D. 398

[47] Claud Rutil. Numatian Itinerar 1 439-448 He afterwards (515-526) mentions a religious madman on the Isle of Gorgona. For such profane remarks, Rutilius and his accomplices are styled by his commentator Barthius, rabiosi canes diaboli Tillemont (Mém. Ecclés. tom xii. p. 471) more calmly observes that the unbelieving poet praises where he means to censure

[48] Orosius, l vii c. 36, p. 564. Augustin commends two of these savage saints of the Isle of Goats (epist lxxxi apud Tillemont, Mém Ecclés tom. xiii p 317, and Baronius, Annal Eccles A D 398, No 51)

[49] Here the first book of the Gildonic war is terminated The rest of Claudian's poem has been lost ; and we are ignorant *how* or *where* the army made good their landing in Africa.

[50] Orosius must be responsible for the account The presumption of Gildo and his various train of Barbarians is celebrated by Claudian (1 Cons. Stil. i. 345-355).

legions of Honorius was too well acquainted with the manners of his countrymen to entertain any serious apprehension of a naked and disorderly host of Barbarians; whose left arm, instead of a shield, was protected only by a mantle; who were totally disarmed as soon as they had darted their javelin from their right hand; and whose horses had never been taught to bear the control, or to obey the guidance, of the bridle.   He fixed his camp of five thousand veterans in the face of a superior enemy, and, after the delay of three days, gave the signal of a general engagement.[51]   As Mascezel advanced before the front with fair offers of peace and pardon, he encountered one of the foremost standard-bearers of the Africans, and, on his refusal to yield, struck him on the arm with his sword.   The arm, and the standard, sunk under the weight of the blow, and the imaginary act of submission was hastily repeated by all the standards of the line.   At this signal, the disaffected cohorts proclaimed the name of their lawful sovereign; the Barbarians, astonished by the defection of their Roman allies, dispersed, according to their custom, in tumultuary flight; and Mascezel obtained the honours of an easy, and almost bloodless, victory.[52] The tyrant escaped from the field of battle to the seashore, and threw himself into a small vessel, with the hope of reaching in safety some friendly port of the empire of the East; but the obstinacy of the wind drove him back into the harbour of Tabraca,[53] which had acknowledged, with the rest of the province, the dominion of Honorius and the authority of his lieutenant. The inhabitants, as a proof of their repentance and loyalty, seized and confined the person of Gildo in a dungeon; and his own despair saved him from the intolerable torture of supporting the presence of an injured and victorious brother.[54]   The captives and the spoils of Africa were laid at the feet of the emperor; but Stilicho, whose moderation appeared more conspicuous and more sincere in the midst of prosperity, still affected to consult the laws of the republic, and referred to the

[Battle of Ardalio]

[Tabarca]

---

[51] St Ambrose, who had been dead about a year, revealed, in a vision, the time and place of the victory   Mascezel afterwards related his dream to Paulinus, the original biographer of the saint, from whom it might easily pass to Orosius.

[52] Zosimus (l v. p 303 [c 11]) supposes an obstinate combat ; but the narrative of Orosius appears to conceal a real fact, under the disguise of a miracle.

[53] Tabraca lay between the two Hippos (Cellarius, tom. ii. p ii. p. 112; d'Anville, tom iii p 84). Orosius has distinctly named the field of battle, but our ignorance cannot define the precise situation

[54] The death of Gildo is expressed by Claudian (i. Cons Stil. l. 357) and his best interpreters, Zosimus and Orosius.

senate and people of Rome the judgment of the most illustrious criminals.[55] Their trial was public and solemn ; but the judges, in the exercise of this obsolete and precarious jurisdiction, were impatient to punish the African magistrates, who had intercepted the subsistence of the Roman people.   The rich and guilty province was impressed by the Imperial ministers, who had a visible interest to multiply the number of the accomplices of Gildo ; and, if an edict of Honorius seems to check the malicious industry of informers, a subsequent edict, at the distance of ten years, continues and renews the prosecution of the offences which had been committed in the time of the general rebellion.[56]   The adherents of the tyrant who escaped the first fury of the soldiers and the judges might derive some consolation from the tragic fate of his brother, who could never obtain his pardon for the extraordinary services which he had performed. After he had finished an important war in the space of a single winter, Mascezel was received at the court of Milan with loud applause, affected gratitude, and secret jealousy ;[57]   and his death, which, perhaps, was the effect of accident, has been considered as the crime of Stilicho.   In the passage of a bridge, the Moorish prince, who accompanied the master-general of the West, was suddenly thrown from his horse into the river ;   the officious haste of the attendants was restrained by a cruel and perfidious smile which they observed on the countenance of Stilicho ; and, while they delayed the necessary assistance, the unfortunate Mascezel was irrecoverably drowned.[58]

The joy of the African triumph was happily connected with the nuptials of the emperor Honorius and of his cousin Maria, the daughter of Stilicho : and this equal and honourable alliance seemed to invest the powerful minister with the authority of a parent over his submissive pupil.   The muse of Claudian was

Marriage and character of Honorius A D 398

[55] Claudian (ii Cons Stilich 99-119) describes their trial (tremuit quos Africa nuper, cernunt rostra reos) and applauds the restoration of the ancient constitution It is here that he introduces the famous sentence, so familiar to the friends of despotism
.   Nunquam libertas gratior exstat
          Quam sub rege pio
But the freedom which depends on royal piety scarcely deserves that appellation

[56] See the Theodosian Code, l. ix. tit xxxix. leg 3, tit xl. leg 19.

[57] Stilicho, who claimed an equal share in all the victories of Theodosius and his son, particularly asserts that Africa was recovered by the wisdom of *his* counsels (see an inscription produced by Baronius)   [Gruter, p 412. See Appendix 13]

[58] I have softened the narrative of Zosimus, which, in its crude simplicity, is almost incredible (l v p. 303 [c. 11])   Orosius damns the victorious general (p. 538 [7, 33]) for violating the right of sanctuary

not silent on this propitious day:[59] he sung, in various and lively strains, the happiness of the royal pair, and the glory of the hero, who confirmed their union and supported their throne. The ancient fables of Greece, which had almost ceased to be the object of religious faith, were saved from oblivion by the genius of poetry The picture of the Cyprian grove, the seat of harmony and love ; the triumphant progress of Venus over her native seas, and the mild influence which her presence diffused in the palace of Milan ; express to every age the natural sentiments of the heart, in the just and pleasing language of allegorical fiction.   But the amorous impatience which Claudian attributes to the young prince [60] must excite the smiles of the court ; and his beauteous spouse (if she deserved the praise of beauty) had not much to fear or to hope from the passions of her lover.   Honorius was only in the fourteenth year of his age ; Serena, the mother of his bride, deferred, by art or persuasion, the consummation of the royal nuptials ; Maria died a virgin, after she had been ten years a wife ; and the chastity of the emperor was secured by the coldness, or perhaps the debility, of his constitution [61]   His subjects, who attentively studied the character of their young sovereign, discovered that Honorius was without passions, and consequently without talents ; and that his feeble and languid disposition was alike incapable of discharging the duties of his rank or of enjoying the pleasures of his age. In his early youth he made some progress in the exercises of riding and drawing the bow : but he soon relinquished these fatiguing occupations, and the amusement of feeding poultry became the serious and daily care of the monarch of the West,[62] who resigned the reins of empire to the firm and

---

[59] Claudian, as the poet laureate, composed a serious and elaborate epithalamium of 340 lines besides some gay Fescennines, which were sung in a more licentious tone on the wedding-night

[60]   .   Calet obvius ire
Jam princeps, tardumque cupit discedere solem
Nobilis haud aliter *sonipes*

(de Nuptiis Honor. et Mariæ, 587) and more freely in the Fescennines (112-126 [iv. 14-29, ed. Koch]).

Dices " *O* " *quotiens*, " hoc mihi dulcius
Quam flavos *decies* vincere Sarmatas "

·   ·   ·   ·   ·   ·   ·

Tum victor madido prosilias toro
Nocturni referens vulnera prœlii.

[61] See Zosimus, l v p 333 [c 28]

[62] Procopius de Bell. Gothico, l i c 2.   I have borrowed the general practice of Honorius, without adopting the singular and, indeed, improbable tale which is related by the Greek historian.

skilful hand of his guardian Stilicho.   The experience of history
will countenance the suspicion that a prince who was born in
the purple received a worse education than the meanest peasant
of his dominions ; and that the ambitious minister suffered him
to attain the age of manhood without attempting to excite his
courage or to enlighten his understanding.[63]   The predecessors
of Honorius were accustomed to animate by their example, or at
least by their presence, the valour of the legions ; and the dates
of their laws attest the perpetual activity of their motions through
the provinces of the Roman world.   But the son of Theodosius
passed the slumber of his life, a captive in his palace, a stranger
in his country, and the patient, almost the indifferent, spectator
of the ruin of the Western empire, which was repeatedly attacked,
and finally subverted, by the arms of the Barbarians.   In the
eventful history of a reign of twenty-eight years, it will seldom
be necessary to mention the name of the emperor Honorius.

[63] The lessons of Theodosius, or rather Claudian (iv Cons Honor. 214-418),
might compose a fine institution for the future prince of a great and free nation.
It was far above Honorius and his degenerate subjects.

CHAPTER XXX

Revolt of the Goths—They plunder Greece—Two great Invasions of
Italy by Alaric and Radagaisus—They are repulsed by Stilicho
—The Germans overrun Gaul—Usurpation of Constantine in the
West—Disgrace and Death of Stilicho

Revolt of the If the subjects of Rome could be ignorant of their obligations
Goths to the great Theodosius, they were too soon convinced how
A.D 395
painfully the spirit and abilities of their deceased emperor had
supported the frail and mouldering edifice of the republic.   He
died in the month of January ; and before the end of the winter
of the same year the Gothic nation was in arms.[1]   The Barbarian
auxiliaries   erected   their   independent   standard ;   and boldly
avowed the hostile designs which they had long cherished in
their ferocious minds.   Their countrymen, who had been condemned by the conditions of the last treaty to a life of tranquillity and labour, deserted their farms at the first sound of the
trumpet, and eagerly resumed the weapons which they had
reluctantly laid down.   The barriers of the Danube were thrown
open ; the savage warriors of Scythia issued from their forests ;
and the uncommon severity of the winter allowed the poet to
remark " that they rolled their ponderous waggons over the
broad and icy back of the indignant river ".[2]   The unhappy
natives of the provinces to the south of the Danube submitted
to the calamities which, in the course of twenty years, were
almost grown familiar to their imagination ;   and the various
troops of Barbarians who gloried in the Gothic name were
irregularly spread from the woody shores of Dalmatia to the

---

[1] The revolt of the Goths and the blockade of Constantinople are distinctly
mentioned by Claudian (in Rufin l ii. 7-100), Zosimus (l. v p. 292 [c. 5]), and
Jornandes (de Rebus Geticis, c 29)   [Alaric approached Constantinople, but did
not blockade it.   Cp. Keller, Stilicho, p 31]
[2] ———Alii per terga ferocis
                Danubii solidata ruunt expertaque remis
                Frangunt stagna rotis [*ib* 26]
Claudian and Ovid often amuse their fancy by interchanging the metaphors and
properties of *liquid* water and *solid* ice   Much false wit has been expended in this
easy exercise.

walls of Constantinople.[3] The interruption, or at least the diminution, of the subsidy which the Goths had received from the prudent liberality of Theodosius was the specious pretence of their revolt; the affront was embittered by their contempt for the unwarlike sons of Theodosius; and their resentment was inflamed by the weakness or treachery of the minister of Arcadius. The frequent visits of Rufinus to the camp of the Barbarians, whose arms and apparel he affected to imitate, were considered as a sufficient evidence of his guilty correspondence: and the public enemy, from a motive either of gratitude or of policy, was attentive, amidst the general devastation, to spare the private estates of the unpopular præfect. The Goths, instead of being impelled by the blind and headstrong passions of their chiefs, were now directed by the bold and artful genius of Alaric. [Born between A D 360 and 370] That renowned leader was descended from the noble race of the Balti;[4] which yielded only to the royal dignity of the Amali: he had solicited the command of the Roman armies; and the Imperial court provoked him to demonstrate the folly of their [Probably made King A D 395] refusal and the importance of their loss. Whatever hopes might be entertained of the conquest of Constantinople, the judicious general soon abandoned an impracticable enterprise. In the midst of a divided court and a discontented people, the Emperor Arcadius was terrified by the aspect of the Gothic arms; but the want of wisdom and valour was supplied by the strength of the city; and the fortifications, both of the sea and land, might securely brave the impotent and random darts of the Barbarians Alaric disdained to trample any longer on the prostrate and ruined countries of Thrace and Dacia, and he resolved to seek a plentiful harvest of fame and riches in a province which had hitherto escaped the ravages of war.[5]

The character of the civil and military officers, on whom [Alaric marches in to Greece A D 396]

[3] Jerom, tom. 1. p 26 [ep. 60]. He endeavours to comfort his friend Heliodorus, bishop of Altinum, for the loss of his nephew Nepotian, by a curious recapitulation of all the public and private misfortunes of the times. See Tillemont, Mém. Ecclés tom xii p 200, &c

[4] *Baltha* or *bold* · origo mirifica, says Jornandes (c 29) [The meaning of the passage of Jordanes may be, as Kopke thinks, that owing to his bravery Alaric was described *inter suos*, as a true Baltha (ορθώνυμος).] This illustrious race long continued to flourish in France, in the Gothic province of Septimania or Languedoc, under the corrupted appellation of *Baux* and a branch of that family afterwards settled in the kingdom of Naples (Grotius in Prolegom ad Hist Gothic p. 53) The lords of Baux, near Arles, and of seventy-nine subordinate places, were independent of the counts of Provence (Longuerue, Description de la France, tom 1. p 357).

[5] Zosimus (l v p 293-295 [c 5]) is our best guide for the conquest of Greece, but the hints and allusion of Claudian are so many rays of historic light.

Rufinus had devolved the government of Greece, confirmed the public suspicion that he had betrayed the ancient seat of freedom and learning to the Gothic invader. The proconsul Antiochus was the unworthy son of a respectable father ; and Gerontius, who commanded the provincial troops, was much better qualified to execute the oppressive orders of a tyrant than to defend, with courage and ability, a country most remarkably fortified by the hand of nature. Alaric had traversed, without resistance, the plains of Macedonia and Thessaly, as far as the foot of Mount Oeta, a steep and woody range of hills, almost impervious to his cavalry. They stretched from East to West, to the edge of the seashore ; and left, between the precipice and the Malian Gulf, an interval of three hundred feet, which, in some places, was contracted to a road capable of admitting only a single carriage.[6] In this narrow pass of Thermopylæ, where Leonidas and the three hundred Spartans had gloriously devoted their lives, the Goths might have been stopped, or destroyed, by a skilful general ; and perhaps the view of that sacred spot might have kindled some sparks of military ardour in the breasts of the degenerate Greeks. The troops which had been posted to defend the streights of Thermopylæ retired, as they were directed, without attempting to disturb the secure and rapid passage of Alaric ;[7] and the fertile fields of Phocis and Bœotia were instantly covered by a deluge of barbarians, who massacred the males of an age to bear arms, and drove away the beautiful females, with the spoil and cattle, of the flaming villages. The travellers who visited Greece several years afterwards could easily discover the deep and bloody traces of the march of the Goths, and Thebes was less indebted for her preservation to the strength of her seven gates than to the eager haste of Alaric, who advanced to occupy the city of Athens and the important harbour of the Piræus. The same impatience urged him to prevent the delay and danger of a siege, by the offer of a capitulation : and, as soon as the Athenians heard the voice of the Gothic herald, they were easily persuaded to deliver the greatest part of their wealth, as the ransom of the city of Minerva and its inhabitants. The treaty was ratified by solemn oaths, and observed with mutual fidelity. The Gothic prince, with a small

---

[6] Compare Herodotus (l. vii. c. 176) and Livy (xxxvi. 15.) The narrow entrance of Greece was probably enlarged by each successive ravisher [The sea has retreated far from the pass.]

[7] He passed, says Eunapius (in Vit. Philosoph. p. 93, edit. Commelin, 1596), through the streights, διὰ τῶν πυλῶν (of Thermopylæ) παρῆλθεν, ὥσπερ διὰ σταδίου καὶ ἱπποκρότου πεδίου τρέχων [On Alaric in Greece, cp .App 15.]

and select train, was admitted within the walls; he indulged
himself in the refreshment of the bath, accepted a splendid
banquet which was provided by the magistrate, and affected to
show that he was not ignorant of the manners of civilised
nations.[8] But the whole territory of Attica, from the promontory
of Sunium to the town of Megara, was blasted by his baleful
presence; and, if we may use the comparison of a contemporary
philsopher, Athens itself resembled the bleeding and empty skin
of a slaughtered victim.   The distance between Megara and
Corinth could not much exceed thirty miles; but the *bad road*,
an expressive name, which it still bears among the Greeks, was,
or might easily have been made, impassable for the march of
an enemy.   The thick and gloomy woods of Mount Cithæron
covered the inland country; the Scironian rocks approached the
water's edge, and hung over the narrow and winding path,
which was confined above six miles along the seashore.[9]   The
passage of those rocks, so infamous in every age, was terminated
by the isthmus of Corinth; and a small body of firm and intrepid
soldiers might have successfully defended a temporary intrench-
ment of five or six miles from the Ionian to the Ægean sea.
The confidence of the cities of Peloponnesus in their natural
rampart had tempted them to neglect the care of their antique
walls; and the avarice of the Roman governors had exhausted
and betrayed the unhappy province.[10]   Corinth, Argos, Sparta,
yielded without resistance to the arms of the Goths; and the
most fortunate of the inhabitants were saved by death from
beholding the slavery of their families and the conflagration of
their cities.[11]   The vases and statues were distributed among the

[8] In obedience to Jerom and Claudian (in Rufin. l. ii. 191), I have mixed some
darker colours in the mild representation of Zosimus, who wished to soften the
calamities of Athens
             Nec fera Cecropias traxissent vincula matres
Synesius (Epist clvi. [*leg* 135], p. 272, edit Petav) observes that Athens, whose
sufferings he imputes to the proconsul's avarice, was at that time less famous for
her schools of philosophy than for her trade of honey.
[9] ————Vallata mari Scironia rupes
    Et duo continuo connectens æquora muro
    Isthmos————
                    Claudian de Bell Getico, 188
The Scironian rocks are described by Pausanias (l. 1 c 44, p. 107, edit Kuhn,
[§ 10]), and our modern travellers, Wheeler (p 436), and Chandler (p. 298)   Hadrian
made the road passable for two carriages
[10] Claudian (in Rufin l ii 186, and de Bello Getico, 611, &c.) vaguely, though
forcibly, delineates the scene of rapine and destruction.
[11] Τρὶς μακαρες Δαναοι καὶ τετρακις, &c   These generous lines of Homer (Odyss
l v 306) were transcribed by one of the captive youths of Corinth; and the tears
of Mummius may prove that the rude conqueror, though he was ignorant of the
value of an original picture, possessed the purest source of good taste, a benevolent
heart (Plutarch, Symposiac. l ix tom. ii. p 737, edit. Wechel).

Barbarians, with more regard to the value of the materials than to the elegance of the workmanship ; the female captives submitted to the laws of war ; the enjoyment of beauty was the reward of valour ; and the Greeks could not reasonably complain of an abuse, which was justified by the example of the heroic times.[12] The descendants of that extraordinary people, who had considered valour and discipline as the walls of Sparta, no longer remembered the generous reply of their ancestors to an invader more formidable than Alaric : "If thou art a god, thou wilt not hurt those who have never injured thee ; if thou art a man, advance :—and thou wilt find men equal to thyself".[13] From Thermopylæ to Sparta, the leader of the Goths pursued his victorious march without encountering any mortal antagonists ; but one of the advocates of expiring Paganism has confidently asserted that the walls of Athens were guarded by the goddess Minerva, with her formidable Ægis, and by the angry phantom of Achilles ;[14] and that the conqueror was dismayed by the presence of the hostile deities of Greece. In an age of miracles, it would perhaps be unjust to dispute the claim of the historian Zosimus to the common benefit ; yet it cannot be dissembled that the mind of Alaric was ill prepared to receive, either in sleeping or waking visions, the impressions of Greek superstition. The songs of Homer and the fame of Achilles had probably never reached the ear of the illiterate *Barbarian ;* and the *Christian* faith, which he had devoutly embraced, taught him to despise the imaginary deities of Rome and Athens. The invasion of the Goths, instead of vindicating the honour, contributed, at least accidentally, to extirpate the last remains, of Paganism ; and the mysteries of Ceres, which had subsisted eighteen hundred years, did not survive the destruction of Eleusis and the calamities of Greece.[15]

He is attacked by Stilicho, A D 397 [396]

The last hope of a people who could no longer depend on their arms, their gods, or their sovereign, was placed in the powerful assistance of the general of the West ; and Stilicho,

---

[12] Homer perpetually describes the exemplary patience of those female captives, who gave their charms, and even their hearts, to the murderers of their fathers, brothers, &c   Such a passion (of Eriphile for Achilles) is touched with admirable delicacy by Racine

[13] Plutarch (in Pyrrho, tom ii. p. 471, edit Brian [c. 26, *ad fin*]) gives the genuine answer in the Laconic dialect   Pyrrhus attacked Sparta, with 25,000 foot, 2000 horse, and 24 elephants : and the defence of that open town is a fine comment on the laws of Lycurgus, even in the last stage of decay.

[14] Such, perhaps, as Homer (Iliad, xx 164) has so nobly painted him

[15] Eunapius (in Vit Philosoph p 90-93) intimates that a troop of Monks betrayed Greece and followed the Gothic camp. [Cp Appendix 15]

who had not been permitted to repulse, advanced to chastise
the invaders of Greece [16] A numerous fleet was equipped in
the ports of Italy ; and the troops, after a short and prosperous
navigation over the Ionian sea, were safely disembarked on the
isthmus, near the ruins of Corinth. The woody and mountainous country of Arcadia, the fabulous residence of Pan and
the Dryads, became the scene of a long and doubtful conflict
between two generals not unworthy of each other. The skill
and perseverance of the Roman at length prevailed ; and the
Goths, after sustaining a considerable loss from disease and
desertion, gradually retreated to the lofty mountain of Pholoe,
near the sources of the Peneus, and on the frontiers of Elis : a
sacred country, which had formerly been exempted from the
calamities of war.[17] The camp of the Barbarians was immediately besieged ; the waters of the river [18] were diverted into
another channel ; and, while they laboured under the intolerable
pressure of thirst and hunger, a strong line of circumvallation
was formed to prevent their escape. After these precautions,
Stilicho, too confident of victory, retired to enjoy his triumph
in the theatrical games and lascivious dances of the Greeks ;
his soldiers, deserting their standards, spread themselves over
the country of their allies, which they stripped of all that had
been saved from the rapacious hands of the enemy. Alaric
appears to have seized the favourable moment to execute one
of those hardy enterprises, in which the abilities of a general
are displayed with more genuine lustre than in the tumult of a
day of battle. To extricate himself from the prison of Peloponnesus, it was necessary that he should pierce the intrenchments
which surrounded his camp ; that he should perform a difficult

[Early in A.D. 396]

---

[16] For Stilicho's Greek war, compare the honest narrative of Zosimus (l. v.
p. 295, 296 [c 7]) with the curious circumstantial flattery of Claudian (i Cons
Stilich. 1 172-186; iv. Cons Hon 459-487) As the event was not glorious, it is
artfully thrown into the shade [See Appendix 14.]

[17] The troops who marched through Elis delivered up their arms This security
enriched the Eleans, who were lovers of a rural life Riches begat pride ; they
disdained their privilege, and they suffered. Polybius advises them to retire once
more within their magic circle. See a learned and judicious discourse on the
Olympic games, which Mr. West has prefixed to his translation of Pindar.

[18] Claudian (in iv. Cons. Hon 480) alludes to the fact, without naming the
river perhaps the Alpheus (i. Cons. Stil. l i. 185)

————Et Alpheus Geticis angustus acervis
Tardior ad Siculos etiamnum pergit amores.

Yet I should prefer the Peneus, a shallow stream in a wide and deep bed, which
runs through Elis, and falls into the sea below Cyllene It had been joined with
the Alpheus, to cleanse the Augean stable (Cellarius, tom. i p 760; Chandler's
Travels, p 286).

and dangerous march of thirty miles as far as the Gulf of
Corinth; and that he should transport his troops, his captives,
and his spoil, over an arm of the sea which, in the narrow
interval between Rhium and the opposite shore, is at least

Escapes to Epirus

half a mile in breadth [19] The operations of Alaric must have
been secret, prudent, and rapid; since the Roman general was
confounded by the intelligence that the Goths, who had eluded
his efforts, were in full possession of the important province of
Epirus.   This unfortunate delay allowed Alaric sufficient time
to conclude the treaty, which he secretly negotiated with the
ministers of Constantinople.   The apprehension of a civil war
compelled Stilicho to retire, at the haughty mandate of his
rivals, from the dominions of Arcadius; and he respected in the
enemy of Rome the honourable character of the ally and servant
of the emperor of the East.

Alaric is declared master general of the Eastern Illyricum, A.D 398

[A.D 399]

A Grecian philosopher,[20] who visited Constantinople soon after
the death of Theodosius, published his liberal opinions concerning the duties of kings and the state of the Roman republic.
Synesius observes and deplores the fatal abuse which the imprudent bounty of the late emperor had introduced into the military
service.   The citizens and subjects had purchased an exemption
from the indispensable duty of defending their country; which
was supported by the arms of Barbarian mercenaries.   The
fugitives of Scythia were permitted to disgrace the illustrious
dignities of the empire; their ferocious youth, who disdained the
salutary restraint of laws, were more anxious to acquire the
riches than to imitate the arts of a people, the object of their contempt and hatred; and the power of the Goths was the stone of
Tantalus, perpetually suspended over the peace and safety of
the devoted state.   The measures which Synesius recommends
are the dictates of a bold and generous patriot.   He exhorts the
emperor to revive the courage of his subjects by the example
of manly virtue; to banish luxury from the court and from the
camp; to substitute in the place of the Barbarian mercenaries,
an army of men interested in the defence of their laws and of
their property; to force, in such a moment of public danger, the

[19] Strabo, l. viii p 517; Plin. Hist. Natur iv 3, Wheeler, p 308;
Chandler, p 275   They measured from different points the distance between the
two lands
[20] Synesius passed three years (A.D 397-400) at Constantinople, as deputy from
Cyrene to the emperor Arcadius.   He presented him with a crown of gold, and
pronounced before him the instructive oration de Regno (p 1-32, edit. Petav. Paris,
1612) [A D. 399].   The philosopher was made bishop of Ptolemais, A D 410, and
died about 430.   See Tillemont, Mém. Ecclés tom. xii. p 499, 554, 683-685.

mechanic from his shop and the philosopher from his school ; to
rouse the indolent citizen from his dream of pleasure, and to
arm, for the protection of agriculture, the hands of the laborious
husbandman.   At the head of such troops, who might deserve
the name, and would display the spirit, of Romans, he animates
the son of Theodosius to encounter a race of Barbarians who
were destitute of any real courage ; and never to lay down his
arms, till he had chased them far away into the solitudes of
Scythia ; or had reduced them to the state of ignominious servitude which the Lacedæmonians formerly imposed on the captive
Helots.[21]   The court of Arcadius indulged the zeal, applauded
the eloquence, and neglected the advice of Synesius.   Perhaps
the philosopher, who addresses the emperor of the East in the
language of reason and virtue which he might have used to
a Spartan king, had not condescended to form a practicable
scheme, consistent with the temper and circumstances of a
degenerate age.   Perhaps the pride of the ministers, whose
business was seldom interrupted by reflection, might reject as
wild and visionary every proposal which exceeded the measure
of their capacity and deviated from the forms and precedents
of office.   While the oration of Synesius and the downfall of
the Barbarians were the topics of popular conversation, an edict
was published at Constantinople, which declared the promotion
of Alaric to the rank of master-general of the Eastern Illyricum.   The Roman provincials and the allies, who had respected
the faith of treaties, were justly indignant that the ruin of
Greece and Epirus should be so liberally rewarded   The
Gothic conqueror was received as a lawful magistrate, in the
cities which he had so lately besieged.   The fathers whose sons
he had massacred, the husbands whose wives he had violated,
were subject to his authority ; and the success of his rebellion
encouraged the ambition of every leader of the foreign mercenaries   The use to which Alaric applied his new command
distinguishes the firm and judicious character of his policy.   He
issued his orders to the four magazines and manufactures of
offensive and defensive arms, Margus, Ratiaria, Naissus, and
Thessalonica, to provide his troops with an extraordinary supply
of shields, helmets, swords, and spears; the unhappy provincials
were compelled to forge the instruments of their own destruction ; and the Barbarians removed the only defect which had

[21] Synesius de Regno, p. 21-26.

sometimes disappointed the efforts of their courage [22]   The birth of Alaric, the glory of his past exploits, and the confidence in his future designs, insensibly united the body of the nation under his victorious standard ; and with the unanimous consent of the Barbarian chieftains, the master-general of Illyricum was elevated, according to ancient custom, on a shield, and solemnly proclaimed king of the Visigoths. [23]   Armed with this double power, seated on the verge of the two empires, he alternately sold his deceitful promises to the courts of Arcadius and Honorius, [24] till he declared and executed his resolution of invading the dominions of the West.   The provinces of Europe which belonged to the Eastern emperor were already exhausted ; those of Asia were inaccessible ; and the strength of Constantinople had resisted his attack.   But he was tempted by the fame, the beauty, the wealth of Italy, which he had twice visited ; and he secretly aspired to plant the Gothic standard on the walls of Rome, and to enrich his army with the accumulated spoils of three hundred triumphs. [25]

and king of the Visigoths

The scarcity of facts [26] and the uncertainty of dates [27] oppose

He invades Italy   A.D 400 403

[22] ————qui fœdera rumpit
Ditatur . qui servat, eget : vastator Achivœ
Gentis, et Epirum nuper populatam multam
Præsidet Illyrico , jam, quos obsedit, amicos
Ingreditur muros   illis responsa daturus
Quorum conjugibus potitur natosque peremit
Claudian in Eutrop. l. ii. 212.   Alaric applauds his own policy (de Bell Getic. 533-543) in the use which he had made of this Illyrian jurisdiction   [The precise title is uncertain ; but Master-General is probable   From de B G , 534, *ducem*, Mr Hodgkin suggests Dux Daciæ ripensis et Mœsiæ primæ.]

[23] Jornandes, c. 29, p 651.   The Gothic historian adds, with unusual spirit, Cum suis deliberans suasit suo labore quærere regna, quam alienis per otium subjacere.   [It is much more probable that he was proclaimed king (*thiudans*) in 395 A D , after the death of Theodosius ; see Hodgkin, i 653   Isidore gives the date 382, which Clinton accepts]

[24] ————Discors odiisque anceps civibus orbis
Non sua vis tutata diu, dum fœdera fallax
Ludit, et alternæ perjuria venditat aulæ.
Claudian de Bell Get , 565.

[25] Alpibus Italiæ ruptis penetrabis ad *Urbem.*   This authentic prediction was announced by Alaric, or at least by Claudian (de Bell Getico, 547), seven years before the event.   But, as it was not accomplished within the term which has been rashly fixed, the interpreters escaped through an ambiguous meaning   [For Claudian's acrostich in this passage, see Appendix 16]

[26] Our best materials are 970 verses of Claudian, in the poem on the Getic war, and the beginning of that which celebrates the sixth consulship of Honorius Zosimus is totally silent ; and we are reduced to such scraps, or rather crumbs, as we can pick from Orosius and the Chronicles

[27] Notwithstanding the gross errors of Jornandes, who confounds the Italian wars of Alaric (c 29), his date of the consulship of Stilicho and Aurelian (A D 400) is firm and respectable   It is certain from Claudian (Tillemont, Hist des Emp. tom v p 804) that the battle of Pollentia was fought A D 403, but we cannot easily fill the interval   [The right date is 402 , see Appendix 17]

our attempts to describe the circumstances of the first invasion of
Italy by the arms of Alaric. His march, perhaps from Thessalonica, through the warlike and hostile country of Pannonia,
as far as the foot of the Julian Alps; his passage of those
mountains, which were strongly guarded by troops and intrenchments; the siege of Aquileia, and the conquest of the provinces
of Istria and Venetia, appear to have employed a considerable
time. Unless his operations were extremely cautious and slow,
the length of the interval would suggest a probable suspicion
that the Gothic king retreated towards the banks of the Danube
and reinforced his army with fresh swarms of Barbarians, before
he again attempted to penetrate into the heart of Italy   Since
the public and important events escape the diligence of the
historian, he may amuse himself with contemplating, for a
moment, the influence of the arms of Alaric on the fortunes of
two obscure individuals, a presbyter of Aquileia and an husbandman of Verona.   The learned Rufinus, who was summoned by
his enemies to appear before a Roman synod,[28] wisely preferred
the dangers of a besieged city; and the Barbarians, who
furiously shook the walls of Aquileia, might save him from the
cruel sentence of another heretic, who, at the request of the
same bishops, was severely whipped and condemned to perpetual exile on a desert island [29]   The *old man*,[30] who had
passed his simple and innocent life in the neighbourhood of
Verona, was a stranger to the quarrels both of kings and of
bishops; *his* pleasures, his desires, his knowledge, were confined
within the little circle of his paternal farm; and a staff supported his aged steps, on the same ground where he had sported
in his infancy. Yet even this humble and rustic felicity (which
Claudian describes with so much truth and feeling) was still
exposed to the undistinguishing rage of war.   His trees, his old
contemporary trees,[31] must blaze in the conflagration of the whole

---

[28] Tantum Romanæ urbis judicium fugis, ut magis obsidionem barbaricam,
quam *pacatæ* urbis judicium velis sustinere.   Jerom, tom. ii. p 239   Rufinus
understood his danger : the *peaceful* city was inflamed by the beldam Marcella and
the rest of Jerom s faction. [Cp Appendix 1]

[29] Jovinian, the enemy of fasts and celibacy, who was persecuted and insulted by
the furious Jerom (Jortin's Remarks, vol. iv. p 104, &c)   See the original edict
of banishment in the Theodosian Code, l xvi tit v. leg 43

[30] This epigram (de Sene Veronensi qui suburbium nusquam egressus est) is one
of the earliest and most pleasing compositions of Claudian   Cowley's imitation
(Hurd's edition, vol. ii p 241) has some natural and happy strokes   but it is
much inferior to the original portrait, which is evidently drawn from the life.

[31] Ingentem meminit parvo qui germine quercum
Æquævumque videt consenuisse nemus

country; a detachment of Gothic cavalry might sweep away his cottage and his family; and the power of Alaric could destroy this happiness which he was not able either to taste or to bestow. "Fame," says the poet, "encircling with terror her gloomy wings, proclaimed the march of the Barbarian army, and filled Italy with consternation," the apprehensions of each individual were increased in just proportion to the measure of his fortune; and the most timid, who had already embarked their valuable effects, meditated their escape to the island of Sicily or the African coast. The public distress was aggravated by the fears and reproaches of superstition.[32] Every hour produced some horrid tale of strange and portentous accidents, the Pagans deplored the neglect of omens and the interruption of sacrifices; but the Christians still derived some comfort from the powerful intercession of the saints and martyrs.[33]

Honorius flies from Milan. A.D 403 The emperor Honorius was distinguished, above his subjects, by the pre-eminence of fear, as well as of rank. The pride and luxury in which he was educated had not allowed him to suspect that there existed on the earth any power presumptuous enough to invade the repose of the successor of Augustus. The arts of flattery concealed the impending danger, till Alaric approached the palace of Milan. But, when the sound of war had awakened the young emperor, instead of flying to arms with the spirit, or even the rashness, of his age, he eagerly listened to those timid counsellors who proposed to convey his sacred person and his faithful attendants to some secure and distant station in the provinces of Gaul. Stilicho alone [34] had courage and authority to resist this disgraceful measure, which would have abandoned Rome and Italy to the Barbarians; but, as the troops of the palace had been lately detached to the Rhætian frontier, and as the resource of new levies was slow and precarious, the general of the West could only promise that, if the court of Milan would maintain their ground during his

A neighbouring wood born with himself he sees,
And loves his old contemporary trees

In this passage, Cowley is perhaps superior to his original; and the English poet, who was a good botanist has concealed the oaks under a more general expression

[32] Claudian de Bell Get 192-266. He may seem prolix but fear and superstition occupied as large a space in the minds of the Italians.

[33] From the passages of Paulinus, which Baronius has produced (Annal. Eccles A D. 403, No. 51) it is manifest that the general alarm had pervaded all Italy, as far as Nola in Campania, where that famous penitent had fixed his abode.

[34] Solus erat Stilicho, &c, is the exclusive commendation which Claudian bestows (de Bell. Get 267) without condescending to except the emperor. How insignificant must Honorius have appeared in his own court!

absence, he would soon return with an army equal to the encounter of the Gothic king. Without losing a moment (while each moment was so important to the public safety) Stilicho hastily embarked on the Larian lake, ascended the mountains of ice and snow, amidst the severity of an Alpine [winter of] winter, and suddenly repressed, by his unexpected presence, A D 401-2 the enemy who had disturbed the tranquillity of Rhætia.[35] The Barbarians, perhaps some tribes of the Alemanni, respected the firmness of a chief who still assumed the language of command ; and the choice which he condescended to make of a select number of their bravest youths was considered as a mark of his esteem and favour. The cohorts, who were delivered from the neighbouring foe, diligently repaired to the Imperial standard ; and Stilicho issued his orders to the most remote troops of the West to advance, by rapid marches, to the defence of Honorius and of Italy. The fortresses of the Rhine were abandoned ; and the safety of Gaul was protected only by the faith of the Germans and the ancient terror of the Roman name. Even the legion which had been stationed to guard the wall [Twentieth of Britain against the Caledonians of the north was hastily Legion] recalled ;[36] and a numerous body of the cavalry of the Alani was persuaded to engage in the service of the emperor, who anxiously expected the return of his general. The prudence and vigour of Stilicho were conspicuous on this occasion, which revealed, at the same time, the weakness of the falling empire. The legions of Rome, which had long since languished in the gradual decay of discipline and courage, were exterminated by the Gothic and civil wars ; and it was found impossible, without exhausting and exposing the provinces, to assemble an army for the defence of Italy

When Stilicho seemed to abandon his sovereign in the He is pursued and besieged unguarded palace of Milan, he had probably calculated the by the Goths term of his absence, the distance of the enemy, and the obstacles that might retard their march. He principally de-

---

[35] The face of the country, and the hardiness of Stilicho, are finely described (de Bell. Get. 340-363) [The danger which Stilicho had to meet in Rætia and Vindelicia was an attack of the Goth Radagaisus, who was in league with Alaric , see Prosper, sub anno 400, a notice which has been improperly confounded with that under 505, and cp Appendix 17]

[36] Venit et extremis legio prætenta Britannis
Quæ Scoto dat frena truci. De Bell. Get. 416
Yet the most rapid march from Edinburgh, or Newcastle, to Milan must have required a longer space of time than Claudian seems willing to allow for the duration of the Gothic war,

pended on the rivers of Italy, the Adige, the Mincius, the Oglio, and the Addua, which, in the winter or spring, by the fall of rains, or by the melting of the snows, are commonly swelled into broad and impetuous torrents.[37]   But the season happened to be remarkably dry; and the Goths could traverse, without impediment, the wide and stony beds, whose centre was faintly marked by the course of a shallow stream.   The bridge and passage of the Addua were secured by a strong detachment of the Gothic army; and, as Alaric approached the walls, or rather the suburbs, of Milan, he enjoyed the proud satisfaction of seeing the emperor of the Romans fly before him.   Honorius, accompanied by a feeble train of statesmen and eunuchs, hastily retreated towards the Alps, with a design of securing his person in the city of Arles, which had often been the royal residence of his predecessors.   But Honorius[38] had scarcely passed the Po, before he was overtaken by the speed of the Gothic cavalry;[39] since the urgency of the danger compelled him to seek a temporary shelter within the fortification of Asta, a town of Liguria or Piemont, situate on the banks of the Tanarus.[40]   The siege of an obscure place, which contained so rich a prize and seemed incapable of a long resistance, was instantly formed and indefatigably pressed by the king of the Goths; and the bold declaration, which the emperor might afterwards make, that his breast had never been susceptible of fear, did not probably obtain much credit, even in his own court.[41]   In the last and almost hopeless extremity, after the Barbarians had already proposed the indignity of a capitulation, the Imperial captive was suddenly relieved by the fame, the approach, and at length the presence of the hero

[Tanaro]

[37] Every traveller must recollect the face of Lombardy (see Fontenelle, tom. v p. 279), which is often tormented by the capricious and irregular abundance of waters.   The Austrians, before Genoa, were incamped in the dry bed of the Polcevera.   "Ne sarebbe" (says Muratori) "mai passato per mente a que' buoni Alemanni, che quel picciolo torrente potesse, per cosi dire, in un instante cangiarsi in un terribil gigante" (Annal d'Italia, tom xvi p 443.   Milan, 1753, 8vo edit)

[38] Claudian does not clearly answer our question, Where was Honorius himself? Yet the flight is marked by the pursuit, and my idea of the Gothic war is justified by the Italian critics, Sigonius (tom L P ii p 369, de Imp Occident, l x) and Muratori (Annali d'Italia, tom iv p 45).

[39] One of the roads may be traced in the Itineraries (p 98, 288, 294, with Wesseling's notes)   Asta lay some miles on the right hand

[40] Asta, or Asti, a Roman colony, is now the capital of a pleasant country, which, in the sixteenth century, devolved to the dukes of Savoy (Leandro Alberti, Descrizzione d'Italia, p 382).   [The town meant by Claudian is Milan, see App. 17]

[41] Nec me timor impulit ullus.   He might hold this proud language the next year at Rome, five hundred miles from the scene of danger (vi Cons. Hon. 449).

whom he had so long expected   At the head of a chosen and
intrepid vanguard, Stilicho swam the stream of the Addua, to
gain the time which he must have lost in the attack of the
bridge ; the passage of the Po was an enterprise of much less
hazard and difficulty ; and the successful action, in which he cut
his way through the Gothic camp under the walls of Asta, revived
the hopes, and vindicated the honour, of Rome.   Instead of
grasping the fruit of his victory, the Barbarian was gradually
invested, on every side, by the troops of the West, who successively issued through all the passes of the Alps ; his quarters
were straitened ; his convoys were intercepted ; and the
vigilance of the Romans prepared to form a chain of fortifications, and to besiege the lines of the besiegers.   A military
council was assembled of the long-haired chiefs of the Gothic
nation ; of aged warriors, whose bodies were wrapped in furs,
and whose stern countenances were marked with honourable
wounds.   They weighed the glory of persisting in their attempt
against the advantage of securing their plunder ; and they
recommended the prudent measure of a seasonable retreat.
In this important debate, Alaric displayed the spirit of the
conqueror of Rome ; and, after he had reminded his countrymen of their achievements and of their designs, he concluded
his animating speech by the solemn and positive assurance that
he was resolved to find in Italy either a kingdom or a grave.[42]

The loose discipline of the Barbarians always exposed them Battle of
Pollentia.
to the danger of a surprise ; but, instead of choosing the dis- A D 403
March 29
solute hours of riot and intemperance, Stilicho resolved to [April 6,
attack the *Christian* Goths, whilst they were devoutly employed A D 402]
in celebrating the festival of Easter.[43]   The execution of the
stratagem, or, as it was termed by the clergy, of the sacrilege,
was entrusted to Saul, a Barbarian and a Pagan, who had
served, however, with distinguished reputation among the
veteran generals of Theodosius.   The camp of the Goths, which

[42] Hanc ego vel victor regno vel morte tenebo
       Victus humum ——
The speeches (de Bell. Get. 479-549) of the Gothic Nestor and Achilles are strong,
characteristic, adapted to the circumstances, and possibly not less genuine than
those of Livy.

[43] Orosius (l vii c 37) is shocked at the impiety of the Romans who attacked,
on Easter Sunday, such pious Christians   Yet, at the same time, public prayers
were offered at the shrine of St Thomas of Edessa, for the destruction of the
Arian robber   See Tillemont (Hist. des Emp tom v p 529), who quotes an
homily, which has been erroneously ascribed to St. Chrysostom   [For date see
Appendix 17.]

[Pollenzo]

[Saulus]

Alaric had pitched in the neighbourhood of Pollentia,[44] was thrown into confusion by the sudden and impetuous charge of the Imperial cavalry; but, in a few moments, the undaunted genius of their leader gave them an order, and a field, of battle; and, as soon as they had recovered from their astonishment, the pious confidence, that the God of the Christians would assert their cause, added new strength to their native valour. In this engagement, which was long maintained with equal courage and success, the chief of the Alani, whose diminutive and savage form concealed a magnanimous soul, approved his suspected loyalty by the zeal with which he fought, and fell, in the service of the republic; and the fame of this gallant Barbarian has been imperfectly preserved in the verses of Claudian, since the poet, who celebrates his virtue, has omitted the mention of his name. His death was followed by the flight and dismay of the squadrons which he commanded; and the defeat of the wing of cavalry might have decided the victory of Alaric, if Stilicho had not immediately led the Roman and Barbarian infantry to the attack. The skill of the general and the bravery of the soldiers surmounted every obstacle. In the evening of the bloody day, the Goths retreated from the field of battle; the intrenchments of their camp were forced, and the scene of rapine and slaughter made some atonement for the calamities which they had inflicted on the subjects of the empire.[45] The magnificent spoils of Corinth and Argos enriched the veterans of the West; the captive wife of Alaric, who had impatiently claimed his promise of Roman jewels and Patrician handmaids,[46] was reduced to implore the mercy of the insulting foe; and many thousand prisoners, released from the Gothic chains, dispersed through the provinces of Italy the praises of their

[44] The vestiges of Pollentia are twenty-five miles to the south-east of Turin *Urbs* [River Urbis = Borbo, see Tillemont, H des Emp v. 530], in the same neighbourhood, was a royal chace of the Kings of Lombardy, and a small river, which excused the prediction, "penetrabis ad urbem". Cluver Ital. Antiq tom 1 p 83-85.

[45] Orosius wishes, in doubtful words, to insinuate the defeat of the Romans. " Pugnantes vicimus, victores victi sumus." Prosper (in Chron.) makes it an equal and bloody battle, but the Gothic writers, Cassiodorius (in Chron) and Jornandes (de Reb Get c 29) claim a decisive victory. [The Goths may have been slightly victorious on the field of battle; but they clearly received a decisive strategic defeat]

[46] Demens Ausonidum gemmata monilia matrum,
    Romanasque alta famulas cervice petebat
                                             De Bell Get 627
[The capture of Alaric's wife is a totally unjustifiable inference from these lines. Cp. Von Wietersheim, Gesch der Volkerwanderung (ed Dahn), 2, 189.]

heroic deliverer. The triumph of Stilicho [47] was compared by the poet, and perhaps by the public, to that of Marius; who, in the same part of Italy, had encountered and destroyed another army of northern Barbarians. The huge bones, and the empty helmets, of the Cimbri and of the Goths would easily be confounded by succeeding generations; and posterity might erect a common trophy to the memory of the two most illustrious generals who had vanquished, on the same memorable ground, the two most formidable enemies of Rome.[48]

The eloquence of Claudian [49] has celebrated with lavish **Boldness** applause the victory of Pollentia, one of the most glorious days **and retreat of Alaric** in the life of his patron; but his reluctant and partial muse bestows more genuine praise on the character of the Gothic king. His name is indeed branded with the reproachful epithets of pirate and robber, to which the conquerors of every age are so justly entitled; but the poet of Stilicho is compelled to acknowledge that Alaric possessed the invincible temper of mind which rises superior to every misfortune and derives new resources from adversity. After the total defeat of his infantry he escaped, or rather withdrew, from the field of battle, with the greatest part of his cavalry entire and unbroken. Without wasting a moment to lament the irreparable loss of so many brave companions, he left his victorious enemy to bind in chains the captive images of a Gothic king; [50] and boldly resolved to break through the unguarded passes of the Apennine, to spread desolation over the fruitful face of Tuscany, and to conquer or die before the gates of Rome.[51] The capital was saved by the active and in-

---

[47] Claudian (de Bell Get 580-647) and Prudentius (in Symmach L ii 694-719) celebrate, without ambiguity, the Roman victory of Pollentia They are poetical and party writers, yet some credit is due to the most suspicious witnesses, who are checked by the recent notoriety of facts.

[48] Claudian's peroration is strong and elegant; but the identity of the Cimbric and Gothic fields must be understood (like Virgil's Philippi, Georgic i 490) according to the loose geography of a poet. Vercellæ and Pollentia are sixty miles from each other, and the latitude is still greater, if the Cimbri were defeated in the wide and barren plain of Verona (Maffei, Verona Illustrata, P. i p 54-62).

[49] Claudian and Prudentius must be strictly examined, to reduce the figures, and extort the historic sense of those poets
[50] Et gravant en airain ses frêles avantages
De mes états conquis enchaîner les images
The practice of exposing in triumph the images of kings and provinces was familiar to the Romans. The bust of Mithridates himself was twelve feet high, of massy gold (Freinsbem Supplement Livian. cm 47).
[51] [Alaric was retreating and had no idea of advancing on Rome He was obliged to retreat towards the Apennines (Claud de vi. Cons Hon 183) Stilicho let him go once more (as before in the Peloponnesus) Cp. von Wietersheim, *op cit.* 2, 230.]

cessant diligence of Stilicho : but he respected the despair of
his enemy ; and, instead of committing the fate of the republic
to the chance of another battle, he proposed to purchase the
absence of the Barbarians.   The spirit of Alaric would have
rejected such terms, the permission of a retreat and the offer of
a pension, with contempt and indignation ; but he exercised a
limited and precarious authority over the independent chieftains,
who had raised him, for *their* service, above the rank of his equals;
they were still less disposed to follow an unsuccessful general,
and many of them were tempted to consult their interest by a
private negotiation with the minister of Honorius.   The king
submitted to the voice of his people, ratified the treaty with the
empire of the West, and repassed the Po, with the remains of the
flourishing army which he had led into Italy.   A considerable
part of the Roman forces still continued to attend his motions ;
and Stilicho, who maintained a secret correspondence with some
of the Barbarian chiefs, was punctually apprized of the designs
that were formed in the camp and council of Alaric.   The king
of the Goths, ambitious to signalise his retreat by some splendid
achievement, had resolved to occupy the important city of
Verona, which commands the principal passage of the Rhætian
Alps; and directing his march through the territories of those
German tribes, whose alliance would restore his exhausted
strength, to invade, on the side of the Rhine, the wealthy and
unsuspecting provinces of Gaul.   Ignorant of the treason, which
had already betrayed his bold and judicious enterprise, he advanced towards the passes of the mountains, already possessed
by the Imperial troops ; where he was exposed, almost at the
same instant, to a general attack in the front, on his flanks, and
in the rear.   In this bloody action, at a small distance from the
walls of Verona,[52] the loss of the Goths was not less heavy than
that which they had sustained in the defeat of Pollentia ; and
their valiant king, who escaped by the swiftness of his horse,
must either have been slain or made prisoner, if the hasty rashness of the Alani had not disappointed the measures of the
Roman general.   Alaric secured the remains of his army on the
adjacent rocks, and prepared himself with undaunted resolution
to maintain a siege against the superior numbers of the enemy,
who invested him on all sides.   But he could not oppose the
destructive progress of hunger and disease; nor was it possible
for him to check the continual desertion of his impatient and

[A.D 403]

[52] [Claudian alone mentions this battle. See, for date, Appendix 17]

capricious Barbarians In this extremity he still found resources in his own courage, or in the moderation of his adversary, and the retreat of the Gothic king was considered as the deliverance of Italy.[53] Yet the people and even the clergy, incapable of forming any rational judgment of the business of peace and war, presumed to arraign the policy of Stilicho, who so often vanquished, so often surrounded, and so often dismissed the implacable enemy of the republic. The first moment of the public safety is devoted to gratitude and joy ; but the second is diligently occupied by envy and calumny.[54]

The citizens of Rome had been astonished by the approach of Alaric ; and the diligence with which they laboured to restore the walls of the capital confessed their own fears and the decline of the empire. After the retreat of the Barbarians, Honorius was directed to accept the dutiful invitation of the senate, and to celebrate in the Imperial city the auspicious æra of the Gothic victory and of his sixth consulship [55] The suburbs and the streets from the Milvian bridge to the Palatine mount, were filled by the Roman people, who, in the space of an hundred years, had only thrice been honoured with the presence of their sovereigns While their eyes were fixed on the chariot where Stilicho was deservedly seated by the side of his royal pupil, they applauded the pomp of a triumph, which was not stained, like that of Constantine, or of Theodosius, with civil blood. The procession passed under a lofty arch, which had been purposely erected. but in less than seven years the Gothic conquerors of Rome might read, if they were able to read, the superb inscription of that monument, which attested the total defeat and destruction of their nation [56] The emperor resided several months in the capital, and every part of his behaviour was regulated with care to conciliate the affection of the clergy, the senate, and the people of Rome. The clergy was edified by his frequent visits and liberal gifts to the shrines of the apostles. The senate, who in the triumphal procession had been excused

The triumph of Honorius at Rome A D 404 (marginal note)

---

[53] The Getic war and the sixth consulship of Honorius obscurely connect the events of Alaric's retreat and losses

[54] Taceo de Alarico .   sæpe victo, sæpe concluso, semperque dimisso Orosius, l vii c 37, p 567.   Claudian (vi Cons Hon. 320) drops the curtain with a fine image.

[55] The remainder of Claudian's poem on the sixth consulship of Honorius describes the journey, the triumph, and the games (330-660)

[56] See the inscription in Mascou's History of the Ancient Germans, viii. 12. The words are positive and indiscreet, Getarum nationem in omne ævum domitam [leg docuere extingui], &c   [C I L 6, 1196. It probably refers to the defeat of Radagaisus, A D 405 See Appendix 13]

from the humiliating ceremony of preceding on foot the Imperial chariot, was treated with the decent reverence which Stilicho always affected for that assembly   The people was repeatedly gratified by the attention and courtesy of Honorius in the public games, which were celebrated on that occasion with a magnificence not unworthy of the spectator. As soon as the appointed number of chariot races was concluded, the decoration of the Circus was suddenly changed, the hunting of wild beasts afforded a various and splendid entertainment, and the chase was succeeded by a military dance, which seems in the lively description of Claudian to present the image of a modern tournament.

The gladiators abolished

In these games of Honorius, the inhuman combats of gladiators [57] polluted, for the last time, the amphitheatre of Rome. The first Christian emperor may claim the honour of the first edict which condemned the art and amusement of shedding human blood, [58] but this benevolent law expressed the wishes of the prince, without reforming an inveterate abuse, which degraded a civilised nation below the condition of savage cannibals Several hundred, perhaps several thousand, victims were annually slaughtered in the great cities of the empire, and the month of December, more peculiarly devoted to the combats of gladiators, still exhibited to the eyes of the Roman people a grateful spectacle of blood and cruelty. Amidst the general joy of the victory of Pollentia, a Christian poet exhorted the emperor to extirpate by his authority the horrid custom which had so long resisted the voice of humanity and religion. [59] The pathetic representations of Prudentius were less effectual than the generous boldness of Telemachus, an Asiatic monk, whose death was more useful to mankind than his life. [60] The Romans were provoked by the interruption of their pleasures ; and the rash monk, who had descended into the arena to separate the gladiators, was overwhelmed under a shower of stones But the

[57] On the curious, though horrid, subject of the gladiators, consult the two books of the Saturnalia of Lipsius, who, as an *antiquarian*, is inclined to excuse the practice of *antiquity* (tom iii p 483-545)
[58] Cod Theodos l xv tit xii leg i   The commentary of Godefroy affords large materials (tom v p 396) for the history of gladiators
[59] See the peroration of Prudentius (in Symmach l ii, 1121-1131), who had doubtless read the eloquent invective of Lactantius (Divin Institut l vi c 20) The Christian apologists have not spared these bloody games, which were introduced in the religious festivals of Paganism.
[60] Theodoret, l v c 26   I wish to believe the story of St Telemachus   Yet no church has been dedicated, no altar has been erected, to the only monk who died a martyr in the cause of humanity   [There is evidence for gladiatorial spectacles some years later.]

madness of the people soon subsided; they respected the memory of Telemachus, who had deserved the honours of martyrdom; and they submitted, without a murmur, to the laws of Honorius, which abolished for ever the human sacrifices of the amphitheatre The citizens who adhered to the manners of their ancestors, might perhaps insinuate that the last remains of a martial spirit were preserved in this school of fortitude, which accustomed the Romans to the sight of blood and to the contempt of death · a vain and cruel prejudice, so nobly confuted by the valour of ancient Greece and of modern Europe [61]

The recent danger to which the person of the emperor had been exposed in the defenceless palace of Milan urged him to seek a retreat in some inaccessible fortress of Italy, where he might securely remain while the open country was covered by a deluge of Barbarians. On the coast of the Hadriatic, about ten or twelve miles from the most southern of the seven mouths of the Po, the Thessalians had founded the ancient colony of RAVENNA,[62] which they afterwards resigned to the natives of Umbria. Augustus, who had observed the opportunity of the place, prepared, at the distance of three miles from the old town, a capacious harbour for the reception of two hundred and fifty ships of war. This naval establishment, which included the arsenals and magazines, the barracks of the troops, and the houses of the artificers, derived its origin and name from the permanent station of the Roman fleet, the intermediate space was soon filled with buildings and inhabitants, and the three extensive and populous quarters of Ravenna gradually contributed to form one of the most important cities of Italy. The principal canal of Augustus poured a copious stream of the waters of the Po through the midst of the city to the entrance of the harbour; the same waters were introduced into the profound ditches that encompassed the walls, they were distributed by a thousand subordinate canals into every part of the city, which they divided into a variety of small islands; the

Honorius fixes his residence at Ravenna
A D 404

---

[61] Crudele gladiatorum spectaculum et inhumanum *nonnullis* videri solet, et *haud scio* an ita sit, ut nunc fit   Cic Tusculan ii 17   He faintly censures the *abuse* and warmly defends the *use* of these sports, oculis nulla poterat esse fortior contra dolorem et mortem disciplina   Seneca (epist vii) shews the feelings of a man

[62] This account of Ravenna is drawn from Strabo (l v p 327 [c 1 § 7]), Pliny (iii 20), Stephen of Byzantium (sub voce ῾Ράβεννα, p 651, edit Berkel), Claudian (in vi Cons Honor. 494, &c), Sidonius Apollinaris (l 1 epist v 8), Jornandes (de Reb Get c 29), Procopius (de Bell Gothic l 1 c 1, p 309, edit Louvre), and Cluverius (Ital. Antiq tom. 1 p 301-307). Yet I still want a local antiquarian, and a good topographical map   [C. Ricci, Ravenna e i suoi dintorni.]

communication was maintained only by the use of boats and bridges ; and the houses of Ravenna, whose appearance may be compared to that of Venice, were raised on the foundation of wooden piles   The adjacent country, to the distance of many miles, was a deep and impassable morass, and the artificial causeway, which connected Ravenna with the continent, might be easily guarded or destroyed on the approach of an hostile army.   These morasses were interspersed, however, with vineyards ; and, though the soil was exhausted by four or five crops, the town enjoyed a more plentiful supply of wine than of fresh water.[63]   The air, instead of receiving the sickly and almost pestilential exhalations of low and marshy grounds, was distinguished, like the neighbourhood of Alexandria, as uncommonly pure and salubrious ; and this singular advantage was ascribed to the regular tides of the Hadriatic, which swept the canals, interrupted the unwholesome stagnation of the waters, and floated every day the vessels of the adjacent country into the heart of Ravenna.   The gradual retreat of the sea has left the modern city at the distance of four miles from the Hadriatic ; and as early as the fifth or sixth century of the Christian æra the port of Augustus was converted into pleasant orchards, and a lonely grove of pines covered the ground where the Roman fleet once rode at anchor.[64]   Even this alteration contributed to increase the natural strength of the place , and the shallowness of the water was a sufficient barrier against the large ships of the enemy.   This advantageous situation was fortified by art and labour ; and in the twentieth year of his age the emperor of the West, anxious only for his personal safety, retired to the perpetual confinement of the walls and morasses of Ravenna. The example of Honorius was imitated by his feeble successors, the Gothic kings, and afterwards the Exarchs, who occupied the throne and palace of the emperors ; and, till the middle of the eighth century, Ravenna was considered as the seat of government and the capital of Italy.[65]

[63] Martial (epigram ni 56, 57) plays on the trick of the knave who had sold him wine instead of water , but he seriously declares that a cistern at Ravenna is more valuable than a vineyard.   Sidonius complains that the town is destitute of fountains and aqueducts, and ranks the want of fresh water among the local evils, such as the croaking of frogs, the stinging of gnats, &c

[64] The fable of Theodore and Honoria, which Dryden has so admirably transplanted from Boccaccio (Giornata, iii novell viii), was acted in the wood of *Chiassi*, a corrupt word from *Classis*, the naval station, which, with the intermediate road or suburb, the *Via Caesaris*, constituted the *triple* city of Ravenna

[65] From the year 404, the dates of the Theodosian Code become sedentary at Constantinople and Ravenna.   See Godefroy's Chronology of the Laws, tom i p cxlviii , &c

The fears of Honorius were not without foundation, nor were his precautions without effect. While Italy rejoiced in her deliverance from the Goths, a furious tempest was excited among the nations of Germany, who yielded to the irresistible impulse that appears to have been gradually communicated from the eastern extremity of the continent of Asia   The Chinese annals, as they have been interpreted by the learned industry of the present age, may be usefully applied to reveal the secret and remote causes of the fall of the Roman empire. The extensive territory to the north of the great wall was possessed, after the flight of the Huns, by the victorious Sien-pi, who were sometimes broken into independent tribes, and re-united under a supreme chief, till at length, styling themselves *Topa*, or masters of the earth, they acquired a more solid consistence and a more formidable power.   The Topa soon compelled the pastoral nations of the eastern desert to acknowledge the superiority of their arms ; they invaded China in a period of weakness and intestine discord ; and these fortunate Tartars, adopting the laws and manners of the vanquished people, founded an Imperial dynasty, which reigned near one hundred and sixty years over the northern provinces of the monarchy.   Some generations before they ascended the throne of China one of the Topa princes had enlisted in his cavalry a slave of the name of Moko, renowned for his valour ; but who was tempted by the fear of punishment to desert his standard and to range the desert at the head of an hundred followers   This gang of robbers and outlaws swelled into a camp, a tribe, a numerous people, distinguished by the appellation of *Geougen ;* and their hereditary chieftains, the posterity of Moko, the slave, assumed their rank among the Scythian monarchs   The youth of Toulun, the greatest of his descendants, was exercised by those misfortunes which are the school of heroes   He bravely struggled with adversity, broke the imperious yoke of the Topa, and became the legislator of his nation and the conqueror of Tartary.   His troops were distributed into regular bands of an hundred and of a thousand men ; cowards were stoned to death , the most splendid honours were proposed as the reward of valour , and Toulun, who had knowledge enough to despise the learning of China, adopted only such arts and institutions as were favourable to the military spirit of his government   His tents, which he removed in the winter season to a more southern latitude, were pitched during the summer on the fruitful banks of the Selinga.   His

[Marginal notes:]
The revolutions of Scythia A D 400

[c A D 300 ?]

[Mukkuru]

[Jeu jen]

[Shelun or Zarun]

[A D 394]

conquests stretched from Corea far beyond the river Irtish. He
vanquished in the country to the North of the Caspian Sea the
nation of the *Huns*, and the new title of *Khan* or *Cagan* expressed the
fame and power which he derived from this memorable victory.[66]

The chain of events is interrupted, or rather is concealed, as
it passes from the Volga to the Vistula, through the dark interval which separates the extreme limits of the Chinese and of
the Roman geography. Yet the temper of the Barbarians and
the experience of successive emigrations sufficiently declare
that the Huns, who were oppressed by the arms of the Geougen,
soon withdrew from the presence of an insulting victor. The
countries towards the Euxine were already occupied by their
kindred tribes; and their hasty flight, which they soon converted into a bold attack, would more naturally be directed
towards the rich and level plains through which the Vistula
gently flows into the Baltic Sea. The North must again have
been alarmed and agitated by the invasion of the Huns; and the
nations who retreated before them must have pressed with incumbent weight on the confines of Germany.[67] The inhabitants
of those regions which the ancients have assigned to the Suevi,
the Vandals, and the Burgundians might embrace the resolution
of abandoning to the fugitives of Sarmatia their woods and
morasses; or at least of discharging their superfluous numbers
on the provinces of the Roman empire.[68] About four years
after the victorious Toulun had assumed the title of Khan of the
Geougen, another Barbarian, the haughty Rhodogast or Radagaisus,[69] marched from the northern extremities of Germany

[Khakhan]

*Emigration of
the northern
Germans
A D 405*

[66] See M de Guignes, Hist des Huns, tom 1 p 179-189, tom 11 p 295, 334-
338 [His empire "extended east and west from Corea to Harashar and south as
far as the country of the Tukuhun and the modern Kan Suh province" "North-
west of Zarun s empire were the remains of the Hiungnu, and they were all gradually annexed by him This modest statement, which precedes the distinct limita-
tion of his dominions in a westerly direction to the north of Harashar—at the
utmost Tarbagatai or Kuldja—is evidently the ground for Gibbon's mistaken
statement that he 'vanquished the Huns to the north of the Caspian'." Mr E
H Parker, A Thousand Years of the Tartars, p 161-2]

[67] Procopius (de Bell Vandal l 1 c 111 p 182) has observed an emigration
from the Palus Mæotis to the north of Germany, which he ascribes to famine.
But his views of ancient history are strangely darkened by ignorance and error

[68] Zosimus (l v p 331 [c 26]) uses the general description of the nations
beyond the Danube and the Rhine Their situation, and consequently their
names, are manifestly shown, even in the various epithets which each ancient
writer may have casually added

[69] The name of Rhadagast was that of a local deity of the Obotrites (in Meck-
lenburgh) A hero might naturally assume the appellation of his tutelar god, but
it is not probable that the Barbarians should worship an unsuccessful hero See
Mascou, Hist of the Germans, viii 14 [His name suggested that Radagaisus
was a Slav, but he is now generally supposed to be a Goth.]

almost to the gates of Rome, and left the remains of his army to achieve the destruction of the West. The Vandals, the Suevi, and the Burgundians formed the strength of this mighty host ; but the Alani, who had found an hospitable reception in their new seats, added their active cavalry to the heavy infantry of the Germans ; and the Gothic adventurers crowded so eagerly to the standard of Radagaisus that, by some historians, he has been styled the king of the Goths. Twelve thousand warriors, distinguished above the vulgar by their noble birth or their valiant deeds, glittered in the van ;[70] and the whole multitude, which was not less than two hundred thousand fighting men, might be increased by the accession of women, of children and of slaves, to the amount of four hundred thousand persons. This formidable emigration issued from the same coast of the Baltic which had poured forth the myriads of the Cimbri and Teutones to assault Rome and Italy in the vigour of the republic   After the departure of those Barbarians, their native country, which was marked by the vestiges of their greatness, long ramparts and gigantic moles,[71] remained during some ages a vast and dreary solitude ; till the human species was renewed by the powers of generation, and the vacancy was filled by the influx of new inhabitants. The nations who now usurp an extent of land which they are unable to cultivate would soon be assisted by the industrious poverty of their neighbours, if the government of Europe did not protect the claims of dominion and property.

The correspondence of nations was in that age so imperfect and precarious that the revolutions of the North might escape the knowledge of the court of Ravenna , till the dark cloud which was collected along the coast of the Baltic burst in thunder upon the banks of the Upper Danube. The emperor of the West, if his ministers disturbed his amusements by the news of the impending danger, was satisfied with being the occasion, and the spectator, of the war [72] The safety of Rome was entrusted to the counsels and the sword of Stilicho , but

Radagaisus invades Italy. A D 406 [405]

---

[70] Olympiodorus (apud Photium, p 180 [F H G iv p 59, fr 9]) uses the Greek word Ὁππιματοι , which does not convey any precise idea   I suspect that they were the princes and nobles, with their faithful companions, the knights with their squires, as they would have been styled some centuries afterwards.

[71] Tacit de Moribus Germanorum, c 37

[72] ——Cujus agendi
      Spectator vel causa fui,
            Claudian, vi Cons. Hon 439,
is the modest language of Honorius, in speaking of the Gothic war, which he had seen somewhat nearer

such was the feeble and exhausted state of the empire that it
was impossible to restore the fortifications of the Danube, or to
prevent, by a vigorous effort, the invasion of the Germans [73]   The
hopes of the vigilant minister of Honorius were confined to the
defence of Italy   He once more abandoned the provinces, recalled the troops, pressed the new levies, which were rigorously
exacted and pusillanimously eluded, employed the most efficacious means to arrest, or allure, the deserters, and offered the gift
of freedom, and of two pieces of gold, to all the slaves who would
enlist. [74]   By these efforts he painfully collected, from the subjects of a great empire, an army of thirty or forty thousand men,
which, in the days of Scipio or Camillus, would have been instantly furnished by the free citizens of the territory of Rome [75]
The thirty legions of Stilicho were reinforced by a large body
of Barbarian auxiliaries , the faithful Alani were personally
attached to his service ; and the troops of Huns and of Goths, who
marched under the banners of their native princes, Huldin and
Sarus, were animated by interest and resentment to oppose the
ambition of Radagaisus.   The king of the confederate Germans
passed, without resistance, the Alps, the Po, and the Apennine,
leaving on one hand the inaccessible palace of Honorius, securely
buried among the marshes of Ravenna, and, on the other, the
camp of Stilicho, who had fixed his headquarters at Ticinum, or
Pavia, but who seems to have avoided a decisive battle, till he
had assembled his distant forces.   Many cities of Italy were
pillaged, or destroyed, and the siege of Florence [76] by Radagaisus is one of the earliest events in the history of that celebrated

[Uldin]

Besieges
Florence

[73] Zosimus (l v p 331 [c 26]) transports the war and the victory of Stilicho
beyond the Danube   A strange error, which is awkwardly and imperfectly cured
by reading Ἄρνον for Ἴστρον (Tillemont, Hist des Emp tom v p 807)   In good
policy, we must use the service of Zosimus, without esteeming or trusting him
[But see Appendix 18]

[74] Codex Theodos l vii tit. xiii leg 16   The date of this law (A D 406,
18th May) satisfies me, as it had done Godefroy (tom ii p 387), of the true year
of the invasion of Radagaisus Tillemont, Pagi, and Muratori prefer the preceding
year , but they are bound, by certain obligations of civility and respect, to St
Paulinus of Nola.   [A D 405 is the true date, given by our best authority,
Prosper]

[75] Soon after Rome had been taken by the Gauls, the senate, on a sudden emergency, armed ten legions, 3000 horse, and 42,000 foot , a force which the city could
not have sent forth under Augustus (Livy, vii 25)   This declaration may puzzle
an antiquary, but it is clearly explained by Montesquieu

[76] Machiavel has explained, at least as a philosopher, the origin of Florence,
which insensibly descended, for the benefit of trade, from the rock of Fæsulæ to
the banks of the Arno (Istoria Fiorentina, tom. i l ii p 36, Londra, 1747)   The
Triumvirs sent a colony to Florence, which, under Tiberius (Tacit Annal i 79),
deserved the reputation and name of a *flourishing* city   See Cluver Ital Antiq
tom i p 507, &c.

republic, whose firmness checked and delayed the unskilful fury
of the Barbarians   The senate and people trembled at their
approach within an hundred and eighty miles of Rome, and
anxiously compared the danger which they had escaped with
the new perils to which they were exposed   Alaric was a
Christian and a soldier, the leader of a disciplined army, who
understood the laws of war, who respected the sanctity of
treaties, and who had familiarly conversed with the subjects of
the empire in the same camps, and the same churches   The
savage Radagaisus was a stranger to the manners, the religion,
and even the language, of the civilised nations of the South
The fierceness of his temper was exasperated by cruel superstition, and it was universally believed that he had bound himself
by a solemn vow to reduce the city into a heap of stones and and threat-
ens Rome
ashes, and to sacrifice the most illustrious of the Roman sena-
tors on the altars of those gods who were appeased by human
blood.   The public danger, which should have reconciled all
domestic animosities, displayed the incurable madness of religious faction.   The oppressed votaries of Jupiter and Mercury
respected, in the implacable enemy of Rome, the character of a
devout Pagan ; loudly declared that they were more apprehensive of the sacrifices than of the arms of Radagaisus, and secretly
rejoiced in the calamities of their country which condemned the
faith of their Christian adversaries [77]

Florence was reduced to the last extremity, and the fainting Defeat and
destruction
of his army
by Stilicho
A D 406
courage of the citizens was supported only by the authority of
St. Ambrose, who had communicated, in a dream, the promise
of a speedy deliverance [78]   On a sudden, they beheld, from their
walls, the banners of Stilicho, who advanced, with his united
force, to the relief of the faithful city, and who soon marked
that fatal spot for the grave of the Barbarian host.   The apparent contradictions of those writers who variously relate the defeat of Radagaisus may be reconciled, without offering much
violence to their respective testimonies   Orosius and Augustin,
who were intimately connected by friendship and religion, ascribe this miraculous victory to the providence of God rather

---

[77] Yet the Jupiter of Radagaisus who worshipped Thor and Woden was very
different from the Olympic or Capitoline Jove   The accommodating temper of
Polytheism might unite those various and remote deities, but the genuine Romans
abhorred the human sacrifices of Gaul and Germany

[78] Paulinus (in Vit Ambros c 50) relates this story, which he received from the
mouth of Pansophia herself, a religious matron of Florence   Yet the archbishop
soon ceased to take an active part in the business of the world, and never became
a popular saint

than to the valour of man [79]   They strictly exclude every idea
of chance, or even of bloodshed, and positively affirm that the
Romans, whose camp was the scene of plenty and idleness, enjoyed the distress of the Barbarians, slowly expiring on the sharp
and barren ridge of the hills of Fæsulæ, which rise above the city of
Florence   Their extravagant assertion that not a single soldier of
the Christian army was killed, or even wounded, may be dismissed
with silent contempt ; but the rest of the narrative of Augustin
and Orosius is consistent with the state of the war and the
character of Stilicho   Conscious that he commanded the *last*
army of the republic, his prudence would not expose it in the
open field to the headstrong fury of the Germans   The method
of surrounding the enemy with strong lines of circumvallation,
which he had twice employed against the Gothic king, was
repeated on a larger scale, and with more considerable effect
The examples of Cæsar must have been familiar to the most
illiterate of the Roman warriors , and the fortifications of Dyrra-
chium, which connected twenty-four castles by a perpetual ditch
and rampart of fifteen miles, afforded the model of an intrench-
ment which might confine and starve the most numerous host
of Barbarians.[80]   The Roman troops had less degenerated from
the industry than from the valour of their ancestors, and, if the
servile and laborious work offended the pride of the soldiers,
Tuscany could supply many thousand peasants who would
labour, though perhaps they would not fight, for the salvation of
their native country   The imprisoned multitude of horses and
men [81] was gradually destroyed by famine rather than by the
sword ; but the Romans were exposed, during the progress of
such an extensive work, to the frequent attacks of an impatient

[79] Augustin de Civitat Dei, v 23   Orosius, l vii c 37, p 567-571   The two
friends wrote in Africa, ten or twelve years after the victory , and their authority is
implicitly followed by Isidore of Seville (in Chron p 713, edit Grot)   How many
interesting facts might Orosius have inserted in the vacant space which is devoted
to pious nonsense !

[80] Franguntur montes, planumque per ardua Cæsar
    Ducit opus   pandit fossas, turritaque summis
    Disponit castella jugis, magnoque recessu
    Amplexus fines , saltus nemorosaque tesqua
    Et silvas vastâque feras indagine claudit
Yet the simplicity of truth (Cæsar, de Bell Civ iii 44) is far greater than the
amplifications of Lucan (Pharsal l vi 29-63)

[81] The rhetorical expressions of Orosius, " In arido et aspero montis jugo," " in
unum ac parvum verticem," are not very suitable to the encampment of a great
army   But Fæsulæ, only three miles from Florence, might afford space for the
headquarters of Radagaisus, and would be comprehended within the circuit of the
Roman lines

enemy. The despair of the hungry Barbarians would precipitate them against the fortifications of Stilicho; the general might sometimes indulge the ardour of his brave auxiliaries, who eagerly pressed to assault the camp of the Germans; and these various incidents might produce the sharp and bloody conflicts which dignify the narrative of Zosimus and the Chronicles of Prosper and Marcellinus [82] A seasonable supply of men and provisions had been introduced into the walls of Florence, and the famished host of Radagaisus was in its turn besieged. The proud monarch of so many warlike nations, after the loss of his bravest warriors, was reduced to confide either in the faith of a capitulation or in the clemency of Stilicho.[83] But the death of the royal captive, who was ignominiously beheaded, disgraced the triumph of Rome and of Christianity, and the short delay of his execution was sufficient to brand the conqueror with the guilt of cool and deliberate cruelty.[84] The famished Germans who escaped the fury of the auxiliaries were sold as slaves, at the contemptible price of as many single pieces of gold; but the difference of food and climate swept away great numbers of those unhappy strangers; and it was observed that the inhuman purchasers, instead of reaping the fruits of their labour, were soon obliged to provide the expense of their interment. Stilicho informed the emperor and the senate of his success, and deserved, a second time, the glorious title of Deliverer of Italy.[85]

The fame of the victory, and more especially of the miracle, has encouraged a vain persuasion that the whole army, or rather nation, of Germans, who migrated from the shores of the Baltic, miserably perished under the walls of Florence. Such indeed was the fate of Radagaisus himself, of his brave and faithful companions, and of more than one third of the various multitude of Sueves and Vandals, of Alani and Burgundians,

The remainder of the Germans invade Gaul A D 406, Dec 31

---

[82] See Zosimus, l v. p 331 [c 26], and the Chronicles of Prosper and Marcellinus.

[83] Olympiodorus (apud Photium, p 180) uses an expression (προσηταιρισατο) which would denote a strict and friendly alliance, and render Stilicho still more criminal [fr 9, F H G iv p 59 The expression refers to Gothic chiefs, not to Radagaisus] The paulisper detentus, deinde interfectus, of Orosius is sufficiently odious

[84] Orosius, piously inhuman, sacrifices the king and people, Agag and the Amalekites, without a symptom of compassion. The bloody actor is less detestable than the cool unfeeling historian

[85] And Claudian's muse, was she asleep? had she been ill paid? Methinks the seventh consulship of Honorius (A D 407) would have furnished the subject of a noble poem. [See below, p 282, and cp. Appendix 1.] Before it was discovered that the state could no longer be saved, Stilicho (after Romulus, Camillus, and Marius) might have been worthily surnamed the fourth founder of Rome.

who adhered to the standard of their general [86]   The union of
such an army might excite our surprise, but the causes of
separation are obvious and forcible ; the pride of birth, the
insolence of valour, the jealousy of command, the impatience
of subordination, and the obstinate conflict of opinions, of
interests, and of passions, among so many kings and warriors,
who were untaught to yield, or to obey.   After the defeat of
Radagaisus, two parts of the German host, which must have
exceeded the number of one hundred thousand men, still
remained in arms, between the Apennine and the Alps, or
between the Alps and the Danube.   It is uncertain whether
they attempted to revenge the death of their general ; but
their irregular fury was soon diverted by the prudence and
firmness of Stilicho, who opposed their march, and facilitated
their retreat ; who considered the safety of Rome and Italy as
the great object of his care, and who sacrificed, with too much
indifference, the wealth and tranquillity of the distant provinces.[87]   The Barbarians acquired, from the junction of some
Pannonian deserters, the knowledge of the country and of the
roads ; and the invasion of Gaul, which Alaric had designed,
was executed by the remains of the great army of Radagaisus.[88]

Yet, if they expected to derive any assistance from the tribes
of Germany, who inhabited the banks of the Rhine, their hopes
were disappointed   The Alemanni preserved a state of inactive neutrality ; and the Franks distinguished their zeal and
courage in the defence of the empire   In the rapid progress
?A D 396]   down the Rhine, which was the first act of the administration
of Stilicho, he had applied himself, with peculiar attention, to
secure the alliance of the warlike Franks, and to remove the
irreconcileable enemies of peace and of the republic.   Marcomir,
one of their kings, was publicly convicted before the tribunal
of the Roman magistrate, of violating the faith of treaties   He

[86] A luminous passage of Prosper's Chronicle, "*In tres partes, per diversos
principes, divisus exercitus,*" reduces the miracle of Florence, and connects the
history of Italy, Gaul and Germany
[87] Orosius and Jerom positively charge him with instigating the invasion
"Excitatæ a Stilichone gentes," &c   They must mean *indirectly*   He saved
Italy at the expense of Gaul
[88] The Count de Buat is satisfied that the Germans who invaded Gaul were the
two thirds that yet remained of the army of Radagaisus   See the Histoire
Ancienne des Peuples de l'Europe (tom vii p 87-121   Paris, 1772), an elaborate
work, which I had not the advantage of perusing till the year 1777   As early as
1771, I find the same idea expressed in a rough draught of the present History
I have since observed a similar intimation in Mascou (viii 15).   Such agreement,
without mutual communication, may add some weight to our common sentiment
[That the invaders of Gaul went forth from Noricum and Vindelicia seems probable.]

was sentenced to a mild, but distant, exile in the province of
Tuscany; and this degradation of the regal dignity was so far
from exciting the resentment of his subjects that they punished
with death the turbulent Sunno, who attempted to revenge his
brother, and maintained a dutiful allegiance to the princes who
were established on the throne by the choice of Stilicho.[89]
When the limits of Gaul and Germany were shaken by the
northern emigration, the Franks bravely encountered the single
force of the Vandals, who, regardless of the lessons of adversity,
had again separated their troops from the standard of their
Barbarian allies. They paid the penalty of their rashness, and
twenty thousand Vandals, with their king Godigisclus, were
slain in the field of battle. The whole people must have been
extirpated if the squadrons of the Alani, advancing to their
relief, had not trampled down the infantry of the Franks, who,
after an honourable resistance, were compelled to relinquish the
unequal contest The victorious confederates pursued their
march; and on the last day of the year, in a season when the [A D 406]
waters of the Rhine were most probably frozen, they entered,
without opposition, the defenceless provinces of Gaul This
memorable passage of the Suevi, the Vandals, the Alani, and
the Burgundians, who never afterwards retreated, may be considered as the fall of the Roman empire in the countries beyond
the Alps; and the barriers, which had so long separated the
savage and the civilised nations of the earth, were from that
fatal moment levelled with the ground.[90]

While the peace of Germany was secured by the attachment Desolation
of the Franks, and the neutrality of the Alemanni, the subjects of Gaul
of Rome, unconscious of their approaching calamities, enjoyed A D 407,
the state of quiet and prosperity, which had seldom blessed the &c
frontiers of Gaul. Their flocks and herds were permitted to
graze in the pastures of the Barbarians, their huntsmen pene-

---

[89]———Provincia missos
    Expellet citius fasces quam Francia reges
    Quos dederis

Claudian (1 Cons Stil. i. 235 [236], &c) is clear and satisfactory These kings of
France are unknown to Gregory of Tours, but the author of the Gesta Francorum
mentions both Sunno and Marcomir, and names the latter as the father of Pharamond (in tom. ii p 543) He seems to write from good materials, which he did
not understand [Mr Hodgkin places this journey of Stilicho in the first half of
A D 396 (i 660). The source for it is Claudian, de iv Cons. Hon 439 *sqq*]

[90] See Zosimus (l vi, p 373 [c 3]). Orosius (l vii c 40, p 576), and the
Chronicles Gregory of Tours (l ii c 9, p 165, in the second volume of the
Historians of France) has preserved a valuable fragment of Renatus Profuturus
Frigeridus, whose three names denote a Christian, a Roman subject, and a Semi-
barbarian

trated, without fear or danger, into the darkest recesses of the Hercynian wood [91] The banks of the Rhine were crowned, like those of the Tiber, with elegant houses, and well-cultivated farms ; and, if a poet descended the river, he might express his doubt on which side was situated the territory of the Romans [92] This scene of peace and plenty was suddenly changed into a desert ; and the prospect of the smoking ruins could alone distinguish the solitude of nature from the desolation of man.

[Mogontia-cum] The flourishing city of Mentz was surprised and destroyed ; and many thousand Christians were inhumanly massacred in the [Borbetoma-gus] church Worms perished after a long and obstinate siege ; [Argentora-tum, Nemetes, Remi, Torna-cum, Atreba-tum, Ambiani] Strasburg, Spires, Rheims, Tournay, Arras, Amiens, experienced the cruel oppression of the German yoke , and the consuming flames of war spread from the banks of the Rhine over the greatest part of the seventeen provinces of Gaul That rich and extensive country, as far as the ocean, the Alps, and the Pyrenees, was delivered to the Barbarians, who drove before them, in a promiscuous crowd, the bishop, the senator, and the virgin, laden with the spoils of their houses and altars.[93] The ecclesiastics, to whom we are indebted for this vague description of the public calamities, embraced the opportunity of exhorting the Christians to repent of the sins which had provoked the Divine Justice, and to renounce the perishable goods of a wretched and deceitful world But, as the Pelagian controversy,[94] which attempts to sound the abyss of grace and predestination, soon became the serious employment of the Latin clergy , the Providence which had decreed, or foreseen, or permitted such a train of moral and natural evils was rashly weighed in the imperfect and fallacious balance of reason The crimes and the mis-

[91] Claudian (1 Cons Stil 1 1 221, &c , 1 11 186) describes the peace and prosperity of the Gallic frontier The Abbé Dubos (Hist Critique, &c , tom 1 p. 174) would read *Alba* (a nameless rivulet of the Ardennes) instead of *Albis*, and expatiates on the danger of the Gallic cattle grazing beyond the *Elbe* Foolish enough ! In poetical geography, the Elbe, and the Hercynian, signify any river, or any wood in Germany Claudian is not prepared for the strict examination of our antiquaries

[92]———— Geminasque viator
        Cum videat ripas, quæ sit Romana requirat

[93] Jerom, tom 1 p 93 See in the 1st vol of the Historians of France, p 777, 782, the proper extracts from the Carmen de Providentiâ Divinâ, and Salvian The anonymous poet was himself a captive, with his bishop and fellow-citizens

[94] The Pelagian doctrine, which was first agitated A D 405, was condemned, in the space of ten years, at Rome and Carthage St Augustin fought and conquered, but the Greek Church was favourable to his adversaries , and (what is singular enough) the people did not take any part in a dispute which they could not understand

fortunes of the suffering people were presumptuously compared
with those of their ancestors ; and they arraigned the Divine
Justice, which did not exempt from the common destruction the
feeble, the guiltless, the infant portion of the human species
These idle disputants overlooked the invariable laws of nature,
which have connected peace with innocence, plenty with industry, and safety with valour.   The timid and selfish policy of the
court of Ravenna might recall the Palatine legions for the protection of Italy ; the remains of the stationary troops might
be unequal to the arduous task , and the Barbarian auxiliaries
might prefer the unbounded licence of spoil to the benefits of a
moderate and regular stipend.   But the provinces of Gaul were
filled with a numerous race of hardy and robust youth, who, in
the defence of their houses, their families, and their altars, if
they had dared to die, would have deserved to vanquish.   The
knowledge of their native country would have enabled them to
oppose continual and insuperable obstacles to the progress of an
invader ; and the deficiency of the Barbarians, in arms as well
as in discipline, removed the only pretence which excuses the
submission of a populous country to the inferior numbers of a
veteran army.   When France was invaded by Charles the Fifth,
he inquired of a prisoner how many *days* Paris might be distant
from the frontier.   " Perhaps *twelve,* but they will be days of
battle ; " [95] such was the gallant answer which checked the
arrogance of that ambitious prince   The subjects of Honorius
and those of Francis I were animated by a very different spirit ;
and in less than two years the divided troops of the savages of
the Baltic, whose numbers, were they fairly stated, would appear
contemptible, advanced without a combat to the foot of the
Pyrenæan mountains.

In the early part of the reign of Honorius, the vigilance of Revolt of the
Stilicho had successfully guarded the remote island of Britain British army.
A D 407
from her incessant enemies of the ocean, the mountains, and the
Irish coast [96]   But those restless Barbarians could not neglect the

---

[95] See Mémoires de Guillaume du Bellay, l vi   In French the original reproof is
less obvious and more pointed, from the double sense of the word *journée,* which
signifies a day's travel or a battle

[96] Claudian (i Cons Stil l ii 250)   It is supposed that the Scots of Ireland
invaded, by sea, the whole western coast of Britain , and some slight credit may
be given even to Nennius and the Irish traditions (Carte's Hist of England, vol i
p 169.   Whitaker's Genuine History of the Britons, p 199).   The sixty-six lives
of St Patrick, which were extant in the ninth century, must have contained as
many thousand lies , yet we may believe that, in one of these Irish inroads, the
future apostle was led away captive (Usher, Antiquit Eccles. Britann. p 431, and
Tillemont, Mém Ecclés. tom. xvi p 456, 782, &c)

fair opportunity of the Gothic war, when the walls and stations of the province were stripped of the Roman troops. If any of the legionaries were permitted to return from the Italian expedition, their faithful report of the court and character of Honorius must have tended to dissolve the bonds of allegiance and to exasperate the seditious temper of the British army. The spirit of revolt, which had formerly disturbed the age of Gallienus, was revived by the capricious violence of the soldiers; and the unfortunate, perhaps the ambitious, candidates, who were the objects of their choice, were the instruments, and at length the victims, of their passion.[97] Marcus was the first whom they placed on the throne, as the lawful emperor of Britain, and of the West. They violated, by the hasty murder of Marcus, the oath of fidelity which they had imposed on themselves; and *their* disapprobation of his manners may seem to inscribe an honourable epitaph on his tomb. Gratian was the next whom they adorned with the diadem and the purple, and, at the end of four months, Gratian experienced the fate of his predecessor. The memory of the great Constantine, whom the British legions had given to the church and to the empire, suggested the singular motive of their third choice. They discovered in the ranks a private soldier of the name of Constantine, and their impetuous levity had already seated him on the throne, before they perceived his incapacity to sustain the weight of that glorious appellation.[98] Yet the authority of Constantine was less precarious, and his government was more successful, than the transient reigns of Marcus and of Gratian. The danger of leaving his inactive troops in those camps which had been twice polluted with blood and sedition urged him to attempt the reduction of the Western provinces. He landed at Boulogne with an inconsiderable force; and, after he had reposed himself some days, he summoned the cities of Gaul, which had escaped the yoke of the Barbarians, to acknowledge their lawful sovereign. They obeyed the summons without reluctance. The neglect of the court of Ravenna had absolved a deserted people from the duty of allegiance; their actual distress en-

[A D 406]

Constantine is acknowledged in Britain and Gaul A D 407

---

[97] The British usurpers are taken from Zosimus (l vi p 371-375 [c 2]), Orosius (l vii c 40, p 576, 577), Olympiodorus (apud Photium, p 180, 181 [fr 12]), the ecclesiastical historians, and the Chronicles. The Latins are ignorant of Marcus [According to Zosimus, the invasion of Gaul by the Vandals caused the revolt in Britain For the usurpers see Appendix 19 and 20]

[98] Cum in Constantino *inconstantiam* execrarentur (Sidonius Apollinaris, l v epist 9, p 139, edit secund Sirmond.) Yet Sidonius might be tempted, by so fair a pun, to stigmatize a prince who had disgraced his grandfather

couraged them to accept any circumstances of change, without apprehension, and perhaps with some degree of hope; and they might flatter themselves that the troops, the authority, and even the name of a Roman emperor, who fixed his residence in Gaul, would protect the unhappy country from the rage of the Barbarians The first successes of Constantine against the detached parties of the Germans were magnified by the voice of adulation into splendid and decisive victories; which the reunion and insolence of the enemy soon reduced to their just value. His negotiations procured a short and precarious truce, and, if some tribes of the barbarians were engaged, by the liberality of his gifts and promises, to undertake the defence of the Rhine, these expensive and uncertain treaties, instead of restoring the pristine vigour of the Gallic frontier, served only to disgrace the majesty of the prince and to exhaust what yet remained of the treasures of the republic. Elated, however, with this imaginary triumph, the vain deliverer of Gaul advanced into the provinces of the South, to encounter a more pressing and personal danger. Sarus the Goth was ordered to lay the head of the rebel at the feet of [A D. 408] the emperor Honorius, and the forces of Britain and Italy were unworthily consumed in this domestic quarrel After the loss of his two bravest generals Justinian and Nevigastes, the former [Neviogast] of whom was slain in the field of battle, the latter in a peaceful and treacherous interview, Constantine fortified himself within the walls of Vienna The place was ineffectually attacked [leg Valentia, cp Zos vi 2] seven days; and the Imperial army supported, in a precipitate retreat, the ignominy of purchasing a secure passage from the freebooters and outlaws of the Alps [99] Those mountains now separated the dominions of two rival monarchs and the fortifications of the double frontier were guarded by the troops of the empire, whose arms would have been more usefully employed to maintain the Roman limits against the Barbarians of Germany and Scythia.

On the side of the Pyrenees, the ambition of Constantine He reduces might be justified by the proximity of danger; but his throne Spain A.D 408 was soon established by the conquest, or rather submission, of Spain, which yielded to the influence of regular and habitual subordination, and received the laws and magistrates of the Gallic præfecture The only opposition which was made to the

[99] *Bagaudæ* is the name which Zosimus applies to them [Βακαυδαις vi 2], perhaps they deserved a less odious character (see Dubos, Hist Critique, tom i p 203, and this History, vol ii p 121) We shall hear of them again [Here they appear as a sort of national militia. Cp Freeman, in Eng Hist Review, i 63]

authority of Constantine proceeded not so much from the powers
of government, or the spirit of the people, as from the private
zeal and interest of the family of Theodosius Four brothers [100]
had obtained by the favour of their kinsman, the deceased
emperor, an honourable rank, and ample possessions, in their
native country, and the grateful youths resolved to risk those
advantages in the service of his son After an unsuccessful
effort to maintain their ground at the head of the stationary
troops of Lusitania, they retired to their estates; where they
armed and levied, at their own expense, a considerable body of
slaves and dependents, and boldly marched to occupy the strong
posts of the Pyrenæan mountains This domestic insurrection
alarmed and perplexed the sovereign of Gaul and Britain; and
he was compelled to negotiate with some troops of Barbarian
auxiliaries, for the service of the Spanish war They were distinguished by the title of *Honorians* ; [101] a name which might have
reminded them of their fidelity to their lawful sovereign, and,
if it should candidly be allowed that the *Scots* were influenced by
any partial affection for a British prince, the *Moors* and *Marcomanni* could be tempted only by the profuse liberality of the
usurper, who distributed among the Barbarians the military, and
even the civil, honours of Spain The nine bands of *Honorians*,
which may be easily traced on the establishment of the Western
empire, could not exceed the number of five thousand men,
yet this inconsiderable force was sufficient to terminate a war
which had threatened the power and safety of Constantine
The rustic army of the Theodosian family was surrounded and
destroyed in the Pyrenees · two of the brothers had the good
fortune to escape by sea to Italy, or the East. the other two,
after an interval of suspense, were executed at Arles; and, if
Honorius could remain insensible of the public disgrace, he
might perhaps be affected by the personal misfortunes of his
generous kinsmen Such were the feeble arms which decided

[100] Verinianus, Didymus, Theodosius, and Lagodius, who, in modern courts,
would be styled princes of the blood, were not distinguished by any rank or
privileges above the rest of their fellow-subjects
[101] These *Honoriani*, or *Honoriaci*, consisted of two bands of Scots, or Attacotti,
two of Moors, two of Marcomanni, the Victores, the Ascarii, and the Gallicani
(Notitia Imperii, sect xxxviii edit Lab) They were part of the sixty-five
Auxilia Palatina, and are properly styled ἐν τῇ αὐλῇ τάξεις by Zosimus (l vi p
374 [c 4]) [Mr Hodgkin rightly observes that it is a mistake to suppose that the
troops of Aux Pal, called Honoriani, formed a single division, or necessarily
acted together The Honoriani in Gaul had nothing to do with the Honoriani in
Illyricum, and Constantine had only to do with the Honoriani in Gaul Moreover
the phrase of Zosimus does not refer to Auxilia Palatina]

the possession of the Western provinces of Europe, from the wall of Antoninus to the columns of Hercules. The events of peace and war have undoubtedly been diminished by the narrow and imperfect view of the historians of the times, who were equally ignorant of the causes and of the effects of the most important revolutions. But the total decay of the national strength had annihilated even the last resource of a despotic government, and the revenue of exhausted provinces could no longer purchase the military service of a discontented and pusillanimous people.

The poet whose flattery has ascribed to the Roman eagle the victories of Pollentia and Verona pursues the hasty retreat of Alaric, from the confines of Italy, with a horrid train of imaginary spectres, such as might hover over an army of Barbarians, which was almost exterminated by war, famine, and disease.[102]   In the course of this unfortunate expedition, the king of the Goths must indeed have sustained a considerable loss, and his harassed forces required an interval of repose, to recruit their numbers and revive their confidence   Adversity had exercised, and displayed, the genius of Alaric ; and the fame of his valour invited to the Gothic standard the bravest of the Barbarian warriors, who, from the Euxine to the Rhine, were agitated by the desire of rapine and conquest. He had deserved the esteem, and he soon accepted the friendship, of Stilicho himself. Renouncing the service of the emperor of the East, Alaric concluded, with the court of Ravenna, a treaty of peace and alliance, by which he was declared master-general of the Roman armies throughout the præfecture of Illyricum ; as it was claimed, according to the true and ancient limits, by the minister of Honorius [103]   The execution of the ambitious design, which was either stipulated, or implied, in the articles of the treaty, appears to have been suspended by the formidable irruption of Radagaisus ; and the neutrality of the Gothic king may perhaps be compared to the indifference of Cæsar, who, in the conspiracy of Catiline, refused either to assist or to oppose the enemy of the republic. After the defeat of the Vandals, Stilicho resumed his pretensions to the provinces of the East, appointed civil magistrates for the

Negotiation of Alaric and Stilicho A D 404 408

---

[102] ——Comitatur euntem
Pallor et atra fames, et saucia lividus ora
Luctus, et inferni stridentes agmine morbi
                    Claudian in vi Cons Hon 321, &c.
[103] These dark transactions are investigated by the Count de Buat (Hist des Peuples de l'Europe, tom vii c iii -viii p 69-206), whose laborious accuracy may sometimes fatigue a superficial reader.

administration of justice, and of the finances ; and declared his
impatience to lead to the gates of Constantinople the united
armies of the Romans and of the Goths. The prudence, however, of Stilicho, his aversion to civil war, and his perfect knowledge of the weakness of the state, may countenance the
suspicion that domestic peace, rather than foreign conquest,
was the object of his policy , and that his principal care was to
employ the forces of Alaric at a distance from Italy. This
design could not long escape the penetration of the Gothic king,
who continued to hold a doubtful, and perhaps a treacherous,
correspondence with the rival courts, who protracted, like a
dissatisfied mercenary, his languid operations in Thessaly and
Epirus, and who soon returned to claim the extravagant reward
[Laibach] of his ineffectual services. From his camp near Æmona,[104] on the
confines of Italy, he transmitted, to the emperor of the West, a
long account of promises, of expenses, and of demands ; called
for immediate satisfaction and clearly intimated the consequences
of a refusal. Yet, if his conduct was hostile, his language was
decent and dutiful   He humbly professed himself the friend of
Stilicho, and the soldier of Honorius , offered his person and
his troops to march, without delay, against the usurper of Gaul ,
and solicited, as a permanent retreat for the Gothic nation, the
possession of some vacant province of the Western empire.

Debates of
the Roman
senate A D.   The political and secret transactions of two statesmen, who
408   laboured to deceive each other and the world, must for ever have
been concealed in the impenetrable darkness of the cabinet, if
the debates of a popular assembly had not thrown some rays
of light on the correspondence of Alaric and Stilicho. The
necessity of finding some artificial support for a government,
which, from a principle, not of moderation, but of weakness,
was reduced to negotiate with its own subjects, had insensibly
revived the authority of the Roman senate ; and the minister of
Honorius respectfully consulted the legislative council of the
republic. Stilicho assembled the senate in the palace of the
Cæsars . represented, in a studied oration, the actual state of
affairs ; proposed the demands of the Gothic king, and submitted to their consideration the choice of peace or war   The
senators, as if they had been suddenly awakened from a dream

104 See Zosimus, l. v p 334, 335 [c 29]   He interrupts his scanty narrative, to
relate the fable of Æmona, and of the ship Argo, which was drawn over from that
place to the Hadriatic   Sozomen (l viii c 25, l ix c 4) and Socrates (l vii.
c, 10) cast a pale and doubtful light , and Orosius (l vii , c 38, p 571) is
abominably partial

of four hundred years, appeared on this important occasion to be inspired by the courage, rather than by the wisdom, of their predecessors. They loudly declared, in regular speeches, or in tumultuary acclamations, that it was unworthy of the majesty of Rome to purchase a precarious and disgraceful truce from a Barbarian king, and that, in the judgment of a magnanimous people, the chance of ruin was always preferable to the certainty of dishonour. The minister, whose pacific intentions were seconded only by the voices of a few servile and venal followers, attempted to allay the general ferment, by an apology for his own conduct, and even for the demands of the Gothic prince. "The payment of a subsidy, which had excited the indignation of the Romans, ought not (such was the language of Stilicho) to be considered in the odious light either of a tribute or of a ransom, extorted by the menaces of a Barbarian enemy. Alaric had faithfully asserted the just pretensions of the republic to the provinces which were usurped by the Greeks of Constantinople; he modestly required the fair and stipulated recompense of his services; and, if he had desisted from the prosecution of his enterprise, he had obeyed, in his retreat, the peremptory though private letters of the emperor himself. These contradictory orders (he would not dissemble the errors of his own family) had been procured by the intercession of Serena. The tender piety of his wife had been too deeply affected by the discord of the royal brothers, the sons of her adopted father; and the sentiments of nature had too easily prevailed over the stern dictates of the public welfare." These ostensible reasons, which faintly disguise the obscure intrigues of the palace of Ravenna, were supported by the authority of Stilicho; and obtained, after a warm debate, the reluctant approbation of the senate. The tumult of virtue and freedom subsided; and the sum of four thousand pounds of gold was granted, under the name of a subsidy, to secure the peace of Italy, and to conciliate the friendship of the king of the Goths. Lampadius alone, one of the most illustrious members of the assembly, still persisted in his dissent; exclaimed with a loud voice, "This is not a treaty of peace, but of servitude"; [105] and escaped the danger of such bold opposition by immediately retiring to the sanctuary of a Christian church.

But the reign of Stilicho drew towards its end, and the proud Intrigues of the palace A D 408, May

[105] Zosimus, l v p 338, 339 [c 29] He repeats the words of Lampadius, as they were spoke in Latin, "Non est ista pax, sed pactio servitutis," and then translates them into Greek for the benefit of his readers

minister might perceive the symptoms of his approaching disgrace The generous boldness of Lampadius had been applauded , and the senate, so patiently resigned to a long servitude, rejected with disdain the offer of invidious and imaginary freedom   The troops, who still assumed the name and prerogatives of the Roman legions, were exasperated by the partial affection of Stilicho for the Barbarians ; and the people imputed to the mischievous policy of the minister the public misfortunes, which were the natural consequence of their own degeneracy.   Yet Stilicho might have continued to brave the clamours of the people, and even of the soldiers, if he could have maintained his dominion over the feeble mind of his pupil But the respectful attachment of Honorius was converted into fear, suspicion, and hatred.   The crafty Olympius,[106] who concealed his vices under the mask of Christian piety, had secretly undermined the benefactor by whose favour he was promoted to the honourable offices of the Imperial palace.   Olympius revealed to the unsuspecting emperor, who had attained the twenty-fifth year of his age, that he was without weight, or authority, in his own government ; and artfully alarmed his timid and indolent disposition by a lively picture of the designs of Stilicho, who already meditated the death of his sovereign, with the ambitious hope of placing the diadem on the head of his son Eucherius   The emperor was instigated, by his new favourite, to assume the tone of independent dignity ; and the minister was astonished to find that secret resolutions were formed in the court and council, which were repugnant to his interest or to his intentions   Instead of residing in the palace at Rome, Honorius declared that it was his pleasure to return to the secure fortress of Ravenna.   On the first intelligence of the death of his brother Arcadius, he prepared to visit Constantinople, and to regulate, with the authority of a guardian, the provinces of the infant Theodosius.[107]   The representation of the difficulty and expense of such a distant expedition checked this

[106] He came from the coast of the Euxine, and exercised a splendid office, λαμπρᾶς δε στρατειας ἐν τοῖς βασιλειοις ἀξιούμειος   His actions justify his character, which Zosimus (l v p 340 [c 32]) exposes with visible satisfaction   Augustin revered the piety of Olympius, whom he styles a true son of the church (Baronius, Annal. Eccles A D. 408, No 19, &c   Tillemont, Mém Ecclés tom viii. p. 467, 468)   But these praises, which the African saint so unworthily bestows, might proceed as well from ignorance as from adulation

[107] Zosimus, l v p 338, 339 [c 31]   Sozomen, l iv c 4   Stilicho offered to undertake the journey to Constantinople, that he might divert Honorius from the vain attempt   The Eastern empire would not have obeyed, and could not have been conquered

strange and sudden sally of active diligence , but the dangerous project of showing the emperor to the camp of Pavia, which was [Ticinum] composed of the Roman troops, the enemies of Stilicho, and his Barbarian auxiliaries, remained fixed and unalterable.   The minister was pressed, by the advice of his confidant Justinian, a Roman advocate of a lively and penetrating genius, to oppose a journey so prejudicial to his reputation and safety   His strenuous, but ineffectual, efforts confirmed the triumph of Olympius ; and the prudent lawyer withdrew himself from the impending ruin of his patron

In the passage of the emperor through Bologna, a mutiny of the guards was excited and appeased by the secret policy of Stilicho , who announced his instructions to decimate the guilty, and ascribed to his own intercession the merit of their pardon After this tumult, Honorius embraced, for the last time, the minister whom he now considered as a tyrant, and proceeded on his way to the camp of Pavia, where he was received by the loyal acclamations of the troops who were assembled for the service of the Gallic war   On the morning of the fourth day, he pronounced, as he had been taught, a military oration in the presence of the soldiers, whom the charitable visits, and artful discourses, of Olympius had prepared to execute a dark and bloody conspiracy.   At the first signal, they massacred the friends of Stilicho, the most illustrious officers of the empire ; two Prætorian præfects, of Gaul, and of Italy ; two masters-general, of the cavalry and infantry ; the master of the offices , the quæstor, the treasurer, and the count of the domestics. Many lives were lost ; many houses were plundered ; the furious sedition continued to rage till the close of the evening ; and the trembling emperor, who was seen in the streets of Pavia with-out his robes or diadem, yielded to the persuasions of his favourite, condemned the memory of the slain, and solemnly approved the innocence and fidelity of their assassins   The in-telligence of the massacre of Pavia filled the mind of Stilicho with just and gloomy apprehensions , and he instantly sum-moned, in the camp of Bologna, a council of the confederate leaders who were attached to his service, and would be involved in his ruin   The impetuous voice of the assembly called aloud for arms, and for revenge . to march, without a moment's delay, under the banners of a hero whom they had so often followed to victory, to surprise, to oppress, to extirpate the guilty Olympius, and his degenerate Romans , and perhaps to fix the diadem on the head of their injured general.   Instead of

Disgrace and death of Stilicho A D 408 Aug 23

executing a resolution, which might have been justified by success, Stilicho hesitated till he was irrecoverably lost. He was still ignorant of the fate of the emperor, he distrusted the fidelity of his own party; and he viewed with horror the fatal consequences of arming a crowd of licentious Barbarians against the soldiers and people of Italy. The confederates, impatient of his timorous and doubtful delay, hastily retired, with fear and indignation. At the hour of midnight, Sarus, a Gothic warrior, renowned among the Barbarians themselves for his strength and valour, suddenly invaded the camp of his benefactor, plundered the baggage, cut in pieces the faithful Huns, who guarded his person, and penetrated to the tent, where the minister, pensive and sleepless, meditated on the dangers of his situation. Stilicho escaped with difficulty from the sword of the Goths, and, after issuing a last and generous admonition to the cities of Italy, to shut their gates against the Barbarians, his confidence, or his despair, urged him to throw himself into Ravenna, which was already in the absolute possession of his enemies. Olympius, who had assumed the dominion of Honorius, was speedily informed that his rival had embraced, as a suppliant, the altar of the Christian church. The base and cruel disposition of the hypocrite was incapable of pity or remorse; but he piously affected to elude, rather than to violate, the privilege of the sanctuary. Count Heraclian, with a troop of soldiers, appeared, at the dawn of day, before the gates of the church of Ravenna. The bishop was satisfied by a solemn oath that the Imperial mandate only directed them to secure the person of Stilicho. but, as soon as the unfortunate minister had been tempted beyond the holy threshold, he produced the warrant for his instant execution. Stilicho supported, with calm resignation, the injurious names of traitor and parricide, repressed the unseasonable zeal of his followers, who were ready to attempt an ineffectual rescue, and, with a firmness not unworthy of the last of the Roman generals, submitted his neck to the sword of Heraclian [108]

His memory persecuted   The servile crowd of the palace, who had so long adored the fortune of Stilicho, affected to insult his fall, and the most distant connexion with the master-general of the West, which had so lately been a title to wealth and honours, was studiously

[108] Zosimus (l. v. p. 336-345 [c. 30]) has copiously, though not clearly, related the disgrace and death of Stilicho. Olympiodorus (apud Phot. p. 177 [fr. 2]), Orosius (l. vii. c. 38, p. 571, 572), Sozomen (l. ix. c. 4), and Philostorgius (l. xi. c. 3, l. xii. c. 2) afford supplemental hints.

denied and rigorously punished.   His family, united by a
triple alliance with the family of Theodosius, might envy the
condition of the meanest peasant   The flight of his son
Eucherius was intercepted, and the death of that innocent youth
soon followed the divorce of Thermantia, who filled the
place of her sister Maria, and who, like Maria, had remained a
virgin in the Imperial bed.[109]   The friends of Stilicho, who had
escaped the massacre of Pavia, were persecuted by the implacable revenge of Olympius, and the most exquisite cruelty was
employed to extort the confession of a treasonable and sacrilegious conspiracy   They died in silence . their firmness justified
the choice,[110] and perhaps absolved the innocence, of their patron,
and the despotic power which could take his life without a trial,
and stigmatize his memory without a proof, has no jurisdiction
over the impartial suffrage of posterity.[111]   The services of Stilicho are great and manifest ; his crimes, as they are vaguely
stated in the language of flattery and hatred, are obscure, at
least, and improbable.   About four months after his death an
edict was published in the name of Honorius to restore the free
communication of the two empires which had been so long interrupted by the *public enemy* [112]   The minister whose fame and
fortune depended on the prosperity of the state was accused of
betraying Italy to the Barbarians, whom he repeatedly vanquished at Pollentia, at Verona, and before the walls of Florence.
His pretended design of placing the diadem on the head of his
son Eucherius could not have been conducted without preparations or accomplices, and the ambitious father would not surely
have left the future emperor, till the twentieth year of his age,
in the humble station of tribune of the notaries   Even the religion of Stilicho was arraigned by the malice of his rival   The
seasonable and almost miraculous deliverance was devoutly cele-

109 Zosimus, l v p 333 [c 28]   The marriage of a Christian with two sisters
scandalizes Tillemont (Hist des Empereurs, tom v p 557), who expects, in vain,
that Pope Innocent I should have done something in the way either of censure or
of dispensation.

110 Two of his friends are honourably mentioned (Zosimus, l v p 346 [c 35]) :
Peter, chief of the school of notaries, and the great chamberlain Deuterius   Stilicho had secured the bedchamber, and it is surprising that, under a feeble prince,
the bedchamber was not able to secure him

111 Orosius (l vii c 38, p 571, 572) seems to copy the false and furious manifes-
toes which were dispersed through the provinces by the new administration

112 See the Theodosian Code, l vii tit. xvi leg 1 , l iv tit xlii leg 22
Stilicho is branded with the name of *praedo publicus*, who employed his wealth *ad*
*omnem ditandam inquietandam*que *Barbariem*   [Especially noteworthy is the
measure of Stilicho, mentioned in C Th vii 16, 1, which closed the ports of Italy
to all comers from the realm of Arcadius.]

brated by the applause of the clergy, who asserted that the
restoration of idols and the persecution of the church would
have been the first measure of the reign of Eucherius   The son
of Stilicho, however, was educated in the bosom of Christianity,
which his father had uniformly professed and zealously supported [113]   Serena had borrowed her magnificent necklace from
the statue of Vesta,[114] and the Pagans execrated the memory of
the sacrilegious minister, by whose order the Sybilline books,
the oracles of Rome, had been committed to the flames [115]   The
pride and power of Stilicho constituted his real guilt.   An
honourable reluctance to shed the blood of his countrymen
appears to have contributed to the success of his unworthy
rival ; and it is the last humiliation of the character of Honorius that posterity has not condescended to reproach him with
his base ingratitude to the guardian of his youth and the support
of his empire

The poet
Claudian

Among the train of dependents whose wealth and dignity
attracted the notice of their own times *our* curiosity is excited
by the celebrated name of the poet Claudian, who enjoyed the
favour of Stilicho, and was overwhelmed in the ruin of his patron.
The titular offices of tribune and notary fixed his rank in the
Imperial court ; he was indebted to the powerful intercession
of Serena for his marriage with a very rich heiress of the province
of Africa,[116] and the statue of Claudian, erected in the forum of
Trajan, was a monument of the taste and liberality of the Roman
senate.[117]   After the praises of Stilicho became offensive and

[113] Augustin himself is satisfied with the effectual laws which Stilicho had enacted
against heretics and idolaters, and which are still extant in the Code   He only
applies to Olympius for their confirmation (Baronius, Annal Eccles A D 408, No
19)

[114] Zosimus, l v p 351 [c 38]   We may observe the bad taste of the age in
dressing their statues with such awkward finery

[115] See Rutilius Numatianus (Itinerar l ii 41-60), to whom religious enthusiasm
has dictated some elegant and forcible lines   Stilicho likewise stripped the gold
plates from the doors of the Capitol, and read a prophetic sentence which was en-
graven under them (Zosimus, l v p 352 [ib])   These are foolish stories   yet the
charge of *impiety* adds weight and credit to the praise, which Zosimus reluctantly
bestows, of his virtues

[116] At the nuptials of Orpheus (a modest comparison ') all the parts of animated
nature contributed their various gifts, and the gods themselves enriched their
favourite.   Claudian had neither flocks, nor herds, nor vines, nor olives   His
wealthy bride was heiress to them all   But he carried to Africa a recommendatory
letter from Serena, his Juno, and was made happy (Epist ii ad Serenam)

[117] Claudian feels the honour like a man who deserved it (in præfat Bell Get)
The original inscription on marble, was found at Rome, in the fifteenth century,
in the house of Pomponius Lætus   [See Appendix 1, in notices of Claudian]   The
statue of a poet, far superior to Claudian, should have been erected during his lifetime by the men of letters, his countrymen, and contemporaries.   It was a noble
design [1]   [See Appendix 21.]

criminal, Claudian was exposed to the enmity of a powerful and unforgiving courtier, whom he had provoked by the insolence of wit. He had compared, in a lively epigram, the opposite characters of two Prætorian præfects of Italy ; he contrasts the innocent repose of a philosopher who sometimes resigned the hours of business to slumber, perhaps to study, with the interested diligence of a rapacious minister, indefatigable in the pursuit of unjust or sacrilegious gain. " How happy," continues Claudian, " how happy might it be for the people of Italy if Mallius could be constantly awake, and if Hadrian would always sleep ! " [118] The repose of Mallius was not disturbed by this friendly and gentle admonition, but the cruel vigilance of Hadrian watched the opportunity of revenge, and easily obtained from the enemies of Stilicho the trifling sacrifice of an obnoxious poet. The poet concealed himself, however, during the tumult of the revolution, and, consulting the dictates of prudence rather than of honour, he addressed, in the form of an epistle, a suppliant and humble recantation to the offended præfect. He deplores, in mournful strains, the fatal indiscretion into which he had been hurried by passion and folly , submits to the imitation of his adversary the generous examples of the clemency of gods, of heroes, and of lions , and expresses his hope that the magnanimity of Hadrian will not trample on a defenceless and contemptible foe, already humbled by disgrace and poverty, and deeply wounded by the exile, the tortures, and the death of his dearest friends.[119] Whatever might be the success of his prayer, or the accidents of his future life, the period of a few years levelled in the grave the minister and the poet : but the name of Hadrian is almost sunk in oblivion, while Claudian is read with pleasure in every country which has retained, or acquired, the knowledge of the Latin language. If

[118] See Epigram xxx
      Mallius indulget somno noctesque diesque :
      Insomnis *Pharius* sacra, profana, rapit
      Omnibus, hoc, Italæ gentes, exposcite votis
      Mallius ut vigilet, dormiat ut Pharius
Hadrian was a Pharian (of Alexandria) See his public life in Godefroy, Cod Theodos tom vi p 364 [Hadrianus was Pr Pr in 405 A D] Mallius did not always sleep He composed some elegant dialogues on the Greek systems of natural philosophy (Claud in Mall Theodor Cons 61-112) [This Hadrian episode is very doubtful , see next note]
[119] See Claudian's first Epistle ' Yet, in some places, an air of irony and indignation betrays his secret reluctance [" (1) The Mss greatly vary as to the heading of this epistle, some even calling it *Deprecatio ad Stilichonem*, (2) there is nothing to connect it with the latter rather than the earlier part of Claudian's career , and (3) the whole piece sounds more like banter than earnest," Hodgkin, i 731]

we fairly balance his merits and his defects, we shall acknowledge that Claudian does not either satisfy or silence our
reason   It would not be easy to produce a passage that
deserves the epithet of sublime or pathetic , to select a verse
that melts the heart or enlarges the imagination.   We should
vainly seek, in the poems of Claudian, the happy invention and
artificial conduct of an interesting fable, or the just and lively
representation of the characters and situations of real life   For
the service of his patron he published occasional panegyrics and
invectives ; and the design of these slavish compositions encouraged his propensity to exceed the limits of truth and nature.
These imperfections, however, are compensated in some degree
by the poetical virtues of Claudian.   He was endowed with the
rare and precious talent of raising the meanest, of adorning the
most barren, and of diversifying the most similar topics ; his
colouring, more especially in descriptive poetry, is soft and
splendid ; and he seldom fails to display, and even to abuse, the
advantages of a cultivated understanding, a copious fancy, an
easy, and sometimes forcible, expression, and a perpetual flow of
harmonious versifications.   To these commendations, independent of any accidents of time and place, we must add the peculiar merit which Claudian derived from the unfavourable circumstances of his birth   In the decline of arts and of empire a
native of Egypt,[120] who had received the education of a Greek,
assumed, in a mature age, the familiar use and absolute command of the Latin language,[121] soared above the heads of his
feeble contemporaries, and placed himself, after an interval of
three hundred years, among the poets of ancient Rome.[122]

[120] National vanity has made him a Florentine, or a Spaniard.   But the first
epistle of Claudian proves him a native of Alexandria (Fabricius, Bibliot Latin
tom III. p 191-202, edit Ernest)
[121] His first Latin verses were composed during the consulship of Probinus,
A D 395
　　　　Romanos bibimus primum, te consule, fontes,
　　　　　　Et Latiæ cessit Graia Thalia togæ
Besides some Greek epigrams, which are still extant, the Latin poet had composed,
in Greek, the antiquities of Tarsus, Anazarbus, Berytus, Nice, &c   It is more
easy to supply the loss of good poetry than of authentic history
[122] Strada (Prolusion v vi)allows him to contend with the five heroic poets, Lucre-
tius, Virgil, Ovid, Lucan, and Statius   His patron is the accomplished courtier
Balthazar Castiglione   His admirers are numerous and passionate   Yet the rigid
critics reproach the exotic weeds, or flowers, which spring too luxuriantly in his
Latian soil,

CHAPTER XXXI

Invasion of Italy by Alaric—Manners of the Roman Senate and People—Rome is thrice besieged and at length pillaged by the Goths—Death of Alaric—The Goths evacuate Italy—Fall of Constantine—Gaul and Spain are occupied by the Barbarians—Independence of Britain

THE incapacity of a weak and distracted government may often assume the appearance, and produce the effects, of a treasonable correspondence with the public enemy.   If Alaric himself had been introduced into the council of Ravenna, he would probably have advised the same measures which were actually pursued by the ministers of Honorius[1]   The king of the Goths would have conspired, perhaps with some reluctance, to destroy the formidable adversary by whose arms, in Italy as well as in Greece, he had been twice overthrown   *Their* active and interested hatred laboriously accomplished the disgrace and ruin of the great Stilicho   The valour of Sarus, his fame in arms, and his personal, or hereditary, influence over the confederate Barbarians could recommend him only to the friends of their country, who despised, or detested, the worthless characters of Turpilio, Varanes, and Vigilantius   By the pressing instances of the new favourites, these generals, unworthy as they had shewn themselves of the name of soldiers,[2] were promoted to the command of the cavalry, of the infantry, and of the domestic troops   The Gothic prince would have subscribed with pleasure the edict which the fanaticism of Olympius dictated to the simple and devout emperor Honorius excluded all persons who were adverse to the catholic church from holding any office in the state , obstinately rejected the service of all those who dissented from his religion ; and rashly disqualified many of his bravest and most skilful

Weakness of the court of Ravenna
A D 408 Sept

---

[1] The series of events from the death of Stilicho to the arrival of Alaric before Rome can only be found in Zosimus, l v p 347-350 [c. 35-37]

[2] The expression of Zosimus is strong and lively . καταφροιησιν ἐμποιῆσαι τοῖς πολεμιοις αρκοῦντας, sufficient to excite the contempt of the enemy

officers, who adhered to the Pagan worship, or who had imbibed the opinions of Arianism.[8] These measures, so advantageous to an enemy, Alaric would have approved, and might
perhaps have suggested , but it may seem doubtful whether
the Barbarian would have promoted his interest at the expense
of the inhuman and absurd cruelty which was perpetrated by
the direction, or at least with the connivance, of the Imperial
ministers. The foreign auxiliaries who had been attached to
the person of Stilicho lamented his death , but the desire of
revenge was checked by a natural apprehension for the safety
of their wives and children, who were detained as hostages
in the strong cities of Italy, where they had likewise deposited
their most valuable effects. At the same hour, and as if by a
common signal, the cities of Italy were polluted by the same
horrid scenes of universal massacre and pillage, which involved,
in promiscuous destruction, the families and fortunes of the
Barbarians. Exasperated by such an injury, which might have
awakened the tamest and most servile spirit, they cast a look
of indignation and hope towards the camp of Alaric, and unanimously swore to pursue, with just and implacable war, the
perfidious nation that had so basely violated the laws of
hospitality By the imprudent conduct of the ministers of
Honorius, the republic lost the assistance, and deserved the
enmity, of thirty thousand of her bravest soldiers ; and the
weight of that formidable army, which alone might have determined the event of the war, was transferred from the scale of
the Romans into that of the Goths.

Alaric
marches to
Rome A D
408, Oct , &c

In the arts of negotiation, as well as in those of war, the
Gothic king maintained his superior ascendant over an enemy
whose seeming changes proceeded from the total want of
counsel and design   From his camp, on the confines of Italy,
Alaric attentively observed the revolutions of the palace,
watched the progress of faction and discontent, disguised the
hostile aspect of a Barbarian invader, and assumed the more
popular appearance of the friend and ally of the great Stilicho ,
to whose virtues, when they were no longer formidable, he
could pay a just tribute of sincere praise and regret. The
pressing invitation of the malcontents, who urged the king of

---

[8] Eos qui catholicæ sectæ sunt inimici intra palatium militare prohibemus
Nullus nobis sit aliquâ ratione conjunctus, qui a nobis fide et religione discordat.
Cod Theodos l xvi tit v leg 42, and Godefroy's Commentary, tom vi. p 164.
This law was applied in the utmost latitude, and rigorously executed   Zosimus,
l v p 361 [c 46]

the Goths to invade Italy, was enforced by a lively sense of his personal injuries; and he might speciously complain that the Imperial ministers still delayed and eluded the payment of the four thousand pounds of gold, which had been granted by the Roman senate either to reward his services or to appease his fury. His decent firmness was supported by an artful moderation, which contributed to the success of his designs. He required a fair and reasonable satisfaction; but he gave the strongest assurances that, as soon as he had obtained it, he would immediately retire. He refused to trust the faith of the Romans, unless Aetius and Jason, the sons of two great officers of state, were sent as hostages to his camp; but he offered to deliver, in exchange, several of the noblest youths of the Gothic nation. The modesty of Alaric was interpreted, by the ministers of Ravenna, as a sure evidence of his weakness and fear. They disdained either to negotiate a treaty or to assemble an army; and with a rash confidence, derived only from their ignorance of the extreme danger, irretrievably wasted the decisive moments of peace and war. While they expected, in sullen silence, that the Barbarians should evacuate the confines of Italy, Alaric, with bold and rapid marches, passed the Alps and the Po; hastily pillaged the cities of Aquileia, Altinum, Concordia, and Cremona, which yielded to his arms;[4] increased his forces by the accession of thirty thousand auxiliaries; and without meeting a single enemy in the field, advanced as far as the edge of the morass which protected the impregnable residence of the emperor of the West. Instead of attempting the hopeless siege of Ravenna, the prudent leader of the Goths proceeded to Rimini, stretched his ravages along the sea-coast of the Hadriatic, and meditated the conquest of the ancient mistress of the world. An Italian hermit, whose zeal and sanctity were respected by the Barbarians themselves, encountered the victorious monarch, and boldly denounced the indignation of heaven against the oppressors of the earth, but the saint himself was so confounded by the solemn asseveration of Alaric, that he felt a secret and præternatural impulse, which directed, and even compelled, his march to the gates of Rome. He felt that his genius and his fortune were equal to the most arduous enterprises, and the enthusiasm which he communicated to the Goths insensibly removed the popular,

[4][That he took and plundered these cities is not implied by the phrase of Zosimus (κατατρεχει) Cp von Wietersheim, Gesch. der Volkerwanderung, 2, 146.]

and almost superstitious, reverence of the nations for the majesty of the Roman name. His troops, animated by the hopes of spoil, followed the course of the Flaminian way, occupied the unguarded passes of the Apennine,[5] descended into the rich plains of Umbria ; and, as they lay encamped on the banks of the Clitumnus, might wantonly slaughter and devour the milk-white oxen, which had been so long reserved for the use of Roman triumphs [6] A lofty situation and a seasonable tempest of thunder and lightning preserved the little city of Narni ; but the king of the Goths, despising the ignoble prey, still advanced with unabated vigour ; and, after he had passed through the stately arches, adorned with the spoils of Barbaric victories, he pitched his camp under the walls of Rome [7]

Hannibal at the gates of Rome

During a period of six hundred and nineteen years, the seat of empire had never been violated by the presence of a foreign enemy The unsuccessful expedition of Hannibal [8] served only to display the character of the senate and people ; of a senate degraded, rather than ennobled, by the comparison of an assembly of kings ; and of a people to whom the ambassador of Pyrrhus ascribed the inexhaustible resources of the Hydra [9] Each of the senators, in the time of the Punic war, had accomplished his term of military service, either in a subordinate or a superior station , and the decree which invested with temporary command all those who had been consuls or censors or dictators gave the republic the immediate assistance of many brave and experienced generals. In the beginning of the war, the Roman people consisted of two

[5] Addison (see his Works, vol ii p 54, edit Baskerville) has given a very picturesque description of the road through the Apennine The Goths were not at leisure to observe the beauties of the prospect , but they were pleased to find that the Saxa Intercisa, a narrow passage which Vespasian had cut through the rock (Cluver. Italia Antiq tom. i p 618), was totally neglected

[6] Hinc albi, Clitumne, greges, et maxima taurus
    Victima, sæpe tuo perfusi flumine sacro
    Romanos ad templa Deum duxere triumphos.

Besides Virgil, most of the Latin poets, Propertius, Lucan, Silius, Italicus, Claudian, &c , whose passages may be found in Cluverius and Addison, have celebrated the triumphal victims of the Clitumnus.

[7] Some ideas of the march of Alaric are borrowed from the journey of Honorius over the same ground (see Claudian in vi Cons Hon 494-522) The measured distance between Ravenna and Rome was 254 Roman miles Itinerar Wesseling, p 126

[8] The march and retreat of Hannibal are described by Livy, l xxvi c 7, 8, 9, 10, 11 , and the reader is made a spectator of the interesting scene

[9] These comparisons were used by Cineas, the counsellor of Pyrrhus, after his return from his embassy, in which he had diligently studied the discipline and manners of Rome. See Plutarch in Pyrrho, tom. ii p 459 [c. 19].

hundred and fifty thousand citizens of an age to bear arms.[10]
Fifty thousand had already died in the defence of their country;
and the twenty-three legions which were employed in the
different camps of Italy, Greece, Sardinia, Sicily, and Spain,
required about one hundred thousand men   But there still
remained an equal number in Rome, and the adjacent territory, who were animated by the same intrepid courage , and
every citizen was trained, from his earliest youth, in the
discipline and exercises of a soldier. Hannibal was astonished
by the constancy of the senate, who, without raising the siege
of Capua or recalling their scattered forces, expected his
approach. He encamped on the banks of the Anio, at the
distance of three miles from the city; and he was soon informed that the ground on which he had pitched his tent was
sold for an adequate price at a public auction and that a body
of troops was dismissed by an opposite road, to reinforce the
legions of Spain [11] He led his Africans to the gates of Rome,
where he found three armies in order of battle, prepared to
receive him; but Hannibal dreaded the event of a combat
from which he could not hope to escape, unless he destroyed
the last of his enemies , and his speedy retreat confessed the
invincible courage of the Romans.

From the time of the Punic war the uninterrupted succession Genealogy
of senators had preserved the name and image of the republic; of the Senators
and the degenerate subjects of Honorius ambitiously derived
their descent from the heroes who had repulsed the arms of
Hannibal and subdued the nations of the earth. The temporal
honours which the devout Paula [12] inherited and despised are

---

[10] In the three *census*, which were made of the Roman people, about the time
of the second Punic war, the numbers stand as follows (see Livy, Epitom 1 xx
Hist 1 xxvii 36, xxix 37), 270, 213, 137, 108, 214,000   The fall of the second,
and the rise of the third, appears so enormous that several critics, notwithstanding the unanimity of the Mss , have suspected some corruption of the text of Livy
(See Drakenborch ad xxvii 36, and Beaufort, République Romaine, tom 1 p
325) They did not consider that the second *census* was taken only at Rome,
and that the numbers were diminished, not only by the death, but likewise by the
absence, of many soldiers   In the third *census*, Livy expressly affirms that the
legions were mustered by the care of particular commissaries   From the numbers
on the list we must always deduct one twelfth above three score and incapable of
bearing arms   See Population de la France, p 72

[11] Livy considers these two incidents as the effects only of chance and
courage   I suspect that they were both managed by the admirable policy of the
senate

[12] See Jerom, tom 1 p 169, 170, ad Eustochium [cp. 108, ed. Migne, 1. p
878], he bestows on Paula the splendid titles of Gracchorum stirps, soboles Scip-
ionum, Pauli hæres, cujus vocabulum trahit, Martiæ Papyriæ Matris Africani vera
et germana propago   This particular description supposes a more solid title than

carefully recapitulated by Jerom, the guide of her conscience and the historian of her life. The genealogy of her father, Rogatus, which ascended as high as Agamemnon, might seem to betray a Grecian origin ; but her mother, Blæsilla, numbered the Scipios, Æmilius Paulus and the Gracchi, in the list of her ancestors, and Toxotius, the husband of Paula, deduced his royal lineage from Æneas, the father of the Julian line. The vanity of the rich who desired to be noble was gratified by these lofty pretensions Encouraged by the applause of their parasites, they easily imposed on the credulity of the vulgar, and were countenanced in some measure by the custom of adopting the name of their patron, which had always prevailed among the freedmen and clients of illustrious families Most of those families, however, attacked by so many causes of external violence or internal decay, were gradually extirpated ; and it would be more reasonable to seek for a lineal descent of twenty generations among the mountains of the Alps, or in the peaceful solitude of Apulia, than on the theatre of Rome, the seat of fortune, of danger, and of perpetual revolutions.   Under each successive reign and from every province of the empire, a crowd of hardy adventurers, rising to eminence by their talents or their vices, usurped the wealth, the honours and the palaces of Rome ; and oppressed or protected the poor and humble remains of consular families ; who were ignorant perhaps of the glory of their ancestors [13]

The Anician family

In the time of Jerom and Claudian, the senators unanimously yielded the pre-eminence to the Anician line ; and a slight view of *their* history will serve to appreciate the rank and antiquity of the noble families which contended only for the second place.[14] During the first five ages of the city the name of the Anicians was unknown , they appear to have derived their origin from Præneste , and the ambition of those new citizens was long

the surname of Julius, which Toxotius shared with a thousand families of the Western provinces   See the Index of Tacitus, of Gruter's Inscriptions, &c.

[13] Tacitus (Annal in 55) affirms that between the battle of Actium and the reign of Vespasian the senate was gradually filled with *new* families from the Municipia and colonies of Italy

[14] Nec quisquam Procerum tentet (licet ære vetusto
Floreat et claro cingatur Roma senatu)
Se jactare parem , sed primâ sede relictâ
Auchenus, de jure licet certare secundo
                    Claud in Prob et Olybrii Coss 18

Such a compliment paid to the obscure name of the Auchenii has amazed the critics ; but they all agree that, whatever may be the true reading, the sense of Claudian can be applied only to the Anician family.

satisfied with the Plebeian honours of tribunes of the people.[15]
One hundred and sixty-eight years before the Christian æra, the
family was ennobled by the prætorship of Anicius, who gloriously
terminated the Illyrian war by the conquest of the nation and
the captivity of their king.[16] From the triumph of that general,
three consulships in distant periods mark the succession of the
Anician name.[17] From the reign of Diocletian to the final extinction of the Western empire that name shone with a lustre
which was not eclipsed in the public estimation by the majesty
of the Imperial purple.[18] The several branches to whom it was
communicated united, by marriage or inheritance, the wealth
and titles of the Annian, the Petronian and the Olybrian houses;
and in each generation the number of consulships was multiplied
by an hereditary claim.[19] The Anician family excelled in faith
and in riches, they were the first of the Roman senate who embraced Christianity; and it is probable that Anicius Julian, who
was afterwards consul and prefect of the city, atoned for his
attachment to the party of Maxentius by the readiness with
which he accepted the religion of Constantine.[20] Their ample
patrimony was increased by the industry of Probus, the chief of
the Anician family; who shared with Gratian the honours of
the consulship, and exercised four times the high office of Præ-

[Præt. Præf.
Italy 368 75,
Gaul 380, Italy
383 Italy 387]

---

[15] The earliest date in the annals of Pighius is that of M Anicius Gallus, Trib
Pl A U C 506 Another Tribune, Q Anicius, A U.C 508, is distinguished by
the epithet of Prænestinus Livy (xlv 43) places the Anicii below the great
families of Rome [Q. Anicius Prænestinus was curule ædile B C 304]

[16] Livy, xliv 30, 31, xlv 3, 26, 43 He fairly appreciates the merit of Anicius
and justly observes that his fame was clouded by the superior lustre of the Macedonian, which preceded the Illyrian, triumph

[17] The dates of the three consulships are, A U C 593, 818, 967, the two last
under the reigns of Nero and Caracalla The second of these consuls distinguished
himself only by his infamous flattery (Tacit Annal xv 74), but even the evidence
of crimes, if they bear the stamp of greatness and antiquity, is admitted without
reluctance to prove the genealogy of a noble house

[18] In the sixth century the nobility of the Anician name is mentioned (Cassiodor
Variar l. x Ep 10, 12) with singular respect by the minister of a Gothic king of
Italy.

[19] ———Fixus in omnes
Cognatos procedit honos, quemcumque requiras
Hâc de stirpe virum, certum est de Consule nasci
Per fasces numerantur Avi, semperque renata
Nobilitate virent, et prolem fata sequuntur
(Claudian in Prob et Olyb Consulat 12, &c.) The Annii, whose name seems to
have merged in the Anician, mark the Fasti with many consulships, from the time
of Vespasian to the fourth century

[20] The title of first Christian senator may be justified by the authority of Pru-
dentius (in Symmach i. 553), and the dislike of the pagans to the Anician family
See Tillemont, Hist des Empereurs, tom iv p. 183, v p. 44 Baron Annal
A D 312, No 78, A D 322, No 2

torian prefect.[21]   His immense estates were scattered over the wide extent of the Roman world ; and, though the public might suspect or disapprove the methods by which they had been acquired, the generosity and magnificence of that fortunate statesman deserved the gratitude of his clients and the admiration of strangers.[22]   Such was the respect entertained for his memory that the two sons of Probus in their earliest youth, and at the request of the senate, were associated in the consular dignity · a memorable distinction without example in the annals of Rome.[23]

" The marbles of the Anician palace " was used as a proverbial expression of opulence and splendour ,[24] but the nobles and senators of Rome aspired in due gradation to imitate that illustrious family. The accurate description of the city, which was composed in the Theodosian age, enumerates one thousand seven hundred and eighty *houses*, the residence of wealthy and honourable citizens [25]   Many of these stately mansions might almost excuse the exaggeration of the poet . that Rome contained a multitude of palaces, and that each palace was equal to a city ; since it included within its own precincts everything which could be subservient either to use or luxury · markets, hippodromes, temples, fountains, baths, porticos, shady groves, and artificial aviaries.[26]   The historian Olympiodorus, who represents the state of Rome when it was besieged by the Goths,[27] continues to observe that several of the richest senators received

---

[21] Probus .   claritudine generis et potentia et opum magnitudine cognitus Orbi Romano, per quem universum pœne patrimonia sparsa possedit, juste an secus non judicioli est nostri.   Ammian. Marcellin xxvii. 11   His children and widow erected for him a magnificent tomb in the Vatican, which was demolished in the time of Pope Nicholas V to make room for the new church of St Peter Baronius, who laments the ruin of this Christian monument, has diligently preserved the inscriptions and basso-relievos   See Annal Eccles A D 395, No. 5-17.

[22] Two Persian Satraps travelled to Milan and Rome to hear St. Ambrose and to see Probus (Paulin in Vit Ambros)   Claudian (in Cons Probin et Olybr 30-60) seems at a loss how to express the glory of Probus

[23] See the poem which Claudian addressed to the two noble youths

[24] Secundinus, the Manichæan, ap Baron Annal Eccles A.D 390, No 34

[25] See Nardini, Roma Antica, p. 89, 498, 500

[26]   Quid loquar inclusas inter laquearia sylvas ,
            Vernula quæ vario carmine ludit avis
                    Claud Rutil Numatian Itinerar ver iiii.
The poet lived at the time of the Gothic invasion   A moderate palace would have covered Cincinnatus's farm of four acres (Val Max iv. 4)   In laxitatem ruris excurrunt, says Seneca, Epist 114   See a judicious note of Mr. Hume, Essays, vol i p 562, last 8vo edition.

[27] This curious account of Rome in the reign of Honorius is found in a fragment of the historian Olympiodorus, ap Photium, p 197 [fr. 43, 44, F H. G iv p. 67]

from their estates an annual income of four thousand pounds of gold, above one hundred and sixty thousand pounds sterling; without computing the stated provision of corn and wine, which, had they been sold, might have equalled in value one-third of the money   Compared to this immoderate wealth, an ordinary revenue of a thousand or fifteen hundred pounds of gold might be considered as no more than adequate to the dignity of the senatorian rank, which required many expenses of a public and ostentatious kind.   Several examples are recorded in the age of Honorius, of vain and popular nobles who celebrated the year of their prætorship by a festival, which lasted seven days and cost above one hundred thousand pounds sterling [28]   The estates of the Roman senators, which so far exceeded the proportion of modern wealth, were not confined to the limits of Italy   Their possessions extended far beyond the Ionian and Ægean seas to the most distant provinces; the city of Nicopolis, which Augustus had founded as an eternal monument of the Actian victory, was the property of the devout Paula, [29] and it is observed by Seneca that the rivers which had divided hostile nations now flowed through the lands of private citizens [30]   According to their temper and circumstances, the estates of the Romans were either cultivated by the labour of their slaves or granted, for a certain and stipulated rent, to the industrious farmer   The economical writers of antiquity strenuously recommend the former method

[28] The sons of Alypius, of Symmachus, and of Maximus, spent during their respective prætorships twelve or twenty or forty *centenaries* (or hundredweight of gold). See Olympiodor ap Phot p 197 [*ib*]   This popular estimation allows some latitude , but it is difficult to explain a law in the Theodosian Code (l. vi. leg 5) which fixes the expense of the first prætor at 25,000, of the second at 20,000, and of the third at 15,000 *folles*   The name of *folles* (see Mém de l'Acad. des Inscriptions, tom xxviii p 727) was equally applied to a purse of 125 pieces of silver, and to a small copper coin of the value of $\frac{1}{2625}$ part of that purse   In the former sense the 25,000 folles would be equal to 150,000 l., in the latter to five or six pounds sterling   The one appears extravagant [but is the true amount], the other is ridiculous   There must have existed some third and middle value which is understood . but ambiguity is an inexcusable fault in the language of laws.

[29] Nicopolis   . in Actiaco littore sita possessionis vestræ nunc pars vel maxima est   Jerom in præfat comment ad Epistol ad Titum, tom ix p 243 [ed Migne, vii p 556]   M de Tillemont supposes, strangely enough, that it was part of Agamemnon's inheritance   Mém Ecclés tom xii p 85.

[30] Seneca, Epist lxxxix   His language is of the declamatory kind , but declamation could scarcely exaggerate the avarice and luxury of the Romans   The philosopher himself deserved some share of the reproach , if it be true that his rigorous exaction of *Quadragenties*, above three hundred thousand pounds, which he had lent at high interest, provoked a rebellion in Britain (Dion Cassius, l. lxii. p 1003 [c 2])   According to the conjecture of Gale (Antoninus's Itinerary in Britain, p 92) the same Faustinus possessed an estate near Bury in Suffolk, and another in the kingdom of Naples

wherever it may be practicable ; but, if the object should be removed by its distance or magnitude from the immediate eye of the master, they prefer the active care of an old hereditary tenant, attached to the soil and interested in the produce to the mercenary administration of a negligent, perhaps an unfaithful, steward [31]

Their manners

The opulent nobles of an immense capital, who were never excited by the pursuit of military glory, and seldom engaged in the occupations of civil government, naturally resigned their leisure to the business and amusements of private life. At Rome, commerce was always held in contempt ; but the senators, from the first age of the republic, increased their patrimony, and multiplied their clients, by the lucrative practice of usury ; and the obsolete laws were eluded, or violated, by the mutual inclinations and interest of both parties [32] A considerable mass of treasure must always have existed at Rome, either in the current coin of the empire or in the form of gold and silver plate ; and there were many sideboards, in the time of Pliny, which contained more solid silver than had been transported by Scipio from vanquished Carthage [33] The greater part of the nobles, who dissipated their fortunes in profuse luxury, found themselves poor in the midst of wealth, and idle in a constant round of dissipation   Their desires were continually gratified by the labour of a thousand hands ; of the numerous train of their domestic slaves, who were actuated by the fear of punishment ; and of the various professions of artificers and merchants, who were more powerfully impelled by the hopes of gain. The ancients were destitute of many of the conveniences of life which have been invented or improved by the progress of industry ; and the plenty of glass and linen has diffused more real comforts among the modern nations of Europe than the senators of Rome could derive from all the refinements of pompous or sensual luxury.[34] Their luxury and their manners

[31] Volusius, a wealthy senator (Tacit Annal iii 30), always preferred tenants born on the estate   Columella, who received this maxim from him, argues very judiciously on the subject De Re Rusticâ, l i c 7, p 408, edit Gesner, Leipsig, 1735

[32] Valesius (ad Ammian xiv 6) has proved from Chrysostom and Augustin that the senators were not allowed to lend money at usury   Yet it appears from the Theodosian Code (see Godefroy ad l ii tit xxxiii tom i p 230-239) that they were permitted to take six per cent or one half of the legal interest ; and, what is more singular, this permission was granted to the *young* senators.

[33] Plin Hist. Natur xxxiii 50   He states the silver at only 4380 pounds, which is increased by Livy (xxx 45) to 100,023   the former seems too little for an opulent city, the latter too much for any private sideboard

[34] The learned Arbuthnot (Tables of Ancient Coins, &c , p 153) has observed with humour, and I believe with truth, that Augustus had neither glass to his

have been the subject of minute and laborious disquisition ; but, as such inquiries would divert me too long from the design of the present work, I shall produce an authentic state of Rome and its inhabitants, which is more peculiarly applicable to the period of the Gothic invasion   Ammianus Marcellinus, who prudently chose the capital of the empire as the residence the best adapted to the historian of his own times, has mixed with the narrative of public events a lively representation of the scenes with which he was familiarly conversant   The judicious reader will not always approve the asperity of censure, the choice of circumstances, or the style of expression ; he will perhaps detect the latent prejudices and personal resentments which soured the temper of Ammianus himself ; but he will surely observe, with philosophic curiosity, the interesting and original picture of the manners of Rome [35]

"The greatness of Rome " (such is the language of the historian) " was founded on the rare and almost incredible alliance of virtue and of fortune   The long period of her infancy was employed in a laborious struggle against the tribes of Italy, the neighbours and enemies of the rising city.   In the strength and ardour of youth, she sustained the storms of war ; carried her victorious arms beyond the seas and the mountains, and brought home triumphal laurels from every country of the globe.   At length, verging towards old age, and sometimes conquering by the terror only of her name, she sought the blessings of ease and tranquillity   The VENERABLE CITY, which had trampled on the necks of the fiercest nations, and established a system of laws, the perpetual guardians of justice and freedom, was content, like a wise and wealthy parent, to devolve on the Cæsars, her favourite sons, the care of governing her ample patrimony.[36]   A secure and profound peace, such as had been once enjoyed in the reign of Numa, succeeded

Character of the Roman nobles, by Ammianus Marcellinus

windows nor a shirt to his back   Under the lower empire, the use of linen and glass became somewhat more common.   [Glass was used in the age of Augustus.]

[35] It is incumbent on me to explain the liberties which I have taken with the text of Ammianus   1 I have melted down into one piece the sixth chapter of the fourteenth, and the fourth of the twenty-eighth, book   2 I have given order and connexion to the confused mass of materials   3 I have softened *some* extravagant hyperboles and pared away some superfluities of the original   4 I have developed some observations which were insinuated rather than expressed   With these allowances, my version will be found, not literal indeed, but faithful and exact

[36] Claudian, who seems to have read the history of Ammianus, speaks of this great revolution in a much less courtly style

Postquam jura ferox in se communia Cæsar
Transtulit , et lapsi mores , desuetaque priscis
Artibus in gremium pacis servile recessi
De Bell. Gildonico, v 49.

to the tumults of a republic ; while Rome was still adored as the
queen of the earth, and the subject nations still reverenced the
name of the people and the majesty of the senate. But this
native splendour" (continues Ammianus) "is degraded and sullied
by the conduct of some nobles ; who, unmindful of their own
dignity and of that of their country, assume an unbounded licence
of vice and folly. They contend with each other in the empty
vanity of titles and surnames ; and curiously select or invent the
most lofty and sonorous appellations, Reburius, or Fabunius,
Pagonius, or Tarrasius,[37] which may impress the ears of the
vulgar with astonishment and respect From a vain ambition of
perpetuating their memory, they affect to multiply their likeness
in statues of bronze and marble , nor are they satisfied, unless
those statues are covered with plates of gold an honourable
distinction, first granted to Acilius the consul, after he had
subdued, by his arms and counsels, the power of king Antiochus
The ostentation of displaying, of magnifying perhaps, the rent-
roll of the estates which they possess in all the provinces, from
the rising to the setting sun, provokes the just resentment of
every man who recollects that their poor and invincible ancestors
were not distinguished from the meanest of the soldiers by the
delicacy of their food or the splendour of their apparel But the
modern nobles measure their rank and consequence according to
the loftiness of their chariots [38] and the weighty magnificence of
their dress Their long robes of silk and purple float in the
wind ; and, as they are agitated, by art or accident, they occasionally discover the under garments, the rich tunics, embroidered

---

[37] The minute diligence of antiquarians has not been able to verify these extraordinary names I am of opinion that they were invented by the historian himself,
who was afraid of any personal satire or application [Not so , Paconius is not
uncommon, cp , for example, C I L xiv 1444, vii 5038, for Reburrus, cp.
xiv 413 , Tarasius is familiar] It is certain, however that the simple denominations of the Romans were gradually lengthened to the number of four, five, or
even seven pompous surnames , as, for instance, Marcus Mæcius Memmius
Furius Balburius Cæcilianus Placidus See Noris, Cenotaph Pisan Dissert iv.
p 438

[38] The *carruca*, or coaches, of the Romans were often of solid silver, curiously
carved and engraved ; and the trappings of the mules or horses were embossed with
gold This magnificence continued from the reign of Nero to that of Honorius ,
and the Appian way was covered with the splendid equipages of the nobles, who
came out to meet St Melania when she returned to Rome, six years before the
Gothic siege (Seneca, epist lxxxvii. ; Plin Hist Natur xxxiii. 49 , Paulin Nolan
apud Baron Annal Eccles A D. 397, No 5) Yet pomp is well exchanged for
convenience , and a plain modern coach that is hung upon springs is much preferable to the silver or gold *carts* of antiquity, which rolled on the axle-tree and were
exposed, for the most part, to the inclemency of the weather.

with the figures of various animals.[39] Followed by a train of
fifty servants, and tearing up the pavement, they move along
the streets with the same impetuous speed as if they travelled
with post horses ; and the example of the senators is boldly
imitated by the matrons and ladies, whose covered carriages are
continually driving round the immense space of the city and
suburbs Whenever these persons of high distinction condescend
to visit the public baths, they assume, on their entrance, a tone
of loud and insolent command, and appropriate to their own use
the conveniencies which were designed for the Roman people.
If, in these places of mixed and general resort, they meet any of
the infamous ministers of their pleasures, they express their
affection by a tender embrace, while they proudly decline the
salutations of their fellow-citizens, who are not permitted to aspire above the honour of kissing their hands or their knees. As soon
as they have indulged themselves in the refreshment of the bath,
they resume their rings, and the other ensigns of their dignity ;
select from their private wardrobe of the finest linen, such as
might suffice for a dozen persons, the garments the most agreeable to their fancy, and maintain till their departure the same
haughty demeanour , which perhaps might have been excused
in the great Marcellus, after the conquest of Syracuse. Sometimes, indeed, these heroes undertake more arduous achievements , they visit their estates in Italy, and procure themselves,
by the toil of servile hands, the amusements of the chase.[40]
If at any time, but more especially on a hot day, they have
courage to sail, in their painted galleys, from the Lucrine lake [41]
to their elegant villas on the sea-coast of Puteoli and Caieta,[42]
they compare their own expeditions to the marches of Cæsar

---

[39] In a homily of Asterius, bishop of Amasia, M de Valois has discovered (ad
Ammian. xx 6), that this was a new fashion , that bears, wolves, lions and tigers,
woods, hunting-matches, &c , were represented in embroidery , and that the more
pious coxcombs substituted the figure or legend of some favourite saint

[40] See Pliny's Epistles, i 6   Three wild boars were allured and taken in the
toils, without interrupting the studies of the philosophic sportsman

[41] The change from the inauspicious word *Avernus*, which stands in the text, is
immaterial   The two lakes, Avernus and Lucrinus, communicated with each
other, and were fashioned by the stupendous moles of Agrippa into the Julian port,
which opened, through a narrow entrance, into the gulf of Puteoli   Virgil, who
resided on the spot, has described (Georgic ii 161) this work at the moment of its
execution, and his commentators, especially Catrou, have derived much light
from Strabo, Suetonius, and Dion   Earthquakes and volcanos have changed the
face of the country, and turned the Lucrine lake, since the year 1538, into the
Monte Nuovo. See Camillo Pellegrino Discorsi della Campania Felice, p 239,
244, &c , Antonii Sanfelicii Campania, p 13, 88

[42] The regna Cumana et Puteolana , loca cæteroqui valde expetenda, interpel-
lantium autem multitudine pœne fugienda   Cicero ad Attic xvi. 17

and Alexander. Yet should a fly presume to settle on the silken folds of their gilded umbrellas, should a sunbeam penetrate through some unguarded and imperceptible chink, they deplore their intolerable hardships, and lament in affected language that they were not born in the land of the Cimmerians,[43] the regions of eternal darkness   In these journeys into the country[44] the whole body of the household marches with their master.   In the same manner as the cavalry and infantry, the heavy and the light armed troops, the advanced guard and the rear, are marshalled by the skill of their military leaders , so the domestic officers, who bear a rod as an ensign of authority, distribute and arrange the numerous train of slaves and attendants   The baggage and wardrobe move in the front; and are immediately followed by a multitude of cooks and inferior ministers employed in the service of the kitchens and of the table   The main body is composed of a promiscuous crowd of slaves, increased by the accidental concourse of idle or dependent plebeians   The rear is closed by the favourite band of eunuchs, distributed from age to youth, according to the order of seniority   Their numbers and their deformity excite the horror of the indignant spectators, who are ready to execrate the memory of Semiramis for the cruel art which she invented of frustrating the purposes of nature and of blasting in the bud the hopes of future generations.   In the exercise of domestic jurisdiction the nobles of Rome express an exquisite sensibility for any personal injury, and a contemptuous indifference for the rest of the human species   When they have called for warm water, if a slave has been tardy in his obedience, he is instantly chastised with three hundred lashes . but should the same slave commit wilful murder, the master will mildly observe that he is a worthless fellow; but that, if he repeats the offence, he shall not escape punishment.   Hospitality was formerly the

[43] The proverbial expression of *Cimmerian darkness* was originally borrowed from the description of Homer (in the eleventh book of the Odyssey), which he applies to a remote and fabulous country on the shores of the ocean   See Erasmi Adagia, in his works, tom 11 p 593, the Leyden edition
[44] We may learn from Seneca, epist cxxiii , three curious circumstances relative to the journeys of the Romans   1 They were preceded by a troop of Numidian light horse, who announced, by a cloud of dust, the approach of a great man 2 Their baggage mules transported not only the precious vases, but even the fragile vessels of crystal and *murra*, which last is almost proved by the learned French translator of Seneca (tom 11 pp 402-422) to mean the porcelain of China and Japan   3 The beautiful faces of the young slaves were covered with a medicated crust or ointment, which secured them against the effects of the sun and frost

virtue of the Romans; and every stranger who could plead
either merit or misfortune was relieved or rewarded by their
generosity At present, if a foreigner, perhaps of no contemptible rank, is introduced to one of the proud and wealthy senators, he is welcome indeed in the first audience, with such warm
professions and such kind inquiries that he retires, enchanted
with the affability of his illustrious friend, and full of regret
that he had so long delayed his journey to Rome, the native
seat of manners as well as of empire. Secure of a favourable
reception, he repeats his visit the ensuing day, and is mortified
by the discovery that his person, his name, and his country are
already forgotten. If he still has resolution to persevere, he is
gradually numbered in the train of dependents, and obtains the
permission to pay his assiduous and unprofitable court to a
haughty patron, incapable of gratitude or friendship, who
scarcely deigns to remark his presence, his departure, or his
return. Whenever the rich prepare a solemn and popular
entertainment; [45] whenever they celebrate, with profuse and
pernicious luxury, their private banquets; the choice of the
guests is the subject of anxious deliberation The modest, the
sober, and the learned are seldom preferred, and the nomen-
clators, who are commonly swayed by interested motives, have
the address to insert, in the list of invitations, the obscure
names of the most worthless of mankind But the frequent and
familiar companions of the great are those parasites who practise the most useful of all arts, the art of flattery; who eagerly
applaud each word and every action of their immortal patron;
gaze with rapture on his marble columns and variegated pave-
ments, and strenuously praise the pomp and elegance which
he is taught to consider as a part of his personal merit At
the Roman tables the birds, the *squirrels*,[46] or the fish, which [*dormice*]

---

[45] Distributio solemnium sportularum The *sportulæ*, or *sportellæ*, were small
baskets, supposed to contain a quantity of hot provisions, of the value of 100
quadrantes, or twelvepence halfpenny, which were ranged in order in the hall, and
ostentatiously distributed to the hungry or servile crowd who waited at the door.
This indelicate custom is very frequently mentioned in the epigrams of Martial and
the satires of Juvenal See likewise Suetonius in Claud c 21, in Neron c 16,
in Domitian c 4, 7 These baskets of provisions were afterwards converted into
large pieces of gold and silver coin or plate, which were mutually given and accepted
even by the persons of the highest rank (see Symmach. epist iv 55, iv 124,
and Miscell p 256) on solemn occasions, of consulships, marriages, &c.

[46] The want of an English name obliges me to refer to the common genus of
squirrels, the Latin *glis*, the French *loir*, a little animal who inhabits the woods,
and remains torpid in cold weather (See Plin Hist Natur viii 82 Buffon,
Hist Naturelle, tom viii. p. 158. Pennant's Synopsis of Quadrupeds, p 289.)
The art of rearing and fattening great numbers of *glires* was practised in Roman

appeal of an uncommon size, are contemplated with curious
attention, a pair of scales is accurately applied to ascertain
their real weight, and, while the more rational guests are dis-
gusted by the vain and tedious repetition, notaries are summoned to attest by an authentic record the truth of such a
marvellous event   Another method of introduction into the
houses and society of the great is derived from the profession
of gaming, or, as it is more politely styled, of play.   The confederates are united by a strict and indissoluble bond of friendship, or rather of conspiracy; a superior degree of skill in the
Tesseraiian art (which may be interpreted the game of dice and
tables[47]) is a sure road to wealth and reputation   A master of
that sublime science, who in a supper or assembly is placed
below a magistrate, displays in his countenance the surprise and
indignation which Cato might be supposed to feel when he was
refused the prætorship by the votes of a capricious people   The
acquisition of knowledge seldom engages the curiosity of the
nobles, who abhor the fatigue and disdain the advantages of
study ; and the only books which they peruse are the satires of
Juvenal, and the verbose and fabulous histories of Marius Maximus.[48]   The libraries which they have inherited from their
fathers are secluded, like dreary sepulchres, from the light of
day.[49]   But the costly instruments of the theatre, flutes, and
enormous lyres, and hydraulic organs, are constructed for their

villas, as a profitable article of rural economy (Varro, de Re Rusticâ, ni.. 15).
The excessive demand of them for luxurious tables was increased by the foolish
prohibitions of the Censors ; and it is reported that they are still esteemed in
modern Rome, and are frequently sent as presents by the Colonna princes   (See
Brotier, the last editor of Pliny, tom ii p 458, apud Barbou, 1779)

[47] This game, which might be translated by the more familiar names of *trictrac*
or *backgammon*, was a favourite amusement of the gravest Romans , and old
Mucius Scævola, the lawyer, had the reputation of a very skilful player   It was
called *ludus duodecim scriptorum*, from the twelve *scripta*, or lines, which equally
divided the *alveolus*, or table   On these the two armies, the white and the black,
each consisting of fifteen men, or *calculi*, were regularly placed, and alternately
moved, according to the laws of the game, and the chances of the *tesseræ*, or
dice   Dr Hyde, who diligently traces the history and varieties of the *nerdiludium*
(a name of Persic etymology) from Ireland to Japan, pours forth, on this trifling
subject, a copious torrent of classic and Oriental learning   See Syntagma Dissertat tom ii p 217-405

[48] Marius Maximus, homo omnium verbosissimus, qui et mythistoricis se volu-
minibus implicavit   Vopiscus, in Hist August p 242 [xxix 1, 2]   He wrote
the lives of the emperors from Trajan to Alexander Severus   See Gerard Vossius
de Historicis Latin l ii c 3, in his works, vol iv p 57

[49] This satire is probably exaggerated   The Saturnalia of Macrobius and the
Epistles of Jerom afford satisfactory proofs that Christian theology and classic
literature were studiously cultivated by several Romans of both sexes and of the
highest rank

use ; and the harmony of vocal and instrumental music is incessantly repeated in the palaces of Rome In those palaces sound is preferred to sense, and the care of the body to that of the mind It is allowed as a salutary maxim that the light and frivolous suspicion of a contagious malady is of sufficient weight to excuse the visits of the most intimate friends ; and even the servants who are dispatched to make the decent inquiries are not suffered to return home till they have undergone the ceremony of a previous ablution Yet this selfish and unmanly delicacy occasionally yields to the more imperious passion of avarice. The prospect of gain will urge a rich and gouty senator as far as Spoleto ; every sentiment of arrogance and dignity is subdued by the hopes of an inheritance, or even of a legacy ; and a wealthy, childless citizen is the most powerful of the Romans The art of obtaining the signature of a favourable testament, and sometimes of hastening the moment of its execution, is perfectly understood, and it has happened that in the same house, though in different apartments, a husband and a wife, with the laudable design of over-reaching each other, have summoned their respective lawyers, to declare, at the same time, their mutual but contradictory intentions The distress which follows and chastises extravagant luxury often reduces the great to the use of the most humiliating expedients. When they desire to borrow, they employ the base and supplicating style of the slave in the comedy ; but, when they are called upon to pay, they assume the royal and tragic declamation of the grandsons of Hercules If the demand is repeated, they readily procure some trusty sycophant, instructed to maintain a charge of poison or magic against the insolent creditor ; who is seldom released from prison till he has signed a discharge of the whole debt. These vices, which degrade the moral character of the Romans, are mixed with a puerile superstition that disgraces their understanding. They listen with confidence to the predictions of haruspices, who pretend to read in the entrails of victims the signs of future greatness and prosperity ; and there are many who do not presume either to bathe, or to dine, or to appear in public, till they have diligently consulted, according to the rules of astrology, the situation of Mercury and the aspect of the moon.[50] It is singular enough that this vain credulity may often be discovered among the profane sceptics,

---

[50] Macrobius, the friend of these Roman nobles, considered the stars as the cause, or at least the signs, of future events (de Somn. Scipion l i c 19, p 68).

who impiously doubt or deny the existence of a celestial power."

In populous cities which are the seat of commerce and manu-factures, the middle ranks of inhabitants, who derive their sub-sistence from the dexterity or labour of their hands, are com-monly the most prolific, the most useful, and in that sense the most respectable part of the community But the plebeians of Rome, who disdained such sedentary and servile arts, had been oppressed from the earliest times, by the weight of debt and usury ; and the husbandman, during the term of his military service, was obliged to abandon the cultivation of his farm.[51] The lands of Italy, which had been originally divided among the families of free and indigent proprietors, were insensibly pur-chased or usurped by the avarice of the nobles , and in the age which preceded the fall of the republic it was computed that only two thousand citizens were possessed of any independent sub-stance.[52] Yet, as long as the people bestowed, by their suffrages, the honours of the state, the command of the legions, and the administration of wealthy provinces, their conscious pride alle-viated, in some measure, the hardships of poverty ; and their wants were seasonably supplied by the ambitious liberality of the candidates, who aspired to secure a venal majority in the thirty-five tribes, or the hundred and ninety-three centuries, of Rome. But, when the prodigal commons had imprudently alienated not only the *use*, but the *inheritance*, of power, they sunk, under the reign of the Cæsars, into a vile and wretched populace which must, in a few generations, have been totally ex-tinguished, if it had not been continually recruited by the manu-mission of slaves and the influx of strangers As early as the time of Hadrian it was the just complaint of the ingenuous natives that the capital had attracted the vices of the universe and the manners of the most opposite nations The intemper-ance of the Gauls, the cunning and levity of the Greeks, the savage obstinacy of the Egyptians and Jews, the servile temper

---

[51] The histories of Livy (see particularly vi. 36) are full of the extortions of the rich, and the sufferings of the poor debtors   The melancholy story of a brave old soldier (Dionys Hal l vi c 26, p 347, edit Hudson, and Livy, ii. 23) must have been frequently repeated in those primitive times, which have been so undeservedly praised.

[52] Non esse in civitate duo milia hominum qui rem haberent Cicero, Offic ii 21, and Comment Paul Manut in edit Græv   This vague computation was made A U.C. 649, in a speech of the tribune Philippus, and it was his object, as well as that of the Gracchi (see Plutarch), to deplore, and perhaps to exaggerate, the misery of the common people

of the Asiatics, and the dissolute, effeminate prostitution of the Syrians, were mingled in the various multitude, which, under the proud and false denomination of Romans, presumed to despise their fellow-subjects, and even their sovereigns, who dwelt beyond the precincts of the ETERNAL CITY [53]

Yet the name of that city was still pronounced with respect : the frequent and capricious tumults of its inhabitants were in-dulged with impunity; and the successors of Constantine, instead of crushing the last remains of the democracy by the strong arm of military power, embraced the mild policy of Augustus, and studied to relieve the poverty, and to amuse the idleness, of an innumerable people.[54] I. For the convenience of the lazy plebeians the monthly distributions of corn were converted into a daily allowance of bread ; a great number of ovens was construct and maintained at the public expense ; and at the appointed hour each citizen who was furnished with a ticket as-cended the flight of steps which had been assigned to his peculiar quarter or division, and received, either as a gift or at a very low price, a loaf of bread of the weight of three pounds for the use of his family. II The forests of Lucania, whose acorns fattened large droves of wild hogs,[55] afforded, as a species of tribute, a plentiful supply of cheap and wholesome meat During five months of the year a regular allowance of bacon was distributed to the poorer citizens ; and the annual consumption of the capital, at a time when it was much declined from its former lustre, was ascertained by an edict of Valentinian the Third, at three

(margin note: Public distribution of bread, bacon, oil, wine, &c)

---

[53] See the third Satire (60-125) of Juvenal, who indignantly complains,

——— Quamvis quota portio fæcis Achæi !
Jampridem Syrus in Tiberim defluxit Orontes,
Et linguam et mores, &c

Seneca, when he proposes to comfort his mother (Consolat ad Helv c 6) by the reflection that a great part of mankind were in a state of exile, reminds her how few of the inhabitants of Rome were born in the city

[54] Almost all that is said of the bread, bacon, oil, wine, &c , may be found in the fourteenth book of the Theodosian Code, which expressly treats of the *police* of the great cities See particularly the titles in iv v xvi xvii xxiv The colla-teral testimonies are produced in Godefroy's Commentary, and it is needless to transcribe them According to a law of Theodosius, which appreciates in money the military allowance, a piece of gold (eleven shillings) was equivalent to eighty pounds of bacon, or to eighty pounds of oil, or to twelve modii (or pecks) of salt (Cod Theod l viii tit iv leg 17) This equation, compared with another, of seventy pounds of bacon for an *amphora* (Cod Theod. l. xiv tit iv. leg. 4), fixes the price of wine at about sixteen pence the gallon

[55] The anonymous author of the Description of the World (p 14 in tom iii Geograph Minor Hudson) observes of Lucania, in his barbarous Latin, Regio obtima, et ipsa omnibus habundans, et lardum multum foras emittit Propter quod est in montibus, cujus æscam animalium variam, &c

millions six hundred and twenty-eight thousand pounds [56]   III
In the manners of antiquity the use of oil was indispensable for
the lamp as well as for the bath ; and the annual tax, which
was imposed on Africa for the benefit of Rome, amounted to the
weight of three millions of pounds, to the measure, perhaps, of
three hundred thousand English gallons   IV The anxiety of
Augustus to provide the metropolis with sufficient plenty of
corn was not extended beyond that necessary article of human
subsistence , and, when the popular clamour accused the dear-
ness and scarcity of wine, a proclamation was issued by the
grave reformer to remind his subjects that no man could reasonably complain of thirst since the aqueducts of Agrippa had
introduced into the city so many copious streams of pure and
salubrious water.[57]   This rigid sobriety was insensibly relaxed ;
and, although the generous design of Aurelian [58] does not appear
to have been executed in its full extent, the use of wine was
allowed on very easy and liberal terms   The administration of
the public cellars was delegated to a magistrate of honourable
rank ; and a considerable part of the vintage of Campania was
reserved for the fortunate inhabitants of Rome

Use of the
public baths

The stupendous aqueducts, so justly celebrated by the praises
of Augustus himself, replenished the *Thermæ*, or baths, which
had been constructed in every part of the city, with Imperial
magnificence   The baths of Antoninus Caracalla, which were
open, at stated hours, for the indiscriminate service of the
senators and the people, contained about sixteen hundred seats
of marble ; and more than three thousand were reckoned in the
baths of Diocletian [59] The walls of the lofty apartments were
covered with curious mosaics, that imitated the art of the pencil
in the elegance of design and the variety of colours   The
Egyptian granite was beautifully incrusted with the precious
green marble of Numidia ; the perpetual stream of hot water
was poured into the capacious basons, through so many wide
mouths of bright and massy silver ; and the meanest Roman
could purchase, with a small copper coin, the daily enjoyment of

[56] See Novell ad calcem Cod Theod D Valent l 1 tit xv   This law was
published at Rome, 29th June, A D 452
[57] Sueton in August c 42   The utmost debauch of the emperor himself, in
his favourite wine of Rhætia, never exceeded a *sextarius* (an English pint) Id c
77   Torrentius ad loc and Arbuthnot's Tables, p 86
[58] His design was to plant vineyards along the sea-coast of Etruria (Vopiscus,
in Hist August p 225 [xxvi 48, 2]), the dreary, unwholesome, uncultivated
Maremme of modern Tuscany
[59] Olympiodor apud Phot p 197 [fr 43]

a scene of pomp and luxury, which might excite the envy
of the kings of Asia.[60]   From these stately palaces issued a
swarm of dirty and ragged plebeians, without shoes, and without a mantle; who loitered away whole days in the street or
Forum, to hear news, and to hold disputes; who dissipated,
in extravagant gaming, the miserable pittance of their wives
and children; and spent the hours of the night in obscure
taverns and brothels in the indulgence of gross and vulgar
sensuality.[61]

But the most lively and splendid amusement of the idle *Games and spectacles*
multitude depended on the frequent exhibition of public games
and spectacles.   The piety of Christian princes had suppressed
the inhuman combats of gladiators; but the Roman people still
considered the Circus as their home, their temple, and the seat
of the republic.   The impatient crowd rushed at the dawn of
day to secure their places, and there were many who passed a
sleepless and anxious night in the adjacent porticos.   From the
morning to the evening, careless of the sun or of the rain,
the spectators, who sometimes amounted to the number of
four hundred thousand, remained in eager attention; their eyes
fixed on the horses and charioteers, their minds agitated with
hope and fear, for the success of the *colours* which they
espoused.   and the happiness of Rome appeared to hang on
the event of a race.[62]   The same immoderate ardour inspired
their clamours and their applause, as often as they were entertained with the hunting of wild beasts and the various modes
of theatrical representation.   These representations in modern
capitals may deserve to be considered as a pure and elegant
school of taste, and perhaps of virtue.   But the Tragic and
Comic Muse of the Romans, who seldom aspired beyond the

[60] Seneca (epistol lxxxvi.) compares the baths of Scipio Africanus, at his villa of
Liternum, with the magnificence (which was continually increasing) of the public
baths of Rome, long before the stately Thermæ of Antoninus and Diocletian were
erected   The *quadrans* paid for admission was the quarter of the *as*, about one
eighth of an English penny.

[61] Ammianus (l. xiv. c. 6, and l. xxviii. c. 4), after describing the luxury and
pride of the nobles of Rome, exposes, with equal indignation, the vices and follies
of the common people.

[62] Juvenal Satir xi. 191, &c.   The expressions of the historian Ammianus are
not less strong and animated than those of the satirist; and both the one and the
other painted from the life   The numbers which the great Circus was capable
of receiving are taken from the *original Notitia* of the city.   The differences
between them prove that they did not transcribe each other; but the sum
may appear incredible, though the country on these occasions flocked to the
city

imitation of Attic genius,[63] had been almost totally silent since the fall of the republic ;[64] and their place was unworthily occupied by licentious farce, effeminate music, and splendid pageantry. The pantomimes,[65] who maintained their reputation from the age of Augustus to the sixth century, expressed, without the use of words, the various fables of the gods and heroes of antiquity, and the perfection of their art, which sometimes disarmed the gravity of the philosopher, always excited the applause and wonder of the people The vast and magnificent theatres of Rome were filled by three thousand female dancers, and by three thousand singers, with the masters of the respective choruses Such was the popular favour which they enjoyed that, in a time of scarcity, when all strangers were banished from the city, the merit of contributing to the public pleasures exempted *them* from a law which was strictly executed against the professors of the liberal arts [66]

Populousness of Rome

It is said that the foolish curiosity of Elagabalus attempted to discover, from the quantity of spiders' webs, the number of the inhabitants of Rome. A more rational method of inquiry might not have been undeserving of the attention of the wisest princes, who could easily have resolved a question so important for the Roman government and so interesting to succeeding ages. The births and deaths of the citizens were duly registered ; and, if any writer of antiquity had condescended to mention the annual amount, or the common average, we might now produce some

---

[63] Sometimes indeed they composed original pieces
——Vestigia Græca
Ausi deserere et celebrare domestica facta.
Horat Epistol ad Pisones, 285, and the learned, though perplexed, note of Dacier, who might have allowed the name of tragedies to the *Brutus* and the *Decius* of Pacuvius, or to the *Cato* of Maternus The *Octavia*, ascribed to one of the Senecas, still remains a very unfavourable specimen of Roman tragedy [This play was not the work of one of the Senecas, as it contains a reference to the death of Nero, but it was probably written soon after that event]

[64] In the time of Quintilian and Pliny, a tragic poet was reduced to the imperfect method of hiring a great room, and reading his play to the company whom he invited for that purpose (see Dialog de Oratoribus, c 9, 11, and Plin. Epistol vii 17)

[65] See the Dialogue of Lucian, intitled, De Saltatione, tom ii. p 265-317, edit Reitz The pantomimes obtained the honourable name of χειροσοφοι, and it was required that they should be conversant with almost every art and science Burette (in the Mém de l'Acad. des Inscrip tom i p 127, &c) has given a short history of the art of pantomimes

[66] Ammianus, l xiv c 6 He complains, with decent indignation, that the streets of Rome were filled with crowds of females, who might have given children to the state, but whose only occupation was to curl and dress their hair, and jactari volubilibus gyris, dum exprimunt innumera simulacra, quæ finxere fabulæ theatrales

satisfactory calculation, which would destroy the extravagant assertions of critics, and perhaps confirm the modest and probable conjectures of philosophers.[67] The most diligent researches have collected only the following circumstances , which, slight and imperfect as they are, may tend, in some degree, to illustrate the question of the populousness of ancient Rome   I   When the capital of the empire was besieged by the Goths, the circuit of the walls was accurately measured by Ammonius, the mathematician, who found it equal to twenty-[Ammon] one miles.[68]   It should not be forgotten that the form of the city was almost that of a circle, the geometrical figure which is known to contain the largest space within any given circumference   II.   The architect Vitruvius, who flourished in the Augustan age, and whose evidence on this occasion has peculiar weight and authority, observes that the innumerable habitations of the Roman people would have spread themselves far beyond the narrow limits of the city; and that the want of ground, which was probably contracted on every side by gardens and villas, suggested the common, though inconvenient, practice of raising the houses to a considerable height in the air.[69]   But the loftiness of these buildings, which often consisted of hasty work and insufficient materials, was the cause of frequent and fatal accidents; and it was repeatedly enacted by Augustus, as well as by Nero, that the height of private edifices within the walls of Rome should not exceed the measure of seventy feet from the ground [70]   III.   Juvenal [71] laments, as it should seem from

[67] Lipsius (tom iii p 423, de Magnitud Romanâ, l iii c 3) and Isaac Vossius (Observat Var p 26-34) have indulged strange dreams of four, eight, or fourteen millions in Rome   Mr Hume (Essays, vol i, p 450-457), with admirable good sense and scepticism, betrays some secret disposition to extenuate the populousness of ancient times

[68] Olympiodor ap Phot p 197 [fr. 43]   See Fabricius, Bibl Græc tom. ix p. 400

[69] In eâ autem majestate urbis et civium infinitâ frequentiâ innumerabiles habitationes opus fuit explicare   Ergo, cum recipere non posset area plana tantam multitudinem [ad habitandum] in urbe, ad auxilium altitudinis ædificiorum res ipsa coegit devenire Vitruv ii 8   This passage, which I owe to Vossius, is clear, strong, and comprehensive

[70] The successive testimonies of Pliny, Aristides, Claudian, Rutilius, &c prove the insufficiency of these restrictive edicts   See Lipsius, de Magnitud Romanâ, l. iii c 4

——Tabulata tibi jam tertia fumant ,
Tu nescis ; nam si gradibus trepidatur ab imis,
Ultimus ardebit quem tegula sola tuetur
A pluviâ.

Juvenal Satir iii 199
[71] Read the whole third satire, but particularly 166, 223, &c   The description of a crowded *insula* or lodging-house in Petronius (c 95, 97) perfectly tallies with the complaints of Juvenal , and we learn from legal authority that in the time of

his own experience, the hardships of the poorer citizens, to whom he addresses the salutary advice of emigrating, without delay, from the smoke of Rome, since they might purchase, in the little towns of Italy, a cheerful, commodious dwelling, at the same price which they annually paid for a dark and miserable lodging. House-rent was therefore immoderately dear; the rich acquired, at an enormous expense, the ground, which they covered with palaces and gardens; but the body of the Roman people was crowded into a narrow space; and the different floors and apartments of the same house were divided, as it is still the custom of Paris and other cities, among several families of plebeians IV. The total number of houses in the fourteen regions of the city is accurately stated in the description of Rome composed under the reign of Theodosius, and they amount to forty-eight thousand three hundred and eighty-two [72] The two classes of *domus* and of *insulæ*, into which they are divided, include all the habitations of the capital, of every rank and condition, from the marble palace of the Anicii, with a numerous establishment of freedmen and slaves, to the lofty and narrow lodging-house, where the poet Codrus and his wife were permitted to hire a wretched garret immediately under the tiles. If we adopt the same average which, under similar circumstances, has been found applicable to Paris,[73] and indifferently allow about twenty-five persons for each house of every degree, we may fairly estimate the inhabitants of Rome at twelve hundred thousand: a number which cannot be thought excessive for the capital of a mighty empire, though it exceeds the populousness of the greatest cities of modern Europe.[74]

[48,392]

Augustus (Heineccius, Hist Juris Roman, c iv p 181) the ordinary rent of the several *cenacula*, or apartments of an *insula*, annually produced forty thousand sesterces, between three and four hundred pounds sterling (Pandect l xix tit ii, No 30), a sum which proves at once the large extent and high value of those common buildings.

[72] This sum total is composed of 1780 [1790] *domus*, or great *houses*, of 46,602 *insulæ*, or plebeian habitations (see Nardini, Roma Antica, l iii p 88), and these numbers are ascertained by the agreement of the texts of the different *Notitiæ*. Nardini, l viii p 498, 500

[73] See that accurate writer M. de Messance, Recherches sur la Population, p. 175-187 From probable or certain grounds, he assigns to Paris 23,565 houses, 71,114 families, and 576,630 inhabitants

[74] This computation is not very different from that which M Brotier, the last editor of Tacitus (tom ii p 380), has assumed from similar principles, though he seems to aim at a degree of precision which it is neither possible nor important to obtain [This computation does not differ much from that of Bunsen, for the age of Augustus 1,300,000, and that of von Wietersheim (1,350,000) Gregorovius puts the population of Rome at the beginning of fifth century as low as 300,000, Mr Hodgkin at about 1,000,000, cp Italy and her Invaders, i p 814]

Such was the state of Rome under the reign of Honorius; at First siege of Rome by the Goths A D 408 the time when the Gothic army formed the siege, or rather the blockade, of the city [75] By a skilful disposition of his numerous forces, who impatiently watched the moment of an assault, Alaric encompassed the walls, commanded the twelve principal gates, intercepted all communication with the adjacent country, and vigilantly guarded the navigation of the Tiber, from which the Romans derived the surest and most plentiful supply of provisions The first emotions of the nobles and of the people were those of surprise and indignation, that a vile Barbarian should dare to insult the capital of the world ; but their arrogance was soon humbled by misfortune ; and their unmanly rage, instead of being directed against an enemy in arms, was meanly exercised on a defenceless and innocent victim. Perhaps in the person of Serena the Romans might have respected the niece of Theodosius, the aunt, nay even the adopted mother, of the reigning emperor · but they abhorred the widow of Stilicho ; and they listened with credulous passion to the tale of calumny which accused her of maintaining a secret and criminal correspondence with the Gothic invader   Actuated, or overawed, by the same popular frenzy, the senate, without requiring any evidence of her guilt, pronounced the sentence of her death. Serena was ignominiously strangled ; and the infatuated multitude were astonished to find that this cruel act of injustice did not immediately produce the retreat of the Barbarians and the deliverance of the city. That unfortunate city gradually ex-Famine perienced the distress of scarcity, and at length the horrid calamities of famine. The daily allowance of three pounds of bread was reduced to one-half, to one-third, to nothing; and the price of corn still continued to rise in a rapid and extravagant proportion. The poorer citizens, who were unable to purchase the necessaries of life, solicited the precarious charity of the rich ; and for a while the public misery was alleviated by the humanity of Læta, the widow of the emperor Gratian, who had fixed her residence at Rome, and consecrated to the use of the indigent the princely revenue which she annually received from the grateful successors of her husband [76] But these private and temporary donatives were insufficient to appease the hunger of

[75] For the events of the first siege of Rome, which are often confounded with those of the second and third, see Zosimus, l v p 350-354 [c 38 *sqq*], Sozomen, l ix c. 6 , Olympiodorus, ap. Phot p 180 [fr 3, F. H G iv] , Philostorgius, l xii c 3 , and Godefroy, Dissertat p 467-745
[76] The mother of Læta was named Pissumena   Her father, family, and country are unknown   Ducange, Fam Byzantin p 59

a numerous people; and the progress of famine invaded the marble palaces of the senators themselves. The persons of both sexes, who had been educated in the enjoyment of ease and luxury, discovered how little is requisite to supply the demands of nature, and lavished their unavailing treasures of gold and silver, to obtain the coarse and scanty sustenance which they would formerly have rejected with disdain. The food the most repugnant to sense or imagination, the aliments the most unwholesome and pernicious to the constitution, were eagerly devoured and fiercely disputed by the rage of hunger A dark suspicion was entertained that some desperate wretches fed on the bodies of their fellow-creatures, whom they had secretly murdered; and even mothers (such was the horrid conflict of the two most powerful instincts implanted by nature in the human breast)—even mothers are said to have tasted the flesh of their slaughtered infants [77] Many thousands of the inhabitants of Rome expired in their houses, or in the streets, for want of sustenance; and, as the public sepulchres without the walls were in the power of the enemy, the stench which arose from so many putrid and unburied carcases infected the air, and the miseries of famine were succeeded and aggravated by the

Plague contagion of pestilential disease. The assurances of speedy and effectual relief, which were repeatedly transmitted from the court of Ravenna, supported for some time the fainting resolution of the Romans, till at length the despair of any human aid

Superstition tempted them to accept the offers of a præternatural deliverance. Pompeianus, præfect of the city, had been persuaded, by the art or fanaticism of some Tuscan diviners, that, by the mysterious force of spells and sacrifices, they could extract the lightning from the clouds, and point those celestial fires against the camp of the Barbarians [78] The important secret was communicated

[77] Ad nefandos cibos erupit esurientium rabies, et sua invicem membra laniarunt, dum mater non parcit lactenti infantiæ, et recipit utero, quem paullo ante effuderat. Jerom ad Principiam, tom 1 p 221 [ep. 127, Migne, 1 p 1094] The same horrid circumstance is likewise told of the sieges of Jerusalem and Paris. For the latter, compare the tenth book of the Henriade, and the Journal de Henri IV tom 1 p. 47-83, and observe that a plain narrative of facts is much more pathetic than the most laboured descriptions of epic poetry.

[78] Zosimus (l v p 355, 356 [c 41]) speaks of these ceremonies like a Greek unacquainted with the national superstition of Rome and Tuscany   I suspect that they consisted of two parts, the secret and the public, the former were probably an imitation of the arts and spells by which Numa had drawn down Jupiter and his thunder on Mount Aventine

> ————Quid agant laquei, quæ carmina dicant,
> Quâque trahant superis sedibus arte Jovem,
> Scire nefas homini.

The *ancilia*, or shields of Mars, the *pignora Imperii*, which were carried in solemn to Innocent, the bishop of Rome; and the successor of St. Peter is accused, perhaps without foundation, of preferring the safety of the republic to the rigid severity of the Christian worship. But, when the question was agitated in the senate, when it was proposed, as an essential condition, that those sacrifices should be performed in the Capitol, by the authority, and in the presence of the magistrates; the majority of that respectable assembly, apprehensive either of the Divine or of the Imperial displeasure, refused to join in an act which appeared almost equivalent to the public restoration of Paganism [79]

The last resource of the Romans was in the clemency, or at least in the moderation, of the king of the Goths. The senate, who in this emergency assumed the supreme powers of government, appointed two ambassadors to negotiate with the enemy. This important trust was delegated to Basilius, a senator, of Spanish extraction, and already conspicuous in the administration of provinces and to John, the first tribune of the notaries, who was peculiarly qualified by his dexterity in business as well as by his former intimacy with the Gothic prince. When they were introduced into his presence, they declared, perhaps in a more lofty style than became their abject condition, that the Romans were resolved to maintain their dignity, either in peace or war ; and that, if Alaric refused them a fair and honourable capitulation, he might sound his trumpets, and prepare to give battle to an innumerable people, exercised in arms and animated by despair. "The thicker the hay, the easier it is moved," was the concise reply of the Barbarian ; and this rustic metaphor was accompanied by a loud and insulting laugh, expressive of his contempt for the menaces of an unwarlike populace, enervated by luxury before they were emaciated by famine He then condescended to fix the ransom, which he would accept as the price of his retreat from the walls of Rome : *all* the gold and silver in the city, whether it were the property of the state or of individuals , *all* the rich and precious moveables ; and *all* the

Alaric accepts a ransom, and raises the siege A D 409 [rather 408]

[Primicerius Notariorum]

procession on the calends of March, derived their origin from this mysterious event (Ovid Fast iii 259-398) It was probably designed to revive this ancient festival, which had been suppressed by Theodosius In that case, we recover a chronological date (March the 1st, A D 409) which has not hitherto been observed   [An improbable guess The siege of Rome was certainly raised in A D 408.]

[79] Sozomen (l ix c 6) insinuates that the experiment was actually, though unsuccessfully, made , but he does not mention the name of Innocent and Tillemont (Mem Eccles tom x p 645) is determined not to believe that a pope could be guilty of such impious condescension [The episode of Pompeianus seems to have taken place *after* the embassy of Basilius and John]

slaves who could prove their title to the name of *Barbarians*.
The ministers of the senate presumed to ask, in a modest and
suppliant tone, " If such, O king ! are your demands, what do
you intend to leave us ?"   " Your lives," replied the haughty
conqueror they trembled and retired   Yet, before they retired,
a short suspension of arms was granted, which allowed some
time for a more temperate negotiation.   The stern features of
Alaric were insensibly relaxed ; he abated much of the rigour of
his terms ; and at length consented to raise the siege, on the
immediate payment of five thousand pounds of gold, of thirty
thousand pounds of silver, of four thousand robes of silk, of three
thousand pieces of fine scarlet cloth,[80] and of three thousand
pounds weight of pepper [81]   But the public treasury was exhausted ; the annual rents of the great estates in Italy and the
provinces were intercepted by the calamities of war , the gold
and gems had been exchanged during the famine for the vilest
sustenance ; the hoards of secret wealth were still concealed by
the obstinacy of avarice ; and some remains of consecrated spoils
afforded the only resource that could avert the impending ruin
of the city.   As soon as the Romans had satisfied the rapacious
demands of Alaric, they were restored, in some measure, to the
enjoyment of peace and plenty.   Several of the gates were
cautiously opened , the importation of provisions from the river
and the adjacent country was no longer obstructed by the Goths ;
the citizens resorted in crowds to the free market, which was
held during three days in the suburbs ; and, while the merchants
who undertook this gainful trade made a considerable profit, the
future subsistence of the city was secured by the ample magazines
which were deposited in the public and private granaries.   A
more regular discipline than could have been expected was
maintained in the camp of Alaric ; and the wise Barbarian
justified his regard for the faith of treaties by the just severity
with which he chastised a party of licentious Goths, who had
insulted some Roman citizens on the road to Ostia   His army,
enriched by the contributions of the capital, slowly advanced into
the fair and fruitful province of Tuscany, where he proposed to
establish his winter-quarters ; and the Gothic standard became

[£225,000]
[£90,000]

[A D 409]

---

[80] [Rather, hides dyed scarlet]

[81] Pepper was a favourite ingredient of the most expensive Roman cookery, and
the best sort commonly sold for fifteen denarii, or ten shillings, the pound   See
Pliny, Hist Natur xii 14   It was brought from India, and the same country,
the coast of Malabar, still affords the greatest plenty . but the improvement of trade
and navigation has multiplied the quantity and reduced the price.   See Histoire
Politique et Philosophique, &c., tom ι p 457

the refuge of forty thousand Barbarian slaves, who had broke their chains, and aspired, under the command of their great deliverer, to revenge the injuries and the disgrace of their cruel servitude About the same time, he received a more honourable reinforcement of Goths and Huns, whom Adolphus,[82] the brother of his wife, had conducted, at his pressing invitation, from the banks of the Danube to those of the Tiber, and who had cut their way, with some difficulty and loss, through the superior numbers of the Imperial troops. A victorious leader, who united the daring spirit of a Barbarian with the art and discipline of a Roman general, was at the head of an hundred thousand fighting men ; and Italy pronounced, with terror and respect, the formidable name of Alaric.[83]

At the distance of fourteen centuries, we may be satisfied with relating the military exploits of the conquerors of Rome without presuming to investigate the motives of their political conduct In the midst of his apparent prosperity, Alaric was conscious, perhaps, of some secret weakness, some internal defect ; or perhaps the moderation which he displayed was intended only to deceive and disarm the easy credulity of the ministers of Honorius The king of the Goths repeatedly declared that it was his desire to be considered as the friend of peace and of the Romans. Three senators, at his earnest request, were sent ambassadors to the court of Ravenna, to solicit the exchange of hostages and the conclusion of the treaty ; and the proposals, which he more clearly expressed during the course of the negotiations, could only inspire a doubt of his sincerity, as they might seem inadequate to the state of his fortune The Barbarian still aspired to the rank of master-general of the armies of the West ; he stipulated an annual subsidy of corn and money ; and he chose the provinces of Dalmatia, Noricum, and Venetia, for the seat of his new kingdom, which would have commanded the important communication between Italy and the Danube. If these modest terms should be rejected, Alaric shewed a disposition to relinquish his pecuniary demands, and even to content himself

(marginal note: Fruitless negotiations for peace A D 409)

---

[82] This Gothic chieftain is called, by Jornandes and Isidore, *Athaulphus*, by Zosimus and Orosius, *Ataulphus*, and by Olympiodorus, *Adaulphus* I have used the celebrated name of *Adolphus*, which seems to be authorized by the practice of the Swedes, the sons or brothers of the ancient Goths

[83] The treaty between Alaric and the Romans, &c , is taken from Zosimus, l v P 354, 355, 358, 359, 362, 363 [41, 42] The additional circumstances are too few and trifling to require any other quotation [Mr Hodgkin conjectures that Alaric s army at this time " ranged between 50,000 and 100,000 men," i p 812]

with the possession of Noricum · an exhausted and impoverished country, perpetually exposed to the inroads of the Barbarians of Germany [84] But the hopes of peace were disappointed by the weak obstinacy, or interested views, of the minister Olympius Without listening to the salutary remonstrances of the senate, he dismissed their ambassadors under the conduct of a military escort, too numerous for a retinue of honour and too feeble for an army of defence Six thousand Dalmatians, the flower of the Imperial legions, were ordered to march from Ravenna to Rome, through an open country, which was occupied by the formidable myriads of the Barbarians These brave legionaries, encompassed and betrayed, fell a sacrifice to ministerial folly; their general, Valens, with an hundred soldiers, escaped from the field of battle; and one of the ambassadors, who could no longer claim the protection of the law of nations, was obliged to purchase his freedom with a ransom of thirty thousand pieces of gold Yet Alaric, instead of resenting this act of impotent hostility, immediately renewed his proposals of peace; and the second embassy of the Roman senate, which derived weight and dignity from the presence of Innocent, bishop of the city, was guarded from the dangers of the road by a detachment of Gothic soldiers [85]

Change and succession of ministers Olympius [86] might have continued to insult the just resentment of a people who loudly accused him as the author of the public calamities, but his power was undermined by the secret intrigues of the palace The favourite eunuchs transferred the government of Honorius and the empire to Jovius, the Prætorian præfect: an unworthy servant, who did not atone by the merit of personal attachment for the errors and misfortunes of his administration The exile or escape of the guilty Olympius reserved him for more vicissitudes of fortune · he experienced the adventures of an obscure and wandering life, he again rose to power; he fell a second time into disgrace, his ears were cut off; he expired under the lash, and his ignominious death afforded a grateful spectacle to the friends of Stilicho After the removal of Olympius, whose character was deeply tainted with religious fanaticism, the Pagans and heretics were delivered

---

[84] Zosimus, l v p 367, 368, 369 [c 48 See below, note 90]

[85] Zosimus, l v p 360, 361, 392 [45] The bishop by remaining at Ravenna, escaped the impending calamities of the city Orosius, l vii c 39, p 573

[86] For the adventures of Olympius and his successors in the ministry, see Zosimus, l v p 363, 365, 366 [45 sqq] and Olympiodor ap Phot p 180, 181 [fr 8, 13]

from the impolitic proscription which excluded them from the
dignities of the state.   The brave Gennerid,[87] a soldier of Barbarian origin who still adhered to the worship of his ancestors,
had been obliged to lay aside the military belt ; and, though he
was repeatedly assured by the emperor himself that laws were
not made for persons of his rank or merit, he refused to accept
any partial dispensation, and persevered in honourable disgrace
till he had extorted a general act of justice from the distress of
the Roman government   The conduct of Gennerid in the important station, to which he was promoted or restored, of master-
general of Dalmatia, Pannonia, Noricum and Rhætia[88] seemed to [Not Mag
revive the discipline and spirit of the republic   From a life of of Illyricum]
idleness and want his troops were soon habituated to severe
exercise and plentiful subsistence ; and his private generosity
often supplied the rewards which were denied by the avarice
or poverty of the court of Ravenna.   The valour of Gennerid,
formidable to the adjacent Barbarians, was the firmest bulwark
of the Illyrian frontier ; and his vigilant care assisted the
empire with a reinforcement of ten thousand Huns, who arrived
on the confines of Italy, attended by such a convoy of provisions
and such a numerous train of sheep and oxen as might have
been sufficient not only for the march of an army but for
the settlement of a colony.   But the court and councils of
Honorius still remained a scene of weakness and distraction, of
corruption and anarchy.   Instigated by the præfect Jovius the
guards rose in furious mutiny, and demanded the heads of two [At Classis]
generals, and of the two principal eunuchs.   The generals,
under a perfidious promise of safety, were sent on shipboard,
and privately executed ; while the favour of the eunuchs procured them a mild and secure exile at Milan and Constantinople.
Eusebius the eunuch and the Barbarian Allobich succeeded to
the command of the bedchamber and of the guards ; and the
mutual jealousy of these subordinate ministers was the cause of
their mutual destruction.   By the insolent order of the count of

---

[87] Zosimus (l v p 364 [46]) relates this circumstance with visible complacency,
and celebrates the character of Gennerid as the last glory of expiring paganism
Very different were the sentiments of the council of Carthage, who deputed four
bishops to the court of Ravenna to complain of the law which had just been
enacted that all conversions to Christianity should be free and voluntary   See
Baronius, Annal Eccles A D 409, No 12, A D 410, No 47, 48

[88] [The opportunity may be seized to correct the text of Zosimus, v. 46, where
the Vatican codex gives ὄντα στρατηγον καὶ τῶν ἄλλων ὁσαι Παιονίας τε τας ἄνω και
Νωρικους και 'Ραιτους ἐφυλαττον   Mendelssohn well suggests ιλῶν for ἄλλων, but we
should keep ἄλλων and read . καὶ τῶν ἄλλων ιλῶν ὁσαι Παιονας τε τους ἄνω καὶ κ,τ.λ]

the domestics the great chamberlain was shamefully beaten to death with sticks before the eyes of the astonished emperor; and the subsequent assassination of Allobich in the midst of a public procession is the only circumstance of his life in which Honorius discovered the faintest symptom of courage or resentment Yet, before they fell, Eusebius and Allobich had contributed their part to the ruin of the empire by opposing the conclusion of a treaty which Jovius, from a selfish and perhaps a criminal motive, had negotiated with Alaric in a personal inter-

[Ariminum] view under the walls of Rimini During the absence of Jovius the emperor was persuaded to assume a lofty tone of inflexible dignity, such as neither his situation nor his character could enable him to support and a letter signed with the name of Honorius was immediately dispatched to the Prætorian præfect, granting him a free permission to dispose of the public money, but sternly refusing to prostitute the military honours of Rome to the proud demands of a Barbarian This letter was imprudently communicated to Alaric himself; and the Goth, who in the whole transaction had behaved with temper and decency, expressed in the most outrageous language his lively sense of the insult so wantonly offered to his person and to his nation The conference of Rimini was hastily interrupted; and the præfect Jovius on his return to Ravenna was compelled to adopt, and even to encourage, the fashionable opinions of the court. By his advice and example the principal officers of the state and army were obliged to swear that, without listening, in *any* circumstances, to *any* condition of peace, they would still persevere in perpetual and implacable war against the enemy of the republic This rash engagement opposed an insuperable bar to all future negotiation The ministers of Honorius were heard to declare that, if they had only invoked the name of the Deity, they would consult the public safety and trust their souls to the mercy of Heaven; but they had sworn by the sacred head of the emperor himself, they had touched in solemn ceremony that august seat of majesty and wisdom, and the violation of their oath would expose them to the temporal penalties of sacrilege and rebellion [89]

[89] Zos 1 v p 367, 368, 369 [48, 49]   This custom of swearing by the head, or life, or safety, or genius of the sovereign was of the highest antiquity, both in Egypt (Genesis, xli 15) and Scythia   It was soon transferred by flattery to the Cæsars; and Tertullian complains that it was the only oath which the Romans of his time affected to reverence   See an elegant Dissertation of the Abbé Massieu on the Oaths of the Ancients, in the Mém de l'Académie des Inscriptions, tom i p 208, 209

Second siege of Rome by the Goths A D 409

While the emperor and his court enjoyed, with sullen pride, the security of the marshes and fortifications of Ravenna, they abandoned Rome almost without defence to the resentment of Alaric   Yet such was the moderation which he still preserved or affected that, as he moved with his army along the Flaminian way, he successfully dispatched the bishops of the towns of Italy to reiterate his offers of peace and to conjure the emperor that he would save the city and its inhabitants from hostile fire and the sword of the Barbarians.[90] These impending calamities were however averted, not indeed by the wisdom of Honorius, but by the prudence or humanity of the Gothic king, who employed a milder, though not less effectual, method of conquest. Instead of assaulting the capital, he successfully directed his efforts against the *Port* of Ostia, one of the boldest and most stupendous works of Roman magnificence.[91] The accidents to which the precarious subsistence of the city was continually exposed in a winter-navigation and an open road had suggested to the genius of the first Cæsar the useful design which was executed under the reign of Claudius. The artificial moles which formed the narrow entrance advanced far into the sea and firmly repelled the fury of the waves, while the largest vessels securely rode at anchor within three deep and capacious basons, which received the northern branch of the Tiber, about two miles from the ancient colony of Ostia.[92] The Roman *Port* insensibly swelled

[90] Zosimus, l. v p 368, 369 [50] I have softened the expressions of Alaric, who expatiates in too florid a manner on the history of Rome [It was now that Alaric offered to be content with Noricum, see above, note 84]

[91] See Sueton. in Claud c. 20, Dion Cassius, l lx p 949, edit Reimar[c 11], and the lively description of Juvenal, Satir xii 75, &c   In the sixteenth century when the remains of this Augustan port were still visible, the antiquarians sketched the plan (see d'Anville, Mém de l'Académie des Inscriptions, tom xxx p 198) and declared with enthusiasm that all the monarchs of Europe would be unable to execute so great a work (Bergier, Hist des grands Chemins des Romains, tom ii p. 356).

[92] The *Ostia Tiberina* (see Cluver Italia Antiq l iii. p 870-879) in the plural number, the two mouths of the Tiber, were separated by the Holy Island, an equilateral triangle, whose sides were each of them computed at about two miles The colony of Ostia was founded immediately beyond the left or southern, and the *Port* immediately beyond the right or northern, branch of the river, and the distance between their remains measures something more than two miles on Cingolani's map   In the time of Strabo, the sand and mud deposited by the Tiber had choked the harbour of Ostia, the progress of the same cause has added much to the size of the Holy Island, and gradually left both Ostia and the Port at a considerable distance from the shore   The dry channels (fiumi morti) and the large estuaries (stagno di Ponente, di Levante) mark the changes of the river and the efforts of the sea   Consult, for the present state of this dreary and desolate tract, the excellent map of the ecclesiastical state by the mathematicians of Benedict XIV , an actual survey of the *Agro Romano*, in six sheets, by Cingolani, which contains 113,819 *rubbia* (about 570,000 acres), and the large topographical map of Ameti in eight sheets   [Cp Procopius, B. G. i. 26 , Cassiodorius, vii. 9 , and the description of Gregorovius, Rome in the Middle Ages, Eng. tr., i. p. 400.]

to the size of an episcopal city,[93] where the corn of Africa was deposited in spacious granaries for the use of the capital. As soon as Alaric was in possession of that important place, he summoned the city to surrender at discretion, and his demands were enforced by the positive declaration that a refusal or even a delay should be instantly followed by the destruction of the magazines, on which the life of the Roman people depended. The clamours of that people and the terror of famine subdued the pride of the senate; they listened without reluctance to the proposal of placing a new emperor on the throne of the unworthy Honorius, and the suffrage of the Gothic conqueror [Priscus Attalus] bestowed the purple on Attalus, præfect of the city. The grateful monarch immediately acknowledged his protector as mastergeneral of the armies of the West, Adolphus, with the rank of count of the domestics, obtained the custody of the person of Attalus, and the two hostile nations seemed to be united in the closest bands of friendship and alliance.[94]

Attalus is created emperor by the Goths and Romans

The gates of the city were thrown open, and the new emperor of the Romans, encompassed on every side by the Gothic arms, was conducted in tumultuous procession, to the palace of Augustus and Trajan. After he had distributed the civil and military dignities among his favourites and followers, Attalus convened an assembly of the senate; before whom, in a formal and florid speech, he asserted his resolution of restoring the majesty of the republic, and of uniting to the empire the provinces of Egypt and the East, which had once acknowledged the sovereignty of Rome. Such extravagant promises inspired every reasonable citizen with a just contempt for the character of an unwarlike usurper; whose elevation was the deepest and most ignominious wound which the republic had yet sustained from the insolence of the Barbarians. But the populace, with their usual levity, applauded the change of masters. The public discontent was favourable to the rival of Honorius; and the sectaries, oppressed by his persecuting edicts, expected some

[93] As early as the third (Lardner's Credibility of the Gospel, part ii vol iii. p 89-92), or at least the fourth, century (Carol à Sancto Paulo, Notit Eccles p. 47), the Port of Rome was an episcopal city, which was demolished, as it should seem, in the ninth century, by Pope Gregory IV during the incursions of the Arabs It is now reduced to an inn, a church and the house or palace of the bishop, who ranks as one of six cardinal bishops of the Romish church See Eschinard, Descrizione di Roma et dell Agro Romano, p 328

[94] For the elevation of Attalus consult Zosimus, l vi p 377-380 [7 sqq], Sozomen, l ix c 8, 9, Olympiodor ap Phot p 180, 181 [fr 13], Philostorg l. xii c 3, and Godefroy, Dissertat p 470

degree of countenance, or at least of toleration, from a prince who, in his native country of Ionia, had been educated in the Pagan superstition, and who had since received the sacrament of baptism from the hands of an Arian bishop [95]   The first days of the reign of Attalus were fair and prosperous   An officer of confidence was sent with an inconsiderable body of troops to secure the obedience of Africa; the greatest part of Italy submitted to the terror of the Gothic powers; and, though the city of Bologna made a vigorous and effectual resistance, the people of Milan, dissatisfied perhaps with the absence of Honorius, accepted, with loud acclamations, the choice of the Roman senate.   At the head of a formidable army Alaric conducted his royal captive almost to the gates of Ravenna; and a solemn embassy of the principal ministers, of Jovius, the Præ- [A D 410] torian præfect, of Valens, master of the cavalry and infantry, of the quæstor Potamius, and of Julian, the first of the notaries, was introduced with martial pomp into the Gothic camp.   In the name of their sovereign they consented to acknowledge the lawful election of his competitor, and to divide the provinces of Italy and the West between the two emperors   Their proposals were rejected with disdain; and the refusal was aggravated by the insulting clemency of Attalus, who condescended to promise that, if Honorius would instantly resign the purple, he should be permitted to pass the remainder of his life in the peaceful exile of some remote island.[96]   So desperate indeed did the situation of the son of Theodosius appear to those who were the best acquainted with his strength and resources, that Jovius and Valens, his minister and his general, betrayed their trust, infamously deserted the sinking cause of their benefactor, and devoted their treacherous allegiance to the service of his more fortunate rival   Astonished by such examples of domestic treason, Honorius trembled at the approach of every servant, at the arrival of every messenger.   He dreaded the secret enemies, who might lurk in his capital, his palace, his bed-chamber; and some ships lay ready in the harbour of Ravenna to transport the

---

[95] We may admit the evidence of Sozomen for the Arian baptism, and that of Philostorgius for the Pagan education, of Attalus   The visible joy of Zosimus, and the discontent which he imputes to the Anician family, are very unfavourable to the Christianity of the new emperor

[96] He carried his insolence so far as to declare that he should mutilate Honorius before he sent him into exile   But this assertion of Zosimus is destroyed by the more impartial testimony of Olympiodorus, who attributes the ungenerous proposal (which was absolutely rejected by Attalus) to the baseness, and perhaps the treachery, of Jovius

abdicated monarch to the dominions of his infant nephew, the emperor of the East.

But there is a Providence (such at least was the opinion of the historian Procopius [97]) that watches over innocence and folly; and the pretensions of Honorius to its peculiar care cannot reasonably be disputed. At the moment when his despair, incapable of any wise or manly resolution, meditated a shameful flight,[98] a seasonable reinforcement of four thousand veterans unexpectedly landed in the port of Ravenna. To these valiant strangers, whose fidelity had not been corrupted by the factions of the court, he committed the walls and gates of the city; and the slumbers of the emperor were no longer disturbed by the apprehension of imminent and internal danger The favourable intelligence which was received from Africa suddenly changed the opinions of men, and the state of public affairs. The troops and officers whom Attalus had sent into that province were defeated and slain, and the active zeal of Heraclian maintained his own allegiance and that of his people. The faithful count of Africa transmitted a large sum of money, which fixed the attachment of the Imperial guards; and his vigilance, in preventing the exportation of corn and oil, introduced famine, tumult, and discontent into the walls of Rome. The failure of the African expedition was the source of mutual complaint and recrimination in the party of Attalus; and the mind of his protector was insensibly alienated from the interest of a prince who wanted spirit to command or docility to obey. The most imprudent measures were adopted, without the knowledge, or against the advice, of Alaric; and the obstinate refusal of the senate to allow, in the embarkation, the mixture even of five hundred Goths betrayed a suspicious and distrustful temper, which, in their situation, was neither generous nor prudent. The resentment of the Gothic king was exasperated by the malicious arts of Jovius, who had been raised to the rank of patrician, and who afterwards excused his double perfidy by declaring, without a blush, that he had only *seemed* to abandon the service of Honorius, more effectually to ruin the cause of the usurper In a large plain near Rimini, and in the presence of an innumerable multitude of Romans and Barbarians, the wretched Attalus was publicly despoiled of the diadem and purple; and those ensigns of royalty were sent by Alaric, as the

[97] Procop de Bell Vandal l i c 2
[98] [So Sozomen, but the text of Zosimus gives '' 6 divisions amounting to 40,000,' a number accepted by Mr Hodgkin, i 788.]

pledge of peace and friendship, to the son of Theodosius [99]   The officers who returned to their duty were reinstated in their employments, and even the merit of a tardy repentance was graciously allowed, but the degraded emperor of the Romans, desirous of life and insensible of disgrace, implored the permission of following the Gothic camp in the train of a haughty and capricious Barbarian [100]

The degradation of Attalus removed the only real obstacle to the conclusion of the peace; and Alaric advanced within three miles of Ravenna, to press the irresolution of the Imperial ministers, whose insolence soon returned with the return of fortune.   His indignation was kindled by the report that a rival chieftain, that Sarus, the personal enemy of Adolphus and the hereditary foe of the house of Balti, had been received into the palace.   At the head of three hundred followers, that fearless Barbarian immediately sallied from the gates of Ravenna; surprised, and cut in pieces, a considerable body of Goths, re-entered the city in triumph; and was permitted to insult his adversary by the voice of a herald, who publicly declared that the guilt of Alaric had for ever excluded him from the friendship and alliance of the emperor [101]   The crime and folly of the court of Ravenna was expiated a third time by the calamities of Rome.   The king of the Goths, who no longer dissembled his appetite for plunder and revenge, appeared in arms under the walls of the capital; and the trembling senate, without any hopes of relief, prepared, by a desperate resistance, to delay the ruin of their country.   But they were unable to guard against the secret conspiracy of their slaves and domestics; who, either from birth or interest, were attached to the cause of the enemy. At the hour of midnight, the Salarian gate was silently opened, and the inhabitants were awakened by the tremendous sound of the Gothic trumpet.   Eleven hundred and sixty-three years after the foundation of Rome, the Imperial city, which had subdued and civilized so considerable a part of mankind, was

Third siege and sack of Rome by the Goths A D 410, Aug 24

---

[99] See the cause and circumstances of the fall of Attalus in Zosimus, l vi. p 380-383 [12], Sozomen, l ix. c 8, Philostorg l xii c 3   The two acts of indemnity in the Theodosian Code, l ix tit xxxviii leg 11, 12, which were published the 12th of February and the 8th of August, A D 410, evidently relate to this usurper

[100] In hoc, Alaricus, imperatore facto, infecto, refecto, ac defecto . . . Mimum risit, et ludum spectavit imperii   Orosius, l vii c, 42, p 582

[101] Zosimus, l. vi p. 384 [13], Sozomen, l ix c. 9, Philostorgius, l xii c 3 In this place the text of Zosimus is mutilated, and we have lost the remainder of his sixth and last book, which ended with the sack of Rome   Credulous and partial as he is, we must take our leave of that historian with some regret

delivered to the licentious fury of the tribes of Germany and Scythia [102]

Respect of the Goths for the Christian religion The proclamation of Alaric, when he forced his entrance into a vanquished city, discovered, however, some regard for the laws of humanity and religion   He encouraged his troops boldly to seize the rewards of valour, and to enrich themselves with the spoils of a wealthy and effeminate people , but he exhorted them at the same time to spare the lives of the unresisting citizens, and to respect the churches of the apostles St Peter and St Paul, as holy and inviolable sanctuaries   Amidst the horrors of a nocturnal tumult, several of the Christian Goths displayed the fervour of a recent conversion ; and some instances of their uncommon piety and moderation are related, and perhaps adorned, by the zeal of ecclesiastical writers [103] While the Barbarians roamed through the city in quest of prey, the humble dwelling of an aged virgin, who had devoted her life to the service of the altar, was forced open by one of the powerful Goths   He immediately demanded, though in civil language, all the gold and silver in her possession ; and was astonished at the readiness with which she conducted him to a splendid hoard of massy plate, of the richest materials and the most curious workmanship.   The Barbarian viewed with wonder and delight this valuable acquisition, till he was interrupted by a serious admonition, addressed to him in the following words : " These," said she, " are the consecrated vessels belonging to St. Peter ; if you presume to touch them, the sacrilegious deed will remain on your conscience   For my part, I dare not keep what I am unable to defend "   The Gothic captain, struck with reverential awe, dispatched a messenger to inform the king of the treasure which

[102] Adest Alaricus, trepidam Romam obsidet, turbat, irrumpit   Orosius, l vii c 39, p 573   He dispatches this great event in seven words , but he employs whole pages in celebrating the devotion of the Goths   I have extracted from an improbable story of Procopius the circumstances which had an air of probability. Procop de Bell Vandal l i c 2   He supposes that the city was surprised while the senators slept in the afternoon , but Jerom, with more authority and more reason, affirms that it was in the night, nocte Moab capta est , nocte cecidit murus ejus, tom i p 121, ad Principiam [ep 16]   [The date, Aug 24, is derived from Theophanes (A M 5903 , Cedrenus gives Aug 26)   Mr Hodgkin, laying stress on the word *irrumpit* in Orosius, rejects the suggestion of treachery, i 794]

[103] Orosius (l vii c 39, p 573-576) applauds the piety of the Christian Goths, without seeming to perceive that the greatest part of them were Arian heretics. Jornandes (c 30, p 653) and Isidore of Seville (Chron p 714, edit Grot), who were both attached to the Gothic cause, have repeated and embellished these edifying tales   According to Isidore, Alaric himself was heard to say that he waged war with the Romans and not with the Apostles   Such was the style of the seventh century , two hundred years before, the fame and merit had been ascribed not to the apostles, but to Christ

he had discovered ; and received a peremptory order from Alaric that all the consecrated plate and ornaments should be transported, without damage or delay, to the church of the apostle From the extremity, perhaps, of the Quirinal hill to the distant quarter of the Vatican, a numerous detachment of Goths, marching in order of battle through the principal streets, protected, with glittering arms, the long train of their devout companions, who bore aloft, on their heads, the sacred vessels of gold and silver ; and the martial shouts of the Barbarians were mingled with the sound of religious psalmody. From all the adjacent houses, a crowd of Christians hastened to join this edifying procession ; and a multitude of fugitives, without distinction of age, or rank, or even of sect, had the good fortune to escape to the secure and hospitable sanctuary of the Vatican   The learned work, concerning the *City of God*, was professedly composed by St Augustin, to justify the ways of Providence in the destruction of the Roman greatness. He celebrates with peculiar satisfaction this memorable triumph of Christ ; and insults his adversaries by challenging them to produce some similar example of a town taken by storm in which the fabulous gods of antiquity had been able to protect either themselves or their deluded votaries.[104]

In the sack of Rome, some rare and extraordinary examples of Barbarian virtue have been deservedly applauded   But the holy precincts of the Vatican and the apostolic churches could receive a very small proportion of the Roman people : many thousand warriors, more especially of the Huns, who served under the standard of Alaric, were strangers to the name, or at least to the faith, of Christ ; and we may suspect, without any breach of charity or candour, that in the hour of savage licence, when every passion was inflamed and every restraint was removed, the precepts of the gospel seldom influenced the behaviour of the Gothic Christians   The writers, the best disposed to exaggerate their clemency, have freely confessed that a cruel slaughter was made of the Romans ;[105] and that the streets of the city were

Pillage and fire of Rome

---

[104] See Augustin, de Civitat Dei, l   1   c   1-6   He particularly appeals to the example of Troy, Syracuse and Tarentum
[105] Jerom (tom   1   p   121, ad Principiam [ep   16]) has applied to the sack of Rome all the strong expressions of Virgil
  Quis cladem illius noctis, quis funera fando,
      Explicet, &c
Procopius (l   1, c   2) positively affirms that great numbers were slain by the Goths Augustin (de Civ   Dei, l   1   c   12, 13) offers Christian comfort for the death of those whose bodies (*multa corpora*) had remained (*in tantâ strage*) unburied Baronius, from the different writings of the Fathers, has thrown some light on the sack of Rome   Annal   Eccles   A D   410, No   16-44

filled with dead bodies, which remained without burial during
the general consternation The despair of the citizens was
sometimes converted into fury ; and, whenever the Barbarians
were provoked by opposition, they extended the promiscuous
massacre to the feeble, the innocent, and the helpless The
private revenge of forty thousand slaves was exercised without
pity or remorse ; and the ignominious lashes, which they had
formerly received, were washed away in the blood of the guilty,
or obnoxious, families The matrons and virgins of Rome were
exposed to injuries more dreadful in the apprehension of chastity
than death itself ; and the ecclesiastical historian has selected
an example of female virtue, for the admiration of future ages [106]
A Roman lady of singular beauty and orthodox faith had excited
the impatient desires of a young Goth, who, according to the
sagacious remark of Sozomen, was attached to the Arian heresy
Exasperated by her obstinate resistance, he drew his sword, and,
with the anger of a lover, slightly wounded her neck. The
bleeding heroine still continued to brave his resentment and to
repel his love, till the ravisher desisted from his unavailing
efforts, respectfully conducted her to the sanctuary of the
Vatican, and gave six pieces of gold to the guards of the church,
on condition that they should restore her inviolate to the arms
of her husband. Such instances of courage and generosity were
not extremely common The brutal soldiers satisfied their
sensual appetites, without consulting either the inclination or
the duties of their female captives , and a nice question of
casuistry was seriously agitated, Whether those tender victims
who had inflexibly refused their consent to the violation which
they sustained had lost, by their misfortune, the glorious crown
of virginity.[107] There were other losses indeed of a more sub-

---

[106] Sozomen, l ix c 10 Augustin (de Civitat Dei, l. 1 c 17) intimates that
some virgins or matrons actually killed themselves to escape violation ; and, though
he admires their spirit, he is obliged by his theology to condemn their rash presumption Perhaps the good bishop of Hippo was too easy in the belief, as well as too
rigid in the censure, of this act of female heroism The twenty maidens (if they
ever existed) who threw themselves into the Elbe, when Magdeburg was taken
by storm, have been multiplied to the number of twelve hundred See Harte's
History of Gustavus Adolphus, vol 1 p 308

[107] See August de Civitat Dei, l 1 c 16, 18 He treats the subject with remarkable accuracy , and, after admitting that there cannot be any crime where
there is no consent, he adds, Sed quia non solum quod ad dolorem, verum etiam
quod ad libidinem, pertinet in corpore alieno perpetrari potest ; quicquid tale
factum fuerit, etsi, retentam constantissimo animo pudicitiam non excutit, pudorem
tamen incutit, ne credatur factum cum mentis etiam voluntate, quod fieri fortasse
sine carnis aliquâ voluptate non potuit In c 18 he makes some curious distinctions between moral and physical virginity

stantial kind and more general concern.   It cannot be presumed
that all the Barbarians were at all times capable of perpetrating
such amorous outrages ; and the want of youth or beauty or
chastity protected the greatest part of the Roman women from
the danger of a rape   But avarice is an insatiate and universal
passion ; since the enjoyment of almost every object that can
afford pleasure to the different tastes and tempers of mankind
may be procured by the possession of wealth.   In the pillage of
Rome, a just preference was given to gold and jewels, which
contain the greatest value in the smallest compass and weight ;
but, after these portable riches had been removed by the more
diligent robbers, the palaces of Rome were rudely stripped of
their splendid and costly furniture.   The sideboards of massy
plate, and the variegated wardrobes of silk and purple, were
irregularly piled in the waggons that always followed the march
of a Gothic army. The most exquisite works of art were roughly
handled or wantonly destroyed : many a statue was melted for
the sake of the precious materials ; and many a vase, in the
division of the spoil, was shivered into fragments by the stroke
of a battle-axe   The acquisition of riches served only to stimulate
the avarice of the rapacious Barbarians, who proceeded by
threats, by blows, and by tortures, to force from their prisoners
the confession of hidden treasure.[108]   Visible splendour and
expense were alleged as the proof of a plentiful fortune ; the
appearance of poverty was imputed to a parsimonious disposition ;
and the obstinacy of some misers, who endured the most cruel
torments before they would discover the secret object of their
affection, was fatal to many unhappy wretches, who expired
under the lash for refusing to reveal their imaginary treasures.
The edifices of Rome, though the damage has been much
exaggerated, received some injury from the violence of the
Goths.   At their entrance through the Salarian gate, they fired
the adjacent houses, to guide their march and to distract the
attention of the citizens ; the flames, which encountered no
obstacle in the disorder of the night, consumed many private
and public buildings ; and the ruins of the palace of Sallust [109]

[108] Marcella, a Roman lady, equally respectable for her rank, her age, and her
piety, was thrown on the ground, and cruelly beaten and whipped, cæsam fustibus
flagellisque, &c.   Jerom, tom 1 p 121, ad Principiam [ep. 16].   See Augustin,
de Civ Dei, l 1 c 10   The modern Sacco di Roma, p 208, gives an idea of the
various methods of torturing prisoners for gold
[109] The historian Sallust, who usefully practised the vices which he has so
eloquently censured, employed the plunder of Numidia to adorn his palace and
gardens on the Quirinal hill   The spot where the house stood is now marked by

remained in the age of Justinian, a stately monument of the Gothic conflagration [110] Yet a contemporary historian has observed that fire could scarcely consume the enormous beams of solid brass, and that the strength of man was insufficient to subvert the foundations of ancient structures Some truth may possibly be concealed in his devout assertion that the wrath of Heaven supplied the imperfections of hostile rage, and that the proud Forum of Rome, decorated with the statues of so many gods and heroes, was levelled in the dust by the stroke of lightning [111]

Captives and fugitives Whatever might be the numbers, of equestrian or plebeian rank, who perished in the massacre of Rome, it is confidently affirmed that only one senator lost his life by the sword of the enemy.[112] But it was not easy to compute the multitudes, who, from an honourable station and a prosperous fortune, were suddenly reduced to the miserable condition of captives and exiles. As the Barbarians had more occasion for money than for slaves, they fixed at a moderate price the redemption of their indigent prisoners, and the ransom was often paid by the benevolence of their friends or the charity of strangers [113] The captives, who were regularly sold, either in open market or by private contract, would have legally regained their native freedom, which it was impossible for a citizen to lose or to

the church of St Susanna, separated only by a street from the baths of Diocletian, and not far distant from the Salarian gate See Nardini, Roma Antica, p 192, 193, and the great Plan of Modern Rome, by Nolli

[110] The expressions of Procopius are distinct and moderate (de Bell Vandal l 1 c 2)   The Chronicle of Marcellinus speaks too strongly, partem urbis Romæ cremavit , and the words of Philostorgius (εν ερειπιοις δε της πολεως κειμενης, l xii c 3) convey a false and exaggerated idea   Bargæus has composed a particular dissertation (see tom iv. Antiquit Rom Græv) to prove that the edifices of Rome were not subverted by the Goths and Vandals   [On the forbearance of the Goths to Rome, see Gregorovius Rome in the Middle Ages, i p. 158 *sqq.* (Eng tr.)]

[111] Orosius, l, ii c 19, p 143   He speaks as if he disapproved *all* statues ; vel Deum vel hominem mentiuntur   They consisted of the kings of Alba and Rome from Æneas, the Romans, illustrious either in arms or arts, and the deified Cæsars The expression which he uses of *Forum* is somewhat ambiguous since there existed *five* principal *Fora* , but, as they were all contiguous and adjacent, in the plain which is surrounded by the Capitoline, the Quirinal, the Esquiline, and the Palatine hills, they might fairly be considered as *one*   See the Roma Antiqua of Donatus p 162-201, and the Roma Antica of Nardini, p 212-273   The former is more useful for the ancient descriptions, the latter for the actual topography

[112] Orosius (l ii c 19, p 142) compares the cruelty of the Gauls and the clemency of the Goths   Ibi vix quemquam inventum senatorem, qui vel absens evascrit , hic vix quemquam requiri, qui forte ut latens perierit   But there is an air of rhetoric, and perhaps of falsehood, in this antithesis , and Socrates (l vii c 10) affirms, perhaps by an opposite exaggeration, that *many* senators were put to death with various and exquisite tortures

[113] Multi .   Christiani in captivitatem ducti sunt, Augustin, de Civ. Dei, l i. c 14 , and the Christians experienced no peculiar hardships

alienate [114] But, as it was soon discovered that the vindication
of their liberty would endanger their lives, and that the Goths,
unless they were tempted to sell, might be provoked to murder,
their useless prisoners, the civil jurisprudence had been already
qualified by a wise regulation that they should be obliged to
serve the moderate term of five years, till they had discharged
by their labour the price of their redemption.[115]   The nations
who invaded the Roman empire had driven before them, into
Italy, whole troops of hungry and affrighted provincials, less
apprehensive of servitude than of famine.   The calamities of
Rome and Italy dispersed the inhabitants to the most lonely,
the most secure, the most distant places of refuge.   While the
Gothic cavalry spread terror and desolation along the sea-coast
of Campania and Tuscany, the little Island of Igilium, separated
by a narrow channel from the Argentarian promontory, repulsed,
or eluded, their hostile attempts; and, at so small a distance
from Rome, great numbers of citizens were securely concealed
in the thick woods of that sequestered spot [116] The ample
patrimonies, which many senatorian families possessed in Africa,
invited them, if they had time and prudence, to escape from the
ruin of their country, to embrace the shelter of that hospitable
province.   The most illustrious of these fugitives was the noble
and pious Proba,[117] the widow of the præfect Petronius.   After

[114] See Heineccius, Antiquitat Juris Roman tom 1 p 96.
[115] Appendix Cod Theodos Avi in Sirmond Opera, tom 1 p 735   This
edict was published the 11th December, A D 408, and is more reasonable than
properly belonged to the ministers of Honorius
[116] Eminus Igili silvosa cacumina miror ;
   Quem fraudare nefas laudis honore suæ
   Hæc proprios nuper tutata est insula saltus,
    Sive loci ingenio seu Domini genio
   Gurgite cum modico victricibus obstitit armis
    Tanquam longinquo dissociata mari
   Hæc multos laceră suscepit ab urbe fugatos,
    Hic fessis posito certa timore salus
   Plurima terreno populaverat æquora bello,
    Contra naturam classe timendus eques
   Unum, mira fides, vario discrimine portum !
    'I am prope Romanis, tam procul esse Getis
       Rutilius, in Itinerar 1 1 325
The island is now called Giglio   See Cluver Ital Antiq 1 ii p 502
[117] As the adventures of Proba and her family are connected with the life of St
Augustin, they are diligently illustrated by Tillemont, Mém Ecclés tom xiii p
620-635   Some time after their arrival in Africa, Demetrias took the veil, and
made a vow of virginity , an event which was considered as of the highest importance to Rome and to the world   All the Saints wrote congratulatory letters to
her ; that of Jerom is still extant (tom 1 p 62-73, ad Demetriad de servandă
Virginitat) and contains a mixture of absurd reasoning, spirited declamation, and
curious facts, some of which relate to the siege and sack of Rome [ep. 130 , Migne,
1. 1107]

the death of her husband, the most powerful subject of Rome, she had remained at the head of the Anician family, and successively supplied, from her private fortune, the expense of the consulships of her three sons When the city was besieged and taken by the Goths, Proba supported, with Christian resignation, the loss of immense riches, embarked in a small vessel, from whence she beheld, at sea, the flames of her burning palace ; and fled with her daughter Læta, and her grand daughter, the celebrated virgin Demetrias, to the coast of Africa The benevolent profusion with which the matron distributed the fruits, or the price, of her estates contributed to alleviate the misfortunes of exile and captivity   But even the family of Proba herself was not exempt from the rapacious oppression of Count Herachan, who basely sold, in matrimonial prostitution, the noblest maidens of Rome to the lust or avarice of the Syrian merchants.   The Italian fugitives were dispersed through the provinces, along the coast of Egypt and Asia, as far as Constantinople and Jerusalem ; and the village of Bethlem, the solitary residence of St. Jerom and his female converts, was crowded with illustrious beggars of either sex and every age, who excited the public compassion by the remembrance of their past fortune [118] This awful catastrophe of Rome filled the astonished empire with grief and terror So interesting a contrast of greatness and ruin disposed the fond credulity of the people to deplore, and even to exaggerate, the afflictions of the queen of cities The clergy, who applied to recent events the lofty metaphors of Oriental prophecy, were sometimes tempted to confound the destruction of the capital and the dissolution of the globe.

Sack of Rome by the troops of Cha. V   There exists in human nature a strong propensity to depreciate the advantages, and to magnify the evils, of the present times. Yet, when the first emotions had subsided, and a fair estimate was made of the real damage, the more learned and judicious contemporaries were forced to confess that infant Rome had formerly received more essential injury from the Gauls than she had now sustained from the Goths in her declining age [119] The experience of eleven centuries has enabled posterity to produce

[118] See the pathetic complaint of Jerom (tom v   p 400), in his preface to the second book of his Commentaries on the prophet Ezekiel
[119] Orosius, though with some theological partiality, states this comparison, l ii c 19, p 142, l vii c 39, p 575   But in the history of the taking of Rome by the Gauls everything is uncertain, and perhaps fabulous   See Beaufort sur l Incertitude, &c , de l Histoire Romaine, p 356 ; and Melot, in the Mém de l'Académie des Inscript. tom xv. p. 1-21

a much more singular parallel; and to affirm with confidence
that the ravages of the Barbarians, whom Alaric had led from
the banks of the Danube, were less destructive than the
hostilities exercised by the troops of Charles the Fifth, a Catholic
prince, who styled himself Emperor of the Romans [120] The Goths
evacuated the city at the end of six days, but Rome remained
above nine months in the possession of the Imperialists; and
every hour was stained by some atrocious act of cruelty, lust, and
rapine The authority of Alaric preserved some order and
moderation among the ferocious multitude, which acknowledged
him for their leader and king; but the constable of Bourbon
had gloriously fallen in the attack of the walls, and the death
of the general removed every restraint of discipline from an
army which consisted of three independent nations, the Italians,
the Spaniards, and the Germans.   In the beginning of the
sixteenth century, the manners of Italy exhibited a remarkable
scene of the depravity of mankind.   They united the sanguinary
crimes that prevail in an unsettled state of society, with the
polished vices that spring from the abuse of art and luxury, and
the loose adventurers, who had violated every prejudice of
patriotism and superstition to assault the palace of the Roman
pontiff, must deserve to be considered as the most profligate of
the *Italians.* At the same æra, the *Spaniards* were the terror
both of the Old and New World; but their high-spirited
valour was disgraced by gloomy pride, rapacious avarice, and
unrelenting cruelty. Indefatigable in the pursuit of fame and
riches, they had improved, by repeated practice, the most
exquisite and effectual methods of torturing their prisoners,
many of the Castilians, who pillaged Rome, were familiars of
the holy inquisition, and some volunteers, perhaps, were lately
returned from the conquest of Mexico. The *Germans* were less
corrupt than the Italians, less cruel than the Spaniards; and the
rustic, or even savage, aspect of those *Tramontane* warriors often
disguised a simple and merciful disposition. But they had
imbibed, in the first fervour of the reformation, the spirit, as well

---

[120] The reader who wishes to inform himself of the circumstances of this famous
event may peruse an admirable narrative in Dr Robertson's History of Charles V
vol II p 283, or consult the Annali d'Italia of the learned Muratori, tom XIV
p. 230-244, octavo edition   If he is desirous of examining the originals, he may
have recourse to the eighteenth book of the great but unfinished history of
Guicciardini   But the account which most truly deserves the name of authentic
and original is a little book, intitled, *Il Sacco di Roma*, composed, within less than
a month after the assault of the city, by the *brother* of the historian Guicciardini,
who appears to have been an able magistrate and a dispassionate writer.

as the principles, of Luther. It was their favourite amusement to insult or destroy the consecrated objects of Catholic superstition, they indulged, without pity or remorse, a devout hatred against the clergy of every denomination and degree, who form so considerable a part of the inhabitants of modern Rome, and then fanatic zeal might aspire to subvert the throne of Antichrist, to purify, with blood and fire, the abominations of the spiritual Babylon.[121]

Alaric evacuates Rome and ravages Italy A D 410, August 29The retreat of the victorious Goths, who evacuated Rome on the sixth day,[122] might be the result of prudence, but it was not surely the effect of fear.[123] At the head of an army, encumbered with rich and weighty spoils, their intrepid leader advanced along the Appian way into the southern provinces of Italy, destroying whatever dared to oppose his passage, and contenting himself with the plunder of the unresisting country. The fate of Capua, the proud and luxurious metropolis of Campania, and which was respected, even in its decay, as the eighth city of the empire,[124] is buried in oblivion; whilst the adjacent town of Nola [125] has been illustrated, on this occasion, by the sanctity of Paulinus,[126] who was successively a consul, a monk, and a bishop At the age of forty, he renounced the enjoyment of wealth and honour, of society and literature, to embrace a life of solitude and penance; and the loud applause of the clergy encouraged him to despise the reproaches of his worldly friends, who ascribed this desperate act to some disorder of the mind or body.[127]

---

[121] The furious spirit of Luther, the effect of temper and enthusiasm, has been forcibly attacked (Bossuet, Hist des Variations des Eglises Protestantes, livre 1 p 20-36), and feebly defended (Seckendorf, Comment de Lutheranismo, especially l 1 No 78, p 120, and l 111 No 122, p 556)

[122] Marcellinus in Chron Orosius (l vii c 39, p 575) asserts that he left Rome on the *third* day, but this difference is easily reconciled by the successive motions of great bodies of troops

[123] Socrates (l vii c 10) pretends, without any colour of truth or reason, that Alaric fled on the report that the armies of the Eastern empire were in full march to attack him

[124] Ausonius de Claris Urbibus, p 233, edit Toll The luxury of Capua had ormerly surpassed that of Sybaris itself See Athenæus, Deipnosophist l. xii p. 528, edit Casaubon

[125] Forty-eight years before the foundation of Rome (about 800 before the Christian æra) the Tuscans built Capua and Nola, at the distance of twenty-three miles from each other, but the latter of the two cities never emerged from a state of mediocrity

[126] Tillemont (Mém Ecclés tom xiv p 1 146) has compiled, with his usual diligence, all that relates to the life and writings of Paulinus, whose retreat is celebrated by his own pen, and by the praises of St Ambrose, St Jerom, St Augustin, Sulpicius Severus, &c, his Christian friends and contemporaries

[127] See the affectionate letters of Ausonius (epist xix -xxv p 650 698, edit Toll) to his colleague, his friend, and his disciple Paulinus The religion of Ausonius is

An early and passionate attachment determined him to fix his humble dwelling in one of the suburbs of Nola, near the miraculous tomb of St. Felix, which the public devotion had already surrounded with five large and populous churches The remains of his fortune, and of his understanding, were dedicated to the service of the glorious martyr, whose praise, on the day of his festival, Paulinus never failed to celebrate by a solemn hymn, and in whose name he erected a sixth church, of superior elegance and beauty, which was decorated with many curious pictures, from the history of the Old and New Testament. Such assiduous zeal secured the favour of the saint,[128] or at least of the people ; and, after fifteen years' retirement, the Roman consul was compelled to accept the bishopric of Nola, a few months before the city was invested by the Goths. During the siege, some religious persons were satisfied that they had seen, either in dreams or visions, the divine form of their tutelar patron ; yet it soon appeared by the event that Felix wanted power, or inclination, to preserve the flock of which he had formerly been the shepherd. Nola was not saved from the general devastation ;[129] and the captive bishop was protected only by the general opinion of his innocence and poverty. Above four years elapsed from the successful invasion of Italy by the arms of Alaric to the voluntary retreat of the Goths under the conduct of his successor Adolphus ; and, during the whole time, they reigned without control over a country which, in the opinion of the ancients, had united all the various excellencies of nature and art. The prosperity, indeed, which Italy had attained in the auspicious age of the Antonines, had gradually declined with the decline of the empire. The fruits of a long peace perished under the rude grasp of the Barbarians, and they themselves were incapable of tasting the more elegant refinements of luxury which had been prepared for the use of the soft and polished Italians Each soldier, however, claimed an ample portion of the substantial plenty, the corn and cattle, oil and wine, that was daily collected and consumed in the Gothic camp ; and the principal warriors insulted the villas and

Possession of Italy by the Goths A D 408 412

still a problem (see Mém de l'Académie des Inscriptions, tom xv p 123-138) I believe that it was such in his own time, and, consequently, that in his heart he was a Pagan' [Cp Appendix 1]

[128] The humble Paulinus once presumed to say that he believed St Felix *did* love him, at least, as a master loves his little dog

[129] See Jornandes, de Reb Get. c 30, p 653 Philostorgius, l xii c 3 Augustin, de Civ Dei, l i. c 10 Baronius, Annal Eccles A D 410, No 45, 46

gardens, one inhabited by Lucullus and Cicero, along the beauteous coast of Campania   Their trembling captives, the sons and daughters of Roman senators, presented in goblets of gold and gems large draughts of Falernian wine to the haughty victors ; who stretched their huge limbs under the shade of plane-trees,[130] artificially disposed to exclude the scorching rays, and to admit the genial warmth, of the sun   These delights were enhanced by the memory of past hardships ; the comparison of their native soil, the bleak and barren hills of Scythia, and the frozen banks of the Elbe and Danube, added new charms to the felicity of the Italian climate [131]

Death of
Alaric
A D 410   Whether fame or conquest or riches were the object of Alaric, he pursued that object with an indefatigable ardour, which could neither be quelled by adversity nor satiated by success   No sooner had he reached the extreme land of Italy than he was attacked by the neighbouring prospect of a fertile and peaceful island. Yet even the possession of Sicily he considered only as an intermediate step to the important expedition which he already meditated against the continent of Africa.   The streights of Rhegium and Messina [132] are twelve miles in length, and in the narrowest passage about one mile and a half broad; and the fabulous monsters of the deep, the rocks of Scylla and the whirlpool of Charybdis, could terrify none but the most timid and unskilful mariners. Yet, as soon as the first division of the Goths had embarked, a sudden tempest arose, which sunk or scattered many of the transports ; their courage was daunted by

---

[130] The *platanus*, or plane-tree, was a favourite of the ancients, by whom it was propagated, for the sake of shade, from the East to Gaul, Pliny, Hist Natur xiii 3, 4, 5   He mentions several of an enormous size, one in the Imperial villa at Velitræ, which Caligula called his nest, as the branches were capable of holding a large table, the proper attendants, and the emperor himself, whom Pliny quaintly styles *pars umbrae*, an expression which might with equal reason be applied to Alaric

[131]   The prostrate South to the destroyer yields
         Her boasted titles, and her golden fields :
         With grim delight the brood of winter view
         A brighter day, and skies of azure hue ,
         Scent the new fragrance of the opening rose,
         And quaff the pendent vintage as it grows.
See Gray's Poems, published by Mr Mason, p 197   Instead of compiling tables of chronology and natural history, why did not Mr Gray apply the powers of his genius to finish the philosophic poem of which he has left such an exquisite specimen ?

[132] For the perfect description of the Streights of Messina, Scylla, Charybdis, &c , see Cluverius (Ital Antiq l iv p 1293, and Sicilia Antiq l i p 60-76), who had diligently studied the ancients and surveyed with a curious eye the actual face of the country

the terrors of a new element; and the whole design was defeated by the premature death of Alaric, which fixed, after a short illness, the fatal term of his conquests.   The ferocious character of the Barbarians was displayed in the funeral of a hero, whose valour and fortune they celebrated with mournful applause.   By the labour of a captive multitude they forcibly diverted the course of the Busentinus, a small river that washes the walls of [Busento] Consentia.   The royal sepulchre, adorned with the splendid spoils and trophies of Rome, was constructed in the vacant bed; the waters were then restored to their natural channel, and the secret spot, where the remains of Alaric had been deposited, was for ever concealed by the inhuman massacre of the prisoners who had been employed to execute the work.[133]

The personal animosities and hereditary feuds of the Barbarians were suspended by the strong necessity of their affairs; and the brave Adolphus, the brother-in-law of the deceased monarch, was unanimously elected to succeed to his throne. The character and political system of the new king of the Goths may be best understood from his own conversation with an illustrious citizen of Narbonne, who afterwards, in a pilgrimage to the Holy Land, related it to St. Jerom, in the presence of the historian Orosius   " In the full confidence of valour and victory I once aspired" (said Adolphus) "to change the face of the universe; to obliterate the name of Rome; to erect on its ruins the dominion of the Goths; and to acquire, like Augustus, the immortal fame of the founder of a new empire   By repeated experiments I was gradually convinced that laws are essentially necessary to maintain and regulate a well-constituted state, and that the fierce untractable humour of the Goths was incapable of bearing the salutary yoke of laws and civil government From that moment I proposed to myself a different object of glory and ambition; and it is now my sincere wish that the gratitude of future ages should acknowledge the merit of a stranger who employed the sword of the Goths, not to subvert, but to restore and maintain, the prosperity of the Roman empire."[134]   With these pacific views the successor of Alaric suspended the operations of war, and seriously negotiated with the Imperial court a treaty of friendship and alliance.   It was the interest of the ministers of Honorius, who were now released

[margin: Adolphus, King of the Goths, concludes a peace with the empire, and marches into Gaul A D 412]

---

[133] Jornandes, de Reb Get c. 30, p 654.
[134] Orosius, l vii c 43, p 584, 585   He was sent by St Augustin, in the year 415, from Africa to Palestine, to visit St Jerom, and to consult with him on the subject of the Pelagian controversy.

from the obligation of their extravagant oath, to deliver Italy from the intolerable weight of the Gothic powers, and they readily accepted their service against the tyrants and barbarians who infested the provinces beyond the Alps Adolphus,[135] assuming the character of a Roman general, directed his march from the extremity of Campania to the southern provinces of Gaul.   His troops, either by force or agreement, immediately occupied the cities of Narbonne, Toulouse, and Bourdeaux, and though they were repulsed by Count Boniface from the walls of Marseilles, they soon extended their quarters from the Mediterranean to the Ocean.   The oppressed provincials might exclaim that the miserable remnant which the enemy had spared was cruelly ravished by their pretended allies ; yet some specious colours were not wanting to palliate, or justify, the violence of the Goths.   The cities of Gaul which they attacked might perhaps be considered as in a state of rebellion against the government of Honorius ; the articles of the treaty, or the secret instructions of the court, might sometimes be alleged in favour of the seeming usurpations of Adolphus; and the guilt of any irregular, unsuccessful act of hostility might always be imputed, with an appearance of truth, to the ungovernable spirit of a Barbarian host, impatient of peace or discipline.   The luxury of Italy had been less effectual to soften the temper than to relax the courage of the Goths ; and they had imbibed the vices, without imitating the arts and institutions, of civilised society [136]

His marriage with Placidia A D 414   The professions of Adolphus were probably sincere, and his attachment to the cause of the republic was secured by the ascendant which a Roman princess had acquired over the heart and understanding of the Barbarian king.   Placidia,[137] the daughter of the great Theodosius and of Galla, his second wife, had received a royal education in the palace of Constantinople ; but the eventful story of her life is connected with the revolutions which agitated the Western empire under the reign of her brother Honorius   When Rome was first invested by the arms

[135] Jornandes supposes, without much probability, that Adolphus visited and plundered Rome a second time (more locustarum erasit)   Yet he agrees with Orosius in supposing that a treaty of peace was concluded between the Gothic prince and Honorius   See Oros l vii, c 43, p 584, 585. Jornandes, de Reb Geticis c 31, p 654, 655
[136] The retreat of the Goths from Italy, and their first transactions in Gaul, are dark and doubtful   I have derived much assistance from Mascou (Hist of the ancient Germans, l. viii c 29, 35, 36, 37), who has illustrated and connected the broken chronicles and fragments of the times
[137] See an account of Placidia in Ducange, Fam Byzant. p 72 , and Tillemont, Hist des Empereurs, tom. i p 260, 386, &c tom. vi p 240

of Alaric, Placidia, who was then about twenty years of age, resided in the city, and her ready consent to the death of her
cousin Serena has a cruel and ungrateful appearance, which,
according to the circumstances of the action, may be aggravated
or excused by the consideration of her tender age [138] The victorious Barbarians detained, either as a hostage or a captive,[139] the
sister of Honorius; but, while she was exposed to the disgrace
of following round Italy the motions of a Gothic camp, she experienced, however, a decent and respectful treatment. The
authority of Jornandes, who praises the beauty of Placidia, may
perhaps be counterbalanced by the silence, the expressive silence,
of her flatterers; yet the splendour of her birth, the bloom of
youth, the elegance of manners, and the dexterous insinuation
which she condescended to employ, made a deep impression on
the mind of Adolphus; and the Gothic king aspired to call himself the brother of the emperor   The ministers of Honorius rejected with disdain the proposal of an alliance so injurious to
every sentiment of Roman pride, and repeatedly urged the
restitution of Placidia as an indispensable condition of the
treaty of peace.   But the daughter of Theodosius submitted,
without reluctance, to the desires of the conqueror, a young and
valiant prince, who yielded to Alaric in loftiness of stature, but
who excelled in the more attractive qualities of grace and beauty.
The marriage of Adolphus and Placidia [140] was consummated be
fore the Goths retired from Italy; and the solemn, perhaps the
anniversary, day of their nuptials was afterwards celebrated in
the house of Ingenuus, one of the most illustrious citizens of
Narbonne in Gaul.   The bride, attired and adorned like a
Roman empress, was placed on a throne of state; and the king
of the Goths, who assumed on this occasion the Roman habit,
contented himself with a less honourable seat by her side   The
nuptial gift, which according to the custom of his nation [141] was

[138] Zosim l v p 350 [38]
[139] Zosim l. vi p 383 [12]   Orosius (l vii c 40, p 576) and the Chronicles
of Marcellinus and Idatius seem to suppose that the Goths did not carry away
Placidia until after the last siege of Rome
    [140] See the pictures of Adolphus and Placidia, and the account of their marriage,
in Jornandes, de Reb Geticis, c 31, p 654, 655   With regard to the place where
the nuptials were stipulated or consummated or celebrated, the Mss. of Jornandes
vary between two neighbouring cities, Forli and Imola (Forum Livii and Forum
Cornelii)   It is fair and easy to reconcile the Gothic historian with Olympiodorus
(see Mascou, l viii. c 46), but Tillemont grows peevish, and swears that it is not
worth while to try to conciliate Jornandes with any good authors   [All the Mss
of Jordanes have *Iuli*, which the ed Basil corrects to *Livii*   Idatius and
Olympiodorus place the marriage at Narbo]
    [141] The Visigoths (the subjects of Adolphus) restrained by subsequent laws the
prodigality of conjugal love   It was illegal for a husband to make any gift or

offered to Placidia, consisted of the rare and magnificent spoils
of her country Fifty beautiful youths, in silken robes, carried
a basin in each hand ; and one of these basins was filled with
pieces of gold, the other with precious stones of an inestimable
value Attalus, so long the sport of fortune and of the Goths,
was appointed to lead the chorus of the Hymenæal song, and
the degraded emperor might aspire to the praise of a skilful
musician The Barbarians enjoyed the insolence of their
triumph ; and the provincials rejoiced in this alliance, which
tempered by the mild influence of love and reason the fierce
spirit of their Gothic lord.[142]

The Gothic
treasures
The hundred basins of gold and gems, presented to Placidia
at her nuptial feast, formed an inconsiderable portion of the
Gothic treasures ; of which some extraordinary specimens may be
selected from the history of the successors of Adolphus. Many
curious and costly ornaments of pure gold, enriched with jewels,
were found in their palace of Narbonne when it was pillaged in
the sixth century by the Franks · sixty cups or chalices ; fifteen
patens, or plates, for the use of the communion; twenty boxes, or
cases, to hold the books of the gospel; this consecrated wealth [143]
was distributed by the son of Clovis among the churches of his
dominions, and his pious liberality seems to upbraid some former
sacrilege of the Goths. They possessed, with more security of
conscience, the famous *missorium*, or great dish for the service of
the table, of massy gold of the weight of five hundred pounds,
and of far superior value from the precious stones, the exquisite
workmanship, and the tradition that it had been presented by
Aetius the patrician to Torismond king of the Goths. One of
the successors of Torismond purchased the aid of the French
monarch by the promise of this magnificent gift. When he
was seated on the throne of Spain, he delivered it with reluct-

settlement for the benefit of his wife during the first year of their marriage, and his
liberality could not exceed the tenth part of his property   The Lombards were
somewhat more indulgent ; they allowed the *morgingcap* immediately after the
wedding-night ; and this famous gift, the reward of virginity, might equal the
fourth part of the husband's substance   Some cautious maidens, indeed, were
wise enough to stipulate beforehand a present, which they were too sure of not
deserving   See Montesquieu, Esprit des Loix, l xix c 25   Muratori, delle
Antichità Italiane, tom i Dissertazione xx p 243
[142] We owe the curious detail of this nuptial feast to the historian Olympiodorus,
ap Photium, p 185, 188 [fr 24]
[143] See in the great collection of the historians of France by Dom Bouquet,
tom ii , Greg Turonens, l iii c 10, p 191 ; Gesta Regum Franc. c 23, p
557.   The anonymous writer, with an ignorance worthy of his times, supposes
that these instruments of Christian worship had belonged to the temple of Solomon
If he has any meaning, it must be that they were found in the sack of Rome
[Procopius, B G i. 12, states that they were taken from Jerusalem by the Romans]

ance to the ambassadors of Dagobert; despoiled them on the road ; stipulated, after a long negotiation, the inadequate ransom of two hundred thousand pieces of gold ; and preserved the *missorium* as the pride of the Gothic treasury.[144] When that treasury, after the conquest of Spain, was plundered by the Arabs, they admired, and they have celebrated, another object still more remarkable : a table of considerable size, of one single piece of solid emerald,[145] encircled with three rows of fine pearls, supported by three hundred and sixty-five feet of gems and massy gold, and estimated at the price of five hundred thousand pieces of gold.[146] Some portion of the Gothic treasures might be the gift of friendship or the tribute of obedience ; but the far greater part had been the fruits of war and rapine, the spoils of the empire, and perhaps of Rome.

After the deliverance of Italy from the oppression of the Goths some secret counsellor was permitted, amidst the factions of the palace, to heal the wounds of that afflicted country.[147] By a wise and humane regulation the eight provinces which had been the most deeply injured, Campania, Tuscany, Picenum, Samnium, Apulia, Calabria, Bruttium, and Lucania, obtained an indulgence of five years : the ordinary tribute was reduced to one-fifth, and even that fifth was destined to restore and support the useful institution of the public posts By another law the lands which had been left without inhabitants or cultivation were granted, with some diminution of taxes, to the neighbours who should occupy, or the strangers who should solicit, them , and the new possessors were secured against the future claims of the fugitive proprietors. About the same time a general amnesty was published in the name of Honorius, to abolish the guilt and memory of all the *involuntary* offences

Laws for the relief of Italy and Rome A D 410 417

[144] Consult the following original testimonies in the Historians of France, tom ii Fredegarii Scholastici Chron c 73, p 441   Fredegar. Fragment. iii. p. 463 Gesta Regis Dagobert c 29, p 587   The accession of Sisenand to the throne of Spain happened A D 631   The 200,000 pieces of gold were appropriated by Dagobert to the foundation of the church of St Denys

[145] The president Goguet (Origine des Loix, &c tom ii p 239) is of opinion that the stupendous pieces of emerald, the statues and columns which antiquity has placed in Egypt, at Gades, at Constantinople, were in reality artificial compositions of coloured glass   The famous emerald dish which is shown at Genoa is supposed to countenance the suspicion

[146] Elmacin, Hist Saracenica, l i p 85   Roderic Tolet Hist Arab c 9 Cardonne, Hist de l'Afrique et de l'Espagne sous les Arabes, tom i p 83   It was called the Table of Solomon according to the custom of the Orientals, who ascribe to that prince every ancient work of knowledge or magnificence

[147] His three laws are inserted in the Theodosian Code, l xi tit xxviii leg 7 L xiii tit xi leg 12   L xv tit xiv leg 14   The expressions of the last are very remarkable, since they contain not only a pardon but an apology.

which had been committed by his unhappy subjects during the
term of the public disorder and calamity. A decent and
respectful attention was paid to the restoration of the capital;
the citizens were encouraged to rebuild the edifices which had been
destroyed or damaged by hostile fire; and extraordinary supplies
of corn were imported from the coast of Africa. The crowds
that so lately fled before the sword of the Barbarians were soon
recalled by the hopes of plenty and pleasure; and Albinus,
præfect of Rome, informed the court, with some anxiety and
surprise, that in a single day he had taken an account of the
arrival of fourteen thousand strangers.[148] In less than seven
years the vestiges of the Gothic invasion were almost obliterated,
and the city appeared to resume its former splendour and tranquillity. The venerable matron replaced her crown of laurel
which had been ruffled by the storms of war, and was still
amused, in the last moment of her decay, with the prophecies
of revenge, of victory, and of eternal dominion.[149]

Revolt and
defeat of
Heraclian,
count of
Africa
A D. 413 This apparent tranquillity was soon disturbed by the approach
of an hostile armament from the country which afforded the
daily subsistence of the Roman people   Heraclian, count of
Africa, who, under the most difficult and distressful circumstances, had supported, with active loyalty, the cause of Honorius,
was tempted, in the year of his consulship, to assume the character of a rebel and the title of emperor   The ports of Africa
were immediately filled with the naval forces, at the head of
which he prepared to invade Italy; and his fleet, when it cast
anchor at the mouth of the Tiber, indeed surpassed the fleets of
Xerxes and Alexander, if all the vessels, including the royal
galley and the smallest boat, did actually amount to the incredible number of three thousand two hundred.[150]   Yet with

---

[148] Olympiodorus ap Phot p 188 [fr 25]   Philostorgius (l vii c 5) observes
that, when Honorius made his triumphal entry, he encouraged the Romans with
his hand and voice (χειρι και γλωττη) to rebuild their city, and the Chronicle of
Prosper commends Heraclian, qui in Romanæ urbis reparationem strenuum ex-
hibuerat ministerium

[149] The date of the voyage of Claudius Rutilius Numatianus [Namatianus] is
clogged with some difficulties, but Scaliger has deduced from astronomical characters that he left Rome the 24th of September and embarked at Porto the 9th of
October, A D 416   See Tillemont, Hist des Empereurs, tom v p. 820   In
this political Itinerary Rutilius (l 1 115, &c) addresses Rome in a high strain of
congratulation —

Erige crinales lauros, seniumque sacrati
Vertices in virides Roma recinge comas, &c

[Rutilius had been magister officiorum and præf urbi of Rome

[150] Orosius composed his history in Africa only two years after the event, yet
his authority seems to be overbalanced by the improbability of the fact   The

such an armament, which might have subverted or restored the greatest empires of the earth, the African usurper made a very faint and feeble impression on the provinces of his rival. As he marched from the port along the road which leads to the gates of Rome, he was encountered, terrified, and routed by one of the Imperial captains, and the lord of this mighty host, deserting his fortune and his friends, ignominiously fled with a single ship.[151] When Heraclian landed in the harbour of Carthage, he found that the whole province, disdaining such an unworthy ruler, had returned to their allegiance. The rebel was beheaded in the ancient temple of Memory; his consulship was abolished,[152] and the remains of his private fortune, not exceeding the moderate sum of four thousand pounds of gold, were granted to the brave Constantius, who had already defended the throne which he afterwards shared with his feeble sovereign. Honorius viewed with supine indifference the calamities of Rome and Italy,[153] but the rebellious attempts of Attalus and Heraclian against his personal safety awakened, for a moment, the torpid instinct of his nature. He was probably ignorant of the causes and events which preserved him from these impending dangers; and, as Italy was no longer invaded by any foreign or domestic enemies, he peaceably existed in the palace of Ravenna, while the tyrants beyond the Alps were repeatedly vanquished in the name, and by the lieutenants, of the son of Theodosius.[154] In the course of a busy and interesting narrative, I might possibly forget to mention the death of such a prince, and I shall

Chronicle of Marcellinus gives Heraclian 700 ships and 3000 men the latter of these numbers is ridiculously corrupt, but the former would please me very much

[151] The Chronicle of Idatius affirms, without the least appearance of truth, that he advanced as far as Otriculum, in Umbria, where he was overthrown in a great battle, with the loss of fifty thousand men

[152] See Cod. Theod. l. xv tit iv leg 13 The legal acts performed in his name, even the manumission of slaves, were declared invalid till they had been formally repealed

[153] I have disdained to mention a very foolish, and probably a false, report (Procop de Bell Vandal l 1 c 2) that Honorius was alarmed by the *loss* of Rome, till he understood that it was not a favourite chicken of that name, but *only* the capital of the world, which had been lost Yet even this story is some evidence of the public opinion

[154] The materials for the lives of all these tyrants are taken from six contemporary historians, two Latins and four Greeks Orosius, l vii c 42, p 581, 582, 583, Renatus Profuturus Frigeridus, apud Gregor Turon l ii c 9, in the historians of France, tom ii p 165, 166, Zosimus, l vi p 370, 371 [2 *sqq*]; Olympiodorus, apud Phot p 180, 181, 184, 185 [fr 12-19], Sozomen, l ix c 12, 13, 14, 15, and Philostorgius, l xii c 5, 6, with Godefroy's Dissertations, p. 477-481; besides the four Chronicles of Prosper Tiro, Prosper of Aquitain, Idatius, and Marcellinus

therefore take the precaution of observing, in this place, that he survived the last siege of Rome about thirteen years

Revolutions of Gaul and Spain. A D 409 413 The usurpation of Constantine, who received the purple from the legions of Britain, had been successful, and seemed to be secure His title was acknowledged, from the wall of Antoninus to the columns of Hercules; and, in the midst of the public disorder, he shared the dominion, and the plunder, of Gaul and Spain with the tribes of Barbarians, whose destructive progress was no longer checked by the Rhine or Pyrenees. Stained with the blood of the kinsmen of Honorius, he extorted from the court of Ravenna, with which he secretly corresponded, the ratification of his rebellious claims   Constantine engaged himself by a solemn promise to deliver Italy from the Goths , advanced as far as the banks of the Po , and, after alarming rather than assisting his pusillanimous ally, hastily returned to the palace of Arles, to celebrate, with intemperate luxury, his vain and ostentatious triumph   But this transient prosperity was soon interrupted and destroyed by the revolt of count Gerontius, the bravest of his generals, who, during the absence of his son Constans, a prince already invested with the Imperial purple, had been left to command in the provinces of Spain.   For some reason of which we are ignorant, Gerontius, instead of assuming the diadem, placed it on the head of his friend Maximus,[155] who fixed his residence at Tarragona, while the active count pressed forwards, through the Pyrenees, to surprise the two emperors, Constantine and Constans, before they could prepare for their [Vienne] defence   The son was made prisoner at Vienna and immediately put to death ; and the unfortunate youth had scarcely leisure to deplore the elevation of his family, which had tempted or compelled him sacrilegiously to desert the peaceful obscurity of the monastic life.   The father maintained a siege within the walls of Arles; but those walls must have yielded to the assailants had not the city been unexpectedly relieved by the approach of an Italian army.   The name of Honorius, the proclamation of a lawful emperor, astonished the contending parties of the rebels Gerontius, abandoned by his own troops, escaped to the confines of Spain, and rescued his name from oblivion by the Roman courage which appeared to animate the last moments of his life   In the middle of the night, a great body of his perfidious soldiers surrounded and attacked his house, which he

---

[155] [A dependent friend Olympiodorus, fr 16, has τὸν ἑαυτοῦ παῖδα, which doubtless means his "servant," not his "son".]

had strongly barricaded   His wife, a valiant friend of the
nation of the Alani, and some faithful slaves were still attached
to his person , and he used with so much skill and resolution a
large magazine of darts and arrows that above three hundred of
the assailants lost their lives in the attempt.   His slaves, when
all the missile weapons were spent, fled at the dawn of day,
and Gerontius, if he had not been restrained by conjugal tenderness, might have imitated their example ; till the soldiers, provoked by such obstinate resistance, applied fire on all sides to
the house   In this fatal extremity, he complied with the request
of his Barbarian friend, and cut off his head   The wife of
Gerontius, who conjured him not to abandon her to a life of
misery and disgrace, eagerly presented her neck to his sword ;
and the tragic scene was terminated by the death of the count
himself, who, after three ineffectual strokes, drew a short dagger,
and sheathed it in his heart.[156]   The unprotected Maximus,
whom he had invested with the purple, was indebted for his
life to the contempt that was entertained of his power and
abilities   The caprice of the Barbarians, who ravaged Spain,
once more seated this Imperial phantom on the throne , but
they soon resigned him to the justice of Honorius ; and the
tyrant Maximus, after he had been shown to the people of
Ravenna and Rome, was publicly executed.   [A.D 422]

The general, Constantius was his name, who raised by his **Character and**
approach the siege of Arles, and dissipated the troops of Geron- **victories of**
tius, was born a Roman , and this remarkable distinction is **the general Constantius.**
strongly expressive of the decay of military spirit among the
subjects of the empire   The strength and majesty which were
conspicuous in the person of that general [157] marked him, in the
popular opinion, as a candidate worthy of the throne which he
afterwards ascended.   In the familiar intercourse of private
life his manners were cheerful and engaging ; nor would he
sometimes disdain, in the licence of convivial mirth, to vie with
the pantomimes themselves in the exercises of their ridiculous
profession.   But, when the trumpet summoned him to arms ;
when he mounted his horse, and, bending down (for such was

---

[156] The praises which Sozomen has bestowed on this act of despair appear
strange and scandalous in the mouth of an ecclesiastical historian   He observes
(p 379) that the wife of Gerontius was a *Christian* , and that her death was worthy
of her religion and of immortal fame   [For death of Maximus, cp App 22]

[157] Εἶδος ἄξιον τυραννίδος, is the expression of Olympiodorus, which he seems to
have borrowed from *Æolus*, a tragedy of Euripides, of which some fragments
only are now extant (Euripid Barnes, tom ii p 443, ver 38)   This allusion
may prove that the ancient tragic poets were still familiar to the Greeks of the fifth
century.

his singular practice) almost upon the neck, fiercely rolled his large animated eyes round the field, Constantius then struck terror into his foes, and inspired his soldiers with the assurance of victory He had received from the court of Ravenna the important commission of extirpating rebellion in the provinces of the West, and the pretended emperor Constantine, after enjoying a short and anxious respite, was again besieged in his capital by the arms of a more formidable enemy Yet this interval allowed time for a successful negotiation with the Franks and Alemanni, and his ambassador, Edobic, soon returned, at the head of an army, to disturb the operations of the siege of Arles. The Roman general, instead of expecting the attack in his lines, boldly, and perhaps wisely, resolved to pass the Rhone, and to meet the Barbarians His measures were conducted with so much skill and secrecy that, while they engaged the infantry of Constantius in the front, they were suddenly attacked, surrounded, and destroyed by the cavalry of his lieutenant Ulphilas, who had silently gained an advantageous post in their rear The remains of the army of Edobic were preserved by flight or submission, and their leader escaped from the field of battle to the house of a faithless friend, who too clearly understood that the head of his obnoxious guest would be an acceptable and lucrative present for the Imperial general. On this occasion, Constantius behaved with the magnanimity of a genuine Roman. Subduing or suppressing every sentiment of jealousy, he publicly acknowledged the merit and services of Ulphilas, but he turned with horror from the assassin of Edobic, and sternly intimated his commands that the camp should no longer be polluted by the presence of an ungrateful wretch, who had violated the laws of friendship and hospitality The usurper, who beheld from the walls of Arles the ruin of his last hopes, was tempted to place some confidence in so generous a conqueror He required a solemn promise for his security, and after receiving, by the imposition of hands, the sacred character of a Christian Presbyter, he ventured to open the gates of the city. But he soon experienced that the principles of honour and integrity, which might regulate the ordinary conduct of Constantius, were superseded by the loose doctrines of political morality. The Roman general, indeed, refused to sully his laurels with the blood of Constantine; but the abdicated emperor and his son Julian were sent under a strong guard into Italy; and before they reached the palace of Ravenna they met the ministers of death

Death of the usurper Constantine A D 411, November 23 [leg Sept 18]

At a time when it was universally confessed that almost every man in the empire was superior in personal merit to the princes whom the accident of their birth had seated on the throne, a rapid succession of usurpers, regardless of the fate of their predecessors, still continued to arise. This mischief was peculiarly felt in the provinces of Spain and Gaul, where the principles of order and obedience had been extinguished by war and rebellion   Before Constantine resigned the purple, and in the fourth month of the siege of Arles, intelligence was received in the Imperial camp that Jovinus had assumed the diadem at Mentz in the Upper Germany, at the instigation of Goar, king of the Alani, and of Guntiarius, king of the Burgundians; and that the candidate on whom they had bestowed the empire advanced with a formidable host of Barbarians from the banks of the Rhine to those of the Rhone   Every circumstance is dark and extraordinary in the short history of the reign of Jovinus   It was natural to expect that a brave and skilful general, at the head of a victorious army, would have asserted in a field of battle the justice of the cause of Honorius   The hasty retreat of Constantius might be justified by weighty reasons , but he resigned, without a struggle, the possession of Gaul · and Dardanus, the Prætorian præfect, is recorded as the only magistrate who refused to yield obedience to the usurper.[158]   When the Goths, two years after the siege of Rome, established their quarters in Gaul, it was natural to suppose that their inclinations could be divided only between the emperor Honorius, with whom they had formed a recent alliance, and the degraded Attalus, whom they reserved in their camp for the occasional purpose of acting the part of a musician or a monarch.   Yet in a moment of disgust (for which it is not easy to assign a cause or a date) Adolphus connected himself with the usurper of Gaul, and imposed on Attalus the ignominious task of negotiating the treaty which ratified his own disgrace   We are again surprised to read that, instead of considering the Gothic alliance as the firmest support of his throne, Jovinus upbraided, in dark and ambiguous language, the officious importunity of Attalus ; that, scorning the advice of

---

[158] Sidonius Apollinaris (l v epist 9, p 139, and Not Sirmond, p 58), after stigmatizing the *inconstancy* of Constantine, the *facility* of Jovinus, the *perfidy* of Gerontius, continues to observe that *all* the vices of these tyrants were united in the person of Dardanus   Yet the præfect supported a respectable character in the world, and even in the church, held a devout correspondence with St Augustin and St Jerom , and was complimented by the latter (tom iii p 66) with the epithets of Christianorum Nobilissime and Nobilium Christianissime

his great ally, he invested with the purple his brother Sebastian ;
and that he most imprudently accepted the service of Sarus,
when that gallant chief, the soldier of Honorius, was provoked
to desert the court of a prince who knew not how to reward or
punish. Adolphus, educated among a race of warriors, who
esteemed the duty of revenge as the most precious and sacred
portion of their inheritance, advanced with a body of ten
thousand Goths to encounter the hereditary enemy of the
house of Balti   He attacked Sarus at an unguarded moment,
when he was accompanied only by eighteen or twenty of his
valiant followers.   United by friendship, animated by despair,
but at length oppressed by multitudes, this band of heroes
deserved the esteem, without exciting the compassion, of their
enemies ; and the lion was no sooner taken in the toils [159] than
he was instantly dispatched   The death of Sarus dissolved the
loose alliance which Adolphus still maintained with the usurpers
of Gaul   He again listened to the dictates of love and
prudence , and soon satisfied the brother of Placidia, by the
assurance that he would immediately transmit to the palace of
Ravenna the heads of the two tyrants, Jovinus and Sebastian
The king of the Goths executed his promise without difficulty
or delay , the helpless brothers, unsupported by any personal
merit, were abandoned by their Barbarian auxiliaries , and the
short opposition of Valentia was expiated by the ruin of one of
the noblest cities of Gaul.   The emperor, chosen by the Roman
senate, who had been promoted, degraded, insulted, restored,
again degraded, and again insulted, was finally abandoned to
his fate ; but, when the Gothic king withdrew his protection,
he was restrained by pity or contempt from offering any violence
to the person of Attalus.   The unfortunate Attalus, who was
left without subjects or allies, embarked in one of the ports of
Spain, in search of some secure and solitary retreat ; but he
was intercepted at sea, conducted to the presence of Honorius,
led in triumph through the streets of Rome or Ravenna, and
publicly exposed to the gazing multitude, on the second step
of the throne of his *invincible* conqueror   The same measure
of punishment with which, in the days of his prosperity, he
was accused of menacing his rival was inflicted on Attalus him-

[159] The expression may be understood almost literally , Olympiodorus says [fr
17], μολις σακκοις ἐζώγρησαν. Σακκος (or σακος) may signify a sack, or a loose
garment , and this method of entangling and catching an enemy, lacinus
contortis, was much practised by the Huns (Ammian xxxi 2)   Il fut pris vif
avec des filets, is the translation of Tillemont, Hist des Empereurs, tom v p.
608

self· he was condemned, after the amputation of two fingers, to a perpetual exile in the isle of Lipari, where he was supplied with the decent necessaries of life   The remainder of the reign of Honorius was undisturbed by rebellion ; and it may be observed that, in the space of five years, seven usurpers had yielded to the fortunes of a prince, who was himself incapable either of counsel or of action

The situation of Spain, separated, on all sides, from the enemies of Rome, by the sea, by the mountains, and by intermediate provinces, had secured the long tranquillity of that remote and sequestered country ; and we may observe, as a sure symptom of domestic happiness, that in a period of four hundred years Spain furnished very few materials to the history of the Roman empire   The footsteps of the Barbarians, who, in the reign of Gallienus, had penetrated beyond the Pyrenees, were soon obliterated by the return of peace ; and in the fourth century of the Christian æra, the cities of Emerita, or Merida, of Corduba, Seville, Bracara, and Tarragona, were numbered with the most illustrious of the Roman world   The various plenty of the animal, the vegetable, and the mineral kingdoms was improved and manufactured by the skill of an industrious people ; and the peculiar advantages of naval stores contributed to support an extensive and profitable trade.[160]   The arts and sciences flourished under the protection of the Emperors ; and, if the character of the Spaniards was enfeebled by peace and servitude, the hostile approach of the Germans, who had spread terror and desolation from the Rhine to the Pyrenees, seemed to rekindle some sparks of military ardour.   As long as the defence of the mountains was entrusted to the hardy and faithful militia of the country, they successfully repelled the frequent attempts of the Barbarians   But no sooner had the national troops been compelled to resign their post to the Honorian bands in the service of Constantine than the gates of Spain were treacherously betrayed to the public enemy, about ten months before the sack of Rome by the Goths.[161]   The con-

Invasion of Spain by the Suevi, Vandals, Alani, &c
A D 409,
October 13
[Sept 28 --
Oct 13]

[160] Without recurring to the more ancient writers, I shall quote three respectable testimonies which belong to the fourth and seventh centuries ; the Expositio totius Mundi (p 16 in the third volume of Hudson's Minor Geographers), Ausonius (de Claris Urbibus, p 242, edit Toll), and Isidore of Seville (Præfat ad Chron. ap Grotium, Hist Goth. p 707)   Many particulars relative to the fertility and trade of Spain may be found in Nonnius, Hispania Illustrata, and in Huet, Hist du Commerce des Anciens, c 40, p 228-234

[161] The date is accurately fixed in the Fasti and the Chronicle of Idatius Orosius (l vii c 40, p 578) imputes the loss of Spain to the treachery of the Honorians, while Sozomen (l ix c 12) accuses only their negligence

sciousness of guilt and the thirst of rapine promoted the mercenary guards of the Pyrenees to desert their station, to invite the arms of the Suevi, the Vandals, and the Alani, and to swell the torrent which was poured with irresistible violence from the frontiers of Gaul to the sea of Africa   The misfortunes of Spain may be described in the language of its most eloquent historian, who has concisely expressed the passionate, and perhaps exaggerated, declamations of contemporary writers [162] "The irruption of these nations was followed by the most dreadful calamities, as the Barbarians exercised their indiscriminate cruelty on the fortunes of the Romans and the Spaniards, and ravaged with equal fury the cities and the open country   The progress of famine reduced the miserable inhabitants to feed on the flesh of their fellow-creatures ; and even the wild beasts, who multiplied, without control, in the desert, were exasperated, by the taste of blood and the impatience of hunger, boldly to attack and devour their human prey.   Pestilence soon appeared, the inseparable companion of famine, a large proportion of the people was swept away, and the groans of the dying excited only the envy of their surviving friends   At length the Barbarians, satiated with carnage and rapine, and afflicted by the contagious evils which they themselves had introduced, fixed their permanent seats in the depopulated country.   The ancient Gallicia, whose limits included the kingdom of Old Castille, was divided between the Suevi and the Vandals : the Alani were scattered over the provinces of Carthagena and Lusitania, from the Mediterranean to the Atlantic Ocean, and the fruitful territory of Bætica was allotted to the Silingi another branch of the Vandalic nation   After regulating this partition, the conquerors contracted with their new subjects some reciprocal engagements of protection and obedience, the lands were again cultivated, and the towns and villages were again occupied by a captive people.   The greatest part of the Spaniards was even disposed to prefer this new condition of poverty and barbarism to the severe oppressions of the Roman government ; yet there were many who still asserted their native freedom ; and who refused, more especially in the mountains of Gallicia, to submit to the Barbarian yoke [163]

[162] Idatius wishes to apply the prophecies of Daniel to these national calamities, and is therefore obliged to accommodate the circumstances of the event to the terms of the prediction
[163] Mariana de Rebus Hispanicis, l v c 1, tom 1 p 148, Hag Comit 1733 He had read, in Orosius (l vii c 41, p 579), that the Barbarians had turned their

The important present of the heads of Jovinus and Sebastian Adolphus,
King of the
Goths,
marches had approved the friendship of Adolphus and restored Gaul into Spain to the obedience of his brother Honorius.   Peace was incom- A D 414 patible with the situation and temper of the king of the Goths.   He readily accepted the proposal of turning his victorious arms against the Barbarians of Spain , the troops of Constantius intercepted his communication with the seaports of Gaul, and gently pressed his march towards the Pyrenees ,[164] he passed the mountains, and surprised, in the name of the emperor, the city of Barcelona.   The fondness of Adolphus for his Roman bride was not abated by time or possession , and the birth of a son, surnamed, from his illustrious grandsire, Theodosius, appeared to fix him for ever in the interest of the republic.   The loss of that infant, whose remains were deposited in a silver coffin in one of the churches near Barcelona, afflicted his parents ; but the grief of the Gothic king was suspended by the labours of the field ; and the course of his victories was soon interrupted by domestic treason.   He had imprudently received into his service one of the followers of Sarus : a Barbarian of a daring spirit, but of a diminutive stature ; whose secret desire of revenging the death of his beloved patron was His death
A D 415, continually irritated by the sarcasms of his insolent master. August Adolphus was assassinated in the palace of Barcelona ; the laws of the succession were violated by a tumultuous faction ;[165] and a stranger to the royal race, Singeric, the brother of Sarus himself, was seated on the Gothic throne   The first act of his reign was the inhuman murder of the six children of Adolphus, the issue of a former marriage, whom he tore, without pity, from the feeble arms of a venerable bishop [166]   The unfortunate Placidia, instead of the respectful compassion which she might have excited in the most savage breasts, was treated with cruel and wanton insult.   The daughter of the emperor Theodosius, confounded among a crowd of vulgar captives, was compelled

swords into ploughshares , and that many of the Provincials preferred inter Barbaros pauperem libertatem quam inter Romanos tributariam solicitudinem sustinere

[164] This mixture of force and persuasion may be fairly inferred from comparing Orosius and Jornandes, the Roman and the Gothic historian   [Force   the words of Orosius (*a Narbona expulit*, and *coegit*) are confirmed by Idatius (Chron ed. Momms p 19 *pulsatus*)]

[165] According to the system of Jornandes (c 33, p 659) the true hereditary right to the Gothic sceptre was vested in the *Amali* , but those princes, who were the vassals of the Huns, commanded the tribes of the Ostrogoths in some distant parts of Germany or Scythia

[166] The murder is related by Olympiodorus , but the number of children is from an epitaph of suspected authority

to march on foot above twelve miles, before the horse of a Barbarian, the assassin of a husband whom Placidia loved and lamented.[167]

The Goths
conquer and
restore Spain
A D 415-418 But Placidia soon obtained the pleasure of revenge, and the view of her ignominious sufferings might rouse an indignant people against the tyrant who was assassinated on the seventh day of his usurpation   After the death of Singeric, the free choice of the nation bestowed the Gothic sceptre on Walha, whose warlike and ambitious temper appeared in the beginning of his reign extremely hostile to the republic   He marched in arms from Barcelona to the shores of the Atlantic Ocean, which the ancients revered and dreaded as the boundary of the world   But, when he reached the southern promontory of Spain,[168] and, from the rock now covered by the fortress of Gibraltar, contemplated the neighbouring and fertile coast of Africa, Walha resumed the designs of conquest which had been interrupted by the death of Alaric.   The winds and waves again disappointed the enterprise of the Goths, and the minds of a superstitious people were deeply affected by the repeated disasters of storms and shipwrecks.   In this disposition, the successor of Adolphus no longer refused to listen to a Roman ambassador, whose proposals were enforced by the real, or supposed, approach of a numerous army under the conduct of the brave Constantius   A solemn treaty was stipulated and observed: Placidia was honourably restored to her brother, six hundred thousand measures of wheat were delivered to the hungry Goths;[169] and Wallia engaged to draw his sword in the service of the empire.   A bloody war was instantly excited among the Barbarians of Spain; and the contending princes are said to have addressed their letters, their ambassadors, and their hostages, to the throne of the Western emperor, exhorting him to remain a tranquil spectator of their contest, the events of which must be favourable to the

[167] The death of Adolphus was celebrated at Constantinople with illuminations and Circensian games   (See Chron Alexandrin)   It may seem doubtful whether the Greeks were actuated, on this occasion, by their hatred of the Barbarians or of the Latins

[168] Quod *Tartessiacis* avus hujus Vallia *terris*
Vandalicas turmas, et juncti Martis Alanos
Stravit, et occiduam texere cadavera *Calpen*
Sidon Apollinar in Panegyr. Anthem 363
p 300, edit Sirmond.

[169] This supply was very acceptable   the Goths were insulted by the Vandals of Spain with the epithet of *Truli*, because, in their extreme distress, they had given a piece of gold for a *trula*, or about half a pound of flour   Olympiod apud Phot. p 189   [A *trula* held somewhat less than ⅓rd of a pint]

Romans, by the mutual slaughter of their common enemies [170]
The Spanish war was obstinately supported, during three campaigns, with desperate valour and various success, and the
martial achievements of Wallia diffused through the empire the
superior renown of the Gothic hero   He exterminated the
Silingi, who had irretrievably ruined the elegant plenty of the
province of Bætica . He slew, in battle, the king of the Alani ;
and the remains of those Scythian wanderers who escaped from
the field, instead of choosing a new leader, humbly sought a
refuge under the standard of the Vandals, with whom they were
ever afterwards confounded.   The Vandals themselves and the
Suevi yielded to the efforts of the invincible Goths   The promiscuous multitude of Barbarians, whose retreat had been intercepted, were driven into the mountains of Gallicia , where they
still continued, in a narrow compass and on a barren soil, to
exercise their domestic and implacable hostilities.   In the pride
of victory, Wallia was faithful to his engagements : he restored
his Spanish conquests to the obedience of Honorius ; and the
tyranny of the Imperial officers soon reduced an oppressed
people to regret the time of their Barbarian servitude   While
the event of the war was still doubtful, the first advantages obtained by the arms of Wallia had encouraged the court of Ravenna
to decree the honours of a triumph to their feeble sovereign   He
entered Rome like the ancient conquerors of nations; and, if the
monuments of servile corruption had not long since met with
the fate which they deserved, we should probably find that a
crowd of poets and orators, of magistrates and bishops, applauded
the fortune, the wisdom, and the invincible courage, of the emperor Honorius.[171]

Such a triumph might have been justly claimed by the ally of
Rome, if Wallia, before he repassed the Pyrenees, had extirpated
the seeds of the Spanish war   His victorious Goths, forty-three
years after they had passed the Danube, were established, according to the faith of treaties, in the possession of the second
Aquitain . a maritime province between the Garonne and the

*Their estab
lishment in
Aquitain
A D 419*

---

[170] Orosius inserts a copy of these pretended letters   Tu cum omnibus pacem
habe, omniumque obsides accipe , nos nobis confligimus, nobis perimus, tibi vin-
cimus , immortalis vero quæstus erat Reipublicæ tuæ, si utrique pereamus   The
idea is just , but I cannot persuade myself that it was entertained, or expressed, by
the Barbarians

[171] Romam triumphans ingreditur, is the formal expression of Prosper's Chronicle
The facts which relate to the death of Adolphus, and the exploits of Wallia, are
related from Olympiodorus (apud Phot. p. 188 [26]), Orosius (l vii c 43, p 584-
587), Jornandes (de Rebus Geticis, c. 31, 32), and the Chronicles of Idatius and
Isidore

Loire, under the civil and ecclesiastical jurisdiction of Bourdeaux. That metropolis, advantageously situated for the trade of the ocean, was built in a regular and elegant form, and its numerous inhabitants were distinguished among the Gauls by their wealth, their learning, and the politeness of their manners. The adjacent province, which has been fondly compared to the garden of Eden, is blessed with a fruitful soil and a temperate climate the face of the country displayed the arts and the rewards of industry ; and the Goths, after their martial toils, luxuriously exhausted the rich vineyards of Aquitain [172] The Gothic limits were enlarged by the additional gift of some neighbouring dioceses , and the successors of Alaric fixed their royal residence at Toulouse, which included five populous quarters, or cities, within the spacious circuit of its walls About the same time, in the last years of the reign of Honorius, the Goths, the Burgundians, and the Franks obtained a permanent seat and dominion in the provinces of Gaul The liberal grant of the usurper Jovinus to his Burgundian allies was confirmed by the lawful emperor ; the lands of the First, or Upper, Germany were ceded to those formidable Barbarians , and they gradually occupied, either by conquest or treaty, the two provinces which still retain, with the titles of *Duchy* and of *County*, the national appellation of Burgundy [173] The Franks, the valiant and faithful allies of the Roman republic, were soon tempted to imitate the invaders, whom they had so bravely resisted Treves, the capital of Gaul, was pillaged by their lawless bands ; and the humble colony, which they so long maintained in the district of Toxandria, in Brabant, insensibly multiplied along the banks of the Meuse and Scheld, till their independent power filled the whole extent of the Second or Lower Germany These facts may be sufficiently justified by historic evidence ; but the foundation of the French monarchy by Pharamond, the conquests, the laws, and even the existence, of that hero, have been justly arraigned by the impartial severity of modern criticism.[174]

The Burgundians

[Augusta Treveror um = Trier = Trèves]

[172] Ausonius (de Claris Urbibus, p 257-262) celebrates Bourdeaux with the partial affection of a native See in Salvian (de Gubern Dei, p 228 Paris, 1608) a florid description of the provinces of Aquitain and Novempopulania

[173] Orosius (l vii c 32, p 550) commends the mildness and modesty of these Burgundians who treated their subjects of Gaul as their Christian brethren Mascou has illustrated the origin of their kingdom in the four first annotations at the end of his laborious History of the ancient Germans, vol ii p 555-572, of the English translation [For the ten Burgundies see Appendix i of Mr Bryce's Holy Roman Empire]

[174] See Mascou, l viii c 43, 44, 45 Except in a short and suspicious line of the Chronicle of Prosper (in tom. i p 638 [pseudo-Prosper, see Mommsen, Chron.

The ruin of the opulent provinces of Gaul may be dated from the establishment of these Barbarians, whose alliance was dangerous and oppressive, and who were capriciously impelled, by interest or passion, to violate the public peace. A heavy and partial ransom was imposed on the surviving provincials, who had escaped the calamities of war; the fairest and most fertile lands were assigned, to the rapacious strangers, for the use of their families, their slaves, and their cattle, and the trembling natives relinquished with a sigh the inheritance of their fathers Yet these domestic misfortunes, which are seldom the lot of a vanquished people, had been felt and inflicted by the Romans themselves, not only in the insolence of foreign conquest, but in the madness of civil discord The Triumvirs proscribed eighteen of the most flourishing colonies of Italy; and distributed their lands and houses to the veterans who revenged the death of Cæsar and oppressed the liberty of their country. Two poets, of unequal fame, have deplored, in similar circumstances, the loss of their patrimony: but the legionaries of Augustus appeared to have surpassed, in violence and injustice, the Barbarians who invaded Gaul under the reign of Honorius It was not without the utmost difficulty that Virgil escaped from the sword of the centurion who had usurped his farm in the neighbourhood of Mantua; [175] but Paulinus of Bourdeaux received a sum of money from his Gothic purchaser, which he accepted with pleasure and surprise; and, though it was much inferior to the real value of his estate, this act of rapine was disguised by some colours of moderation and equity [176] The odious name of conquerors, was softened into the mild and friendly appellation of the *guests*, of the Romans; and the Barbarians of Gaul, more especially the Goths, repeatedly declared that they were bound to the people by the ties of hospitality and to the emperor by the duty of

Min. 1. p 656]) the name of Pharamond is never mentioned before the seventh [8th] century. The author of the Gesta Francorum (in tom 11 p 543) suggests, probably enough, that the choice of Pharamond, or at least of a king, was recommended to the Franks by his father Marcomir, who was an exile in Tuscany

[175] O Lycida, vivi pervenimus advena nostri
(Quod nunquam veriti sumus) ut possessor agelli
Diceret Hæc mea sunt, veteres migrate coloni
Nunc victi tristes, &c

See the whole of the ninth Eclogue, with the useful Commentary of Servius Fifteen miles of the Mantuan territory were assigned to the veterans, with a reservation, in favour of the inhabitants, of three miles round the city Even in this favour they were cheated by Alfenus Varus, a famous lawyer, and one of the commissioners, who measured eight hundred paces of water and morass

[176] See the remarkable passage of the Eucharisticon of Paulinus, 575, apud Mascou, l viii c 42 [See Appendix 1]

allegiance and military service.   The title of Honorius and his successors, their laws, and their civil magistrates, were still respected in the provinces of Gaul of which they had resigned the possession to the Barbarian allies ; and the kings, who exercised a supreme and independent authority over their native subjects, ambitiously solicited the more honourable rank of master-generals of the Imperial armies.[177]   Such was the involuntary reverence which the Roman name still impressed on the minds of those warriors who had borne away in triumph the spoils of the Capitol.

Revolt of
Britain and
Armorica
A.D 409   Whilst Italy was ravaged by the Goths and a succession of feeble tyrants oppressed the provinces beyond the Alps, the British island separated itself from the body of the Roman empire   The regular forces, which guarded that remote province, had been gradually withdrawn , and Britain was abandoned, without defence, to the Saxon pirates and the savages of Ireland and Caledonia.   The Britons, reduced to this extremity, no longer relied on the tardy and doubtful aid of a declining monarch   They assembled in arms, repelled the invaders, and rejoiced in the important discovery of their own strength [178] Afflicted by similar calamities and actuated by the same spirit, the Armorican provinces (a name which comprehended the maritime countries of Gaul between the Seine and the Loire [179]) resolved to imitate the example of the neighbouring island. They expelled the Roman magistrates who acted under the authority of the usurper Constantine ; and a free government was established among a people who had so long been subject to the arbitrary will of a master   The independence of Britain and Armorica was soon confirmed by Honorius himself, the lawful emperor of the West, and the letters, by which he committed to the new states the care of their own safety, might be interpreted as an absolute and perpetual abdication of the exercise and rights of sovereignty.   This interpretation was, in some measure, justified by the event.   After the usurpers of Gaul had

---

[177] This important truth is established by the accuracy of Tillemont (Hist des Emp tom v p 641) and by the ingenuity of the Abbé Dubos (Hist de l'Etablissement de la Monarchie Françoise dans les Gaules, tom 1 p 259)

[178] Zosimus (l vi p 376, 383 [5 and 10]) relates in a few words the revolt of Britain and Armorica   Our antiquarians, even the great Cambden himself, have been betrayed into many gross errors by their imperfect knowledge of the history of the continent

[179] The limits of Armorica are defined by two national geographers, Messieurs de Valois and d'Anville, in their *Notitias* of Ancient Gaul   The word had been used in a more extensive, and was afterwards contracted to a much narrower, signification

successively fallen, the maritime provinces were restored to the empire. Yet their obedience was imperfect and precarious: the vain, inconstant, rebellious disposition of the people was incompatible either with freedom or servitude,[180] and Armorica, though it could not long maintain the form of a republic,[181] was agitated by frequent and destructive revolts. Britain was irrecoverably lost.[182] But, as the emperors wisely acquiesced in the independence of a remote province, the separation was not embittered by the reproach of tyranny or rebellion; and the claims of allegiance and protection were succeeded by the mutual and voluntary offices of national friendship.[183]

This revolution dissolved the artificial fabric of civil and military State of government; and the independent country, during a period of Britain. A D 409-449 forty years, till the descent of the Saxons, was ruled by the authority of the clergy, the nobles, and the municipal towns.[184] I. Zosimus, who alone has preserved the memory of this singular transaction, very accurately observes that the letters of Honorius were addressed to the *cities* of Britain [185] Under the protection of the Romans, ninety-two considerable towns had arisen in the several parts of that great province ; and, among these, thirty-three cities were distinguished above the rest by their superior

---

[180] Gens inter geminos nótissima clauditur amnes,
    Armoricana prius veteri cognomine dicta.
    Torva, ferox, ventosa, procax, incauta, rebellis
    Inconstans, disparque sibi novitatis amore ,
    Prodiga verborum, sed non et prodiga facti.
Erricus Monach. in Vit St Germani, l v apud Vales   Notit Galliarum, p 43. Valesius alleges several testimonies to confirm this character; to which I shall add the evidence of the presbyter Constantine (A D 488), who, in the life of St. Germain, calls the Armorican rebels mobilem et indisciplinatum populum   See the Historians of France, tom 1 p. 643

[181] I thought it necessary to enter my protest against this part of the system of the Abbé Dubos, which Montesquieu has so vigorously opposed   See Esprit des Loix, l. xxx. c. 24.

[182] Βρεταννίαν μέντοι Ῥωμαῖοι ἀνασωσασθαι οὐκετι εἶχον are the words of Procopius (de Bell Vandal l 1. c 2, p 181, Louvre edition) in a very important passage which has been too much neglected   Even Bede (Hist. Gent. Anglican. l 1. c. 12, p. 50, edit. Smith) acknowledges that the Romans finally left Britain in the reign of Honorius.   Yet our modern historians and antiquaries extend the term of their dominion , and there are some who allow only the interval of a few months between their departure and the arrival of the Saxons.

[183] Bede has not forgot the occasional aid of the legions against the Scots and Picts , and more authentic proof will hereafter be produced that the independent Britains raised 12,000 men for the service of the emperor Anthemius in Gaul

[184] I owe it to myself, and to historic truth, to declare that some *circumstances* in the paragraph are founded only on conjecture and analogy   The stubbornness of our language has sometimes forced me to deviate from the *conditional* into the *indicative* mood

[185] Πρὸς τὰς ἐν Βρεταννίᾳ πόλεις. Zosimus, l. vi. p 383 [10].

privileges and importance.[186]   Each of these cities, as in all the other provinces of the empire, formed a legal corporation, for the purpose of regulating their domestic policy ; and the powers of municipal government were distributed among annual magistrates, a select senate, and the assembly of the people, according to the original model of the Roman constitution.[187]   The management of a common revenue, the exercise of civil and criminal jurisdiction, and the habits of public counsel and command were inherent to these petty republics ; and, when they asserted their independence, the youth of the city and of the adjacent districts would naturally range themselves under the standard of the magistrate.   But the desire of obtaining the advantages, and of escaping the burdens, of political society is a perpetual and inexhaustible source of discord ; nor can it reasonably be presumed that the restoration of British freedom was exempt from tumult and faction.   The pre-eminence of birth and fortune must have been frequently violated by bold and popular citizens ; and the haughty nobles, who complained that they were become the subjects of their own servants,[188] would sometimes regret the reign of an arbitrary monarch.   II. The jurisdiction of each city over the adjacent country was supported by the patrimonial influence of the principal senators ; and the smaller towns, the villages, and the proprietors of land consulted their own safety by adhering to the shelter of these rising republics.   The sphere of their attraction was proportioned to the respective degrees of their wealth and populousness ; but the hereditary lords of ample possessions, who were not oppressed by the neighbourhood of any powerful city, aspired to the rank of independent princes, and boldly exercised the rights of peace and war.   The gardens and villas, which exhibited some faint imitation of Italian elegance, would soon be converted into strong castles, the refuge, in time of danger, of the adjacent country ; [189] the produce of the land was applied to purchase

[186] Two cities of Britain were *municipia*, nine *coloniae*, ten *Latii jure donatae*, twelve *stipendiariae* of eminent note   This detail is taken from Richard of Cirencester, de Situ Britanniæ, p 36, and, though it may not seem probable that he wrote from the Mss of a Roman general, he shews a genuine knowledge of antiquity, very extraordinary for a monk of the fourteenth century. [The treatise is a forgery of the 18th century, by one Bertram , cp. vol. i. Appendix 2]
[187] See Maffei, Verona Illustrata, part i l. v p 83-106
[188] Leges restituit, libertatemque reducit,
    Et servos famulis non sinit esse suis
                                    Itinerar Rutil. L i 215
[189] An inscription (apud Sirmond., Not ad Sidon. Apollinar. p. 59) describes a castle, cum muris et portis, tuitioni omnium, erected by Dardanus [Praet. Praef.

arms and horses, to maintain a military force of slaves, of peasants, and of licentious followers; and the chieftain might assume, within his own domain, the powers of a civil magistrate. Several of these British chiefs might be the genuine posterity of ancient kings; and many more would be tempted to adopt this honourable genealogy, and to vindicate their hereditary claims, which had been suspended by the usurpation of the Cæsars.[190] Their situation and their hopes would dispose them to affect the dress, the language, and the customs of their ancestors.   If the *princes* of Britain relapsed into barbarism, while the *cities* studiously preserved the laws and manners of Rome, the whole island must have been gradually divided by the distinction of two national parties; again broken into a thousand subdivisions of war and faction, by the various provocations of interest and resentment.   The public strength, instead of being united against a foreign enemy, was consumed in obscure and intestine quarrels; and the personal merit which had placed a successful leader at the head of his equals might enable him to subdue the freedom of some neighbouring cities, and to claim a rank among the *tyrants* [191] who infested Britain after the dissolution of the Roman government. III. The British church might be composed of thirty or forty bishops,[192] with an adequate proportion of the inferior clergy; and the want of riches (for they seem to have been poor [193]) would compel them to deserve the public esteem by a decent and exemplary behaviour.   The interest, as well as the temper, of the clergy was favourable to the peace and union of their distracted country; those salutary lessons might be

of Gaul in 409 and 411-13] on his own estate near Sisteron, in the second Narbonnese, and named by him Theopolis. [See C I L. xii 1524, the stone is on the road from Sister on to St Genies in Provence.   Dardanus is not stated to have given its name to the village or castle of Theopolis (now hamlet of Théon), but to have given it walls and gates]

[190] The establishment of their power would have been easy indeed, if we could adopt the impracticable scheme of a lively and learned antiquarian; who supposes that the British monarchs of the several tribes continued to reign, though with subordinate jurisdiction, from the time of Claudius to that of Honorius.   See Whitaker's History of Manchester, vol. i. p. 247-257.

[191] Ἀλλ᾿ οὖσα ὑπὸ τυράννοις ἀπ᾿ αὐτοῦ ἔμενε.   Procopius, de Bell. Vandal. l. i. c. 2, p. 181   Britannia fertilis provincia tyrannorum, was the expression of Jerom, in the year 415 (tom. ii p 255, ad Ctesiphont)   By the pilgrims, who resorted every year to the Holy Land, the Monk of Bethlem received the earliest and most accurate intelligence.

[192] See Bingham's Eccles. Antiquities, vol i. l. ix. c. 6, p. 394.   [A discreet and important paper on Early British Christianity by Mr. F. Haverfield appeared in Eng. Hist. Review, July, 1896.   The archæological evidence is mustered]

[193] It is reported of *three* British bishops who assisted at the council of Rimini, A D. 359, tam pauperes fuisse ut nihil [proprium] haberent   Sulpicius Severus, Hist. Sacra, l. ii. p. 420 [c. 41].   Some of their brethren, however, were in better circumstances.

frequently inculcated in their popular discourses; and the episcopal synods were the only councils that could pretend to the weight and authority of a national assembly. In such councils, where the princes and magistrates sat promiscuously with the bishops, the important affairs of the state, as well as of the church, might be freely debated; differences reconciled, alliances formed, contributions imposed, wise resolutions often concerted, and sometimes executed; and there is reason to believe that, in moments of extreme danger, a *Pendragon*, or Dictator, was elected by the general consent of the Britons. These pastoral cares, so worthy of the episcopal character, were interrupted, however, by zeal and superstition; and the British clergy incessantly laboured to eradicate the Pelagian heresy, which they abhorred as the peculiar disgrace of their native country.[194]

Assembly of the seven provinces of Gaul. A.D 418

It is somewhat remarkable, or rather it is extremely natural, that the revolt of Britain and Armorica should have introduced an appearance of liberty into the obedient provinces of Gaul. In a solemn edict,[195] filled with the strongest assurances of that paternal affection which princes so often express and so seldom feel, the emperor Honorius promulgated his intention of convening an annual assembly of the *seven provinces*: a name peculiarly appropriated to Aquitain, and the ancient Narbonnese, which had long since exchanged their Celtic rudeness for the useful and elegant arts of Italy.[196] Arles, the seat of government and commerce, was appointed for the place of the assembly; which regularly continued twenty-eight days, from the fifteenth of August to the thirteenth of September, of every year. It consisted of the Prætorian præfect of the Gauls; of seven provincial governors, one consular and six presidents; of the magistrates, and perhaps the bishops, of about sixty cities; and of a competent, though indefinite, number of the most honourable and opulent *possessors* of land, who might justly be considered as the representatives of their country. They were empowered to interpret and communicate the laws of their

[194] Consult Usher, de Antiq Eccles. Britannicar c. 8-12

[195] See the correct text of this edict, as published by Sirmond (Not. ad Sidon. Apolln. p 147) Hincmar of Rheims, who assigns a place to the *bishops*, had probably seen (in the ninth century) a more perfect copy Dubos, Hist. Critique de la Monarchie Françoise, tom. i. p 241-255

[196] It is evident from the *Notitia* that the seven provinces were the Viennensis, the maritime Alps, the first and second Narbonnese, Novempopulania, and the first and second Aquitain. In the room of the first Aquitain, the Abbé Dubos, on the authority of Hincmar, desires to introduce the first Lugdunensis, or Lyonnese. [The Seven Provinces are not to be confused with Septimania; cp. Appendix 23]

sovereign; to expose the grievances and wishes of their constituents; to moderate the excessive or unequal weight of taxes; and to deliberate on every subject of local or national importance, that could tend to the restoration of the peace and prosperity of the seven provinces. If such an institution, which gave the people an interest in their own government, had been universally established by Trajan or the Antonines, the seeds of public wisdom and virtue might have been cherished and propagated in the empire of Rome. The privileges of the subject would have secured the throne of the monarch; the abuses of an arbitrary administration might have been prevented, in some degree, or corrected, by the interposition of these representative assemblies; and the country would have been defended against a foreign enemy by the arms of natives and freemen. Under the mild and generous influence of liberty, the Roman empire might have remained invincible and immortal; or, if its excessive magnitude and the instability of human affairs had opposed such perpetual continuance, its vital and constituent members might have separately preserved their vigour and independence. But in the decline of the empire, when every principle of health and life had been exhausted, the tardy application of this partial remedy was incapable of producing any important or salutary effects. The Emperor Honorius expresses his surprise that he must compel the reluctant provinces to accept a privilege which they should ardently have solicited. A fine of three or even five pounds of gold was imposed on the absent representatives; who seem to have declined this imaginary gift of a free constitution, as the last and most cruel insult of their oppressors.[197]

[197] [Guizot, in his Histoire de la Civilisation en Europe (c 2), translates this edict. It interests him as an unsuccessful attempt at representative government and centralisation, which were contrary to the nature of a society in which the municipal spirit was predominant. Chateaubriand had already described the institution of the assembly as "un très grand fait historique qui annonce le passage à une nouvelle espèce de liberté". These and other writers have exaggerated the importance of the edict and ascribed to Honorius and his ministers ideas which were foreign to them. There was certainly no question of anything like a national representation. For recent discussions of the document, see Guiraud, Les assemblées provinciales dans l'Empire romain, and Carette, Les assemblées provinciales de la Gaule romaine. The main objects of Honorius were probably, as M. Carette says, p 249, to multiply the points of contact between the chief of his Gallic subjects and his governors; and to facilitate the administrative business of the provinces by centralisation. For diocesan, as distinct from provincial, concilia, see C. Th. 12, 12, 9.]

CHAPTER XXXII

Arcadius Emperor of the East—Administration and Disgrace of Eutropius—Revolt of Gainas—Persecution of St. John Chrysostom—Theodosius II. Emperor of the East—His Sister Pulcheria —His Wife Eudocia—The Persian War, and Division of Armenia

The empire of the East. A.D 395 1453

Reign of Arcadius A.D 395-408

THE division of the Roman world between the sons of Theodosius marks the final establishment of the empire of the East, which, from the reign of Arcadius to the taking of Constantinople by the Turks, subsisted one thousand and fifty-eight years, in a state of premature and perpetual decay. The sovereign of that empire assumed, and obstinately retained, the vain, and at length fictitious, title of Emperor of the Romans; and the hereditary appellations of Cæsar and Augustus continued to declare that he was the legitimate successor of the first of men, who had reigned over the first of nations. The palace of Constantinople rivalled, and perhaps excelled, the magnificence of Persia; and the eloquent sermons of St. Chrysostom[1] celebrate, while they condemn, the pompous luxury of the reign of Arcadius. "The emperor," says he, "wears on his head either a diadem or a crown of gold, decorated with precious stones of inestimable value. These ornaments and his purple garments are reserved for his sacred person alone; and his robes of silk are embroidered with the figures of golden dragons. His throne is of massy gold. Whenever he appears in public, he is surrounded by his courtiers, his guards, and his attendants. Their spears, their shields, their cuirasses, the bridles and trappings of their horses, have either the substance or the appearance of gold; and the large splendid boss in the midst of their shield is encircled with smaller bosses,

---

[1] Father Montfaucon, who, by the command of his Benedictine superiors, was compelled (see Longueruana, tom. i. p. 205) to execute the laborious edition of St. Chrysostom, in thirteen volumes in folio (Paris, 1738), amused himself with extracting, from that immense collection of morals, some curious *antiquities*, which illustrate the manners of the Theodosian age (see Chrysostom. Opera, tom. xiii p. 192-196, and his French Dissertation, in the Mémoires de l'Acad des Inscriptions, tom. xiii p. 474-490) [A. Puech has recently devoted a whole book to the same subject: St. Jean Chrysostome et les moeurs de son temps, 1891.]

which represent the shape of the human eye. The two mules
that draw the chariot of the monarch are perfectly white, and
shining all over with gold.   The chariot itself, of pure and solid
gold, attracts the admiration of the spectators, who contemplate
the purple curtains, the snowy carpet, the size of the precious
stones, and the resplendent plates of gold, that glitter as they
are agitated by the' motion of the carriage.   The Imperial
pictures are white on a blue ground; the emperor appears
seated on his throne, with his arms, his horses, and his guards
beside him; and his vanquished enemies in chains at his feet "
The successors of Constantine established their perpetual residence in the royal city which he had erected on the verge of
Europe and Asia   Inaccessible to the menaces of their enemies,
and perhaps to the complaints of their people, they received,
with each wind, the tributary productions of every climate;
while the impregnable strength of their capital continued for
ages to defy the hostile attempts of the Barbarians   Their
dominions were bounded by the Hadriatic and Tigris; and the
whole interval of twenty-five days' navigation, which separated
the extreme cold of Scythia from the torrid zone of Ethiopia,[2]
was comprehended within the limits of the empire of the East
The populous countries of that empire were the seat of art and
learning, of luxury and wealth ; and the inhabitants, who had
assumed the language and manners of Greeks, styled themselves,
with some appearance of truth, the most enlightened and
civilized portion of the human species.   The form of government was a pure and simple monarchy ; the name of the ROMAN
REPUBLIC, which so long preserved a faint tradition of freedom,
was confined to the Latin provinces; and the princes of Constantinople measured their greatness by the servile obedience of
their people.   They were ignorant how much this passive disposition enervates and degrades every faculty of the mind.   The
subjects, who had resigned their will to the absolute commands
of a master, were equally incapable of guarding their lives and
fortunes against the assaults of the Barbarians or of defending
their reason from the terrors of superstition.

[2] According to the loose reckoning that a ship could sail, with a fair wind,
1000 stadia, or 125 miles, in the revolution of a day and night , Diodorus Siculus
computes ten days from the Palus Mæotis to Rhodes, and four days from Rhodes
to Alexandria. The navigation of the Nile, from Alexandria to Syene, under the
tropic of Cancer, required, as it was against the stream, ten days more. Diodor.
Sicul tom. 1. 1 iii p. 200, edit. Wesseling   He might, without much impro-
priety, measure the extreme heat from the verge of the torrid zone , but he speaks
of the Mæotis in the 47th degree of northern latitude, as if it lay within the polar
circle. [On rates of sea travelling see Appendix 24]

Administra-
tion and
character of
Eutropius
A.D. 395-399
The first events of the reign of Arcadius and Honorius are so
intimately connected that the rebellion of the Goths and the
fall of Rufinus have already claimed a place in the history of the
West.   It has already been observed that Eutropius,[3] one of the
principal eunuchs of the palace of Constantinople, succeeded the
haughty minister whose ruin he had accomplished, and whose
vices he soon imitated   Every order of the state bowed to the
new favourite ; and their tame and obsequious submission encouraged him to insult the laws, and, what is still more difficult
and dangerous, the manners, of his country   Under the weakest
of the predecessors of Arcadius, the reign of the eunuchs had
been secret and almost invisible.   They insinuated themselves
into the confidence of the prince ; but their ostensible functions
were confined to the menial service of the wardrobe and Imperial bed-chamber.   They might direct, in a whisper, the public
counsels, and blast, by their malicious suggestions, the fame
and fortunes of the most illustrious citizens ; but they never
presumed to stand forward in the front of empire,[4] or to profane
the public honours of the state.   Eutropius was the first of his
artificial sex, who dared to assume the character of a Roman
magistrate and general.[5]   Sometimes in the presence of the blush-
ing senate he ascended the tribunal, to pronounce judgment or
to repeat elaborate harangues ; and sometimes appeared on
horseback, at the head of his troops, in the dress and armour of
a hero.   The disregard of custom and decency always betrays
a weak and ill-regulated mind ; nor does Eutropius seem to have

---

[3] Barthius, who adored his author with the blind superstition of a commentator,
gives the preference to the two books which Claudian composed against Eutropius,
above all his other productions (Baillet, Jugemens des Savans, tom iv p 227)
They are indeed a very elegant and spirited satire ; and would be more valuable
in an historical light, if the invective were less vague and more temperate.

[4] After lamenting the progress of the eunuchs in the Roman palace and defining
their proper functions, Claudian adds,

———A fronte recedant
Imperii   In Eutrop i 422

Yet it does not appear that the eunuch had assumed any of the efficient offices of
the empire, and he is styled only Præpositus sacri cubiculi, in the edict of his
banishment   See Cod Theod l iv tit xl leg 17

[5] Jamque oblita sui, nec sobria divitiis mens
In miseras leges hominumque negotia ludit
Judicat eunuchus. . . . .
Arma etiam violare parat   .

Claudian (i 229-270), with that mixture of indignation and humour which always
pleases in a satiric poet, describes the insolent folly of the eunuch, the disgrace of
the empire, and the joy of the Goths,

———Gaudet, cum viderit hostis,
Et sentit jam deesse viros

compensated for the folly of the design by any superior merit or ability in the execution   His former habits of life had not introduced him to the study of the laws or the exercises of the field; his awkward and unsuccessful attempts provoked the secret contempt of the spectators; the Goths expressed their wish that such a general might always command the armies of Rome; and the name of the minister was branded with ridicule, more pernicious perhaps than hatred to a public character. The subjects of Arcadius were exasperated by the recollection that this deformed and decrepid eunuch,[6] who so perversely mimicked the actions of a man, was born in the most abject condition of servitude; that, before he entered the Imperial palace, he had been successively sold and purchased by an hundred masters, who had exhausted his youthful strength in every mean and infamous office, and at length dismissed him, in his old age, to freedom and poverty.[7]   While these disgraceful stories were circulated, and perhaps exaggerated, in private conversations, the vanity of the favourite was flattered with the most extraordinary honours.   In the senate, in the capital, in the provinces, the statues of Eutropius were erected in brass or marble, decorated with the symbols of his civil and military virtues, and inscribed with the pompous title of the third founder of Constantinople.   He was promoted to the rank of *patrician*, which began to signify, in a popular and even legal acceptation, the father of the emperor; and the last year of the fourth century was polluted by the *consulship* of an eunuch and a slave. This strange and inexpiable prodigy[8] awakened, however, the prejudices of the Romans.   The effeminate consul was rejected

[6] The poet's lively description of his deformity (l. 110 125) is confirmed by the authentic testimony of Chrysostom (tom iii. p. 384, edit Montfaucon), who observes that, when the paint was washed away, the face of Eutropius appeared more ugly and wrinkled than that of an old woman.   Claudian remarks (i. 469), and the remark must have been founded on experience, that there was scarcely any interval between the youth and the decrepid age of an eunuch.

[7] Eutropius appears to have been a native of Armenia or Assyria.   His three services, which Claudian more particularly describes, were these   1. He spent many years as the catamite of Ptolemy, a groom or soldier of the Imperial stables. 2 Ptolemy gave him to the old general Arintheus, for whom he very skilfully exercised the profession of a pimp. 3 He was given, on her marriage, to the daughter of Arintheus, and the future consul was employed to comb her hair, to present the silver ewer, to wash and to fan his mistress in hot weather. See l. i. 31-137.

[8] Claudian (l. 1 in Eutrop. 1-22), after enumerating the various prodigies of monstrous birds, speaking animals, showers of blood or stones, double suns, &c , adds, with some exaggeration,——Omnia cesserunt eunucho consule monstra. The first book concludes with a noble speech of the goddess of Rome to her favourite Honorius, deprecating the *new* ignominy to which she was exposed.

by the West, as an indelible stain to the annals of the republic ; and, without invoking the shades of Brutus and Camillus, the colleague of Eutropius, a learned and respectable magistrate,[9] sufficiently represented the different maxims of the two administrations.

His venality and injustice

The bold and vigorous mind of Rufinus seems to have been actuated by a more sanguinary and revengeful spirit; but the avarice of the eunuch was not less insatiate than that of the præfect.[10] As long as he despoiled the oppressors who had enriched themselves with the plunder of the people, Eutropius might gratify his covetous disposition without much envy or injustice, but the progress of his rapine soon invaded the wealth which had been acquired by lawful inheritance or laudable industry. The usual methods of extortion were practised and improved, and Claudian has sketched a lively and original picture of the public auction of the state. "The impotence of the eunuch" (says that agreeable satirist) "has served only to stimulate his avarice : the same hand which, in his servile condition, was exercised in petty thefts, to unlock the coffers of his master, now grasps the riches of the world, and this infamous broker of the empire appreciates and divides the Roman provinces, from Mount Hæmus to the Tigris. One man, at the expense of his villa, is made proconsul of Asia; a second purchases Syria with his wife's jewels; and a third laments that he has exchanged his paternal estate for the government of Bithynia. In the anti-chamber of Eutropius, a large tablet is exposed to public view, which marks the respective prices of the provinces. The different value of Pontus, of Galatia, of Lydia, is accurately distinguished. Lycia may be obtained for so many thousand pieces of gold ; but the opulence of Phrygia will require a more considerable sum. The eunuch wishes to obliterate, by the general disgrace, his personal ignominy ; and, as he has been sold himself, he is desirous of selling the rest of mankind. In the eager contention, the balance, which contains the fate and fortunes of the province, often trembles on the beam ; and, till one of the scales is inclined, by a superior weight,

<hr/>

[9] Fl. Mallius Theodorus, whose civil honours, and philosophical works, have been celebrated by Claudian [who by the change of one letter has transformed Mallius into a member of the ancient Manlian family].

[10] Μεθύων δε ἤδη τῷ πλούτῳ, drunk with riches, is the forcible expression of Zosimus (l. v. p. 301 [10]) ; and the avarice of Eutropius is equally execrated in the Lexicon of Suidas and the Chronicle of Marcellinus. Chrysostom had often admonished the favourite, of the vanity and danger of immoderate wealth, tom. iii. p. 381.

the mind of the impartial judge remains in anxious suspense.[11]
Such " (continues the indignant poet) "are the fruits of Roman
valour, of the defeat of Antiochus, and of the triumph of Pompey." This venal prostitution of public honours secured the
impunity of *future* crimes; but the riches which Eutropius
derived from confiscation were *already* stained with injustice;
since it was decent to accuse, and to condemn, the proprietors of
the wealth which he was impatient to confiscate. Some noble
blood was shed by the hand of the executioner; and the most
inhospitable extremities of the empire were filled with innocent
and illustrious exiles. Among the generals and consuls of the Ruin of Abun-
East, Abundantius [12] had reason to dread the first effects of the dantius
resentment of Eutropius. He had been guilty of the unpardonable crime of introducing that abject slave to the palace of
Constantinople; and some degree of praise must be allowed to
a powerful and ungrateful favourite, who was satisfied with the
disgrace of his benefactor. Abundantius was stripped of his
ample fortunes by an Imperial rescript, and banished to Pityus
on the Euxine, the last frontier of the Roman world; where he
subsisted by the precarious mercy of the Barbarians, till he
could obtain, after the fall of Eutropius, a milder exile at Sidon
in Phœnicia. The destruction of Timasius [13] required a more of Timasius
serious and regular mode of attack. That great officer, the
master-general of the armies of Theodosius, had signalized his
valour by a decisive victory, which he obtained over the Goths
of Thessaly; but he was too prone, after the example of his
sovereign, to enjoy the luxury of peace, and to abandon his
confidence to wicked and designing flatterers. Timasius had
despised the public clamour, by promoting an infamous depend-

---

11 ————certantum sæpe duorum
    Diversum suspendit onus   cum pondere Judex
    Vergit, et in geminas nutat provincia lances.
Claudian (i. 192-209) so curiously distinguishes the circumstances of the sale that
they all seem to allude to particular anecdotes.

12 Claudian (i. 154-170) mentions the *guilt* and exile of Abundantius, nor
could he fail to quote the example of the artist who made the first trial of the
brazen bull which he presented to Phalaris. See Zosimus, l. v. p 302 [10]
Jerom, tom. i. p. 26 [ep. 60; Migne, i. 600]. The difference of place is easily
reconciled; but the decisive authority of Asterius of Amasia (Orat. iv p. 76 apud
Tillemont, Hist des Empereurs, tom v. p 435) must turn the scale in favour of
Pityus

13 Suidas (most probably, from the history of Eunapius) has given a very unfavourable picture of Timasius. The account of his accuser, the judges, trial, &c.
is perfectly agreeable to the practice of ancient and modern courts (See Zosimus,
l. v p 298, 299, 300 [9 *sqq*].) I am almost tempted to quote the romance of a
great master (Fielding's Works, vol. iv. p. 47, &c. 8vo edit.), which may be considered as the history of human nature.

ent to the command of a cohort; and he deserved to feel the
ingratitude of Bargus, who was secretly instigated by the favourite to accuse his patron of a treasonable conspiracy. The general
was arraigned before the tribunal of Arcadius himself; and
the principal eunuch stood by the side of the throne, to suggest
the questions and answers of his sovereign. But, as this form
of trial might be deemed partial and arbitrary, the farther
inquiry into the crimes of Timasius was delegated to Saturninus
and Procopius: the former of consular rank, the latter still
respected as the father-in-law of the emperor Valens. The
appearances of a fair and legal proceeding were maintained by
the blunt honesty of Procopius; and he yielded with reluctance
to the obsequious dexterity of his colleague, who pronounced
a sentence of condemnation against the unfortunate Timasius.
His immense riches were confiscated, in the name of the emperor, and for the benefit of the favourite; and he was doomed
to perpetual exile at Oasis, a solitary spot in the midst of the
sandy deserts of Libya.[14] Secluded from all human converse,
the master-general of the Roman armies was lost for ever to the
world; but the circumstances of his fate have been related in a
various and contradictory manner. It is insinuated that Eutropius dispatched a private order for his secret execution.[15] It
was reported that, in attempting to escape from Oasis, he perished
in the desert, of thirst and hunger; and that his dead body was
found on the sands of Libya.[16] It has been asserted with more
confidence that his son Syagrius, after successfully eluding the
pursuit of the agents and emissaries of the court, collected a
band of African robbers; that he rescued Timasius from the
place of his exile; and that both the father and son disappeared
from the knowledge of mankind.[17] But the ungrateful Bargus,
instead of being suffered to possess the reward of guilt, was
soon afterwards circumvented and destroyed by the more power-

[14] The great Oasis was one of the spots in the sands of Libya watered with
springs, and capable of producing wheat, barley, and palm-trees. It was about
three days' journey from north to south, about half a day in breadth, and at the
distance of about five days' march to the west of Abydus on the Nile. See
d'Anville, Description de l'Egypte, p. 186, 187, 188. The barren desert which
encompasses Oasis (Zosimus, l. v. p. 300) has suggested the idea of comparative
fertility, and even the epithet of the *happy island* (Herodot. lii. 26).

[15] The line of Claudian, in Eutrop. l. i. 180:

Marmaricus claris violatur cædibus Hammon,

evidently alludes to *his* persuasion of the death of Timasius.

[16] Sozomen, l. viii. c. 7. He speaks from report ὡς τινος ἐπυθόμην.

[17] Zosimus, l. v. p. 300 [9 *ad fin.*]. Yet he seems to suspect that this rumour
was spread by the friends of Eutropius.

ful villany of the minister himself; who retained sense and spirit enough to abhor the instrument of his own crimes.

The public hatred and the despair of individuals continually threatened, or seemed to threaten, the personal safety of Eutropius; as well as of the numerous adherents who were attached to his fortune and had been promoted by his venal favour. For their mutual defence, he contrived the safeguard of a law, which violated every principle of humanity and justice.[18] I. It is enacted, in the name and by the authority of Arcadius, that all those who shall conspire, either with subjects or with strangers, against the lives of any of the persons whom the emperor considers as the members of his own body, shall be punished with death and confiscation. This species of fictitious and metaphorical treason is extended to protect, not only the *illustrious* officers of the state and army, who are admitted into the sacred consistory, but likewise the principal domestics of the palace, the senators of Constantinople, the military commanders, and the civil magistrates of the provinces: a vague and indefinite list, which, under the successors of Constantine, included an obscure and numerous train of subordinate ministers. II. This extreme severity might perhaps be justified, had it been only directed to secure the representatives of the sovereign from any actual violence in the execution of their office. But the whole body of Imperial dependents claimed a privilege, or rather impunity, which screened them, in the loosest moments of their lives, from the hasty, perhaps the justifiable, resentment of their fellow-citizens; and, by a strange perversion of the laws, the same degree of guilt and punishment was applied to a private quarrel and to a deliberate conspiracy against the emperor and the empire. The edict of Arcadius most positively and most absurdly declares that in such cases of treason *thoughts* and *actions* ought to be punished with equal severity; that the knowledge of a mischievous intention, unless it be instantly revealed, becomes equally criminal with the intention itself;[10]

A cruel and unjust law of treason. A.D. 397, Sept 4

---

[18] See the Theodosian Code, l ix. tit 14, ad legem Corneliam de Sicariis, leg. 3, and the Code of Justinian, l ix tit viii ad legem Juliam de Majestate, leg. 5. The alteration of the *title*, from murder to treason, was an improvement of the subtle Tribonian. Godefroy, in a formal dissertation which he has inserted in his Commentary, illustrates this law of Arcadius, and explains all the difficult passages which had been perverted by the jurisconsults of the darker ages. See tom iii. p 88-111.

[19] Bartolus understands a simple and naked consciousness, without any sign of approbation or concurrence For this opinion, says Baldus, he is now roasting in hell. For my own part, continues the discreet Heineccius (Element Jur. Civil. l. iv. p 411), I must approve the theory of Bartolus, but in practice I should

and that those rash men who shall presume to solicit the pardon of traitors shall themselves be branded with public and perpetual infamy.   III. "With regard to the sons of the traitors" (continues the emperor), "although they ought to share the punishment, since they will probably imitate the guilt, of their parents, yet, by the special effect of our Imperial lenity, we grant them their lives ; but, at the same time, we declare them incapable of inheriting, either on the father's or on the mother's side, or of receiving any gift or legacy from the testament either of kinsmen or of strangers. Stigmatized with hereditary infamy, excluded from the hopes of honours or fortune, let them endure the pangs of poverty and contempt, till they shall consider life as a calamity, and death as a comfort and relief " In such words, so well adapted to insult the feelings of mankind, did the emperor, or rather his favourite eunuch, applaud the moderation of a law which transferred the same unjust and inhuman penalties to the children of all those who had seconded, or who had not disclosed, these fictitious conspiracies   Some of the noblest regulations of Roman jurisprudence have been suffered to expire; but this edict, a convenient and forcible engine of ministerial tyranny, was carefully inserted in the codes of Theodosius and Justinian , and the same maxims have been revived in modern ages, to protect the electors of Germany and the cardinals of the church of Rome.[20]

Rebellion of
Tribigild.
A.D 399   Yet these sanguinary laws, which spread terror among a disarmed and dispirited people, were of too weak a texture to restrain the bold enterprise of Tribigild [21] the Ostrogoth. The colony of that warlike nation, which had been planted by Theodosius in one of the most fertile districts of Phrygia,[22] impatiently compared the slow returns of laborious husbandry

incline to the sentiments of Baldus. Yet Bartolus was gravely quoted by the lawyers of Cardinal Richelieu , and Eutropius was indirectly guilty of the murder of the virtuous de Thou.

[20] Godefroy, tom III. p. 89.   It is, however, suspected that this law, so repugnant to the maxims of Germanic freedom, has been surreptitiously added to the golden bull.

[21] A copious and circumstantial narrative (which he might have reserved for more important events) is bestowed by Zosimus (l. v p 304-312 [13 *sqq.*]) on the revolt of Tribigild and Gainas. See likewise Socrates, l vi. c. 6, and Sozomen, l viii c. 4.   The second book of Claudian against Eutropius is a fine, though imperfect, piece of history.

[22] Claudian (in Eutrop l. ii. 237-250) very accurately observes that the ancient name and nation of the Phrygians extended very far on every side, till their limits were contracted by the colonies of the Bithynians of Thrace, of the Greeks, and at last of the Gauls.   His description (ii. 257-272) of the fertility of Phrygia, and of the four rivers that produce gold, is just and picturesque.

with the successful rapine and liberal rewards of Alaric ; and their leader resented, as a personal affront, his own ungracious reception in the palace of Constantinople. A soft and wealthy province, in the heart of the empire, was astonished by the sound of war ; and the faithful vassal, who had been disregarded or oppressed, was again respected, as soon as he resumed the hostile character of a Barbarian. The vineyards and fruitful fields, between the rapid Marsyas and the winding Mæander,[23] were consumed with fire ; the decayed walls of the city crumbled into dust, at the first stroke of an enemy ; the trembling inhabitants escaped from a bloody massacre to the shores of the Hellespont ; and a considerable part of Asia Minor was desolated by the rebellion of Tribigild. His rapid progress was checked by the resistance of the peasants of Pamphylia ; and the Ostrogoths, attacked in a narrow pass, between the city of Selgæ,[24] a deep morass, and the craggy cliffs of Mount Taurus, were defeated with the loss of their bravest troops. But the spirit of their chief was not daunted by misfortune ; and his army was continually recruited by swarms of Barbarians and outlaws, who were desirous of exercising the profession of robbery, under the more honourable names of war and conquest. The rumours of the success of Tribigild might for some time be suppressed by fear or disguised by flattery ; yet they gradually alarmed both the court and the capital. Every misfortune was exaggerated in dark and doubtful hints ; and the future designs of the rebels became the subject of anxious conjecture. Whenever Tribigild advanced into the inland country, the Romans were inclined to suppose that he meditated the passage of Mount Taurus and the invasion of Syria. If he descended towards the sea, they imputed, and perhaps suggested, to the Gothic chief the more dangerous project of arming a fleet in the harbours of Ionia, and of extending his depredations along the maritime coast, from the mouth of the Nile to the port of Constantinople. The approach of danger, and the obstinacy of Tribigild, who refused all terms of accommodation, compelled Eutropius to summon a council of

[23] Xenophon, Anabasis, l. i. p. 11, 12, edit. Hutchinson, Strabo, l. xii. p. 865, edit. Amstel [8, 15], Q. Curt. l. iii c. 1. Claudian compares the junction of the Marsyas and Mæander to that of the Saône and the Rhone ; with this difference, however, that the smaller of the Phrygian rivers is not accelerated, but retarded, by the larger.

[24] Selgæ, a colony of the Lacedæmonians, had formerly numbered twenty thousand citizens ; but in the age of Zosimus it was reduced to a πολίχνη, or small town. See Cellarius, Geograph. Antiq. tom. ii. p. 117.

war.[25] After claiming for himself the privilege of a veteran soldier, the eunuch entrusted the guard of Thrace and the Hellespont to Gainas the Goth; and the command of the Asiatic army to his favourite Leo two generals who differently, but effectually, promoted the cause of the rebels. Leo,[26] who, from the bulk of his body and the dulness of his mind, was surnamed the Ajax of the East, had deserted his original trade of a wool comber, to exercise, with much less skill and success, the military profession, and his uncertain operations were capriciously framed and executed, with an ignorance of real difficulties and a timorous neglect of every favourable opportunity. The rashness of the Ostrogoths had drawn them into a disadvantageous position between the rivers Melas and Eurymedon, where they were almost besieged by the peasants of Pamphylia; but the arrival of an Imperial army, instead of completing their destruction, afforded the means of safety and victory. Tribigild surprised the unguarded camp of the Romans, in the darkness of the night; seduced the faith of the greater part of the Barbarian auxiliaries; and dissipated, without much effort, the troops which had been corrupted by the relaxation of discipline and the luxury of the capital. The discontent of Gainas, who had so boldly contrived and executed the death of Rufinus, was irritated by the fortune of his unworthy successor, he accused his own dishonourable patience under the servile reign of an eunuch; and the ambitious Goth was convicted, at least in the public opinion, of secretly fomenting the revolt of Tribigild, with whom he was connected by a domestic, as well as by a national, alliance [27] When Gainas passed the Hellespont, to unite under his standard the remains of the Asiatic troops, he skilfully adapted his motions to the wishes of the Ostrogoths; abandoning, by his retreat, the country which they desired to invade; or facilitating, by his approach, the desertion of the Barbarian auxiliaries. To the Imperial court he repeatedly magnified the valour, the genius, the inexhaustible resources

[25] The council of Eutropius, in Claudian, may be compared to that of Domitian in the fourth satire of Juvenal The principal members of the former were: juvenes protervi lascivique senes; one of them had been a cook, a second a woolcomber The language of their original profession exposes their assumed dignity; and their trifling conversation about tragedies, dancers, &c is made still more ridiculous by the importance of the debate.

[26] Claudian (l ii 376-461) has branded him with infamy, and Zosimus, in more temperate language, confirms his reproaches. L v. p. 305 [14]

[27] The *conspiracy* of Gainas and Tribigild, which is attested by the Greek historian, had not reached the ears of Claudian, who attributes the revolt of the Ostrogoth to his own *martial* spirit and the advice of his wife.

of Tribigild; confessed his own inability to prosecute the war; and extorted the permission of negotiating with his invincible adversary. The conditions of peace were dictated by the haughty rebel, and the peremptory demand of the head of Eutropius revealed the author and the design of this hostile conspiracy.

The bold satirist, who has indulged his discontent by the partial and passionate censure of the Christian emperors, violates the dignity rather than the truth of history, by comparing the son of Theodosius to one of those harmless and simple animals who scarcely feel that they are the property of their shepherd. Two passions, however, fear and conjugal affection, awakened the languid soul of Arcadius: he was terrified by the threats of a victorious Barbarian; and he yielded to the tender eloquence of his wife Eudoxia, who, with a flood of artificial tears, presenting her infant children to their father, implored his justice for some real or imaginary insult which she imputed to the audacious eunuch [28] The emperor's hand was directed to sign the condemnation of Eutropius; the magic spell, which during four years had bound the prince and the people, was instantly dissolved, and the acclamations that so lately hailed the merit and fortune of the favourite were converted into the clamours of the soldiers and the people, who reproached his crimes and pressed his immediate execution. In this hour of distress and despair his only refuge was in the sanctuary of the church, whose privileges he had wisely, or profanely, attempted to circumscribe; and the most eloquent of the saints, John Chrysostom, enjoyed the triumph of protecting a prostrate minister, whose choice had raised him to the ecclesiastical throne of Constantinople. The archbishop, ascending the pulpit of the cathedral, that he might be distinctly seen and heard by an innumerable crowd of either sex and of every age, pronounced a seasonable and pathetic discourse on the forgiveness of injuries and the instability of human greatness. The agonies of the pale and affrighted wretch, who lay grovelling under the table of the altar, exhibited a solemn and instructive spectacle; and the orator, who was afterwards accused of insulting the misfortunes of Eutropius, laboured to excite the contempt, that he might assuage the fury, of the

(margin note:) Fall of Eutropius A.D. 399

---

[28] This anecdote, which Philostorgius alone has preserved (l. xi c 6, and Gothofred. Dissertat p 451-456), is curious and important, since it connects the revolt of the Goths with the secret intrigues of the palace.

people [29] The powers of humanity, of superstition, and of eloquence, prevailed. The empress Eudoxia was restrained, by her own prejudices, or by those of her subjects, from violating the sanctuary of the church ; and Eutropius was tempted to capitulate, by the milder arts of persuasion, and by an oath that his life should be spared.[30] Careless of the dignity of their sovereign, the new ministers of the palace immediately published an edict, to declare that his late favourite had disgraced the names of consul and patrician, to abolish his statues, to confiscate his wealth, and to inflict a perpetual exile in the island of Cyprus [31] A despicable and decrepid eunuch could no longer alarm the fears of his enemies ; nor was he capable of enjoying what yet remained, the comforts of peace, of solitude, and of a happy climate. But their implacable revenge still envied him the last moments of a miserable life, and Eutropius had no sooner touched the shores of Cyprus than he was hastily recalled. The vain hope of eluding, by a change of place, the obligation of an oath engaged the empress to transfer the scene of his trial and execution from Constantinople to the adjacent suburb of Chalcedon. The consul Aurelian pronounced the sentence ; and the motives of that sentence expose the jurisprudence of a despotic government. The crimes which Eutropius had committed against the people might have justified his death ; but he was found guilty of harnessing to his chariot the *sacred* animals, who, from their breed or colour, were reserved for the use of the emperor alone.[32]

[29] See the Homily of Chrysostom, tom. iii p 381-386, of which the exordium is particularly beautiful. Socrates, l vi c 5, Sozomen, l. viii c. 7. Montfaucon (in his Life of Chrysostom, tom xiii p 135) too hastily supposes that Tribigild was *actually* in Constantinople ; and that he commanded the soldiers who were ordered to seize Eutropius. Even Claudian, a Pagan poet (Præfat. ad l. ii. in Eutrop p 27), has mentioned the flight of the eunuch to the sanctuary.
> Suppliciterque pias humilis prostratus ad aras
> Mitigat iratas voce tremente nurus

[30] Chrysostom, in another homily (tom iii p 386), affects to declare that Eutropius would not have been taken, had he not deserted the church Zosimus (l v. p. 313 [18]), on the contrary, pretends that his enemies forced him ἐξαρπάσαντες αὐτόν from the sanctuary Yet the promise is an evidence of some treaty, and the strong assurance of Claudian (Præfat ad l. ii 46),
> Sed tamen exemplo non feriere tuo,
may be considered as an evidence of some promise.

[31] Cod Theod. l ix. tit xi leg 14 [*leg.* tit. xl. leg. 17]. The date of that law (Jan 17, A D. 399) is erroneous and corrupt ; since the fall of Eutropius could not happen till the autumn of the same year See Tillemont, Hist des Empereurs, tom v p. 780.

[32] Zosimus, l. v. p. 313 [18] Philostorgius, l vi c. 6. [Not using imperial animals (βοσκήμασιν), but imperial decorations (κοσμήμασιν). See note of Valesius, on the passage of Philostorgius (Migne, vol. 65, p. 600).]

While this domestic revolution was transacted, Gainas [33] Conspiracy and fall of Gainas A.D. openly revolted from his allegiance; united his forces, at Thyatira 400 in Lydia, with those of Tribigild; and still maintained his superior ascendant over the rebellious leader of the Ostrogoths. The confederate armies advanced, without resistance, to the streights of the Hellespont and the Bosphorus; and Arcadius was instructed to prevent the loss of his Asiatic dominions by resigning his authority and his person to the faith of the Barbarians. The church of the holy martyr Euphemia, situate on a lofty eminence near Chalcedon,[34] was chosen for the place of the interview. Gainas bowed, with reverence, at the feet of the emperor, whilst he required the sacrifice of Aurelian and Saturninus, two ministers of consular rank; and their naked necks were exposed, by the haughty rebel, to the edge of the sword, till he condescended to grant them a precarious and disgraceful respite. The Goths, according to the terms of the agreement, were immediately transported from Asia into Europe; and their victorious chief, who accepted the title of master-general of the Roman armies, soon filled Constantinople with his troops, and distributed among his dependents the honours and rewards of the empire. In his early youth, Gainas had passed the Danube as a suppliant and a fugitive; his elevation had been the work of valour and fortune; and his indiscreet, or perfidious, conduct was the cause of his rapid downfall. Notwithstanding the vigorous opposition of the archbishop, he importunately claimed, for his Arian sectaries, the possession of a peculiar church; and the pride of the Catholics was offended by the public toleration of heresy.[35] Every quarter of Constantinople was filled with tumult and disorder; and the Barbarians gazed with such ardour on the rich shops of the jewellers, and the tables of the bankers, which were covered with gold and silver, that it was judged prudent to remove those dangerous tempta-

[33] Zosimus (l. v. p. 313-323 [18 *sqq.*]), Socrates (l vi. c. 4), Sozomen (l viii. c 4), and Theodoret (l. v c. 32, 33) represent, though with some various circumstances, the conspiracy, defeat, and death of Gainas   [Tribigild's death is only mentioned by Philostorgius (xi. 8) · " having crossed over to Thrace he perishes soon after "]

[34] Ὁσίας Εὐφημίας μαρτύριον, is the expression of Zosimus himself (l. v. p 314 [18]), who inadvertently uses the fashionable language of the Christians. Evagrius describes (l ii c 3) the situation, architecture, relics, and miracles of that celebrated church, in which the general council of Chalcedon was afterwards held [See Appendix 27]

[35] The pious remonstrances of Chrysostom, which do not appear in his own writings, are strongly urged by Theodoret, but his insinuation that they were successful is disproved by facts   Tillemont (Hist. des Empereurs, tom. v. 383) has discovered that the emperor, to satisfy the rapacious demands of Gainas, melted the plate of the church of the Apostles.

tions from their sight.   They resented the injurious precaution ;
and some alarming attempts were made, during the night, to
attack and destroy with fire the Imperial palace.[36]   In this state
of mutual and suspicious hostility, the guards and the people
of Constantinople shut the gates, and rose in arms to prevent, or
to punish, the conspiracy of the Goths.   During the absence of
Gainas, his troops were surprised and oppressed , seven thousand
Barbarians perished in this bloody massacre.   In the fury of the
pursuit, the catholics uncovered the roof, and continued to throw
down flaming logs of wood, till they overwhelmed their adversaries, who had retreated to the church or conventicle of
the Arians.   Gainas was either innocent of the design or too
confident of his success ; he was astonished by the intelligence
that the flower of his army had been ingloriously destroyed ;
that he himself was declared a public enemy ; and that his
countryman, Fravitta, a brave and loyal confederate, had
assumed the management of the war by sea and land   The
enterprises of the rebel against the cities of Thrace were
encountered by a firm and well-ordered defence ; his hungry
soldiers were soon reduced to the grass that grew on the margin
of the fortifications ; and Gainas, who vainly regretted the wealth
and luxury of Asia, embraced a desperate resolution of forcing
the passage of the Hellespont.   He was destitute of vessels ; but
the woods of the Chersonesus afforded materials for rafts, and his
intrepid Barbarians did not refuse to trust themselves to the
waves.   But Fravitta attentively watched the progress of their
undertaking.   As soon as they had gained the middle of the
stream, the Roman galleys,[37] impelled by the full force of oars,
of the current, and of the favourable wind, rushed forwards in
compact order and with irresistible weight , and the Hellespont was covered with the fragments of the Gothic shipwreck.
After the destruction of his hopes, and the loss of many thousands
of his bravest soldiers, Gainas, who could no longer aspire to
govern, or to subdue, the Romans, determined to resume the

July 20

Dec 23

[36] The ecclesiastical historians, who sometimes guide, and sometimes follow,
the public opinion, most confidently assert that the palace of Constantinople was
guarded by legions of angels

[37] Zosimus (l. v. p 319 [20, cp Eunap. fi. 81]) mentions these galleys by the
name of *Liburnians*, and observes that they were as swift (without explaining the
difference between them) as the vessels with fifty oars ; but that they were far
inferior in speed to the *triremes*, which had been long disused.   Yet he reasonably
concludes, from the testimony of Polybius, that galleys of a still larger size had
been constructed in the Punic wars.   Since the establishment of the Roman
empire over the Mediterranean, the useless art of building large ships of war had
probably been neglected and at length forgotten.

independence of a savage life. A light and active body of Barbarian horse, disengaged from their infantry and baggage, might perform, in eight or ten days, a march of three hundred miles from the Hellespont to the Danube; [38] the garrisons of that important frontier had been gradually annihilated; the river, in the month of December, would be deeply frozen; and the unbounded prospect of Scythia was opened to the ambition of Gainas. This design was secretly communicated to the national troops, who devoted themselves to the fortunes of their leader; and, before the signal of departure was given, a great number of provincial auxiliaries, whom he suspected of an attachment to their native country, were perfidiously massacred. The Goths advanced, by rapid marches, through the plains of Thrace; and they were soon delivered from the fear of a pursuit by the vanity of Fravitta, who, instead of extinguishing the war, hastened to enjoy the popular applause and to assume the peaceful honours of the consulship. But a formidable ally appeared in arms to vindicate the majesty of the empire and to guard the peace and liberty of Scythia. [39] The superior forces of Uldin, king of the Huns, opposed the progress of Gainas; an hostile and ruined country prohibited his retreat; he disdained to capitulate; and, after repeatedly attempting to cut his way through the ranks of the enemy, he was slain, with his desperate followers, in the field of battle. Eleven days after the naval victory of the Hellespont, the head of Gainas, the inestimable gift of the conqueror, was received at Constantinople with the most liberal expressions of gratitude, and the public deliverance was celebrated by festivals and illuminations. The triumphs of Arcadius became the subject of epic poems; [40] and the monarch, no longer oppressed by any hostile terrors, resigned himself to the mild and absolute dominion of his wife, the fair and artful

A D 401, January 3

[38] Chishul (Travels, p. 61-63, 72-76) proceeded from Gallipoli, through Hadrianople, to the Danube, in about fifteen days. He was in the train of an English ambassador, whose baggage consisted of seventy-one waggons. That learned traveller has the merit of tracing a curious and unfrequented route.

[39] The narrative of Zosimus, who actually leads Gainas beyond the Danube, must be corrected by the testimony of Socrates and Sozomen, that he was killed in *Thrace;* and, by the precise and authentic dates of the Alexandrian, or Paschal, Chronicle, p 307 The naval victory of the Hellespont is fixed to the month Apellæus, the tenth of the calends of January (December 23); the head of Gainas was brought to Constantinople the third of the nones of January (January 3), in the month Audynæus. [These dates imply too short an interval; the second is probably wrong; and we may accept from Marcellinus the notice that Gainas was killed early in February]

[40] Eusebius Scholasticus acquired much fame by his poem on the Gothic war, in which he had served Near forty years afterwards, Ammonius recited another poem on the same subject, in the presence of Theodosius. See Socrates, l. vi. c. 6.

Eudoxia ; who has sullied her fame by the persecution of St. John Chrysostom.

Election and merit of Chry-sostom A.D. 398, Feb 26 [397] After the death of the indolent Nectarius, the successor of Gregory Nazianzen, the church of Constantinople was distracted by the ambition of rival candidates, who were not ashamed to solicit, with gold or flattery, the suffrage of the people, or of the favourite   On this occasion, Eutropius seems to have deviated from his ordinary maxims ; and his uncorrupted judgment was determined only by the superior merit of a stranger.   In a late journey into the East, he had admired the sermons of John, a native and presbyter of Antioch, whose name has been dis-tinguished by the epithet of Chrysostom, or the Golden Mouth.[41] A private order was dispatched to the governor of Syria ; and, as the people might be unwilling to resign their favourite preacher, he was transported with speed and secrecy, in a post-chariot, from Antioch to Constantinople.   The unanimous and unsolicited consent of the court, the clergy, and the people, ratified the choice of the minister ; and, both as a saint and as an orator, the new archbishop surpassed the sanguine expecta-tions of the public.   Born of a noble and opulent family, in the capital of Syria, Chrysostom had been educated by the care of a tender mother, under the tuition of the most skilful masters. He studied the art of rhetoric in the school of Libanius, and that celebrated sophist, who soon discovered the talents of his disciple, ingenuously confessed that John would have deserved to succeed him, had he not been stolen away by the Christians. His piety soon disposed him to receive the sacrament of baptism ; to renounce the lucrative and honourable profession of the law ; and to bury himself in the adjacent desert, where he subdued the lusts of the flesh by an austere penance of six years.   His

[41] The sixth book of Socrates, the eighth of Sozomen, and the fifth of Theodoret, afford curious and authentic materials for the life of John Chrysostom   Besides those general historians, I have taken for my guides the four principal biographers of the saint.   1 The author of a partial and passionate Vindication of the Archbishop of Constantinople, composed in the form of a dialogue, and under the name of his zealous partizan Palladius, bishop of Helenopolis (Tillemont, Mém. Ecclés tom xi. p 500-533).   It is inserted among the works of Chrysostom, tom. xiii. p. 1-90, edit. Montfaucon.   2   The moderate Erasmus (tom iii epist. MCL. p. 1331-1347, edit Ludg Bat).   His vivacity and good sense were his own , his errors, in the uncultivated state of ecclesiastical antiquity, were almost irrevitable   3 The learned Tillemont (Mém. Ecclésiastiques, tom. xi. p. 1-405, 547-626, &c. &c) ; who compiles the lives of the saints with incredible patience and religious accuracy.   He has minutely searched the voluminous works of Chrysostom himself   4. Father Montfaucon, who has perused those works with the curious diligence of an editor, discovered several new homilies, and again reviewed and composed the life of Chrysostom (Opera Chrysostom, tom. xiii. p. 91-177). [For modern works see Appendix 1.]

infirmities compelled him to return to the society of mankind; and the authority of Meletius devoted his talents to the service of the church; but in the midst of his family, and afterwards on the archiepiscopal throne, Chrysostom still persevered in the practice of the monastic virtues. The ample revenues, which his predecessors had consumed in pomp and luxury, he diligently applied to the establishment of hospitals; and the multitudes, who were supported by his charity, preferred the eloquent and edifying discourses of their archbishop to the amusements of the theatre or the circus. The monuments of that eloquence, which was admired near twenty years at Antioch and Constantinople, have been carefully preserved, and the possession of near one thousand sermons, or homilies, has authorized the critics [42] of succeeding times to appreciate the genuine merit of Chrysostom. They unanimously attribute to the Christian orator the free command of an elegant and copious language; the judgment to conceal the advantages which he derived from the knowledge of rhetoric and philosophy; an inexhaustible fund of metaphors and similitudes, of ideas and images, to vary and illustrate the most familiar topics; the happy art of engaging the passions in the service of virtue; and of exposing the folly as well as the turpitude of vice, almost with the truth and spirit of a dramatic representation.

The pastoral labours of the archbishop of Constantinople provoked, and gradually united against him, two sorts of enemies; the aspiring clergy, who envied his success, and the obstinate sinners, who were offended by his reproofs. When Chrysostom thundered, from the pulpit of St. Sophia, against the degeneracy of the Christians, his shafts were spent among the crowd, without wounding, or even marking, the character of any individual. When he declaimed against the peculiar vices of the rich, poverty might obtain a transient consolation from his invectives; but the guilty were still sheltered by their numbers, and the reproach itself was dignified by some ideas of superiority and enjoyment. But, as the pyramid rose towards the summit, it insensibly diminished to a point; and the magistrates, the ministers, the favourite eunuchs, the ladies of the court, [43] the empress *His administration and defects A.D. 398-403*

---

[42] As I am *almost* a stranger to the voluminous sermons of Chrysostom, I have given my confidence to the two most judicious and moderate of the ecclesiastical critics, Erasmus (tom. iii. p. 1344) and Dupin (Bibliotheque Ecclésiastique, tom. iii. p 38), yet the good taste of the former is sometimes vitiated by an excessive love of antiquity, and the good sense of the latter is always restrained by prudential considerations.

[43] The females of Constantinople distinguished themselves by their enmity or

Eudoxia herself, had a much larger share of guilt to divide among a smaller proportion of criminals. The personal applications of the audience were anticipated, or confirmed, by the testimony of their own conscience; and the intrepid preacher assumed the dangerous right of exposing both the offence and the offender to the public abhorrence.   The secret resentment of the court encouraged the discontent of the clergy and monks of Constantinople, who were too hastily reformed by the fervent zeal of their archbishop.   He had condemned, from the pulpit, the domestic females of the clergy of Constantinople, who, under the name of servants or sisters, afforded a perpetual occasion either of sin or of scandal   The silent and solitary ascetics who had secluded themselves from the world were intitled to the warmest approbation of Chrysostom ; but he despised and stigmatized, as the disgrace of their holy profession, the crowd of degenerate monks, who, from some unworthy motives of pleasure or profit, so frequently infested the streets of the capital   To the voice of persuasion the archbishop was obliged to add the terrors of authority ; and his ardour, in the exercise of ecclesiastical jurisdiction, was not always exempt from passion ; nor was it always guided by prudence.   Chrysostom was naturally of a choleric disposition.[44]   Although he struggled, according to the precepts of the gospel, to love his private enemies, he indulged himself in the privilege of hating the enemies of God and of the church ; and his sentiments were sometimes delivered with too much energy of countenance and expression.   He still maintained, from some considerations of health or abstinence, his former habits of taking his repasts alone ; and this inhospitable custom,[45] which his enemies imputed to pride, contributed,

their attachment to Chrysostom.   Three noble and opulent widows, Marsa, Castricia, and Eugraphia, were the leaders of the persecution (Pallad Dialog. tom xiii p 14)   It was impossible that they should forgive a preacher who reproached their affectation to conceal, by the ornaments of dress, their age and ughness (Pallad p 27)   Olympias, by equal zeal, displayed in a more pious cause, has obtained the title of saint.   See Tillemont, Mém Ecclés tom. xi. 416-440.

[44] Sozomen, and more especially Socrates, have defined the real character of Chrysostom with a temperate and impartial freedom, very offensive to his blind admirers.   Those historians lived in the next generation, when party violence was abated, and had conversed with many persons intimately acquainted with the virtues and imperfections of the saint.

[45] Palladius (tom. xiii. p 40, &c) very seriously defends the archbishop : 1 He never tasted wine.   2 The weakness of his stomach required a peculiar diet. 3 Business, or study, or devotion, often kept him fasting till sunset   4 He detested the noise and levity of great dinners   5 He saved the expense for the use of the poor   6 He was apprehensive, in a capital like Constantinople, of the envy and reproach of partial invitations.

at least, to nourish the infirmity of a morose and unsocial humour. Separated from that familiar intercourse which facilitates the knowledge and the dispatch of business, he reposed an unsuspecting confidence in his deacon Serapion; and seldom applied his speculative knowledge of human nature to the particular characters either of his dependents or of his equals. Conscious of the purity of his intentions, and perhaps of the superiority of his genius, the archbishop of Constantinople extended the jurisdiction of the Imperial city that he might enlarge the sphere of his pastoral labours; and the conduct which the profane imputed to an ambitious motive appeared to Chrysostom himself in the light of a sacred and indispensable duty.   In his visitation through the Asiatic provinces, he deposed thirteen bishops of Lydia and Phrygia; and indiscreetly declared that 'a deep corruption of simony and licentiousness had infected the whole episcopal order.[46] If those bishops were innocent, such a rash and unjust condemnation must excite a well-grounded discontent.   If they were guilty, the numerous associates of their guilt would soon discover that their own safety depended on the ruin of the archbishop; whom they studied to represent as the tyrant of the Eastern church.

This ecclesiastical conspiracy was managed by Theophilus,[47] archbishop of Alexandria, an active and ambitious prelate, who displayed the fruits of rapine in monuments of ostentation.   His national dislike to the rising greatness of a city which degraded him from the second to the third rank in the Christian world was exasperated by some personal disputes with Chrysostom himself.[48] By the private invitation of the empress, Theophilus landed at Constantinople, with a stout body of Egyptian mariners, to encounter the populace; and a train of attendant bishops, to secure, by their voices, the majority of a synod.   The synod [49] was convened in the suburb of Chalcedon, surnamed the *Oak*,

Chrysostom is persecuted by the empress Eudoxia.
A.D. 403

[46] Chrysostom declares his free opinion (tom IV hom III in Act. Apostol p. 29) that the number of bishops who might be saved bore a very small proportion to those who would be damned.

[47] See Tillemont, Mém Ecclés. tom XI. p. 441-500.

[48] I have purposely omitted the controversy which arose among the monks of Egypt concerning Origenism and Anthropomorphism; the dissimulation and violence of Theophilus, his artful management of the simplicity of Epiphanius, the persecution and flight of the *long*, or tall, brothers, the ambiguous support which they received at Constantinople from Chrysostom, &c. &c.

[49] Photius (p. 53-60) has preserved the original acts of the synod of the Oak [Mansi, Concil. III p. 1148]; which destroy the false assertion [of Palladius; see Mansi, Concil. III. 1153] that Chrysostom was condemned by no more than thirty-six bishops, of whom twenty-nine were Egyptians. Forty-five bishops subscribed his sentence. See Tillemont, Mém. Ecclés tom XI. p. 595.

where Rufinus had erected a stately church and monastery, and their proceedings were continued during fourteen days, or sessions. A bishop and a deacon accused the archbishop of Constantinople ; but the frivolous or improbable nature of the forty-seven articles which they presented against him may justly be considered as a fair and unexceptionable panegyric. Four successive summons were signified to Chrysostom, but he still refused to trust either his person or his reputation in the hands of his implacable enemies, who, prudently declining the examination of any particular charges, condemned his contumacious disobedience, and hastily pronounced a sentence of deposition. The synod of the *Oak* immediately addressed the emperor to ratify and execute their judgment, and charitably insinuated that the penalties of treason might be inflicted on the audacious preacher who had reviled, under the name of Jezebel, the empress Eudoxia herself. The archbishop was rudely arrested, and conducted through the city, by one of the Imperial messengers, who landed him, after a short navigation, near the entrance of the Euxine ; from whence, before the expiration of two days, he was gloriously recalled.

Popular tumults a Constantinople

The first astonishment of his faithful people had been mute and passive ; they suddenly rose with unanimous and irresistible fury Theophilus escaped ; but the promiscuous crowd of monks and Egyptian mariners were slaughtered without pity in the streets of Constantinople.[50] A seasonable earthquake justified the interposition of heaven , the torrent of sedition rolled forwards to the gates of the palace ; and the empress, agitated by fear or remorse, threw herself at the feet of Arcadius, and confessed that the public safety could be purchased only by the restoration of Chrysostom. The Bosphorus was covered with innumerable vessels ; the shores of Europe and Asia were profusely illuminated ; and the acclamations of a victorious people accompanied, from the port to the cathedral, the triumph of the archbishop; who, too easily, consented to resume the exercise of his functions, before his sentence had been legally reversed by the authority of an ecclesiastical synod. Ignorant or careless of the impending danger, Chrysostom indulged his zeal, or per-

[50] Palladius owns (p 30) that, if the people of Constantinople had found Theophilus, they would certainly have thrown him into the sea. Socrates mentions (l vi c. 17) a battle between the mob and the sailors of Alexandria in which many wounds were given and some lives were lost. The massacre of the monks is observed only by the Pagan Zosimus (l v p 324 [23]), who acknowledges that Chrysostom had a singular talent to lead the illiterate multitude ἦν γὰρ ὁ ἄνθρωπος ἄλογον ὄχλον ὑπαγαγέσθαι δεινός,

haps his resentment ; declaimed with peculiar asperity against *female* vices ; and condemned the profane honours which were addressed almost in the precincts of St. Sophia, to the statue of the empress.   His imprudence tempted his enemies to inflame the haughty spirit of Eudoxia by reporting, or perhaps inventing, the famous exordium of a sermon : " Herodias is again furious ; Herodias again dances ; she once more requires the head of John : " an insolent allusion, which, as a woman and a sovereign, it was impossible for her to forgive.[51]   The short interval of a perfidious truce was employed to concert more effectual measures for the disgrace and ruin of the archbishop.   A numerous council of the Eastern prelates, who were guided from a distance by the advice of Theophilus, confirmed the validity, without examining the justice, of the former sentence ; and a detachment of Barbarian troops was introduced into the city, to suppress the emotions of the people.   On the vigil of Easter, the solemn administration of baptism was rudely interrupted by the soldiers, who alarmed the modesty of the naked catechumens, and violated, by their presence, the awful mysteries of the Christian worship.   Arsacius occupied the church of St. Sophia and the archiepiscopal throne.   The catholics retreated to the baths of Constantine, and afterwards to the fields ; where they were still pursued and insulted by the guards, the bishops, and the magistrates.   The fatal day of the second and final exile of Chrysostom was marked by the conflagration of the cathedral, of the senate house, and of the adjacent buildings ; and this calamity was imputed, without proof but not without probability, to the despair of a persecuted faction.[52]

Cicero might claim some merit, if his voluntary banishment preserved the peace of the republic ;[53] but the submission of Chrysostom was the indispensable duty of a Christian and a subject.   Instead of listening to his humble prayer that he might be permitted to reside at Cyzicus or Nicomedia, the inflexible empress assigned for his exile the remote and desolate town of Cucusus, among the ridges of Mount Taurus, in the Lesser Armenia.

Exile of Chrysostom A D 404, June 20

---

[51] See Socrates, l. vi c. 18.   Sozomen, l. viii. c. 20   Zosimus (l. v p 324, 327 [23, 24]) mentions, in general terms, his invectives against Eudoxia.   The homily, which begins with those famous words, is rejected as spurious.   Montfaucon, tom xiii. p 151   Tillemont, Mém Ecclés tom. xi. p. 603.

[52] We might naturally expect such a charge from Zosimus (l. v. p. 327 [24]), but it is remarkable enough that it should be confirmed by Socrates, l vi. c 18, and the Paschal Chronicle, p 307   [Cp Cod. Th. 16, 2, 37]

[53] He displays those specious motives (Post Reditum, c. 13, 14) in the language of an orator and a politician

A secret hope was entertained that the archbishop might perish in a difficult and dangerous march of seventy days in the heat of summer through the provinces of Asia Minor, where he was continually threatened by the hostile attacks of the Isaurians and the more implacable fury of the monks   Yet Chrysostom arrived in safety at the place of his confinement ; and the three years which he spent at Cucusus and the neighbouring town of Arabissus were the last and most glorious of his life.   His character was consecrated by absence and persecution , the faults of his administration were no longer remembered ; but every tongue repeated the praises of his genius and virtue, and the respectful attention of the Christian world was fixed on a desert spot among the mountains of Taurus.   From that solitude the archbishop, whose active mind was invigorated by misfortunes, maintained a strict and frequent correspondence [54] with the most distant provinces, exhorted the separate congregation of his faithful adherents to persevere in their allegiance ; urged the destruction of the temples of Phœnicia, and the extirpation of heresy in the isle of Cyprus ; extended his pastoral care to the missions of Persia and Scythia , negotiated, by his ambassadors, with the Roman pontiff and the emperor Honorius ; and boldly appealed, from a partial synod, to the supreme tribunal of a free and general council.   The mind of the illustrious exile was still independent ; but his captive body was exposed to the revenge of the oppressors, who continued to abuse the name and authority of Arcadius.[55]   An order was dispatched for the instant removal of Chrysostom to the extreme desert of Pityus : and his guards so faithfully obeyed their cruel instructions that, before he reached the sea-coast of the Euxine, he expired at Comana, in Pontus, in the sixtieth year of his age. The succeeding generation acknowledged his innocence and merit. The archbishops of the East, who might blush that their predecessors

His death.
A.D 407,
September 14

---

[54] Two hundred and forty-two of the epistles of Chrysostom are still extant (Opera, tom. iii p 528-736)   They are addressed to a great variety of persons, and show a firmness of mind much superior to that of Cicero in his exile.   The fourteenth epistle contains a curious narrative of the dangers of his journey

[55] After the exile of Chrysostom, Theophilus published an *enormous* and *horrible* volume against him, in which he perpetually repeats the polite expressions of hostem humanitatis, sacrilegorum principem, immundum dæmonem , he affirms that John Chrysostom had delivered his soul to be adulterated by the devil, and wishes that some farther punishment, adequate (if possible) to the magnitude of his crimes, may be inflicted on him.   St. Jerom, at the report of his friend Theophilus, translated this edifying performance from Greek into Latin   See Facundus Herman Defens. pro iii Capitul l. vi. c. 5, published by Sirmond, Opera, tom ii p 595, 596, 597.

had been the enemies of Chrysostom, were gradually disposed, by the firmness of the Roman pontiff, to restore the honours of that venerable name.[56] At the pious solicitation of the clergy and people of Constantinople, his relics, thirty years after his death, were transported from their obscure sepulchre to the royal city.[57] The emperor Theodosius advanced to receive them as far as Chalcedon; and, falling prostrate on the coffin, implored, in the name of his guilty parents, Arcadius and Eudoxia, the forgiveness of the injured saint.[58]

His relics transported to Constantinople A D 438, January 27

Yet a reasonable doubt may be entertained, whether any stain of hereditary guilt could be derived from Arcadius to his successor. Eudoxia was a young and beautiful woman, who indulged her passions and despised her husband; count John enjoyed, at least, the familiar confidence of the empress; and the public named him as the real father of Theodosius the younger.[59] The birth of a son was accepted, however, by the pious husband, as an event the most fortunate and honourable to himself, to his family, and to the eastern world; and the royal infant, by an unprecedented favour, was invested with the titles of Cæsar and Augustus. In less than four years afterwards, Eudoxia, in the bloom of youth, was destroyed by the consequences of a miscarriage; and this untimely death confounded the prophecy of a holy bishop,[60] who, amidst the universal joy, had ventured

The death of Arcadius A D 408, May 1

[56] His name was inserted by his successor Atticus in the Diptychs of the church of Constantinople, A.D. 418. Ten years afterwards he was revered as a saint. Cyril, who inherited the place, and the passions, of his uncle, Theophilus, yielded with much reluctance. See Facund. Hermian l. iv. c 1. Tillemont, Mém. Ecclés. tom. xiv. p. 277-283.

[57] Socrates, l. vii c 45. Theodoret, l v c. 36 This event reconciled the Joannites, who had hitherto refused to acknowledge his successors During his lifetime the Joannites were respected by the catholics as the true and orthodox communion of Constantinople. Their obstinacy gradually drove them to the brink of schism.

[58] According to some accounts (Baronius, Annal. Eccles. A.D. 438, No. 9, 10) the emperor was forced to send a letter of invitation and excuses before the body of the ceremonious saint could be moved from Comana

[59] Zosimus, l. v, p 315 [18]. The chastity of an empress should not be impeached without producing a witness; but it is astonishing that the witness should write and live under a prince whose legitimacy he dared to attack. We must suppose that his history was a party libel, privately read and circulated by the Pagans. [For date of Zosimus see above, vol ii. p. 538] Tillemont (Hist des Empereurs, tom. v. p. 782) is not averse to brand the reputation of Eudoxia.

[60] Porphyry of Gaza. His zeal was transported by the order which he had obtained for the destruction of eight Pagan temples of that city. See the curious details of his life (Baronius, A D. 401, No 17-51), originally written in Greek, or perhaps in Syriac, by a monk, one of his favourite deacons. [The Greek text was first published by Haupt in the Abhandlungen of the Berlin Academy, 1874; and it has been re-edited by the Soc Philol Bonnensis Sodales, 1895. For an account of the visit of Porphyry to Constantinople, see Bury, Later Roman Empire, i. p. 200 sqq.]

to foretell that she should behold the long and auspicious reign of her glorious son   The catholics applauded the justice of heaven, which avenged the persecution of St. Chrysostom , and perhaps the emperor was the only person who sincerely bewailed the loss of the haughty and rapacious Eudoxia.   Such a domestic misfortune afflicted *him* more deeply than the public calamities of the East ;[61] the licentious excursions, from Pontus to Palestine, of the Isaurian robbers, whose impunity accused the weakness of the government ; and the earthquakes, the conflagrations, the famine, and the flights of locusts,[62] which the popular discontent was equally disposed to attribute to the incapacity of the monarch.   At length, in the thirty-first year of his age, after a reign (if we may abuse that word) of thirteen years, three months, and fifteen days, Arcadius expired in the palace of Constantinople.   It is impossible to delineate his character ; since, in a period very copiously furnished with historical materials, it has not been possible to remark one action that properly belongs to the son of the great Theodosius.

His supposed testament   The historian Procopius [63] has indeed illuminated the mind of the dying emperor with a ray of human prudence or celestial wisdom. Arcadius considered, with anxious foresight, the helpless condition of his son Theodosius, who was no more than seven years of age, the dangerous factions of a minority, and the aspiring spirit of Jezdegerd, the Persian monarch   Instead of tempting the allegiance of an ambitious subject by the participation of supreme power, he boldly appealed to the magnanimity of a king ; and placed, by a solemn testament, the sceptre of the East in the hands of Jezdegerd himself.   The royal guardian accepted and discharged this honourable trust with unexampled fidelity ; and the infancy of Theodosius was protected by the arms and councils of Persia.   Such is the singular narrative of Procopius ; and his veracity is not disputed by Agathias,[64] while he presumes to dissent from his judgment and to arraign the wisdom of a Christian emperor, who so rashly, though so fortu-

[61] Philostorg. l xi c 8, and Godefroy, Dissertat p. 457

[62] Jerom (tom. vi p 73, 76) describes, in lively colours, the regular and destructive march of the locusts, which spread a dark cloud, between heaven and earth, over the land of Palestine.   Seasonable winds scattered them, partly into the Dead Sea, and partly into the Mediterranean.

[63] Procopius, de Bell Persic l i c. 2, p 8, edit Louvre.

[64] Agathias, l iv p 136, 137[c. 26].   Although he confesses the prevalence of the tradition, he asserts that Procopius was the first who had committed it to writing Tillemont (Hist. des Empereurs, tom vi p. 597) argues very sensibly on the merits of this fable.   His criticism was not warped by any ecclesiastical authority : both Procopius and Agathias are half Pagans.   [The whole tone of Agathias in regard to the story is sceptical.]

nately, committed his son and his dominions to the unknown
faith of a stranger, a rival, and a heathen. At the distance of one
hundred and fifty years, this political question might be debated
in the court of Justinian; but a prudent historian will refuse to
examine the *propriety*, till he has ascertained the *truth*, of the
testament of Arcadius. As it stands without a parallel in the
history of the world, we may justly require that it should be
attested by the positive and unanimous evidence of contemporaries. The strange novelty of the event, which excites our
distrust, must have attracted their notice; and their universal
silence annihilates the vain tradition of the succeeding age.

The maxims of Roman jurisprudence, if they could fairly be Administration of Anthe-
mius A D
408 415
transferred from private property to public dominion, would
have adjudged to the emperor Honorius the guardianship of his
nephew, till he had attained, at least, the fourteenth year of his
age. But the weakness of Honorius and the calamities of his
reign disqualified him from prosecuting this natural claim; and
such was the absolute separation of the two monarchies, both in
interest and affection, that Constantinople would have obeyed
with less reluctance the orders of the Persian, than those of the
Italian, court. Under a prince whose weakness is disguised by
the external signs of manhood and discretion the most worthless
favourites may secretly dispute the empire of the palace, and
dictate to submissive provinces the commands of a master whom
they direct and despise. But the ministers of a child who is
incapable of arming them with the sanction of the royal name
must acquire and exercise an independent authority. The great
officers of the state and army, who had been appointed before
the death of Arcadius, formed an aristocracy, which might have
inspired them with the idea of a free republic; and the government of the eastern empire was fortunately assumed by the
præfect Anthemius,[65] who obtained, by his superior abilities, a
lasting ascendant over the minds of his equals. The safety of
the young emperor proved the merit and integrity of Anthemius;
and his prudent firmness sustained the force and reputation of
an infant reign Uldin, with a formidable host of Barbarians,
was encamped in the heart of Thrace: he proudly rejected all
terms of accommodation; and, pointing to the rising sun,

[65] Socr l. vii c i   Anthemius was the grandson of Philip, one of the ministers of Constantius, and the grandfather of the emperor Anthemius. After his
return from the Persian embassy, he was appointed consul and Prætorian præfect
of the East, in the year 405; and held the præfecture about ten years See his
honours and praises in Godefroy, Cod. Theod. tom vi p 350. Tillemont, Hist.
des Emp. tom vi p. i, &c.

declared to the Roman ambassadors that the course of that planet should alone terminate the conquests of the Huns. But the desertion of his confederates, who were privately convinced of the justice and liberality of the Imperial ministers, obliged Uldin to repass the Danube ; the tribe of the Scyrri, which composed his rear-guard, was almost extirpated ; and many thousand captives were dispersed to cultivate, with servile labour, the fields of Asia.[66] In the midst of the public triumph, Constantinople was protected by a strong enclosure of new and more extensive walls ; the same vigilant care was applied to restore the fortifications of the Illyrian cities ; and a plan was judiciously conceived, which, in the space of seven years, would have secured the command of the Danube, by establishing on that river a perpetual fleet of two hundred and fifty armed vessels [67]

Character and administration of Pulcheria. A D 414-453

But the Romans had so long been accustomed to the authority of a monarch, that the first, even among the females, of the Imperial family who displayed any courage or capacity was permitted to ascend the vacant throne of Theodosius. His sister Pulcheria,[68] who was only two years older than himself, received at the age of sixteen the title of *Augusta ;* and, though her favour might be sometimes clouded by caprice or intrigue, she continued to govern the Eastern empire near forty years ; during the long minority of her brother, and, after his death, in her own name, and in the name of Marcian, her nominal husband. From a motive, either of prudence or religion, she embraced a life of celibacy ; and, notwithstanding some aspersions on the chastity of Pulcheria,[69] this resolution, which she communicated to her sisters Arcadia and Marina, was celebrated by the Christian world, as the sublime effort of heroic piety. In the presence of the clergy and people, the three daughters of Arcadius [70] dedicated their virginity to God ; and the obligation of their solemn vow was inscribed on a tablet of gold and gems ; which

[66] Sozomen, l. ix c. 5 He saw some Scyrri at work near Mount Olympus, in Bithynia, and cherished the vain hope that those captives were the last of the nation

[67] Cod Theod l. vii tit xvii l. xv. tit. i. leg 49

[68] Sozomen has filled three chapters with a magnificent panegyric of Pulcheria (L ix. c. 1, 2, 3) ; and Tillemont (Mémoires Eccles tom xv. p. 171-184) has dedicated a separate article to the honour of St. Pulcheria, virgin and empress.

[69] Suidas (Excerpta, p. 68 in Script. Byzant) pretends, on the credit of the Nestorians, that Pulcheria was exasperated against their founder, because he censured her connexion with the beautiful Paulinus and her incest with her brother Theodosius

[70] See Ducange, Famil. Byzantin. p. 70 Flaccilla, the eldest daughter, either died before Arcadius, or, if she lived to the year 431 (Marcellin. Chron.), some defect of mind or body must have excluded her from the honours of her rank.

they publicly offered in the great church of Constantinople.
Their palace was converted into a monastery; and all males,
except the guides of their conscience, the saints who had forgotten the distinction of sexes, were scrupulously excluded from
the holy threshold.   Pulcheria, her two sisters, and a chosen train
of favourite damsels formed a religious community   they renounced the vanity of dress; interrupted, by frequent fasts, their
simple and frugal diet, allotted a portion of their time to works
of embroidery; and devoted several hours of the day and night to
the exercises of prayer and psalmody   The piety of a Christian
virgin was adorned by the zeal and liberality of an empress.
Ecclesiastical history describes the splendid churches which
were built at the expense of Pulcheria, in all the provinces of the
East; her charitable foundations for the benefit of strangers and
the poor; the ample donations which she assigned for the
perpetual maintenance of monastic societies, and the active
severity with which she laboured to suppress the opposite
heresies of Nestorius and Eutyches   Such virtues were supposed
to deserve the peculiar favour of the Deity; and the relics of
martyrs, as well as the knowledge of future events, were communicated in visions and revelations to the Imperial saint [71]   Yet
the devotion of Pulcheria never diverted her indefatigable
attention from temporal affairs; and she alone, among all the
descendants of the great Theodosius, appears to have inherited
any share of his manly spirit and abilities.   The elegant and
familiar use which she had acquired both of the Greek and
Latin languages was readily applied to the various occasions of
speaking or writing on public business; her deliberations were
maturely weighed; her actions were prompt and decisive, and,
while she moved, without noise or ostentation, the wheel of
government, she discreetly attributed to the genius of the
emperor the long tranquillity of his reign.   In the last years of
his peaceful life Europe was indeed afflicted by the arms of
Attila; but the more extensive provinces of Asia still continued
to enjoy a profound and permanent repose.   Theodosius the
younger was never reduced to the disgraceful necessity of

*   [71] She was admonished, by repeated dreams, of the place where the relics of the
forty martyrs had been buried   The ground had successively belonged to the
house and garden of a woman of Constantinople, to a monastery of Macedonian
monks, and to a church of St Thyrsus, erected by Cæsarius, who was consul, A D
397; and the memory of the relics was almost obliterated   Notwithstanding the
charitable wishes of Dr Jortin (Remarks, tom iv p 234) it is not easy to acquit
Pulcheria of some share in the pious fraud, which must have been transacted when
she has more than five and thirty years of age

encountering and punishing a rebellious subject ; and, since we cannot applaud the vigour, some praise may be due to the mildness and prosperity, of the administration of Pulcheria.

Education and character of Theodosius the younger

The Roman world was deeply interested in the education of its master. A regular course of study and exercise was judiciously instituted , of the military exercises of riding and shooting with the bow ; of the liberal studies of grammar, rhetoric, and philosophy , the most skilful masters of the East ambitiously solicited the attention of their royal pupil ; and several noble youths were introduced into the palace, to animate his diligence by the emulation of friendship   Pulcheria alone discharged the important task of instructing her brother in the arts of government , but her precepts may countenance some suspicion of the extent of her capacity or of the purity of her intentions   She taught him to maintain a grave and majestic deportment ; to walk, to hold his robes, to seat himself on his throne, in a manner worthy of a great prince ; to abstain from laughter ; to listen with condescension ; to return suitable answers ; to assume, by turns, a serious or a placid countenance , in a word, to represent with grace and dignity the external figure of a Roman emperor   But Theodosius [72] was never excited to support the weight and glory of an illustrious name , and, instead of aspiring to imitate his ancestors, he degenerated (if we may presume to measure the degrees of incapacity) below the weakness of his father and his uncle.   Arcadius and Honorius had been assisted by the guardian care of a parent whose lessons were enforced by his authority and example.   But the unfortunate prince who is born in the purple must remain a stranger to the voice of truth , and the son of Arcadius was condemned to pass his perpetual infancy, encompassed only by a servile train of women and eunuchs   The ample leisure, which he acquired by neglecting the essential duties of his high office, was filled by idle amusements and unprofitable studies   Hunting was the only active pursuit that could tempt him beyond the limits of the palace , but he most assiduously laboured, sometimes by the light of a midnight lamp,

[72] There is a remarkable difference between the two ecclesiastical historians, who in general bear so close a resemblance   Sozomen (l ix c 1) ascribes to Pulcheria the government of the empire and the education of her brother , whom he scarcely condescends to praise   Socrates, though he affected disclaims all hopes of favour or fame, composes an elaborate panegyric on the emperor, and cautiously suppresses the merits of his sister (l vii c 22, 42)   Philostorgius (l vii c 7) expresses the influence of Pulcheria in gentle and courtly language, τας βασιλικας σημειωσεις υπηρετουμενη και διευθυνουσα   Suidas (Excerpt p 53) gives a true character of Theodosius, and I have followed the example of Tillemont (tom vi p 25) in borrowing some strokes from the modern Greeks

in the mechanic occupations of painting and carving ; and the elegance with which he transcribed religious books entitled the Roman emperor to the singular epithet of *Calligraphes*, or a fair writer   Separated from the world by an impenetrable veil, Theodosius trusted the persons whom he loved , he loved those who were accustomed to amuse and flatter his indolence ; and, as he never perused the papers that were presented for the royal signature, the acts of injustice the most repugnant to his character were frequently perpetrated in his name.   The emperor himself was chaste, temperate, liberal, and merciful , but these qualities, which can only deserve the name of virtues when they are supported by courage and regulated by discretion, were seldom beneficial, and they sometimes proved mischievous, to mankind   His mind, enervated by a royal education, was oppressed and degraded by abject superstition ; he fasted, he sung psalms, he blindly accepted the miracles and doctrines with which his faith was continually nourished.   Theodosius devoutly worshipped the dead and living saints of the Catholic church ; and he once refused to eat, till an insolent monk, who had cast an excommunication on his sovereign, condescended to heal the spiritual wound which he had inflicted.[73]

The story of a fair and virtuous maiden, exalted from a private condition to the Imperial throne, might be deemed an incredible romance, if such a romance had not been verified in the marriage of Theodosius.   The celebrated Athenais [74] was educated by her father Leontius in the religion and sciences of the Greeks ; and so advantageous was the opinion which the Athenian philosopher entertained of his contemporaries, that he divided his patrimony between his two sons, bequeathing to his daughter a small legacy of one hundred pieces of gold, in the lively confidence that her beauty and merit would be a sufficient portion.   The jealousy and avarice of her brothers

Character and adventures of the empress Eudocia A D 421-460

[73] Theodoret, l v c 37   The bishop of Cyrrhus, one of the first men of his age for his learning and piety, applauds the obedience of Theodosius to the divine laws

[74] Socrates (l vii c 21) mentions her name (Athenais, the daughter of Leontius, an Athenian sophist), her baptism, marriage, and poetical genius   The most ancient account of her history is in John Malala (part ii p 20, 21, edit Venet 1743), and in the Paschal Chronicle (p 311, 312)   Those authors had probably seen original pictures of the empress Eudocia   The modern Greeks, Zonaras, Cedrenus, &c have displayed the love, rather than the talent, of fiction   From Nicephorus, indeed, I have ventured to assume her age   The writer of a romance would not have *imagined* that Athenais was near twenty-eight years old when she inflamed the heart of a young emperor   [Her story has been told agreeably by Gregorovius in his Athenais (ed 3, 1892).   The same empress is the subject of monograph by W. Wiegand . Eudocia, 1871

soon compelled Athenais to seek a refuge at Constantinople; and with some hopes, either of justice or favour, to throw herself at the feet of Pulcheria That sagacious princess listened to her eloquent complaint ; and secretly destined the daughter of the philosopher Leontius for the future wife of the emperor of the East, who had now attained the twentieth year of his age   She easily excited the curiosity of her brother by an interesting picture of the charms of Athenais ; large eyes, a well-proportioned nose, a fair complexion, golden locks, a slender person, a graceful demeanour, an understanding improved by study, and a virtue tried by distress   Theodosius, concealed behind a curtain in the apartment of his sister, was permitted to behold the Athenian virgin , the modest youth immediately declared his pure and honourable love , and the royal nuptials were celebrated amidst the acclamations of the capital and the provinces.   Athenais, who was easily persuaded to renounce the errors of Paganism, received at her baptism the Christian name of Eudocia ; but the cautious Pulcheria withheld the title of Augusta, till the wife of Theodosius had approved her fruitfulness by the birth of a daughter, who espoused, fifteen years afterwards, the emperor of the West.   The brothers of Eudocia obeyed, with some anxiety, her Imperial summons ; but, as she could easily forgive their fortunate unkindness, she indulged the tenderness, or perhaps the vanity, of a sister by promoting them to the rank of consuls and præfects   In the luxury of the palace, she still cultivated those ingenuous arts which had contributed to her greatness ; and wisely dedicated her talents to the honour of religion and of her husband.   Eudocia composed a poetical paraphrase of the first eight books of the old Testament, and of the prophecies of Daniel and Zachariah ; a cento of the verses of Homer, applied to the life and miracles of Christ , the legend of St. Cyprian, and a panegyric on the Persian victories of Theodosius , and her writings, which were applauded by a servile and superstitious age, have not been disdained by the candour of impartial criticism [75]   The fondness of the emperor was not abated by time and possession , and Eudocia, after the

---

[75] Socrates, l vii c 21 , Photius, p 413-420   The Homeric cento is still extant, and has been repeatedly printed, but the claim of Eudocia to that insipid performance is disputed by the critics   See Fabricius, Bibhoth Græc tom i p 357.   The *Ionia*, a miscellaneous dictionary of history and fable, was compiled by another empress of the name of Eudocia, who lived in the eleventh century , and the work is still extant in manuscript   [The Ionia has been edited by H Flach   The works of the earlier Eudocia have been recently published by A Ludwich, 1893]

marriage of her daughter, was permitted to discharge her grateful vows by a solemn progress to Jerusalem. Her ostentatious progress through the East may seem inconsistent with the spirit of Christian humility ; she pronounced, from a throne of gold and gems, an eloquent oration to the senate of Antioch, declared her royal intention of enlarging the walls of the city, bestowed a donative of two hundred pounds of gold to restore the public baths, and accepted the statues which were decreed by the gratitude of Antioch   In the Holy Land, her alms and pious foundations exceeded the munificence of the great Helena ; and, though the public treasure might be impoverished by this excessive liberality, she enjoyed the conscious satisfaction of returning to Constantinople with the chains of St Peter, the right arm of St. Stephen, and an undoubted picture of the Virgin, painted by St. Luke.[76]   But this pilgrimage was the fatal term of the glories of Eudocia. Satiated with empty pomp, and unmindful, perhaps, of her obligations to Pulcheria, she ambitiously aspired to the government of the Eastern empire , the palace was distracted by female discord ; but the victory was at last decided by the superior ascendant of the sister of Theodosius.   The execution of Paulinus, master of the offices, and the disgrace of Cyrus, Prætorian præfect of the East, convinced the public that the favour of Eudocia was insufficient to protect her most faithful friends , and the uncommon beauty of Paulinus encouraged the secret rumour that his guilt was that of a successful lover.[77] As soon as the empress perceived that the affection of Theodosius was irretrievably lost, she requested the permission of retiring to the distant solitude of Jerusalem.   She obtained her request ; but the jealousy of Theodosius, or the vindictive spirit of Pulcheria, pursued her in her last retreat ; and Saturninus, count of the domestics, was directed to punish with death two ecclesiastics, her most favoured servants.   Eudocia instantly revenged them by the assassination of the count , the furious passions, which she indulged on this suspicious occasion, seemed to justify the severity of Theodosius ; and the empress,

---

[76] Baronius (Annal Eccles A D 438, 439) is copious and florid , but he is accused of placing the lies of different ages on the same level of authenticity
[77] In this short view of the disgrace of Eudocia, I have imitated the caution of Evagrius (l 1 c 21) and 'count Marcellinus (in Chron A D 440 and 444)   The two authentic dates assigned by the latter overturn a great part of the Greek fictions , and the celebrated story of the *apple*, &c is fit only for the Arabian Nights, where something not very unlike it may be found

ignominiously stript of the honours of her rank,[78] was disgraced, perhaps unjustly, in the eyes of the world. The remainder of the life of Eudocia, about sixteen years, was spent in exile and devotion ; and the approach of age, the death of Theodosius, the misfortunes of her only daughter, who was led a captive from Rome to Carthage, and the society of the Holy Monks of Palestine, insensibly confirmed the religious temper of her mind   After a full experience of the vicissitudes of human life, the daughter of the philosopher Leontius expired at Jerusalem, in the sixty-seventh year of her age ; protesting, with her dying breath, that she had never transgressed the bounds of innocence and friendship [79]

The Persian war A.D 422   The gentle mind of Theodosius was never inflamed by the ambition of conquest or military renown ; and the slight alarm of a Persian war scarcely interrupted the tranquillity of the East.   The motives of this war were just and honourable   In the last year of the reign of Jezdegerd, the supposed guardian of Theodosius, a bishop, who aspired to the crown of martyrdom, destroyed one of the fire temples of Susa.[80]   His zeal and obstinacy were revenged on his brethren , and the Magi excited a cruel persecution , and the intolerant zeal of Jezdegerd was imitated by his son Vararanes, or Bahram, who soon afterwards ascended the throne.   Some Christian fugitives, who escaped to the Roman frontier, were sternly demanded and generously refused , and the refusal, aggravated by commercial disputes, soon kindled a war between the rival monarchies   The mountains of Armenia and the plains of Mesopotamia were filled with hostile armies ; but the operations of two successive campaigns were not productive of any decisive or memorable events. Some engagements were fought, some towns were besieged, with various and doubtful success ; and, if the Romans failed

---

[78] Priscus (in Excerpt Legat p 69 [Muller, F H G iv p 94]), a contemporary, and a courtier, divly mentions her Pagan and Christian names, without adding any title of honour or respect

[79] For the two pilgrimages of Eudocia, and her long residence at Jerusalem, her devotion, alms, &c , see Socrates (l vii c 47), and Evagrius (l i c 20, 21, 22). The Paschal Chronicle may sometimes deserve regard , and, in the domestic history of Antioch, John Malala becomes a writer of good authority   The Abbé Guenée, in a Memoir on the fertility of Palestine, of which I have only seen an extract, calculates the gifts of Eudocia at 20,488 pounds of gold, above 800,000 pounds sterling

[80] Theodoret, l v. c. 39   Tillemont, Mém Ecclés tom vii. p 356-364 Assemanni, Bibliot Oriental tom iii p 396, tom iv p 61   Theodoret blames the rashness of Abdas, but extols the constancy of his martyrdom.   Yet I do not clearly understand the casuistry which prohibits our repairing the damage which we have unlawfully committed

in their attempt to recover the long lost possession of Nisibis, the Persians were repulsed from the walls of a Mesopotamian city by the valour of a martial bishop, who pointed his thundering engine in the name of St. Thomas the Apostle. Yet the splendid victories, which the incredible speed of the messenger Palladius repeatedly announced to the palace of Constantinople, were celebrated with festivals and panegyrics From these panegyrics the historians[81] of the age might borrow their extraordinary and, perhaps, fabulous tales ; of the proud challenge of a Persian hero, who was entangled by the net, and dispatched by the sword, of Areobindus the Goth; of the ten thousand *Immortals*, who were slain in the attack of the Roman camp, and of the hundred thousand Arabs, or Saracens, who were impelled by a panic of terror to throw themselves headlong into the Euphrates. Such events may be disbelieved or disregarded ; but the charity of a bishop, Acacius of Amida, whose name might have dignified the saintly calendar, shall not be lost in oblivion Boldly declaring that vases of gold and silver are useless to a God who neither eats nor drinks, the generous prelate sold the plate of the church of Amida , employed the price in the redemption of seven thousand Persian captives ; supplied their wants with affectionate liberality , and dismissed them to their native country, to inform the king of the true spirit of the religion which he persecuted. The practice of benevolence in the midst of war must always tend to assuage the animosity of contending nations ; and I wish to persuade myself that Acacius contributed to the restoration of peace In the conference which was held on the limits of the two empires, the Roman ambassadors degraded the personal character of their sovereign by a vain attempt to magnify the extent of his power , when they seriously advised the Persians to prevent, by a timely accommodation, the wrath of a monarch who was yet ignorant of this distant war. A truce of one hundred years was solemnly ratified , and, although the revolutions of Armenia might threaten the public tranquillity, the essential conditions of this treaty were respected near fourscore years by the successors of Constantine and Artaxerxes.

Since the Roman and Parthian standards first encountered on the banks of the Euphrates, the kingdom of Armenia[82] was *Armenia divided between the Persians and the Romans*

[81] Socrates (l vii c 18, 19, 20, 21) is the best author for the Persian war We may likewise consult the three Chronicles, the Paschal, and those of Marcellinus and Malala. [For the succession of the Persian kings, see Appendix 5]
[82] This account of the ruin and division of the kingdom of Armenia is taken from the third book of the Armenian history of Moses of Chorene Deficient as

alternately oppressed by its formidable protectors; and, in the
course of this History, several events, which inclined the balance
of peace and war, have been already related.   A disgraceful
treaty had resigned Armenia to the ambition of Sapor, and the
scale of Persia appeared to preponderate.   But the royal race of
Arsaces impatiently submitted to the house of Sassan; the turbulent nobles asserted or betrayed their hereditary independence, and the nation was still attached to the *Christian* princes
of Constantinople.   In the beginning of the fifth century, Armenia was divided by the progress of war and faction,[83] and
the unnatural division precipitated the downfall of that ancient
monarchy   Chosroes, the Persian vassal, reigned over the
Eastern and most extensive portion of the country, while the

[son of Pap] Western province acknowledged the jurisdiction of Arsaces and
the supremacy of the emperor Arcadius   After the death of
Arsaces, the Romans suppressed the regal government and imposed on their allies the condition of subjects   The military
command was delegated to the count of the Armenian frontier;
the city of Theodosiopolis [84] was built and fortified in a strong
situation, on a fertile and lofty ground near the sources of the
Euphrates, and the dependent territories were ruled by five
satraps, whose dignity was marked by a peculiar habit of gold
and purple   The less fortunate nobles, who lamented the loss
of their king and envied the honours of their equals, were provoked to negotiate their peace and pardon at the Persian court;
and, returning, with their followers, to the palace of Artaxata,
acknowledged Chosroes for their lawful sovereign   About thirty
years afterwards, Artasires, the nephew and successor of Chosroes, fell under the displeasure of the haughty and capricious
nobles of Armenia; and they unanimously desired a Persian
governor in the room of an unworthy king.   The answer of the

he is of every qualification of a good historian, his local information, his passions,
and his prejudices are strongly expressive of a native and contemporary   Procopius
(de Edificiis, l viii c i 5) relates the same facts in a very different manner, but
I have extracted the circumstances the most probable in themselves and the least
inconsistent with Moses of Chorene   [For the division of Armenia see Appendix 25]

[83] The western Armenians used the Greek language and characters in their
religious offices, but the use of that hostile tongue was prohibited by the Persians
in the eastern provinces, which were obliged to use the Syriac, till the invention of
the Armenian letters by Mesrobes in the beginning of the fifth century and the
subsequent version of the Bible into the Armenian language, an event which relaxed the connexion of the church and nation with Constantinople

[84] Moses Choren. l iii. c 59, p 309, and p 358   Procopius, de Aedificiis, l iii c
5   Theodosiopolis stands, or rather stood, about thirty-five miles to the east of
Arzeroum, the modern capital of Turkish Armenia   See d'Anville, Géographie
Ancienne, tom ii p 99, 100

archbishop Isaac, whose sanction they earnestly solicited, is ex- [Sahag] pressive of the character of a superstitious people.   He deplored the manifest and inexcusable vices of Artasires; and declared that he should not hesitate to accuse him before the tribunal of a Christian emperor who would punish, without destroying, the sinner.   "Our king," continued Isaac, "is too much addicted to licentious pleasures, but he has been purified in the holy waters of baptism   He is a lover of women, but he does not adore the fire or the elements   He may deserve the reproach of lewdness, but he is an undoubted Catholic;   and his faith is pure, though his manners are flagitious.   I will never consent to abandon my sheep to the rage of devouring wolves;   and you would soon repent your rash exchange of the infirmities of a believer for the specious virtues of an heathen "[85]   Exasperated by the firmness of Isaac, the factious nobles accused both the king and the archbishop as the secret adherents of the emperor;   and absurdly rejoiced in the sentence of condemnation, which, after a partial hearing, was solemnly pronounced by Bahram himself. . The descendants of Arsaces were degraded from the royal dignity,[86] which they had possessed above five hundred and sixty years, [87] [580] and the dominions of the unfortunate Artasires, under the new and significant appellation of Persarmenia, were reduced into the form of a province.   This usurpation excited the jealousy of [c A D 428] the Roman government;   but the rising disputes were soon terminated by an amicable, though unequal, partition of the ancient kingdom of Armenia, and a territorial acquisition, which Augustus might have despised, reflected some lustre on the declining empire of the younger Theodosius.

[85] Moses Choren 1 iii c 63, p 316   According to the institution of St Gregory the apostle of Armenia, the archbishop was always of the royal family , a circumstance which, in some degree, corrected the influence of the sacerdotal character, and united the mitre with the crown

[86] A branch of the royal house of Arsaces still subsisted with the rank and possessions (as it should seem) of Armenian satraps   See Moses Choren i iii c 65, p 321

[87] Valarsaces was appointed king of Armenia by his brother the Parthian monarch, immediately after the defeat of Antiochus Sidetes (Moses Choren 1 ii c ii. p 85), one hundred and thirty years before Christ   Without depending on the various and contradictory periods of the reigns of the last kings, we may be assured that the ruin of the Armenian kingdom happened after the council of Chalcedon, A D 431 (1 iii c 61, p 312), and under Veramus or Bahram, king of Persia (1 iii c 64, p 317), who reigned from A D 420 to 440 [see Appendix 25] See Assemanni, Bibliot Oriental, tom iii p 396

CHAPTER XXXIII

Death of Honorius—Valentinian III. Emperor of the West—Administration of his Mother Placidia—Aetius and Boniface—Conquest of Africa by the Vandals

Last years
and death of
Honorius
A D 423,
August 27

During a long and disgraceful reign of twenty-eight years, Honorius, emperor of the West, was separated from the friendship of his brother, and afterwards of his nephew, who reigned over the East, and Constantinople beheld, with apparent indifference and secret joy, the calamities of Rome. The strange adventures of Placidia[1] gradually renewed and cemented the alliance of the two empires. The daughter of the great Theodosius had been the captive and the queen of the Goths; she lost an affectionate husband, she was dragged in chains by his insulting assassin; she tasted the pleasure of revenge, and was exchanged, in the treaty of peace, for six hundred thousand measures of wheat. After her return from Spain to Italy, Placidia experienced a new persecution in the bosom of her family. She was averse to a marriage which had been stipulated without her consent, and the brave Constantius, as a noble reward for the tyrants whom he had vanquished, received, from the hand of Honorius himself, the struggling and reluctant hand of the widow of Adolphus But her resistance ended with the

[A D 317]

ceremony of the nuptials, nor did Placidia refuse to become the mother of Honoria and Valentinian the Third, or to assume and exercise an absolute dominion over the mind of her grateful husband The generous soldier, whose time had hitherto been divided between social pleasure and military service, was taught new lessons of avarice and ambition; he extorted the title of Augustus, and the servant of Honorius was associated to the empire of the West The death of Constantius, in the seventh

[A D 321]

month of his reign, instead of diminishing, seemed to increase, the power of Placidia; and the indecent familiarity[2] of her

---

[1] See p 334-348

[2] Τα συνεχη κατα στομα φιληματα, is the expression of Olympiodorus (apud Photium, p 197 [fr 40]), who means, perhaps, to describe the same caresses which

brother, which might be no more than the symptoms of a childish affection, were [2a] universally attributed to incestuous love. On a sudden, by some base intrigues of a steward and a nurse, this excessive fondness was converted into an irreconcileable quarrel, the debates of the emperor and his sister were not long confined within the walls of the palace, and, as the Gothic soldiers adhered to their queen, the city of Ravenna was agitated with bloody and dangerous tumults, which could only be appeased by the forced or voluntary retreat of Placidia and her children The royal exiles landed at Constantinople, soon after the marriage of Theodosius, during the festival of the Persian victories They were treated with kindness and magnificence; but, as the statues of the emperor Constantius had been rejected by the Eastern court, the title of Augusta could not decently be allowed to his widow. Within a few months after the arrival of Placidia, a swift messenger announced the death of Honorius, the consequence of a dropsy, but the important secret was not divulged, till the necessary orders had been dispatched for the march of a large body of troops to the sea-coast of Dalmatia. The shops and the gates of Constantinople remained shut during seven days; and the loss of a foreign prince, who could neither be esteemed nor regretted, was celebrated with loud and affected demonstrations of the public grief.

While the ministers of Constantinople deliberated, the vacant throne of Honorius was usurped by the ambition of a stranger. Elevation and fall of the usurper John A D 423-425 The name of the rebel was John; he filled the confidential office of *Primicerius*, or principal secretary, and history has attributed to his character more virtues than can easily be reconciled with the violation of the most sacred duty Elated by the submission of Italy and the hope of an alliance with the Huns, John presumed to insult, by an embassy, the majesty of the Eastern emperor; but, when he understood that his agents had been banished, imprisoned, and at length chased away with deserved ignominy, John prepared to assert, by arms, the injustice of his claims. In such a cause, the grandson of the great Theodosius should have marched in person, but the young emperor was easily diverted, by his physicians, from so rash and hazardous a design; and the conduct of the Italian expedition was pru-

---

Mahomet bestowed on his *daughter* Phatemah Quando (says the prophet himself) quando subit mihi desiderium Paradisi, osculor eam, et ingero linguam meam in os ejus But this sensual indulgence was justified by miracle and mystery, and the anecdote has been communicated to the public by the Reverend Father Maracci, in his Version and Confutation of the Koran, tom ı p 32.

[2a] [*Symptoms* in the relative clause seems to have caused the irregular plural]

dently entrusted to Ardabunus and his son Aspar, who had already signalized their valour against the Persians It was resolved that Ardabunus should embark with the infantry; whilst Aspar, at the head of the cavalry, conducted Placidia and her son Valentinian along the sea-coast of the Hadriatic. The march of the cavalry was performed with such active diligence that they surprised, without resistance, the important city of Aquileia, when the hopes of Aspar were unexpectedly confounded by the intelligence that a storm had dispersed the Imperial fleet; and that his father, with only two galleys, was taken and carried a prisoner into the port of Ravenna. Yet this incident, unfortunate as it might seem, facilitated the conquest of Italy. Ardabunus employed, or abused, the courteous freedom which he was permitted to enjoy, to revive among the troops a sense of loyalty and gratitude, and, as soon as the conspiracy was ripe for execution, he invited, by private messages, and pressed the approach of, Aspar. A shepherd, whom the popular credulity transformed into an angel, guided the Eastern cavalry, by a secret and, it was thought, an impassable road, through the morasses of the Po, the gates of Ravenna, after a short struggle, were thrown open; and the defenceless tyrant was delivered to the mercy, or rather to the cruelty, of the conquerors His right hand was first cut off, and, after he had been exposed, mounted on an ass, to the public derision, John was beheaded in the circus of Aquileia. The emperor Theodosius, when he received the news of the victory, interrupted the horse-races; and, singing, as he marched through the streets, a suitable psalm, conducted his people from the Hippodrome to the church, where he spent the remainder of the day in grateful devotion [3]

Valentinian III emperor of the West A D 425 455   In a monarchy, which, according to various precedents, might be considered as elective, or hereditary, or patrimonial, it was impossible that the intricate claims of female and collateral succession should be clearly defined,[4] and Theodosius, by the right of consanguinity or conquest, might have reigned the sole

[3] For these revolutions of the Western Empire, consult Olympiodor apud Phot p 192, 193, 196, 197, 200 [fr 41, 44, 45, 46]   Sozomen, l iv c 16   Socrates, l vii 23, 24   Philostorgius, l. vii. c 10, 11, and Godefroy, Dissertat p 486 Procopius, de Bell Vandal l i c 3, p 182, 183   Theophanes, in Chronograph p 72, 73, and the Chronicles
[4] See Grotius de Jure Belli et Pacis, l ii c 7   He has laboriously, but vainly, attempted to form a reasonable system of jurisprudence, from the various and discordant modes of royal succession, which have been introduced by fraud or force, by time or accident

legitimate emperor of the Romans. For a moment, perhaps, his eyes were dazzled by the prospect of unbounded sway, but his indolent temper gradually acquiesced in the dictates of sound policy   He contented himself with the possession of the East; and wisely relinquished the laborious task of waging a distant and doubtful war against the Barbarians beyond the Alps; or of securing the obedience of the Italians and Africans, whose minds were alienated by the irreconcileable difference of language and interest. Instead of listening to the voice of ambition, Theodosius resolved to imitate the moderation of his grandfather, and to seat his cousin Valentinian on the throne of the West. The royal infant was distinguished at Constantinople by the title of *Nobilissimus*, he was promoted, before his departure from Thessalonica, to the rank and dignity of *Cæsar*; and, after the conquest of Italy, the patrician Helion, by the authority of Theodosius, and in the presence of the senate, saluted Valentinian the Third by the name of Augustus, and solemnly invested him with the diadem and the Imperial purple [5] By the agreement of the three females who governed the Roman world, the son of Placidia was betrothed to Eudoxia, the daughter of Theodosius and Athenais; and, as soon as the lover and his bride had attained the age of puberty, this honourable alliance was faithfully accomplished. At the same time, as a compensation, perhaps, for the expenses of the war, the Western Illyricum was detached from the Italian dominions and yielded to the throne of Constantinople.[6] The emperor of the East acquired the useful dominion of the rich and maritime province of Dalmatia, and the dangerous sovereignty of Pannonia and Noricum, which had been filled and ravaged above twenty years by a promiscuous crowd of Huns, Ostrogoths, Vandals, and *Bavarians*. Theodosius and Valentinian continued to respect the obligations of their public and domestic alliance; but the unity of the Roman government was finally dissolved. By a positive declaration, the validity of all future laws was limited to the dominions of their peculiar author, unless he should think proper to com-

---

[5] The original writers are not agreed (see Muratori, Annali d'Italia, tom. iv. p 139) whether Valentinian received the Imperial diadem at Rome or Ravenna In this uncertainty, I am willing to believe that some respect was shown to the senate

[6] The Count de Buat (Hist des Peuples de l'Europe, tom vii p 292-300) has established the reality, explained the motives, and traced the consequences of this remarkable cession   [Cp Appendix 14.]

municate them, subscribed with his own hand, for the approbation of his independent colleague [7]

Administration of his mother Placidia A D 425-450

Valentinian, when he received the title of Augustus, was no more than six years of age ; and his long minority was intrusted to the guardian care of a mother, who might assert a female claim to the succession of the Western Empire Placidia envied, but she could not equal, the reputation and virtues of the wife and sister of Theodosius the elegant genius of Eudocia, the wise and successful policy of Pulcheria The mother of Valentinian was jealous of the power, which she was incapable of exercising ; [8] she reigned twenty-five years, in the name of her son ; and the character of that unworthy emperor gradually countenanced the suspicion that Placidia had enervated his youth by a dissolute education and studiously diverted his attention from every manly and honourable pursuit. Amidst the decay of military spirit, her armies were commanded by two generals, Aetius [9] and Boniface,[10] who may be deservedly named as the last of the Romans Their union might have supported a sinking empire , their discord was the fatal and immediate cause of the loss of Africa The invasion and defeat of Attila has immortalized the fame of Aetius ; and, though time has thrown a shade over the exploits of his rival, the defence of Marseilles and the deliverance of Africa [11] attest

Her two generals, Aetius and Boniface

[A D 412]

[A D 422]

---

[7] See the first *Novel* of Theodosius, by which he ratifies and communicates (A D 438) the Theodosian Code About forty years before that time, the unity of legislation had been proved by an exception The Jews, who were numerous in the cities of Apulia and Calabria, produced a law of the East to justify their exemption from municipal offices (Cod Theod 1 xvi tit viii leg 13); and the Western emperor was obliged to invalidate by a special edict, the law quam constat meis partibus esse damnosam. Cod. Theod 1 xi [*leg* xii], tit i leg 158

[8] Cassiodorus (Varior. l. xi epist 1 p 238) has compared the regencies of Placidia and Amalasuntha He arraigns the weakness of the mother of Valentinian, and praises the virtues of his royal mistress On this occasion flattery seems to have spoken the language of truth

[9] Philostorgius, l xii c 12, and Godefroy's Dissertat p 493, &c , and Renatus Frigeridus, apud Gregor Turon l ii c 8, in tom ii. p 163 The father of Aetius was Gaudentius, an illustrious citizen of the province of Scythia, and master-general of the cavalry , his mother was a rich and noble Italian From his earliest youth, Aetius, as a soldier and a hostage, had conversed with the Barbarians

[10] For the character of Boniface, see Olympiodorus, apud Phot p 196 [F H G iv fr 42] , and St Augustin, apud Tillemont, Mémoires Ecclés tom. xiii p 712-715, 886 The bishop of Hippo at length deplored the fall of his friend, who, after a solemn vow of chastity, had married a second wife of the Arian sect, and who was suspected of keeping several concubines in his house.

[11] [From the invasions of Moorish tribes , he went to Africa from Spain in 422 A D , without a regular commission]

the military talents of Count Boniface. In the field of battle,
in partial encounters, in single combats, he was still the terror of
the Barbarians ; the clergy, and particularly his friend Augustin,
were edified by the Christian piety which had once tempted
him to retire from the world , the people applauded his spotless
integrity , the army dreaded his equal and inexorable justice,
which may be displayed in a very singular example   A peasant,
who complained of the criminal intimacy between his wife and
a Gothic soldier, was directed to attend his tribunal the following day , in the evening the count, who had diligently informed
himself of the time and place of the assignation, mounted his
horse, rode ten miles into the country, surprised the guilty
couple, punished the soldier with instant death, and silenced
the complaints of the husband by presenting him, the next
morning, with the head of the adulterer   The abilities of
Aetius and Boniface might have been usefully employed against
the public enemies, in separate and important commands ; but
the experience of their past conduct should have decided the
real favour and confidence of the empress Placidia   In the
melancholy season of her exile and distress, Boniface alone had
maintained her cause with unshaken fidelity ; and the troops
and treasures of Africa had essentially contributed to extinguish
the rebellion. The same rebellion had been supported by the
zeal and activity of Aetius, who brought an army, of sixty
thousand Huns from the Danube to the confines of Italy, for the
service of the usurper. The untimely death of John compelled
him to accept an advantageous treaty , but he still continued,
the subject and the soldier of Valentinian, to entertain a secret,
perhaps a treasonable, correspondence with his Barbarian allies,
whose retreat had been purchased by liberal gifts and more
liberal promises. But Aetius possessed an advantage of singular
moment in a female reign : he was present ; he besieged, with
artful and assiduous flattery, the palace of Ravenna ; disguised
his dark designs with the mask of loyalty and friendship ; and
at length deceived both his mistress and his absent rival by a
subtle conspiracy, which a weak woman and a brave man could
not easily suspect. He secretly persuaded [12] Placidia to recal   Error and re
Boniface from the government of Africa ; he secretly advised   volt of Boni
face in Africa
A D 427

[12] Procopius (de Bell Vandal 1 1 c 3, 4, p 182-186) relates the fraud of
Aetius, the revolts of Boniface, and the loss of Africa   This anecdote, which is
supported by some collateral testimony (see Ruinart, Hist Persecut Vandal p
420, 421), seems agreeable to the practice of ancient and modern courts, and would
be naturally revealed by the repentance of Boniface

Boniface to disobey the Imperial summons : to the one he represented the order as a sentence of death ; to the other he stated the refusal as a signal of revolt, and, when the credulous and unsuspectful count had armed the province in his defence, Aetius applauded his sagacity in foreseeing the rebellion which his own perfidy had excited. A temperate inquiry into the real motives of Boniface would have restored a faithful servant to his duty and to the republic, but the arts of Aetius still continued to betray and to inflame, and the count was urged by persecution to embrace the most desperate counsels The success with which he eluded or repelled the first attacks could not inspire a vain confidence that, at the head of some loose, disorderly Africans, he should be able to withstand the regular forces of the West, commanded by a rival whose military character it was impossible for him to despise. After some hesitation, the last struggles of prudence and loyalty, Boniface dispatched a [Guntheric] trusty friend to the court, or rather to the camp, of Gonderic, king of the Vandals, with the proposal of a strict alliance, and the offer of an advantageous and perpetual settlement.

He invites the Vandals A D 428 After the retreat of the Goths, the authority of Honorius had obtained a precarious establishment in Spain, except only in the province of Gallicia, where the Suevi and the Vandals had [A D 419] fortified their camps, in mutual discord and hostile independence. The Vandals prevailed ; and their adversaries were besieged in [A D 420] the Nervasian hills, between Leon and Oviedo, till the approach of Count Asterius compelled, or rather provoked, the victorious Barbarians to remove the scene of the war to the plains of Baetica The rapid progress of the Vandals soon required a [A D 422] more effectual opposition ; and the master-general Castinus marched against them with a numerous army of Romans and Goths Vanquished in battle by an inferior enemy, Castinus [Tarraco] fled with dishonour to Tarragona ; and this memorable defeat, which has been represented as the punishment, was most [Hispalis Nova Carthago] probably the effect, of his rash presumption.[13] Seville and Carthagena became the reward, or rather the prey, of the ferocious conquerors, and the vessels which they found in the harbour of Carthagena might easily transport them to the isles [A D 425] of Majorca and Minorca, where the Spanish fugitives, as in a secure recess, had vainly concealed their families and their fortunes

---

[13] See the Chronicles of Prosper and Idatius Salvian (de Gubernat Dei, l vii p 246, Paris, 1608) ascribes the victory of the Vandals to their superior piety They fasted, they prayed, they carried a Bible in the front of the Host, with the design, perhaps, of reproaching the perfidy and sacrilege of their enemies

The experience of navigation, and perhaps the prospect of Africa, encouraged the Vandals to accept the invitation which they received from Count Boniface , and the death of Gonderic served only to forward and animate the bold enterprise   In the room of a prince, not conspicuous for any superior powers of the mind or body, they acquired his bastard brother, the terrible Genseric :[14] a name which, in the destruction of the Roman empire, has deserved an equal rank with the names of Alaric and Attila.   The king of the Vandals is described to have been of a middle stature, with a lameness in one leg, which he had contracted by an accidental fall from his horse.   His slow and cautious speech seldom declared the deep purposes of his soul : he disdained to imitate the luxury of the vanquished ; but he indulged the sterner passions of anger and revenge.   The ambition of Genseric was without bounds, and without scruples ; and the warrior could dexterously employ the dark engines of policy to solicit the allies who might be useful to his success, or to scatter among his enemies the seeds of hatred and contention.   Almost in the moment of his departure he was informed that Heimanric, king of the Suevi, had presumed to ravage the Spanish territories, which he was resolved to abandon.   Impatient of the insult, Genseric pursued the hasty retreat of the Suevi as far as Merida ; precipitated the king and his army into the river Anas , and calmly returned to the sea-shore, to embark his victorious troops.   The vessels which transported the Vandals over the modern Streights of Gibraltar, a channel only twelve miles in breadth,[15] were furnished by the Spaniards, who anxiously wished their departure, and by the African general, who had implored their formidable assistance [16]

Genseric, king of the Vandals

[Emerita]

[Guadiana]

He lands in Africa, A D 429, May

[14] Gizericus (his name is variously expressed) staturâ mediocris et equi casu claudicans, animo profundus, sermone rarus, luxuriæ contemptor, irâ turbidus habendi, cupidus, ad solicitandas gentes providentissimus, semina contentionum jacere, odia miscere paratus   Jornandes, de Rebus Geticis, c. 33, p 657   This portrait, which is drawn with some skill, and a strong likeness, must have been copied from the Gothic history of Cassiodorius   [The right form of the name, now universally accepted, is *Gaiseric* (Idatius , *Geiseric*, Prosper and Victor Vitensis)   The nasalized form appears first in writers of the sixth century   Unfortunately there are no coins of this king , see Friedlander's Die Munzen der Vandalen]

[15] [It seems far more probable that the Vandals sailed directly to Cæsarea than that they crossed the straits and undertook the long land march through the deserts of western Mauritania , notwithstanding the statement of Victor Vitensis, i. 1]

[16] See the Chronicle of Idatius   That bishop, a Spaniard and a contemporary, places the passage of the Vandals in the month of May, of the year of Abraham (which commences in October) 2444   This date, which coincides with A D 429, is confirmed [rather, adopted] by Isidore, another Spanish bishop, and is justly preferred to the opinion of those writers who have marked for that event one of the preceding years   See Pagi, Critica, tom ii p 205, &c   [So too Clinton   But

and reviews
his army.
A.D. 429
Our fancy, so long accustomed to exaggerate and multiply
the martial swarms of Barbarians that seemed to issue from the
North, will perhaps be surprised by the account of the army
which Genseric mustered on the coast of Mauritania. The
Vandals, who in twenty years had penetrated from the Elbe to
Mount Atlas, were united under the command of their warlike
king; and he reigned with equal authority over the Alani, who
had passed, within the term of human life, from the cold of
Scythia to the excessive heat of an African climate. The hopes
of the bold enterprise had excited many brave adventurers of
the Gothic nation; and many desperate provincials were
tempted to repair their fortunes by the same means which had
occasioned their ruin. Yet this various multitude amounted
only to fifty thousand effective men; and, though Genseric
artfully magnified his apparent strength, by appointing eighty
chiliarchs, or commanders of thousands, the fallacious increase of
old men, of children, and of slaves, would scarcely have swelled
his army to the number of fourscore thousand persons.[17] But
his own dexterity, and the discontents of Africa, soon fortified
the Vandal powers by the accession of numerous and active
The Moors   allies. The parts of Mauritania, which border on the great
desert and the Atlantic ocean, were filled with a fierce and untractable race of men, whose savage temper had been exasperated, rather than reclaimed, by their dread of the Roman
arms. The wandering Moors,[18] as they gradually ventured to
approach the sea-shore and the camp of the Vandals, must have
viewed with terror and astonishment the dress, the armour, the
martial pride and discipline of the unknown strangers, who had
landed on their coast; and the fair complexions of the blue-eyed
warriors of Germany formed a very singular contrast with the

Mr. Hodgkin, ii. 292, makes out a good case for the date 428, given in the Chron.
Pasch. and perhaps really implied by Idatius.]
[17] Compare Procopius (de Bell. Vandal. l. i. c. 5, p. 190) and Victor Vitensis
(de Persecutione Vandal. l. i. c. 1, p. 3, edit. Ruinart). We are assured by
Idatius that Genseric evacuated Spain, cum Vandalis *omnibus* eorumque
familiis; and Possidius (in Vit. Augustin. c. 28, apud Ruinart, p. 427) describes
his army as manus ingens immanium gentium Vandalorum et Alanorum,
commixtam secum habens Gothorum gentem, aliarumque diversarum personas.
[To reconcile the 50,000 fighting men of Procopius with the 80,000 (including old
men and *parvuli*) of Victor, Mr. Hodgkin supposes that females were excluded in
Victor's enumeration (ii. 231).]
[18] For the manners of the Moors, see Procopius (de Bell. Vandal. l. ii. c. 6,
p. 249); for their figure and complexion, M. de Buffon (Histoire Naturelle, tom.
iii. p. 430). Procopius says in general that the Moors had joined the Vandals
before the death of Valentinian (de Bell. Vandal. l. i. c. 5, p. 190), and it is
probable that the independent tribes did not embrace any uniform system of policy.

swarthy or olive hue which is derived from the neighbourhood of the torrid zone. After the first difficulties had in some measure been removed, which arose from the mutual ignorance of their respective language, the Moors, regardless of any future consequence, embraced the alliance of the enemies of Rome ; and a crowd of naked savages rushed from the woods and valleys of Mount Atlas, to satiate their revenge on the polished tyrants who had injuriously expelled them from the native sovereignty of the land.

The persecution of the Donatists [19] was an event not less favourable to the designs of Genseric. Seventeen years before he landed in Africa, a public conference was held at Carthage, by the order of the magistrate. The Catholics were satisfied that, after the invincible reasons which they had alleged, the obstinacy of the schismatics must be inexcusable and voluntary ; and the emperor Honorius was persuaded to inflict the most rigorous penalties on a faction which had so long abused his patience and clemency. Three hundred bishops,[20] with many thousands of the inferior clergy, were torn from their churches, stripped of their ecclesiastical possessions, banished to the islands, and proscribed by the laws, if they presumed to conceal themselves in the provinces of Africa. Their numerous congregations, both in cities and in the country, were deprived of the rights of citizens, and of the exercise of religious worship. A regular scale of fines, from ten to two hundred pounds of silver, was curiously ascertained, according to the distinctions of rank and fortune, to punish the crime of assisting at a schismatic conventicle ; and, if the fine had been levied five times, without subduing the obstinacy of the offender, his future punishment was referred to the discretion of the Imperial court.[21] By these severities, which obtained the warmest approbation of St. Augustin,[22] great numbers of Donatists were reconciled to the

[19] See Tillemont, Mémoires Ecclés tom xiii p 516-558, and the whole series of the persecution in the original monuments, published by Dupin at the end of Optatus, p 323-515

[20] The Donatist bishops, at the conference of Carthage, amounted to 279, and they asserted that their whole number was not less than 400. The Catholics had 286 present, 120 absent, besides sixty-four vacant bishoprics

[21] The fifth title of the sixteenth book of the Theodosian Code exhibits a series of the Imperial laws against the Donatists, from the year 400 to the year 428. Of these the 54th law, promulgated by Honorius A D 514, is the most severe and effectual

[22] St Augustin altered his opinion with regard to the proper treatment of heretics. His pathetic declaration of pity and indulgence for the Manichæens has been inserted by Mr. Locke (vol iii p 469) among the choice specimens of his commonplace book. Another philosopher, the celebrated Bayle (tom ii. p. 445-496), has refuted, with superfluous diligence and ingenuity, the arguments by which the bishop of Hippo justified, in his old age, the persecution of the Donatists

Catholic church ; but the fanatics, who still persevered in their opposition, were provoked to madness and despair, the distracted country was filled with tumult and bloodshed; the armed troops of Circumcellions alternately pointed their rage against themselves or against their adversaries ; and the calendar of martyrs received on both sides a considerable augmentation [23] Under these circumstances, Genseric, a Christian, but an enemy of the orthodox communion, showed himself to the Donatists as a powerful deliverer, from whom they might reasonably expect the repeal of the odious and oppressive edicts of the Roman emperors [24] The conquest of Africa was facilitated by the active zeal, or the secret favour, of a domestic faction; the wanton outrages against the churches and the clergy, of which the Vandals are accused, may be fairly imputed to the fanaticism of their allies ; and the intolerant spirit, which disgraced the triumph of Christianity, contributed to the loss of the most important province of the West.[25]

Tardy re pentance of Boniface A D 430 The court and the people were astonished by the strange intelligence that a virtuous hero, after so many favours and so many services, had renounced his allegiance, and invited the Barbarians to destroy the province entrusted to his command The friends of Boniface, who still believed that his criminal behaviour might be excused by some honourable motive, solicited, during the absence of Aetius, a free conference with the count of Africa, and Darius, an officer of high distinction, was named for the important embassy [26] In their first interview at Car-

[23] See Tillemont, Mém Ecclés tom xiii p 586-592, 806   The Donatists boasted of *thousands* of these voluntary martyrs   Augustin asserts, and concludes with truth, that these numbers were much exaggerated , but he sternly maintains that it was better that *some* should burn themselves in this world than that *all* should burn in hell flames

[24] According to St Augustin and Theodoret the Donatists were inclined to the principles, or at least to the party, of the Arians, which Genseric supported Tillemont, Mém. Ecclés tom vi p 68

[25] See Baronius, Annal Ecclés A D 428, No 7, A D 439, No 35   The cardinal, though more inclined to seek the cause of great events in heaven than on the earth, has observed the apparent connexion of the Vandals and the Donatists Under the reign of the Barbarians, the schismatics of Africa enjoyed an obscure peace of one hundred years , at the end of which, we may again trace them by the light of the Imperial persecutions   See Tillemont, Mém Ecclés. tom vi p 192, &c

[26] In a confidential letter to Count Boniface, St Augustin, without examining the grounds of the quarrel, piously exhorts him to discharge the duties of a Christian and a subject , to extricate himself without delay from his dangerous and guilty situation , and even, if he could obtain the consent of his wife, to embrace a life of celibacy and penance (Tillemont, Mém Ecclés tom xiii p 890) The bishop was intimately connected with Darius, the minister of peace (Id tom xiii p 928)

thage, the imaginary provocations were mutually explained; the opposite letters of Aetius were produced and compared, and the fraud was easily detected. Placidia and Boniface lamented their fatal error, and the count had sufficient magnanimity to confide in the forgiveness of his sovereign or to expose his head to her future resentment   His repentance was fervent and sincere; but he soon discovered that it was no longer in his power to restore the edifice which he had shaken to its foundations Carthage, and the Roman garrisons, returned with their general to the allegiance of Valentinian ; but the rest of Africa was still distracted with war and faction, and the inexorable king of the Vandals, disdaining all terms of accommodation, sternly refused to relinquish the possession of his prey   The band of veterans, who marched under the standard of Boniface, and his hasty levies of provincial troops, were defeated with considerable loss ; the victorious Barbarians insulted the open country, and Carthage, Cirta, and Hippo Regius were the only cities that appeared to rise above the general inundation.

    The long and narrow tract of the African coast was filled with frequent monuments of Roman art and magnificence, and the respective degrees of improvement might be accurately measured by the distance from Carthage and the Mediterranean   A simple reflection will impress every thinking mind with the clearest idea of fertility and cultivation : the country was extremely populous; the inhabitants reserved a liberal subsistence for their own use ; and the annual exportation, particularly of wheat, was so regular and plentiful that Africa deserved the name of the common granary of Rome and of mankind.   On a sudden the seven fruitful provinces, from Tangier to Tripoli, were overwhelmed by the invasion of the Vandals, whose destructive rage has perhaps been exaggerated by popular animosity, religious zeal, and extravagant declamation   War, in its fairest form, implies a perpetual violation of humanity and justice; and the hostilities of Barbarians are inflamed by the fierce and lawless spirit which incessantly disturbs their peaceful and domestic society   The Vandals, where they found resistance, seldom gave quarter, and the deaths of their valiant countrymen were expiated by the ruin of the cities under whose walls they had fallen   Careless of the distinctions of age, or sex, or rank, they employed every species of indignity and torture, to force from the captives a discovery of their hidden wealth   The stern policy of Genseric justified his frequent examples of military execution. he was not always the master of his own passions, or

of those of his followers; and the calamities of war were aggra
vated by the licentiousness of the Moors and the fanaticism of
the Donatists. Yet I shall not easily be persuaded that it was
the common practice of the Vandals to extirpate the olives, and
other fruit trees, of a country where they intended to settle;
nor can I believe that it was a usual stratagem to slaughter
great numbers of their prisoners before the walls of a besieged
city, for the sole purpose of infecting the air and producing a
pestilence of which they themselves must have been the first
victims.[27]

Siege of
Hippo A D
430, May

The generous mind of Count Boniface was tortured by the
exquisite distress of beholding the ruin which he had occasioned,
and whose rapid progress he was unable to check. After the
loss of a battle he retired into Hippo Regius, where he was
immediately besieged by an enemy who considered him as the
real bulwark of Africa The maritime colony of *Hippo*,[28] about
two hundred miles westward of Carthage, had formerly acquired
the distinguishing epithet of *Regius*, from the residence of
Numidian kings; and some remains of trade and populousness
still adhere to the modern city, which is known in Europe by
the corrupted name of Bona The military labours and anxious
reflections of Count Boniface were alleviated by the edifying
conversation of his friend St Augustin;[29] till that bishop, the
light and pillar of the Catholic church, was gently released, in

Death of
Augustin
A D 430,
August 28

the third month of the siege, and in the seventy-sixth year of
his age, from the actual and the impending calamities of his
country. The youth of Augustin had been stained by the vices
and errors which he so ingenuously confesses, but from the

---

[27] The original complaints of the desolation of Africa are contained 1 In a
letter from Capreolus, bishop of Carthage, to excuse his absence from the council
of Ephesus (ap Ruinart, p 429) 2 In the life of St Augustin, by his friend and
colleague Possidius (ap Ruinart, p 427) 3 In the History of the Vandalic Persecution, by Victor Vitensis (l. 1 c 1, 2, 3, edit Ruinart) The last picture, which
was drawn sixty years after the event, is more expressive of the author's passions
than of the truth of facts

[28] See Cellarius, Geograph Antiq tom ii part ii p 112, Leo African in
Ramusio, tom i fol 70, L'Afrique de Marmol tom ii p 434, 437; Shaw's
Travels, p 46, 47 The old Hippo Regius was finally destroyed by the Arabs in
the seventh century, but a new town, at the distance of two miles, was built with
the materials, and it contained, in the sixteenth century, about three hundred families of industrious, but turbulent, manufacturers The adjacent territory is renowned for a pure air, a fertile soil, and plenty of exquisite fruits

[29] The life of St Augustin, by Tillemont, fills a quarto volume (Mém Eccles.
tom xiii) of more than one thousand pages, and the diligence of that learned
Jansenist was excited on this occasion by factious and devout zeal for the founder
of his sect,

moment of his conversion to that of his death the manners of
the bishop of Hippo were pure and austere ; and the most con
spicuous of his virtues was an ardent zeal against heretics of
every denomination : the Manichæans, the Donatists, and the
Pelagians, against whom he waged a perpetual controversy
When the city, some months after his death, was burnt by the
Vandals, the library was fortunately saved, which contained his
voluminous writings. two hundred and thirty-two separate
books, or treatises, on theological subjects, besides a complete
exposition of the psalter and the gospel, and a copious magazine
of epistles and homilies.[30]   According to the judgment of the
most impartial critics, the superficial learning of Augustin was
confined to the Latin language ; [31] and his style, though sometimes animated by the eloquence of passion, is usually clouded
by false and affected rhetoric.   But he possessed a strong, capacious, argumentative mind ; he boldly sounded the dark abyss
of grace, predestination, free-will, and original sin ; and the rigid
system of Christianity, which he framed or restored,[32] has been
entertained, with public applause and secret reluctance, by the
Latin church [33]

By the skill of Boniface, and perhaps by the ignorance of the
Vandals, the siege of Hippo was protracted above fourteen
months ; the sea was continually open, and, when the adjacent

Defeat and retreat of Boniface A D 431

[30] Such at least is the account of Victor Vitensis (de Persecut. Vandal l 1 c 3),
though Gennadius seems to doubt whether any person had read, or even collected,
all the works of St Augustin (see Hieronym Opera, tom 1 p 319, in Catalog
Scriptor Eccles)   They have been repeatedly printed , and Dupin (Bibliothèque
Ecclés tom 111 p 158-257) has given a large and satisfactory abstract of them,
as they stand in the last edition of the Benedictines   My personal acquaintance
with the bishop of Hippo does not extend beyond the *Confessions* and the *City of
God*

[31] In his early youth (Confess 1 14) St Augustin disliked and neglected the
study of Greek, and he frankly owns that he read the Platonists in a Latin version
(Confess vii 9)   Some modern critics have thought that his ignorance of Greek
disqualified him from expounding the Scriptures, and Cicero or Quintilian would
have required the knowledge of that language in a professor of rhetoric

[32] These questions were seldom agitated from the time of St Paul to that of St
Augustin   I am informed that the Greek fathers maintain the natural sentiments
of the Semi-Pelagians , and that the orthodoxy of St Augustin was derived from
the Manichæan school

[33] The church of Rome has canonized Augustin, and reprobated Calvin   Yet, as
the *real* difference between them is invisible even to a theological microscope, the
Molinists are oppressed by the authority of the saint, and the Jansenists are disgraced by their resemblance to the heretic   In the meanwhile the Protestant
Arminians stand aloof, and deride the mutual perplexity of the disputants (see a
curious Review of the Controversy, by Le Clerc, Bibliothèque Universelle, tom
xiv p 144-398)   Perhaps a reasoner still more independent may smile in *his*
turn, when he peruses an Arminian Commentary on the Epistle to the Romans

country had been exhausted by irregular rapine, the besiegers themselves were compelled by famine to relinquish their enterprise The
importance and danger of Africa were deeply felt by the regent
of the West   Placidia implored the assistance of her eastern
ally; and the Italian fleet and army were reinforced by Aspar,
who sailed from Constantinople with a powerful armament   As soon
as the force of the two empires was united under the command of
Boniface he boldly marched against the Vandals, and the loss of a
second battle irretrievably decided the fate of Africa He embarked
with the precipitation of despair, and the people of Hippo were
permitted, with their families and effects, to occupy the vacant
place of the soldiers, the greatest part of whom were either
slain or made prisoners by the Vandals   The count, whose
fatal credulity had wounded the vitals of the republic, might
enter the palace of Ravenna with some anxiety, which was soon
removed by the smiles of Placidia   Boniface accepted with
[Magister gratitude the rank of patrician, and the dignity of master-general
atriusque of the Roman armies , but he must have blushed at the sight of
militiae] those medals in which he was represented with the name and
attributes of victory [34] The discovery of his fraud, the displeasure of the empress, and the distinguished favour of his
rival, exasperated the haughty and perfidious soul of Aetius
He hastily returned from Gaul to Italy, with a retinue, or rather
with an army, of Barbarian followers ; and such was the weakness of the government that the two generals decided their
private quarrel in a bloody battle.   Boniface was successful; but
he received in the conflict a mortal wound from the spear of his
His death. adversary, of which he expired within a few days, in such Chris-
A D 432 tian and charitable sentiments that he exhorted his wife, a rich
heiress of Spain, to accept Aetius for her second husband   But
Aetius could not derive any immediate advantage from the
generosity of his dying enemy; he was proclaimed a rebel by
the justice of Placidia, and, though he attempted to defend
some strong fortresses erected on his patrimonial estate, the
Imperial power soon compelled him to retire into Pannonia, to
the tents of his faithful Huns.   The republic was deprived, by

[34] Ducange, Fam Byzant p 67   On one side the head of Valentinian , on
the reverse, Boniface, with a scourge in one hand, and a palm in the other, standing
in a triumphal car, which is drawn by four horses, or, in another medal, by four
stags : an unlucky emblem !   I should doubt whether another example can be
found of the head of a subject on the reverse of an Imperial medal   See Science
des Médailles, by the Pere Jobert, tom 1 p 132-150, edit of 1739, by the Baron
de la Bastie   [Eckhel, 8, 293, explains these as private medals issued in honour of
a charioteer named Bonifatius]

their mutual discord, of the service of her two most illustrious champions [35]

It might naturally be expected, after the retreat of Boniface, that the Vandals would achieve, without resistance or delay, the conquest of Africa   Eight years however elapsed from the evacuation of Hippo to the reduction of Carthage.   In the midst of that interval the ambitious Genseric, in the full tide of apparent prosperity, negotiated a treaty of peace, by which he gave his son Hunneric for an hostage, and consented to leave the Western emperor in the undisturbed possession of the three Mauritanias.[36]   This moderation, which cannot be imputed to the justice, must be ascribed to the policy, of the conqueror. His throne was encompassed with domestic enemies, who accused the baseness of his birth and asserted the legitimate claims of his nephews, the sons of Gonderic   Those nephews, indeed, he sacrificed to his safety ; and their mother, the widow of the deceased king, was precipitated, by his order, into the river Ampsaga.   But the public discontent burst forth in dangerous and frequent conspiracies ; and the warlike tyrant is supposed to have shed more Vandal blood by the hand of the executioner than in the field of battle.[37]   The convulsions of Africa, which had favoured his attack, opposed the firm establishment of his power, and the various seditions of the Moors and Germans, the Donatists and Catholics, continually disturbed, or threatened, the unsettled reign of the conqueror.   As he advanced towards Carthage, he was forced to withdraw his troops from the Western provinces ; the sea-coast was exposed to the naval enterprises of the Romans of Spain and Italy ; and, in the heart of Numidia, the strong inland city of Cirta still persisted in obstinate inde- [Constantine]

(marginal notes: Progress of the Vandals in Africa A D 431 439 ;   [A D 435, Feb 11])*

---

[35] Procopius (de Bell Vandal. 1 1. c. 3, p   185) continues the history of Boniface no farther than his return to Italy   His death is mentioned by Prosper [ad ann. 432] and Marcellinus , the expression of the latter, that Aetius, the day before, had provided himself with a *longer* spear, implies something like a regular duel   [So Mr. Hodgkin, 1 879, who sees here " the influence of Teutonic usages "   See further, Appendix 26]

[36] See Procopius, de Bell Vandal 1 1 c 4, p 186   Valentinian published several humane laws, to relieve the distress of his Numidian and Mauritanian subjects , he discharged them, in a great measure, from the payment of their debts, reduced their tribute to one-eighth, and gave them a right of appeal from their provincial magistrates to the præfect of Rome   Cod Theod tom vi Novell p. 11, 12   [By the treaty of 435 the Vandals ſseem to have been recognized in the possession of Numidia, Byzacena, and Proconsularis, with the exception of Carthage and the adjacent region   It is doubtful what happened at Hippo]

[37] Victor Vitensis, de Persecut Vandal 1 11 c 5, p 26   The cruelties of Genseric towards his subjects are strongly expressed in Prosper s Chronicle, A D. 442.

pendence [38]   These difficulties were gradually subdued by the
spirit, the perseverance, and the cruelty of Genseric, who alternately applied the arts of peace and war to the establishment of
his African kingdom.   He subscribed a solemn treaty, with the
hope of deriving some advantage from the term of its continuance and the moment of its violation   The vigilance of his
enemies was relaxed by the protestations of friendship which
concealed his hostile approach ; and Carthage was at length surprised by the Vandals, five hundred and eighty-five years after
the destruction of the city and republic by the younger Scipio.[39]

They surprise
Carthage
A D 439, Octo-
ber 9 [19 or 23]

A new city had arisen from its ruins, with the title of a
colony ; and, though Carthage might yield to the royal preroga
tives of Constantinople, and perhaps to the trade of Alexandria
or the splendour of Antioch, she still maintained the second
rank in the West, as the *Rome* (if we may use the style of contemporaries) of the African world   That wealthy and opulent
metropolis [40] displayed, in a dependent condition, the image of
a flourishing republic.   Carthage contained the manufactures,
the arms, and the treasures of the six provinces   A regular
subordination of civil honours gradually ascended from the procurators of the streets and quarters of the city to the tribunal of
the supreme magistrate, who, with the title of proconsul, represented the state and dignity of a consul of ancient Rome
Schools and *gymnasia* were instituted for the education of the
African youth, and the liberal arts and manners, grammar,
rhetoric, and philosophy, were publicly taught in the Greek and
Latin languages   The buildings of Carthage were uniform and
magnificent , a shady grove was planted in the midst of the
capital ; the *new* port, a secure and capacious harbour, was subservient to the commercial industry of citizens and strangers ,
and the splendid games of the circus and theatre were exhibited
almost in the presence of the Barbarians.   The reputation of the
Carthaginians was not equal to that of their country, and the
reproach of Punic faith still adhered to their subtle and faithless

[38] Possidius, in Vit Augustin c 28, apud Ruinart, p 428
[39] See the Chronicles of Idatius, Isidore, Prosper, and Marcellinus [and Chron
Pasch]   They mark the same year, but different days, for the surprisal of Carthage
[40] The picture of Carthage, as it flourished in the fourth and fifth centuries, is
taken from the Expositio totius Mundi, p 17, 18, in the third volume of Hudson's
Minor Geographers, from Ausonius de Claris Urbibus, p 228, 229, and principally
from Salvian, de Gubernatione Dei, l vii p 257, 258 [§ 67 *qq*].   I am surprised
that the *Notitia* should not place either a mint or an arsenal at Carthage, but
only a gynæceum or female manufacture

character [41]   The habits of trade and the abuse of luxury had
corrupted their manners ; but their impious contempt of monks
and the shameless practice of unnatural lusts are the two abominations which excite the pious vehemence of Salvian, the
preacher of the age.[42] The king of the Vandals severely reformed
the vices of a voluptuous people ; and the ancient, noble, ingenuous
freedom of Carthage (these expressions of Victor are not without
energy) was reduced by Genseric into a state of ignominious
servitude. After he had permitted his licentious troops to
satiate their rage and avarice, he instituted a more regular system
of rapine and oppression   An edict was promulgated, which
enjoined all persons, without fraud or delay, to deliver their
gold, silver, jewels, and valuable furniture or apparel, to the
royal officers ; and the attempt to secrete any part of their
patrimony was inexorably punished with death and torture, as
an act of treason against the state   The lands of the procon-
sular province, which formed the immediate district of Carthage,
were accurately measured and divided among the Barbarians, and
the conqueror reserved for his peculiar domain, the fertile territory of Byzacium, and the adjacent parts of Numidia and Getulia.[43]

It was natural enough that Genseric should hate those whom *African exiles and captives* he had injured ; the nobility and senators of Carthage were exposed to his jealousy and resentment ; and all those who refused the ignominious terms, which their honour and religion
forbade them to accept, were compelled by the Arian tyrant to
embrace the condition of perpetual banishment   Rome, Italy,
and the provinces of the East were filled with a crowd of exiles,
of fugitives, and of ingenuous captives, who solicited the public
compassion ; and the benevolent epistles of Theodoret still preserve the names and misfortunes of Cælestian and Maria.[44]   The

[41] The anonymous author of the Expositio totius Mundi compares, in his barbarous Latin, the country and the inhabitants , and after stigmatizing their want
of faith, he coolly concludes . Difficile autem inter eos invenitur bonus, tamen in
multis pauci boni esse possunt   P 18

[42] He declares that the peculiar vices of each country were collected in the sink
of Carthage (l vii 257 [§ 74])   In the indulgence of vice the Africans applauded
their manly virtue   Et illi se magis virilis fortitudinis esse crederent, qui maxime
viros fœminei usus probrositate fregissent (p. 268 [§ 87])   The streets of Carthage
were polluted by effeminate wretches, who publicly assumed the countenance, the
dress, and the character of women (p. 264 [§ 83])   If a monk appeared in the city, the
holy man was pursued with impious scorn and ridicule ; detestantibus ridentium
cachinnis ([cachinnis et d r. sibilis] p 289 [viii 22])

[43] Compare Procopius de Bell Vandal l 1 c 5, p 189, 190, and Victor
Vitensis, de Persecut Vandal. L 1 c 4

[44] Ruinart (p 444-457) has collected from Theodoret, and other authors, the misfortunes, real and fabulous, of the inhabitants of Carthage

Syrian bishop deplores the misfortunes of Cælestian, who, from the state of a noble and opulent senator of Carthage, was reduced, with his wife and family, and servants, to beg his bread in a foreign country, but he applauds the resignation of the Christian exile, and the philosophic temper which, under the pressure of such calamities, could enjoy more real happiness than was the ordinary lot of wealth and prosperity The story of Maria, the daughter of the magnificent Eudæmon, is singular and interesting. In the sack of Carthage, she was purchased from the Vandals by some merchants of Syria, who afterwards sold her as a slave in their native country. A female attendant, transported in the same ship, and sold in the same family, still continued to respect a mistress whom fortune had reduced to the common level of servitude; and the daughter of Eudæmon received from her grateful affection the domestic services which she had once required from her obedience This remarkable behaviour devulged the real condition of Maria, who, in the absence of the bishop of Cyrrhus, was redeemed from slavery by the generosity of some soldiers of the garrison The liberality of Theodoret provided for her decent maintenance; and she passed ten months among the deaconesses of the church; till she was unexpectedly informed that her father, who had escaped from the ruin of Carthage, exercised an honourable office in one of the western provinces Her filial impatience was seconded by the pious bishop : Theodoret, in a letter still extant, recommends Maria to the bishop of Ægæ, a maritime city of Cilicia, which was frequented, during the annual fair, by the vessels of the West, most earnestly requesting that his colleague would use the maiden with a tenderness suitable to her birth, and that he would intrust her to the care of such faithful merchants as would esteem it a sufficient gain if they restored a daughter, lost beyond all human hope, to the arms of her afflicted parent

Fable of the seven sleepers Among the insipid legend of ecclesiastical history, I am tempted to distinguish the memorable fable of the SEVEN SLEEPERS; [45] whose imaginary date corresponds with the reign of the younger Theodosius and the conquest of Africa by

[45] The choice of fabulous circumstances is of small importance , yet I have confined myself to the narrative which was translated from the Syriac by the care of Gregory of Tours (de Gloriâ Martyrum, l 1 c 95, in Max Bibliothecâ Patrum, tom xi p 856), to the Greek acts of their martyrdom (apud Photium, p 1400, 1401), and to the Annals of the Patriarch Eutychius (tom i p 391, 531, 532, 535 Vers Pocock)

the Vandals [46]   When the emperor Decius persecuted the Christians, seven noble youths of Ephesus concealed themselves in a spacious cavern in the side of an adjacent mountain; where they were doomed to perish by the tyrant, who gave orders that the entrance should be firmly secured with a pile of huge stones.   They immediately fell into a deep slumber, which was miraculously prolonged, without injuring the powers of life, during a period of one hundred and eighty-seven years. At the end of that time, the slaves of Adolius, to whom the inheritance of the mountain had descended, removed the stones, to supply materials for some rustic edifice; the light of the sun darted into the cavern, and the seven sleepers were permitted to awake.   After a slumber, as they thought, of a few hours, they were pressed by the calls of hunger; and resolved that Jamblichus, one of their number, should secretly return to the city, to purchase bread for the use of his companions   The youth (if we may still employ that appellation) could no longer recognise the once familiar aspect of his native country; and his surprise was increased by the appearance of a large cross, triumphantly erected over the principal gate of Ephesus.   His singular dress and obsolete language confounded the baker, to whom he offered an ancient medal of Decius as the current coin of the empire; and Jamblichus, on the suspicion of a secret treasure, was dragged before the judge.   Their mutual inquiries produced the amazing discovery that two centuries were almost elapsed since Jamblichus and his friends had escaped from the rage of a Pagan tyrant   The bishop of Ephesus, the clergy, the magistrates, the people, and, as it is said, the emperor Theodosius himself, hastened to visit the cavern of the Seven Sleepers, who bestowed their benediction, related their story, and at the same instant peaceably expired.   The origin of this marvellous fable cannot be ascribed to the pious fraud and credulity of the *modern* Greeks, since the authentic tradition may be traced within half a century of the supposed miracle. James of Sarug, a Syrian bishop, who was born only two years after the death of the younger Theodosius, has devoted one of

[46] Two Syriac writers, as they are quoted by Assemanni (Bibliot. Oriental tom i. p. 336, 338), place the resurrection of the Seven Sleepers in the year 736 (A D 425) or 748 (A D 437) of the æra of the Seleucides Their Greek acts, which Photius had read, assign the date of the thirty-eighth year of the reign of Theodosius, which may coincide either with A D 439, or 446 The period which had elapsed since the persecution of Decius is easily ascertained; and nothing less than the ignorance of Mahomet, or the legendaries, could suppose an interval of three or four hundred years

his two hundred and thirty homilies to the praise of the young
men of Ephesus [47] Their legend, before the end of the sixth
century, was translated from the Syriac into the Latin language,
by the care of Gregory of Tours   The hostile communions
of the East preserve their memory with equal reverence ; and
their names are honourably inscribed in the Roman, the
Abyssinian, and the Russian calendar.[48] Nor has their reputation been confined to the Christian world   This popular tale,
which Mahomet might learn when he drove his camels to the
fairs of Syria, is introduced, as a divine revelation, into the
Koran [49] The story of the Seven Sleepers has been adopted,
and adorned, by the nations, from Bengal to Africa, who profess the Mahometan religion , [50] and some vestiges of a similar
tradition have been discovered in the remote extremities of
Scandinavia [51] This easy and universal belief, so expressive of
the sense of mankind, may be ascribed to the genuine merit of
the fable itself. We imperceptibly advance from youth to age,
without observing the gradual, but incessant, change of human
affairs, and, even in our larger experiences of history, the imagination is accustomed, by a perpetual series of causes and
effects, to unite the most distant revolutions.   But, if the
interval between two memorable æras could be instantly an-

[47] James, one of the orthodox fathers of the Syrian church, was born A D 452 ,
he began to compose his sermons, A.D 474 , he was |made bishop of Batnæ, in
the district of Sarug, and province of Mesopotamia, A D 519, and died A D 521
(Assemanni, tom 1 p 288, 289) For the homily *de Pueris Ephesinis*, see p
335-339 : though I could wish that Assemanni had translated the text of James of
Sarug, instead of answering the objections of Baronius
[48] See the *Acta Sanctorum* of the Bollandists (Mensis Julii, tom vi p 375-397).
This immense calendar of saints, in one hundred and twenty-six years (1644-1770),
and in fifty volumes in folio, has advanced no farther than the 7th day of October
The suppression of the Jesuits has most probably checked an undertaking, which,
through the medium of fable and superstition, communicates much historical and
philosophical instruction   [After a long interval, from 1794 to 1845, it was continued, and has now reached November 4rth (1894)]
[49] See Maracci Alcoran , Sura, xviii. tom 11 p 420-427, and tom 1 part iv.
p 103   With such an ample privilege, Mahomet has not shewn much taste or ingenuity.   He has invented the dog (Al Rakim) of the Seven Sleepers , the respect
of the sun, who altered his course twice a day that he might shine into the cavern ,
and the care of God himself, who preserved their bodies from putrefaction, by
turning them to the right and left
[50] See D'Herbelot, Bibliothèque Orientale, p 139 , and Renaudot, Hist.
Patriarch Alexandrin, p 39, 40
[51] Paul, the deacon of Aquileia (de Gestis Langobardorum, l 1 c 4, p 745,
746, edit Grot), who lived towards the end of the eighth century, has placed in a
cavern under a rock, on the shore of the ocean, the Seven Sleepers of the North,
whose long repose was respected by the Barbarians   Their dress declared them
to be Romans , and the deacon conjectures that they were reserved by Providence
as the future apostles of those unbelieving countries.

nihilated; if it were possible, after a momentary slumber of
two hundred years, to display the *new* world to the eyes of a
spectator, who still retained a lively and recent impression of
the *old;* his surprise and his reflections would furnish the
pleasing subject of a philosophical romance The scene could
not be more advantageously placed than in the two centuries
which elapsed between the reigns of Decius and of Theodosius
the younger   During this period, the seat of government had
been transported from Rome to a new city on the banks of the
Thracian Bosphorus; and the abuse of military spirit had been
suppressed by an artificial system of tame and ceremonious
servitude   The throne of the persecuting Decius was filled
by a succession of Christian and orthodox princes, who had
extirpated the fabulous gods of antiquity; and the public devotion of the age was impatient to exalt the saints and martyrs
of the Catholic church on the altars of Diana and Hercules.
The union of the Roman empire was dissolved ; its genius was
humbled in the dust , and armies of unknown Barbarians,
issuing from the frozen regions of the North, had established
their victorious reign over the fairest provinces of Europe and
Africa.

CHAPTER XXXIV

*The Character, Conquests, and Court of Attila, King of the Huns—
Death of Theodosius the Younger—Elevation of Marcian to the
Empire of the East*

The Huns
A D 376-433

THE western world was oppressed by the Goths and Vandals,
who fled before the Huns ; but the achievements of the Huns
themselves were not adequate to their power and prosperity.
Their victorious hords had spread from the Volga to the
Danube ; but the public force was exhausted by the discord of
independent chieftains; their valour was idly consumed in
obscure and predatory excursions ; and they often degraded
their national dignity by condescending, for the hopes of spoil,
to enlist under the banners of their fugitive enemies.   In the
reign of ATTILA,[1] the Huns again became the terror of the
world ; and I shall now describe the character and actions of
that formidable Barbarian, who alternately insulted and invaded the East and the West, and urged the rapid downfall of
the Roman empire

Their estab
lishment
in modern
Hungary

In the tide of emigration which impetuously rolled from the
confines of China to those of Germany, the most powerful and
populous tribes may commonly be found on the verge of the
Roman provinces.   The accumulated weight was sustained for
a while by artificial barriers , and the easy condescension of
the emperors invited, without satisfying, the insolent demands
of the Barbarians, who had acquired an eager appetite for the
luxuries of civilized life.   The Hungarians, who ambitiously

[1] The authentic materials for the history of Attila may be found in Jornandes
(de Rebus Geticis, c 34-50, p 660-688, edit Grot) and Priscus (Excerpta de
Legationibus, p 33-76, Paris, 1648 [fr 1 *sqq* in F H G vol iv])   I have not
seen the lives of Attila, composed by Juvencus Cœlius Calanus Dalmatinus, in the
twelfth century , or by Nicholas Olahus, archbishop of Gran, in the sixteenth
See Mascou's History of the Germans, iv 23, and Maffei, Osservazioni Litterarie,
tom 1 p 88, 89   Whatever the modern Hungarians have added, must be
fabulous , and they do not seem to have excelled in the art of fiction   They
suppose that, when Attila invaded Gaul and Italy, married innumerable wives, &c
he was one hundred and twenty years of age   Thewrocz, Chron p 1 c 22, in
Script Hungar tom 1 p 76

insert the name of Attila among their native kings, may affirm
with truth that the hordes which were subject to his uncle
Roas, or Rugilas, had formed their encampments within the [Roaa]
limits of modern Hungary,[2] in a fertile country which liberally supplied the wants of a nation of hunters and shepherds.
In this advantageous situation, Rugilas and his valiant brothers,
who continually added to their power and reputation, commanded the alternative of peace or war with the two empires
His alliance with the Romans of the West was cemented by
his personal friendship for the great Aetius, who was always
secure of finding in the Barbarian camp a hospitable reception
and a powerful support   At his solicitation, in the name of John
the usurper, sixty thousand Huns advanced to the confines of [A D 425]
Italy, their march and their retreat were alike expensive to the
state ; and the grateful policy of Aetius abandoned the possession
of Pannonia to his faithful confederates   The Romans of the
East were not less apprehensive of the arms of Rugilas, which
threatened the provinces, or even the capital. Some ecclesiastical
historians have destroyed the Barbarians with lightning and
pestilence,[3] but Theodosius was reduced to the more humble
expedient of stipulating an annual payment of three hundred [£14,000]
and fifty pounds of gold, and of disguising this dishonourable
tribute by the title of general, which the king of the Huns
condescended to accept   The public tranquillity was frequently
interrupted by the fierce impatience of the Barbarians and the
perfidious intrigues of the Byzantine court   Four dependent
nations, among whom we may distinguish the Bavarians, disclaimed the sovereignty of the Huns ; and their revolt was encouraged and protected by a Roman alliance, till the just
claims and formidable power of Rugilas were effectually urged [A D 432]
by the voice of Eslaw his ambassador Peace was the unanimous wish of the senate ; their decree was ratified by the
emperor ; and two ambassadors were named, Plinthas, a general

[2] Hungary has been successfully occupied by three Scythian colonies 1, The
Huns of Attila , 2, the Abares, in the sixth century ; and 3, the Turks or Magyars,
A D 889 the immediate and genuine ancestors of the modern Hungarians, whose
connexion with the two former is extremely faint and remote   The *Prodromus*
and *Notitia* of Matthew Belius appear to contain a rich fund of information concerning ancient and modern Hungary I have seen the extracts in Bibliothèque
Ancienne et Moderne, tom xxii p 1-51, and Bibliothèque Raisonnée, tom xvi
p 127-175
[3] Socrates, l vii c 43   Theodoret, l v c. 36   Tillemont, who always depends on the faith of his ecclesiastical authors, strenuously contends (Hist des
Emp tom vi p 136, 607) that the wars and personages were not the same

of Scythian extraction, but of consular rank, and the quæstor Epigenes, a wise and experienced statesman, who was recommended to that office by his ambitious colleague.

The death of Rugilas suspended the progress of the treaty His two nephews, Attila and Bleda, who succeeded to the throne of their uncle, consented to a personal interview with the ambassadors of Constantinople; but, as they proudly refused to dismount, the business was transacted on horseback, in a spacious plain near the city of Margus in the Upper Mæsia.   The kings of
the Huns assumed the solid benefits, as well as the vain honours, of the negotiation   They dictated the conditions of peace, and each condition was an insult on the majesty of the empire. Besides the freedom of a safe and plentiful market on the banks of the Danube, they required that the annual contribution should be augmented from three hundred and fifty to seven hundred pounds of gold; that a fine, or ransom, of eight pieces of gold should be paid for every Roman captive who had escaped from his Barbarian master; that the emperor should renounce all treaties and engagements with the enemies of the Huns; and that all the fugitives, who had taken refuge in the court or provinces of Theodosius, should be delivered to the justice of their offended sovereign   This justice was rigorously inflicted on some unfortunate youths of a royal race.   They were crucified on the territories of the empire, by the command of Attila · and, as soon as the king of the Huns had impressed the Romans with the terror of his name, he indulged them in a short and arbitrary respite, whilst he subdued the rebellious or independent nations of Scythia and Germany [4]

Attila, the son of Mundzuk, deduced his noble, perhaps his regal, descent [5] from the ancient Huns, who had formerly contended with the monarchs of China   His features, according to the observation of a Gothic historian, bore the stamp of his national origin : and the portrait of Attila exhibits the genuine deformity of a modern Calmuck . [6] a large head, a swarthy complexion, small, deep-seated eyes, a flat nose, a few hairs in the place of a beard, broad shoulders, and a short square body, of

---

[4] See Priscus, p 47, 48 [fr. 1], and Hist des Peuples de l'Europe, tom vii c xii xiii xiv xv.

[5] Priscus, p 39 [fr. 12]   The modern Hungarians have deduced his genealogy, which ascends, in the thirty-fifth degree, to Ham the son of Noah; yet they are ignorant of his father's real name (de Guignes, Hist des Huns, tom ii p 297)

[6] Compare Jornandes (c 35, p 661) with Buffon, Hist Naturelle, tom. iii. p 380   The former had a right to observe, originis suæ signa restituens   The character and portrait of Attila are probably transcribed from Cassiodorius.

nervous strength, though of a disproportioned form.   The
haughty step and demeanour of the king of the Huns expressed
the consciousness of his superiority above the rest of mankind ;
and he had a custom of fiercely rolling his eyes, as if he wished
to enjoy the terror which he inspired   Yet this savage hero
was not inaccessible to pity · his suppliant enemies might confide in the assurance of peace or pardon , and Attila was considered by his subjects as a just and indulgent master.   He
delighted in war ; but, after he had ascended the throne in a
mature age, his head, rather than his hand, achieved the conquest of the North ; and the fame of an adventurous soldier was
usefully exchanged for that of a prudent and successful general.
The effects of personal valour are so inconsiderable, except in
poetry or romance, that victory, even among Barbarians, must
depend on the degree of skill with which the passions of the
multitude are combined and guided for the service of a single
man   The Scythian conquerors, Attila and Zingis, surpassed
their rude countrymen in art rather than in courage , and it
may be observed that the monarchies, both of the Huns and of
the Moguls, were erected by their founders on the basis of
popular superstition   The miraculous conception, which fraud
and credulity ascribed to the virgin-mother of Zingis, raised him
above the level of human nature , and the naked prophet, who,
in the name of the Deity, invested him with the empire of the
earth, pointed the valour of the Moguls with irresistible enthusiasm [7]   The religious arts of Attila were not less skilfully
adapted to the character of his age and country   It was natural
enough that the Scythians should adore, with peculiar devotion,
the god of war ; but, as they were incapable of forming either
an abstract idea or a corporeal representation, they worshipped
their tutelar deity under the symbol of an iron cimeter.[8]   One
of the shepherds of the Huns perceived that a heifer, who was
grazing, had wounded herself in the foot, and curiously followed
the track of the blood, till he discovered, among the long grass,

He discovers the sword of Mars

[7] Abulpharag. Dynast. vers Pocock, p 281   Genealogical History of the
Tartars, by Abulghazi Bahadar Khan, part iii c 15, part iv c 3   Vie de
Gengiscan, par Petit de la Croix, l 1 c 1, 6   The relations of the missionaries
who visited Tartary in the thirteenth century (see the seventh volume of the
Histoire des Voyages) express the popular language and opinions ; Zingis is styled
the Son of God, &c , &c

[8] Nec templum apud eos visitur aut delubrum, ne tugurium quidem culmo
tectum cerni usquam potest; sed *gladius* Barbarico ritu humi figitur nudus,
eumque ut Martem regionum quas circumcircant præsulum verecundius colunt
Ammian. Marcellin xxxi. 2, and the learned Notes of Lindenbrogius and
Valesius.

the point of an ancient sword, which he dug out of the ground and presented to Attila That magnanimous, or rather that artful, prince accepted, with pious gratitude, this celestial favour, and, as the rightful possessor of the *sword of Mars*, asserted his divine and indefeasible claim to the dominion of the earth [9] If the rights of Scythia were practised on this solemn occasion, a lofty altar or rather pile of faggots, three hundred yards in length and in breadth, was raised in a spacious plain; and the sword of Mars was placed erect on the summit of this rustic altar, which was annually consecrated by the blood of sheep, horses, and of the hundredth captive.[10] Whether human sacrifices formed any part of the worship of Attila, or whether he propitiated the god of war with the victims which he continually offered in the field of battle, the favourite of Mars soon acquired a sacred character, which rendered his conquests more easy, and more permanent; and the Barbarian princes confessed, in the language of devotion and flattery, that they could not presume to gaze, with a steady eye, on the divine majesty of the king of the Huns [11] His

[A.D 445]

brother Bleda, who reigned over a considerable part of the nation, was compelled to resign his sceptre and his life.   Yet even this cruel act was attributed to a supernatural impulse; and the vigour with which Attila wielded the sword of Mars convinced the world that it had been reserved alone for his invincible arm [12] But the extent of his empire affords the only remaining evidence of the number and importance of his victories; and the Scythian monarch, however ignorant of the value of science and philosophy, might, perhaps, lament that his illiterate subjects were destitute of the art which could perpetuate the memory of his exploits

and acquires the empire of Scythia and Germany If a line of separation were drawn between the civilized and the savage climates of the globe; between the inhabitants of

---

[9] Priscus relates this remarkable story, both in his own text (p 65 [p. 90]) and in the quotation made by Jornandes (c 35, p 662) He might have explained the tradition, or fable, which characterized this famous sword, and the name as well as attributes of the Scythian deity, whom he has translated into the Mars of the Greeks and Romans

[10] Herodot l iv. c 62   For the sake of economy, I have calculated by the smallest stadium   In the human sacrifices, they cut off the shoulder and arm of the victim, which they threw up into the air, and drew omens and presages from the manner of their falling on the pile

[11] Priscus, p 55 [F H G iv p 83]   A more civilized hero, Augustus himself, was pleased if the person on whom he fixed his eyes seemed unable to support their divine lustre, Sueton in August c 79

[12] The count de Buat (Hist des Peuples de l'Europe, tom vii p 428, 429) attempts to clear Attila from the murder of his brother, and is almost inclined to reject the concurrent testimony of Jornandes and the contemporary Chronicles

cities, who cultivated the earth, and the hunters and shepherds, who dwelt in tents ; Attila might aspire to the title of supreme and sole monarch of the Barbarians [13] He alone, among the conquerors of ancient and modern times, united the two mighty kingdoms of Germany and Scythia ; and those vague appellations, when they are applied to his reign, may be understood with an ample latitude Thuringia, which stretched beyond its actual limits as far as the Danube, was in the number of his provinces ; he interposed, with the weight of a powerful neighbour, in the domestic affairs of the Franks , and one of his lieutenants chastised, and almost exterminated, the Burgundians of the Rhine. He subdued the islands of the ocean, the kingdoms of Scandinavia, encompassed and divided by the waters of the Baltic ; and the Huns might derive a tribute of furs from that northern region which has been protected from all other conquerors by the severity of the climate and the courage of the natives Towards the East, it is difficult to circumscribe the dominion of Attila over the Scythian deserts , yet we may be assured that he reigned on the banks of the Volga ; that the king of the Huns was dreaded, not only as a warrior, but as a magician ; [14] that he insulted and vanquished the Khan of the formidable Geougen ; and that he sent ambassadors to negotiate an equal alliance with the empire of China. In the proud review of the nations who acknowledged the sovereignty of Attila, and who never entertained, during his lifetime, the thought of a revolt, the Gepidæ and the Ostrogoths were distinguished by their numbers, their bravery, and the personal merit of their chiefs. The renowned Ardaric, king of the Gepidæ, was the faithful and sagacious counsellor of the monarch, who esteemed his intrepid genius, whilst he loved the mild and discreet virtues of the noble Walamir, king of the Ostrogoths The crowd of vulgar kings, the leaders of so many martial tribes, who served under the standard of Attila, were ranged in the submissive order of guards and domestics, round the person of their master They watched his nod ; they trembled at his frown, and, at the first signal of his

---

[13] Fortissimarum gentium dominus, qui, inauditâ ante se potentiâ, solus Scythica et Germanica regna possedit Jornandes, c 49, p 684 Priscus, p 64, 65 [F H G iv p 90] M de Guignes, by his knowledge of the Chinese, has acquired (tom ii p 295-301) an adequate idea of the empire of Attila
[14] See Hist des Huns, tom ii p 296 The Geougen believed that the Huns could excite at pleasure storms of wind and rain This phenomenon was produced by the stone Gezi , to whose magic power the loss of a battle was ascribed by the Mahometan Tartars of the fourteenth century See Cherefeddin Ali, Hist. de Timur Bec, tom i p 82, 83

will, they executed, without murmur or hesitation, his stern and absolute commands   In time of peace, the dependent princes, with their national troops, attended the royal camp in regular succession , but, when Attila collected his military force, he was able to bring into the field an army of five, or according to another account of seven, hundred thousand Barbarians.[15]

The Huns invade Persia
A.D 430-440

The ambassadors of the Huns might awaken the attention of Theodosius, by reminding him that they were his neighbours both in Europe and Asia ; since they touched the Danube on one hand, and reached, with the other, as far as the Tanais   In the reign of his father Arcadius, a band of adventurous Huns had ravaged the provinces of the East; from whence they brought away rich spoils and innumerable captives [16]

They advanced, by a secret path, along the shores of the Caspian sea ; traversed the snowy mountains of Armenia ; passed the Tigris, the Euphrates, and the Halys , recruited their weary cavalry with the generous breed of Cappadocian horses ; occupied the hilly country of Cilicia ; and disturbed the festal songs and dances of the citizens of Antioch. Egypt trembled at their approach , and the monks and pilgrims of the Holy Land prepared to escape their fury by a speedy embarkation   The memory of this invasion was still recent in the minds of the Orientals   The subjects of Attila might execute, with superior forces, the design which these adventurers had so boldly attempted ; and it soon became the subject of anxious conjecture, whether the tempest would fall on the dominions of Rome or of Persia   Some of the great vassals of the king of the Huns, who were

---

[15] Jornandes, c 35, p 661, c 37, p 667   See Tillemont's Hist des Empereurs, tom vi p 129, 138   Corneille has represented the pride of Attila to his subject kings , and his tragedy opens with these two ridiculous lines
    Ils ne sont pas venus, nos deux rois¹ qu on leur die
    Qu'ils se font trop attendre, et qu' Attila s'ennuie
The two kings of the Gepidæ and the Ostrogoths are profound politicians and sentimental lovers , and the whole piece exhibits the defects, without the genius, of the poet

[16] ———— alii per Caspia claustra
    Armeniasque nives inopino tramite ducti
    Invadunt Orientis opes   jam pascua fumant
    Cappadocum, volucrumque parens Argæus equorum
    Jam rubet altus Halys, nec se defendit iniquo
    Monte Cilix , Syriæ tractus vastantur amœni ,
    Assuetumque choris et lætâ plebe canorum
    Proterit imbellem sonipes hostilis Orontem
                 Claudian, in Rufin. l ii 28-35
See likewise, in Eutrop l i 243-251, and the strong description of Jerom, who wrote from his feelings, tom i p 26, ad Heliodor [ep 60], p 220, ad Ocean [ep 77]   Philostorgius (l ix c. 8) mentions this irruption.

themselves in the rank of powerful princes, had been sent to ratify an alliance and society of arms with the emperor, or rather with the general, of the West. They related, during their residence at Rome, the circumstances of an expedition which they had lately made into the East.   After passing a desert and a morass, supposed by the Romans to be the lake Mæotis, they penetrated through the mountains, and arrived, at the end of fifteen days' march, on the confines of Media; where they advanced as far as the unknown cities of Basic and Cursic [17] They encountered the Persian army in the plains of Media; and the air, according to their own expression, was darkened by a cloud of arrows. But the Huns were obliged to retire, before the numbers of the enemy.   Their laborious retreat was effected by a different road, they lost the greatest part of their booty, and at length returned to the royal camp, with some knowledge of the country, and an impatient desire of revenge.   In the free conversation of the Imperial ambassadors, who discussed, at the court of Attila, the character and designs of their formidable enemy, the ministers of Constantinople expressed their hope that his strength might be diverted and employed in a long and doubtful contest with the princes of the house of Sassan.   The more sagacious Italians admonished their Eastern brethren of the folly and danger of such a hope, and convinced them *that* the Medes and Persians were incapable of resisting the arms of the Huns, and *that* the easy and important acquisition would exalt the pride, as well as power, of the conqueror   Instead of contenting himself with a moderate contribution, and a military title which equalled him only to the generals of Theodosius, Attila would proceed to impose a disgraceful and intolerable yoke on the necks of the prostrate and captive Romans, who would then be encompassed, on all sides, by the empire of the Huns.[18]

While the powers of Europe and Asia were solicitous to avert the impending danger, the alliance of Attila maintained the Vandals in the possession of Africa   An enterprise had been conceited between the courts of Ravenna and Constantinople, for the recovery of that valuable province; and the ports of Sicily were already filled with the military and naval forces of Theodosius   But the subtle Genseric, who spread his negotiations round the world, prevented their designs by exciting the king of the Huns to invade the Eastern empire; and a trifling

They attack the Eastern empire, A D 441, &c

----

[17] [Basich and Cursich are not names of cities, but of two men, commanders of large bands of the Huns who invaded Persia   Gibbon misunderstood Priscus]
[18] See the original conversation in Priscus, p 64, 65 [p 90]

incident soon became the motive, or pretence, of a destructive war.[19] Under the faith of the treaty of Margus, a free market was held on the northern side of the Danube, which was protected by a Roman fortress surnamed Constantia. A troop of Barbarians violated the commercial security, killed, or dispersed, the unsuspecting traders, and levelled the fortress with the ground The Huns justified this outrage as an act of reprisal; alleged that the bishop of Margus had entered their territories, to discover and steal a secret treasure of their kings; and sternly demanded the guilty prelate, the sacrilegious spoil, and the fugitive subjects, who had escaped from the justice of Attila The refusal of the Byzantine court was the signal of war, and the Mœsians at first applauded the generous firmness of their sovereign But they were soon intimidated by [Kostolatz] the destruction of Viminacium and the adjacent towns; and the people were persuaded to adopt the convenient maxim that a private citizen, however innocent or respectable, may be justly sacrificed to the safety of his country. The bishop of Margus, who did not possess the spirit of a martyr, resolved to prevent the designs which he suspected. He boldly treated with the princes of the Huns, secured, by solemn oaths, his pardon and reward; posted a numerous detachment of Barbarians, in silent ambush, on the banks of the Danube; and at the appointed hour opened, with his own hand, the gates of his episcopal city. This advantage, which had been obtained by treachery, served as a prelude to more honourable and decisive victories The Illyrian frontier was covered by a line of castles and fortresses, and, though the greatest part of them consisted only of a single tower, with a small garrison, they were commonly sufficient to repel, or to intercept, the inroads of an enemy who was ignorant of the art, and impatient of the delay, of a regular siege. But these slight obstacles were instantly swept away by the inundation of the Huns[20] They destroyed, with fire and sword, the

[19] Priscus, p 331 [leg p 33, fr 1, F H G. iv p 72, fr 2] His history contained a copious and elegant account of the war (Evagrius, l 1 c 17), but the extracts which relate to the embassies are the only parts that have reached our times The original work was accessible, however, to the writers from whom we borrow our imperfect knowledge Jornandes, Theophanes, Count Marcellinus, Prosper-Tiro, and the author of the Alexandrian, or Paschal, Chronicle M de Buat (Hist des Peuples de l Europe, tom vii c xv) has examined the cause, the circumstances, and the duration, of this war; and will not allow it to extend beyond the year four hundred and forty-four
[20] Procopius, de Ædificiis, l iv c 5 These fortresses were afterwards restored, strengthened, and enlarged, by the emperor Justinian, but they were soon destroyed by the Abares, who succeeded to the power and possessions of the Huns

populous cities of Sirmium and Singidunum, of Ratiaria [20a] and Marcianopolis, of Naissus and Sardica ; where every circumstance, in the discipline of the people and the construction of the buildings, had been gradually adapted to the sole purpose of defence   The whole breadth of Europe, as it extends above *and ravage Europe as far* five hundred miles from the Euxine to the Hadriatic, was at *as Constantinople* once invaded, and occupied, and desolated, by the myriads of Barbarians whom Attila led into the field   The public danger and distress could not, however, provoke Theodosius to interrupt his amusements and devotion, or to appear in person at the head of the Roman legions.   But the troops which had been sent against Genseric were hastily recalled from Sicily ; the garrisons on the side of Persia were exhausted ; and a military force was collected in Europe, formidable by their arms and numbers, if the generals had understood the science of command, and their soldiers the duty of obedience   The armies of the Eastern empire were vanquished in three successive engagements ; and the progress of Attila may be traced by the fields of battle. The two former, on the banks of the Utus, and under the walls of Marcianopolis, were fought in the extensive plains between the Danube and Mount Hæmus.   As the Romans were pressed by a victorious enemy, they gradually, and unskilfully, retired towards the Chersonesus of Thrace ; and that narrow peninsula, the last extremity of the land, was marked by their third, and irreparable, defeat.   By the destruction of this army, Attila acquired the indisputable possession of the field   From the Hellespont to Thermopylæ and the suburbs of Constantinople, he ravaged, without resistance, and without mercy, the provinces of Thrace and Macedonia.   Heraclea and Hadrianople might, perhaps, escape this dreadful irruption of the Huns , but the words the most expressive of total extirpation and erasure are applied to the calamities which they inflicted on seventy cities of the Eastern empire [21]   Theodosius, his court, and the unwarlike people, were protected by the walls of Constantinople ; but those walls had been shaken by a recent earthquake, and the fall of fifty-eight towers had opened a large and tremendous breach   The damage indeed was speedily repaired , but this accident was aggravated by a superstitious fear that Heaven itself had delivered the Imperial city to the shepherds of

[20a] [Ratiaria was near the modern Ardscher below Widdin (Bononia)]
[21] Septuaginta civitates (says Prosper-Tiro) deprædatione vastatæ   The language of count Marcellinus is still more forcible.   Pene totam Europam, invasis *excisisque* civitatibus atque castellis, *conrasit.*

Scythia, who were strangers to the laws, the language, and the religion, of the Romans.[22]

In all their invasions of the civilized empires of the South, the Scythian shepherds have been uniformly actuated by a savage and destructive spirit   The laws of war, that restrain the exercise of national rapine and murder, are founded on two principles of substantial interest : the knowledge of the permanent benefits which may be obtained by a moderate use of conquest ; and a just apprehension lest the desolation which we inflict on the enemy's country may be retaliated on our own. But these considerations of hope and fear are almost unknown in the pastoral state of nations   The Huns of Attila may, without injustice, be compared to the Moguls and Tartars, before their primitive manners were changed by religion and luxury ; and the evidence of Oriental history may reflect some light on the short and imperfect annals of Rome   After the Moguls had subdued the northern provinces of China, it was seriously proposed, not in the hour of victory and passion, but in calm deliberate council, to exterminate all the inhabitants of that populous country, that the vacant land might be converted to the pasture of cattle.   The firmness of a Chinese mandarin,[23] who insinuated some principles of rational policy into the mind of Zingis, diverted him from the execution of this horrid design But in the cities of Asia, which yielded to the Moguls, the inhuman abuse of the rights of war was exercised, with a regular form of discipline, which may, with equal reason, though not with equal authority, be imputed to the victorious Huns.   The inhabitants, who had submitted to their discretion, were ordered to evacuate their houses, and to assemble in some plain adjacent to the city, where a division was made of the vanquished into three parts   The first class consisted of the soldiers of the garrison, and of the young men capable of bearing arms, and their fate was instantly decided   they were either enlisted among the Moguls, or they were massacred on the spot by the

[22] Tillemont (Hist des Empereurs, tom vi p 106, 107) has paid great attention to this memorable earthquake, which was felt as far from Constantinople as Antioch and Alexandria, and is celebrated by all the ecclesiastical writers   In the hands of a popular preacher, an earthquake is an engine of admirable effect

[23] He represented to the emperor of the Moguls, that the four provinces (Petchlei, Chantong, Chansi, and Leaotong) which he already possessed might annually produce, under a mild administration, 500,000 ounces of silver, 400,000 measures of rice, and 800,000 pieces of silk   Gaubil, Hist de la Dynastie des Mongous, p 58, 59   Yelutchousay (such was the name of the mandarin) was a wise and virtuous minister, who saved his country, and civilized the conquerors. See p 102, 103

troops, who, with pointed spears and bended bows, had formed a circle round the captive multitude. The second class, composed of the young and beautiful women, of the artificers of every rank and profession, and of the more wealthy or honourable citizens, from whom a private ransom might be expected, was distributed in equal or proportionable lots. The remainder, whose life or death was alike useless to the conquerors, were permitted to return to the city; which, in the meanwhile, had been stripped of its valuable furniture; and a tax was imposed on those wretched inhabitants for the indulgence of breathing their native air. Such was the behaviour of the Moguls, when they were not conscious of any extraordinary rigour.[24] But the most casual provocation, the slightest motive of caprice or convenience, often provoked them to involve a whole people in an indiscriminate massacre, and the ruin of some flourishing cities was executed with such unrelenting perseverance that, according to their own expression, horses might run, without stumbling, over the ground where they had once stood. The three great capitals of Khorasan, Maru, Neisabour, and Herat, were destroyed by the armies of Zingis, and the exact account which was taken of the slain amounted to four millions three hundred and forty-seven thousand persons.[25] Timur, or Tamerlane, was educated in a less barbarous age, and in the profession of the Mahometan religion, yet, if Attila equalled the hostile ravages of Tamerlane,[26] either the Tartar or the Hun might deserve the epithet of the Scourge of God.[27]

It may be affirmed, with bolder assurance, that the Huns depopulated the provinces of the empire, by the number of Roman   State of captives

[24] Particular instances would be endless, but the curious reader may consult the life of Gengiscan, by Petit de la Croix, the Histoire des Mongous, and the fifteenth book of the History of the Huns

[25] At Maru, 1,300,000, at Herat, 1,600,000; at Neisabour, 1,747,000 D'Herbelot, Bibliothèque Orientale, p 380, 381 I use the orthography of d'Anville's maps It must, however, be allowed that the Persians were disposed to exaggerate their losses, and the Moguls to magnify their exploits

[26] Cherefeddin Ali, his servile panegyrist, would afford us many horrid examples. In his camp before Delhi, Timur massacred 100,000 Indian prisoners, who had *smiled* when the army of their countrymen appeared in sight (Hist de Timur Bec, tom iii p 90) The people of Ispahan supplied 70,000 human sculls for the structure of several lofty towers (id tom i p 434) A similar tax was levied on the revolt of Bagdad (tom iii p 370), and the exact account, which Cherefeddin was not able to procure from the proper officers, is stated by another historian (Ahmed Arabsiada, tom ii p 175, vers Manger) at 90,000 heads.

[27] The ancients, Jornandes, Priscus, &c are ignorant of this epithet The modern Hungarians have imagined that it was applied, by a hermit of Gaul, to Attila, who was pleased to insert it among the titles of his royal dignity Mascou, ix 23, and Tillemont, Hist des Empereurs, tom. vi. p. 143

subjects whom they led away into captivity In the hands of a
wise legislator, such an industrious colony might have contributed
to diffuse through the deserts of Scythia, the rudiments of the
useful and ornamental arts , but these captives, who had been
taken in war, were accidently dispersed among the hordes that
obeyed the empire of Attila   The estimate of their respective
value was formed by the simple judgment of unenlightened and
unprejudiced Barbarians.   Perhaps they might not understand
the merit of a theologian, profoundly skilled in the controversies
of the Trinity and the Incarnation , yet they respected the
ministers of every religion ; and the active zeal of the Christian
missionaries, without approaching the person or the palace of
the monarch, successfully laboured in the propagation of the
gospel [28]   The pastoral tribes, who were ignorant of the distinction of landed property, must have disregarded the use, as well
as the abuse, of civil jurisprudence , and the skill of an eloquent
lawyer could excite only their contempt, or their abhorrence [29]
The perpetual intercourse of the Huns and the Goths had communicated the familiar knowledge of the two national dialects ;
and the Barbarians were ambitious of conversing in Latin, the
military idiom even of the Eastern empire.[30]   But they disdained
the language, and the sciences, of the Greeks , and the vain
sophist, or grave philosopher, who had enjoyed the flattering
applause of the schools, was mortified to find that his robust
servant was a captive of more value and importance than
himself.   The mechanic arts were encouraged and esteemed, as
they tended to satisfy the wants of the Huns.   An architect, in
the service of Onegesius, one of the favourites of Attila, was
employed to construct a bath ; but this work was a rare example of private luxury; and the trades of the smith, the
carpenter, the armourer, were much more adapted to supply a
wandering people with the useful instruments of peace and war

[28] The missionaries of St. Chrysostom had converted great numbers of the
Scythians, who dwelt beyond the Danube in tents and waggons.   Theodoret, l.
v c 31, Photius, p 1517   The Mahometans, the Nestorians, and the Latin Christians thought themselves secure of gaining the sons and grandsons of Zingis, who
treated the rival missionaries with impartial favour

[29] The Germans, who exterminated Varus and his legions, had been particularly
offended with the Roman laws and lawyers   One of the Barbarians, after the
effectual precautions of cutting out the tongue of an advocate and sewing up his
mouth, observed with much satisfaction that the viper could no longer hiss
Florus, iv 12

[30] Priscus, p 59 [p. 86]   It should seem that the Huns preferred the Gothic
and Latin language to their own, which was probably a harsh and barren
idiom

But the merit of the physician was received with universal favour and respect; the Barbarians, who despised death, might be apprehensive of disease; and the haughty conqueror trembled in the presence of a captive, to whom he ascribed, perhaps, an imaginary power of prolonging, or preserving, his life.[31] The Huns might be provoked to insult the misery of their slaves, over whom they exercised a despotic command;[32] but their manners were not susceptible of a refined system of oppression; and the efforts of courage and diligence were often recompensed by the gift of freedom. The historian Priscus, whose embassy is a course of curious instruction, was accosted, in the camp of Attila, by a stranger, who saluted him in the Greek language, but whose dress and figure displayed the appearance of a wealthy Scythian. In the siege of Viminacium, he had lost, according to his own account, his fortune and liberty; he became the slave of Onegesius; but his faithful services, against the Romans and the Acatzires, had gradually raised him to the rank of the native Huns, to whom he was attached by the domestic pledges of a new wife and several children. The spoils of war had restored and improved his private property; he was admitted to the table of his former lord; and the apostate Greek blessed the hour of his captivity, since it had been the introduction to an happy and independent state; which he held by the honourable tenure of military service This reflection naturally produced a dispute on the advantages, and defects, of the Roman government, which was severely arraigned by the apostate, and defended by Priscus in a prolix and feeble declamation. The freedom of Onegesius exposed, in true and lively colours, the vices of a declining empire, of which he had so long been the victim; the cruel absurdity of the Roman princes, unable to protect their subjects against the public enemy, unwilling to trust them with arms for their own defence; the intolerable weight of taxes, rendered still more oppressive by the intricate or arbitrary modes of collection;

[31] Philip de Comines, in his admirable picture of the last moments of Lewis XI (Mémoires, l vi c 12), represents the insolence of his physician, who, in five months, extorted 54,000 crowns, and a rich bishopric, from the stern, avaricious tyrant

[32] Priscus (p 61 [p 88]) extols the equity of the Roman laws, which protected the life of a slave Occidere solent (says Tacitus of the Germans) non disciplinâ et severitate, sed impetu et irâ, ut inimicum, nisi quod impune De Moribus Germ c 25 The Heruli, who were the subjects of Attila, claimed, and exercised, the power of life and death over their slaves. See a remarkable instance in the second book of Agathias

the obscurity of numerous and contradictory laws; the tedious and expensive forms of judicial proceedings; the partial administration of justice; and the universal corruption, which increased the influence of the rich, and aggravated the misfortunes of the poor A sentiment of patriotic sympathy was at length revived in the breast of the fortunate exile, and he lamented, with a flood of tears, the guilt or weakness of those magistrates who had perverted the wisest and most salutary institutions.[33]

Treaty of peace between Attila and the Eastern empire A D 446

The timid, or selfish, policy of the Western Romans had abandoned the Eastern empire to the Huns.[34] The loss of armies, and the want of discipline or virtue, were not supplied by the personal character of the monarch Theodosius might still affect the style, as well as the title, of *Invincible Augustus*, but he was reduced to solicit the clemency of Attila, who imperiously dictated these harsh and humiliating conditions of peace. I. The emperor of the East resigned, by an express or tacit convention, an extensive and important territory, which stretched along the southern banks of the Danube, from Singidunum, or Belgrade, as far as Novæ, in the diocese of Thrace The breadth was defined by the vague computation of fifteen days' journey; but, from the proposal of Attila to remove the situation of the national market, it soon appeared that he comprehended the ruined city of Naissus within the limits of his dominions II The king of the Huns required and obtained, that his tribute or subsidy should be augmented from seven hundred pounds of gold to the annual sum of two thousand one hundred; and he stipulated the immediate payment of six thousand pounds of gold to defray the expenses, or to expiate the guilt, of the war. One might imagine that such a demand, which scarcely equalled the measure of private wealth, would have been readily discharged by the opulent empire of the East, and the public distress affords a remarkable proof of the impoverished, or at least of the disorderly, state of the finances A large proportion of the taxes, extorted from the people, was detained and intercepted in their passage, through the foulest channels, to the treasury of Constantinople. The revenue was dissipated by Theodosius and his favourites in wasteful and profuse luxury; which was disguised by the names

[Sistova]

[Nitzch]

[£270,000]

---

[33] See the whole conversation in Priscus, p 59 62 [p 86-89]

[34] Nova iterum Orienti assurgit [*leg* consurgit] ruina . . . quum nulla ab Occidentalibus ferrentur auxilia [Chron Gall A D. 452, ed Mommsen, Chron. Min. i p 662, ad ann 447] Prosper-Tiro [see App i] composed his Chronicle in the West, and his observation implies a censure

of Imperial magnificence or Christian charity. The immediate
supplies had been exhausted by the unforeseen necessity of
military preparations. A personal contribution, rigorously, but
capriciously, imposed on the members of the senatorian order,
was the only expedient that could disarm, without loss of time,
the impatient avarice of Attila ; but the poverty of the nobles
compelled them to adopt the scandalous resource of exposing
to public auction the jewels of their wives and the hereditary
ornaments of their palaces [35] III   The king of the Huns
appears to have established, as a principle of national jurisprudence, that he could never lose the property which he had
once acquired in the persons who had yielded either a voluntary
or reluctant submission to his authority   From this principle
he concluded, and the conclusions of Attila were irrevocable
laws, that the Huns who had been taken prisoners in war should
be released without delay and without ransom ; that every Roman captive who had presumed to escape should purchase his
right to freedom at the price of twelve pieces of gold , and that [£7]
all the Barbarians who had deserted the standard of Attila
should be restored, without any promise, or stipulation, of
pardon   In the execution of this cruel and ignominious treaty,
the Imperial officers were forced to massacre several loyal and
noble deserters, who refused to devote themselves to certain
death , and the Romans forfeited all reasonable claims to the
friendship of any Scythian people, by this public confession that
they were destitute either of faith or power to protect the
suppliants who had embraced the throne of Theodosius.[36]

The firmness of a single town, so obscure that, except on this Spirit of the
Azimuntines
occasion, it has never been mentioned by any historian or
geographer, exposed the disgrace of the emperor and empire.
Azimus, or Azimuntium, a small city of Thrace on the Illyrian [Asemus]
borders,[37] had been distinguished by the martial spirit of its

[35] According to the description or rather invective of Chrysostom, an auction of
Byzantine luxury must have been very productive   Every wealthy house possessed a semicircular table of massy silver, such as two men could scarcely lift,
a vase of solid gold of the weight of forty pounds, cups, dishes of the same
metal

[36] The articles of the treaty, expressed without much order or precision, may be
found in Priscus (p 34, 35, 36, 37, 53, [&c fr 2-4, and fr 8, p 81])   Count
Marcellinus dispenses some comfort by observing, 1st, *That* Attila himself
solicited the peace and presents which he had formerly refused , and, 2dly, *That*,
about the same time, the ambassadors of India presented a fine large tame tiger
to the emperor Theodosius

[37] Priscus, p 35, 36 [fr 5]   Among the hundred and eighty-two forts, or castles,
of Thrace, enumerated by Procopius (de Aedificiis, l iv c xi tom ii p 92, edit

youth, the skill and reputation of the leaders whom they had chosen, and their daring exploits against the innumerable host of the Barbarians. Instead of tamely expecting their approach, the Azimuntines attacked, in frequent and successful sallies, the troops of the Huns, who gradually declined the dangerous neighbourhood ; rescued from their hands the spoil and the captives , and recruited their domestic force by the voluntary association of fugitives and deserters. After the conclusion of the treaty, Attila still menaced the empire with implacable war, unless the Azimuntines were persuaded, or compelled, to comply with the conditions which their sovereign had accepted. The ministers of Theodosius confessed with shame, and with truth, that they no longer possessed any authority over a society of men, who so bravely asserted their natural independence ; and the king of the Huns condescended to negotiate an equal exchange with the citizens of Azimus   They demanded the restitution of some shepherds, who, with their cattle, had been accidently surprised   A strict, though fruitless, inquiry was allowed ; but the Huns were obliged to swear that they did not detain any prisoners belonging to the city, before they could recover two surviving countrymen, whom the Azimuntines had reserved as pledges for the safety of their lost companions. Attila, on his side, was satisfied, and deceived, by their solemn asseveration that the rest of the captives had been put to the sword . and that it was their constant practice immediately to dismiss the Romans and the deserters, who had obtained the security of the public faith.   This prudent and officious dissimulation may be condemned or excused by the casuists, as they incline to the rigid decree of St Augustin or to the milder sentiment of St. Jerom and St. Chrysostom : but every soldier, every statesman, must acknowledge that, if the race of the Azimuntines had been encouraged and multiplied, the Barbarians would have ceased to trample on the majesty of the empire.[38]

Paris) there is one of the name of *Esimontou*, whose position is doubtfully marked in the neighbourhood of Anchialus and the Euxine Sea   The name and walls of Azimuntium might subsist till the reign of Justinian, but the race of its brave defenders had been carefully extirpated by the jealousy of the Roman princes [But the town appears again in the reign of Maurice , and there—c xlvi. footnote 36—Gibbon corrects his statement here]

[38] The peevish dispute of St Jerom and St Augustin, who laboured, by different expedients, to reconcile the *seeming* quarrel of the two apostles St Peter and St Paul, depends on the solution of an important question (Middleton's Works, vol ii p 5-10) which has been frequently agitated by Catholic and Protestant divines, and even by lawyers and philosophers of every age

It would have been strange, indeed, if Theodosius had pur- chased, by the loss of honour, a secure and solid tranquillity , or if his tameness had not invited the repetition of injuries.   The Byzantine court was insulted by five or six successive embassies;[39] and the ministers of Attila were uniformly instructed to press the tardy or imperfect execution of the last treaty ; to produce the names of fugitives and deserters, who were still protected by the empire ; and to declare, with seeming moderation, that, unless their sovereign obtained complete and immediate satis- faction, it would be impossible for him, were it even his wish, to check the resentment of his warlike tribes   Besides the motives of pride and interest which might prompt the king of the Huns to continue this train of negotiation, he was influenced by the less honourable view of enriching his favourites at the expense of his enemies   The Imperial treasury was exhausted, to pro- cure the friendly offices of the ambassadors and their principal attendants, whose favourable report might conduce to the maintenance of peace.   The Barbarian monarch was flattered by the liberal reception of his ministers; he computed with pleasure the value and splendour of their gifts, rigorously exacted the performance of every promise which would contribute to their private emolument, and treated as an important business of state the marriage of his secretary Constantius [40]   That Gallic adven- turer, who was recommended by Aetius to the king of the Huns, had engaged his service to the ministers of Constantinople, for the stipulated reward of a wealthy and noble wife ; and the daughter of count Saturninus was chosen to discharge the obligations of her country   The reluctance of the victim, some domestic troubles, and the unjust confiscation of her fortune, cooled the ardour of her interested lover; but he still demanded, in the name of Attila, an equivalent alliance ; and, after many ambiguous delays and excuses, the Byzantine court was com- pelled to sacrifice to this insolent stranger the widow of Armatius, whose birth, opulence, and beauty placed her in the most illus- trious rank of the Roman matrons   For these importunate and

[39] Montesquieu (Considérations sur la Grandeur, &c c xix) has delineated, with a bold and easy pencil, some of the most striking circumstances of the pride of Attila, and the disgrace of the Romans   He deserves the praise of having read the Fragments of Priscus, which have been too much disregarded
[40] See Priscus, p 69, 71, 72, &c [F H G iv. p 93, 97, 98]   I would fain believe that this adventurer was afterwards crucified by the order of Attila, on a suspicion of treasonable practices , but Priscus (p 57 [p 84]) has too plainly dis- tinguished *two* persons of the name of Constantius, who, from the similar events of their lives, might have been easily confounded

oppressive embassies, Attila claimed a suitable return; he weighed, with suspicious pride, the character and station of the Imperial envoys; but he condescended to promise that he would advance as far as Sardica, to receive any ministers who had been invested with the consular dignity. The council of Theodosius eluded this proposal by representing the desolate and ruined condition of Sardica; and even ventured to insinuate that every officer of the army or household was qualified to treat with the most powerful princes of Scythia. Maximin,[41] a respectable courtier, whose abilities had been long exercised in civil and military employments, accepted with reluctance the troublesome, and, perhaps, dangerous commission of reconciling the angry spirit of the king of the Huns. His friend, the historian Priscus,[42] embraced the opportunity of observing the Barbarian hero in the peaceful and domestic scenes of life; but the secret of the embassy, a fatal and guilty secret, was entrusted only to the interpreter Vigilius. The two last ambassadors of the Huns, Orestes, a noble subject of the Pannonian province, and Edecon, a valiant chieftain of the tribe of the Scyri, returned at the same time from Constantinople to the royal camp. Their obscure names were afterwards illustrated by the extraordinary fortune and the contrast of their sons, the two servants of Attila became the fathers of the last Roman emperor of the West and of the first Barbarian king of Italy.

The embassy of Maximin to Attila A D 448

[Sofia]

The ambassadors, who were followed by a numerous train of men and horses, made their first halt at Sardica, at the distance of three hundred and fifty miles, or thirteen days' journey, from Constantinople. As the remains of Sardica were still included within the limits of the empire, it was incumbent on the Romans to exercise the duties of hospitality. They provided, with the assistance of the provincials, a sufficient number of sheep and oxen, and invited the Huns to a splendid, or at least a plentiful, supper. But the harmony of the entertainment was soon

---

[41] In the Persian treaty, concluded in the year 422, the wise and eloquent Maximin had been the assessor of Ardaburius (Socrates, l vii c. 20) When Marcian ascended the throne, the office of Great Chamberlain was bestowed on Maximin, who is ranked, in a public edict, among the four principal ministers of state (Novell ad Calc Cod Theod p 31) He executed a civil and military commission in the Eastern provinces, and his death was lamented by the savages of Ethiopia, whose incursions he had repressed See Priscus, p 40, 41

[42] Priscus was a native of Panium in Thrace, and deserved, by his eloquence, an honourable place among the sophists of the age His Byzantine history, which related to his own times, was comprised in seven books See Fabricius, Bibliot. Graec tom vi p 235, 236 Notwithstanding the charitable judgment of the critics, I suspect that Priscus was a Pagan.

disturbed by mutual piejudice and indiscretion.   The greatness
of the emperor and the empire was warmly maintained by their
ministers ; the Huns, with equal ardour, asserted the superiority
of their victorious monarch.   the dispute was inflamed by the
rash and unseasonable flattery of Vigilius, who passionately
rejected the comparison of a mere mortal with the divine
Theodosius ; and it was with extreme difficulty that Maximin
and Priscus were able to divert the conversation, or to soothe
the angry minds of the Barbarians.   When they rose from table,
the Imperial ambassador presented Edecon and Orestes with
rich gifts of silk robes and Indian pearls, which they thankfully
accepted.   Yet Orestes could not forbear insinuating that *he*
had not always been treated with such respect and liberality ;
the offensive distinction which was implied between his civil
office and the hereditary rank of his colleague seems to have
made Edecon a doubtful friend, and Orestes an irreconcileable
enemy   After this entertainment, they travelled about one
hundred miles from Sardica to Naissus.   That flourishing city, [Nisch]
which had given birth to the great Constantine, was levelled
with the ground ; the inhabitants were destroyed or dispersed ;
and the appearance of some sick persons, who were still permitted to exist among the ruins of the churches, served only to
increase the horror of the prospect.   The surface of the country
was covered with the bones of the slain ; and the ambassadors,
who directed their course to the north-west, were obliged to pass
the hills of modern Servia, before they descended into the flat
and marshy grounds which are terminated by the Danube.   The
Huns were masters of the great river, their navigation was
performed in large canoes, hollowed out of the trunk of a single
tree ; the ministers of Theodosius were safely landed on the
opposite bank ; and their Barbarian associates immediately
hastened to the camp of Attila, which was equally prepared for
the amusements of hunting or of war.   No sooner had Maximin
advanced about two miles from the Danube, than he began to
experience the fastidious insolence of the conqueror   He was
sternly forbid to pitch his tents in a pleasant valley, lest he
should infringe the distant awe that was due to the royal
mansion.   The ministers of Attila pressed him to communicate
the business and the instructions, which he reserved for the ear
of their sovereign.   When Maximin temperately urged the
contrary practice of nations, he was still more confounded to
find that the resolutions of the Sacred Consistory, those secrets
(says Priscus) which should not be revealed to the gods them-

selves, had been treacherously disclosed to the public enemy.
On his refusal to comply with such ignominious terms, the Imperial envoy was commanded instantly to depart, the order was
recalled; it was again repeated, and the Huns renewed their
ineffectual attempts to subdue the patient firmness of Maximin.
At length, by the intercession of Scotta, the brother of Onegesius, whose friendship had been purchased by a liberal gift, he
was admitted to the royal presence. but, instead of obtaining
a decisive answer, he was compelled to undertake a remote
journey towards the North, that Attila might enjoy the proud
satisfaction of receiving, in the same camp, the ambassadors of
the Eastern and Western empires   His journey was regulated
by the guides, who obliged him to halt, to hasten his march, or
to deviate from the common road, as it best suited the convenience of the King.   The Romans who traversed the plains
of Hungary suppose that they passed *several* navigable rivers,
either in canoes or portable boats; but there is reason to suspect
that the winding stream of the Theiss, or Tibiscus, might present
itself in different places, under different names.   From the
contiguous villages they received a plentiful and regular supply
of provisions; mead instead of wine, millet in the place of bread,
and a certain liquor named *camus*, which, according to the report
of Priscus, was distilled from barley.[43]   Such fare might appear
coarse and indelicate to men who had tasted the luxury of Constantinople · but, in their accidental distress, they were relieved
by the gentleness and hospitality of the same Barbarians, so
terrible and so merciless in war.   The ambassadors had encamped on the edge of a large morass.   A violent tempest of
wind and rain, of thunder and lightning, overturned their tents,
immersed their baggage and furniture in the water, and scattered
their retinue, who wandered in the darkness of the night, uncertain of their road, and apprehensive of some unknown danger,
till they awakened by their cries the inhabitants of a neighbouring village, the property of the widow of Bleda   A bright
illumination, and, in a few moments, a comfortable fire of reeds,
was kindled by their officious benevolence; the wants, and even
the desires, of the Romans were liberally satisfied; and they

---

[43] The Huns themselves still continued to despise the labours of agriculture,
they abused the privilege of a victorious nation, and the Goths, their industrious
subjects who cultivated the earth, dreaded their neighbourhood, like that of so
many ravenous wolves (Priscus, p 45 [p 108])   In the same manner the Sarts
and Tadgics provide for their own subsistence, and for that of the Usbec Tartars,
their lazy and rapacious sovereigns   See Genealogical History of the Tartars,
p 423, 455, &c

seem to have been embarrassed by the singular politeness of Bleda's widow, who added to her other favours the gift, or at least the loan, of a sufficient number of beautiful and obsequious damsels. The sunshine of the succeeding day was dedicated to repose ; to collect and dry the baggage, and to the refreshment of the men and horses but, in the evening, before they pursued their journey, the ambassadors expressed their gratitude to the bounteous lady of the village, by a very acceptable present of silver cups, red fleeces, dried fruits, and Indian pepper. Soon after this adventure, they rejoined the march of Attila, from whom they had been separated about six days ; and slowly proceeded to the capital of an empire which did not contain, in the space of several thousand miles, a single city.

As far as we may ascertain the vague and obscure geography The royal village and palace of Priscus, this capital appears to have been seated between the Danube, the Theiss, and the Carpathian hills, in the plains of Upper Hungary, and most probably in the neighbourhood of Jazberin, Agria, or Tokay [44] In its origin it could be no more than an accidental camp, which, by the long and frequent residence of Attila, had insensibly swelled into a huge village, for the reception of his court, of the troops who followed his person, and of the various multitude of idle or industrious slaves and retainers.[45]   The baths, constructed by Onegesius, were the only edifice of stone , the materials had been transported from Pannonia ; and, since the adjacent country was destitute even of large timber, it may be presumed that the meaner habitations of the royal village consisted of straw, of mud, or of canvas. The wooden houses of the more illustrious Huns were built and adorned with rude magnificence, according to the rank, the fortune, or the taste of the proprietors. They seem to have been distributed with some degree of order and symmetry ; and each spot became more honourable, as it approached the person

[44] It is evident that Priscus passed the Danube and the Theiss, and that he did not reach the foot of the Carpathian Hills Agria, Tokay, and Jazberin, are situated in the plains circumscribed by this definition M de Buat (Histoire des Peuples, &c tom vii p 461) has chosen Tokay Otrokosci (p 180, apud Mascou, ix 23), a learned Hungarian, has preferred Jazberin, a place about thirty-six miles westward of Buda and the Danube [Jász-Berény]

[45] The royal village of Attila may be compared to the city of Karacorum, the residence of the successors of Zingis, which, though it appears to have been a more stable habitation, did not equal the size or splendour of the town and abbeys of St Denys, in the thirteenth century (see Rubruquis, in the Histoire Générale des Voyages, tom vii p 286)   The camp of Aurengzebe, as it is so agreeably described by Bernier (tom ii p 217-235), blended the manners of Scythia with the magnificence and luxury of Hindostan

of the sovereign. The palace of Attila, which surpassed all other houses in his dominions, was built entirely of wood, and covered an ample space of ground   The outward enclosure was a lofty wall, or palisade of smooth square timber, intersected with high towers, but intended rather for ornament than defence. This wall, which seems to have encircled the declivity of a hill, comprehended a great variety of wooden edifices, adapted to the uses of royalty.   A separate house was assigned to each of the numerous wives of Attila; and, instead of the rigid and illiberal confinement imposed by Asiatic jealousy, they politely admitted the Roman ambassadors to their presence, their table, and even to the freedom of an innocent embrace.   When [leg Creca] Maximin offered his presents to Cerca, the principal queen, he admired the singular architecture of her mansion, the height of the round columns, the size and beauty of the wood, which was curiously shaped, or turned, or polished, or carved, and his attentive eye was able to discover some taste in the ornaments, and some regularity in the proportions.   After passing through the guards who watched before the gate, the ambassadors were introduced into the private apartment of Cerca   The wife of Attila received their visit sitting, or rather lying, on a soft couch; the floor was covered with a carpet; the domestics formed a circle round the queen; and her damsels, seated on the ground, were employed in working the variegated embroidery which adorned the dress of the Barbaric warriors.   The Huns were ambitious of displaying those riches which were the fruit and evidence of their victories · the trappings of their horses, their swords, and even their shoes, were studded with gold and precious stones; and their tables were profusely spread with plates, and goblets, and vases of gold and silver, which had been fashioned by the labour of Grecian artists   The monarch alone assumed the superior pride of still adhering to the simplicity of his Scythian ancestors.[46] The dress of Attila, his arms, and the furniture of his horse were plain, without ornament, and of a single colour   The royal table was served in wooden cups and platters, flesh was his only food, and the conqueror of the North never tasted the luxury of bread

The behaviour of Attila to the Roman ambassadors   When Attila first gave audience to the Roman ambassadors on the banks of the Danube, his tent was encompassed with a

[46] When the Moguls displayed the spoils of Asia, in the diet of Toncat, the throne of Zingis was still covered with the original black felt carpet on which he had been seated when he was raised to the command of his warlike countrymen See Vie de Gengiscan, l iv c 9

formidable guard   The monarch himself was seated in a wooden chair.   His stern countenance, angry gestures, and impatient tone astonished the firmness of Maximin ; but Vigilius had more reason to tremble, since he distinctly understood the menace that, if Attila did not respect the law of nations, he would nail the deceitful interpreter to a cross and leave his body to the vultures   The Barbarian condescended, by producing an accurate list, to expose the bold falsehood of Vigilius, who had affirmed that no more than seventeen deserters could be found.   But he arrogantly declared that he apprehended only the disgrace of contending with his fugitive slaves ; since he despised their impotent efforts to defend the provinces which Theodosius had entrusted to their arms. "For what fortress" (added Attila), " what city, in the wide extent of the Roman Empire, can hope to exist, secure and impregnable, if it is our pleasure that it should be erased from the earth ? "   He dismissed, however, the interpreter, who returned to Constantinople with his peremptory demand of more complete restitution and a more splendid embassy.   His anger gradually subsided, and his domestic satisfaction in a marriage which he celebrated on the road with the daughter of Eslam [47] might perhaps contribute to mollify the native fierceness of his temper   The entrance of Attila into the royal village was marked by a very singular ceremony   A numerous troop of women came out to meet their hero, and their king   They marched before him, distributed into long and regular files ; the intervals between the files were filled by white veils of thin linen, which the women on either side bore aloft in their hands, and which formed a canopy for a chorus of young virgins, who chanted hymns and songs in the Scythian language. The wife of his favourite Onegesius, with a train of female attendants, saluted Attila at the door of her own house, on his way to the palace ; and offered, according to the custom of the country, her respectful homage, by entreating him to taste the wine and meat which she had prepared for his reception   As soon as the monarch had graciously accepted her hospitable gift, his domestics lifted a small silver table to a convenient height, as he sat on horseback ; and Attila, when he had touched the goblet with his lips, again saluted the wife of Onegesius, and continued his march.   During his residence at the seat of empire, his hours were not wasted in the recluse idleness of a

[47] [Eskam ἐν ᾗ γαμεῖν θυγατερα Ἐσκαμ ἐβούλετο   Milman asks whether this means " his own daughter, Eskam " or " the daughter of Eskam "   The fact that Priscus passes no comment is in favour of the second interpretation]

seraglio ; and the king of the Huns could maintain his superior dignity, without concealing his person from the public view. He frequently assembled his council, and gave audience to the ambassadors of the nations : and his people might appeal to the supreme tribunal, which he held at stated times, and, according to the eastern custom, before the principal gate of his wooden palace. The Romans, both of the East and of the West, were

twice invited to the banquets, where Attila feasted with the princes and nobles of Scythia   Maximin and his colleagues were stopped on the threshold, till they had made a devout libation to the health and prosperity of the king of the Huns ; and were conducted, after this ceremony, to their respective seats in a spacious hall   The royal table and couch, covered with carpets and fine linen, was raised by several steps in the midst of the hall , and a son, an uncle, or perhaps a favourite king, were admitted to share the simple and homely repast of Attila.   Two lines of small tables, each of which contained three or four guests, were ranged in order on either hand ; the right was esteemed the most honourable, but the Romans ingenuously confess that they were placed on the left ; and that Beric, an unknown chieftain, most probably of the Gothic race, preceded the representatives of Theodosius and Valentinian.   The Barbarian monarch received from his cup-bearer a goblet filled with wine, and courteously drank to the health of the most distinguished guest, who rose from his seat and expressed, in the same manner, his loyal and respectful vows   This ceremony was successively performed for all, or at least for the illustrious persons of the assembly ; and a considerable time must have been consumed, since it was thrice repeated, as each course or service was placed on the table   But the wine still remained after the meat had been removed , and the Huns continued to indulge their intemperance long after the sober and decent ambassadors of the two empires had withdrawn themselves from the nocturnal banquet.   Yet before they retired, they enjoyed a singular opportunity of observing the manners of the nation in their convivial amusements   Two Scythians stood before the couch of Attila, and recited the verses which they had composed, to celebrate his valour and his victories. A profound silence prevailed in the hall , and the attention of the guests was captivated by the vocal harmony, which revived and perpetuated the memory of their own exploits   a martial ardour flashed from the eyes of the warriors, who were impatient for battle ; and the tears of the old men expressed their generous despair that they could no longer partake the danger and glory of the field [48] This entertainment, which might be considered as a school of military virtue, was succeeded by a farce that debased the dignity of human nature   A Moorish and a Scythian buffoon successively excited the mirth of the rude spectators, by their deformed figure, ridiculous dress, antic gestures, absurd speeches, and the strange unintelligible confusion of the Latin, the Gothic, and the Hunnic languages ; and the hall resounded with loud and licentious peals of laughter.   In the midst of this intemperate riot, Attila alone, without a change of countenance, maintained his stedfast and inflexible gravity ; which was never relaxed, except on the entrance of Irnac, the youngest of his sons . he embraced the boy with a smile of paternal tenderness, gently pinched him by the cheek, and betrayed a partial affection, which was justified by the assurance of his prophets that Irnac would be the future support of his family and empire.   Two days afterwards, the ambassadors received a second invitation ; and they had reason to praise the politeness as well as the hospitality of Attila   The king of the Huns held a long and familiar conversation with Maximin , but his civility was interrupted by rude expressions, and haughty reproaches , and he was provoked, by a motive of interest, to support, with unbecoming zeal, the private claims of his secretary Constantius   "The emperor " (said Attila) " has long promised him a rich wife ; Constantius must not be disappointed ; nor should a Roman emperor deserve the name of liar." On the third day, the ambassadors were dismissed , the freedom of several captives was granted, for a moderate ransom, to their pressing entreaties ; and, besides the royal presents, they were permitted to accept from each of the Scythian nobles the honourable and useful gift of a horse.   Maximin returned, by the same road, to Constantinople ; and though he was involved in an accidental dispute with Beric, the new ambassador of Attila, he flattered himself that he had contributed, by the laborious journey, to confirm the peace and alliance of the two nations.[49]

[48] If we may believe Plutarch (in Demetrio, tom v p 24 [c 19]), it was the custom of the Scythians, when they indulged in the pleasures of the table, to awaken their languid courage by the martial harmony of twanging their bowstrings

[49] The curious narrative of this embassy, which required few observations, and was not susceptible of any collateral evidence, may be found in Priscus, p 49-70 [fr 8]   But I have not confined myself to the same order , and I had previously extracted the historical circumstances, which were less intimately connected with the journey, and business, of the Roman ambassadors

Conspiracy of the Romans against the life of Attila

But the Roman ambassador was ignorant of the treacherous design, which had been concealed under the mask of the public faith. The surprise and satisfaction of Edecon, when he contemplated the splendour of Constantinople, had encouraged the interpreter Vigilius to procure for him a secret interview with the eunuch Chrysaphius,[50] who governed the emperor and the empire. After some previous conversation, and a mutual oath of secrecy, the eunuch, who had not, from his own feelings or experience, imbibed any exalted notions of ministerial virtue, ventured to propose the death of Attila, as an important service, by which Edecon might deserve a liberal share of the wealth and luxury which he admired. The ambassador of the Huns listened to the tempting offer, and professed, with apparent zeal, his ability, as well as readiness, to execute the bloody deed; the design was communicated to the master of the offices, and the devout Theodosius consented to the assassination of his invincible enemy. But this perfidious conspiracy was defeated by the dissimulation, or the repentance, of Edecon; and, though he might exaggerate his inward abhorrence for the treason, which he seemed to approve, he dexterously assumed the merit of an early and voluntary confession. If we *now* review the embassy of Maximin, and the behaviour of Attila, we must applaud the Barbarian, who respected the laws of hospitality, and generously entertained and dismissed the minister of a prince who had conspired against his life. But the rashness of Vigilius will appear still more extraordinary, since he returned, conscious of his guilt and danger, to the royal camp; accompanied by his son, and carrying with him a weighty purse of gold, which the favourite eunuch had furnished, to satisfy the demands of Edecon, and to corrupt the fidelity of the guards. The interpreter was instantly seized, and dragged before the tribunal of Attila, where he asserted his innocence with specious firmness, till the threat of inflicting instant death on his son extorted from him a sincere discovery of the criminal transaction. Under the name of ransom or confiscation, the rapacious king of the Huns accepted two hundred pounds of gold for the life of a traitor, whom he disdained to punish. He pointed his just

He reprimands and forgives the Emperor

---

[50] M. de Tillemont has very properly given the succession of Chamberlains who reigned in the name of Theodosius. Chrysaphius was the last and, according to the unanimous evidence of history, the worst of these favourites (see Hist. des Empereurs, tom. vi. p. 117-119. Mém. Ecclés. tom. xv. p. 438). His partiality for his godfather, the heresiarch Eutyches, engaged him to persecute the orthodox party.

indignation against a nobler object   His ambassadors Eslaw and Orestes were immediately dispatched to Constantinople with a peremptory instruction, which it was much safer for them to execute than to disobey.   They boldly entered the Imperial presence, with the fatal purse hanging down from the neck of Orestes : who interrogated the eunuch Chrysaphius, as he stood beside the throne, whether he recognised the evidence of his guilt.   But the office of reproof was reserved for the superior dignity of his colleague Eslaw, who gravely addressed the Emperor of the East in the following words . "Theodosius is the son of an illustrious and respectable parent ; Attila likewise is descended from a noble race ; and *he* has supported, by his actions, the dignity which he inherited from his father Mundzuk. But Theodosius has forfeited his paternal honours, and, by consenting to pay tribute, has degraded himself to the condition of a slave.   It is therefore just that he should reverence the man whom fortune and merit have placed above him , instead of attempting, like a wicked slave, clandestinely to conspire against his master."   The son of Arcadius, who was accustomed only to the voice of flattery, heard with astonishment the severe language of truth ; he blushed and trembled , nor did he presume directly to refuse the head of Chrysaphius, which Eslajv and Orestes were instructed to demand   A solemn embassy, armed with full powers and magnificent gifts, was hastily sent to deprecate the wrath of Attila ; and his pride was gratified by the choice of Nomius and Anatolius, two ministers of consular or [Nomus] patrician rank, of whom the one was great treasurer, and the other was master-general of the armies of the East.   He condescended to meet these ambassadors on the banks of the river Drenco , and, though he at first affected a stern and haughty [?Drav] demeanour, his anger was insensibly mollified by their eloquence and liberality.   He condescended to pardon the emperor, the eunuch, and the interpreter ; bound himself by an oath to observe the conditions of peace ; to release a great number of captives ; abandoned the fugitives and deserters to their fate ; and resigned a large territory to the south of the Danube, which he had already exhausted of its wealth and its inhabitants.   But this treaty was purchased at an expense which might have supported a vigorous and successful war ; and the subjects of Theodosius were compelled to redeem the safety of a worthless favourite by oppressive taxes, which they would more cheerfully have paid for his destruction.[51]

[51] This secret conspiracy and its important consequences may be traced in the

The emperor Theodosius did not long survive the most humiliating circumstance of an inglorious life. As he was riding, or hunting, in the neighbourhood of Constantinople, he was thrown from his horse into the river Lycus ; the spine of the back was injured by the fall ; and he expired some days afterwards, in the fiftieth year of his age, and the forty-third of his reign.[52] His sister Pulcheria, whose authority had been controlled both in civil and ecclesiastical affairs by the pernicious influence of the eunuchs, was unanimously proclaimed empress of the East ; and the Romans, for the first time, submitted to a female reign. No sooner had Pulcheria ascended the throne than she indulged her own and the public resentment by an act of popular justice. Without any legal trial, the eunuch Chrysaphius was executed before the gates of the city ; and the immense riches which had been accumulated by the rapacious favourite served only to hasten and to justify his punishment.[53] Amidst the general acclamations of the clergy and people, the empress did not forget the prejudice and disadvantage to which her sex was exposed ; and she wisely resolved to prevent their murmurs by the choice of a colleague, who would always respect the superior rank and virgin chastity of his wife. She gave her hand to Marcian, a senator, about sixty years of age, and the nominal husband of Pulcheria was solemnly invested with the Imperial purple. The zeal which he displayed for the orthodox creed, as it was established by the council of Chalcedon, would alone have inspired the grateful eloquence of the Catholics. But the behaviour of Marcian in a private life, and afterwards on the throne, may support a more rational belief that he was qualified to restore and invigorate an empire which had been almost dissolved by the successive weakness of two hereditary monarchs. He was born in Thrace, and educated to the profession of arms ; but Marcian's youth had been severely exercised by poverty and misfortune, since his only resource, when he first arrived at

fragments of Priscus, p. 37, 38, 39 [fr. 7 ; 8 ad init.], 54 [p. 82], 70, 71, 72 [p. 95, 96, 97]. The chronology of that historian is not fixed by any precise date ; but the series of negotiations between Attila and the Eastern empire must be included between the three or four years which are terminated, A.D. 450, by the death of Theodosius.

[52] Theodorus the Reader (see Vales. Hist. Eccles. tom. iii. p. 563) and the Paschal Chronicle mention the fall, without specifying the injury ; but the consequence was so likely to happen, and so unlikely to be invented, that we may safely give credit to Nicephorus Callistus, a Greek of the fourteenth century.

[53] Pulcheriæ nutu (says Count Marcellinus) suâ cum avaritiâ interemptus est. She abandoned the eunuch to the pious revenge of a son whose father had suffered at his instigation.

Constantinople, consisted in two hundred pieces of gold, which he had borrowed of a friend.   He passed nineteen years in the domestic and military service of Aspar and his son Ardaburius ; followed those powerful generals to the Persian and African wars ; and obtained, by their influence, the honourable rank of tribune and senator.   His mild disposition, and useful talents, without alarming the jealousy, recommended Marcian to the esteem and favour, of his patrons ; he had seen, perhaps he had felt, the abuses of a venal and oppressive administration , and his own example gave weight and energy to the laws which he promulgated for the reformation of manners.[54]

[54] Procopius, de Bell Vandal l. 1 c 4   Evagrius, 1 11 c 1   Theophanes, p 90, 91.   Novell ad Calcem Cod Theod tom vi p 30   The praises which St Leo and the Catholics have bestowed on Marcian are diligently transcribed, by Baronius, as an encouragement for future princes

CHAPTER XXXV

*Invasion of Gaul by Attila—He is repulsed by Aetius and the Visi-
goths—Attila invades and evacuates Italy—The deaths of
Attila, Aetius, and Valentinian the Third*

Attila
threatens
both empires
and prepares
to invade
Gaul. A D
450

IT was the opinion of Marcian that war should be avoided, as
long as it is possible to preserve a secure and honourable peace ;
but it was likewise his opinion that peace cannot be honourable
or secure, if the sovereign betrays a pusillanimous aversion to
war   This temperate courage dictated his reply to the demands
of Attila, who insolently pressed the payment of the annual
tribute. The emperor signified to the Barbarians that they must
no longer insult the majesty of Rome, by the mention of a
tribute ; that he was disposed to reward with becoming liberality

Marcia-
A

the faithful friendship of his allies ; but that if they presumed
to violate the public peace, they should feel that he possessed
troops, and arms, and resolution, to repel their attacks   The
same language, even in the camp of the Huns, was used by his
ambassador Apollonius, whose bold refusal to deliver the presents, till he had been admitted to a personal interview, displayed a sense of dignity, and a contempt of danger, which
Attila was not prepared to expect from the degenerate Romans.[1] He threatened to chastise the rash successor of Theodosius ; but he hesitated whether he should first direct his
invincible arms against the Eastern or the Western empire.
While mankind awaited his decision with awful suspense, he
sent an equal defiance to the courts of Ravenna and Constantinople, and his ministers saluted the two emperors with the
same haughty declaration.   "Attila, *my* Lord, and *thy* lord,
commands thee to provide a palace for his immediate reception." [2] But, as the Barbarian despised, or affected to despise,

---

[1] See Priscus, p 39 [fr 15], [2] [fr 18]
[2] The Alexandrian or Pascal Chronicle, which introduces this haughty message during the lifetime of Theodosius, may have anticipated the date , but the
dull annalist was incapable of venting the original and genuine style of Attila
[The story is also mentioned by John Malalas]

the Romans of the East, whom he had so often vanquished, he
soon declared his resolution of suspending the easy conquest,
till he had achieved a more glorious and important enterprise.
In the memorable invasions of Gaul and Italy, the Huns were
naturally attracted by the wealth and fertility of those provinces;
but the particular motives and provocations of Attila can only
be explained by the state of the Western empire under the reign
of Valentinian, or, to speak more correctly, under the administration of Aetius.[3]

After the death of his rival Boniface, Aetius had prudently retired to the tents of the Huns; and he was indebted to their alliance for his safety and his restoration. Instead of the suppliant
language of a guilty exile, he solicited his pardon at the head of
sixty thousand Barbarians; and the empress Placidia confessed,
by a feeble resistance, that the condescension, which might have
been ascribed to clemency, was the effect of weakness or fear.
She delivered herself, her son Valentinian, and the Western empire, into the hands of an insolent subject; nor could Placidia
protect the son-in-law of Boniface, the virtuous and faithful
Sebastian,[4] from the implacable persecution, which urged him
from one kingdom to another, till he miserably perished in the
service of the Vandals. The fortunate Aetius, who was immediately promoted to the rank of patrician, and thrice invested
with the honours of the consulship, assumed, with the title of
master of the cavalry and infantry, the whole military power of
the state, and he is sometimes styled, by contemporary writers,
the Duke, or General, of the Romans of the West. His prudence,
rather than his virtue, engaged him to leave the grandson of
Theodosius in the possession of the purple; and Valentinian was
permitted to enjoy the peace and luxury of Italy, while the
patrician appeared in the glorious light of a hero and a patriot
who supported near twenty years the ruins of the Western
empire. The Gothic historian ingenuously confesses that Aetius

Character and administra- tion of Aetius

A.D. 433-454

---

[3] The second book of the Histoire Critique de l'Etablissement de la Monarchie
Françoise, tom. i. p 189-424, throws great light on the state of Gaul, when it was
invaded by Attila, but the ingenious author, the Abbé Dubos, too often bewilders
himself in system and conjecture.
[4] Victor Vitensis (de Persecut. Vandal. l. i c 6, p 8, ed t. Ruinart) calls him,
acer consilio et strenuus in bello, but his courage, when he became unfortunate,
was censured as desperate rashness, and Sebastian deserved, or obtained, the
epithet of *praeceps* (Sidon. Apoll nar Carmen. ix. 131 [*leg* 280]). His adventures
at Constantinople, in Sicily, Gaul, Spain and Africa, are faintly marked in the
Chronicles of Marcellinus and Idatius In his distress he was always followed by
a numerous train; since he could ravage the Hellespont and Propontis and seize
the city of Barcelona.

was born for the salvation of the Roman republic,[5] and the following portrait, though it is drawn in the fairest colours, must be allowed to contain a much larger proportion of truth than of flattery. "His mother was a wealthy and noble Italian, and his father Gaudentius, who held a distinguished rank in the province of Scythia, gradually rose from the station of a military *domestic* to the dignity of master of the cavalry. Their son, who was enrolled almost in his infancy in the guards, was given as a hostage, first to Alaric, and afterwards to the Huns, and he successively obtained the civil and military honours of the palace, for which he was equally qualified by superior merit. The graceful figure of Aetius was not above the middle stature, but his manly limbs were admirably formed for strength, beauty, and agility, and he excelled in the martial exercises of managing a horse, drawing the bow, and darting the javelin. He could patiently endure the want of food or of sleep; and his mind and body were alike capable of the most laborious efforts. He possessed the genuine courage that can despise not only dangers but injuries; and it was impossible either to corrupt, or deceive, or intimidate, the firm integrity of his soul"[6] The Barbarians who had seated themselves in the Western provinces were insensibly taught to respect the faith and valour of the patrician Aetius. He soothed their passions, consulted their prejudices, balanced their interests, and checked their ambition. A seasonable treaty, which he concluded with Genseric, protected Italy from the depredations of the Vandals; the independent Britons implored and acknowledged his salutary aid; the Imperial authority was restored and maintained in Gaul and Spain; and he compelled the Franks and the Suevi, whom he had vanquished in the field, to become the useful confederates of the republic.

His connexion with the Huns and Alani

From a principle of interest, as well as gratitude, Aetius assiduously cultivated the alliance of the Huns. While he resided in their tents as a hostage or an exile, he had familiarly conversed with Attila himself, the nephew of his benefactor; and

---

[5] Reipublicæ Romanæ singulariter natus, qui superbiam Suevorum, Francorumque barbariem immensis cædibus servire Imperio Romano coegisset   Jornandes de Rebus Geticis, c 34, p 660

[6] This portrait is drawn by Renatus Profuturus Frigeridus, a contemporary historian, known only by some extracts, which are preserved by Gregory of Tours (l ii c 8, in tom ii p 163) It was probably the duty, or at least the interest, of Renatus to magnify the virtues of Aetius, but he would have shewn more dexterity, if he had not insisted on his patient, *forgiving* disposition   [See further the panegyric of Aetius by Merobaudes, ed by Bekker   Cp Appendix 1]

the two famous antagonists appear to have been connected by a personal and military friendship, which they afterwards confirmed by mutual gifts, frequent embassies, and the education of Carpilio, the son of Aetius, in the camp of Attila. By the specious professions of gratitude and voluntary attachment, the patrician might disguise his apprehensions of the Scythian conqueror, who pressed the two empires with his innumerable armies. His demands were obeyed or eluded. When he claimed the spoils of a vanquished city, some vases of gold, which had been fraudulently embezzled, the civil and military governors of Noricum were immediately dispatched to satisfy his complaints,[7] and it is evident from their conversation with Maximin and Priscus in the royal village, that the valour and prudence of Aetius had not saved the Western Romans from the common ignominy of tribute. Yet his dexterous policy prolonged the advantages of a salutary peace, and a numerous army of Huns and Alani, whom he had attached to his person, was employed in the defence of Gaul. Two colonies of these Barbarians were judiciously fixed in the territories of Valence and Orleans;[8] [Valentia, Aureliani] and their active cavalry secured the important passages of the Rhone and of the Loire. These savage allies were not indeed less formidable to the subjects than to the enemies of Rome. Their original settlement was enforced with the licentious violence of conquest; and the province through which they marched was exposed to all the calamities of an hostile invasion.[9] Strangers to the emperor or the republic, the Alani of

[7] The embassy consisted of Count Romulus, of Promotus, president of Noricum, and of Romanus, the military duke They were accompanied by Tatullus, an illustrious citizen of Petovio [Pettau] in the same province, and father of Orestes, who had married the daughter of Count Romulus See Priscus, p 57, 65 [p 84, 91]. Cassiodorius (Variar 1 4) mentions another embassy, which was executed by his father and Carpilio, the son of Aetius, and, as Attila was no more, he could safely boast of their manly intrepid behaviour in his presence

[8] Deserta Valentinæ urbis rura Alanis partienda traduntur Prosper Tironis Chron [ad ann 440] in Historiens de France, tom 1 p 639 A few lines afterwards, Prosper observes that lands in the *ulterior* Gaul were assigned to the Alani Without admitting the correction of Dubos (tom 1 p 300), the reasonable supposition of *two* colonies or garrisons of Alani will confirm his arguments and remove his objections [Cp Dahn, Kon der Germanen, 1 264 Von Wietersheim argues for only one settlement in the neighbourhood of Orleans, Volkerw ii p 213 (ed Dahn) The gratuitous correction of Dubos was *Aurelianae urbis*]

[9] See Prosper Tiro, p 639 Sidonius (Panegyr Avit 246) complains, in the name of Auvergne, his native country,

Litorius Scythicos equites tunc [*leg* tum] forte subacto
Celsus Aremorico, Geticum rapiebat in agmen
Per terras, Arverne, tuas, qui proxima quæque

Gaul were devoted to the ambition of Aetius; and, though he might suspect that, in a contest with Attila himself, they would revolt to the standard of their national king, the patrician laboured to restrain, rather than to excite, their zeal and resentment against the Goths, the Burgundians, and the Franks.

The Visigoths in Gaul under the reign of Theodoric A.D. 419-451

The kingdom established by the Visigoths in the southern provinces of Gaul had gradually acquired strength and maturity, and the conduct of those ambitious Barbarians, either in peace or war, engaged the perpetual vigilance of Aetius   After the death of Wallia the Gothic sceptre devolved to Theodoric, the son of the great Alaric [10] and his prosperous reign, of more than thirty years, over a turbulent people, may be allowed to prove that his prudence was supported by uncommon vigour, both of mind and body   Impatient of his narrow limits, Theodoric aspired to the possession of Arles, the wealthy seat of

[Arelate]

government and commerce; but the city was saved by the timely approach of Aetius; and the Gothic king, who had raised the siege with some loss and disgrace, was persuaded, for an adequate subsidy, to divert the martial valour of his subjects in a Spanish war.   Yet Theodoric still watched, and eagerly seized, the favourable moment of renewing his hostile attempts.

A.D. 435-439 [Narbo Martius]

The Goths besieged Narbonne, while the Belgic provinces were invaded by the Burgundians, and the public safety was threatened on every side by the apparent union of the enemies of Rome   On every side, the activity of Aetius, and his Scythian cavalry, opposed a firm and successful resistance.   Twenty thousand Burgundians were slain in battle; and the remains of the nation humbly accepted a dependent seat in the mountains of Savoy [11]   The walls of Narbonne had been shaken by the

Discursu, flammis, ferro, feritate, rapinis,
Delebant, pacis fallentes nomen inane.
Another poet Paulinus of Perigord, confirms the complaint
Nam socium vix ferre queas, qui durior hoste
See Dubos, tom i p 330

[10] Theodoric II, the son of Theodoric I, declares to Avitus his resolution of repairing or expiating the fault which his *grandfather* had committed
Quæ *noster* peccavit *avus*, quem fuscat id unu.n,
Quod te, Roma, capit ———
Sidon Panegyric Avit 505
This character, applicable only to the great Alaric, establishes the genealogy of the Gothic kings, which has hitherto been unnoticed   [The reference to Alaric is clear, cp Luetjohann in his ed of Sidonius, p 418   But *avus* is used loosely If Theodoric I were Alaric's son, the fact must have been otherwise known]

[11] The name of *Sapaudiae*, the origin of *Savoy*, is first mentioned by Ammianus Marcellinus [xv 11, 17], and two military posts are ascertained, by the Notitia,

battering engines, and the inhabitants had endured the last
extremities of famine, when count Litorius, approaching in
silence, and directing each horseman to carry behind him two
sacks of flour, cut his way through the entrenchments of the
besiegers The siege was immediately raised; and the more
decisive victory, which is ascribed to the personal conduct of
Aetius himself, was marked with the blood of eight thousand
Goths. But in the absence of the- patrician, who was hastily
summoned to Italy by some public or private interest, count
Litorius succeeded to the command ; and his presumption soon
discovered that far different talents are required to lead a wing
of cavalry, or to direct the operations of an important war.   At
the head of an army of Huns, he rashly advanced to the gates
of Toulouse, full of careless contempt for an enemy whom his [Tolosa
misfortunes had rendered prudent and his situation made
desperate.   The predictions of the augurs had inspired Litorius
with the profane confidence that he should enter the Gothic
capital in triumph ; and the trust which he reposed in his Pagan
allies encouraged him to reject the fair conditions of peace,
which were repeatedly proposed by the bishops in the name of
Theodoric.   The king of the Goths exhibited in his distress the
edifying contrast of Christian piety and moderation ; nor did he
lay aside his sackcloth and ashes till he was prepared to arm for
the combat.   His soldiers, animated with martial and religious
enthusiasm, assaulted the camp of Litorius.   The conflict was
obstinate ; the slaughter was mutual.   The Roman general,
after a total defeat, which could be imputed only to his unskilful rashness, was actually led through the streets of Toulouse,
not in his own, but in a hostile triumph , and the misery which
he experienced, in a long and ignominious captivity, excited the
compassion of the Barbarians themselves.[12] Such a loss, in a
country whose spirit and finances were long since exhausted,
could not easily be repaired ; and the Goths, assuming, in their
turn, the sentiments of ambition and revenge, would have
planted their victorious standards on the banks of the Rhone,
if the presence of Aetius had not restored strength and disci-

within the limits of that province a cohort was stationed at Grenoble [Gratiano-
polis] in Dauphiné , and Ebredunum, or Iverdun, sheltered a fleet of small vessels,
which commanded the lake of Neufchâtel   See Valesius, Notit Galliarum, p
503   D'Anville, Notice de l'Ancienne Gaule, p. 284, 579

[12] Salvian has attempted to explain the moral government of the Deity ; a task
which may be readily performed by supposing that the calamities of the wicked
are *judgments*, and those of the righteous, *trials*

plinc to the Romans.[13] The two armies expected the signal of
a decisive action ; but the generals, who were conscious of each
other's force, and doubtful of their own superiority, prudently
sheathed their swords in the field of battle ; and their reconciliation was permanent and sincere Theodoric, king of the
Visigoths, appears to have deserved the love of his subjects, the
confidence of his allies, and the esteem of mankind. His throne
was surrounded by six valiant sons, who were educated with
equal care in the exercises of the Barbarian camp and in those
of the Gallic schools ; from the study of the Roman jurisprudence, they acquired the theory, at least, of law and justice ;
and the harmonious sense of Virgil contributed to soften the
asperity of their native manners.[14] The two daughters of the
Gothic king were given in marriage to the eldest sons of the
kings of the Suevi and of the Vandals, who reigned in Spain
and Africa ; but these illustrious alliances were pregnant with
guilt and discord. The queen of the Suevi bewailed the death
of an husband, inhumanly massacred by her brother. The
princess of the Vandals was the victim of a jealous tyrant,
whom she called her father The cruel Genseric suspected
that his son's wife had conspired to poison him ; the supposed crime was punished by the amputation of her nose
and ears ; and the unhappy daughter of Theodoric was
ignominiously returned to the court of Toulouse in that deformed and mutilated condition This horrid act, which must
seem incredible to a civilized age, drew tears from every spectator ; but Theodoric was urged, by the feelings of a parent and
a king, to revenge such irreparable injuries The Imperial
ministers, who always cherished the discord of the Barbarians,
would have supplied the Goths with arms and ships and

[13] ——Capto terrarum damna patebant
Litorio, in Rhodanum proprios producere fines,
Theudoridæ fixum ; nec erat pugnare necesse,
Sed migrare Getis Rabidam trux asperat iram
Victor, quod sensit Scythicum sub mœnibus hostem,
Imputat, et nihil est gravius, si forsitan unquam
Vincere contingat, trepido——
Panegyr. Avit 300, &c
Sidonius then proceeds, according to the duty of a panegyrist, to transfer the
whole merit from Aetius to his minister Avitus

[14] Theodoric II revered, in the person of Avitus, the character of his preceptor
——Mihi Romula dudum
Per te jura placent, parvumque ediscere jussit
Ad tua verba pater, docili quo prisca *Maronis*
Carmine molliret Scythicos mihi pagina mores
Sidon Panegyr Avit 495, &c

treasures for the African war; and the cruelty of Genseric might have been fatal to himself, if the artful Vandal had not armed, in his cause, the formidable power of the Huns. His rich gifts and pressing solicitations inflamed the ambition of Attila, and the designs of Aetius and Theodoric were prevented by the invasion of Gaul.[15]

The Franks, whose monarchy was still confined to the neighbourhood of the Lower Rhine, had wisely established the right of hereditary succession in the noble family of the Merovingians.[16] These princes were elevated on a buckler, the symbol of military command;[17] and the royal fashion of long hair was the ensign of their birth and dignity. Their flaxen locks, which they combed and dressed with singular care, hung down in flowing ringlets on their back and shoulders; while the rest of the nation were obliged, either by law or custom, to shave the hinder part of their head, to comb their hair over the forehead, and to content themselves with the ornament of two small whiskers.[18] The lofty stature of the Franks, and their blue eyes, denoted a Germanic origin; their close apparel accurately expressed the figure of their limbs, a weighty sword was suspended from a broad belt; their bodies were protected by a large shield, and these warlike Barbarians were trained, from their earliest youth, to run, to leap, to swim; to dart the javelin or

(margin note:) The Franks in Gaul under the Merovingian kings A D 420 451

[15] Our authorities for the reign of Theodoric I are · Jornandes de Rebus Geticis, c 34, 36, and the Chronicles of Idatius, and the two Prospers, inserted in the Historians of France, tom 1 p 612-640   To these we may add Salvian de Gubernatione Dei, 1 vii p 243, 244, 245, and the Panegyric of Avitus, by Sidonius

[16] Reges *Crinitos* [super] se creavisse de primâ, et ut ita dicam nobiliori suorum familiâ (Greg Turon 1 ii c 9, p 166 of the second volume of the Historians of France)   Gregory himself does not mention the *Merovingian* name, which may be traced, however, to the beginning of the seventh century as the distinctive appellation of the royal family, and even of the French monarchy   An ingenious critic has deduced the Merovingians from the great Maroboduus, and he has clearly proved that the prince who gave his name to the first race was more ancient than the father of Childeric   See the Mémoires de l'Académie des Inscriptions, tom xx p 52-90, tom xxx p 557-587

[17] This German custom, which may be traced from Tacitus to Gregory of Tours, was at length adopted by the emperors of Constantinople   From a Ms of the tenth century Montfaucon has delineated the representation of a similar ceremony, which the ignorance of the age had applied to king David   See Monuments de la Monarchie Françoise, tom 1 Discourse Préliminaire

[18] Cæsaries prolixa   crinium flagellis per terga dimissis, &c.   See the Preface to the third volume of the Historians of France, and the Abbé Le Bœuf (Dissertat tom iii p 47-79)   This peculiar fashion of the Merovingians has been remarked by natives and strangers, by Priscus (tom 1 p 608), by Agathias (tom ii. p 49 [i c 3]) and by Gregory of Tours, 1 iii 18, vi 24, viii. 10, tom ii. p. 196, 278, 316 [For the short hair of the other Franks cp. Claudian's *detonsa Sigambria* (in Eutr i. 383) and Sidon Apoll Epist 8, 9]

battle-axe with unerring aim; to advance, without hesitation, against a superior enemy; and to maintain, either in life or death, the invincible reputation of their ancestors [19] Clodion, the first of the long-haired kings whose name and actions are mentioned in authentic history, held his residence at Dispargum,[20] a village or fortress whose place may be assigned between Louvain and Brussels From the report of his spies the king of the Franks was informed that the defenceless state of the second Belgic must yield, on the slightest attack, to the valour of his subjects. He boldly penetrated through the thickets and morasses of the Carbonarian forest ;[21] occupied Tournay and Cambray, the only cities which existed in the fifth century ; and extended his conquests as far as the river Somme, over a desolate country, whose cultivation and populousness are the effects of more recent industry.[22] While Clodion lay encamped in the plains of Artois,[23] and celebrated with vain and ostentatious security the marriage, perhaps, of his son, the nuptial feast was interrupted by the unexpected and unwelcome presence of Aetius, who had passed the Somme at the head of his light cavalry. The tables, which had been spread under the shelter of a hill, along the banks of a pleasant stream, were rudely overturned ; the Franks were oppressed before they could recover their arms, or their ranks ; and their unavailing valour was fatal only to themselves The loaded waggons which had followed their march afforded a rich booty ; and the virgin bride, with her female attendants, submitted to the new lovers who were imposed on them by the

[Cameracum, Tornacum]

[19] See an original picture of the figure, dress, arms, and temper of the ancient Franks in Sidonius Apollinaris (Panegyr Majorian. 238-254) , and such pictures, though coarsely drawn, have a real and intrinsic value Father Daniel (Hist de la Milice Françoise, tom 1 p 2-7) has illustrated the description
[20] Dubos, Hist Critique, &c tom 1 p 271, 272 Some geographers have placed Dispargum on the German side of the Rhine See a note of the Benedictine Editors to the Historians of France, tom ii p 166 [Greg ii 9 (p 77, ed M G H) The site of Dispargum is uncertain Cp Longnon, Géogr de la Gaule, p 619 Some identify it with Duisburg]
[21] The Carbonarian wood was that part of the great forest of the Ardennes, which lay between the Escaut, or Scheld, and the Meuse Vales Notit Gall p 126 [Cp Longnon, op cit p 154]
[22] Gregor Turon l ii c 9, in tom ii p 166, 167 Fredegar. Epitom c 9, p 395 Gesta Reg Francor c 5, in tom ii p 544 Vit St Remig ab Hincmar, in tom iii p 373
[23] ———— Francus qua Cloio patentes
    Atrebatum terras pervaserat ————
                                          Panegyr Majorian 212.
The precise spot was a town or village called Vicus Helena [ib 215], and both the name and the place are discovered by modern geographers at Lens [Longnon suggests Hélenne Sirmond sought the place at Vieil-Hesdin] See Vales Notit Gall p 246 Longuerue, Description de la France, tom. ii. p 88.

chance of war.   This advantage, which had been obtained by
the skill and activity of Aetius, might reflect some disgrace on
the military prudence of Clodion ; but the king of the Franks
soon regained his strength and reputation, and still maintained
the possession of his Gallic kingdom from the Rhine to the
Somme [24] Under his reign, and most probably from the enter-
prising spirit of his subjects, the three capitals, Mentz, Treves,
and Cologne, experienced the effects of hostile cruelty and
avarice   The distress of Cologne was prolonged by the perpetual dominion of the same Barbarians, who evacuated the ruins
of Treves ; and Treves, which, in the space of forty years, had
been four times besieged and pillaged, was disposed to lose the
memory of her afflictions in the vain amusements of the circus [25]
The death of Clodion, after a reign of twenty years, exposed his
kingdom to the discord and ambition of his two sons.   Meroveus,
the younger,[26] was persuaded to implore the protection of
Rome ; he was received at the Imperial court as the ally of
Valentinian and the adopted son of the patrician Aetius ; and
dismissed to his native country with splendid gifts and the
strongest assurances of friendship and support.   During his absence, his elder brother had solicited, with equal ardour, the formidable aid of Attila : and the king of the Huns embraced an
alliance which facilitated the passage of the Rhine and justified,
by a specious and honourable pretence, the invasion of Gaul.[27]

When Attila declared his resolution of supporting the cause   The adven-
of his allies, the Vandals and the Franks, at the same time, and   princess
almost in the spirit of romantic chivalry, the savage monarch   Honoria

[24] See a vague account of the action in Sidonius, Panegyr Majorian 212-230
The French critics, impatient to establish their monarchy in Gaul, have drawn a
strong argument from the silence of Sidonius, who dares not insinuate that the
vanquished Franks were compelled to repass the Rhine   Dubos, tom 1 p 322
[25] Salvian (de Gubernat Dei, 1 vi) has expressed, in vague and declamatory
language, the misfortunes of these three cities, which are distinctly ascertained by
the learned Mascou, Hist of the Ancient Germans, ix 21
[26] Priscus, in relating the contest, does not name the two brothers , the second
of whom he had seen at Rome, a beardless youth, with long flowing hair (Historians of France, tom 1 p 607, 608)   The Benedictine Editors are inclined
to believe that they were the sons of some unknown king of the Franks who
reigned on the banks of the Necker ,   but the arguments of M de Foncemagne (Mém de l'Académie, tom viii p 464) seem to prove that the succession
of Clodion was disputed by his two sons, and that the younger was Meroveus, the
father of Childeric   [Of Merovech, Gregory says merely that, according to some,
he was of the race of Chlojo (de hujus stirpe)]
[27] Under the Merovingian race the throne was hereditary , but all the sons of
the deceased monarch were equally entitled to their share of his treasures and
territories   See the Dissertations of M. de Foncemagne in the sixth and eighth
volumes of the Mémoires de l'Académie   [Cp Waitz, Deutsche Verfassungs-
geschichte, ii , 1 , 139 sqq.]

[Born A D
418]

professed himself the lover and the champion of the princess Honoria   The sister of Valentinian was educated in the palace of Ravenna ; and, as her marriage might be productive of some danger to the state, she was raised, by the title of *Augusta*,[28] above the hopes of the most presumptuous subject.   But the fair Honoria had no sooner attained the sixteenth year of her age than she detested the importunate greatness which must for ever exclude her from the comforts of honourable love , in the

[A.D 434]

midst of vain and unsatisfactory pomp, Honoria sighed, yielded to the impulse of nature, and threw herself into the arms of her chamberlain Eugenius   Her guilt and shame (such is the absurd language of imperious man) were soon betrayed by the appearances of pregnancy , but the disgrace of the royal family was published to the world by the imprudence of the empress Placidia ; who dismissed her daughter, after a strict and shameful confinement, to a remote exile at Constantinople   The unhappy princess passed twelve or fourteen years in the irksome society of the sisters of Theodosius, and their chosen virgins ; to whose *crown* Honoria could no longer aspire, and whose monastic assiduity of prayer, fasting, and vigils, she reluctantly imitated.   Her impatience of long and hopeless celibacy urged her to embrace a strange and desperate resolution   The name of Attila was familiar and formidable at Constantinople , and his frequent embassies entertained a perpetual intercourse between his camp and the Imperial palace. In the pursuit of love, or rather of revenge, the daughter of Placidia sacrificed every duty and every prejudice , and offered to deliver her person into the arms of a Barbarian, of whose language she was ignorant, whose figure was scarcely human, and whose religion and manners she abhorred   By the ministry of a faithful eunuch, she transmitted to Attila a ring, the pledge of her affection ; and earnestly conjured him to claim her as a lawful spouse, to whom he had been secretly betrothed. These indecent advances were received, however, with coldness and disdain ; and the king of the Huns continued to multiply the number of his wives, till his love was awakened by the more forcible passions of ambition and avarice   The invasion

[A D 450]

of Gaul was preceded, and justified, by a formal demand of the princess Honoria, with a just and equal share of the Imperial

---

[28] A medal is still extant, which exhibits the pleasing countenance of Honoria, with the title of Augusta , and on the reverse the improper legend of *Salus Reipublicæ* round the monogram of Christ   See Ducange, Famil Byzantin p 67, 73   [Obverse D N IVST GRAT HONORIA P F AVG , see Eckhel, Doctr Num 8, 189]

patiimony. His piedecessors, the ancient Tanjous, had often addressed, in the same hostile and peremptory manner, the daughters of China ; and the pretensions of Attila were not less offensive to the majesty of Rome. A firm, but temperate, refusal was communicated to his ambassadors   The right of female succession, though it might derive a specious argument from the recent examples of Placidia and Pulcheria, was strenuously denied , and the indissoluble engagements of Honoria were opposed to the claims of her Scythian lover [29]   On the discovery of her connexion with the king of the Huns, the guilty princess had been sent away, as an object of horror, from Constantinople to Italy ; her life was spared , but the ceremony of her marriage was performed with some obscure and nominal husband, before she was immured in a perpetual prison, to bewail those crimes and misfortunes which Honoria might have escaped, had she not been born the daughter of an emperor.[30]

A native of Gaul and a contemporary, the learned and eloquent Sidonius, who was afterwards bishop of Clermont, had made a promise to one of his friends that he would compose a regular history of the war of Attila   If the modesty of Sidonius had not discouraged him from the prosecution of this interesting work,[31] the historian would have related, with the simplicity of truth, those memorable events to which the poet, in vague and doubtful metaphors, has concisely alluded.[32] The kings

(margin note: Attila in vades Gaul and besieges Orleans A D 451 *)*

[29] See Priscus, p 39, 40 [fr 15, 16]}   It might be fairly alleged that, if females could succeed to the throne, Valentinian himself, who had married the daughter and heiress of the younger Theodosius, would have asserted her right to the eastern empire

[30] The adventures of Honoria are imperfectly related by Jornandes, de Successione Regn c 97, and de Reb Get c 42, p 674, and in the Chronicles of Prosper and Marcellinus , but they cannot be made consistent, or probable, unless we separate, by an interval of time and place, her intrigue with Eugenius and her invitation of Attila

[31] Exegeras mihi, ut promitterem tibi Attilæ bellum stylo nie posteris intimaturum   cœperam scribere, sed operis arrepti fasce perspecto tæduit inchoasse Sidon Apoll. l viii epist 15, p 246

[32] —— Subito cum rupta tumultu
Barbaries totas in te transfuderat aictos,
Gallia   Pugnacem Rugum comitante Gelono
Gepida trux sequitur , Scyrum Buigundio cogit
Chunus, Bellonotus, Neurus, Bastaina, *Toringus,*
Bructerus, ulvosâ vel quem Nicer alluit undâ
Prorumpit Francus   Cecidit cito secta bipenni
Hercynia in lintres, et Rhenum texuit alno
Et jam terrificis diffuderat Attila turmis
In campos se, Belga, tuos ——
                              Panegyr Avit 319, &c
[The Bellonoti are unknown   Cp Valer Flaccus, vi 160 *Balloniti*]

and nations of Germans and Scythia, from the Volga perhaps to the Danube, obeyed the warlike summons of Attila. From the royal village, in the plains of Hungary, his standard moved towards the West ; and, after a march of seven or eight hundred miles, he reached the conflux of the Rhine and the Necker; [Ripuarian Franks] where he was joined by the Franks, who adhered to his ally, the elder of the sons of Clodion   A troop of light Barbarians, who roamed in quest of plunder, might choose the winter for the convenience of passing the river on the ice ; but the innumerable cavalry of the Huns required such plenty of forage and provisions, as could be procured only in a milder season ; the Hercynian forest supplied materials for a bridge of boats ; and the hostile myriads were poured, with resistless violence, into the Belgic provinces [33]   The consternation of Gaul was universal ; and the various fortunes of its cities have been adorned [Tricasses] by tradition with martyrdom and miracles.[34]   Troyes was saved by the merits of St. Lupus ; St Servatius was removed [Tungri] from the world, that he might not behold the ruin of Tongres ; and the prayers of St Genevieve diverted the march of Attila [Parisii] from the neighbourhood of Paris.   But, as the greatest part of the Gallic cities were alike destitute of saints and soldiers, they were besieged and stormed by the Huns , who practised, in the [Mettis] example of Metz,[35] their customary maxims of war   They in-

---

[33] The most authentic and circumstantial account of this war is contained in Jornandes (de Reb Geticis, c 36-41, p 662-672), who has sometimes abridged, and sometimes transcribed, the larger history of Cassiodorus   Jornandes, a quotation which it would be superfluous to repeat, may be corrected and illustrated by Gregory of Tours, l 2, c 5, 6, 7, and the Chronicles of Idatius, Isidore, and the two Prospers   All the ancient testimonies are collected and inserted in the Historians of France , but the reader should be cautioned against a supposed extract from the Chronicle of Idatius (among the fragments of Fredegarius, tom ii p 462), which often contradicts the genuine text of the Gallician bishop

[34] The *ancient* legendaries deserve some regard, as they are obliged to connect their fables with the real history of their own times   See the lives of St Lupus, St Anianus, the bishops of Metz, St Genevieve, &c , in the Historians of France, tom i p 644, 645, 649, tom iii p 369   [Mr Hodgkin places the visit of the Huns to Troyes on their retreat eastward after the relief of Orleans (ii 122). It is impossible to base any certainty on the vague narrative of our authority (Life of St Lupus), but he thinks that the words " Rheni etiam fluenta visurum " look " as if Attila's face was now set Rhinewards '

[35] The scepticism of the Count de Buat (Hist des Peuples, tom vii p 539, 540) cannot be reconciled with any principles of reason or criticism   Is not Gregory of Tours precise and positive in his account of the destruction of Metz ? At the distance of no more than 100 years, could he be ignorant, could the people be ignorant, of the fate of a city, the actual residence of his sovereigns, the kings of Austrasia ? The learned Count, who seems to have undertaken the apology of Attila and the Barbarians, appeals to the false Idatius, *parcens civitatibus* Germaniæ et Galliæ, and forgets that the true Idatius had explicitly affirmed,

volved, in a promiscuous massacre, the priests who served at the altar, and the infants, who, in the hour of danger, had been providently baptized by the bishop; the flourishing city was delivered to the flames, and a solitary chapel of St. Stephen marked the place where it formerly stood   From the Rhine and the Moselle, Attila advanced into the heart of Gaul; crossed the Seine at Auxerre; and, after a long and laborious march, fixed his camp under the walls of Orleans.   He was desirous of [Aurelianum] securing his conquests by the possession of an advantageous post, which commanded the passage of the Loire; and he depended on the secret invitation of Sangiban, king of the Alani, who had promised to betray the city, and to revolt from the service of the empire   But this treacherous conspiracy was detected and disappointed, Orleans had been strengthened with recent fortifications; and the assaults of the Huns were vigorously repelled by the faithful valour of the soldiers, or citizens, who defended the place.   The pastoral diligence of Anianus, a bishop of primitive sanctity and consummate prudence, exhausted every art of religious policy to support their courage, till the arrival of the expected succours [36]   After an obstinate siege, the walls were shaken by the battering rams, the Huns had already occupied the suburbs, and the people, who were incapable of bearing arms, lay prostrate in prayer   Anianus, who anxiously counted the days and hours, dispatched a trusty messenger to observe, from the rampart, the face of the distant country   He returned twice without any intelligence that could inspire hope or comfort; but, in his third report, he mentioned a small cloud, which he had faintly descried at the extremity of the horizon. " It is the aid of God ! " exclaimed the bishop, in a tone of pious confidence, and the whole multitude repeated after him, " It is the aid of God ".   The remote object, on which every eye was fixed, became each moment larger and more distinct; the Roman and Gothic banners were gradually perceived, and a favourable wind, blowing aside the dust, discovered, in deep array, the impatient squadrons of Aetius and Theodoric, who pressed forwards to the relief of Orleans.

The facility with which Attila had penetrated into the heart Alliance of of Gaul may be ascribed to his insidious policy as well as to the Romans and Visigoths the terror of his arms.   His public declarations were skilfully

plurimæ civitates *effractæ*, among which he enumerates Metz   [See Mommsen's edition, Chron Min ii p 26   Rheims (Remi) also endured a Hunnic occupation]

[36] [See Life of St Anianus in Duchesne, Hist Fr. Scr, vol i.]

mitigated by his private assurances; he alternately soothed
and threatened the Romans and the Goths; and the courts
of Ravenna and Toulouse, mutually suspicious of each other's
intentions, beheld with supine indifference the approach of
their common enemy   Aetius was the sole guardian of the
public safety, but his wisest measures were embarrassed by a
faction which, since the death of Placidia, infested the Imperial
palace; the youth of Italy trembled at the sound of the trumpet, and the Barbarians who, from fear or affection, were inclined to the cause of Attila awaited, with doubtful and venal
faith, the event of the war.   The patrician passed the Alps at
the head of some troops, whose strength and numbers scarcely
deserved the name of an army.[37]   But on his arrival at Arles, or
Lyons, he was confounded by the intelligence that the Visigoths,
refusing to embrace the defence of Gaul, had determined to expect, within their own territories, the formidable invader, whom
they professed to despise   The senator Avitus, who, after the
honourable exercise of the prætorian Præfecture, had retired to
his estate in Auvergne, was persuaded to accept the important
embassy, which he executed with ability and success   He represented to Theodoric that an ambitious conqueror, who aspired
to the dominion of the earth, could be resisted only by the firm
and unanimous alliance of the powers whom he laboured to
oppress.   The lively eloquence of Avitus inflamed the Gothic
warriors, by the description of the injuries which their ancestors
had suffered from the Huns, whose implacable fury still pursued them from the Danube to the foot of the Pyrenees.   He
strenuously urged that it was the duty of every Christian to
save from sacrilegious violation the churches of God and the
relics of the saints, that it was the interest of every Barbarian
who had acquired a settlement in Gaul to defend the fields and
vineyards, which were cultivated for his use, against the desolation of the Scythian shepherds   Theodoric yielded to the evidence of truth; adopted the measure at once the most prudent
and the most honourable; and declared that, as the faithful
ally of Aetius and the Romans, he was ready to expose his life
and kingdom for the common safety of Gaul [38]   The Visigoths,

---

[37] —— Vix liquerat Alpes
   Aetius, tenue et rarum sine milite ducens
   Robur in auxilis, Geticum male credulus agmen
   Incassum propriis præsumens adfore castris
                              Panegyr Avit 328, &c
[38] The policy of Attila, of Aetius, and of the Visigoths, is imperfectly described
in the Panegyric of Avitus and the thirty-sixth chapter of Jornandes   The poet

who at that time were in the mature vigour of their fame and power, obeyed with alacrity the signal of war, prepared their arms and horses, and assembled under the standard of their aged king, who was resolved, with his two-eldest sons, Torismond and Theodoric, to command in person his numerous and valiant people. The example of the Goths determined several tribes or nations that seemed to fluctuate between the Huns and the Romans. The indefatigable diligence of the patrician gradually collected the troops of Gaul and Germany, who had formerly acknowledged themselves the subjects or soldiers of the republic, but who now claimed the rewards of voluntary service and the rank of independent allies ; the Læti, the Armoricans, the Breones, the Saxons, the Burgundians, the Sarmatians or Alani, the Ripuarians, and the Franks who followed Meroveus as their lawful prince. Such was the various army, which, under the conduct of Aetius and Theodoric, advanced, by rapid marches, to relieve Orleans, and to give battle to the innumerable host of Attila.[39]

On their approach the king of the Huns immediately raised the siege, and sounded a retreat to recal the foremost of his troops from the pillage of a city which they had already entered [40] The valour of Attila was always guided by his prudence ; and, as he foresaw the fatal consequences of a defeat in the heart of Gaul, he repassed the Seine and expected the enemy in the plains of Châlons, whose smooth and level surface was adapted to the operations of his Scythian cavalry. But in this tumultuary retreat the vanguard of the Romans and their

Attila retires to the plains of Champagne [June 24]

and the historian were both biassed by personal or national prejudices The former exalts the merit and importance of Avitus, orbis, Avite, salus, &c. ! The latter is anxious to show the Goths in the most favourable light. Yet their agreement, when they are fairly interpreted, is a proof of their veracity

[39] The review of the army of Aetius is made by Jornandes, c 36, p 664, edit Grot tom ii p. 23, of the Historians of France, with the notes of the Benedictine Editor The *Læti* were a promiscuous race of Barbarians, born or naturalized in Gaul; and the Riparii, or *Ripuarii*, derived their name from their posts on the three rivers, the Rhine, the Meuse, and the Moselle; the *Armoricans* possessed the independent cities between the Seine and the Loire A colony of *Saxons* had been planted in the diocese of Bayeux, the *Burgundians* were settled in Savoy, and the *Breones* were a warlike tribe of Rhætians, to the east of the lake of Constance [The list in Jordanes is. " Franci, Sarmatæ, Armoriciani, Liticiani, Burgundiones, Saxones, Ripari, Olibriones, aliæque nonnulli Celticæ vel Germaniæ nationes" The Sarmatæ are probably the Alans who were settled round Valence, the Liticiani may be the Læti, the Ripari the Ripuarian Franks The Olibriones are quite uncertain]

[40] Aurelianensis urbis obsidio, oppugnatio, irruptio, nec direptio, l v Sidon Apollin l viii epist 15, p 246 The preservation of Orleans might be easily turned into a miracle, obtained and foretold by the holy bishop

allies continually pressed, and sometimes engaged the troops whom Attila had posted in the rear, the hostile columns, in the darkness of the night, and the perplexity of the roads, might encounter each other without design ; and the bloody conflict of the Franks and Gepidæ, in which fifteen thousand [41] Barbarians were slain, was a prelude to a more general and decisive action. The Catalaunian fields [42] spread themselves round Châlons, and extend, according to the vague measurement of Jornandes, to the length of one hundred and fifty, and the breadth of one hundred, miles, over the whole province, which is intitled to the appellation of a *champaign* country. [43]   This spacious plain was distinguished, however, by some inequalities of ground ; and the importance of an height, which commanded the camp of Attila, was understood, and disputed, by the two generals. The young and valiant Torismond first occupied the summit, the Goths rushed with irresistible weight on the Huns, who laboured to ascend from the opposite side ; and the possession of this advantageous post inspired both the troops and their leaders with a fair assurance of victory.   The anxiety of Attila prompted him to consult his priests and haruspices   It was reported that, after scrutinizing the entrails of victims and scraping their bones, they revealed, in mysterious language, his own defeat, with the death of his principal adversary ; and that the Barbarian, by accepting the equivalent, expressed his involuntary esteem for the superior merit of Aetius.   But the unusual despondency, which seemed to prevail among the Huns, engaged Attila to use the expedient, so familiar to the generals of antiquity, of animating his troops by a military oration ; and his language was that of a king who had often fought and conquered at their head [44]   He pressed them to consider their

[41] The common editions read XCM, but there is some authority of manuscripts (and almost any authority is sufficient) for the more reasonable number of XVM

[42] Châlons or Duro-Catalaunum, afterwards *Catalauni*, had formerly made a part of the territory of Rheims, from whence it is distant only twenty-seven miles   See Vales Notit Gall. p 136   D'Anville, Notice de l'Ancienne Gaule, p. 212, 279   [See Appendix 28]

[43] The name of Campania, or Champagne, is frequently mentioned by Gregory of Tours, and that great province, of which Rheims was the capital, obeyed the command of a duke   Vales Notit. p 120-123

[44] I am sensible that these military orations are usually composed by the historian, yet the old Ostrogoths, who had served under Attila, might repeat his discourse to Cassiodorius   the ideas, and even the expressions, have an original Scythian cast, and I doubt whether an Italian of the sixth century would have thought of the hujus certaminis *gaudia*

past glory, their actual danger, and their future hopes. The same fortune which opened the deserts and morasses of Scythia to their unarmed valour, which had laid so many warlike nations prostrate at their feet, had reserved the *joys* of this memorable field for the consummation of their victories. The cautious steps of their enemies, their strict alliance, and their advantageous posts, he artfully represented as the effects, not of prudence, but of fear. The Visigoths alone were the strength and nerves of the opposite army; and the Huns might securely trample on the degenerate Romans, whose close and compact order betrayed their apprehensions, and who were equally incapable of supporting the dangers or the fatigues of a day of battle. The doctrine of predestination, so favourable to martial virtue, was carefully inculcated by the king of the Huns, who assured his subjects that the warriors, protected by Heaven, were safe and invulnerable amidst the darts of the enemy; but that the unerring Fates would strike their victims in the bosom of inglorious peace. "I myself," continued Attila, "will throw the first javelin, and the wretch who refuses to imitate the example of his sovereign is devoted to inevitable death" The spirit of the Barbarians was rekindled by the presence, the voice, and the example, of their intrepid leader; and Attila, yielding to their impatience, immediately formed his order of battle. At the head of his brave and faithful Huns he occupied in person the centre of the line. The nations subject to his empire, the Rugians, the Heruli, the Thuringians, the Franks, the Burgundians, were extended, on either hand, over the ample space of the Catalaunian fields; the right wing was commanded by Ardaric, king of the Gepidæ; and the three valiant brothers who reigned over the Ostrogoths were posted on the left to oppose the kindred tribes of the Visigoths. The disposition of the allies was regulated by a different principle. Sangiban, the faithless king of the Alani, was placed in the centre; where his motions might be strictly watched, and his treachery might be instantly punished. Aetius assumed the command of the left, and Theodoric of the right wing; while Torismond still continued to occupy the heights which appear to have stretched on the flank, and perhaps the rear, of the Scythian army. The nations from the Volga to the Atlantic were assembled on the plain of Châlons; but many of these nations had been divided by faction, or conquest, or emigration, and the appearance of similar arms and ensigns, which threatened each other, presented the image of a civil war.

Battle of
Chalons
[Summer
(July ?) A D
451]
The discipline and tactics of the Greeks and Romans form an interesting part of their national manners   The attentive study of the military operations of Xenophon, or Cæsar, or Frederic, when they are described by the same genius which conceived and executed them, may tend to improve (if such improvement can be wished) the art of destroying the human species. But the battle of Châlons can only excite our curiosity by the magnitude of the object ; since it was decided by the blind impetuosity of Barbarians, and has been related by partial writers, whose civil or ecclesiastical profession secluded them from the knowledge of military affairs   Cassiodorius, however, had familiarly conversed with many Gothic warriors, who served in that memorable engagement ; "a conflict," as they informed him, "fierce, various, obstinate and bloody ; such as could not be paralleled either in the present or in past ages"   The number of the slain amounted to one hundred and sixty-two thousand, or, according to another account, three hundred thousand persons ; [45] and these incredible exaggerations suppose a real and effective loss, sufficient to justify the historian's remark that whole generations may be swept away, by the madness of kings, in the space of a single hour   After the mutual and repeated discharge of missile weapons, in which the archers of Scythia might signalize their superior dexterity, the cavalry and infantry of the two armies were furiously mingled in closer combat. The Huns, who fought under the eyes of their king, pierced through the feeble and doubtful centre of the allies, separated their wings from each other, and wheeling, with a rapid effort, to the left, directed their whole force against the Visigoths   As Theodoric rode along the ranks to animate his troops, he received a mortal stroke from the javelin of Andages, a noble Ostrogoth, and immediately fell from his horse. The wounded king was oppressed in the general disorder, and trampled under the feet of his own cavalry, and this important death served to explain the ambiguous prophecy of the haruspices. Attila already exulted in the confidence of victory, when the valiant Torismond descended from the hills, and verified the remainder of the

[45] The expressions of Jornandes, or rather of Cassiodorius [Mommsen, Pref to ed of Jordanes, p xxxvi , regards Priscus as the source], are extremely strong Bellum atrox, multiplex immane, pertinax, cui simili nulla usquam narrat antiquitas ‧ ubi talia gesta referuntur, ut nihil esset quod in vitâ suâ conspicere potuisset egregius, qui hujus miraculi privaretur aspectu   Dubos (Hist Critique, tom i p 392, 393) attempts to reconcile the 162,000 of Jornandes with the 300,000 of Idatius and Isidore, by supposing that the larger number included the total destruction of the war, the effects of disease, the slaughter of the unarmed people, &c

prediction. The Visigoths, who had been thrown into confusion by the flight, or defection, of the Alani, gradually restored their order of battle ; and the Huns were undoubtedly vanquished, since Attila was compelled to retreat   He had exposed his person with the rashness of a private soldier , but the intrepid troops of the centre had pushed forwards beyond the rest of the line ; their attack was faintly supported , their flanks were unguarded ; and the conquerors of Scythia and Germany were saved by the approach of the night from a total defeat. They retired within the circle of waggons that fortified their camp ; and the dismounted squadrons prepared themselves for a defence, to which neither their arms nor their temper were adapted.   The event was doubtful ; but Attila had secured a last and honourable resource.   The saddles and rich furniture of the cavalry were collected by his order into a funeral pile , and the magnanimous Barbarian had resolved, if his intrenchments should be forced, to rush headlong into the flames, and to deprive his enemies of the glory which they might have acquired by the death or captivity of Attila [46]

But his enemies had passed the night in equal disorder and anxiety.   The inconsiderate courage of Torismond was tempted to urge the pursuit, till he unexpectedly found himself, with a few followers, in the midst of the Scythian waggons   In the confusion of a nocturnal combat, he was thrown from his horse ; and the Gothic prince must have perished like his father, if his youthful strength, and the intrepid zeal of his companions, had not rescued him from this dangerous situation.   In the same manner, but on the left of the line, Aetius himself, separated from his allies, ignorant of their victory, and anxious for their fate, encountered and escaped the hostile troops that were scattered over the plains of Châlons ; and at length reached the camp of the Goths, which he could only fortify with a slight rampart of shields, till the dawn of day   The Imperial general was soon satisfied of the defeat of Attila, who still remained inactive within his intrenchments ; and, when he contemplated the bloody scene, he observed, with secret satisfaction, that the loss had principally fallen on the Barbarians.   The body of Theodoric, pierced with honourable wounds, was discovered under a heap of the slain : his subjects bewailed the death of

Retreat of Attila

[46] The Count de Buat (Hist des Peuples, &c tom vii p 554-573), still depending on the *false*, and again rejecting the *true*, Idatius, has divided the defeat of Attila into two great battles the former near Orleans, the latter in Champagne · in the one, Theodoric was slain , in the other, he was revenged

their king and father, but their tears were mingled with songs and acclamations, and his funeral rites were performed in the face of a vanquished enemy The Goths, clashing their arms, elevated on a buckler his eldest son Torismond, to whom they justly ascribed the glory of their success, and the new king accepted the obligation of revenge as a sacred portion of his paternal inheritance Yet the Goths themselves were astonished by the fierce and undaunted aspect of their formidable antagonist; and their historian has compared Attila to a lion encompassed in his den, and threatening his hunters with redoubled fury. The kings and nations, who might have deserted his standard in the hour of distress, were made sensible that the displeasure of their monarch was the most imminent and inevitable danger. All his instruments of martial music incessantly sounded a loud and animating strain of defiance; and the foremost troops who advanced to the assault were checked, or destroyed, by showers of arrows from every side of the intrenchments. It was determined in a general council of war, to besiege the king of the Huns in his camp, to intercept his provisions, and to reduce him to the alternative of a disgraceful treaty or an unequal combat. But the impatience of the Barbarians soon disdained these cautious and dilatory measures, and the mature policy of Aetius was apprehensive that, after the extirpation of the Huns, the republic would be oppressed by the pride and power of the Gothic nation. The patrician exerted the superior ascendant of authority and reason, to calm the passions which the son of Theodoric considered as a duty; represented, with seeming affection, and real truth, the dangers of absence and delay, and persuaded Torismond to disappoint, by his speedy return, the ambitious designs of his brothers, who might occupy the throne and treasures of Toulouse.[47] After the departure of the Goths and the separation of the allied army, Attila was surprised at the vast silence that reigned over the plains of Châlons; the suspicion of some hostile stratagem detained him several days within the circle of his waggons, and his retreat beyond the Rhine confessed the last victory which was achieved in the name of the Western empire. Meroveus and his Franks, observing a

---

[47] Jornandes de Rebus Geticis, c 41, p 671. The policy of Aetius and the behaviour of Torismond are extremely natural; and the patrician, according to Gregory of Tours (l ii c 7, p 163), dismissed the prince of the Franks, by suggesting to him a similar apprehension The false Idatius ridiculously pretends that Aetius paid a clandestine nocturnal visit to the kings of the Huns and of the Visigoths, from each of whom he obtained a bribe of ten thousand pieces of gold as the price of an undisturbed retreat

piudent distance, and magnifying the opinion of their strength by the numerous fires which they kindled every night, continued to follow the rear of the Huns, till they reached the confines of Thuringia.   The Thuringians served in the army of Attila ; they traversed, both in their march and in their return, the territories of the Franks ; and it was perhaps in this war that they exercised the cruelties which, about fourscore years afterwards, were revenged by the son of Clovis.   They massacred their hostages, as well as their captives . two hundred young maidens were tortured with exquisite and unrelenting rage ; their bodies were torn asunder by wild horses, or their bones were crushed under the weight of rolling waggons ; and their unburied limbs were abandoned on the public roads, as a prey to dogs and vultures.   Such were those savage ancestors, whose imaginary virtues have sometimes excited the praise and envy of civilised ages.[48]

Neither the spirit nor the forces nor the reputation of Attila were impaired by the failure of the Gallic expedition.   In the ensuing spring, he repeated his demand of the princess Honoria and her patrimonial treasures.[48a]   The demand was again rejected, or eluded ; and the indignant lover immediately took the field, passed the Alps, invaded Italy, and besieged Aquileia with an innumerable host of Barbarians.   Those Barbarians were unskilled in the methods of conducting a regular siege, which, even among the ancients, required some knowledge, or at least some practice, of the mechanic arts.   But the labour of many thousand provincials and captives, whose lives were sacrificed without pity, might execute the most painful and dangerous work.   The skill of the Roman artists might be corrupted to the destruction of their country.   The walls of Aquileia were assaulted by a formidable train of battering rams, moveable turrets, and engines, that threw stones, darts, and fire ,[49] and

(margin note: Invasion of Italy by Attila A D 452)

---

[48] These cruelties, which are passionately deplored by Theodoric, the son of Clovis (Gregory of Tours, l iii c 10, p 190), suit the time and circumstances of the invasion of Attila   His residence in Thuringia was long attested by popular tradition , and he is supposed to have assembled a *couroultai*, or diet, in the territory of Eisenach   See Mascou, iv 30, who settles with nice accuracy the extent of ancient Thuringia, and derives its name from the Gothic tribe of the Thervingi

[48a] [There seems to be no authority for this statement]

[49] Machinis constructis, omnibusque tormentorum generibus adhibitis   Jornandes, c 42, p 673   In the thirteenth century, the Moguls battered the cities of China with large engines constructed by the Mahometans or Christians in their service, which threw stones from 150 to 300 pounds weight   In the defence of their country, the Chinese used gunpowder, and even bombs, above an hundred years before they were known in Europe , yet even those celestial, or infernal, arms were insufficient to protect a pusillanimous nation   See Gaubil, Hist des Mongous, p 70, 71, 155, 157, &c

the monarch of the Huns employed the forcible impulse of hope, fear, emulation, and interest, to subvert the only barrier which delayed the conquest of Italy. Aquileia was at that period one of the richest, the most populous, and the strongest of the maritime cities of the Hadriatic coast. The Gothic auxiliaries, who appear to have served under their native princes Alaric and Antala, communicated their intrepid spirit; and the citizens still remembered the glorious and successful resistance, which their ancestors had opposed to a fierce, inex- [Maximin] orable Barbarian, who disgraced the majesty of the Roman purple. Three months were consumed without effect in the siege of Aquileia; till the want of provisions, and the clamours of his army, compelled Attila to relinquish the enterprise, and reluctantly to issue his orders that the troops should strike their tents the next morning and begin their retreat But, as he rode round the walls, pensive, angry, and disappointed, he observed a stork preparing to leave her nest, in one of the towers, and to fly with her infant family towards the country. He seized, with the ready penetration of a statesman, this trifling incident, which chance had offered to superstition , and exclaimed, in a loud and cheerful tone, that such a domestic bird, so constantly attached to human society, would never have abandoned her ancient seats, unless those towers had been devoted to impending ruin and solitude.[50] The favourable omen inspired an assurance of victory; the siege was renewed, and prosecuted with fresh vigour; a large breach was made in the part of the wall from whence the stork had taken her flight; the Huns mounted to the assault with irresistible fury; and the succeeding generation could scarcely discover the ruins of Aquileia [51] After this dreadful chastisement, Attila pursued his march, and, as he passed, the cities of Altinum, Concordia, [Patavium] and Padua, were reduced into heaps of stones and ashes. The [Vincentia] [Bergamum] inland towns, Vicenza, Verona, and Bergamo, were exposed to [Mediolanum Ticinum] the rapacious cruelty of the Huns Milan and Pavia submitted, without resistance, to the loss of their wealth , and applauded

[50] The same story is told by Jornandes, and by Procopius (de Bell Vandal 1 1. c 4, p 187, 188). nor is it easy to decide which is the original But the Greek historian is guilty of an inexcusable mistake in placing the siege of Aquileia *after* the death of Aetius

[51] Jornandes, about an hundred years afterwards, affirms that Aquileia was so completely ruined, ita ut vix ejus vestigia, ut appareant, reliquerint See Jornandes de Reb Geticis, c 42, p 673 Paul Diacon l ii c 14, p 785 Liutprand, Hist l iii c 2 The name of Aquileia was sometimes applied to Forum Julii (Civitad del Friuli), the more recent capital of the Venetian province

the unusual clemency, which preserved from the flames the public, as well as private, buildings ; and spared the lives of the captive multitude. The popular traditions of Comum, Turin, or Modena, may justly be suspected, yet they concur [Taurini, Mutina] with more authentic evidence to prove that Attila spread his ravages over the rich plains of modern Lombardy : which are divided by the Po, and bounded by the Alps and Apennine.[52] When he took possession of the royal palace of Milan, he was surprised, and offended, at the sight of a picture, which represented the Cæsars seated on their throne and the princes of Scythia prostrate at their feet. The revenge which Attila inflicted on this monument of Roman vanity was harmless and ingenious   He commanded a painter to reverse the figures and the attitudes; and the emperors were delineated on the same canvas, approaching in a suppliant posture to empty their bags of tributary gold before the throne of the Scythian monarch.[53] The spectators must have confessed the truth and propriety of the alteration ; and were perhaps tempted to apply, on this singular occasion, the well-known fable of the dispute between the lion and the man.[54]

It is a saying worthy of the ferocious pride of Attila, that the [Foundation of the republic of Venice] grass never grew on the spot where his horse had trod. Yet the savage destroyer undesignedly laid the foundations of a republic which revived, in the feudal state of Europe, the art and spirit of commercial industry. The celebrated name of Venice, or Venetia,[55] was formerly diffused over a large and fertile province of Italy, from the confines of Pannonia to the

[52] In describing this war of Attila, a war so famous, but so imperfectly known, I have taken for my guides two learned Italians, who considered the subject with some peculiar advantages Sigonius, de Imperio Occidentali, l xiii in his works, tom i p 495-502 ; and Muratori, Annali d'Italia, tom iv p 229-236, 8vo edition

[53] This anecdote may be found under two different articles (μεδιολανον and κόρυκος) of the miscellaneous compilation of Suidas.

[54] Leo respondit, humanâ hoc pictum manu
Videres hominem dejectum, si pingere
Leones scirent   Appendix ad Phædrum, Fab xxv
The lion in Phædrus very foolishly appeals from pictures to the amphitheatre, and I am glad to observe that the native taste of La Fontaine (l iii fable x) has omitted this most lame and impotent conclusion

[55] Paul the Deacon (de Gestis Langobard, l ii c 14, p 784) describes the provinces of Italy about the end of the eighth century Venetia non solum in paucis insulis quas nunc Venetias dicimus constat, sed ejus terminus a Pannoniæ finibus usque Adduam fluvium protelatur The history of that province till the age of Charlemagne forms the first and most interesting part of the Verona Illustrata (p 1-388), in which the marquis Scipio Maffei has shewn himself equally capable of enlarged views and minute disquisitions,

river Addua, and from the Po to the Rhætian and Julian Alps.
Before the irruption of the Barbarians, fifty Venetian cities
flourished in peace and prosperity, Aquileia was placed in the
most conspicuous station; but the ancient dignity of Padua
was supported by agriculture and manufactures; and the
property of five hundred citizens, who were entitled to the
equestrian rank, must have amounted, at the strictest computation, to one million seven hundred thousand pounds   Many
families of Aquileia, Padua, and the adjacent towns, who fled
from the sword of the Huns, found a safe, though obscure,
refuge in the neighbouring islands.[56]   At the extremity of the
Gulf, where the Hadriatic feebly imitates the tides of the
ocean, near an hundred small islands are separated by shallow
water from the continent, and protected from the waves by
several long slips of land, which admit the entrance of vessels
through some secret and narrow channels.[57]   Till the middle
of the fifth century, these remote and sequestered spots remained without cultivation, with few inhabitants, and almost
without a name   But the manners of the Venetian fugitives,
their arts and their government, were gradually formed by
their new situation, and one of the epistles of Cassiodorus,[58]
which describes their condition about seventy years afterwards,
may be considered as the primitive monument of the republic.   The minister of Theodoric compares them, in his quaint
declamatory style, to water-fowl, who had fixed their nests on
the bosom of the waves, and, though he allows that the
Venetian provinces had formerly contained many noble families,
he insinuates that they were now reduced by misfortune to the
same level of humble poverty.   Fish was the common, and
almost the universal, food of every rank, their only treasure

A D 451

[56] This emigration is not attested by any contemporary evidence, but the fact
is proved by the event, and the circumstances might be preserved by tradition.
The citizens of Aquileia retired to the isle of Gradus, those of Padua to Rivus
Altus, or Rialto, where the city of Venice was afterwards built, &c   [On the
forged decree of the Senate of Patavium and the supposed foundation of a church
of St James on the Rivus Altus in A D 421, see Hodgkin, Italy, ii 182 *sqq*]
[57] The topography and antiquities of the Venetian islands, from Gradus to
Clodia, or Chioggia, are accurately stated in the Dissertatio Chronographica de
Italiâ Medii Ævi, p. 151-155
[58] Cassiodor Variar l xii epist 24.   Maffei (Verona Illustrata, part i p
240-254) has translated and explained this curious letter, in the spirit of a learned
antiquarian and a faithful subject, who considered Venice as the only legitimate
offspring of the Roman republic   He fixes the date of the epistle, and consequently
the præfecture, of Cassiodorus, A D 523 [? 537 A D], and the marquis's authority
has the more weight, as he had prepared an edition of his works, and actually
published a Dissertation on the true orthography of his name   See Osservazioni
Letterarie, tom ii p 290-339

consisted in the plenty of salt, which they extracted from the sea ; and the exchange of that commodity, so essential to human life, was substituted in the neighbouring markets to the currency of gold and silver A people, whose habitations might be doubtfully assigned to the earth or water, soon became alike familiar with the two elements , and the demands of avarice succeeded to those of necessity The islanders, who, from Grado to Chiozza, were intimately connected with each other, penetrated into the heart of Italy by the secure, though laborious, navigation of the rivers and inland canals. Their vessels, which were continually increasing in size and number, visited all the harbours of the Gulf ; and the marriage, which Venice annually celebrates with the Hadriatic, was contracted in her early infancy. The epistle of Cassiodorius, the Prætorian praefect, is addressed to the maritime tribunes ; and he exhorts them, in a mild tone of authority, to animate the zeal of their countrymen for the public service, which required their assistance to transport the magazines of wine and oil from the province of Istria to the royal city of Ravenna The ambiguous office of these magistrates is explained by the tradition that, in the twelve principal islands, twelve tribunes, or judges, were created by an annual and popular election. The existence of the Venetian republic under the Gothic kingdom of Italy is attested by the same authentic record, which annihilates their lofty claim of original and perpetual independence [59] The Italians, who had long since renounced the exercise of arms, were surprised, after forty years' peace, by the approach of a formidable Barbarian, whom they abhorred, as the enemy of their religion as well as of their republic. Amidst the general consternation, Aetius alone was incapable of fear ; but it was impossible that he should achieve, alone and unassisted, any military exploits worthy of his former renown The Barbarians who had defended Gaul refused to march to the relief of Italy , and the succours promised by the Eastern emperor were distant and doubtful. Since Aetius, at the head of his domestic troops, still maintained the field, and harassed or retarded the march of Attila, he never shewed himself more truly great than at the time when his conduct was blamed by an ignorant and

Attila gives peace to the Romans

[59] See, in the second volume of Amelot de la Houssaie, Histoire du Gouvernement de Vénise, a translation of the famous *Squittinio* This book, which has been exalted far above its merits, is stained in every line with the disingenuous malevolence of party , but the principal evidence, genuine and apocryphal, is brought together, and the reader will easily choose the fair medium.

ungrateful people.[60]   If the mind of Valentinian had been
susceptible of any generous sentiments, he would have chosen
such a general for his example and his guide.   But the timid
grandson of Theodosius, instead of sharing the dangers, escaped
from the sound, of war, and his hasty retreat from Ravenna to
Rome, from an impregnable fortress to an open capital, betrayed
his secret intention of abandoning Italy as soon as the danger
should approach his Imperial person.   This shameful abdication
was suspended, however, by the spirit of doubt and delay,
which commonly adheres to pusillanimous counsels, and sometimes corrects their pernicious tendency.   The Western emperor,
with the senate and people of Rome, embraced the more
salutary resolution of deprecating, by a solemn and suppliant
embassy, the wrath of Attila.   This important commission was
accepted by Avienus, who, from his birth and riches, his consular
dignity, the numerous train of his clients, and his personal
abilities, held the first rank in the Roman senate.   The specious
and artful character of Avienus [61] was admirably qualified to
conduct a negotiation either of public or private interest, -his
colleague Trigetius had exercised the Prætorian præfecture of
Italy ; and Leo, bishop of Rome, consented to expose his life
for the safety of his flock.   The genius of Leo [62] was exercised
and displayed in the public misfortunes ; and he has deserved
the appellation of *Great* by the successful zeal with which he
laboured to establish his opinions and his authority, under the
venerable names of orthodox faith and ecclesiastical discipline.
The Roman ambassadors were introduced to the tent of Attila,
as he lay encamped at the place where the slow-winding
Mincius is lost in the foaming waves of the lake Benacus,[63] and

[Mincio]
[L. Garda]

[60] Sirmond (Not ad Sidon Apollin p 19) has published a curious passage
from the Chronicle of Prosper Attila redintegratis viribus, quas in Gallia amiserat,
Italiam ingredi per Pannonias intendit ; nihil duce nostro Aetio secundum prioris
belli opera prospiciente, &c   He reproaches Aetius with neglecting to guard the
Alps, and with a design to abandon Italy, but this rash censure may at least be
counterbalanced by the favourable testimonies of Idatius and Isidore   [Isidore,
Hist. Goth 27, merely repeats Idatius, but leaves out the words *Aetio duce*]

[61] See the original portraits of Avienus and his rival Basilius, delineated and
contrasted in the epistles (i 9, p 22) of Sidonius He had studied the characters
of the two chiefs of the senate, but he attached himself to Basilius, as the more
solid and disinterested friend

[62] The character and principles of Leo may be traced in one hundred and forty-
one original epistles, which illustrate the ecclesiastical history of his long and
busy pontificate, from A D 440 to 461   See Dupin, Bibliothèque Ecclésiastique,
tom iii part ii p 120-165

[63] —— tardis ingens ubi flexibus errat
Mincius, et tenerâ prætexit arundine ripas

Anne lacus tantos, te Lari maxime, teque
Fluctibus, et fremitu assurgens *Benace* marino

trampled, with his Scythian cavalry, the farms of Catullus and
Virgil [64] The Barbarian monarch listened with favourable, and
even respectful, attention; and the deliverance of Italy was
purchased by the immense ransom, or dowry, of the princess
Honoria. The state of his army might facilitate the treaty,
and hasten his retreat. Their martial spirit was relaxed by
the wealth and indolence of a warm climate. The shepherds
of the North, whose ordinary food consisted of milk and raw
flesh, indulged themselves too freely in the use of bread, of
wine, and of meat prepared and seasoned by the arts of cookery;
and the progress of disease revenged in some measure the injuries of the Italians.[65] When Attila declared his resolution of
carrying his victorious arms to the gates of Rome, he was admonished by his friends, as well as by his enemies, that Alaric
had not long survived the conquest of the eternal city. His
mind, superior to real danger, was assaulted by imaginary
terrors; nor could he escape the influence of superstition, which
had so often been subservient to his designs.[66] The pressing
eloquence of Leo, his majestic aspect and sacerdotal robes, excited the veneration of Attila for the spiritual father of the
Christians. The apparition of the two apostles, St. Peter and
St. Paul, who menaced the Barbarian with instant death, if he
rejected the prayer of their successor, is one of the noblest
legends of ecclesiastical tradition The safety of Rome might
deserve the interposition of celestial beings; and some indulgence is due to a fable which has been represented by the
pencil of Raphael and the chisel of Algardi.[67]

[64] The Marquis Maffei (Verona Illustrata, part i p 95, 129, 221, part ii p ii
6) has illustrated with taste and learning this interesting topography He places
the interview of Attila and St Leo near Ariolica, or Ardelica, now Peschiera, at
the conflux of the lake and river , ascertains the villa of Catullus, in the delightful
peninsula of Sirmio , and discovers the Andes of Virgil, in the village of Bandes,
precisely situate quâ se subducere colles incipiunt, where the Veronese hills
imperceptibly slope down into the plain of Mantua [Muratori (Ann d'Italia,
iii 154) placed the interview at Governolo, a village situated where the Mincio joins
the Po]
[65] Si statim infesto agmine urbem petiissent, grande discrimen esset sed in
Venetiâ quo fere tractu Italia mollissima est, ipsâ soli cælique clementiâ robur
elanguit Ad hoc panis usu carnisque coctæ, et dulcedine vini mitigatos, &c This
passage of Florus (iii 3) is still more applicable to the Huns than to the Cimbri,
and it may serve as a commentary on the *celestial* plague, with which Idatius and
Isidore have afflicted the troops of Attila
[66] The historian Priscus had positively mentioned the effect which this example
produced on the mind of Attila Jornandes, c 42, p 673
[67] The picture of Raphael is in the Vatican , the basso (or perhaps the alto)
relievo of Algardi, on one of the altars of St Peter (see Dubos, Reflexions sur la
Poésie et sur la Peinture, tom. i p 519, 520) Baronius (Annal Eccles A D 452,
No 57, 58) bravely sustains the truth of the apparition , which is rejected however,
by the most learned and pious Catholics

The death of
Attila.
A D 453 Before the king of the Huns evacuated Italy, he threatened
to return more dreadful and more implacable, if his bride, the
princess Honoria, were not delivered to his ambassadors within
the term stipulated by the treaty   Yet, in the meanwhile, Attila
relieved his tender anxiety by adding a beautiful maid, whose
name was Ildico, to the list of his innumerable wives [68]   Their
marriage was celebrated with barbaric pomp and festivity at his
wooden palace beyond the Danube ; and the monarch, oppressed with wine and sleep, retired, at a late hour, from the
banquet to the nuptial bed   His attendants continued to respect his pleasures, or his repose, the greatest part of the ensuing
day, till the unusual silence alarmed their fears and suspicions ;
and, after attempting to awaken Attila by loud and repeated cries,
they at length broke into the royal apartment   They found the
trembling bride sitting by the bedside, hiding her face with
her veil, and lamenting her own danger as well as the death of
the king, who had expired during the night.[69]   An artery had
suddenly burst , and, as Attila lay in a supine posture, he was
suffocated by a torrent of blood, which, instead of finding a
passage through the nostrils, regurgitated into the lungs and
stomach.   His body was solemnly exposed in the midst of the
plain, under a silken pavilion ; and the chosen squadrons of the
Huns, wheeling round in measured evolutions, chanted a funeral
song to the memory of a hero, glorious in his life, invincible in
his death, the father of his people, the scourge of his enemies,
and the terror of the world.   According to their national custom, the Barbarians cut off a part of their hair, gashed their
faces with unseemly wounds, and bewailed their valiant leader
as he deserved, not with the tears of women, but with the blood
of warriors.   The remains of Attila were enclosed within three

---

[68] Attila, ut Priscus historicus refert, extinctionis suæ tempore puellam Ildico
nomine, decoram valde, sibi [in] matrimonium post innumerabiles uxores
socians   Jornandes, c 49, p 683, 684   He afterwards adds (c 50, p 686) Filii
Attilæ, quorum per licentiam libidinis pœne populus fuit.—Polygamy has been
established among the Tartars of every age   The rank of plebeian wives is
regulated only by their personal charms and the faded matron prepares, without
a murmur, the bed which is destined for her blooming rival. But in royal families
the daughters of Khans communicate to their sons a prior right of inheritance
See Genealogical History, p 406, 407, 408

[69] The report of her *guilt* reached Constantinople, where it obtained a very
different name ; and Marcellinus observes that the tyrant of Europe was slain in
the night by the hand and the knife of a woman   Corneille, who has adapted
the genuine account to his tragedy, describes the irruption of blood in forty bom-
bast lines, and Attila exclaims with ridiculous fury —

———— S'il veut s'arrêter (*his blood*),
(Dit il) on me payera ce qui m'en va coûter.

coffins, of gold, of silver, and of iron, and privately buried in the night · the spoils of nations were thrown into his grave ; the captives who had opened the ground were inhumanly massacred; and the same Huns, who had indulged such excessive grief, feasted, with dissolute and intemperate mirth, about the recent sepulchre of their king It was reported at Constantinople that on the fortunate night in which he expired Marcian beheld in a dream the bow of Attila broken asunder; and the report may be allowed to prove how seldom the image of that formidable Barbarian was absent from the mind of a Roman emperor.[70]

The revolution which subverted the empire of the Huns established the fame of Attila, whose genius alone had sustained the huge and disjointed fabric. After his death, the boldest chieftains aspired to the rank of kings ; the most powerful kings refused to acknowledge a superior , and the numerous sons, whom so many various mothers bore to the deceased monarch, divided and disputed, like a private inheritance, the sovereign command of the nations of Germany and Scythia The bold Ardaric felt and represented the disgrace of this servile partition , and his subjects, the warlike Gepidæ, with the Ostrogoths, under the conduct of three valiant brothers, encouraged their allies to vindicate the rights of freedom and royalty. In a bloody and decisive conflict on the banks of the river Netad, in Pannonia, the lance of the Gepidæ, [Neaao] the sword of the Goths, the arrows of the Huns, the Suevic infantry, the light arms of the Heruli, and the heavy weapons of the Alani, encountered or supported each other, and the victory of Ardaric was accompanied with the slaughter of thirty thousand of his enemies. Ellac, the eldest son of Attila, lost his life and crown in the memorable battle of Netad · his early valour had raised him to the throne of the Acatzires, a Scythian people, whom he subdued ; and his father, who loved the superior merit, would have envied the death, of Ellac.[71] His brother

Destruction of his empire

---

[70] The curious circumstances of the death and funeral of Attila are related by Jornandes (c 49, p 683, 684, 685), and were probably [those of the death, confessedly] transcribed from Priscus

[71] See Jornandes, de Rebus Geticis, c 50, p 685, 686, 687, 688 His distinction of the national arms is curious and important Nam ibi admirandum reor fuisse spectaculum, ubi cernere erat cunctis pugnantem Gothum ense furentem, Gepidam in vulnere suorum cuncta tela frangentem, Suevum pede Hunnum sagittâ præsumere, Alanum gravi, Herulum levi, armaturâ aciem instruere I am not precisely informed of the situation of the river Netad [The best Mss give the name Nedao (see Mommsen's Jordanis, c 50) It has not been identified]

Dengisich with an army of Huns, still formidable in their flight and ruin, maintained his ground above fifteen years on the banks of the Danube. The palace of Attila, with the old country of Dacia, from the Carpathian hills to the Euxine, became the seat of a new power, which was erected by Ardaric, king of the Gepidæ. The Pannonian conquests, from Vienna to Sirmium, were occupied by the Ostrogoths ; and the settlements of the tribes, who had so bravely asserted their native freedom, were irregularly distributed, according to the measure of their respective strength. Surrounded and oppressed by the multitude of his father's slaves, the kingdom of Dengisich was confined to the circle of his waggons; his desperate courage urged him to invade the Eastern empire ; he fell in battle ; and his head, ignominiously exposed in the Hippodrome, exhibited a grateful spectacle to the people of Constantinople. Attila had fondly or superstitiously believed that Irnac, the youngest of his sons, was destined to perpetuate the glories of his race. The character of that prince, who attempted to moderate the rashness of his brother Dengisich, was more suitable to the declining condition of the Huns, and Irnac, with his subject hordes, retired into the heart of the Lesser Scythia. They were soon overwhelmed by a torrent of new Barbarians, who followed the same road which their own ancestors had formerly discovered. The *Geougen*, or Avares, whose residence is assigned by the Greek writers to the shores of the ocean, impelled the adjacent tribes , till at length the Igours of the North, issuing from the cold Siberian regions, which produce the most valuable furs, spread themselves over the desert, as far as the Borysthenes and Caspian gates ; and finally extinguished the empire of the Huns.[72]

Such an event might contribute to the safety of the Eastern empire, under the reign of a prince who conciliated the friendship, without forfeiting the esteem, of the Barbarians. But the emperor of the West, the feeble and dissolute Valentinian, who had reached his thirty-fifth year without attaining the age of reason or courage, abused this apparent security, to undermine the foundations of his own throne by the murder of the patrician Aetius. From the instinct of a base and jealous mind, he hated the man who was universally celebrated as the terror of the

[Marginal notes: [Vindobona] ; [Dobrudza] ; Valentinian murders the patrician Aetius, A.D. 454]

---

[72] Two modern historians have thrown much new light on the ruin and division of the empire of Attila. M. de Buat, by his laborious and minute diligence (tom. viii. p. 3-31, 68-94), and M. de Guignes, by his extraordinary knowledge of the Chinese language and writers. See Hist. des Huns, tom. ii. p. 315-319.

Barbarians and the support of the republic; and his new favourite, the eunuch Heraclius, awakened the emperor from the supine lethargy, which might be disguised, during the life of Placidia,[73] by the excuse of filial piety The fame of Aetius, his wealth and dignity, the numerous and martial train of Barbarian followers, his powerful dependents, who filled the civil offices of the state, and the hopes of his son Gaudentius,[74] who was already contracted to Eudoxia, the emperor's daughter, had raised him above the rank of a subject. The ambitious designs, of which he was secretly accused, excited the fears, as well as the resentment, of Valentinian. Aetius himself, supported by the consciousness of his merit, his services, and perhaps his innocence, seems to have maintained a haughty and indiscreet behaviour. The patrician offended his sovereign by an hostile declaration; he aggravated the offence by compelling him to ratify, with a solemn oath, a treaty of reconciliation and alliance; he proclaimed his suspicions, he neglected his safety; and, from a vain confidence that the enemy, whom he despised, was incapable even of a manly crime, he rashly ventured his person in the palace of Rome. Whilst he urged, perhaps with intemperate vehemence, the marriage of his son, Valentinian, drawing his sword, the first sword he had ever drawn, plunged it in the breast of a general who had saved his empire; his courtiers and eunuchs ambitiously struggled to imitate their master; and Aetius, pierced with an hundred wounds, fell dead in the royal presence. Boethius, the Prætorian præfect, was killed at the same moment, and, before the event could be divulged, the principal friends of the patrician were summoned to the palace, and separately murdered. The horrid deed, palliated by the specious names of justice and necessity, was immediately communicated by the emperor to his soldiers, his subjects, and his allies. The nations, who were strangers or enemies to Aetius, generously deplored the unworthy fate of a hero, the Barbarians, who had been attached to his service, dissembled their grief and resentment, and the public contempt which had been so long entertained for Valentinian was at once

[73] Placidia died at Rome, November 27, A D 450 She was buried at Ravenna where her sepulchre, and even her corpse, seated in a chair of cypress wood, were preserved for ages [Her Mausoleum (the church of S Nazario and S Celso) and her alabaster sarcophagus are still preserved; but her embalmed corpse was accidentally burned by some children in A D 1577] The empress received many compliments from the orthodox clergy, and St Peter Chrysologus assured her that her zeal for the Trinity had been recompensed by an august trinity of children See Tillemont, Hist des Emp tom vi. p. 240

[74] [Aetius had another son named Carpilio, who was for years a hostage at the court of Attila, as we learn from Priscus]

converted into deep and universal abhorrence. Such sentiments seldom pervade the walls of a palace, yet the emperor was confounded by the honest reply of a Roman, whose approbation he had not disdained to solicit "I am ignorant, sir, of your motives or provocations, I only know that you have acted like a man who cuts off his right hand with his left".[75]

and ravishes the wife of Maximus The luxury of Rome seems to have attracted the long and frequent visits of Valentinian; who was consequently more despised at Rome than in any other part of his dominions A republican spirit was insensibly revived in the senate, as their authority, and even their supplies, became necessary for the support of his feeble government The stately demeanour of an hereditary monarch offended their pride, and the pleasures of Valentinian were injurious to the peace and honour of noble families. The birth of the empress Eudoxia was equal to his own, and her charms and tender affection deserved those testimonies of love which her inconstant husband dissipated in vague and unlawful amours. Petronius Maximus, a wealthy senator of the Anician family, who had been twice consul, was possessed of a chaste and beautiful wife. her obstinate resistance served only to irritate the desires of Valentinian, and he resolved to accomplish them either by stratagem or force Deep gaming was one of the vices of the court; the emperor, who, by chance or contrivance, had gained from Maximus a considerable sum, uncourteously exacted his ring as a security for the debt; and sent it by a trusty messenger to his wife, with an order, in her husband's name, that she should immediately attend the empress Eudoxia The unsuspecting wife of Maximus was conveyed in her litter to the Imperial palace; the emissaries of her impatient lover conducted her to a remote and silent bedchamber, and Valentinian violated, without remorse, the laws of hospitality. Her tears, when she returned home, her deep affliction, and her bitter reproaches against her husband, whom she considered as the accomplice of his own shame, excited Maximus to a just revenge; the desire of revenge was stimulated by ambition; and he might reasonably aspire, by the free suffrage of the Roman senate, to the throne of a detested and despicable rival. Valentinian, who supposed that every human breast was devoid, like his own, of friendship and gratitude, had im-

---

[75] Aetium Placidus mactavit semivir amens, is the expression of Sidonius (Panegyr Avit 359) The poet knew the world, and was not inclined to flatter a minister who had injured or disgraced Avitus and Majorian, the successive heroes of his song.

prudently admitted among his guards several domestics and followers of Aetius. Two of these, of Barbarian race, were persuaded to execute a sacred and honourable duty, by punishing with death the assassin of their patron; and their intrepid courage did not long expect a favourable moment. Whilst Valentinian amused himself in the field of Mars with the spectacle of some military sports, they suddenly rushed upon him with drawn weapons, dispatched the guilty Heraclius, and stabbed the emperor to the heart, without the least opposition from his numerous train, who seemed to rejoice in the tyrant's death   Such was the fate of Valentinian the Third,[76] the last Roman emperor of the family of Theodosius.   He faithfully imitated the hereditary weakness of his cousin and his two uncles, without inheriting the gentleness, the purity, the innocence, which alleviate, in their characters, the want of spirit and ability. Valentinian was less excusable, since he had passions, without virtues; even his religion was questionable; and, though he never deviated into the paths of heresy, he scandalized the pious Christians by his attachment to the profane arts of magic and divination. ^{Death of Valentinian. A D 455, March 16}

As early as the time of Cicero and Varro, it was the opinion of the Roman augurs that the *twelve vultures*, which Romulus had seen, represented the *twelve centuries*, assigned for the fatal period of his city.[77]   This prophecy, disregarded perhaps in the season of health and prosperity, inspired the people with gloomy apprehensions, when the twelfth century, clouded with disgrace and misfortune, was almost elapsed;[78] and even posterity must ^{Symptoms of decay and ruin}

---

[76] With regard to the cause and circumstances of the deaths of Aetius and Valentinian, our information is dark and imperfect   Procopius (de Bell Vandal l 1 c 4, p 186, 187, 188) is a fabulous writer for the events which precede his own memory   His narrative must therefore be supplied and corrected by five or six Chronicles, none of which were composed in Rome or Italy, and which can only express, in broken sentences, the popular rumours, as they were conveyed to Gaul, Spain, Africa, Constantinople, or Alexandria   [John of Antioch is important for these events   See Appendix 26]

[77] This interpretation of Vettius, a celebrated augur, was quoted by Varro, in the xviiith book of his Antiquities. Censorinus, de Die Natali, c 17, p 90, 91, edit. Havercamp

[78] According to Varro, the twelfth century would expire A D 447, but the uncertainty of the true æra of Rome might allow some latitude of anticipation or delay   The poets of the age, Claudian (de Bell Getico, 265) and Sidonius (in Panegyr Avit 357), may be admitted as fair witnesses of the popular opinion
  Jam reputant annos, interceptoque volatu
  Vulturis incidunt properatis sæcula metis

  Jam prope fata tui bissenas vulturis alas
  Implebant; scis namque tuos, scis, Roma, labores
See Dubos, Hist Critique, tom 1 p 340-346

acknowledge with some surprise that the arbitrary interpretation of an accidental or fabulous circumstance has been seriously verified in the downfall of the Western empire   But its fall was announced by a clearer omen than the flight of vultures . the Roman government appeared every day less formidable to its enemies, more odious and oppressive to its subjects [79] The taxes were multiplied with the public distress; economy was neglected in proportion as it became necessary , and the injustice of the rich shifted the unequal burden from themselves to the people, whom they defrauded of the *indulgencies* that might sometimes have alleviated their misery   The severe inquisition, which confiscated their goods and tortured their persons, compelled the subjects of Valentinian to prefer the more simple tyranny of the Barbarians, to fly to the woods and mountains, or to embrace the vile and abject condition of mercenary servants. They abjured and abhorred the name of Roman citizens, which had formerly excited the ambition of mankind.   The Armorican provinces of Gaul, and the greatest part of Spain, were thrown into a state of disorderly independence, by the confederations of the Bagaudæ , and the Imperial ministers pursued with proscriptive laws, and ineffectual arms, the rebels whom they had made.[60] If all the Barbarian conquerors had been annihilated in the same hour, their total destruction would not have restored the empire of the West ; and, if Rome still survived, she survived the loss of freedom, of virtue, and of honour.

[79] The fifth book of Salvian is filled with pathetic lamentations and vehement invectives   His immoderate freedom serves to prove the weakness, as well as the corruption, of the Roman government   His book was published after the loss of Africa (A D 439) and before Attila's war (A D 451)

[80] The Bagaudæ of Spain, who fought pitched battles with the Roman troops, are repeatedly mentioned in the Chronicle of Idatius   Salvian has described their distress and rebellion in very forcible language   Itaque nomen civium Romanorum   nunc ultro repudiatur ac fugitur, nec vile tamen sed etiam abominabile pœnæ habetur   Et hinc est ut etiam hi qui ad Barbaros non confugiunt Barbari tamen esse coguntur, scilicet ut est pars magna Hispanorum, et non minima Gallorum   De Bagaudis nunc mihi sermo est, qui per malos judices et cruentos spoliati, afflicti, necati, post quam jus Romanæ libertatis amiserant, etiam honorem Romani nominis perdiderunt   Vocamus rebelles, vocamus perditos quos esse compulimus criminosos   De Gubernat Dei, l v p 158, 159

APPENDIX

ADDITIONAL NOTES BY THE EDITOR

1. AUTHORITIES

For the works of LIBANIUS, cp. vol. ii. Appendix 1, p. 535. The chronology of the most important of his later orations is determined by Sievers as follows :

A.D. 381. Or. ii , πρὸς τοὺς βαρὺν αὐτὸν καλοῦντας. He contrasts the present with the reign of Julian ; and refers to the Battle of Hadrianople

A.D. 386. Or. xxxi. Against Tisamenos (consularis of Syria). An interesting indictment of the governor's exactions and oppression

A.D. 387 (March). Or. xix., περὶ τῆς στάσεως On the sedition at Antioch, a petition to Theodosius for mercy

A.D. 387. Or. xxxiv., κατὰ τῶν πεφευγότων. Against those who fled from the city during the sedition. It was written during the sedition but μετὰ δικαστήρια καὶ κρίσιν καὶ δεσμόν.

A.D. 387. Or. xx., προς Θεοδόσιον ἐπὶ ταῖς διαλλαγαῖς. The story of the sedition and the pardon is narrated.

A.D. 387. Or. xxi., πρὸς Καισάριον Μάγιστρον A thanksgiving to Caesarius for his good offices in obtaining the pardon from Theodosius.

A.D. 387. Or. xxii., πρὸς Ἐλλεβιχον. Describing the inquiry into the sedition, conducted by Ellebichus.

A.D. 383 (?). Or. xxx , πρὸς Θρασυδαῖον. Deals with events connected with the sedition

After A D 388 Or xxviii , περὶ τῶν ἱερῶν. A complaint that although the offering of incense in pagan temples was not forbidden [by Cod. Theod. xvi. 10, 9. A.D. 385], the monks destroyed the temples.

There can be no question that Or. xxviii. on the Temples and many other of the orations of Libanius were not publicly delivered (in the Emperor's presence, for instance), but were merely read to a private audience of sympathizers, or circulated as pamphlets

For THEMISTIUS, cp vol. ii. Appendix 1, p. 535. The orations which concern the present volume are :

A.D. 364 Or v. On the consulship of Jovian. Claims toleration for both Christians and pagans.

A.D. 364. Or. vi., φιλάδελφοι. To Valentinian and Valens on their accession.

A D 367 Or. vii., περὶ τῶν ἠτυχηκότων ἐπι Οὐαλεντος. On the victory of Valens over Procopius. Praises the Emperor's clemency.

A D. 368. Or. viii , πενταετηρικος. On the quinquennalia of Valens.

A.D. 369. Or. ix., προτρεπτικός Οὐαλεντινιανῷ τῷ νεῳ. To Valentinian the younger, son of Valens, consul this year.

A.D. 370. Or. x , ἐπὶ τῆς εἰρήνης, pronounced before the Senate of Constantinople, congratulating Valens on his peace with the Goths.

A.D. 373 Or xi , δεκετηρικός (March 28). On the decennalia of Valens, who was then in Syria.

A.D. 374 Or xii. An appeal for religious toleration.

A.D. 377. Or. xiii., ἐρωτικός, pronounced in honour of Gratian at Rome, whither Themistius was sent by Valens.

A.D. 379. Or. xiv., πρεσβευτικος εἰς Θεοδόσιον αὐτοκράτορα (early in the year), pronounced at Thessalonica by Themistius as delegate of the Senate of Constantinople.

A.D. 381. Or. xv., εἰς Θεοδόσιον (February or March)   On the virtues of a king.

A.D. 383. Or xvi, χαριστηριος τῳ αὐτοκράτορι ὑπὲρ τῆς εἰρήνης και τῆς ὑπατειας τοῦ στρατηγοῦ Σατορνίνου (January).   On the peace with the Goths in 382.

A.D. 384. Or. xvii , ἐπι τῇ χειροτονιᾳ τῆς πολιαρχίας.   Returning thanks for his own appointment to the Prefecture of Constantinople (c. Sept. 1 ?).

A D. 384. Or xviii., περι τῆς τοῦ βασιλέως φιληκοίας.   Panegyric of Theodosius

A D 385 Or. xix , ἐπι τῇ φιλανθρωπιᾳ τοῦ αὐτοκράτορος Θεοδοσίου, pronounced in the Senate ; praises the clemency of Theodosius (before Sept. 14).

SYNESIUS of Cyrene (born 360-70 A D) studied first at Alexandria, afterwards at Athens. When he had completed his academical course he returned to the Pentapolis and led the life of a cultivated country gentleman. In 397 A.D. he arrived in Constantinople to plead the cause of Cyrene at the court, and stayed there some years, where he enjoyed the friendship of Aurelian.   During that time he delivered his speech on the office of king (see above, p 246), and witnessed the fall of Aurelian and rebellion of Gainas.   He afterwards made these events the subject of a bold political "squib," entitled "The Egyptians".   For the light which this throws on the political parties and intrigues in Constantinople, see below, Appendix 27

After the Gainas episode, Aurelian returned, and by his influence the petition of Synesius was granted   Synesius then returned to Africa (probably in 402 to Alexandria, and 404 to Cyrene , so Seeck, who has revised the chronology of the letters of Synesius in a very valuable study in *Philologus*, 52, p. 458 *sqq* , 1893). Translation of his interesting descriptions of the pleasures of country life will be found in Mr. Halcomb s excellent article on "Synesius," in the Dict. of Chr Biography. These descriptions occur in his letters, of which 156 are extant[1] (included in the Epistolographi Græci of Hercher).   The Cyrenaica, however, was exposed to the depredation of the nomads, owing to the incompetence of the governor Cerealis, and Synesius took an active part in defending the province. In 403 he had married a Christian wife ; he came under the influence of Theophilus, Bishop of Alexandria (where he resided a couple of years) ; and was gradually converted to Christianity   In 410 he yielded to the wishes of the people of Ptolemais and became a bishop   He died a few years later   His works, which included philosophical poems, may be most conveniently consulted in Migne's edition (Monograph , Volkmann, Synesios von Cyrene, 1869.   See also A. Nieri, La Cirenaica nel secolo quinto giusta le lettere di Sinesio, in the Revista di filologia, 21, 220 *sqq*. (1892)).

PALLADIUS, Bishop of Helenopolis, wrote a biographical work on John Chrysostom (of whom he was a supporter) under the title "A Dialogue with Theodore the Deacon".   After Chrysostom's banishment, not being safe in Constantinople, he went to Rome and explained to the Pope the true facts of Chrysostom's treatment.   Afterwards returning to the east he was thrown into prison, and then banished to a remote part of Egypt   At a later time his sentence was revoked , he seems to have been restored to Helenopolis, and was then translated to the See of Aspuna in Galatia I. (Socrates, vii. 36).   A strict ascetic himself, he dedicated to Lausus the Chamberlain (of Theodosius ii ?) a compilation of short biographies of men and women of his time who had embraced the ascetic life.   It is known as the *Historia Lausiaca* (written about 420 A.D), more will be said of it in considering the sources for the growth of monasticism, in an appendix to vol. iv.

To what has been said of EUNAPIUS in vol. ii Appendix 1 (p. 537) I must here add a reference to a paper of C. de Boor (in Rheinisches Museum, vol. xlvii. (1892) p 321-3) on the new edition of the history of Eunapius, which, softened down and mutilated so as not to shock the susceptibilities of Christian readers, was subsequently issued (by the book-trade ?).   The Procemium in the

[1] Among them, letters to Hypatia

Excerpta de Sententiis was copied down from this expurgated edition, and is not the work of Eunapius but is the editor's preface. Guldenpenning has attempted to explain the extraordinary fact that Zosimus does not even mention the greatest blot on the reign of Theodosius the Great—the massacre of Thessalonica—by supposing that he used the expurgated Eunapius This seems hardly probable.

The History (λόγοι ἱστορικοι) of the pagan OLYMPIODORUS (of the Egyptian Thebes) in twenty-two books was a highly important work. It embraced eighteen years of contemporary history (A.D. 407-425). It is unluckily lost, but valuable fragments are preserved in the Bibliotheca of Photius (amongst others a curious account of the initiation of new students at the university of Athens, fr. 28). The work was used as a source by the somewhat later writers, Philostorgius, Socrates, Sozomen, and later still by Zosimus, so that our historical material for the reign of Honorius and the first half of the reign of Theodosius II. depends more largely on Olympiodorus than might be inferred from the extent of the Photian fragments. He himself described his work as material (ὕλη) for history He dedicated it to Theodosius II. The most convenient edition of the fragments is that in Muller's Fragmenta, Hist. Græc., IV. p. 57 sqq

In the same place (69 sqq.) will be found the fragments of PRISCUS of Panium in Thrace, whose history probably began about A.D. 433 and ended at 474 The most famous is the account of his embassy to Hunland, but other very valuable notices from his work are preserved. So far as we can judge from these remains he was perhaps the best historian of the fifth century.

Q. Aurelius SYMMACHUS (of a rich but not an ancient family [2]) was born not long after 340. The details of his career are rehearsed on the base of a statue which his son set up in his house :

Q. Aur(elio) Symmacho v(iro)c(larissimo) quaest(ori) pret(ori) pontifici maiori, correctori Lucaniae et Brittiorum, comiti ordinis tertii, procons(uli) Africae, praef(ecto) urb(i), co(nsuli) ordinario, oratori disertissimo, Q. Fab(ius) Memm(ius) Symmachus v(ir) c(larissimus) patri optimo.

On the occasion of the quinquennalia of Valentinian (A.D. 369, Feb 25) he carried the Senate's congratulations and aurum oblaticium to the Emperor and pronounced panegyrics on Valentinian and Gratian, of which fragments remain (Or. 1. and Or. III., ed. Seeck, p. 318 and 330). He remained with the court, and accompanied the Emperors on their Alamannic expedition in 369 (like Ausonius). He celebrated the campaign in a second panegyric in honour of Valentinian's third consulship, A.D. 370 (Orat. ii). He was proconsul of Africa at the time of the revolt of Firmus (373-375). He was prefect of Rome in 384, and his appointment probably marks a revival of the pagan influence after Gratian's death.[3] In the same year he drew up the celebrated third Relatio to Theodosius for the restoration of the Altar of Victory, which had been removed by Gratian in 382. In 388, as the spokesman of the senate, he pronounced a panegyric on the tyrant Maximus, when he invaded Italy, and for this he was accused of treason on Valentinian's restoration, and with difficulty escaped punishment. The Panegyric and the Apology to Theodosius which he wrote after his pardon are mentioned by Socrates (v. 14), but have not survived. In 391 he was consul, and took the occasion of a panegyric which he pronounced in the presence of Theodosius to recommend to him a petition which the Roman senate had recently preferred for the restoration of the Altar of Victory The result is described by Gibbon (p. 191). Next year Symmachus made another unsuccessful attempt with Valentinian. He probably survived the year 404 (see below, p. 486).

His works have been edited by Seeck (in M. G. H.) They consist of nine Books of Letters, and the Relationes (which used to be numbered as a tenth Book

---

[2] His father, L Aurelius Avianius Symm. (consul 330), was prefect of Rome in A D 364-5. Statues were set up to him both in Rome and Constantinople, as is recorded in an inscription, where the public offices which he held are enumerated He was princeps senatus. C. I L , 6, 1698

[3] For the Panegyric (A.D. 389) of Drepanius Latinus PACATUS, see p 166.

of Letters) ; and fragmentary remains of eight Orations (first published by Mai, and unknown to Gibbon).

The poems of Decimus Magnus Ausonius (born c 310 at Burdigala) are more important for the literary than for the political history of the century. His uncle and praeceptor Arborius, with whom he lived at Tolosa (320-28), had the honour of being for a time teacher of one of Constantine's sons (Constantine or Constantius). He became a teacher of grammar (about 334) and soon afterwards of rhetoric, in his native town, and married about the same time   About 364 A D. he was summoned to the court of Trier to instruct Gratian. In 368 and 369 he accompanied Valentinian and Gratian on their Alamannic campaigns. He refers to their victories in his Mosella (written at Trier in 370-1) :

> Hostibus exactis Nicrum super et Lupodunum
> Et fontem Latiis ignotum annalibus Histri (423-4).

In 370 he obtained the rank of *comes* and in 375 was promoted to be *quæstor sacri palatii*. His son Hesperius (A.D 376 proconsul of Africa) became in 377 prætorian prefect of Italy, while his son-in-law Thalassius became in 378 proconsul of Africa. Ausonius himself was appointed Prætorian prefect of Gaul in first months of 378 (see Cod Th. 8 5, 35)   But in his *Epicedion in Patrem* he describes his son Hesperius as,

> Praefectus Gallis et Libyæ et Latio

By coupling this with words in the *Gratiarum Actio* to Gratian, § 7, ad praefecturæ collegium filius cum patre coniunctus, and *Liber Protrept. ad Nepotem,* v 91, praefecturam duplicem, it has been concluded (see Peiper's preface to his ed. p. ci) that, in consequence of the relationship between the two praefects, the praefectures of Gaul and Italy were temporarily united into a single administration under the collegial government of father and son, and, when Ausonius laid down the office in the last month of 379, again divided   In 379 he was consul. His death occurred later than 393. One of his most intimate friends was his pupil Pontius Paulinus, and he was in touch with many other men of literary importance, such as Symmachus and Drepanius Pacatus. His son-in-law Thalassius was the father (by a first wife) of the poet Paulinus of Pella. The works of Ausonius have been edited by Schenkl (in Mon. Germ. Hist.) and by Peiper (1886)

Of Pontius Paulinus of Nola, the most important of various people of the same name (to be distinguished from (1) Paulinus of Pella, (2) the author of the Life of St Ambrose, and (3) Paulinus of Périgueux, who in the latter half of fifth century wrote a Life of St Martin), there are extant various works both poetical and, in prose, epistles and a panegyric on Theodosius I. Born about 354, he retired to Nola in 394 and died 431 (there is an account of his death in a letter of Uranius to Pacatus, printed in Migne, Patr. Lat., vol. 53). His descriptions of Churches at Nola, in Epistle 32 and in some of his poems (18, 21, 27, 28), are of great importance for the history of Christian architecture. A new edition of his works is much wanted   That in Migne's Patrologia is most convenient for reference (Monograph A. Bose, Paulin und seine Zeit, 1856).

Paulinus of Pella (his father, a native of Burdigala, was Praetorian Praefect of Illyricum ; which explains the birth of Paulinus in Macedonia) is known by his poem entitled *Eucharisticon Deo sub ephemeridis meæ textu* (published in De la Bigne, Bibliot Patr , Appendix col. 281, ed 1579) ; contains one or two important notices of events in Aquitania at the time of Ataulf s invasion   The poet, thirty years old then, was appointed comes largitionum by the tyrant Attalus,

> Ut me conquirens solacia vana tyrannus
> Attalus absentem casso oneraret honoris
> Nomine, privatae comitivae largitionis.

Burdigala was burnt down by the Goths, who, not knowing that he held this dignity, stripped him and his mother of their property. He went to the neighbouring Vasates; induced the Alans to separate from the Goths and undertake the Roman cause; and the town was delivered by their intervention

It is probable that Claudius CLAUDIANUS was born in Egypt and certain that he belonged to Alexandria and spent his early years there (cp Sidonius Apoll. ix 275, and Birt's preface to his ed. of Claudian, ad. init) His father Claudian (cp C. I. L., 6, 1710) may be identical with Claudian the brother of the philosopher Maximus, Julian's teacher (Eunapius, Vit. Soph., p 47 and 101, ed Boiss , Birt, ib. p. vi). At Alexandria he wrote poems in Greek, and a fragment of his Γιγαντομαχία has been preserved (There seems to have been another Greek poet of the same name, who wrote in the reign of Theodosius ii., and to him may be ascribed perhaps some Christian epigrams. But it is certain that the great Claudian wrote in Greek,[4] and his authorship of the Γιγαντομαχια has been successfully vindicated by Birt.) He seems to have come to Italy in or before A.D. 394, where he obtained a small post in one of the departments (scrinia) under the control of the magister officiorum; and his poetical talents were discovered in the senatorial circles of Rome. He was patronized by Rufinus Synesius Hadrianus, a countryman of his own, who held the post of Count of the Sacred Largesses (A.D 395; he was Mag. Offic , 397-399, and subsequently Praet. Praef of Italy), and by members of the great Anician family, in the years 394 and 395, before he was discovered and "taken up" by Stilicho and the court of Honorius. From 396 to 404 he was a sort of poet laureate to the Imperial court; Honorius was his Augustus, Stilicho his Maecenas. His fame and favour did not bring any remarkable advancement in his career in the civil service; by the year 400 he had become tribune and notary But he enjoyed the ample honour of having his statue erected (perhaps at the beginning of A.D. 400; Birt, op. cit , xliv.) in the Forum of Trajan, and the inscription of this statue is preserved in the Museum of Naples. It is printed in C. I. L. 6, 1710, and runs as follows .

```
CL] CLAVDIANI V C
CLA]VDIO CLAVDIANO V C TRI
BV]NO ET NOTARIO INTER CETERAS
DE]CENTES ARTES PRAEGLORIOSISSIMO
PO] ETARVM LICET AD MEMORIAM SEM
PITERNAM SVFFICIANT ADTAMEN
TESTIMONII CRATIA OB IVDICII SVI
EIDEM DDNN ARCADIVS ET HONORIVS
EELICISSIMI AC DOCTISSIMI
IMPERATORES SENATV PETENTE
STATVAM IN FORO DIVI TRAIANI
ERIGI COLLOCARIQVE IVSSERVNT
EIN ENI BIPΓIAIOIO NOON KAI MOYCAN OMHPOY
KAAYΔIANON PΩMH KAI BACIAHC EΘECAN
```

We have no record of Claudian's death; but it is a probability closely approaching certainty that he died in A D. 404 (so Birt, p. lix). The silence of his muse after this date, amidst the public events which ensued, is unintelligible on any other supposition. Here, if ever, a conclusion from silence is justified.

CHRONOLOGICAL TABLE OF CLAUDIAN'S POEMS (AFTER BIRT).

Γιγαντομαχια	A.D. 394, or shortly before.
Panegyricus dictus Probino et Olybrio consulibus	A.D. 394 between Sept. and Dec.
Letters to Olybrius and Probinus (= Carm. Min , 40, 41)	A D. 395
Raptus Proserpinae	between A.D. 395 and 397.
Panegyr. de iii. consulatu Honorii	A D. 395 between Sept. and Dec.
In Rufinum Libri i. and ii.	between A.D. 395 Dec. and A.D. 396 July

[4] He attests it himself, Carm. Min., 41, 14, et Latiae accessit Graia Thalia togae.

APPENDIX

CHRONOLOGICAL TABLE OF CLAUDIAN'S POEMS (AFTER BIRT)—(cont.)

Carm. Min., 32	A.D. 396 or later.
Carm. Min., 21, 22	A D 396.
Carm Min., 19	A D. 397 or later.
Præfatio to Bk. II. in Rufinum, and the whole work published	A.D. 397.
Panegyricus de IV. cons. Honorii	A D 397 between Sept. and Dec
Epithalamium de nuptiis Honorii, and Fescennina de nupt. Hon.	A.D. 398 Jan , Feb.
Carm. Min , 45, 46, 47	between A D. 398 and A D. 404.
De Bello Gildonico	A D. 398 Aug , Sept
Panegyricus dictus Manlio Theodoro consuli	A D. 398 between Oct. and Dec.
In Eutropium Bk. I., written and published by itself	A.D. 399 between Jan and June
In Eutropium Bk. II. and Præfatio	A D. 399 between June and Sept.
Carm. Min , 25 (Epithalamium dict Palladio)	A.D. 399.
De consul. Stilichonis and Præfatio	between A.D. 399 Sept. and A.D. 400 Jan.
Carm. Min., 48, Carm. Min., appendix 4	between A.D. 400 and 404.
Carm. Min , 41	A.D 400 or 401
Carm Min , 20	before A D 401.
Carm. Min , 50	autumn 401.
De bello Gothico	A.D. 402 April, May.
Panegyr dict. de vi. cons. Honorii	A.D. 403 between Sept. and Dec.
Carm. Min , 30 and 53	A D. 404 early months.

This table may be found convenient by those who have the older editions of Claudian. More details, and the proofs of the chronology, will be found in Th. Birt's Preface to his complete and admirable edition of Claudian (in Mon. Germ. Hist) A handy text founded on Birt's work has been published by I Koch (1893). Cp. also Jeep, Cl. Claudiani Carmina, 1876-9. Vogt, de Claudiani carminum quæ Stiliconem prædicant fide historica, 1863. Ney, Vindiciæ Claudianeæ, 1865.

Aurelius PRUDENTIUS Clemens—the first distinctly Christian Latin poet—was a Spaniard by birth (born A D 348) He gave up a secular career at the age of fifty-seven and spent the remainder of his life in composing Christian poetry. For historical purposes his most important work is the *Contra Symmachum* in two Books, on the question of the Altar of Victory. It is important to determine the date of this work. It seems decisive (as Birt has observed in his Preface to Claudian) that in Bk. II. Prudentius sings of the victory over Alaric at Pollentia but does not mention the triumph of Verona (see below, Appendix 17) It follows that the work *Contra Symmachum* appeared between May 402 and August 403 ; another inference is that Symmachus was alive (cp. Gibbon, chap xxvii. n 22) in the year 402-3. (Birt points out a number of verbal echoes which show that the muse of the Christian poet was stimulated by the "Gothic War" of the pagan) It seems highly probable that this controversial poem was called forth by an actual permission granted by Honorius to restore the Altar of Victory in A D. 399. At least this is a very plausible inference from a line (19) of Claudian in the Præf. to *De cons. Stil.* III (a poem of that year)·

advexit reduces secum Victoria Musas,

combined with *de vi. cons. Hon.* 597 :

adfuit ipse suis ales Victoria templis
Romanae tutela togae : quae divite penna
Patricii reverenda fovet sacraria cœtus

> castrorumque eadem comes indefessa tuorum
> nunc tandem fruitur votis atque omne futurum
> te Romae seseque tibi promittit in aevum.

(Edition of Prudentius: H. Dressel, 1860. "Translations from Prudentius," Rev. F. St. J. Thackeray, 1890)

The most distinguished poet[5] in the reign of Valentinian iii., before the rise of Sidonius, was the Spaniard, Flavius MEROBAUDES. Sidonius mentions, without naming him, in Carm. ix. 296 *sqq.*, as one who was honoured (like Claudian) by a statue in the Forum of Trajan.

> sed nec tertius ille nunc legetur
> Baetin qui patrium semel relinquens
> undosae petiit sitim Ravennae,
> plosores cui fulgidam Quirites
> et carus popularitate princeps
> Traiano statuam foro locarunt.

Sirmondus brilliantly guessed the identity of the poet referred to in these lines, and his guess was confirmed by the discovery of the basis of the statue, with the full inscription, beginning: Fl. Merobaudi vs com. sc., and ending · dedicata iv. kal. Aug. Conss. $\overline{DD}$ $\overline{NN}$ Theodosio xv. et Valentiniano iv. About the same time fragments of a poet of that age were discovered in a Ms of St Gall, and the text of the Inscription enabled Niebuhr (by means of verbal similarities) to establish that these relics belonged to Merobaudes. First edited by Niobuhr, they were printed by Bekker in the Bonn Corpus Byz. (in the same volume as Corippus). The following are some of the points of historical interest in these fragments:

Carmina I. and II reflect the establishment of Galla Placidia and her son Valentinian in the West after the overthrow of the usurper John by the help of Theodosius ii. The verse on the child Valentinian (I., 11)

> hic ubi sacra parens *placidi* petit oscula nati,

has a curious interest owing to the epithet. The child who is here *placidus* (with a play on his mother's name) is destined to be more familiar as the mature, effeminate *placidus*, branded for ever with infamy by another poet

> Aetium Placidus mactavit semivir amens.

The victory over John and the betrothal of Valentinian with Eudoxia are thus referred to (l. 9):

> cui natura dedit, victoria reddidit orbem
> claraque longinquos praebuit aula toros.

For the intimate relation between the courts of Ravenna and Constantinople, such a full and candid expression of gratitude to the Eastern sovereign, as the following, on the part of a poet of Ravenna, is of much significance, C ii., 13, 14 ·

> sic dominos secura sui de stemmate regni
> continuat proprios dum creat aula novos.

C. iv. is a hendecasyllabic poem on the birthday of Gaudentius the son of Aetius The sojourn of Aetius as a hostage with the Goths is mentioned:

> vix puberibus pater sub annis
> objectus Geticis puer catenis,
> bellorum mora, fœderis sequester.

The most important fragment is that of the Panegyric on the third consulship of Aetius (A D 446) with a Preface in prose. He refers to his exploits against the Armorici (l. 8):

> lustrat Aremoricos iam mitior incola saltus;

[5] There was another contemporary poet, Quintianus a Ligurian, who also sang the praises of Aetius. Sidonius, c. ix 289 *sqq*

he describes the peace of A.D 442 with Gaiseric (*insessor Libyes*) and alludes to the marriage of Huneric with Eudoxia (ll. 24-30)

> 27 nunc hostem exutus pactis proprioribus arsit
> Romanam vincire fidem Latiosque parentes
> adnumerare sibi sociamque intexere prolem

The death of the father of Aetius and the story of that general's youth are narrated (l. 110 *sqq*), and the suppression of troubles in Gaul, probably caused by the *bagaudae*, is celebrated (148 *sqq*).[6] The deliverance of Narbo is specially emphasized (l 20):

> sed belliger ultor
> captivum reseravit iter clausasque recepit
> expulso praedone vias, &c.

PROSPER TIRO, of Aquitaine, lived in the first half of the fifth century. He was probably in holy orders, and was an admirer of St Augustine He compiled an *Epitome chronicon*, based almost entirely on Jerome's chronicle, and published it in A.D. 433 (*first edition*). (1) From the crucifixion forward, Prosper added the consuls of each year, derived from a consular list (2) He continued the chronicle of Jerome to A D. 433, the year of publication. (3) He introduced notices from some of St. Augustine's works The *second* edition appeared A.D 443, the *third* A.D. 445, the *fourth* (which some of the extant Mss represent) A D 451, in each case brought down to the date of publication The *fifth* and last edition appeared A.D. 455, after the death of Valentinian, which it records. The compilation has been very carelessly done, both in the earlier part which is based on Jerome and in the later independent part, A D. 378-455. But in lack of other sources Prosper is very important for the first half of the fifth century. The authoritative edition is that of Mommsen (in Chronica Minora, 1 p. 343 *sqq*., 1892), on whose preface this notice is based

From the true Prosper Tiro (whom Gibbon always cites as Prosper) we must carefully distinguish another chronicle, which for some time went under Prosper's name. This is what used to be called the Chronicon Imperiale [7] It ended with the year 452, and was ascribed to Prosper, because the last notices of Prosper's chronicle, A.D. 453-455, were added to it in the Mss But it came to be seen that the two chronicles were not from the same author ; the Chronicon Imperiale gives Imperial not Consular years ; and the strange practice was adopted of distinguishing it from the work of the true Prosper by giving it the true Prosper's full name—"Prosper Tiro". This practice was followed by Gibbon. It must therefore be carefully remembered that in Gibbon's references "Prosper" means Prosper Tiro, while "Prosper Tiro" means a totally distinct chronicle with which neither Prosper Tiro nor any one of Prosper's name had anything to do

This anonymous chronicle has been printed by Mommsen in Chron Min i p. 617 *sqq*, along with another anonymous chronicle[8] (which goes down to A D 511), under the title CHRONICA GALLICA The earlier part is based on Jerome's chronicle. The compiler also used the additions made by Rufinus to the Ecclesiastical History of Eusebius ; some works of Ambrose, Augustine and Cassian , and the Life of Ambrose by Paulinus From A D 395 to the end he either used written sources now lost or verbal information He is quite independent of Prosper, and sympathizes with the opponents of Augustine in the Pelagian controversy His work contains two important notices on the Saxon conquest of Britain (A.D 408 and 441)

This later part of the work represents a Gallic chronicle, perhaps written at Massilia (cp Mommsen, p. 628), which was used by the compiler of the other

---

[6] Cp Chron Gall ad 437 A D (Mommsen, Chron Min 1 p 660)
[7] Also Pithoeanum, having been first published (at Paris in 1588) by Petrus Pithoeus. The best Ms is in the British Museum
[8] Preserved in a Ms at Madrid, under the name of Sulpicius Severus It has been discussed by O. Holder-Egger, Ueber die Weltchronik des sogenannten Severus Sulpitius, &c., 1875

chronicle, mentioned above, which goes down to A D 511 The later part of this chronicle is taken doubtless from a continuation of the Gallic chronicle. The author of the chronicle of A D 511 drew also upon Orosius and Idatius and upon the Chronicle of Constantinople (Mommsen, p 627).

In future it would be convenient to refer to Gibbon's "Prosper Tiro" and this second chronicle as the CHRONICLE OF 452 and the CHRONICLE OF 511. The South-Gallic Annals were continued in the sixth century and were used by Marius of Avenches, Maximus of Saragossa, and Isidore of Seville See vol IV , Appendix 1. With the South-Gallic Chronicles Mommsen has published (from a Brussels and a Madrid Ms.) a short untitled NARRATION concerning Emperors of the Valentinianean and Theodosian House (Valentinian, Valens, Gratian, Theodosius, Arcadius and Honorius), written by a "contemporary and admirer" of Theodosius II. It contains no new historical fact ; but is interesting in having the notice that Honorius died of dropsy, which is found in no other Latin record, and among Greek writers only in Philostorgius (12, 13).

The second of the two fragments which, accidentally joined together in an Ms and hence falsely supposed to belong to the same work, go under the name of ANONYMUS VALESII,[9] is highly important for events in Italy for the period which it covers from A.D. 475 to 526, that is to say, for Odovacar and Theodoric. It is a fragment of annals written at Ravenna in the sixth century, when that city had been recovered by the Empire The fragment (of which more will be said in vol. IV Appendix 1) is mentioned here, because it is edited by Mommsen (in Chronica Minora, I. p 259 sqq) as belonging to one of a series of annals and chronicles which had a common source in a lost document which he calls CHRONICA ITALICA and which had formerly been called by Waitz the Ravennate Annals, a name which disguises the fact that the compilation had been begun before Ravenna became the seat of the western Emperors

The other chief documents which contain the material for arriving at the original constitution of the Chronica Italica are as follows .

FASTI VINDOBONENSES, preserved in a Vienna Ms. in two recensions (distinguished as *priores* and *posteriores*), to which are to be added some excerpts in a St Gall Ms. (excerpta Sangallensia). This chronicle used to be known as the Anonymus Cuspiniani, having been first published in 1553 The *prior* recension comes down to A D. 493, the *posterior* to A D 539, but both are mutilated, the *prior* omitting the years 404-454

The CONTINUATION OF PROSPER, preserved in a Copenhagen Ms.[10] (compiled in the seventh century towards the end of the reign of Heraclius, probably in Italy). In the later part of his work he made use of the chronicle of Isidore (who himself used the Chronica Italica) and the Chronica Italica.

The Latin version of a Greek chronicle (written at Alexandria after A.D. 387), known as the BARBARUS of Scaliger.

Excerpts in the Liber Pontificalis of Ravenna, written by Agnellus in the ninth century.

These documents are edited by Mommsen in parallel columns in vol 1. of Chronica Minora. But as the Chronica Italica were utilized by Prosper, Marcellinus Comes, Cassiodorius, Marius of Aventicum, Isidore, Paulus Diaconus. Theophanes, these authors must be also taken into account. The "Chronica Italica" seems to have been first published in A D. 387, and its basis was the chronicle of Constantinople. Afterwards it was from time to time brought up to date, perhaps, as Mommsen suggests, by the care of booksellers. In the sixth century it was probably re-edited and carried on, after the overthrow of the Gothic kingdom, by Archbishop Maximian of Ravenna, whose "chronicle" is cited by Agnellus. But there is no reason to suppose that he had anything to do with the illiterate fragment of the so-called Anonymus Valesii

The so-called HISTORIA MISCELLA is made up of three distinct works of different ages : (1) Books 1-10 = the history of Eutropius, coming down to the

---

[9] For the first fragment see vol II , Appendix, p 533

[10] The new material contained in it was first edited by G. Hille (1866) under the title Prosperi Aquitani Chronici continuator Havniensis.

death of Julian; cp vol i. Appendix 1; (2) Books 11-16, the work of Paulus Diaconus, who lived at the end of the eighth century and is more famous by his History of the Lombards; (3) the continuation of Landulfus Sagax, who lived more than 200 years later. The second part, which concerns us here, is compiled from Prosper, Orosius, Jordanes and others, but contains some notices drawn from lost sources. The work may be consulted in Muratori's Scriptores Rerum Italicarum, vol i, or in Migne's Patrol Lat, vol xcv

Paulus OROSIUS of Tarraco in Spain dedicated to his friend St Augustine his *Historiae adversum Paganos* in 7 Books He was young when, at St. Augustine's suggestion, he wrote the work shortly after A.D. 417. It was intended to illustrate and vindicate the Divine dispensation of a history of the world from the deluge to his own day, and to show that Christianity was not the cause of the evil times (see below on Salvian). The only part of importance as historical material is the last portion of Bk vii, which deals with the latter part of the fourth, and first seventeen years of the fifth, century His spirit is that of a narrow-minded provincial bigot, but he has some very important entries for the history of his own time—for example on the campaign of Pollentia and the invasion of Radagaisus [Edition C Zangemeister in the Corpus Script. Eccles. Lat. 1882; and text (Teubner) by same editor 1889]

The importance of the work of SALVIAN on the Divine Government (*De Gubernatione Dei*, in 8 Books) for the state of the Empire in the fifth century is not adequately realized by Gibbon It is (as Mr Hodgkin justly says, i p. 918, in his admirable chapter on the book) "one of our most valuable sources of information as to the inner life of the dying Empire and the moral character of its foes". Salvian was a presbyter of Massilia He was married, but after the birth of a daughter he and his wife took a vow of chastity for life. He seems to have been born c. 400 and was still living in 480. He wrote his book before the middle of the century.

The purpose of this book was to answer the great problem which at that time was perplexing thoughtful people · Why is civilized society dissolving and breaking up before the barbarians, if there is a Divine governance of the world? This question had been dealt with before by Augustine in the De Civitate Dei, and by Orosius in the Hist adversus Paganos Their various answers have been well compared by Mr. Hodgkin Augustine's answer was merely negative . the evils which had come upon Rome were not the effect of the introduction of Christianity. Orosius denied the existence of the evils. But a good deal had happened between 417 and 440; and in 440 even Orosius could hardly have ventured to maintain his thesis. Salvian's answer was : these evils are the effects of our vices. He draws a vivid and highly exaggerated contrast between Roman vices and Teutonic virtues. He dwells especially on a matter which came very directly within his own knowledge, the abuses and unjust exactions practised by Gallic officials

So far as Salvian's arguments are concerned there is nothing to be added to Gibbon's criticism (xxxv n. 12): "Salvian has attempted to explain the moral government of the Deity . a task which may be readily performed by supposing that the calamities of the wicked are *judgments*, and those of the righteous *trials*".

Tyrannius RUFINUS (born at Concordia c A D. 345, died in Sicily, A D 410) lived in Egypt for some time, where he was thrown into prison, on the occasion of the persecution which was conducted with the permission of the Emperor Valens, by Lucius, the Arian successor of Athanasius at Alexandria. Having quitted Egypt, on his release, he spent nearly twenty years as a monk on the Mount of Olives During this period he became acquainted with Bacurius the first Christian king of the Iberians, and with Oedesius the companion of Frumentius, the apostle of the Ethiopians He returned to Italy in 397 and spent the later part of his life at Aquileia. This period was troubled by a famous controversy with his friend Jerome. Rufinus translated many Greek works into Latin, among others Origen's treatise περὶ ἀρχῶν The controversy arose out of certain references to Jerome in the Preface to this translation, and it was represented that Rufinus misused the authority of Jerome's name to cover heretical doctrines of Origen. The most important works of Rufinus are his Ecclesiastical History in two Books, being a continuation of that of Eusebius, which he rendered into Latin ; and his history of Egyptian Anchorets For the origin of monasticism the latter work is of considerable importance.

MODERN WORKS. Besides those mentioned in the Appendices to vol i and ii. : H Richter, Das westromische Reich, besonders unter den Kaisern Gratian, Valentinian II. und Maximus (375-388), 1865 ; J. Ifland and A. Guldenpenning, der Kaiser Theodosius der Grosse, 1878 ; A. Guldenpenning, Geschichte des ostromischen Reiches unter den Kaisern Arcadius und Theodosius ii , 1885. V Schultze, Geschichte des Untergangs des griechisch-romischen Heidentums, 1887

For the barbarian invasions and the Teutonic Kingdoms· Hodgkin, Italy and her Invaders, vol. i. and ii. (ed. 2, 1892) ; F. Dahn, Konige der Germanen ; and the same writer's Urgeschichte der germanischen und romanischen Volker ; R Pallmann's Geschichte der Volkerwanderung ; E von Wietersheim's Geschichte der Volkerwanderung (ed. 2 by Dahn, 1880-1) ; Kopke's Anfange des Konigthums bei den Gothen There are also special histories of the chief German invaders : I. Aschbach, Geschichte der Westgothen ; F. Papencordt's Geschichte der vandalischen Herrschaft in Afrika ; C. Binding's Geschichte des burgundisch-romanischen Konigreichs. The work of Zeuss : Die Deutschen und die Nachbarstamme, is a most valuable storehouse of references.

Special Monographs : on Stilicho (cp. above, under Claudian) : R. Keller, Stilicho, 1884 ; Rosenstein, Alarich und Stilicho, in Forsch. zur deutschen Geschichte, vol. 3, 1863 ; Vogt, Die politischen Bestrebungen Stilichos, 1870 ; on Chrysostom : F. Ludwig, Der heilige Johannes Chrys. in seinem Verhaltniss zum byzantinischen Hof, 1883, and Rev. W. R. W. Stephens, Life and Times of John Chrysostom (Others are referred to in the footnotes)

2 PICTS AND SCOTS—(P. 42, 43)

"Cæsar tells us that the inhabitants of Britain in his day painted themselves with a dye extracted from wood ; by the time, however, of British independence under Carausius and Allectus, in the latter part of the third century, the fashion h'd so far fallen off in Roman Britain that the word *Picti*, Picts, or painted men, h'ad got to mean the peoples beyond the Northern Wall, and the people on the Solway were probably included under the same name, though they also went by the separate denomination of Atecotti. Now all these Picts were natives of Britain, and the word Picti is found applied to them for the first time in a panegyric by Eumenius, in the year 296 , but in the year 360 another painted people appeared on the scene. They came from Ireland, and to distinguish these two sets of painted foes from one another Latin historians left the painted natives to be called Picti, as had been done before, and for the painted invaders from Ireland they retained, untranslated, a Celtic word of the same (or nearly the same) meaning, namely *Scotti*. Neither the Picts nor the Scotti probably owned these names, the former of which is to be traced to Roman authors, while the latter was probably given the invaders from Ireland by the Brythons, whose country they crossed the sea to ravage. The Scots, however, did recognize a national name, which described them as painted or tattooed men . . . This word was Cruithnig, which is found applied equally to the painted people of both Islands " "The portion of Ireland best known to history as Pictish was a pretty well defined district consisting of the present county of Antrim and most of that of Down." (Professor Rhŷs, Early Britain, p. 235 *sqq*) But Professor Rhŷs now takes another view of *Picti*, which he regards not as Latin, but as native and connected with the Gallic *Pictones*. See *Scottish Review*, July, 1891.

Ammianus (278) divided the inhabitants of the North of Britain (the Picts) into two nations, the Dicalidonæ and Verturiones. "Under the former name, which seems to mean the people of the two Caledonias, we appear to have to do with the Caledonias proper . . . while in later times the word Verturiones yielded in Goidelic the well-known name of the Brythons of the kingdom of

Fortrenn they were possibly the people previously called Boresti, but that is by no means certain." (Rhŷs, *ib.* p 93)

The Atecotti seem to have occupied part of the land between the walls of Hadrian and Antoninus, where the Maeatae dwelled (see Mr. Haverfield's map of Roman Britain, in Poole's Historical Atlas of Modern Europe) Prof. Rhŷs proposes to identify them with the earlier Genunians (Γενουνια μοίρα of Pausanias, 8, 43) and the later Picts of Galloway (*ib.* p 89, 90).

3. THE DEATH OF COUNT THEODOSIUS—(P. 50)

The cause of the sudden execution of Theodosius at Carthage in 396 A D. is obscure We can only suppose that he had powerful enemies—friends of the governor Romanus. H. Richter (das westromische Reich, p. 401) imputes the responsibility to Merobaudes. But Merobaudes was the minister of Gratian in Gaul, and not of Justina and Valentinian in Mediolanum (as Mr. Hodgkin observes). Mr Hodgkin conjectures that the blow came not from Mediolanum but from Antioch. The name of Theodosius began with the four fatal letters Θ ε ο δ, "and it seems therefore allowable to suppose that the incantation scene at Antioch four years previously—the laurel tripod, the person in linen mantle and with linen socks, who shook the magic cauldron and made the ring dance up and down among the twenty-four letters of the alphabet—were links in the chain of causation which led the blameless veteran to his doom" (Italy and her Invaders, 1. p 292) And certainly we can well imagine that the superstitious Valens watched with apprehension the career of every eminent officer whose name began with those four letters, and observing the distinguished services of the Count of Africa used influence at Milan to procure his fall.

4. MELLOBAUDES—(P. 50, 67)

Gibbon has confused Mellobaudes with the more eminent Merobaudes in two places (p. 50 and 67). Mellobaudes (or Mallobaudes vary) was a Frank king and held the post of comes domesticorum under Gratian. See Ammian, 30, 3, 7, and 31, 10, 6.

This Mellobaudes must also be distinguished from another less important Mellobaudes (or Mallobaudes), a Frank who was *tribunus armaturarum* under Constantius ; see Ammian, 14, 11, 21, and 15, 5, 6. These namesakes are confounded in the index of Gardthausen's Ammianus. See Richter, Das westromische Reich, p. 283.

Merobaudes deserves prominence as the first of a series of men of barbarian origin who rose to power in the Imperial service ; Merobaudes, Arbogast, Stilicho, Aetius, Ricimer. He married into the family of Valentinian (Victor, *Epit.* 45), and was consul in A.D. 377.

5. LIST OF KINGS OF PERSIA, FROM SAPOR II. TO KOBAD—(P. 55)

Sapor (Shāpūr) ii dies A.D 379.
Ardashir ii. succeeds A.D. 379, Aug. 19.
Sapor iii   ,,   A D. 383, Aug. 18.
Bahrām iv.   ,,   A.D. 388, Aug. 16.
Yezdegerd i.   ,,   A D 399, Aug 14
Bahrām v.   ,,   A.D 420, Aug 8
Yezdegerd ii.   ,,   A.D 438, Aug. 4.
Hormizd iii.   ,,   A.D 457, July 30.
Pēröz came to the throne in 459, but counted from the first year of Hormizd, whom he deposed.
Balāsh succeeds A.D 484, July 23.
Kobad (Kavādh) succeeds A.D. 488, July 22 ; died Sept. 13, A D. 531

The dates given are those of the beginning of the Persian year in which the king succeeded and from which he counted, not the actual days of accession ; and are taken from Noldeke, Excurs 1 to his Geschichte der Perser und Araber zur Zeit der Sassaniden. Thus Bahrām v. did not actually possess the throne till 421 (spring).

6. THE ORIGIN OF THE HUNS—(C. XXVI.)

Excerpts of ethnological interest from the voluminous Annals of the Han dynasty (in about a hundred volumes)[1] were translated by Mr. Wylie (at Sir H. Howorth's request) and published in the third and fourth volumes of the Journal of the Anthropol. Institute. Sir H. Howorth wrote a preface, arguing that the Hiung-Nu cannot be identified with the Huns. His argument is : the Hiung-Nu were Turks ; the Huns were Ugrians ; therefore the Huns were not Hiung-Nu "The Huns, as I have elsewhere argued, were a race of Ugrians led by a caste of another race now represented by some of the Lesghian tribes of the Caucasus. The Hiung-Nu were not Ugrians. It was Klaproth, whose grasp of the whole subject of the ethnography of Northern Asia was most masterly, and who, notwithstanding some failures, I hold to have been *facile princeps* among Asiatic ethnologists, first proved that the Hiung-Nu were Turks, and his conclusions were endorsed by the very competent authority of Abel Remusat, and since by other scholars."

That the Hiung-Nu were a Turkic race (the correct way of stating it is . the Turks were Hiung-Nu) may indeed be regarded as certain , but so much cannot be said of Sir H. Howorth's other premiss, that the Huns were Ugrians.

For Klaproth's proof that the Huns were Lesghians, see his Tableaux historiques de l'Asie, and Howorth, Journal Anth Inst iii. p. 453-4. His comparative list of Hunnic and Lesghian names presents such strikingly close resemblances that it is hard to resist his conclusions ; and his identification of the Hunnic *var* "river" (Jordanes, *Get.* 52) with Lesghian *or, ouor,* is plausible. While admitting that the Huns may be connected with this Caucasian race, I cannot follow Sir H. Howorth in his further speculations, or admit that an affinity has been proved with the Finno-Ugrian languages. Sir H Howorth's comparative table of Hunnic with Hungarian names (p 470) is quite unconvincing.

On the other hand I cannot accept as proven, or as more than a brilliant conjecture, the identification of the Huns with the Hiung-Nu. The thesis has been recently defended by Mr. E. H Parker, a Chinese scholar, whose work I have used and referred to in additional footnotes on Gibbon's account of the Hiung-Nu in this volume In "A Thousand Years of the Tartars," p. 99, Mr Parker puts it thus : The Northern Hiung-Nu, unable to maintain their ground against various enemies, "disappeared far away to the North, many of them no doubt finding their way by the upper waters of the Selinga and the Irtysh to Issekul, the Aral, and the Caspian, struggling with the Bashkirs, the Alans, and the unknown tribes then occupying Russia into Europe". And again in an article on "The Origin of the Turks" in the English Hist Review, July, 1896, p 434, he defends the view that "the Hiung-Nu were in fact the Huns, who afterwards appeared as the Hunni in Europe".

While I am not convinced that on the ethnographical side there is any a priori objection to the identification of the Huns with the "Hiung" slaves—Mr. Parker observes that to this day Hiung "is in some parts of China still pronounced *Hun*"—I cannot, from the historical side, see the justification for asserting the identity. The resemblance of the name is in fact the only proof. It is a mortal leap from the kingdom of the northern Zenghi to the steppes of Russia, and he who takes it is supported on the wings of fancy, not on the ground of fact. On this question research in the Chinese annals has added nothing to the data which were so ably manipulated by Deguignes.

The Geougen, who will be more important afterwards in connexion with the Turks (see chapter xlii), were wrongly identified with the Avars by Deguignes. Mr. Parker (Eng. Hist. Rev. *loc. cit.* p 435) is unable to decide whether they were of Hunnic or Tungusic origin, and suspects a mixture of both races.

The close connexion of the Huns and Avars seems clear. Professor Vámbéry

---

[1] There is a Russian translation of the entire work.

in his *A Magyarok Eredete* (1882), p. 415 *sqq*, has collected the Hun and Avar words and names that can be gleaned from literature, and attempted to interpret them by the help of Turkish. His list however is not complete.

7. THE SARMATIAN WAR OF A.D. 378—(P. 120, n. 112)

A Sarmatian campaign of Theodosius in 378 A D. after his recall from Spain si mentioned by Theodoret, v. 5, and Theodoret's statement, which has been questioned by some, is confirmed, as H. Richter has pointed out (das weströmische Reich, p. 691), by Themistius and Pacatus. In his Panegyric of A.D. 379 Themistius refers to it thus (xiv. 182 C): ἐξ ἐκείνου δε και σε ἐκάλουν ἐπι τὴν βασιλειαν Ῥωμαίοι, ἐξοτου Σαυρομάτας λυττῶντας και τὴν προς τῷ ποταμῷ γῆν ἄρασαν ἐπιδραμόντας μόνος ἀνεστειλας κ.τ λ. Pacatus, c 10: vix tecta Hispana susceperas, iam Sarmatias tabernaculis tegebaris, vix emerita arma suspenderas, iam hosti armatus instabas; vix Iberum tuum videras, iam Istro prætendebas. Cp. Ifland, p. 59, and Kaufmann, *Philologus*, 31, p 472 *sqq*

8. CHRONOLOGY OF THE PACIFICATION OF THE GOTHS, A.D. 379, 380—(P. 123 *sqq*.)

The account given in our sources of the warfare in Thrace and Illyricum during the years 379-80 and the subjugation of the Goths is very confused, and Gibbon has made no attempt to distinguish the events of the two years With the help of laws in the Codex Theod. (of which the dates however cannot be implicitly trusted) Ifland has extracted with some pains the following chronology from Zosimus, Jordanes, and the ecclesiastical historians, with an occasional indication from Ambrose (Der Kaiser Theodosius, p. 65-86).

379, Spring: Theodosius with Gratian at Sirmium.
,, before middle of June · Theodosius at Thessalonica (c. Th. x. 1, 12);
           Embassy of senate of Constantinople greets Theodosius there,
           Themistius delivers his panegyric, written for the occasion, some weeks later (Or. 14).
           Having organized his army Theodosius divides his forces One part he leads northward to act against the Goths in Dacia and Moesia , the other under Modares is to operate in Thrace
,, 6 July: Theodosius at Scupi (c. Th. vi. 30, 2).
,, Modares gains a great victory in Thrace.
,, Aug · Theodosius at Vicus Augusti (on the Danube?), c Th xii. 13, 4
,, Roman victories during autumn (see chronicles of Idatius and Prosper, Aur. Victor, 48, Socrates, 5, 6, Sozomen, vii 4),
,, foedus made with the Goths, who give hostages (Sozomen, vii 4);
,, Nov 17 proclamation of Roman victories over Goths, Alans and Huns (Idatius Fasti, ad ann)
380, January Theodosius again in Thessalonica (c. Th. ix. 27, 1).
,, February · illness of Theodosius (Feb. 27, his intolerant edict, C. Th. xvi. 1, 2), his illness lasts during the summer.
,, Goths begin new hostilities; two movements distinguished : (1) West Gothic under Fritigern against Epirus, Thessaly, Achaia, (2) East Gothic under Alatheus and Safrax against Pannonia and Upper Moesia.
,, Difficulties of Theodosius in coping with the Goths Gratian sends troops to his aid, under Bauto and Arbogastes. Cp. Zosimus, iv 33.
,, Second half of year Fritigern disappears; Athanaric crosses the Danube into Roman territory, Gratian himself acts against the Goths in Pannonia (Zos, ib., Jordanes, 27)
,, 17 August: Theodosius at Hadrianople; 8 September, at Sirmium.
,, 14 or 24 November: Theodosius enter s Constantinople in triumph (cp. above p. 146, n. 37).

9. THEOLOGY IN THE MARKET-PLACES OF CONSTANTINOPLE—
(P 143)

The humorous description of the interest taken in theological subtleties by the mechanics and slaves of Constantinople is quoted by Gibbon on the authority of Jortin, but Gibbon acknowledges that he does not know where it comes from, and implies that Jortin does not state his source.

A striking instance of the slumbers of Homer. Jortin indeed omits to give the reference, but he expressly ascribes the passage to "Gregory," that is, Gregory of Nyssa, with whom he is dealing in the context. It would seem from Gibbon's note that he took Gregory to be the Nazianzen.

The passage occurs in Gregory Nyssen's Oratio de deitate Filii et Spiritus Sancti (Migne, Patr. Gr., 46, p. 557) and runs as follows :

ἐὰν περὶ τῶν ὀβολῶν ἐρωτήσῃς ὁ δὲ σοι περὶ γεννητοῦ καὶ ἀγεννήτου ἐφιλοσόφησε κἄν περὶ τιμήματος ἄρτου πύθοιο, Μείζων ὁ πατήρ, ἀποκρίνεται, καὶ ὁ υἱὸς ὑποχείριος. εἰ δέ, Τὸ λουτρὸν ἐπιτηδειόν ἐστιν, εἴποις, ὁ δὲ ἐξ οὐκ τὸν υἱὸν εἶναι διωρίσατο·

10 DID THEODOSIUS VISIT ROME IN A.D. 394?—(P 184)

According to Zosimus (iv. 59 and v 30), Theodosius went to Rome after the battle of the Frigidus This is likewise attested by Prudentius (against Symm., 1), and is implied in Theodoret's statement, in reference to the visit of A.D 389, χρόνου δὲ συχνοῦ διελθόντος εἰς τὴν Ῥώμην ἀφικομένος πάλιν ὁ βασιλεύς. This evidence has been accepted by Jeep, but the objections urged by Tillemont against it seem quite decisive, and it is rejected by Clinton and most authorities. It is a case of a confusion between the suppression of Maximus and the suppression of Eugenius ; the visit to Rome after the second war is merely a duplicate of the visit to Rome after the first war. Guldenpenning thinks that Theodosius sent a message to the senate signifying his will that pagan worship should cease (Der Kaiser Theodosios, p. 229-30).

11 THE LIBRARIES OF ALEXANDRIA—(P 199, 201)

"The valuable library of Alexandria was pillaged or destroyed." That is, the lesser library in the Serapeum, which was situated in the Rhacôtis quarter of the city. Gibbon has failed to distinguish it from the great Library of the Brucheum, of which Zenodotus, Callimachus and other famous scholars were librarians. This Library is said to have been burnt down when Caesar was in Alexandria (but see Mahaffy, Egypt under the Ptolemies, p 454).

For the distinction of the two libraries see Epiphanius, de mensuris et ponderibus, 168 (Migne, Patr Gr. vol. 43, p 256): ἔτι δὲ ὕστερον καὶ ἑτέρα ἐγένετο βιβλιοθήκη ἐν τῷ Σεραπίῳ [sic] μικρότερα τῆς πρώτης, ἥτις καὶ θυγατὴρ ὠνομάσθη αὐτῆς. For the first or mother library, see ib. 166 (Migne, p. 249). For other references see Susemihl, Geschichte der alexandrinischen Litteratur, i. p. 336.

But is it an attested fact that the lesser or daughter library was destroyed in A D 391? The sanctuary of Serapis was demolished, but does that imply the demolition of all the buildings connected with the Serapeum?[1] The only evidence on which Gibbon's statement rests is the sentence which he quotes from Orosius (p 201, n. 53). But Orosius does not mention the Serapeum or speak of a large library. He merely says that he had seen bookcases in temples (which he does not name) ; and that, since then, he had been informed that the temples had been pillaged and the bookcases emptied. It seems to me highly improbable that Orosius is thinking either of the Alexandrian library or of the Serapeum. There is no reason to suppose that the library was in the temple I conclude then that there is no evidence that the library of the Serapeum did not survive till the Saracen conquest, notwithstanding the verdict of Susemihl (ib. 344). "Omar fand 642 schwerlich noch Bucher in Alexandreia zu verbrennen ".

[1] The statement of Eunapius in the Vita Aedesii καὶ τὸ Σαραπεῖον ἱερὸν διεσκεδάννυτο οὐχ ἡ θεραπεία μόνον ἀλλὰ καὶ τὰ οἰκοδομήματα, cannot be pressed to mean more than that not only was the worship suppressed but the temple itself was demolished

12. WORSHIP OF RELICS—(P. 210)

In Gregory Nyssen's Encomium of St. Theodore (Migne, vol 46 736 *sqq.* there are passages, which, coming from such an eminent and learned ecclesiastic, are an important illustration of the growth of the veneration of relics. For example, he says:—ει δε και κονιν τις δοίη φερειν τὴν ἐπικειμένην τῇ ἐπιφανεία τῆς αιαπαυσεως, δῶρον ο χοῦς λαμβανεται, καὶ ὡς κειμήλιον ἡ γῆ θησαυριζεται. τὸ γὰρ αὐτοῦ τοῦ λειψάνου προσαψασθαι, εἰ ποτέ τις ἐπιτυχία τοιαύτη παρασχοι τὴν ἐξουσίαν, ὅπως ἐστι πολυποθητον, καὶ εὐχῆς τῆς ἀνωτάτω το δῶρον ἰσασιν οἱ πεπειραμενοι καὶ τῆς τοιαυτης ἐπιθυμίας ἐμφορηθεντες . . . το μεν ἁπλῶς ἀποθανον ῥίπτεται ὡς τὸ τυχόν· τὸ δε τῷ παθει τοῦ μαρτυριου χαριτωθὲν, οὕτως ἐστιν ἐράσμιον καὶ ἀμφισβητησιμον, ὡς ο προλαβὼν λόγος ἐδιδαξεν (p. 740).

13. STILICHO IN INSCRIPTIONS—(P. 225, 237, 257)

The inscription celebrating the rescue of Africa by Stilicho, referred to by Gibbon, p. 225 (note) ad p. 237 (note), will be found in C. I. L. vi. 1730. It runs as follows:

> Flavio Stilichoni illustrissimo viro, magistro equitum peditumque
> comiti domesticorum, tribuno prætoriano, et ab ineunte aetate
> per gradus clarissimæ militiæ ad columen sempiternæ
> et regiæ adfinitatis evecto, progenero Divi Theodosi, comiti
> Divi Theodosi in omnibus bellis adque victoriis et ab eo in
> adfinitatem regiam cooptato itemque socero D. N. Honori
> Augusti Africa consiliis siius et provisione liberata.

For inscriptions referring to the restoration of the "walls, gates and towers of Rome, undertaken through Stilicho's influence before Alaric's first invasion of Italy, see C. I. L vi 1188-1190

Another inscription records Stilicho's victory over Radagaisus C. I L 6, 1196 (p 249). Gibbon (after Mascou) refers it to the Gothic war of 402-3, and expresses surprise at the description of Alaric's defeat as the total extinction of the Gothic nation (p 243). Pallmann took the same view (Volkerwand p 243), but the title is rightly referred in the Corpus (*loc cit*) to the events of 405.

> Imppp clementissimis felicissimis toto orbe victoribus DDD NN*n*
> Arcadio Honorio Theodosio Auggg ad perenne indicium triumph*orum*
> quod Getarum nationem in omne ævum docu*ere* extin*gui*
> arcum simulacris eorum tropæisq decora*tum*
> S P Q R totius operis splendore

14. THE TWO EASTERN EXPEDITIONS OF STILICHO AND HIS ILLYRIC POLICY—(P 227, 245)

An unwary reader of Gibbon might fail to realize that on two separate occasions Stilicho came, an unwelcome helper, to the assistance of Arcadius in the Illyric peninsula. As there has been a difficulty about the dates, and as Zosimus inverts the order of events, it is important to grasp this clearly. On the first occasion (A.D. 395) Stilicho started from Italy in spring (Claudian, *in Rufin.* 2, 101), came up with Alaric in Thessaly, and was then commanded to return, before he had accomplished anything, by an order of Arcadius. Gainas and the Eastern troops went to Constantinople, and Rufinus met his fate; while Stilicho returned to Italy. In the following year (A.D. 396), when Alaric was in Southern Greece, Stilicho again came to help the realm of Arcadius, landed at Corinth, blockaded Alaric in Pholoe, and allowed him to escape (Zosimus v. 7, places the blockade of Pholoe before the death of Rufinus. The charge of Zosimus that Stilicho indulged in debauchery in Elis cannot safely be pressed; for the phrase he uses is borrowed from Julian's Misopogon. See Mendelssohn *ad loc.*)

A D. 395. Claudian represents Alaric as shutting himself up in a fortified camp on the news of Stilicho's approach (in Ruf 2, 124-9). Stilicho arrives in Thessaly (implet Thessaliam ferri nitor, l. 179) and prepares to attack the enemy. If he had been permitted to do so, the invasion of Greece would have been averted (186 *sqq*), but alas ! *regia mandata* arrive from Arcadius, and he has to sacrifice the "publica commoda" to the duty of obedience. This must have been about the beginning of November, if Rufinus was slain on 27th November (as Socrates states, vi 1 ; cp. Chron. Pasch. ad ann). Thus the advance of Stilicho from Italy to Thessaly would have occupied more than six months. What was the cause of this delay ? It is significant that the charge brought against Rufinus by Claudian of having incited the Visigoths to the invasion of Greece is uttered only as a suspicion by Socrates (*loc. cit.*, δοξαν εἰχεν ως κ τ·λ. "was supposed to have," &c), in the following century the suspicion has developed into a positive statement in the chronicle of Count Marcellinus ad ann. (Alaricum . . . infestum reipublicae fecit et in Graeciam misit).

A D 396 (Gibbon wrongly places the events of this year in A D 397. It is not clear why he deserts the guidance of Tillemont.) Stilicho landed at the Isthmus (Zosimus, 5, 7), and is said to have had Alaric at his mercy at Pholoe Three views have been held as to the escape of Alaric : (1) he outwitted Stilicho, who was culpably negligent (cp. Zosimus) ; (2) the suggestion of Claudian (B G. 516) that Arcadius and his ministers, jealous of Stilicho's intervention, treated with Alaric and secured his retreat, might be supported by the circumstance that Arcadius created him Master of Soldiers in Illyricum soon afterwards ; (3) Stilicho is supposed to have made a secret treaty with Alaric, and permitted his retreat, for purposes of his own.

It is certain that Stilicho's assertion of the unity of the Empire by appearing with armed forces in the Praefecture of Illyricum was viewed with suspicion and distrust at Constantinople. The feeling at the court of Arcadius is aptly expressed in words which Claudian has put into the mouth of Rufinus (in Ruf. 2, 161) :

> Deserat (sc Stilicho) Illyrici fines, Eoa remittat
> agmina, fraternas ex aequo dividat hastas

It is certain too that Stilicho afterwards, if not in A.D 396, made it the aim of his policy to detach Illyricum from Arcadius and add it to the realm of Honorius. This is stated in so many words by Zosimus (v. 26), and it was doubtless Stilicho's object from the beginning. This is the view of Jung (Romer and Romanen, p. 188 : ich sehe darin vielmehr die consequente Verfolgung der durch Stilicho von Anfang an beabsichtigten Politik), who has some good remarks on the geographical importance of Illyricum ; the unsatisfactoriness of the line of division of 395 which cut off Dalmatia from the rest of the Balkan peninsula (p 186), and the circumstance that all northern Illyricum belonged to the Latin-speaking part of the Empire.

After the first invasion of Italy, Stilicho intended to use the help of Alaric for this purpose, and established him on the borders of the territory on which he had designs ; but the execution of the plan was continually deferred, on account of other events which claimed the care of Stilicho Alaric during this time was playing his own game, between the courts of Ravenna and Constantinople. His object was to obtain permanently Dalmatia, Noricum, Istria and Venetia, with a regular grant of money from the Empire This was what he asked in 410 (Zos. v 48), and his aim throughout was doubtless a settlement of this kind.

The certainty that from A D. 402 forward Stilicho made use of Alaric for his Illyric designs rouses the suspicion that he was playing with Alaric, with the same intent, in A.D. 395 and 396. The famous words of Orosius (vii. 37) · Alarico rege cum Gothis suis saepe victo saepe concluso semperque dimisso, are strikingly true of Pollentia, of Verona, and of Pholoe ; I suspect that they are also true of the campaign of A D 395, and that the unaccountable delay between Stilicho's start in the spring and his return to Italy in Oct.-Nov was due to diplomatic dallyings with Alaric. Of course nothing would be said of that by Claudian.

494

APPENDIX

While Stilicho aimed at annexing Eastern Illyricum, the court of Constantinople aimed at the acquisition of Dalmatia Olympiodorus says that Stilicho employed Alaric to defend it (fr 3). The object was pursued in the reign of Theodosius ii. and was finally attained at the marriage of Eudoxia with Valentinian iii., when the boundary was changed to the advantage of the East. Compare Cassiodorius, Var. ep 1, Guldenpenning, das ostrom. Reich, p. 310 But even as early as A D. 414-15 there is epigraphic evidence suggesting the conclusion that at that time Salonae was under the government of Constantinople. See Jung, *op. cit.* p. 187 note.

It is possible to regard (with Keller ; Stilicho, p. 27) Stilicho's special Illyric policy and his relations with Alaric as part of a larger policy which had two chief aims : to maintain the unity of the Empire, under two emperors, and to infuse new blood into it by absorbing barbarians. Stilicho s policy has been generally misunderstood A monograph appeared in the year 1805 with the curious title : Flavius Stilicho, ein Wallenstein der Vorwelt (by C. F. Schulz).

15. ALARIC IN GREECE—(P 242-4)

Though no record tells that Alaric burnt down the Temple of Eleusis, it is certain that the invasion of the Goths was coincident with the end of the Eleusinian mysteries. The sanctuary of the two goddesses must have already suffered much under Jovian and Theodosius. The cult, restored by Julian, was suppressed by Jovian, but renewed again under Valentinian through the intervention of Praetextatus, proconsul of Achaia It must have been affected by the intolerant edicts of Theodosius ; certainly the demonstration of the Christian section of the Athenian community forced the last Eumolpid high priest to resign Subsequently—probably on the death of Theodosius—the pagan party felt themselves strong enough to appoint, as hierophant, a priest of Mithras from Thespiae, and he presided at Eleusis at the time of Alaric's invasion.

See Gregorovius, Hat Alarich die Nationalgotter Griechenlands zerstort? (Kleine Schriften, vol. i.), and Geschichte der Stadt Athen im Mittelalter, i. p. 35 *sqq.*

As for Athens, there is no doubt that it capitulated and was spared by Alaric, and that the Goths did not destroy or rob its art treasures. Athens suffered, as Gregorovius remarks, less in the invasion of Alaric than in the invasion in the time of Dexippus. There were of course acts of cruelty ; some are recorded in the *Vita Prisci* of Eunapius But we must not press the words of Claudian (in Rufin. ii. 189) : nec fera Cecropiae traxissent vincula matres, further than at the most to interpret it of the rural inhabitants of Attica. Gregorovius observes that in the other passages where the devastation of Greece is mentioned (iv. Cons. Hon. 471, Eutrop. 2, 199, cons. Stil. i. 180), there is not a word about Athens.

As to the Zeus-temple of Olympia, it is supposed that the Phidiac statue of Zeus had been removed about two years before the Gothic invasion (in A D. 394, when Theodosius suppressed the Olympic games) to Constantinople and was afterwards burned in the Palace of Lausus. Cp Cedrenus, i. p. 364 (Gregorovius i. p. 43). The temple of Olympia was burnt down in the reign of Theodosius ii.

The general conclusion of Gregorovius is that it is a gross exaggeration to ascribe to the Goths the deliberate destruction of the temples and sanctuaries of Greece.

16 PENETRABIS AD URBEM—(P. 248)

The clear voice which Alaric heard in the grove uttered an acrostich with the help of Claudian's art. It has been pointed out that the first and last letters of the two verses (B G. 546-7) spell RÓMA.

> R umpe omnes, Alarice moras ; hoc impiger annO
> A lpibus Italiae ruptis penetrabis ad urbeM.

So it is printed in Koch's edition.

17 ALARIC'S FIRST INVASION OF ITALY—(P. 248, 253 *sqq.*)

That the battle of Pollentia was fought in 402 is now universally agreed by all competent historians, there is no conflict of evidence on the matter, and there is nothing to be said for 403.[1] But there is still room for difference of opinion as to the date of Alaric's entry into Italy, and possibly as to the date of the battle of Verona.

(1) We have to set the statements of two chronicles against each other. On one hand Prosper, sub ann. 400 · Gothi Italiam . . . ingressi (see next Appendix). On the other, the Fasti Vindobonenses (Chronica Italica; see above, App 1) have, sub anno 401, the more precise notice: et intravit Alaricus in Italiam, xiv. kl December [2]

Pallmann (followed by Hodgkin) accepts the date of Prosper. Tillemont, also accepting Prosper, but putting (in spite of Prosper) the battle of Pollentia in 403, found himself driven to assume that Alaric having invaded Italy in 400 was driven out of it in 401 and returned in 402—in fact a double invasion.

As there is little or nothing to choose between Prosper and the Fasti Vindobonenses—both being equally prone to error—we may be disposed to allow the argument of Seeck[3] (approved by Birt) to determine us in preferring the date of the Fasti Vindobonenses   In describing the entry of the Goths Claudian speaks of constant eclipses of the moon among the terrors which preyed upon men's minds :

> territat adsiduus lunæ labor atraque Phœbe
> noctibus aerisonas crebris ululata per urbes.
> nec credunt vetito fraudatam Sole sororem
> telluris subeunte globo sed castra secutas
> barbara Thessalidas patriis lunare venenis
> incestare iubar. (B G , 233 *sqq.*)

These data (cp. *adsiduus*) are satisfied by the two lunar eclipses which took place on June 21 and December 6, A.D. 401.

After Pollentia, there must have been another engagement at Asta (vi cons. Hon , 203). Keller thinks that this took place before that of Pollentia. In any case Gibbon is wrong in supposing that Asta was the town in which Honorius was shut up, till delivered by Stilicho. Honorius was in Milan, as is clear from Claudian's description (*ib.* 456 *sqq*)   To reach Asta Stilicho would have had to cross not only the Addua (488), but the Padus (which is not mentioned).

(2) That the battle of Verona did not take place later than A.D. 403 is proved by the fact that it is celebrated in the Panegyric composed by Claudian before the end of that year for the sixth consulate of Honorius, which began on Jan. 1, A D 404   That it took place in summer is proved by a line of that poem (our only source for the battle) :

> sustinet accensos aestivo pulvere soles (vi. cons., 215)

Those therefore who like Tillemont and Gibbon set P lentia in spring 403 were obliged to set Verona in the summer of the same year. The question therefore arises whether, when we have moved Pollentia a year back, we are to move Verona along with it. Pallmann leaves Verona where it was in 403, and he is followed hesitatingly by Mr. Hodgkin. That the victory of Verona was won in 403, and that more than a year elapsed between the two battles, has, I think, been proved convincingly by Birt (Preface to ed. of Claudian, liv -v.). The argument is that, if Verona had been fought in 402, the long interval of sixteen

---

[1] " The date 403 seems to have originally obtained currency from a simple mistake on the part of Baronius, a mistake fully acknowledged by Tillemont (v 804) "   Hodgkin, i p 736

[2] The Additamenta to Prosper in the Cod Havn. give the date x kal. Sept. (Mommsen, Chron. Min , i p 299)

[3] Forschungen zur deutschen Geschichte, 24, p 182 *sqq* (1884).

months would have stultified the whole tone of Claudian's poem, which breathes the triumph of a recent victory. Such a line as

et sextas Getica praevelans fronde secures (647)

is inconceivable on any save the first First of January following the victory. Cp also lines 406, 580, 653. The transition in l. 201 is suggestive of a considerable interval between the two battles

> te quoque non parvum Getico, Verona, triumpho
> adiungis cumulum nec plus Pollentia rebus
> contulit Ausoniis aut moenia vindicis Hastae.

The resulting chronology is .

A.D. 401. Alaric enters Italy (Venetia) in November ; at the same time Radagai-
sus (see next Appendix) invades Raetia. Stilicho advances against
Radagaisus.
A.D. 402. Battle of Pollentia on Easter Day
A.D. 402-403. Alaric in Istria
A.D. 403, Summer. Alaric again moves westward , Battle of Verona.

18 RADAGAISUS—(P 263)

Radagaisus invaded Italy in 405 A.D., at the head of an army of barbarians. He was defeated by Stilicho on the hills of Faesulae. There is no doubt about these facts, in which our Western authorities agree, Orosius (vii. 37), Prosper, ad ann. 405, and Paulinus (Vita Ambrosii, c 50). Prosper's notice is Radagaisus in Tuscia multis Gothorum milibus caesis, ducente exercitum Stilichone, superatus et captus est But Zosimus (v. 26) places the defeat of Radagaisus on the Ister "A strange error," Gibbon remarks, "which is awkwardly and imperfectly cured by reading "Αρνον for 'Ιστρον." Awkwardly and contrariwise to every principle of criticism It is an emendation of Leunclavius and Reitemeier's 'Ηριδανον is no better. But Zosimus knew where the Danube was, and the critic has to explain his mistake.

From Gibbon's narrative one would draw the conclusion that this invasion of Italy in 405 (406 Gibbon incorrectly ; see Clinton, ad ann.) was the first occasion on which Radagaisus appeared on the stage of Imperial events. But he appeared before. A notice of Prosper, which there is not the smallest cause to question, represents him as co-operating with Alaric, when Alaric invaded Italy Under the year 400 (there may be reason for questioning the year ; see last Appendix) in his Chronicle we find the record : Gothi Italiam Alarico et Rada-gaiso ducibus ingressi. It is perfectly arbitrary to assume that the notice of the action of Radagaisus on this occasion is a mere erroneous duplication of his action, which is separately and distinctly recorded under the year 405. Pallmann emphasized the importance of the earlier notice of Prosper, and made a suggestion which has been adopted and developed by Mr Hodgkin (i. p. 711, 716, 736), that Alaric and Radagaisus combined to attack Italia, Alaric operating in Venetia and his confederate in Raetia in A D. 400-1, and that the winter campaign of Stilicho in Raetia in A.D. 401-2, of which Claudian speaks, was directed against Radagaisus This combination has everything to recommend it The passages in Claudian are as follows :

Bell. Goth, 279 sqq. Non si perfidia nacti penetrabile tempus
> inrupero Getae, nostras dum Raetia vires
> occupat atque alio desudant Marte cohortes
> idcirco spes omnis abit, &c

,,   ,,   329 sqq   sublimis in Arcton
> prominet Hercyniae confinis Raetia silvae
> quae se Danuvii iactat Rhenique parentem
> utraque Romuleo praetendens flumina regno : &c.

Bell. Goth, 363 *sqq.*   iam foedera gentes
                                     exuerant Latiique audita clade feroces
                                     Vindelicos saltus et Norica rura tenebant, &c.
 ,,   ,,   414, 5.   adcurrit vicina manus, quam Raetia nuper
                                     Vandalicis auctam spoliis defensa probavit.

Leaving aside the question whether (as Birt thinks) the barbarians whom Rada-gaisus headed in Raetia were the Vandals and Alans who invaded Gaul in 406, we may without hesitation accept the conclusion that in 401 Radagaisus was at the head of Vandals and other barbarians in Raetia Birt points out the state-ment that Radagaisus had intended to cross into Italy (εἰς τὴν Ἰταλίαν ὥρμητο διαβῆναι), with which Zosimus introduces his account of the overthrow of Rada-gaisus by Stilicho ; and proposes to refer that statement not to the campaign of 405 but to that of 401.

It was satisfactory to find that Birt had already taken a step in a direction in which I had been led before I studied his Preface to Claudian. The fact is that *Zosimus really recounts the campaign of 401, as if it were the campaign of 405.* His story is that Radagaisus prepared to invade Italy. The news created great terror, and Stilicho broke up with the army from Ticinum, and with as many Alans and Huns as he could muster, without waiting for the attack, crossed the Ister, and assailing the barbarians unexpectedly utterly destroyed their host. This *is* the campaign of the winter of 401-2, of which we know from Claudian's *Gothic War ;* only that (1) Zosimus, placing it in 405, has added one feature of the actual campaign in 405, namely the all but total annihilation of the army of Radagaisus, and that (2) Zosimus, in placing the final action beyond the Danube, differs from Claudian, who places it in Noricum or Vindelicia (I. 365, cited above) and does not mention that Stilicho crossed the river. But the winter campaign was in Danubian regions , and the main difficulty, the appearance of the Danube in the narrative of Zosimus, seems to be satisfactorily accounted for by the assump-tion of this confusion between the two Radagaisus episodes, a confusion which must be ascribed to Zosimus himself rather than to his source Olympiodorus.

19. THE SECOND CARAUSIUS—(P. 272)

A new tyrant in Britain at the beginning of the fifth century was discovered by Mr. Arthur Evans through a coin found at Richborough (Rutupiae). See Numismatic Chronicle, 3rd ser. vol. vii. p. 191 *sqq* , 1887. The obverse of this bronze coin "presents a head modelled in a somewhat barbarous fashion on that of a fourth century Emperor, diademed and with the bust draped in the paludamentum". The legend is : DOMINO CARAVS IO CES. "The reverse presents a familiar bronze type of Constans or Constantius ii. The Emperor holding phoenix and labarum standard stands at the prow of a vessel, the rudder of which is held by Victory. In the present case, however, in place of the usual legend that accompanies this reverse—FEL. TEMP. REPARATIO—appears the strange and unparalleled inscription :

DOMIN . . . CONTA . . . NO "

This coin cannot be ascribed to the well-known Carausius of Diocletian's reign , for the type of the reverse is never found before the middle of the fourth century. The DOMINO (without a pronoun—*nostro*) on the obverse is quite unexampled on a Roman coin Mr. Evans conjectures that CONSTANTINO is to be read on the reverse and makes it probable that this obscure Carausius was colleague of Constantine iii., left behind by him, with the title of Caesar, to hold the island while he was himself absent in Gaul ; and would refer the issue of the coin to A.D. 409. "The memory of the brave Carausius, who first raised Britain to a position of maritime supremacy, may have influenced the choice of this obscure Caesar, at a moment when the Romano-British population was about to assert as it had never done before its independence of Continental Empire."

Whether chosen by Constantine or not the coin "may at least be taken as evidence that the new Caesar stood forth as the representative of the interests of the Constantinian dynasty in the island as against the faction of the rebel Gerontius and his barbarian allies ".

20. THE TYRANT CONSTANTINE—(P. 272)

The best account of the rise, reign, and fall of the tyrant Constantine, ruler of Britain, Gaul and Spain, will be found in Mr. Freeman's article, "Tyrants of Britain, Gaul and Spain," in English Historical Review, vol. 1. (1886) p. 53 *sqq.*

At first, in 407, Constantine's Gallic dominions "must have consisted of a long and narrow strip of eastern Gaul, from the Channel to the Mediterranean, which could not have differed very widely from the earliest and most extended of the many uses of the word Lotharingia". That he was acknowledged in Trier is proved by the evidence of coins (Eckhel, 8, 176). Then he moves down to the land between Rhone and Alps, which becomes the chief theatre of operations, and Arelate becomes his capital. His son Constans he creates *Caesar*, and a younger son Julian *nobilissimus*. Early in 408 Sarus is sent against him by Stilicho. Sarus gains a victory over Constantine's officer (Justinian); and lays siege to Valentia in which Constantine secured himself. But he raises the siege on the seventh day, on account of the approach of Constantine's able general Gerontius, from whom he with difficulty escapes (by coming to an understanding with the *Bagaudae*, who appear to act as a sort of national militia) into Italy.

Constantine's next step is to extend his rule over the rest of the Gallic prefecture,—Spain. We are left quite in the dark as to his relations with the Barbarians who in these years (407-9) were ravaging Gaul. Spain at first submitted to those whom Constantine sent; but very soon the influential Theodosian family organized a revolt against it. The main part of the resistance came from Lusitania, where the four Theodosian brothers had most influence. The rustic army that was collected was set to guard the Pyrenees. To put down the rising, Constantine sent troops a second time into Spain—this time under the Caesar Constans, who was accompanied by Gerontius and by Apollinaris (grandfather of the poet Sidonius), who accepted the office of Praetorian Prefect from Constantine. The Theodosian revolt was suppressed; Constans set up his court in Caesaraugusta (Zaragoza), but soon returned to Gaul, leaving Gerontius to defend Spain.

The sources for this story are Orosius, Sozomen and Zosimus. For the Spanish events we have no fragments of Olympiodorus. "On the other hand the local knowledge of Orosius goes for something, and Sozomen seems to have gained, from some quarter or other, a singular knowledge of detail of some parts of the story" (Freeman, p. 65). It is practically certain that Sozomen's source (as well as that of Zosimus) was Olympiodorus (cp. above, vol. ii., Appendix 1).

Thus master of the West, Constantine forces Honorius, then (A.D. 409) too weak to resist, to acknowledge him as his colleague and legitimate Augustus. Later in the year he enters Italy with an army, avowedly to help Honorius against Alaric (so Olympiodorus), his real motive being to annex Italy to his own realm (Soz. ix. 12). At this time he probably raised Constans to the rank of Augustus. It appears that Constantine was in league with Allobich, the general of Honorius, to compass his treasonable designs. They were discovered, Allobich was cut down, and then Constantine, who had not yet reached Ravenna, turned back.

Meanwhile the revolt of Gerontius in Spain had broken out, and Constans went to put it down. Gibbon's account of the revolt is inadequate, in so far as he does not point out its connexion with the invasion of Spain by the Vandals, Sueves and Alans. There is no doubt that Gerontius and Maximus invited them to cross the Pyrenees. (Cp. Olymp.; Oros. 7, 28; Sozom. ix. 113; Zos. 6, 5; Renatus, in Gregory of Tours, 2, 9; Freeman, p. 74: "The evidence seems to go for direct dealings between Gerontius and the invaders, and his treaty with them is more likely to have followed the proclamation of Maximus than to have gone before it") The dominion of Maximus was practically confined to the north-western corner, the seat of his rule was Tarraco. As for the relation of Maximus to Gerontius, it is very doubtful whether παῖδα in Olympiodorus is to be interpreted *son* and not rather *servant* or *retainer*.

The rest of the episode of Constantine's reign—the sieges of Vienna (which, some have suspected, is a mistake for Narbo) and Arelate—have been well told by Gibbon. These events must be placed in the year 411, for Constantine's head arrived at Ravenna on 18th September (Idatius ad ann.), and it was in the fourth month of the siege of Arelate that Edobich's troops came on the scene (Renatus ap. Greg Tur. ii 9).

Mr. Freeman thus contrasts the position of Constantine with that of contemporary tyrants:

"Constantine and Maximus clearly leagued themselves with the barbarians; but they were not mere puppets of the barbarians; they were not even set up by barbarian help. Each was set up by a movement in an army which passed for Roman. But the tyrants who appear in Gaul in the following year, Jovinus, Sebastian and Attalus—Attalus, already known in Italy, is fresh in Gaul—are far more closely connected with the invaders of the provinces. Attalus was a mere puppet of the Goths, set up and put down at pleasure; his story is merely a part of the marches of Ataulf in Gaul and Spain. Jovinus was set up by Burgundian and Alan help; his elevation to the Empire and the earliest Burgundian settlement in Gaul are simply two sides of one event. Even Maximus was not in this way the mere creature of the invaders of Spain, though he found it convenient at least to connive at their invasion."

21. "THE STATUE OF A POET FAR SUPERIOR TO CLAUDIAN"—(P 282)

Other readers may, like myself, have been puzzled by this reference of Gibbon. Professor Dowden has supplied me with what must, I believe, be the true explanation. The statue of Voltaire by Pigalle (now in the Institut) was executed in 1770. The actress Mlle. Clairon opened a subscription for it See Desnoiresterres, Voltaire et la Société au xviii. Siècle, vii., p. 312 *sqq*

22. DEATH OF MAXIMUS—(P. 341)

The chronicle of Count Marcellinus states that the tyrants Maximus and Jovinus were brought in chains from Spain (to Ravenna) and executed in the year 422, on the occasion of the tricennalia of Honorius (sub ann. 422, p. 75, ed. Mommsen, Chron. Min vol ii). This, like some other unique notices in Marcellinus, was doubtless taken by him from the Consularia Italica (see above, Appendix 1), which have come down in a mutilated condition (cp. Mommsen, *ib.* p. 46). It is borne out by Orosius, who, writing in 417, says (vii 425): Maximus exutus purpura destitutusque a militibus Gallicanis—nunc inter barbaros in Hispania egens exulat; which alone is of sufficient authority to refute the statements of the Eastern writers followed by Gibbon.

23. SEPTIMANIA—(P. 356)

An error prevails in regard to the name Septimania It first occurs in Sidonius Apollinaris, Ep iii, 1, 4, where it is said of the Goths of the kingdom of Tolosa. Septimaniam suam fastidiunt vel refundunt, modo invidiosi huius anguli (that is, Arverni) etiam desolata proprietate potiantur. In his Index Locorum to Luetjohann's ed of Sidonius, Mommsen points out that Septimania is not derived from *septem* (the etymon is *septimus*) and therefore did not signify either the Seven Provinces of the Viennese Diocese, or seven cities granted to the Goths (Greg. Tur, 2, 20). It means the coast line from the Pyrenees to the Rhone, in Sidonius as well as in Gregory of Tours and later writers; Sidonius means that the Goths declared themselves ready to exchange this coast district (including towns of Narbo, Tolosa, Bæterræ, Nemausus, Luteva) for Arverni. Bæterræ was a town of the Septimani; hence Septimania.

24 RATE OF TRAVELLING BY SEA—(P. 359)

In connexion with Gibbon's note on the length of journeys by sea in the reign of Arcadius, I have found some contemporary data in the Life of Porphyry of Gaza by the deacon Marcus   (1) From Ascalon, in Palestine, to Thessalonica . 13 days, p 6, ed. Teubner   (2) Back from Thessalonica to Ascalon: 12 days, p 7.   (3) From Gaza to Constantinople · 20 days, p. 24   (4) Back from Constantinople to Gaza . 10 days, p 25   (5) From Cæsarea (Palæst.) to Rhodes: 10 days in winter, p. 30.   (6) From Rhodes to Constantinople . 10 days, winter, p 33.   (7) From Constantinople (starting 18th April) to Rhodes . 5 days, p 47. It must be remembered that we are not informed about intermediate stoppages. These references may be added to those in Friedländer's Sittengeschichte, II. 13-17. With a good wind one could sail 11 or 12 hundred stadia in 24 hours.

25 ARMENIAN AFFAIRS—(P. 392, 393)

Gibbon wrongly places the division of the Armen an kingdom into Roman and Persian Armenia in the fifth century. This division was arranged between Theodosius the Great and the Persian King   See Saint Martin, Mémoires, p 316.   Persarmenia was at least two-thirds of the whole kingdom   Arsaces, who had already reigned 5 years over all Armenia, continued after the division to rule over Roman Armenia for 2½ years; while Chosrov (a Christian) was appointed by Persia as king of Persian Armenia   On the death of Arsaces, Theodosius committed the rule of the Roman part to a native general, who was induced to recognize the authority of Chosrov; while Chosrov, in order to secure his position in Roman Armenia, acknowledged the suzerainty of the Roman Empire. This did not please Persia, and Jezdegird, son of the Persian king, overthrew him, after he had reigned 5 years. Jezdegird then gave Armenia to Chosrov's brother; but Chosrov was subsequently restored through the influence of the archbishop Isaac, and reigned about a year   He was succeeded by Sapor, a royal prince of Persia, who made himself hated and attempted to proselytize the Armenians   On his father's death he returned to Persia, endeavoured to win the crown, failed, and perished. After an interval Ardeshir (Gibbon's Artasires) was appointed—the last of the Armenian kings   His deposition is described by Gibbon. The government was then placed in the hands of Persian *marztans*

26. PROCOPIAN LEGENDS—(P. 408, 478)

(1) Boniface and Aetius; (2) Valentinian and Maximus.

In his *Italy and her Invaders*, vol ii. (p. 206 *sqq*, ed 2) Mr Hodgkin has discussed and rejected the romantic story connected with the death of Valentinian, the elevation of Maximus and his marriage with Eudoxia   The story is told by Procopius (de B. V. i 4); and, in accordance with Gibbon's criticism that "Procopius is a fabulous writer for the events which precede his own memory," Mr Hodgkin relegates it to "the fables of Procopius".

In the *English Historical Review* for July, 1887 (p 417-465), Mr. Freeman published a long criticism of the historical material for the careers of Aetius and Boniface.   He held the account of Procopius (B. V. i 3) to be "legend of the sixth century and not trustworthy history of the fifth," and tried to "recover the true story as it may be put together from the annalists, the writings of St. Augustine, and other more trustworthy authorities".   In this case Mr. Hodgkin takes a completely different view and argues (ib., vol. i. p. 889 *sqq*, ed 2) that the Procopian legend "has still a reasonable claim to be accepted as history," while admitting that in some points it has been shaken by Mr. Freeman.

Now, while the two stories need not stand on the same footing so far as historical credibility is concerned, while it may be possible to follow Mr. Hodgkin in rejecting the one and accepting the main part of the other, there is a preliminary question which must be discussed before we attempt to decide the ultimate question of historical fact. Procopius is not the only authority for these stories. They are also found in the Salmasian Excerpts, which were first printed by Cramer in his Anecdota Parisina, ii. 383 *sqq*, and afterwards included among the fragments of John of Antioch by C. Muller, in the Fragmenta Hist. Græc, vol. iv. p. 535 *sqq*. The fragments in question are 196 and 200. It was a serious flaw in Mr. Freeman's essay that he was not aware either of the Salmasian Excerpt 196, or of the Constantinian Excerpt 201, which also bears on the question of Aetius and Boniface. Mr. Hodgkin refers to fr. 196, which (with Muller) he ascribes to Joannes Antiochenus, and says. "Though a comparatively late author (he probably lived in the seventh century) and though he certainly used Procopius freely in his compilation, he had also some good contemporary authorities before him, especially Priscus, and there seems some probability, though I would not state it more strongly than this, that he may have found the story in one of them as well as in Procopius".

But Mr. Hodgkin, while he takes account of fr. 196 in defending one "Procopian legend," takes no account of fr. 200 in rejecting the other "Procopian legend," though fr. 200 bears to the latter the same relation which fr. 196 bears to the former.

Now in the first place it must be clearly understood that the author of the work from which the Salmasian Excerpts are derived cannot have been the same as the author of the work from which the Constantinian Excerpts are derived. There is no question about this, and it could be proved merely by comparing the two (Salmasian) fragments under consideration (frags. 196 and 200) with (the Constantinian) fragment 201. If then we accept the Constantinian Excerpts under the name Joannes of Antioch, we must be careful not to ascribe the Salmasian Excerpts to that writer. Which is the true Joannes, is a question still *sub judice*. (See below, vol. iv. Appendix 1.)

The vital question then is whether Procopius was the source of S (as we may designate the author of these Excerpts) for these fragments or not. For if he was, S. adds no weight to the authority of Procopius and may be disregarded; if he were not, his statements have to be reckoned with too. From a careful comparison of the passages, I find myself in complete agreement with C. de Boor (who has dealt with the question in Byz. Ztsch. ii. 204 *sqq*.) that Procopius was *not* the source of S. but that the accounts of both authors were derived from a common source [1] The proof in the case of fr. 200 is very complete; because we happen to have in Suidas *sub voce* Θλαδιας (see Muller *ad loc.*) a fragment of what was evidently that common source.

The inference, for historical purposes, is important. We cannot speak with Mr. Freeman of "Procopian legend" or "legend of the sixth century". Procopius cannot be described in these cases as setting down "the received tale that he *heard*". He was using a literary source; and there is not the slightest proof that this literary source belonged to the sixth century. It seems more probable that it was a fifth century source. It *may* have been Priscus or it may not.

These two episodes therefore depend on the authority of a writer (who has so far not been identified) earlier than Procopius and distinct from John of Antioch. They may for all we know have very early authority, and they cannot be waived away as "Procopian legend". Each must be judged on its own merits

It seems to me that there was probably a certain foundation of truth in both stories, but that they have been dressed out with fictitious details (like the story of the Empress Eudocia and Paulinus). I do not feel prepared to reject the main facts implied, that Aetius intrigued against Bonifacius and that Valentinian seduced the wife of Maximus.

[1] Cp further E Gleye in Byz. Ztsch v 460 *sqq*, where some other of the Excerpts (esp fr. 12) are treated in their relation to Procopius, with the same result

The story of the single combat of Aetius and Boniface is derived from Marcellinus (like Procopius, a writer of the sixth century) But rightly interpreted it contains nothing improbable. It does not imply a duel, but a single combat *in a battle*. It is however important to observe that "John of Antioch" (fr. 201, Müller, p. 615) says nothing of Boniface's wound but states that he was *out-generalled* by Aetius, and that he died of diseases due to depression and chagrin

τον δε Βονιφάτιον συν πολλη διαβάντα χειρι από της Διβυης κατεστρατηγησεν, ώστε έκεινον μεν ύπα φροντιδων νόσφ τελευτήσαι·

It remains to be added that the essay of Mr Freeman throws great light on the career of Boniface in Africa and the doings of Castinus, Felix and Sigisvult.

27. THE "EGYPTIAN" OF SYNESIUS—(P. 371)

The interpretation of the Egyptian allegory of Synesius has caused a good deal of trouble, owing to the fact that our other sources supply such meagre material as to the details of the political transactions at Constantinople in the reign of Arcadius It had long been recognized that Egypt stood for the Empire, and Thebes for Constantinople, and the Praetorian Praefect Aurelian had been detected under the veil of Osiris. But no certainty had been attained as to the identity of Typhos, the wicked brother of Osiris It was chiefly in consequence of this lacuna that the able attempt of Guldenpenning to reconstruct the history of the years A.D 399 and 400 on the basis of the work of Synesius (cp my Later Roman Empire, i. p 79 *sqq*) did not carry complete conviction But O. Seeck has recently succeeded in proving the identity of Typhos and in interpreting the allegory more fully (*Philologus*, 52, p. 442 *sqq.*, 1894) His results must be briefly noted.

1. *Taurus.*—Synesius states in the Preface that the name of the father of Osiris and Typhos was Taurus There can be no question that he is the Taurus who appears in the Consular Fasti of A.D 361. He was quaestor in 353, and became praetorian prefect in 355. He held this office (the μεγάλη άρχή of Synes. c. 2, p 1213, ed Migne) till 361. He was appointed to decide a theological disputation (Epiphanius, *de Haer* 71, 1); and presided at the Council of Ariminum (359). He was an author as well as an official. The arguments of Borghesi and Seeck establish his identity with Palladius Rutilius Taurus Aemilianus, the author of 14 Books *De re rustica* Taurus had a son named Harmonius who was killed by Arbogastes 392 (John Ant , fr. 187)

2 *Aurelian.*—He appears first about 383 as builder of a Church (Acta Sanctorum, 6th May, p. 610). In 393 we find him (C. Th 2, 8, 23, &c.) Prefect of Constantinople before Rufinus held that office. Then after the fall of Eutropius, he appears as Praetorian Prefect of the East (399-400). In 400 the revolt of Gainas causes his fall (see above, p 371) But he was to rise again and become Prefect a third time (402-404), as Seeck has shown from two letters of Synesius (31 and 38: cp Cod Th. 4, 2, 1, and 5, 1, 5, where the false dates have to be amended) He is therein described as τρισεπαρχον, "thrice Praefect," in an epigram (Anth Plan 4, 73) on a gilt statue dedicated to him by the senate. His son's name was Taurus (Synes., *epist* , 31), which confirms the identification.

Osiris (i c. 3, p 1217) held a post which is described as έπιστάτης δορυφόρων γενόμενος καὶ άκοας πιστευθείς, explained by Seeck to be that of magister officiorum ; he was then Prefect of the city (πολιαρχήσας, *ib.*) ; he was consul (ii. 4, p 1272), and he twice held the μεγάλη άρχή or praetorian prefecture,—the second time μετὰ συνθήματος μείζονος (*ib*), which means the Patriciate What happened to Osiris on his fall corresponds even more strikingly to that which happened to Aurelian. The leader of the foreign mercenaries is on the other side of a stream (like Gainas), Aurelian crosses it (p. 1252) and is spared His companions in misfortune (Saturninus and Johannes) are alluded to, p. 1268.

3 *Arcadius* —The insignificance of Arcadius is reflected in the myth by the fact that he is never mentioned except in one passage (p 1268) where he appears as the High Priest. The person who through his influence over the Emperor had the real power appears in the myth as holding the kingly office—*e g.* Osiris while he was in power.

4. *Caesarius.*—In the allegory Typhos is in close alliance with the barbarian mercenaries, and instigates their attack on Thebes in order to overthrow his brother Osiris. When Osiris surrenders himself to the barbarian leader, Typhos urges that he should be put to death. Typhos then receives the kingdom and administers it tyrannically; nor is his position shaken by the fall of the barbarian leader. Before the first rise of Osiris to power [1] he had filled a post which gave him patronage in distributing offices, the power of oppressing towns (p. 1217), and the duty of regulating measures in connexion with the payment of taxes in kind (p 1219). These hints taken along with the mention (*ib*) of torch-bearing attendants show that the office was no less than that of Praetorian Prefect. It follows that Typhos was Praetorian Prefect before 399, and again in 400.

Eutropius had endeavoured to reduce the power of Praetorian Prefect of the East by making it a collegial office ; and Eutychianus appears as holding that office (1) along with Caesarius while Eutropius was in power ; (2) along with Aurelian, 399-400 ; (3) along with Aurelian when he was restored 402 It may be assumed that he also held it between 400 and 402.

It follows that Caesarius, whom we find Praetorian Prefect from 396-398, and again in 400 and 401, was the prototype of Typhos, the son of Taurus and the brother of Aurelian. Some other points confirm the conclusion. The tendency to Arianism, of which Typhos is accused, is illustrated by C Th 16, 5, 25, and the passion of Typhos for his wife by a notice in Sozomen, 9, 2.

The great political object of Aurelian was to break the power of the Germans in the army and at the court—the policy for which Synesius pleaded in his *De regno*. The question arises · What was the attitude of the Empress Eudoxia to this policy ? The fall of Eutropius which she brought about (Phil 11, 6) led to the rise of Aurelian, and when Aurelian fell, her intimate friend—scandal said, her lover—Count John, fell with him.[2] Further, Seeck makes it probable that the second Praetorian Prefecture of Aurelian ended, and Anthemius succeeded to that post, about end of 404 ; and it was on 6th October, 404, that the Empress died. We are thus led to infer a close political union between Eudoxia and Aurelian ; and, if the inference is right, it is noteworthy that the Empress of German origin, the daughter of the Frank Bauto, should have allied herself with a statesman whose policy was anti-German.

28. THE BATTLE OF MAURICA, COMMONLY CALLED THE BATTLE OF CHÂLONS—(P. 462)

The scene of the battle by which the invasion of Attila was checked has been the subject of some perplexity. The statements which have to be considered are the following :

1. Idatius : in campis Catalaunicis haud longe de civitate quam effregerant Mettis.

2. An insertion in the text of Prosper, found in the Codex Havniensis, and doubtless representing an entry in the Chronica Italica. Mommsen, Chron. Min , 1 , p. 302 and 481 · pugnatum est in quinto milliario de Trecas, loco numcupato Maurica in Campania

3 Chron. A.D. 511 (see above, App. 1), Mommsen, Chron Min. 1., p. 663: Tricassis pugnat loco Mauriacos.

4a. Jordanes c 36: convenitur itaque in campos Catalaunicos, qui et Mauriaci nominantur, centum leuvas ut Galli vocant in longum tenentes et septuaginta in latum. (A gallic *leuva* or league = 1½ Roman miles).

4b Gregory of Tours, 2, 7 : Mauriacum campum adiens se præcingit ad bellum [Attila]. The accounts of the episode in Jordanes and Gregory are not independent ; cp. Mommsen, Pref. to Jordanes, p. xxxvi.

The traditional view that the battle was fought near Duro-Catalaunum or Châlons on Marne is not borne out by the data. That town is not mentioned,

---

[1] He also held a financial post —Seeck conjectures that of a *rationalis* of a diocese

[2] Further ; Castricia, wife of Saturninus, who was banished with Aurelian, had influence with Eudoxia, as we know from Palladius, Life of Chrysostom.

and the notice of Jordanes shows that its proximity is not implied by the name "Catalaunian Plains," for Maurica might have been at the other extremity. Setting aside Idatius, whose statement is discredited by the words "not far from Metz," we find the other notices agreeing in the designation of the battle-field as the Mauriac Plain, or a place named Maurica, and one of them gives the precise distance from Troyes. The name *Maurica, Mauriac*, has been identified with great probability with Mery (on Seine), about twenty miles from Troyes. There seems therefore every likelihood that the battle was fought between Troyes and Mery, and the solution, for which Mr. Hodgkin well argues (Italy, 1. p. 143-5), is confirmed, as he observes, by the strategical importance of Troyes, which was at the centre of many roads.

An interesting discovery was made in 1842 at the village of Pouan, about 10 miles from Mery-on-Seine. A skeleton was found with a two-edged sword and a cutlass, both adorned with gold, and a number of gold ornaments, one of them a ring with the inscription HEVA. They are the subject of a memoir by M. Peigné Delacourt (1860) who claimed the grave as the tomb of the Visigothic king Theodoric See Hodgkin (*ib* p 140). In any case the remains may well be connected with the great battle

ABERDEEN UNIVERSITY PRESS.

A CATALOGUE OF BOOKS AND ANNOUNCEMENTS OF METHUEN AND COMPANY PUBLISHERS : LONDON 36 ESSEX STREET W.C.

CONTENTS

	PAGE
FORTHCOMING BOOKS,	2
POETRY,	8
BELLES LETTRES, ANTHOLOGIES, ETC ,	9
ILLUSRTATED BOOKS,	10
HISTORY,	11
BIOGRAPHY,	14
TRAVEL, ADVENTURE AND TOPOGRAPHY,	15
NAVAL AND MILITARY,	17
GENERAL LITERATURE,	18
SCIENCE AND TECHNOLOGY,	20
PHILOSOPHY,	20
THEOLOGY,	21
FICTION,	24
BOOKS FOR BOYS AND GIRLS,	34
THE PEACOCK LIBRARY,	34
UNIVERSITY EXTENSION SERIES,	35
SOCIAL QUESTIONS OF TO-DAY	36
CLASSICAL TRANSLATIONS	37
EDUCATIONAL BOOKS,	37

OCTOBER 1898

MESSRS. METHUEN'S
ANNOUNCEMENTS

————•—•————

Travel and Adventure

NORTHWARD OVER THE GREAT ICE By R E. PEARY With over 800 Illustrations, Maps and Diagrams. *Two Volumes. Royal 8vo* 32s *net*

In this important work Lieutenant Peary tells the story of his travels and adventures in the Arctic regions His extraordinary sledge journey and his experiences among the Eskimos are fully described, and this book is a complete record of his Arctic work, for which the Royal Geographical Society has this year awarded him their Gold Medal

The fact that Lieutenant Peary is about to start on a determined effort to reach the North Pole lends a special interest to this book

THROUGH ASIA By SVEN HEDIN With over 250 Illustrations from Sketches and Photographs by the Author, and 10 Maps *Two volumes. Royal 8vo* 36s *net*

In this book Dr Sven Hedin, the distinguished Swedish explorer, describes his four years' experiences and his extraordinary adventures in Central Asia Dr Hedin is an accomplished artist, and his drawings are full of vigour and interest

In adventurous interest and substantial results in various departments of knowledge, Dr Hedin's journey will bear comparison with the travels of the great explorers of the past, from Marco Polo downwards

The Gold Medals of the Royal Geographical Society and of the Russian Geographical Society have been conferred upon him for this journey.

THE HIGHEST ANDES By E. A FITZGERALD With 40 Illustrations, 10 of which are Photogravures, and a Large Map. *Royal 8vo* 30s *net*.

Also, a Small Edition on Handmade Paper, limited to 50 Copies, *4to* £5, 5s.

A narrative of the highest climb yet accomplished The illustrations have been reproduced with the greatest care, and the book, in addition to its adventurous interest, contains appendices of great scientific value

CHITRAL The Story of a Minor Siege By SIR G S. ROBERTSON, K.C S I With Numerous Illustrations and a Map *Demy 8vo* 21s *net*.

Sir George Robertson, who was at the time British Agent at Gilgit, has written the story of Chitral from the point of view of one actually besieged in the fort The book is of considerable length, and has an Introductory part explaining the series of events which culminated in the famous siege, also an account of Ross's disaster in the KORAGH defile, the heroic defence of RESHUN, and Kelly's great march It has numerous illustrations—plans, pictures and portraits—and a map, and will give a connected narrative of the stirring episodes on the Chitral frontier in 1895

TWENTY YEARS IN THE NEAR EAST. By A HULME
BEAMAN. With Portrait. *Demy 8vo.* 10s 6d.

A personal narrative of experiences in Syria, Egypt, Turkey and the Balkan States,
including adventures in the Lebanon, during the bombardment of Alexandra, the
first Egyptian Campaign, the Donogla Expedition, the Cretan Insurrection, etc
The book also contains several chapters on Turkey, its people and its Sultan

Theology

DOCTRINE AND DEVELOPMENT. By HASTINGS RASH-
DALL, M A., Fellow and Tutor of New College, Oxford. *Crown 8vo.*
6s.

This volume consists of twenty sermons, preached chiefly before the University of
Oxford They are an attempt to translate into the language of modern thought
some of the leading ideas of Christian theology and ethics

CLOVELLY SERMONS. By WILLIAM HARRISON, M A., late
Rector of Clovelly. With a Preface by LUCAS MALET. *Crown 8vo*
3s. 6d.

A volume of Sermons by a son-in-law of Charles Kingsley

APOSTOLIC CHRISTIANITY· As Illustrated by the Epistles
of S. Paul to the Corinthians. By H. H. HENSON, M.A., Fellow
of All Souls', Oxford. *Crown 8vo* 6s.

Handbooks of Theology.

General Editor, A. ROBERTSON, D D , Principal of King's College,
London.

THE XXXIX ARTICLES OF THE CHURCH OF ENG-
LAND. Edited with an Introduction by E. C. S. GIBSON, D D ,
Vicar of Leeds, late Principal of Wells Theological College *Revised
and Cheaper Edition in One Volume. Demy 8vo.* 12s. 6d.

AN INTRODUCTION TO THE HISTORY OF THE
CREEDS. By A E. BURN, Examining Chaplain to the Bishop of
Lichfield. *Demy 8vo.* 10s. 6d.

The Churchman's Library.

Edited by J. H. BURN, B.D.

A series of books by competent scholars on Church History, Institutions, and Doctrine, for the use of clerical and lay readers

THE KINGDOM OF HEAVEN HERE AND HERE-
AFTER. By Canon WINTERBOTHAM, M.A., B.Sc , LL B.
Crown 8vo. 3s 6d.

Oxford Commentaries.

General Editor, WALTER LOCK, D.D , Warden of Keble College,
Dean Ireland's Professor of Exegesis in the
University of Oxford.

Messrs. METHUEN propose to issue a series of Commentaries upon such
Books of the Bible as still seem to need further explanation.

The object of each Commentary is primarily exegetical, to interpret
the author's meaning to the present generation   The editors will not
deal, except very subordinately, with questions of textual criticism or
philology , but taking the English text in the Revised Version as their
basis, they will try to combine a hearty acceptance of critical principles
with loyalty to the Catholic Faith.   It is hoped that in this way the series
may be of use both to theological students and to the clergy, and also to
the growing number of educated laymen and laywomen who wish to read
the Bible intelligently and reverently.

THE BOOK OF JOB.   Edited, with Introduction and Notes,
by E. C S. GIBSON, D D , Vicar of Leeds.   *Demy 8vo.   6s*

The Library of Devotion.

Pott 8vo, cloth, 2s ; leather , 2s 6d net.
NEW VOLUMES

A SERIOUS CALL TO A DEVOUT AND HOLY LIFE
By WILLIAM LAW.   Edited, with an Introduction, Analysis, and
Notes, by C. BIGG, D.D.   *Pott 8vo*

A BOOK OF DEVOTIONS. By J W. STANBRIDGE, M A ,
Rector of Bainton, Canon of York, and sometime Fellow of St
John's College, Oxford   *Pott 8vo.*

This book contains devotions, Eucharistic, daily and occasional, for the use of members of the English Church, sufficiently diversified for those who possess other
works of the kind   It is intended to be a companion in private and public worship,
and is in harmony with the thoughts of the best Devotional writers

History and Biography

MEMOIRS OF ADMIRAL THE RIGHT HONBLE. SIR
ASTLEY COOPER KEY   By Vice-Admiral P. H. COLOMB.
With Portrait. *Demy 8vo.   16s.*

This life of a great sailor throws a considerable light on the evolution of the Navy
during the last fifty years

THE DECLINE AND FALL OF THE ROMAN EMPIRE
By EDWARD GIBBON.   A New Edition, edited with Notes,
Appendices, and Maps by J. B. BURY, LL.D , Fellow of Trinity
College, Dublin   *In Seven Volumes. Demy 8vo, gilt top.   8s. 6d.
each. Crown 8vo.   6s each.   Vol. VI.*

A HISTORY OF EGYPT, FROM THE EARLIEST TIMES TO
  THE PRESENT DAY. Edited by W. M. FLINDERS PETRIE, D C L,
  LL D., Professor of Egyptology at University College. *Fully Illus-
  trated   In Six Volumes.   Crown 8vo.   6s. each*
Vol. IV. THE EGYPT OF THE PTOLEMIES.   J. P. MAHAFFY
Vol. V. ROMAN EGYPT.   J. G. MILNE.

THE CANON LAW IN ENGLAND.   By F. W. MAITLAND,
  LL D., Downing Professor of the Laws of England in the University
  of Cambridge.   *Royal 8vo   7s. 6d.*
  A volume of Essays on the History of the Canon Law in England   These Essays
  deal chiefly with the measure of authority attributed in medieval England to the
  papal law-books, and one entitled (1) *William Lyndwood*, (2) *Church, State and
  Decretals*, (3) *William of Drogheda and the Universal Ordinary*, (4) *Henry II
  and the Criminous Clerks*, (5) *Execrabilis in the Common Pleas*, and (6) *The
  Deacon and the Jewess*

A HISTORY OF SHREWSBURY SCHOOL   By G. W
  FISHER, M.A., Assistant Master   With Numerous Illustrations
  Demy 8vo   7s 6d.

A HISTORY OF WESTMINSTER SCHOOL.   By J. SAR-
  GEAUNT, M.A., Assistant Master.   With Numerous Illustrations.
  Demy 8vo.   7s. 6d.

ANNALS OF ETON COLLEGE.   By W STERRY, M.A
  With Numerous Illustrations.   *Demy 8vo   7s 6d.*

General Literature

THE PILGRIM'S PROGRESS. By JOHN BUNYAN. Edited,
  with an Introduction, by C. H FIRTH, M.A. With 39 Illustrations
  by R. ANNING BELL   *Crown 8vo.   6s*
  This book contains a long Introduction by Mr Firth, whose knowledge of the period
  is unrivalled ; and it is lavishly illustrated

AN OLD ENGLISH HOME   By S. BARING GOULD   With
  Numerous Plans and Illustrations   *Crown 8vo.   6s.*
  This book describes the life and environment of an old English family.

CAMBRIDGE AND ITS COLLEGES.   By A. HAMILTON
  THOMPSON.   With Illustrations by E. H. NEW.   *Pott 8vo   Cloth,
  3s.   Leather, 4s.*
  This book is uniform with Mr Wells's very successful book, 'Oxford and its Colleges'

UNIVERSITY AND SOCIAL SETTLEMENTS.   By W.
  REASON, M.A.   *Crown 8vo.   2s. 6d.*   [*Social Question Series.*

DANTE'S GARDEN.   By ROSEMARY COTES.   With a frontis-
  piece   *Fcap 8vo   2s 6d*
  An account of the flowers mentioned by Dante, with their legends

READING AND READERS   By CLIFFORD HARRISON.
  Fcap. 8vo   2s. 6d
  A little book of principles and hints by the most distinguished of living reciters

VENTURES IN VERSE. By B. J. WILLIAMS   *Cr. 8vo.   3s 6d.*

Educational

VOLUMETRIC ANALYSIS By J B RUSSELL, Science Master at Burnley Grammar School *Crown 8vo* 1s.

A small Manual, containing all the necessary rules, etc , on a subject which has hitherto only been treated in expensive volumes

A KEY TO STEDMAN'S EASY FRENCH EXERCISES By G A SCHRUMPF *Crown 8vo* 3s. net

A SHORTER GREEK PRIMER. By A. M. M. STEDMAN, M A *Crown 8vo.* 1s. 6d.

A book which contains the elements of Accidence and Syntax.

CARPENTRY AND JOINERY By F. C. WEBBER With many Illustrations. *Crown 8vo* 3s 6d

[*Text-books of Technology.*

A Manual for technical classes and self instruction

PRACTICAL MECHANICS. By SIDNEY H WELLS Illustrated *Crown 8vo* 3s. 6d [*Text-books of Technology*

A CLASS-BOOK OF DICTATION PASSAGES. By W. WILLIAMSON, M A *Crown 8vo.* 1s 6d

The passages are culled from recognised authors, and a few newspaper passages are included The lists of appended words are drawn up mainly on the principle of comparison and contrast, and will form a repertoire of over 2000 words, embracing practically all the difficulties felt by the pupil

AN ENTRANCE GUIDE TO THE PROFESSIONS AND BUSINESS. By HENRY JONES. *Crown 8vo.* 1s. 6d.

[*Commercial Series.*

Byzantine Texts

Edited by J B. BURY, LL.D , Professor of Modern History at Trinity College, Dublin

EVAGRIUS. Edited by PROFESSOR LÉON PARMENTIER of Liége and M BIDEZ of Gand. *Demy 8vo*

Cheaper Editions

BRITISH CENTRAL AFRICA By Sir H H. JOHNSTON, K C B With nearly Two Hundred Illustrations, and Six Maps. *Revised and Cheaper Edition* *Crown 4to.* 21s net

' The book is crowded with important information, and written in a most attractive style , it is worthy, in short, of the author s established reputation '—*Standard*

VAILIMA LETTERS By ROBERT LOUIS STEVENSON. With an Etched Portrait by WILLIAM STRANG, and other Illustrations *Cheaper Edition. Crown 8vo. Buckram.* 6s.

A BOOK OF CHRISTMAS VERSE Edited by H C BEECHING, M A , and Illustrated by WALTER CRANE *Cheaper Edition. Crown 8vo, gilt top* 3s 6d

A collection of the best verse inspired by the birth of Christ from the Middle Ages to the present day

LYRA SACRA   An Anthology of Sacred Verse   Edited by H. C. BEECHING, M A. *Cheaper Edition   Crown 8vo   Buckram   3s 6d*
'A charming selection, which maintains a lofty standard of excellence'—*Times*

Fiction

THE BATTLE OF THE STRONG. By GILBERT PARKER, Author of 'The Seats of the Mighty.' *Crown 8vo   6s*
A romance of 1798

THE TOWN TRAVELLER   By GEORGE GISSING, Author of 'Demos,' 'In the Year of Jubilee,' etc   *Crown 8vo   6s.*

THE COUNTESS TEKLA. By ROBERT BARR, Author of 'The Mutable Many.' *Crown 8vo. 6s.*
A historical romance

THINGS THAT HAVE HAPPENED. By DOROTHEA GERARD, Author of 'Lady Baby,' 'Orthodox,' etc. *Crown 8vo   6s.*

DOMITIA. By S. BARING GOULD, Author of 'The Broom Squire,' etc. *Crown 8vo. 6s.*
A romance of imperial Rome

FROM THE EAST UNTO THE WEST   By JANE BARLOW, Author of 'Irish Idylls,' 'A Creel of Irish Stories,' etc   *Crown 8vo   6s*

TO ARMS! By ANDREW BALFOUR, Author of 'By Stroke of Sword' Illustrated. *Crown 8vo. 6s.*
A romance of 1715

THE JOURNALIST   By C. F. KEARY. *Crown 8vo. 6s*
A story of modern literary life

PEGGY OF THE BARTONS   By B M CROKER, Author of 'Proper Pride.' *Crown 8vo. 6s*

A VENDETTA OF THE DESERT   By W C SCULLY. *Crown 8vo. 3s. 6d.*
A South African romance

CORRAGEEN IN '98   By Mrs. ORPEN. *Crown 8vo. 6s.*
A romance of the Irish Rebellion

AN ENEMY TO THE KING. By R. N STEPHENS   *Crown 8vo. 6s.*

THE PLUNDERPIT. By J KEIGHLEY SNOWDEN   *Crown 8vo. 6s.*
A romance of adventure

DEADMAN'S. By MARY GAUNT, Author of 'Kirkham's Find' *Crown 8vo. 6s.*
An Australian story

WILLOWBRAKE. By R MURRAY GILCHRIST   *Crown 8vo   6s*

THE ANGEL OF THE COVENANT. By J MACLAREN COBBAN. *Crown 8vo   6s.*
A historical romance, of which Montrose is the hero

OWD BOB, THE GREY DOG OF KENMUIR. By ALFRED OLLIVANT. *Crown 8vo   6s*
A story of the Cumberland dales

ANANIAS. By the Hon. Mrs ALAN BRODRICK   *Crown 8vo   6s.*

ADVENTURES IN WALLYPUG LAND. By G E. FARROW. With Illustrations by ALAN WRIGHT   *Crown 8vo. Gilt top   5s.*

MESSRS. METHUEN'S
PUBLICATIONS

Poetry

Rudyard Kipling BARRACK-ROOM BALLADS. By
RUDYARD KIPLING. *Fourteenth Edition. Crown 8vo. 6s.*

Mr Kipling's verse is strong, vivid, full of character Unmistakable genius rings in every line '—*Times*

'The ballads teem with imagination, they palpitate with emotion We read them with laughter and tears, the metres throb in our pulses, the cunningly ordered words tingle with life; and if this be not poetry, what is?'—*Pall Mall Gazette*

Rudyard Kipling THE SEVEN SEAS By RUDYARD
KIPLING *Fourth Edition Crown 8vo Buckram, gilt top 6s*

'The new poems of Mr Rudyard Kipling have all the spirit and swing of their predecessors Patriotism is the solid concrete foundation on which Mr Kipling has built the whole of his work '—*Times*

'The Empire has found a singer; it is no depreciation of the songs to say that statesmen may have, one way or other, to take account of them '—*Manchester Guardian*

'Animated through and through with indubitable genius.'—*Daily Telegraph.*

"Q." POEMS AND BALLADS. By "Q" *Crown 8vo. 3s 6d.*
'This work has just the faint, ineffable touch and glow that make poetry '—*Speaker*

"Q." GREEN BAYS: Verses and Parodies. By "Q," Author
of 'Dead Man's Rock,' etc. *Second Edition. Crown 8vo. 3s. 6d.*

E Mackay. A SONG OF THE SEA By ERIC MACKAY
Second Edition. Fcap 8vo. 5s
'Everywhere Mr Mackay displays himself the master of a style marked by all the characteristics of the best rhetoric '—*Globe*

H Ibsen. BRAND. A Drama by HENRIK IBSEN. Translated
by WILLIAM WILSON. *Second Edition. Crown 8vo 3s 6d*
'The greatest world-poem of the nineteenth century next to "Faust" It is in the same set with "Agamemnon," with "Lear," with the literature that we now instinctively regard as high and holy '—*Daily Chronicle*

"A. G." VERSES TO ORDER. By "A G." *Cr. 8vo. 2s. 6d. net*
'A capital specimen of light academic poetry '—*St James's Gazette*

J. G. Cordery. THE ODYSSEY OF HOMER A Translation by J G. CORDERY. *Crown 8vo 7s 6d*

Belles Lettres, Anthologies, etc.

R. L. Stevenson VAILIMA LETTERS By ROBERT LOUIS STEVENSON. With an Etched Portrait by WILLIAM STRANG, and other Illustrations. *Second Edition. Crown 8vo. Buckram. 6s*
'A fascinating book '—*Standard*
'Full of charm and brightness '—*Spectator*
'A gift almost priceless '—*Speaker*
'Unique in literature '—*Daily Chronicle*

George Wyndham. THE POEMS OF WILLIAM SHAKE-SPEARE. Edited with an Introduction and Notes by GEORGE WYNDHAM, M.P *Demy 8vo. Buckram, gilt top* 10s. 6d
This edition contains the 'Venus,' 'Lucrece,' and Sonnets, and is prefaced with an elaborate introduction of over 140 pp
'One of the most serious contributions to Shakespearian criticism that has been published for some time '—*Times*
'One of the best pieces of editing in the language '—*Outlook*
'This is a scholarly and interesting contribution to Shakespearian literature '—*Literature.*
'We have no hesitation in describing Mr George Wyndham's introduction as a masterly piece of criticism, and all who love our Elizabethan literature will find a very garden of delight in it '—*Spectator.*
'Mr Wyndham's notes are admirable, even indispensable '—*Westminster Gazette*
'The standard edition of Shakespeare's poems '—*World*
'The book is written with critical insight and literary felicity '—*Standard*

W. E. Henley. ENGLISH LYRICS. Selected and Edited by W. E. HENLEY. *Crown 8vo Buckram., gilt top. 6s*
'It is a body of choice and lovely poetry '—*Birmingham Gazette*

Henley and Whibley. A BOOK OF ENGLISH PROSE Collected by W. E. HENLEY and CHARLES WHIBLEY. *Crown 8vo. Buckram, gilt top. 6s.*
'Quite delightful A greater treat for those not well acquainted with pre-Restoration prose could not be imagined '—*Athenæum*

H. C Beeching. LYRA SACRA An Anthology of Sacred Verse Edited by H. C. BEECHING, M.A. *Crown 8vo. Buckram. 6s.*
'A charming selection, which maintains a lofty standard of excellence '—*Times*

"Q." THE GOLDEN POMP: A Procession of English Lyrics. Arranged by A. T. QUILLER COUCH. *Crown 8vo. Buckram. 6s.*
'A delightful volume · a really golden "Pomp "'—*Spectator*

W. B. Yeats. AN ANTHOLOGY OF IRISH VERSE. Edited by W. B. YEATS. *Crown 8vo 3s. 6d.*
'An attractive and catholic selection.'—*Times.*

G. W. Steevens. MONOLOGUES OF THE DEAD. By G. W STEEVENS. *Foolscap 8vo 3s. 6d.*
'The effect is sometimes splendid, sometimes bizarre, but always amazingly clever '—*Pall Mall Gazette*

W. M. Dixon. A PRIMER OF TENNYSON. By W. M. DIXON, M A., Professor of English Literature at Mason College. *Crown 8vo. 2s. 6d.*
'Much sound and well-expressed criticism. The bibliography is a boon '—*Speaker.*

W A Craigie. A PRIMER OF BURNS   By W. A CRAIGIE
Crown 8vo   2s   6d
'A valuable addition to the literature of the poet '—*Times*

L Magnus. A PRIMER OF WORDSWORTH   By LAURIE
MAGNUS   *Crown 8vo*   2s. 6d
'A valuable contribution to Wordsworthian literature '—*Literature*

Sterne. THE LIFE AND OPINIONS OF TRISTRAM
SHANDY   By LAWRENCE STERNE. With an Introduction by
CHARLES WHIBLEY, and a Portrait   2 *vols.*   7s.
'Very dainty volumes are these; the paper, type, and light green binding are all
very agreeable to the eye '—*Globe*

Congreve. THE COMEDIES OF WILLIAM CONGREVE.
With an Introduction by G S. STREET, and a Portrait   2 *vols.*   7s.

Morier. THE ADVENTURES OF HAJJI BABA OF
ISPAHAN   By JAMES MORIER   With an Introduction by E G
BROWNE, M.A , and a Portrait   2 *vols*   7s

Walton. THE LIVES OF DONNE, WOTTON, HOOKER,
HERBERT, AND SANDERSON. By IZAAK WALTON. With
an Introduction by VERNON BLACKBURN, and a Portrait   3s 6d

Johnson. THE LIVES OF THE ENGLISH POETS   By
SAMUEL JOHNSON, LL D   With an Introduction by J. H. MILLAR,
and a Portrait   3 *vols.*   10s. 6d

Burns. THE POEMS OF ROBERT BURNS.   Edited by
ANDREW LANG and W A. CRAIGIE   With Portrait   *Demy 8vo*,
gilt top.   6s
This edition contains a carefully collated Text, numerous Notes, critical and textual,
a critical and biographical Introduction, and a Glossary
'Among editions in one volume, this will take the place of authority '—*Times*

F. Langbridge. BALLADS OF THE BRAVE · Poems of
Chivalry, Enterprise, Courage, and Constancy   Edited by Rev. F.
LANGBRIDGE. *Second Edition. Crown 8vo.*   3s. 6d   *School Edition*
2s 6d.
'A very happy conception happily carried out   These "Ballads of the Brave" are
intended to suit the real tastes of boys, and will suit the taste of the great majority '
—*Spectator*   'The book is full of splendid things '—*World.*

Illustrated Books

F. D. Bedford. NURSERY RHYMES. With many Coloured
Pictures. By F. D BEDFORD. *Super Royal 8vo*   5s
'An excellent selection of the best known rhymes, with beautifully coloured pictures
exquisitely printed '—*Pall Mall Gazette*

S Baring Gould. A BOOK OF FAIRY TALES retold by S
BARING GOULD. With numerous illustrations and initial letters by
ARTHUR J. GASKIN. *Second Edition Crown 8vo. Buckram.*   6s
'Mr Baring Gould is deserving of gratitude, in re-writing in simple style the old
stories that delighted our fathers and grandfathers '—*Saturday Review*

S. Baring Gould OLD ENGLISH FAIRY TALES. Collected and edited by S BARING GOULD. With Numerous Illustrations by F. D. BEDFORD. *Second Edition. Crown 8vo. Buckram. 6s.*
'A charming volume The stories have been selected with great ingenuity from various old ballads and folk-tales, and now stand forth, clothed in Mr Baring Gould's delightful English, to enchant youthful readers '—*Guardian*

S. Baring Gould A BOOK OF NURSERY SONGS AND RHYMES. Edited by S. BARING GOULD, and Illustrated by the Birmingham Art School. *Buckram, gilt top. Crown 8vo.* 6s.
'The volume is very complete in its way, as it contains nursery songs to the number of 77, game rhymes, and jingles To the student we commend the sensible introduction, and the explanatory notes '—*Birmingham Gazette*

H. C Beeching. A BOOK OF CHRISTMAS VERSE. Edited by H C. BEECHING, M A., and Illustrated by WALTER CRANE. *Crown 8vo, gilt top.* 5s
An anthology which, from its unity of aim and high poetic excellence, has a better right to exist than most of its fellows '—*Guardian*

History

Gibbon. THE DECLINE AND FALL OF THE ROMAN EMPIRE. By EDWARD GIBBON A New Edition, Edited with Notes, Appendices, and Maps, by J B BURY, LL D., Fellow of Trinity College, Dublin. *In Seven Volumes. Demy 8vo. Gilt top. 8s 6d each Also crown 8vo. 6s each Vols. I, II, III, IV., and V.*
'The time has certainly arrived for a new edition of Gibbon's great work . Professor Bury is the right man to undertake this task His learning is amazing, both in extent and accuracy The book is issued in a handy form, and at a moderate price, and it is admirably printed '—*Times*
'This edition, is a marvel of erudition and critical skill, and it is the very minimum of praise to predict that the seven volumes of it will supersede Dean Milman's as the standard edition of our great historical classic '—*Glasgow Herald*
'At last there is an adequate modern edition of Gibbon The best edition the nineteenth century could produce '—*Manchester Guardian*

Flinders Petrie A HISTORY OF EGYPT. FROM THE EARLIEST TIMES TO THE PRESENT DAY Edited by W. M FLINDERS PETRIE, D C L, LL D, Professor of Egyptology at University College. *Fully Illustrated. In Six Volumes. Crown 8vo 6s each*
Vol I PREHISTORIC TIMES TO XVITH DYNASTY. W. M F Petrie. *Third Edition.*
Vol. II THE XVIITH AND XVIIITH DYNASTIES. W. M F Petrie. *Second Edition*
'A history written in the spirit of scientific precision so worthily represented by Dr Petrie and his school cannot but promote sound and accurate study, and supply a vacant place in the English literature of Egyptology '—*Times*

Flinders Petrie. RELIGION AND CONSCIENCE IN ANCIENT EGYPT. By W M FLINDERS PETRIE, D.C.L., LL D. Fully Illustrated. *Crown 8vo* 2s. 6d.
'The lectures will afford a fund of valuable information for students of ancient ethics. —*Manchester Guardian*

Flinders Petrie SYRIA AND EGYPT, FROM THE TELL EL AMARNA TABLETS. By W. M. FLINDERS PETRIE, D C L, LL D   *Crown 8vo   2s 6d.*

'A marvellous record The addition made to our knowledge is nothing short of amazing '—*Times*

Flinders Petrie. EGYPTIAN TALES   Edited by W. M. FLINDERS PETRIE. Illustrated by TRISTRAM ELLIS. *In Two Volumes. Crown 8vo   3s 6d each.*

'A valuable addition to the literature of comparative folk-lore The drawings are really illustrations in the literal sense of the word '—*Globe*
'Invaluable as a picture of life in Palestine and Egypt '—*Daily News*

Flinders Petrie. EGYPTIAN DECORATIVE ART. By W. M FLINDERS PETRIE. With 120 Illustrations. *Cr. 8vo   3s. 6d*

' In these lectures he displays rare skill in elucidating the development of decorative art in Egypt, and in tracing its influence on the art of other countries '—*Times*

C. W. Oman. A HISTORY OF THE ART OF WAR Vol. II . The Middle Ages, from the Fourth to the Fourteenth Century. By C W. OMAN, M A , Fellow of All Souls', Oxford Illustrated   *Demy 8vo.   21s.*

' The book is based throughout upon a thorough study of the original sources, and will be an indispensable aid to all students of mediæval history '—*Athenæum*
'The whole art of war in its historic evolution has never been treated on such an ample and comprehensive scale, and we question if any recent contribution to the exact history of the world has possessed greater and more enduring value '—*Daily Chronicle*

S Baring Gould THE TRAGEDY OF THE CÆSARS. With numerous Illustrations from Busts, Gems, Cameos, etc. By S BARING GOULD. *Fourth Edition   Royal 8vo.   15s.*

' A most splendid and fascinating book on a subject of undying interest. The great feature of the book is the use the author has made of the existing portraits of the Caesars, and the admirable critical subtlety he has exhibited in dealing with this line of research It is brilliantly written, and the illustrations are supplied on a scale of profuse magnificence '—*Daily Chronicle.*

H. de B. Gibbins INDUSTRY IN ENGLAND : HISTORICAL OUTLINES By H DE B GIBBINS, M A., D.Litt With 5 Maps. *Second Edition. Demy 8vo.   10s. 6d.*

H. E. Egerton. A HISTORY OF BRITISH COLONIAL POLICY. By H. E EGERTON, M.A. *Demy 8vo.   12s. 6d.*

' It is a good book, distinguished by accuracy in detail, clear arrangement of facts, and a broad grasp of principles '—*Manchester Guardian*
' Able, impartial, clear . A most valuable volume.'—*Athenæum*

Albert Sorel. THE EASTERN QUESTION IN THE EIGHTEENTH CENTURY. By ALBERT SOREL, of the French Academy. Translated by F. C. BRAMWELL, M.A., with an Introduction by R. C L FLETCHER, Fellow of Magdalen College, Oxford. With a Map   *Crown 8vo*   4s 6d.

'The author's insight into the character and motives of the leading actors in the drama gives the work an interest uncommon in books based on similar material '—*Scotsman.*

C. H. Grinling. A HISTORY OF THE GREAT NORTHERN RAILWAY, 1845-95. By CHARLES H. GRINLING. With Maps and Illustrations   *Demy 8vo.*   10s 6d.

'Admirably written, and crammed with interesting facts '—*Daily Mail*
'The only adequate history of a great English railway company that has as yet appeared '—*Times*
'Mr Grinling has done for the history of the Great Northern what Macaulay did for English History '—*The Engineer*

A. Clark. THE COLLEGES OF OXFORD. Their History and their Traditions   By Members of the University.   Edited by A. CLARK, M A., Fellow and Tutor of Lincoln College.   *8vo.*   12s. 6d.

'A work which will certainly be appealed to for many years as the standard book on the Colleges of Oxford.'—*Athenæum*

Perrens THE HISTORY OF FLORENCE FROM 1434 TO 1492. By F. T. PERRENS.   *8vo.*   12s. 6d.

A history of Florence under the domination of Cosimo, Piero, and Lorenzo de Medicis

J. Wells   A SHORT HISTORY OF ROME. By J. WELLS, M.A, Fellow and Tutor of Wadham Coll., Oxford.   With 4 Maps.   *Crown 8vo.*   3s. 6d

This book is intended for the Middle and Upper Forms of Public Schools and for Pass Students at the Universities   It contains copious Tables, etc.
'An original work written on an original plan, and with uncommon freshness and vigour.'—*Speaker*

O Browning. A SHORT HISTORY OF MEDIÆVAL ITALY, A.D. 1250-1530. By OSCAR BROWNING, Fellow and Tutor of King's College, Cambridge.   *Second Edition.   In Two Volumes   Crown 8vo.*   5s each.

VOL I   1250-1409 —Guelphs and Ghibellines.
VOL. II. 1409-1530. —The Age of the Condottieri.

'Mr. Browning is to be congratulated on the production of a work of immense labour and learning '—*Westminster Gazette.*

O'Grady   THE STORY OF IRELAND. By STANDISH O'GRADY, Author of 'Finn and his Companions.'   *Cr 8vo.*   2s 6d.

'Most delightful, most stimulating   Its racy humour, its original imaginings, make it one of the freshest, breeziest volumes '—*Methodist Times.*

Biography

S. Baring Gould. THE LIFE OF NAPOLEON BONA-
PARTE. By S. BARING GOULD With over 450 Illustrations in
the Text and 12 Photogravure Plates. *Large quarto. Gilt top* 36s.

'The best biography of Napoleon in our tongue, nor have the French as good a
biographer of their hero A book very nearly as good as Southey's "Life of
Nelson"'—*Manchester Guardian.*
'The main feature of this gorgeous volume is its great wealth of beautiful photogravures and finely executed wood engravings, constituting a complete pictorial
chronicle of Napoleon I 's personal history from the days of his early childhood
at Ajaccio to the date of his second interment '—*Daily Telegraph*
'Nearly all the illustrations are real contributions to history '—*Westminster Gazette*

Morris Fuller. THE LIFE AND WRITINGS OF JOHN
DAVENANT, D D (1571-1641), Bishop of Salisbury. By MORRIS
FULLER, B D. *Demy 8vo* 10s 6d.

J. M. Rigg. ST ANSELM OF CANTERBURY : A CHAPTER
IN THE HISTORY OF RELIGION. By J M RIGG. *Demy 8vo.* 7s. 6d.
Mr Rigg has told the story of the life with scholarly ability, and has contributed
an interesting chapter to the history of the Norman period '—*Daily Chronicle*

F. W. Joyce THE LIFE OF SIR FREDERICK GORE
OUSELEY. By F. W. JOYCE, M A. 7s. 6d.
'This book has been undertaken in quite the right spirit, and written with sympathy,
insight, and considerable literary skill '—*Times*

W. G. Collingwood. THE LIFE OF JOHN RUSKIN. By
W. G COLLINGWOOD, M A. With Portraits, and 13 Drawings by
Mr Ruskin *Second Edition.* 2 vols. 8vo. 32s.
'No more magnificent volumes have been published for a long time '—*Times*
'It is long since we had a biography with such delights of substance and of form.
Such a book is a pleasure for the day, and a joy for ever '—*Daily Chron cle*

C. Waldstein. JOHN RUSKIN. By CHARLES WALDSTEIN,
M.A. With a Photogravure Portrait. *Post 8vo.* 5s.
'A thoughtful and well-written criticism of Ruskin's teaching.'—*Daily Chronicle*

A M F. Darmesteter. THE LIFE OF ERNEST RENAN. By
MADAME DARMESTETER. With Portrait. *Second Edition.* Cr. 8vo. 6s
'A polished gem of biography, superior in its kind to any attempt that has been made
of recent years in England. Madame Darmesteter has indeed written for English
readers "*The Life of Ernest Renan*"'—*Athenæum*
'It is a fascinating and biographical and critical study, and an admirably finished
work of literary art '—*Scotsman*
'It is interpenetrated with the dignity and charm, the mild, bright, classical grace of
form and treatment that Renan himself so loved , and it fulfils to the uttermost
the delicate and difficult achievement it sets out to accomplish '—*Academy*

W H Hutton. THE LIFE OF SIR THOMAS MORE. By
W. H. HUTTON, M A. *With Portraits. Crown 8vo.* 5s.
'The book lays good claim to high rank among our biographies. It is excellently,
even lovingly, written '—*Scotsman.*   'An excellent monograph '—*Times*

Travel, Adventure and Topography

H H. Johnston. BRITISH CENTRAL AFRICA By Sir
H H JOHNSTON, K C.B. With nearly Two Hundred Illustrations,
and SIX Maps *Second Edition. Crown 4to.* 30s. *net.*

'A fascinating book, written with equal skill and charm—the work at once of a
literary artist and of a man of action who is singularly wise, brave, and experienced It abounds in admirable sketches from pencil '—*Westminster Gazette*

'A delightful book . collecting within the covers of a single volume all that is
known of this part of our African domains The voluminous appendices are of
extreme value '—*Manchester Guardian*

'The book takes front rank as a standard work by the one man competent to write
it '—*Daily Chronicle.*

L Decle THREE YEARS IN SAVAGE AFRICA. By
LIONEL DECLE With 100 Illustrations and 5 Maps *Second
Edition. Demy 8vo* 21s.

'A fine, full book '—*Pall Mall Gazette*

'Abounding in thrilling adventures.'—*Daily Telegraph*

'His book is profusely illustrated, and its bright pages give a better general survey
of Africa from the Cape to the Equator than any single volume that has yet been
published '—*Times*

'A delightful book '—*Academy*

'Astonishingly frank Every page deserves close attention '—*Literature*

'Unquestionably one of the most interesting books of travel which have recently
appeared.'—*Standard*

'The honest impressions of a keen-eyed and intrepid traveller '—*Scotsman*

'Appealing powerfully to the popular imagination '—*Globe.*

Henri of Orleans. FROM TONKIN TO INDIA. By PRINCE
HENRI OF ORLEANS. Translated by HAMLEY BENT, M.A. With
100 Illustrations and a Map. *Crown 4to, gilt top.* 25s

'A welcome contribution to our knowledge The narrative is full and interesting,
– and the appendices give the work a substantial value '—*Times*

'The Prince's travels are of real importance his services to geography have been
considerable The volume is beautifully illustrated '—*Athenæum*

R. S. S. Baden-Powell. THE DOWNFALL OF PREMPEH.
A Diary of Life in Ashanti, 1895 By Colonel BADEN-POWELL
With 21 Illustrations and a Map *Cheaper Edition. Large Crown
8vo.* 6s

'A compact, faithful, most readable record of the campaign '—*Daily News.*

R. S. S. Baden-Powell THE MATABELE CAMPAIGN, 1896.
By Colonel BADEN-POWELL With nearly 100 Illustrations. *Cheaper
Edition. Large Crown 8vo.* 6s.

'As a straightforward account of a great deal of plucky work unpretentiously done,
this book is well worth reading '—*Times*

S. L Hinde. THE FALL OF THE CONGO ARABS. By
S L. HINDE. With Plans, etc *Demy 8vo.* 12s. 6d.

'The book is full of good things, and of sustained interest '—*St James's Gazette*

'A graphic sketch of one of the most exciting and important episodes in the struggle
for supremacy in Central Africa between the Arabs and their European rivals.'—
Times

A. St. H Gibbons. EXPLORATION AND HUNTING IN CENTRAL AFRICA By Major A St H Gibbons, F.R.G.S. With 8 full-page Illustrations by C Whymper, 25 Photographs and Maps *Demy Svo.* 15s.

'His book is a grand record of quiet, unassuming, tactful resolution. His adventures were as various as his sporting exploits were exciting '—*Times*

E. H. Alderson. WITH THE MOUNTED INFANTRY AND MASHONALAND FIELD FORCE, 1896. By Lieut.-Colonel Alderson. With numerous Illustrations and Plans *Demy Svo* 10s.6d.

'An interesting contribution to the story of the British Empire's growth '—*Daily News*
'A clear, vigorous, and soldier-like narrative '—*Scotsman*

Seymour Vandeleur CAMPAIGNING ON THE UPPER NILE AND NIGER. By Lieut Seymour Vandeleur. With an Introduction by Sir G. Goldie, K C.M G With 4 Maps, Illustrations, and Plans. *Large Crown Svo.* 10s. 6d.

Upon the African question there is no book procurable which contains so much of value as this one '—*Guardian*

Lord Fincastle. A FRONTIER CAMPAIGN. By the Viscount Fincastle, V C., and Lieut P. C. Elliott-Lockhart. With a Map and 16 Illustrations *Second Edition.* *Crown Svo.* 6s.

'An admirable book, combining in a volume a piece of pleasant reading for the general reader, and a really valuable treatise on frontier war.'—*Athenæum*

J. K. Trotter THE NIGER SOURCES By Colonel J K. Trotter, R A With a Map and Illustrations. *Crown Svo.* 5s.

'A most interesting as well as a lucidly and modestly written book '—*Spectator*

Michael Davitt. LIFE AND PROGRESS IN AUSTRAL-ASIA By Michael Davitt, M.P. With 2 Maps *Crown Svo.* 6s. 500 pp.

'An interesting and suggestive work '—*Daily Chronicle*
'Contains an astonishing amount of practical information '—*Daily Mail.*
'One of the most valuable contributions to our store of Imperial literature that has been published for a very long time.'—*Pall Mall Gazette*

W. Crooke. THE NORTH-WESTERN PROVINCES OF INDIA. Their Ethnology and Administration By W Crooke. With Maps and Illustrations. *Demy Svo* 10s 6d.

' A carefully and well written account of one of the most important provinces of the Empire Mr Crooke deals with the land in its physical aspect, the province under Hindoo and Mussulman rule, under British rule, its ethnology and sociology, its religious and social life, the land and its settlement, and the native peasant The illustrations are good, and the map is excellent '—*Manchester Guardian*

A. Boisragon. THE BENIN MASSACRE. By Captain Boisragon. *Second Edition.* *Crown Svo* 3s 6d

'If the story had been written four hundred years ago it would be read to-day as an English classic '—*Scotsman*
'If anything could enhance the horror and the pathos of this remarkable book it is the simple style of the author, who writes as he would talk, unconscious of his own heroism, with an artlessness which is the highest art '—*Pall Mall Gazette*

H. S. Cowper. THE HILL OF THE GRACES : OR, THE GREAT STONE TEMPLES OF TRIPOLI By H S. COWPER, F.S A. With Maps, Plans, and 75 Illustrations. *Demy 8vo.* 10s. 6d.
'Forms a valuable chapter of what has now become quite a large and important branch of antiquarian research.'—*Times*

W. Kinnaird Rose WITH THE GREEKS IN THESSALY. By W. KINNAIRD ROSE, Reuter's Correspondent. With Plans and 23 Illustrations *Crown 8vo.* 6s.

W. B. Worsfold SOUTH AFRICA By W. B. WORSFOLD, M.A. *With a Map Second Edition Crown 8vo.* 6s.
'A monumental work compressed into a very moderate compass '—*World*

Naval and Military

G. W. Steevens. NAVAL POLICY. By. G. W. STEEVENS. *Demy 8vo.* 6s.
This book is a description of the British and other more important navies of the world, with a sketch of the lines on which our naval policy might possibly be developed
'An extremely able and interesting work.'—*Daily Chronicle*

D. Hannay. A SHORT HISTORY OF THE ROYAL NAVY, FROM EARLY TIMES TO THE PRESENT DAY By DAVID HANNAY. Illustrated 2 *Vols Demy 8vo* 7s. 6d each. Vol 1, 1200-1688
'We read it from cover to cover at a sitting, and those who go to it for a lively and brisk picture of the past, with all its faults and its grandeur, will not be disappointed The historian is endowed with literary skill and style '—*Standard*
'We can warmly recommend Mr Hannay's volume to any intelligent student of naval history Great as is the merit of Mr Hannay's historical narrative, the merit of his strategic exposition is even greater '—*Times*

C. Cooper King. THE STORY OF THE BRITISH ARMY. By Colonel COOPER KING, Illustrated. *Demy 8vo.* 7s 6d
An authoritative and accurate story of England's military progress '—*Daily Mail.*
'This handy volume contains, in a compendious form, a brief but adequate sketch of the story of the British army '—*Daily News*

R. Southey ENGLISH SEAMEN (Howard, Clifford, Hawkins, Drake, Cavendish). By ROBERT SOUTHEY. Edited, with an Introduction, by DAVID HANNAY. *Second Edition Crown 8vo.* 6s.
'Admirable and well-told stories of our naval history '—*Army and Navy Gazette*
'A brave, inspiring book.'—*Black and White*

W. Clark Russell. THE LIFE OF ADMIRAL LORD COL-LINGWOOD By W CLARK RUSSELL, With Illustrations by F. BRANGWYN *Third Edition Crown 8vo.* 6s
'A book which we should like to see in the hands of every boy in the country '—*St James's Gazette* 'A really good book.'—*Saturday Review*

E. L S Horsburgh. THE CAMPAIGN OF WATERLOO. By E. L. S. HORSBURGH, B.A. *With Plans. Crown 8vo* 5s.
'A brilliant essay—simple, sound, and thorough '—*Daily Chronicle*

A 3

H B. George. BATTLES OF ENGLISH HISTORY By H B
GEORGE, M A , Fellow of New College, Oxford   With numerous
Plans   *Third Edition.   Crown 8vo   6s*
'Mr George has undertaken a very useful task—that of making military affairs in-
telligible and instructive to non-military readers—and has executed it with laud-
able intelligence and industry, and with a large measure of success.'—*Times*

General Literature

S Baring Gould. OLD COUNTRY LIFE. By S BARING
GOULD. With Sixty seven Illustrations. *Large Crown 8vo   Fifth
Edition. 6s.*
'"Old Country Life," as healthy wholesome reading, full of breezy life and move
ment, full of quaint stories vigorously told, will not be excelled by any book to be
published throughout the year   Sound, hearty, and English to the core.'—*World*

S. Baring Gould. HISTORIC ODDITIES AND STRANGE
EVENTS. By S. BARING GOULD *Fourth Edition. Crown 8vo. 6s.*
'A collection of exciting and entertaining chapters   The whole volume is delightful
reading '—*Times.*

S Baring Gould FREAKS OF FANATICISM By S BARING
GOULD   *Third Edition. Crown 8vo.   6s*
'A perfectly fascinating book '—*Scottish Leader*

S. Baring Gould. A GARLAND OF COUNTRY SONG :
English Folk Songs with their Traditional Melodies. Collected and
arranged by S. BARING GOULD and H F. SHEPPARD. *Demy 4to. 6s*

S Baring Gould. SONGS OF THE WEST · Traditional
Ballads and Songs of the West of England, with their Melodies
Collected by S BARING GOULD, M.A., and H F. SHEPPARD,
M.A. In 4 Parts. *Parts I , II., III., 3s each. Part IV., 5s.
In one Vol., French morocco, 15s.*
'A rich collection of humour, pathos, grace, and poetic fancy '—*Saturday Review*

S. Baring Gould. YORKSHIRE ODDITIES AND STRANGE
EVENTS. By S. BARING GOULD. *Fourth Edition   Crown 8vo.
6s.*

S Baring Gould. STRANGE SURVIVALS AND SUPER-
STITIONS. By S. BARING GOULD *Crown 8vo Second Edition.
6s.*

S Baring Gould. THE DESERTS OF SOUTHERN
FRANCE. By S. BARING·GOULD. *2 vols. Demy 8vo. 32s*

Cotton Minchin. OLD HARROW DAYS. By J. G. COTTON
MINCHIN. *Crown 8vo. Second Edition. 5s.*
'This book is an admirable record.'—*Daily Chronicle*

W. E Gladstone. THE SPEECHES OF THE RT. HON
W. E. GLADSTONE, M.P. Edited by A. W HUTTON, M A.,
and H. J. COHEN, M.A. With Portraits *Demy 8vo. Vols. IX
and X.* 12s. 6d. each.

E V. Zenker ANARCHISM. By E V. ZENKER. *Demy 8vo*
7s. 6d
'Well-written, and full of shrewd comments.'—*The Speaker.*
'Herr Zenker has succeeded in producing a careful and critical history of the growth
of Anarchist theory He is to be congratulated upon a really interesting work '—
Literature

H. G Hutchinson. THE GOLFING PILGRIM. By HORACE
G HUTCHINSON. *Crown 8vo* 6s.
'Full of useful information with plenty of good stories '—*Truth*
'Without this book the golfer's library will be incomplete '—*Pall Mall Gazette.*
'We can recommend few books as better company '—*St James's Gazette*
'It will charm all golfers '—*Times.*
'Decidedly pleasant reading '—*Athenæum*

J. Wells OXFORD AND OXFORD LIFE. By Members of
the University Edited by J WELLS, M.A , Fellow and Tutor of
Wadham College. *Second Edition. Crown 8vo* 3s. 6d
'We congratulate Mr Wells on the production of a readable and intelligent account
of Oxford as it is at the present time, written by persons who are possessed of a
close acquaintance with the system and life of the University '—*Athenæum*

J Wells. OXFORD AND ITS COLLEGES By J. WELLS, M A.,
Fellow and Tutor of Wadham College Illustrated by E H NEW
\ *Second Edition. Fcap. 8vo.* 3s. *Leather.* 3s. 6d. net.
'An admirable and accurate little treatise, attractively illustrated '—*World*
'A luminous and tasteful little volume.'—*Daily Chronicle.*
'Exactly what the intelligent visitor wants '—*Glasgow Herald*

C. G Robertson. VOCES ACADEMICÆ. By C. GRANT
ROBERTSON, M A., Fellow of All Souls', Oxford. *With a Frontis-
piece. Pott 8vo.* 3s 6d
'Decidedly clever and amusing '—*Athenæum*
'A clever and entertaining little book '—*Pall Mall Gazette*

L Whibley. GREEK OLIGARCHIES · THEIR ORGANISA-
TION AND CHARACTER. By L. WHIBLEY, M.A , Fellow
of Pembroke College, Cambridge *Crown 8vo.* 6s.
'An exceedingly useful handbook . a careful and well-arranged study '—*Times.*

L. L. Price. ECONOMIC SCIENCE AND PRACTICE.
By L L PRICE, M A , Fellow of Oriel College, Oxford. *Crown
8vo.* 6s.

J. S Shedlock. THE PIANOFORTE SONATA: Its Origin
and Development. By J. S. SHEDLOCK. *Crown 8vo* 5s.
'This work should be in the possession of every musician and amateur. A concise
and lucid history and a very valuable work for reference '—*Athenæum*

E M Bowden THE EXAMPLE OF BUDDHA Being Quota-
tions from Buddhist Literature for each Day in the Year. Compiled
by E. M. BOWDEN. *Third Edition* 16mo. 2s. 6d.

Science and Technology

Freudenreich. DAIRY BACTERIOLOGY. A Short Manual for the Use of Students   By Dr. ED VON FREUDENREICH. Translated by J R. AINSWORTH DAVIS, B.A.   *Crown 8vo.*   *2s. 6d.*

Chalmers Mitchell. OUTLINES OF BIOLOGY. By P. CHALMERS MITCHELL, M A., *Illustrated*   *Crown 8vo.*   *6s.*
A text-book designed to cover the new Schedule issued by the Royal College of Physicians and Surgeons

G. Massee. A MONOGRAPH OF THE MYXOGASTRES. By GEORGE MASSEE. With 12 Coloured Plates.   *Royal 8vo.*   *18s. net*
'A work much in advance of any book in the language treating of this group of organisms   Indispensable to every student of the Myxogastres '—*Nature*

Stephenson and Suddards   ORNAMENTAL DESIGN FOR WOVEN FABRICS   By C. STEPHENSON, of The Technical College, Bradford, and F. SUDDARDS, of The Yorkshire College, Leeds   With 65 full-page plates. *Demy 8vo.*   *7s 6d*
'The book is very ably done, displaying an intimate knowledge of principles, good taste, and the faculty of clear exposition '—*Yorkshire Post*

TEXT-BOOKS OF TECHNOLOGY.
Edited by PROFESSORS GARNETT and WERTHEIMER.
HOW TO MAKE A DRESS   By J A E. WOOD
Illustrated.   *Crown 8vo*   *1s 6d*
A text-book for students preparing for the City and Guilds examination, based on the syllabus   The diagrams are numerous
'Though primarily intended for students, Miss Wood's dainty little manual may be consulted with advantage by any girls who want to make their own frocks   The directions are simple and clear, and the diagrams very helpful '—*Literature*
'A splendid little book '—*Evening News*

Philosophy

L T. Hobhouse. THE THEORY OF KNOWLEDGE   By L. T. HOBHOUSE, Fellow of C C C, Oxford   *Demy 8vo.*   *21s.*
' The most important contribution to English philosophy since the publication of Mr Bradley's "Appearance and Reality"'—*Glasgow Herald*
'A brilliantly written volume '—*Times.*

W H Fairbrother. THE PHILOSOPHY OF T. H. GREEN. By W H FAIRBROTHER, M A   *Crown 8vo*   *3s 6d.*
'In every way an admirable book '—*Glasgow Herald*

F. W. Bussell. THE SCHOOL OF PLATO   By F W. BUSSELL, D.D., Fellow of Brasenose College, Oxford. *Demy 8vo.*   *10s. 6d.*
'A highly valuable contribution to the history of ancient thought '—*Glasgow Herald*
'A clever and stimulating book,—*Manchester Guardian*

F. S. Granger. THE WORSHIP OF THE ROMANS. By F S. GRANGER, M A., Litt D., Professor of Philosophy at University College, Nottingham. *Crown 8vo.* 6s.

A scholarly analysis of the religious ceremonies, beliefs, and superstitions of ancient Rome, conducted in the new light of comparative anthropology '—*Times*

Theology

Handbooks of Theology.

General Editor, A. ROBERTSON, D D., Principal of King's College, London.

THE XXXIX ARTICLES OF THE CHURCH OF ENG-LAND. Edited with an Introduction by E C S GIBSON, D.D., Vicar of Leeds, late Principal of Wells Theological College. *Second and Cheaper Edition in One Volume. Demy 8vo* 12s. 6d.

' Dr Gibson is a master of clear and orderly exposition And he has in a high degree a quality very necessary, but rarely found, in commentators on this topic, that of absolute fairness His book is pre eminently honest '—*Times*

'After a survey of the whole book, we can bear witness to the transparent honesty of purpose, evident industry, and clearness of style which mark its contents They maintain throughout a very high level of doctrine and tone '—*Guardian*

' The most convenient and most acceptable commentary '—*Expository Times.*

AN INTRODUCTION TO THE HISTORY OF RELIGION. By F B JEVONS, M A , Litt.D., Principal of Bishop Hatfield's Hall *Demy 8vo.* 10s. 6d.

' Dr Jevons has written a notable work, which we can strongly recommend to the serious attention of theologians and anthropologists '—*Manchester Guardian*

' The merit of this book lies in the penetration, the singular acuteness and force of the author's judgment He is at once critical and luminous, at once just and suggestive A comprehensive and thorough book '—*Birmingham Post*

THE DOCTRINE OF THE INCARNATION. By R L. OTTLEY, M.A , late fellow of Magdalen College, Oxon , and Principal of Pusey House *In Two Volumes. Demy 8vo.* 15s.

'Learned and reverent : lucid and well arranged '—*Record*

'A clear and remarkably full account of the main currents of speculation Scholarly precision genuine tolerance . . . intense interest in his subject—are Mr Ottley's merits —*Guardian*

The Churchman's Library.

Edited by J. H BURN, B.D.

THE BEGINNINGS OF ENGLISH CHRISTIANITY By W. E COLLINS, M A , Professor of Ecclesiastical History at King's College, London. With Map. *Crown 8vo.* 3s. 6d.

An investigation in detail, based upon original authorities, of the beginnings of the English Church, with a careful account of earlier Celtic Christianity Some very full appendices treat of a number of special subjects

' An excellent example of thorough and fresh historical work '—*Guardian*

SOME NEW TESTAMENT PROBLEMS. By ARTHUR WRIGHT, Fellow of Queen's College, Cambridge *Crown 8vo.* 6s

' Bold and outspoken , earnest and reverent.'—*Glasgow Herald*

S R. Driver. SERMONS ON SUBJECTS CONNECTED WITH THE OLD TESTAMENT By S R. DRIVER, D D, Canon of Christ Church, Regius Professor of Hebrew in the University of Oxford. *Crown 8vo.* 6s
'A welcome companion to the author's famous 'Introduction '—*Guardian*

T. K. Cheyne. FOUNDERS OF OLD TESTAMENT CRITICISM. By T K. CHEYNE, D D., Oriel Professor at Oxford. *Large crown 8vo* 7s 6d.
A historical sketch of O T Criticism
'A very learned and instructive work '—*Times*

H H Henson. DISCIPLINE AND LAW. By H HENSLEY HENSON, B D, Fellow of All Souls', Oxford; Incumbent of St Mary's Hospital, Ilford; Chaplain to the Bishop of St Albans. *Fcap 8vo* 2s 6d
'An admirable little volume of Lent addresses We warmly commend the general drift of Mr Henson's book '—*Guardian*

H H. Henson. LIGHT AND LEAVEN . HISTORICAL AND SOCIAL SERMONS. By H HENSLEY HENSON, M A. *Crown 8vo* 6s
'They are always reasonable as well as vigorous '—*Scotsman*

W. H. Bennett. A PRIMER OF THE BIBLE By Prof W H. BENNETT *Second Edition. Crown 8vo* 2s 6d.
'The work of an honest, fearless, and sound critic, and an excellent guide in a small compass to the books of the Bible —*Manchester Guardian,*
'A unique primer '—*English Churchman*

C H Prior. CAMBRIDGE SERMONS. Edited by C. H. PRIOR, M A , Fellow and Tutor of Pembroke College. *Crown 8vo.* 6s.
A volume of sermons preached before the University of Cambridge by various preachers, including the late Archbishop of Canterbury and Bishop Westcott

Cecilia Robinson. THE MINISTRY OF DEACONESSES. By Deaconess CECILIA ROBINSON. With an Introduction by the Lord Bishop of Winchester and an Appendix by Professor ARMITAGE ROBINSON *Crown 8vo* 3s 6d
'A learned and interesting book, combining with no ordinary skill the authority of learned research with the practical utility of a descriptive manual of parish work' —*Scotsman*

E. B Layard. RELIGION IN BOYHOOD. Notes on the Religious Training of Boys. By E. B. LAYARD, M.A. *18mo.* 1s

W. Yorke Fausset. THE *DE CATECHIZANDIS RUDIBUS* OF ST. AUGUSTINE. Edited, with Introduction, Notes, etc., by W YORKE FAUSSET, M.A. *Crown 8vo.* 3s. 6d.
An edition of a Treatise on the Essentials of Christian Doctrine, and the best methods of impressing them on candidates for baptism

F Weston THE HOLY SACRIFICE. By F. WESTON, M A., Curate of St. Matthew's, Westminster. *Pott 8vo.* 1s
A small volume of devotions at the Holy Communion, especially adapted to the needs of servers and those who do not communicate

À Kempis. THE IMITATION OF CHRIST. - By THOMAS À KEMPIS. With an Introduction by DEAN FARRAR. Illustrated by C. M. GERE, and printed in black and red. *Second Edition. Fcap. 8vo Buckram. 3s 6d. Padded morocco, 5s.*
Amongst all the innumerable English editions of the " Imitation," there can have been few which were prettier than this one, printed in strong and handsome type, with all the glory of red initials '—*Glasgow Herald*

J. Keble. THE CHRISTIAN YEAR By JOHN KEBLE. With an Introduction and Notes by W LOCK, D D , Warden of Keble College, Ireland Professor at Oxford. Illustrated by R ANNING BELL. *Second Edition. Fcap. 8vo. Buckram. 3s. 6d Padded morocco, 5s*
'The present edition is annotated with all the care and insight to be expected from Mr. Lock The progress and circumstances of its composition are detailed in the Introduction There is an interesting Appendix on the MSS of the "Christian Year," and another giving the order in which the poems were written. A " Short Analysis of the Thought " is prefixed to each, and any difficulty in the text is explained in a note '—*Guardian.*

The Library of Devotion.

Pott 8vo. 2s.; leather, 2s 6d net

'This series is excellent '—THE BISHOP OF LONDON
'A very delightful edition '—THE BISHOP OF BATH AND WELLS
'Well worth the attention of the Clergy '—THE BISHOP OF LICHFIELD
'The new " Library of Devotion " is excellent '—THE BISHOP OF PETERBOROUGH
'Charming '—*Record*
'Delightful '—*Church Bells*

THE CONFESSIONS OF ST. AUGUSTINE Newly Translated, with an Introduction and Notes, by C. BIGG, D D , late Student of Christ Church.
'The translation is an excellent piece of English, and the introduction is a masterly exposition We augur well of a series which begins so satisfactorily '—*Times*
'No translation has appeared in so convenient a form, and none, we think, evidencing so true, so delicate, so feeling a touch '—*Birmingham Post*
'Dr. Bigg has made a new and vigorous translation, and has enriched the text with a luminous introduction and pithy notes '—*Speaker*

THE CHRISTIAN YEAR. By JOHN KEBLE. With Introduction and Notes by WALTER LOCK, D.D , Warden of Keble College, Ireland Professor at Oxford.
No prettier book could be desired '—*Manchester Guardian.*
'The volume is very prettily bound and printed, and may fairly claim to be an advance on any previous editions '—*Guardian*
'The introduction is admirable, and admirers of Keble will be greatly interested in the chronological list of the poems '—*Bookman* '

THE IMITATION OF CHRIST. A Revised Translation, with an Introduction, by C. BIGG, D.D , late Student of Christ Church
Dr Bigg has made a practically new translation of this book, which the reader will have, almost for the first time, exactly in the shape in which it left the hands of the author
'The text is at once scholarly in its faithful reproduction in English of the sonorous Church Latin in which the original is composed, and popular in the sense of being simple and intelligible.'—*Scotsman.*

Leaders of Religion

Edited by H. C. BEECHING, M.A   *With Portraits, crown 8vo.*   3s. 6d.

A series of short biographies of the most prominent leaders of religious life and thought of all ages and countries.

The following are ready—

CARDINAL NEWMAN. By R. H. HUTTON.
JOHN WESLEY. By J H. OVERTON, M.A.
BISHOP WILBERFORCE. By G. W. DANIEL, M.A
CARDINAL MANNING. By A W. HUTTON, M.A.
CHARLES SIMEON. By H. C. G MOULE, D D
JOHN KEBLE. By WALTER LOCK, D D
THOMAS CHALMERS. By Mrs OLIPHANT.
LANCELOT ANDREWES. By R. L. OTTLEY, M.A
AUGUSTINE OF CANTERBURY. By E L. CUTTS, D.D.
WILLIAM LAUD By W. H HUTTON, B.D.
JOHN KNOX By F. M'CUNN.
JOHN HOWE By R F. HORTON, D D.
BISHOP KEN. By F. A CLARKE, M A
GEORGE FOX, THE QUAKER. By T. HODGKIN, D.C L. '
JOHN DONNE. By AUGUSTUS JESSOPP, D D
THOMAS CRANMER By A J. MASON

Other volumes will be announced in due course.

Fiction

SIX SHILLING NOVELS

Marie Corelli's Novels

Crown 8vo   6s. *each.*

A ROMANCE OF TWO WORLDS.   *Eighteenth Edition*
VENDETTA.   *Fourteenth Edition.*
THELMA.   *Nineteenth Edition.*
ARDATH.   *Eleventh Edition.*
THE SOUL OF LILITH   *Ninth Edition*
WORMWOOD.   *Ninth Edition*
BARABBAS : A DREAM OF THE WORLD'S TRAGEDY. *Thirty-second Edition.*

'The tender reverence of the treatment and the imaginative beauty of the writing have reconciled us to the daring of the conception, and the conviction is forced on us that even so exalted a subject cannot be made too familiar to us, provided it be presented in the true spirit of Christian faith The amplifications of the Scripture narrative are often conceived with high poetic insight, and this "Dream of the World's Tragedy" is a lofty and not inadequate paraphrase of the supreme climax of the inspired narrative '—*Dublin Review.*

THE SORROWS OF SATAN.   *Thirty-ninth Edition*

'A very powerful piece of work . . . The conception is magnificent, and is likely to win an abiding place within the memory of man . . The author has immense command of language, and a limitless audacity This interesting and re-markable romance will live long after much of the ephemeral literature of the day is forgotten . A literary phenomenon . novel, and even sublime.'—W T STEAD in the *Review of Reviews*

Anthony Hope's Novels
Crown 8vo 6s each

THE GOD IN THE CAR. *Eighth Edition.*
'A very remarkable book, deserving of critical analysis impossible within our limit; brilliant, but not superficial; well considered, but not elaborated, constructed with the proverbial art that conceals, but yet allows itself to be enjoyed by readers to whom fine literary method is a keen pleasure '— *The World*

A CHANGE OF AIR. *Fifth Edition.*
'A graceful, vivacious comedy, true to human nature The characters are traced with a masterly hand '—*Times*

A MAN OF MARK. *Fourth Edition.*
'Of all Mr Hope's books, "A Man of Mark" is the one which best compares with "The Prisoner of Zenda "'—*National Observer*

THE CHRONICLES OF COUNT ANTONIO. *Third Edition.*
'It is a perfectly enchanting story of love and chivalry, and pure romance The Count is the most constant, desperate, and modest and tender of lovers, a peerless gentleman, an intrepid fighter, a faithful friend, and a magnanimous foe '— *Guardian.*

PHROSO. Illustrated by H R MILLAR *Third Edition.*
'The tale is thoroughly fresh, quick with vitality, stirring the blood, and humorously, dashingly told '—*St James's Gazette.*
'A story of adventure, every page of which is palpitating with action '—*Speaker*
'From cover to cover "Phroso" not only engages the attention, but carries the reader in little whirls of delight from adventure to adventure '—*Academy*

SIMON DALE. By ANTHONY HOPE. Illustrated *Third Edition. Crown 8vo. 6s.*
'"Simon Dale" is one of the best historical romances that have been written for a long while '—*St James's Gazette*
'A bright and gallant story '—*Graphic*
'A brilliant novel The story is rapid and most excellently told. As for the hero, he is a perfect hero of romance—he is brave, witty, adventurous, and a good lover '—*Athenæum*
'There is searching analysis of human nature, with a most ingeniously constructed plot Mr. Hope has drawn the contrasts of his women with marvellous subtlety and delicacy This love-story of 200 years ago makes the man and the woman live again '—*Times.*

S. Baring Gould's Novels
Crown 8vo 6s. each.

'To say that a book is by the author of "Mehalah" is to imply that it contains a story cast on strong lines, containing dramatic possibilities, vivid and sympathetic descriptions of Nature, and a wealth of ingenious imagery '—*Speaker.*
'That whatever Mr Baring Gould writes is well worth reading, is a conclusion that may be very generally accepted His views of life are fresh and vigorous, his language pointed and characteristic, the incidents of which he makes use are striking and original, his characters are life-like, and though somewhat exceptional people, are drawn and coloured with artistic force Add to this that his descriptions of scenes and scenery are painted with the loving eyes and skilled hands of a master of his art, that he is always fresh and never dull, and it is no wonder that readers have gained confidence in his power of amusing and satisfying them, and that year by year his popularity widens '—*Court Circular*

ARMINELL. *Fourth Edition.*

URITH. *Fifth Edition.*

IN THE ROAR OF THE SEA *Sixth Edition.*

MRS. CURGENVEN OF CURGENVEN. *Fourth Edition.*

CHEAP JACK ZITA. *Fourth Edition*

THE QUEEN OF LOVE   *Fourth Edition*

MARGERY OF QUETHER   *Third Edition*

JACQUETTA   *Third Edition*

KITTY ALONE. *Fifth Edition.*

NOÉMI. Illustrated by R. C. WOODVILLE   *Third Edition*

THE BROOM-SQUIRE. Illustrated by F DADD   *Fourth Edition.*

THE PENNYCOMEQUICKS   *Third Edition.*

DARTMOOR IDYLLS.

GUAVAS THE TINNER   Illustrated by Γ DADD.   *Second Edition*

BLADYS. Illustrated   *Second Edition.*

Gilbert Parker's Novels
Crown 8vo   6s. each.

PIERRE AND HIS PEOPLE. *Fourth Edition.*

'Stories happily conceived and finely executed   There is strength and genius in Mr Parker's style '—*Daily Telegraph*

MRS. FALCHION   *Fourth Edition*

'A splendid study of character '—*Athenæum*
'But little behind anything that has been done by any writer of our time '—*Pall Mall Gazette*   'A very striking and admirable novel '—*St. James's Gazette*

THE TRANSLATION OF A SAVAGE.

'The plot is original and one difficult to work out, but Mr Parker has done it with great skill and delicacy   The reader who is not interested in this original, fresh, and well-told tale must be a dull person indeed '—*Daily Chronicle*

THE TRAIL OF THE SWORD. *Illustrated Sixth Edition*

'A rousing and dramatic tale. A book like this, in which swords flash, great surprises are undertaken, and daring deeds done, in which men and women live and love in the old passionate way, is a joy inexpressible '—*Daily Chronicle*

WHEN VALMOND CAME TO PONTIAC. The Story of a Lost Napoleon. *Fourth Edition*

'Here we find romance—real, breathing, living romance. The character of Valmond is drawn unerringly   The book must be read, we may say re-read, for any one thoroughly to appreciate Mr Parker's delicate touch and innate sympathy with humanity '—*Pall Mall Gazette*

AN ADVENTURER OF THE NORTH· The Last Adventures of ' Pretty Pierre '   *Second Edition.*

'The present book is full of fine and moving stories of the great North, and it will add to Mr Parker's already high reputation.'—*Glasgow Herald*

THE SEATS OF THE MIGHTY. *Illustrated. Ninth Edition*

'The best thing he has done, one of the best things that any one has done lately '—*St James's Gazette*
'Mr Parker seems to become stronger and easier with every serious novel that he attempts. He shows the matured power which his former novels have led us to expect, and has produced a really fine historical novel '—*Athenæum*
'A great book '—*Black and White*
'One of the strongest stories of historical interest and adventure that we have read for many a day. . . . A notable and successful book.'—*Speaker*

THE POMP OF THE LAVILETTES. *Second Edition.* 3s. 6d.

'Living, breathing romance, genuine and unforced pathos, and a deeper and more subtle knowledge of human nature than Mr Parker has ever displayed before It is, in a word, the work of a true artist '—*Pall Mall Gazette*

Conan Doyle. ROUND THE RED LAMP. By A. CONAN DOYLE *Sixth Edition Crown 8vo. 6s.*

'The book is far and away the best view that has been vouchsafed us behind the scenes of the consulting-room '—*Illustrated London News*

Stanley Weyman. UNDER THE RED ROBE By STANLEY WEYMAN, Author of 'A Gentleman of France.' With Illustrations by R C. Woodville *Fourteenth Edition. Crown 8vo. 6s.*

'A book of which we have read every word for the sheer pleasure of reading, and which we put down with a pang that we cannot forget it all and start again '— *Westminster Gazette*

'Every one who reads books at all must read this thrilling romance, from the first page of which to the last the breathless reader is haled along An inspiration of manliness and courage '—*Daily Chronicle.*

Lucas Malet. THE WAGES OF SIN. By LUCAS MALET. *Thirteenth Edition. Crown 8vo 6s*

Lucas Malet. THE CARISSIMA By LUCAS MALET, Author of 'The Wages of Sin,' etc. *Third Edition. Crown 8vo. 6s.*

S. R. Crockett. LOCHINVAR. By S. R CROCKETT, Author of 'The Raiders,' etc. Illustrated. *Second Edition Crown 8vo. 6s*

'Full of gallantry and pathos, of the clash of arms, and brightened by episodes of humour and love Mr Crockett has never written a stronger or better book ' —*Westminster Gazette*

S R. Crockett. THE STANDARD BEARER. By S. R. CROCKETT *Crown 8vo. 6s*

'A delightful tale in his best style.'—*Speaker*
'Mr Crockett at his best '—*Literature*
'Enjoyable and of absorbing interest '—*Scotsman.*

Arthur Morrison. TALES OF MEAN STREETS. By ARTHUR MORRISON. *Fifth Edition Crown 8vo 6s.*

'Told with consummate art and extraordinary detail In the true humanity of the book lies its justification, the permanence of its interest, and its indubitable triumph '—*Athenæum.*

'A great book The author's method is amazingly effective, and produces a thrilling sense of reality The writer lays upon us a master hand. The book is simply appalling and irresistible in its interest It is humorous also, without humour it would not make the mark it is certain to make '—*World*

Arthur Morrison. A CHILD OF THE JAGO. By ARTHUR MORRISON. *Third Edition Crown 8vo. 6s.*

'The book is a masterpiece.'—*Pall Mall Gazette*
'Told with great vigour and powerful simplicity '—*Athenæum.*

Mrs Clifford. A FLASH OF SUMMER. By Mrs. W. K. CLIF-
FORD, Author of ' Aunt Anne,' etc   *Second Edition. Crown 8vo. 6s.*
' The story is a very beautiful one, exquisitely told.'—*Speaker*

Emily Lawless. HURRISH   By the Honble EMILY LAW-
LESS, Author of ' Maelcho,' etc   *Fifth Edition. Crown 8vo. 6s*

Emily Lawless. MAELCHO : a Sixteenth Century Romance.
By the Honble EMILY LAWLESS. *Second Edition   Crown 8vo   6s.*
' A really great book.'—*Spectator*
' There is no keener pleasure in life than the recognition of genius   A piece of work
of the first order, which we do not hesitate to describe as one of the most
remarkable literary achievements of this generation '—*Manchester Guardian*

Emily Lawless. TRAITS AND CONFIDENCES. By The
Honble. EMILY LAWLESS. *Crown 8vo. 6s.*
' A very charming little volume   A book which cannot be read without pleasure and
profit, written in excellent English, full of delicate spirit, and a keen appreciation
of nature, human and inanimate '—*Pall Mall Gazette*

Jane Barlow. A CREEL OF IRISH STORIES. By JANE
BARLOW, Author of ' Irish Idylls.' *Second Edition. Crown 8vo. 6s*
' Vivid and singularly real '—*Scotsman*

J. H. Findlater. THE GREEN GRAVES OF BALGOWRIE.
By JANE H. FINDLATER. *Fourth Edition. Crown 8vo. 6s*
' A powerful and vivid story '—*Standard.*
' A beautiful story, sad and strange as truth itself '—*Vanity Fair*
' A very charming and pathetic tale '—*Pall Mall Gazette*
' A singularly original, clever, and beautiful story '—*Guardian*
' Reveals to us a new writer of undoubted faculty and reserve force '—*Spectator*
' An exquisite idyll, delicate, affecting, and beautiful '—*Black and White*

J. H. Findlater   A DAUGHTER OF STRIFE. By JANE
HELEN FINDLATER   *Crown 8vo   6s.*
' A story of strong human interest '—*Scotsman*
' Her thought has solidity and maturity '—*Daily Mail*

Mary Findlater. OVER THE HILLS By MARY FINDLATER
Second Edition   Crown 8vo. 6s.
' A strong and fascinating piece of work '—*Scotsman.*
' A charming romance, and full of incident   The book is fresh and strong '—*Speaker*
' Will make the author's name loved in many a household '—*Literary World*
' A strong and wise book of deep insight and unflinching truth '—*Birmingham Post*

H G. Wells. THE STOLEN BACILLUS, and other Stories.
By H G WELLS. *Second Edition. Crown 8vo. 6s.*
' They are the impressions of a very striking imagination, which, it would seem, has
a great deal within its reach '—*Saturday Review*

H. G. Wells. THE PLATTNER STORY AND OTHERS. By H. G. WELLS. *Second Edition. Crown 8vo. 6s.*

'Weird and mysterious, they seem to hold the reader as by a magic spell '—*Scotsman*
'No volume has appeared for a long time so likely to give equal pleasure to the simplest reader and to the most fastidious critic '—*Academy*

Sara Jeanette Duncan. A VOYAGE OF CONSOLATION. By SARA JEANETTE DUNCAN, Author of 'An American Girl in London ' Illustrated   *Third Edition   Crown 8vo   6s*

'Humour, pure and spontaneous and irresistible '—*Daily Mail*
'A most delightfully bright book '—*Daily Telegraph*
'Eminently amusing and entertaining '—*Outlook*
' The dialogue is full of wit '—*Globe*
'Laughter lurks in every page '—*Daily News*

E F. Benson. DODO : A DETAIL OF THE DAY. By E F BENSON. *Sixteenth Edition   Crown 8vo.   6s.*

'A delightfully witty sketch of society '—*Spectator*
' A perpetual feast of epigram and paradox '—*Speaker.*

E F. Benson. THE RUBICON. By E. F. BENSON, Author of ' Dodo.' *Fifth Edition. Crown 8vo. 6s.*

E F. Benson. THE VINTAGE. By E. F. BENSON. Author of ' Dodo.' Illustrated by G P. JACOMB-HOOD. Third Edition *Crown 8vo. 6s.*

'An excellent piece of romantic literature , a very graceful and moving story   We are struck with the close observation of life in Greece '—*Saturday Review*
' Full of fire, earnestness, and beauty '—*The World*
'An original and vigorous historical romance '—*Morning Post*

Mrs. Oliphant. SIR ROBERT'S FORTUNE.   By Mrs OLIPHANT. *Crown 8vo. 6s.*

' Full of her own peculiar charm of style and character-painting '—*Pall Mall Gazette*

Mrs. Oliphant. THE TWO MARYS By Mrs. OLIPHANT. *Second Edition. Crown 8vo   6s.*

Mrs. Oliphant. THE LADY'S WALK. By Mrs. OLIPHANT. *Second Edition   Crown 8vo. 6s.*
'A story of exquisite tenderness, of most delicate fancy '—*Pall Mall Gazette*

W E Norris MATTHEW AUSTIN. By W. E. NORRIS, Author of ' Mademoiselle de Mersac,' etc. *Fourth Edition. Crown 8vo. 6s.*

'An intellectually satisfactory and morally bracing novel '—*Daily Telegraph.*

W. E. Norris. HIS GRACE. By W. E. NORRIS. *Third Edition. Crown 8vo. 6s.*
'Mr Norris has drawn a really fine character in the Duke of Hurstbourne —*Athenæum*

W. E. Norris. THE DESPOTIC LADY AND OTHERS. By W. E. NORRIS. *Crown 8vo. 6s.*

' A budget of good fiction of which no one will tire.'—*Scotsman.*

W. E. Norris. CLARISSA FURIOSA By W. E. NORRIS, *Crown 8vo. 6s.*

'As a story it is admirable, as a *jeu d'esprit* it is capital, as a lay sermon studded with gems of wit and wisdom it is a model '—*The World*

W. Clark Russell. MY DANISH SWEETHEART By W. CLARK RUSSELL *Illustrated Fourth Edition. Crown 8vo. 6s.*

Robert Barr. IN THE MIDST OF ALARMS. By ROBERT BARR. *Third Edition. Crown 8vo. 6s.*

'A book which has abundantly satisfied us by its capital humour '—*Daily Chronicle.*
'Mr Barr has achieved a triumph '—*Pall Mall Gazette*

Robert Barr. THE MUTABLE MANY By ROBERT BARR, Author of 'In the Midst of Alarms,' 'A Woman Intervenes,' etc *Second Edition Crown 8vo 6s*

'Very much the best novel that Mr Barr has yet given us There is much insight in it, and much excellent humour '—*Daily Chronicle*
'An excellent story It contains several excellently studied characters.'—*Glasgow Herald*

J. Maclaren Cobban. THE KING OF ANDAMAN · A Saviour of Society. By J. MACLAREN COBBAN. *Crown 8vo. 6s.*

'An unquestionably interesting book It contains one character, at least, who has in him the root of immortality.'—*Pall Mall Gazette*

J. Maclaren Cobban WILT THOU HAVE THIS WOMAN ? By J M. COBBAN, Author of 'The King of Andaman ' *Crown 8vo 6s*

M. E Francis. MISS ERIN By M. E. FRANCIS, Author of 'In a Northern Village.' *Second Edition Crown 8vo 6s.*

'A clever and charming story '—*Scotsman*
'Perfectly delightful '—*Daily Mail*
'An excellently fancied love tale '—*Athenæum*

Robert Hichens BYEWAYS By ROBERT HICHENS Author of 'Flames,' etc *Second Edition Crown 8vo 6s*

'A very high artistic instinct and striking command of language raise Mr Hichens' work far above the ruck '—*Pall Mall Gazette.*
'The work is undeniably that of a man of striking imagination '—*Daily News*

Percy White. A PASSIONATE PILGRIM. By PERCY WHITE, Author of 'Mr Bailey-Martin ' *Crown 8vo 6s.*

'A work which it is not hyperbole to describe as of rare excellence '—*Pall Mall Gazette*
'The clever book of a shrewd and clever author '—*Athenæum*

W Pett Ridge. SECRETARY TO BAYNE, M P By W PETT RIDGE. *Crown 8vo. 6s.*

'Sparkling, vivacious, adventurous —*St James's Gazette*
'Ingenious, amusing, and especially smart '—*World*

J S Fletcher. THE BUILDERS By J S FLETCHER, Author of 'When Charles I was King ' *Second Edition. Crown 8vo. 6s.*

'Replete with delightful descriptions '—*Vanity Fair*
'The background of country life has never been sketched more realistically '—*World*

Andrew Balfour BY STROKE OF SWORD By ANDREW
BALFOUR. Illustrated by W. CUBITT COOKE. *Fourth Edition Crown
8vo 6s.*
'A banquet of good things '—*Academy.*
'A recital of thrilling interest told with unflagging vigour '—*Globe.*
'An unusually excellent example of a semi-historic romance '—*World*
'Manly, healthy, and patriotic '—*Glasgow Herald*

J B Burton. IN THE DAY OF ADVERSITY By J BLOUN-
DELLE-BURTON ' *Second Edition Crown 8vo. 6s*
'Unusually interesting and full of highly dramatic situations —*Guardian.*

J. B Burton DENOUNCED. By J BLOUNDELLE-BURTON
Second Edition Crown 8vo 6s.

J. B Burton. THE CLASH OF ARMS By J. BLOUNDELLE-
BURTON *Second Edition Crown 8vo. 6s.*
'A brave story—brave in deed, brave in word, brave in thought '—*St. James's Gazette*
'A fine, manly, spirited piece of work '—*World*

J B. Burton ACROSS THE SALT SEAS By J. BLOUN-
DELLE-BURTON. *Crown 8vo 6s*
'The very essence of the true romantic spirit '—*Truth*
'An ingenious and exciting story '—*Manchester Guardian*
'Singularly well written '—*Athenæum*

W. C. Scully. THE WHITE HECATOMB By W C.
SCULLY, Author of ' Kaffir Stories ' *Crown 8vo 6s.*
'Reveals a marvellously intimate understanding of the Kaffir mind.'—*African Critic.*

W. C Scully BETWEEN SUN AND SAND. By W C.
SCULLY, Author of 'The White Hecatomb.' *Crown 8vo 6s.*
'The reader will find the interest of absolute novelty '—*The Graphic*
'The reader passes at once into the very atmosphere of the African desert. the
inexpressible space and stillness swallow him up, and there is no world for him
but that immeasurable waste '—*Athenæum*
'Strong, simple, direct '—*Daily Chronicle*
'One of the most enthralling tales we have read '—*World*

Victor Waite CROSS TRAILS. By VICTOR WAITE. Illus-
trated. *Crown 8vo. 6s*
'Every page is enthralling '—*Academy*
'Full of strength and reality '—*Athenæum*
'The book is exceedingly powerful '—*Glasgow Herald*

I. Hooper. THE SINGER OF MARLY By I. HOOPER.
Illustrated by W CUBITT COOKE *Crown 8vo 6s*
'The characters are all picturesque '—*Scotsman*
'A novel as vigorous as it is charming '—*Literary World*

M. C. Balfour THE FALL OF THE SPARROW. By
M. C. BALFOUR. *Crown 8vo 6s*
'It is unusually powerful, and the characterization is uncommonly good '—*World*

H. Morrah. A SERIOUS COMEDY. By HERBERT MORRAH.
Crown 8vo. 6s.

H. Morrah. THE FAITHFUL CITY. By HERBERT MORRAH, Author of 'A Serious Comedy.' *Crown 8vo 6s*

L. B. Walford SUCCESSORS TO THE TITLE By Mrs WALFORD, Author of 'Mr Smith,' etc. *Second Edition. Crown 8vo. 6s.*

Mary Gaunt KIRKHAM'S FIND By MARY GAUNT, Author of 'The Moving Finger' *Crown 8vo 6s.*
'A really charming novel '—*Standard*

M. M Dowie. GALLIA By MENIE MURIEL DOWIE, Author of 'A Girl in the Karpathians' *Third Edition Crown 8vo 6s.*
'The style is generally admirable, the dialogue not seldom brilliant, the situations surprising in their freshness and originality.'—*Saturday Review*

M M Dowie THE CROOK OF THE BOUGH By MENIE MURIEL DOWIE. *Crown 8vo. 6s*
'An exceptionally clever and well written book '—*Daily Telegraph*
'An excellent story with shrewd humour and bright writing The author is delightfully witty '—*Pall Mall Gazette.*
'Strong, suggestive, and witty.'—*Daily News*

J A Barry IN THE GREAT DEEP. By J. A. BARRY. Author of 'Steve Brown's Bunyip.' *Crown 8vo. 6s.*
'A collection of really admirable short stories of the sea '—*Westminster Gazette.*

Julian Corbett. A BUSINESS IN GREAT WATERS By JULIAN CORBETT. *Second Edition Crown 8vo 6s*

J. B Patton BIJLI, THE DANCER By JAMES BLYTHE PATTON. Illustrated. *Crown 8vo 6s.*
'Powerful and fascinating '—*Pall Mall Gazette*
'A true and entrancing book '—*Country Life Illustrated.*
'A remarkable book '—*Bookman*
'A vivid picture of Indian life '—*Academy*

Norma Lorimer JOSIAH'S WIFE By NORMA LORIMER *Second Edition Crown 8vo. 6s.*
'Written in a bright and witty style '—*Pall Mall Gazette*

Lucy Maynard THE PHILANTHROPIST. By LUCY MAYNARD. *Crown 8vo. 6s*
'It contains many graphic sketches of the private life of a charitable institution '—*Glasgow Herald*

L. Cope Cornford. CAPTAIN JACOBUS. A ROMANCE OF THE ROAD. By L COPE CORNFORD Illustrated. *Crown 8vo 6s*
'An exceptionally good story of adventure and character '—*World*

L Cope Cornford SONS OF ADVERSITY. By L COPE CORNFORD, Author of 'Captain Jacobus' *Crown 8vo. 6s.*
'A very stirring and spirited sketch of the spacious times of Queen Elizabeth '—*Pall Mall Gazette*
'Packed with incident '—*Outlook.*

F. Brune VAUSSORE. By FRANCIS BRUNE   *Crown 8vo.*
6s
'A subtle, complete achievement '—*Pall Mall Gazette*
'This story is strangely interesting '—*Manchester Guardian*

OTHER SIX-SHILLING NOVELS
Crown 8vo.

THE KING OF ALBERIA   By LAURA DAINTREY
THE DAUGHTER OF ALOUETTE   By MARY A OWEN.
CHILDREN OF THIS WORLD.   By ELLEN F. PINSENT.
AN ELECTRIC SPARK   By G MANVILLE FENN.
UNDER SHADOW OF THE MISSION.   By L. S.
   McCHESNEY
THE SPECULATORS.   By J F. BREWER
THE SPIRIT OF STORM.   By RONALD ROSS.
THE QUEENSBERRY CUP   By CLIVE P WOLLEY.
A HOME IN INVERESK.   By T. L PATON
MISS ARMSTRONG'S AND OTHER CIRCUMSTANCES.
   By JOHN DAVIDSON.
DR CONGALTON'S LEGACY.   By HENRY JOHNSTON
TIME AND THE WOMAN.   By RICHARD PRYCE.
THIS MAN'S DOMINION.   By the Author of 'A High
   Little World '
DIOGENES OF LONDON.   By H. B. MARRIOTT WATSON.
THE STONE DRAGON.   By MURRAY GILCHRIST.
A VICAR'S WIFE.   By EVELYN DICKINSON
ELSA.   By E. M'QUEEN GRAY.

THREE-AND-SIXPENNY NOVELS
Crown 8vo.

DERRICK VAUGHAN, NOVELIST   By EDNA LYALL.
THE KLOOF BRIDE.   By ERNEST GLANVILLE
SUBJECT TO VANITY.   By MARGARET BENSON
THE SIGN OF THE SPIDER.   By BERTRAM MITFORD
THE MOVING FINGER.   By MARY GAUNT
JACO TRELOAR.   By J H PEARCE
THE DANCE OF THE HOURS   By 'VERA.'
A WOMAN OF FORTY   By ESMÉ STUART.
A CUMBERER OF THE GROUND   By CONSTANCE SMITH
THE SIN OF ANGELS   By EVELYN DICKINSON.
AUT DIABOLUS AUT NIHIL.   By X L
THE COMING OF CUCULAIN.   By STANDISH O'GRADY.
THE GODS GIVE MY DONKEY WINGS   By ANGUS EVAN ABBOTT.
THE STAR GAZERS   By G MANVILLE FENN
THE POISON OF ASPS   By R ORTON PROWSE
THE QUIET MRS. FLEMING   By R PRYCE.
DISENCHANTMENT.   By F. MABEL ROBINSON.

THE SQUIRE OF WANDALES   By A SHIELD
A REVEREND GENTLEMAN   By J M CORBAN
A DEPLORABLE AFFAIR.   By W E NORRIS
A CAVALIER S LADYE.   By Mrs DICKER.
THE PRODIGALS   By Mrs OLIPHANT
THE SUPPLANTER   By P NEUMANN
A MAN WITH BLACK EYELASHES   By H A KENNEDY.
A HANDFUL OF EXOTICS   By S GORDON
AN ODD EXPERIMENT   By HANNAH LYNCH
SCOTTISH BORDER LIFE   By JAMES C DIBDIN

HALF-CROWN NOVELS
Crown 8vo.

HOVENDEN, V C,   By F MABEL ROBINSON
THE PLAN OF CAMPAIGN   By F MABEL ROBINSON
MR BUTLER S WARD.   By F. MABEL ROBINSON
ELI'S CHILDREN.   By G MANVILLE FENN
A DOUBLE KNOT   By G MANVILLE FENN
DISARMED   By M BETHAM EDWARDS
A MARRIAGE AT SEA   By W. CLARK RUSSELL
IN TENT AND BUNGALOW   By the Author of 'Indian Idylls'
MY STEWARDSHIP   By E M'QUEEN GRAY
JACK'S FATHER   By W E NORRIS
A LOST ILLUSION   By LESLIE KEITH

THE TRUE HISTORY OF JOSHUA DAVIDSON, Christian and Communist   By E LYNN LYNTON   *Eleventh Edition.   Post 8vo*   1s

Books for Boys and Girls
A Series of Books by well-known Authors, well illustrated.

THREE-AND-SIXPENCE EACH

THE ICELANDER'S SWORD   By S BARING GOULD
TWO LITTLE CHILDREN AND CHING.   By EDITH E CUTHELL
TODDLEBEN'S HERO   By M M BLAKE
ONLY A GUARD-ROOM DOG.   By EDITH E. CUTHELL.
THE DOCTOR OF THE JULIET   By HARRY COLLINGWOOD
MASTER ROCKAFELLAR'S VOYAGE.   By W CLARK RUSSELL
SYD BELTON   Or, The Boy who would not go to Sea.   By G. MANVILLE FENN
THE WALLYPUG IN LONDON.   By G E FARROW.

The Peacock Library
A Series of Books for Girls by well-known Authors, handsomely bound, and well illustrated.

THREE-AND-SIXPENCE EACH

A PINCH OF EXPERIENCE   By L B WALFORD
THE RED GRANGE   By Mrs. MOLESWORTH
THE SECRET OF MADAME DE MONLUC   By the Author of 'Mdle Mori'

DUMPS By Mrs PARR
OUT OF THE FASHION, By L T MEADE
A GIRL OF THE PEOPLE. By L. T MEADE
HEPSY GIPSY By L. T MEADE 2s 6d
THE HONOURABLE MISS By L T MEADE.
MY LAND OF BEULAH By Mrs LEITH ADAMS

University Extension Series

A series of books on historical, literary, and scientific subjects, suitable for extension students and home-reading circles. Each volume is complete in itself, and the subjects are treated by competent writers in a broad and philosophic spirit.

Edited by J. E. SYMES, M.A.,

Principal of University College, Nottingham.
Crown 8vo. Price (with some exceptions) 2s. 6d.

The following volumes are ready —

THE INDUSTRIAL HISTORY OF ENGLAND By H DE B. GIBBINS, D Litt , M A , late Scholar of Wadham College, Oxon , Cobden Prizeman. *Fifth Edition, Revised With Maps and Plans 3s.*

'A compact and clear story of our industrial development A study of this concise but luminous book cannot fail to give the reader a clear insight into the principal phenomena of our industrial history The editor and publishers are to be congratulated on this first volume of their venture, and we shall look with expectant interest for the succeeding volumes of the series '—*University Extension Journal.*

A HISTORY OF ENGLISH POLITICAL ECONOMY. By L L PRICE, M.A , Fellow of Oriel College, Oxon. *Second Edition*

PROBLEMS OF POVERTY. An Inquiry into the Industrial Conditions of the Poor By J. A. HOBSON, M A. *Third Edition.*

VICTORIAN POETS. By A SHARP.

THE FRENCH REVOLUTION By J E SYMES, M A.

PSYCHOLOGY. By F S GRANGER, M A. *Second Edition*

THE EVOLUTION OF PLANT LIFE. Lower Forms. By G. MASSEE. *With Illustrations*

AIR AND WATER. By V B LEWES, M A. *Illustrated*

THE CHEMISTRY OF LIFE AND HEALTH By C. W. KIMMINS, M A *Illustrated*

THE MECHANICS OF DAILY LIFE By V P SELLS, M A *Illustrated.*

ENGLISH SOCIAL REFORMERS By H. DE B GIBBINS, D Litt., M A

ENGLISH TRADE AND FINANCE IN THE SEVENTEENTH CENTURY. By W. A S HEWINS, B A.

THE CHEMISTRY OF FIRE. The Elementary Principles of Chemistry By M. M PATTISON MUIR, M A *Illustrated*

A TEXT-BOOK OF AGRICULTURAL BOTANY By M C POTTER, M A , F L S *Illustrated 3s 6d*

THE VAULT OF HEAVEN. A Popular Introduction to Astronomy. By R A. GREGORY *With numerous Illustrations*

METEOROLOGY. The Elements of Weather and Climate. By H N. DICKSON, F R S E , F R Met Soc *Illustrated.*

A MANUAL OF ELECTRICAL SCIENCE. By GEORGE J. BURCH, M.A *With numerous Illustrations 3s*

THE EARTH   An Introduction to Physiography   By EVAN SMALL, M A
   Illustrated.

INSECT LIFE   By F W THEOBALD, M A   *Illustrated*

ENGLISH POETRY FROM BLAKE TO BROWNING   By W. M
   DIXON, M A.

ENGLISH LOCAL GOVERNMENT.   By E. JLNKS, M A , Professor of
   Law at University College, Liverpool

THE GREEK VIEW OF LIFE   By G L DICKINSON, Fellow of King's
   College, Cambridge.   *Second Edition.*

Social Questions of To-day

Edited by H DE B. GIBBINS, D.Litt , M A.

Crown 8vo.   2s. 6d

A series of volumes upon those topics of social, economic, and industrial
interest that are at the present moment foremost in the public mind
Each volume of the series is written by an author who is an acknowledged authority upon the subject with which he deals

The following Volumes of the Series are ready :—

TRADE UNIONISM—NEW AND OLD   By G HOWELL   *Second
   Edition*

THE CO-OPERATIVE MOVEMENT TO-DAY   By G J. HOLYOAKE,
   Second Edition

MUTUAL THRIFT   By Rev J FROME WILKINSON, M A

PROBLEMS OF POVERTY.   By J A HOBSON, M A.   *Third Edition*

THE COMMERCE OF NATIONS   By C. F. BASTABLE, M A , Professor
   of Economics at Trinity College, Dublin

THE ALIEN INVASION.   By W H WILKINS, B A.

THE RURAL EXODUS   By P. ANDERSON GRAHAM

LAND NATIONALIZATION   By HAROLD COX, B A

A SHORTER WORKING DAY   By H DE B GIBBINS, D Litt., M A.,
   and R. A HADFIELD, of the Hecla Works, Sheffield

BACK TO THE LAND   An Inquiry into the Cure for Rural Depopulation.
   By H E MOORE

TRUSTS, POOLS AND CORNERS   By J STEPHEN JEANS

THE FACTORY SYSTEM   By R. W. COOKE-TAYLOR

THE STATE AND ITS CHILDREN.   By GERTRUDE TUCKWELL

WOMEN'S WORK   By LADY DILKE, Miss BULLEY, and Miss WHITLEY

MUNICIPALITIES AT WORK   The Municipal Policy of Six Great
   Towns, and its Influence on their Social Welfare   By FREDERICK DOLMAN

SOCIALISM AND MODERN THOUGHT.   By M. KAUFMANN.

THE HOUSING OF THE WORKING CLASSES   By E BOWMAKER.

MODERN CIVILIZATION IN SOME OF ITS ECONOMIC ASPECTS By W. CUNNINGHAM, D D , Fellow of Trinity College, Cambridge
THE PROBLEM OF THE UNEMPLOYED   By J A. HOBSON, B.A ,
LIFE IN WEST LONDON. By ARTHUR SHERWELL, M A *Second Edition*
RAILWAY NATIONALIZATION   By CLEMENT EDWARDS
WORKHOUSES AND PAUPERISM. By LOUISA TWINING.

Classical Translations

Edited by H. F. FOX, M.A , Fellow and Tutor of Brasenose College, Oxford.

ÆSCHYLUS—Agamemnon, Choephoroe, Eumenides Translated by LEWIS CAMPBELL, LL D , late Professor of Greek at St Andrews, 5s

CICERO—De Oratore I   Translated by E. N P MOOR, M A   3s 6d

CICERO — Select Orations (Pro Milone, Pro Murena, Philippic II , In Catilinam) Translated by H E D. BLAKISTON, M A , Fellow and Tutor of Trinity College, Oxford. 5s

CICERO—De Natura Deorum   Translated by F. BROOKS, M A , late Scholar of Balliol College, Oxford. 3s 6d

HORACE : THE ODES AND EPODES. Translated by A. GODLEY, M.A , Fellow of Magdalen College, Oxford 2s.

LUCIAN—Six Dialogues (Nigrinus, Icaro-Menippus, The Cock, The Ship, The Parasite, The Lover of Falsehood) Translated by S T IRWIN, M A , Assistant Master at Clifton , late Scholar of Exeter College, Oxford 3s 6d

SOPHOCLES—Electra and Ajax. Translated by E D. A MORSHEAD, M A , Assistant Master at Winchester 2s 6d

TACITUS—Agricola and Germania Translated by R B TOWNSHEND, late Scholar of Trinity College, Cambridge. 2s 6d

Educational Books

CLASSICAL

PLAUTI BACCHIDES   Edited with Introduction, Commentary, and Critical Notes by J M'COSH, M A   Fcap 4to   12s 6d
'The notes are copious, and contain a great deal of information that is good and useful '—*Classical Review*

PASSAGES FOR UNSEEN TRANSLATION   By E. C MARCHANT, M A , Fellow of Peterhouse, Cambridge , and A M COOK, M A , late Scholar of Wadham College, Oxford , Assistant Masters at St. Paul's School. *Crown 8vo.* 3s. 6d.
' A capital selection, and of more variety and value than such books usually are '—*Athenæum*
'A judiciously compiled book which will be found widely convenient '—*Schoolmaster.*
'We know no book of this class better fitted for use in the higher forms of schools.'—*Guardian.*

TACITI AGRICOLA   With Introduction, Notes, Map, etc   By R. F. DAVIS, M A , Assistant Master at Weymouth College *Crown 8vo*   2s.

TACITI GERMANIA. By the same Editor. *Crown 8vo*   2s.

HERODOTUS EASY SELECTIONS   With Vocabulary   By A. C. LIDDELL, M A *Fcap 8vo*   1s. 6d.

SELECTIONS FROM THE ODYSSEY   By E D STONE, M A., late Assistant Master at Eton   *Fcap 8vo.*   1s 6d

PLAUTUS · THE CAPTIVI   Adapted for Lower Forms by J. H FREESE, M A , late Fellow of St John's, Cambridge   1s 6d

DEMOSTHENES AGAINST CONON AND CALLICLES   Edited with Notes and Vocabulary, by F. DARWIN SWIFT, M A., formerly Scholar of Queen's College, Oxford.   *Fcap 8vo*   2s

EXERCISES IN LATIN ACCIDENCE   By S E WINBOLT, Assistant Master in Christ's Hospital   *Crown 8vo*   1s 6d
An elementary book adapted for Lower Forms to accompany the shorter Latin primer
'Skilfully arranged '—*Glasgow Herald*
'Accurate and well arranged '—*Athenæum*

NOTES ON GREEK AND LATIN SYNTAX.   By G BUCKLAND GREEN, M A , Assistant Master at Edinburgh Academy, late Fellow of St John's College, Oxon   *Crown 8vo.*   3s 6d.
Notes and explanations on the chief difficulties of Greek and Latin Syntax, with numerous passages for exercise
'Supplies a gap in educational literature.'—*Glasgow Herald*

GERMAN

A COMPANION GERMAN GRAMMAR   By H DE B GIBBINS, D Litt , M A , Assistant Master at Nottingham High School   *Crown 8vo.*   1s 6d

GERMAN PASSAGES FOR UNSEEN TRANSLATION   By E M'QUEEN GRAY   *Crown 8vo.*   2s 6d

SCIENCE

THE WORLD OF SCIENCE   Including Chemistry, Heat, Light, Sound, Magnetism, Electricity, Botany, Zoology, Physiology, Astronomy, and Geology   By R ELLIOTT STEEL, M A , F C S   147 Illustrations.   *Second Edition*   *Crown 8vo*   2s 6d

ELEMENTARY LIGHT   By R. E STEEL.   With numerous Illustrations.   *Crown 8vo*   4s 6d

ENGLISH

ENGLISH RECORDS   A Companion to the History of England.   By H. E MALDEN, M A.   *Crown 8vo*   3s 6d
A book which aims at concentrating information upon dates, genealogy, officials, constitutional documents, etc , which is usually found scattered in different volumes

THE ENGLISH CITIZEN   HIS RIGHTS AND DUTIES   By H E MALDEN, M A.   1s 6d.

A DIGEST OF DEDUCTIVE LOGIC.   By JOHNSON BARKER, B A   *Crown 8vo*   2s 6d

TEST CARDS IN EUCLID AND ALGEBRA   By D S CALDERWOOD, Headmaster of the Normal School, Edinburgh   In three packets of 40, with Answers.   1s.

A set of cards for advanced pupils in elementary schools.

'They bear all the marks of having been prepared by a teacher of experience who knows the value of careful grading and constant repetition Sums are specially inserted to meet all likely difficulties The papers set at the various public examinations have been largely drawn upon in preparing the cards '—*Glasgow Herald.*

METHUEN'S COMMERCIAL SERIES

Edited by H. DE B. GIBBINS, D Litt., M A.

BRITISH COMMERCE AND COLONIES FROM ELIZABETH TO VICTORIA By H DE B GIBBINS, D Litt., M A 2s *Second Edition*

COMMERCIAL EXAMINATION PAPERS. By H. DE B GIBBINS, D Litt , M A , 1s 6d

THE ECONOMICS OF COMMERCE By H. DE B GIBBINS, D Litt , M A 1s 6d

FRENCH COMMERCIAL CORRESPONDENCE By S E BALLY, Modern Language Master at the Manchester Grammar School 2s *Second Edition*

GERMAN COMMERCIAL CORRESPONDENCE. By S. E BALLY, 2s 6d.

A FRENCH COMMERCIAL READER By S E BALLY 2s.

COMMERCIAL GEOGRAPHY, with special reference to the British Empire By L W LYDE, M A, of the Academy, Glasgow. 2s *Second Edition*

A PRIMER OF BUSINESS By S JACKSON, M A. 1s. 6d *Second Edition*

COMMERCIAL ARITHMETIC. By F G TAYLOR, M A. 1s. 6d

PRÉCIS WRITING AND OFFICE CORRESPONDENCE By E. E WHITFIELD, M.A. 2s.

WORKS BY A. M. M. STEDMAN, M A

INITIA LATINA Easy Lessons on Elementary Accidence *Second Edition* *Fcap* 8vo 1s

FIRST LATIN LESSONS. *Fourth Edition.* *Crown* 8vo 2s.

FIRST LATIN READER With Notes adapted to the Shorter Latin Primer and Vocabulary *Fourth Edition revised* 18mo 1s 6d

EASY SELECTIONS FROM CAESAR Part I. The Helvetian War *Second Edition* 18mo 1s

EASY SELECTIONS FROM LIVY Part 1 The Kings of Rome 18mo 1s 6d

EASY LATIN PASSAGES FOR UNSEEN TRANSLATION *Fifth Edition* *Fcap* 8vo 1s 6d

EXEMPLA LATINA. First Lessons in Latin Accidence With Vocabulary *Crown* 8vo 1s

EASY LATIN EXERCISES ON THE SYNTAX OF THE SHORTER AND REVISED LATIN PRIMER With Vocabulary *Seventh and cheaper Edition re-written.* *Crown* 8vo 1s 6d Issued with the consent of Dr Kennedy

THE LATIN COMPOUND SENTENCE Rules and Exercises *Crown* 8vo 1s 6d With Vocabulary 2s.

NOTANDA QUAEDAM Miscellaneous Latin Exercises on Common Rules and Idioms *Third Edition* *Fcap* 8vo 1s 6d. With Vocabulary 2s

LATIN VOCABULARIES FOR REPETITION : Arranged according to Subjects *Seventh Edition.* *Fcap.* 8vo. 1s 6d.

A VOCABULARY OF LATIN IDIOMS AND PHRASES. 18mo. *Second
Edition.* 1s

STEPS TO GREEK. 18mo 1s

A SHORTER GREEK PRIMER *Crown 8vo* 1s 6d

EASY GREEK PASSAGES FOR UNSEEN TRANSLATION *Third
Edition Revised* *Fcap 8vo* 1s 6d

GREEK VOCABULARIES FOR REPETITION Arranged according to
Subjects. *Second Edition* *Fcap 8vo.* 1s 6d.

GREEK TESTAMENT SELECTIONS For the use of Schools *Third
Edition* With Introduction, Notes, and Vocabulary *Fcap. 8vo* 2s 6d

STEPS TO FRENCH *Third Edition* 18mo 8d

FIRST FRENCH LESSONS *Third Edition Revised.* *Crown 8vo* 1s

EASY FRENCH PASSAGES FOR UNSEEN TRANSLATION. *Third
Edition revised.* *Fcap 8vo* 1s 6d

EASY FRENCH EXERCISES ON ELEMENTARY SYNTAX With
Vocabulary *Second Edition* *Crown 8vo* 2s. 6d. KEY 3s *net*

FRENCH VOCABULARIES FOR REPETITION Arranged according to
Subjects. *Sixth Edition* *Fcap. 8vo* 1s.

SCHOOL EXAMINATION SERIES

EDITED BY A M. M STEDMAN, M A. *Crown 8vo.* 2s. 6d.

FRENCH EXAMINATION PAPERS IN MISCELLANEOUS GRAM-
MAR AND IDIOMS By A. M M STEDMAN, M A *Ninth Edition*
A KEY, issued to Tutors and Private Students only, to be had on
application to the Publishers *Fourth Edition* *Crown 8vo* 6s. *net.*

LATIN EXAMINATION PAPERS IN MISCELLANEOUS GRAM-
MAR AND IDIOMS. By A M M STEDMAN, M A *Eighth Edition*
KEY (*Third Edition*) issued as above 6s *net*

GREEK EXAMINATION PAPERS IN MISCELLANEOUS GRAM-
MAR AND IDIOMS By A M M STEDMAN, M A *Fifth Edition*
KEY (*Second Edition*) issued as above 6s. *net.*

GERMAN EXAMINATION PAPERS IN MISCELLANEOUS GRAM-
MAR AND IDIOMS By R J MORICH, Manchester *Fifth Edition.*
KEY (*Second Edition*) issued as above 6s *net*

HISTORY AND GEOGRAPHY EXAMINATION PAPERS By C H
SPENCE, M A , Clifton College. *Second Edition*

SCIENCE EXAMINATION PAPERS By R E STEEL, M A , F C S ,
Chief Natural Science Master, Bradford Grammar School *In two vols*
Part I Chemistry , Part II Physics

GENERAL KNOWLEDGE EXAMINATION PAPERS. By A. M. M.
STEDMAN, M A. *Third Edition*
KEY (*Second Edition*) issued as above 7s. *net.*

———

Lightning Source UK Ltd.
Milton Keynes UK
UKHW022207270223
417761UK00005B/206